LINCOLNWOOD PUBLIC LIBRARY

W9-APX-603

Lincolnwood Public Library
4000 W. Pratt Ave.
Lincolnwood, IL 60712

THE COMING OF THE TERROR

IN THE

FRENCH REVOLUTION

944.04
TAC

The Coming of the Terror
in the
French Revolution

TIMOTHY TACKETT

THE BELKNAP PRESS OF HARVARD UNIVERSITY PRESS

Cambridge, Massachusetts, and London, England

2015

Copyright © 2015 by the President and Fellows of Harvard College

All rights reserved

Printed in the United States of America

First printing

Library of Congress Cataloging-in-Publication Data

Tackett, Timothy, 1945–

  The coming of the terror in the French Revolution / Timothy Tackett.

    pages cm

  Includes bibliographical references and index.

  ISBN 978-0-674-73655-9 (alk. paper)

  1. France—History—Reign of Terror, 1793–1794. 2. France—History—Revolution, 1789–1799. I. Title.

  DC183.T26 2015

  944.04—dc23

2014023992

Contents

	List of Illustrations	*vii*
	List of Maps	*ix*
	Introduction: The Revolutionary Process	*1*
1	The Revolutionaries and Their World in 1789	*13*
2	The Spirit of '89	*39*
3	The Breakdown of Authority	*70*
4	The Menace of Counterrevolution	*96*
5	Between Hope and Fear	*121*
6	The Factionalization of France	*142*
7	Fall of the Monarchy	*172*
8	The First Terror	*192*
9	The Convention and the Trial of the King	*217*
10	The Crisis of '93	*245*
11	Revolution and Terror until Victory	*280*
12	The Year II and the Great Terror	*312*
	Conclusion: Becoming a Terrorist	*340*
	Abbreviations	*351*
	Notes	*353*
	Sources and Bibliography	*419*
	Acknowledgments	*447*
	Index	*449*

Illustrations

The Tennis Court Oath   *50*

Attack on the Bastille   *56*

Market women leave Paris en route to Versailles   *67*

Federation Ball   . *93*

Confrontation between Catholics and Protestants in Montauban   *106*

The king's flight halted by the national guard in Varennes   *115*

Maximilien Robespierre   *156*

Jacques-Pierre Brissot   *157*

Storming of the Tuileries Palace   *189*

A pro-Montagnard image of the people entering the
  Legislative Assembly   *194*

Memorial service for the patriots killed in the attack
  on the Tuileries   *201*

Enrollment of volunteers in Paris   *218*

Trial of Louis XVI   *237*

The representative on mission, Jean-Baptiste Milhaud   *266*

A surveillance committee during the Terror   *269*

Assassination of Marat by Charlotte Corday   *290*

Brissot and the Girondins sentenced to death by the
  Revolutionary Tribunal   *310*

Festival of the Supreme Being   *318*

Nine emigrants are guillotined after they had returned to France   *331*

9 Thermidor Year II in the Convention   *337*

Maps

France in 1789   *14*

Revolutionary France in 1791   *15*

Paris in 1792   *143*

What the hammer? what the chain?
In what furnace was thy brain?
What the anvil? What dread grasp
Dare its deadly terrors clasp

When the stars threw down their spears,
And water'd heaven with their tears,
Did He smile His work to see?
Did He who made the lamb make thee?

William Blake, "The Tyger" (1794)

It is not power that corrupts but fear.

Aung San Suu Kyi (1991)

The Revolutionary Process

For the French men and women who lived through it, the period from 1793 to 1794 was a deeply troubling and frightening time. Only four years earlier they had witnessed the beginning of an extraordinary Revolution that utterly transformed the state and the relationship of the government to its citizens. A National Assembly, created in the name of popular sovereignty, abolished a "feudal system" that had held sway in France for a thousand years. It also proclaimed a series of basic "human rights": freedom of speech, freedom of the press, religious tolerance, careers determined by talent rather than by blood, and equal justice before the law. It then proceeded to draft Europe's first written constitution. Fueled by an ever-expanding conception of liberty and equality, the Revolutionaries would subsequently broaden individual rights to include universal male suffrage, greatly expanded rights for women, the abolition of slavery, and the goals of universal education and social welfare. By the middle of 1793, however, a darker side of the Revolution had emerged. An increasingly dictatorial government was promoting denunciation and repression, while surveillance committees were everywhere rooting out "suspects" and purported traitors. Thousands of citizens were arrested, and hundreds of others, tried before "Revolutionary Tribunals" without appeal, were executed. The king himself and several major political leaders, whom people once thought they could trust, had been accused of treason and sent to the guillotine. Tragically some of those subjected to capital punishment were men and women who still claimed to be fervent supporters of the Revolution. No less than eighty-two deputies to the National Convention—over 10 percent of the total—would be executed or die in prison through 1794.[1] As the contemporary phrase would have it, terror had become "the order of the day."

How had this happened? How had the high ideals of 1789 turned to the violence and terror of 1793? "Future centuries," wrote the deputy and minister Dominique Garat, "will be astonished by the horrors that we committed; they will also be astonished by our virtues. What will always remain incomprehensible is the incredible contrast between our principles and our follies."[2] For well over 200 years, historians have struggled to understand this strange bipolarism of the Revolution. How can one explain the swing toward state-sponsored intolerance and repression? How was it that the Revolutionaries began killing one another? Of all the issues concerning the period, the origins of the Terror is perhaps the most difficult, the most mysterious.

Throughout the nineteenth century both historians and many French political figures attempted to come to terms with their nation's violent past. François Guizot, Adolphe Thiers, Alphonse de Lamartine, Alexis de Tocqueville, Edgar Quinet, Victor Hugo, Jean Jaurès—all wrote extensively on the Revolution. In the twentieth century three generations of exceptionally talented historians—from Alphonse Aulard, Albert Mathiez, and Georges Lefebvre through Albert Soboul and Michel Vovelle—explained the Terror by emphasizing the powerful contingencies of foreign invasion and counterrevolution that Revolutionary leaders were compelled to confront.[3] The assumption was that the Terror was a rationally calculated option, that it was always conceived as provisional, that the liberal achievements of the early Revolution were temporarily and self-consciously set aside—until threats to the new regime's very survival could be beaten back and overcome. But another group of historians, more conservative in their orientation—from Hippolyte Taine and Augustin Cochin through François Furet—would explain Revolutionary violence and terror in terms of internal politics and above all ideology. Deeply immersed in the philosophy of the Enlightenment, so the argument went, the patriots of 1789 naively adopted a utopian plan to remake society from top to bottom on the basis of reason. Deprived of any direct experience in the exercise of power, they had "nothing to fall back on but first principles," and above all on the political theories of Jean-Jacques Rousseau.[4] Of particular influence was Rousseau's theory of the "general will," according to which any variation from that will, any political opposition, any concept of political pluralism could be viewed as intrinsically pernicious and counterrevolutionary. In this sense the violence of 1793 was already inherent in the ideology of 1789. The National Assembly of that year, in Norman Hampson's phrase, was but the "prelude to Terror."[5]

At the turn of the twenty-first century a number of historians attempted to move away from the stark dichotomy between "circumstances" and "ideology." Arno Mayer, David Andress, Jean-Clément Martin, Donald Sutherland, Dan Edelstein, and Marisa Linton—among others—have written probing and complex analyses of the Terror and the events leading up to it.[6] Building on the work of such scholars and taking into account a considerable amount of new documentation, the present study seeks to entirely reexamine the question. Although "the Terror" can be defined in many ways, here it refers above all to state policy during the period 1793–1794 that used institutionalized violence and the threat of violence—primarily executions—both to punish and intimidate the purported enemies of the nation.[7] While the book is conceived as a general interpretation of events in France from the onset of the Revolution through the fall of Robespierre, it focuses above all on the development of a political culture of violence among the leadership, on the attitude or *mentalité,* it will be argued, that preceded the Terror and made the option of "state-sponsored violence on an unprecedented scale" seem almost inevitable and necessary.[8] In some respects, the book might be seen as a continuation of general reflections on the course of the French Revolution. Whereas an earlier study examined how the French became Revolutionaries, this work seeks to understand how they became terrorists.[9]

Three aspects of the book's approach to the subject need to be underlined from the outset. First, in the exploration of the origins of a political culture of violence, considerable emphasis is placed on the *process* of the Revolution. Part of the difficulty in understanding the Revolutionaries is that theirs was a moving reality in which values, perceptions, and ideologies were continually developing and transforming, often in a quite unpredictable manner. The Revolution was an extraordinarily innovative and protean period in which little if anything was scripted in advance. New perspectives and understandings were pieced together from a wide array of materials from the past or were entirely innovated. Language was set adrift, as the relationship between words and things was transformed. A great many leaders were themselves extraordinarily volatile, inconsistent, and vacillating in their positions from week to week and from month to month. Even social identities and the values on which those identities were

3

based were frequently reexamined and sometimes reformed. Indeed, it seems likely that in the Revolutionary dynamic no single array of factors was operative at all times. The Revolution evolved, rather, in an irregular fashion through a series of "phase changes," each initiated by unanticipated crises or events, each entailing a distinct configuration of cause and consequence.

Many historians and social scientists over the years have gone astray by vaulting directly from the beginning of the Revolution to the Terror, with the unquestioned assumption that the first led directly to the second and with little appreciation for the importance of context and sequence. Between interpretations based on the *longue durée* of ideology or class struggle and on the short term of immediate and imperious "circumstances," it is essential to explore the "middle term," and consider the extent to which attitudes underlying the Terror developed out of the Revolution itself. The military officer Lazare Carnot, deputy to the National Convention and member of the Committee of Public Safety during the Terror, put it succinctly: "A man does not begin as a revolutionary; he becomes one."[10]

Second, while the present study takes into account the full range of French urban and rural society, it focuses in particular on the political elites. Invariably our definition of such elites must be somewhat elastic. We will consider under this rubric all those men who were elected to national, regional, or local offices after 1789 or who joined political clubs. Two generations of scholarship have demonstrated that the vast majority of leadership positions in the Revolution were held by the urban "middle class" of the Old Regime: nonprivileged male commoners—those who were neither nobles nor clergymen—whose occupations did not involve physical labor. To be sure, a certain number of nobles and priests also attained political positions in the Revolution, and there was some variation between those holding posts of national responsibility in Paris and those serving in regional, town, or neighborhood administrations. Municipal elites might include a minority of artisans and petty merchants, and at the village level, leadership was often dominated by wealthy landowning farmers. Moreover, there was a certain evolution over time that brought to power individuals somewhat lower in the social hierarchy. For the most part, however, the Revolutionary political class was composed of "respectable, urban professionals and tradesmen," well educated and generally born in the 1740s or 1750s.[11] The most important political clubs were dominated by the same social group. Even the leadership of the neighborhood councils or "sections" of Paris—commonly associated with the *sans-culottes*—are known to have come primarily from the educated middle classes.[12] This dominance of male social elites is scarcely surprising. Through 1792 elected positions at all levels were restricted by law to men who paid a significant minimum tax. Even after that date leadership was often limited to those who could afford to devote sufficient time to public functions and who were not tied to the day-to-day necessities of making a living. It was also limited to those who possessed functional literacy. In fact, on the eve of the Revolution, only slightly over one-half of all men in France were able to sign their names on their acts of marriage, and only a far smaller percentage had the schooling necessary to assume positions of civic responsibility. Overall, those individuals capable of holding leadership posts represented only about one-fifth of the male population of Revolutionary Paris and a substantially smaller proportion elsewhere in the country.[13]

As for women, there can be no doubt that those of all classes closely followed the Revolution. On occasion, through their writings, through their participation in popular societies, through their presence in demonstrations and revolts, they measurably influenced the course of events. Indeed, we will underscore the veritable "feminist moment" in the spring and summer of 1793, when a significant number of women in Paris and the larger provincial towns achieved a remarkable level of political consciousness and activism. During these years they were granted social and economic rights that would have been scarcely imaginable in 1789. But women never attained—and only rarely sought—the right to vote or hold office. While they must and will be taken into account, the primary focus will be on the Revolution's male institutional leadership.

Third, the present study examines not only the political and institutional activities of the elites but also the evolving mindset that motivated and energized those activities. In order to understand the development of a political culture of violence, we will argue, it is necessary to explore the psychology of the Revolutionary leaders—as others have attempted to understand the psychology of the masses and the crowds. In broaching this issue, we do not intend to adopt a preconceived theoretical framework. "Psychology" is used here in a general sense to evoke the mental states and emotions, the *mentalité* of those who lived through the period. Historians often assume that the behavior of the Revolutionary leaders was always rationally calculated, whether in the effort to logically reconstruct the state and society, to advance their career or faction, or to implement one or another coherent ideology. Yet emotion could play a significant role in actions and decisions. For those who have never lived through a revolution, it is easy to overlook how disconcerting, unsettling, and painful such an experience can be. At a time when so many everyday assumptions were being reassessed or overthrown, anxiety and fear, anger and the desire for revenge, shame and humiliation could all come into play in both individual and collective behavior. Indeed, during periods of great stress, there was often a volatility of emotions among both the elites and the masses, a rapid alternation between joy and anguish, empathy and hatred.

The French Revolution, we shall argue, was quite unanticipated, at least before 1787, and the men to whom power devolved, the architects of the new regime, were long forced to grope for a consistent policy and a coherent ideology. The great majority might agree on the general goals of "liberty" and "equality," and they might adopt those goals with all the conviction and enthusiasm of the newly converted. But the application of these principles in a society quite unaccustomed to the reality of such values, the determination of the boundaries of liberty, the limits of equality, and the reconstruction of a new regime in the midst of an old would all prove extraordinarily challenging. All major revolutions are invariably destabilizing, because they involve a process of tearing down and transition, with lengthy periods of interregnum when the old regime has been discredited but the new is still struggling to assert its legitimacy. The task can become even more daunting with the emergence of counterrevolutionary movements that fundamentally repudiate the new value system. While some revolutionaries rapidly evolve into confident true believers, a great many others are plagued by doubts, uncertainty, and mistrust.

Both social psychologists and neuroscientists have underscored the tight link in human behavior between cognition and affect, between reason and emotion. Such emotions are mediated by cultural rules and expectations and are modified over time through close interaction between individuals in an "emotional community"—to use the concept elaborated by Barbara Rosenwein. Moreover, collective emotions are part and parcel of the phenomenon of rumor—its generation, its propagation, and its transformation within the society. In times of great stress such rumors can transcend sociocultural class and cross between emotional communities that are normally separate. Thus, the fear, suspicion, and anger of the masses can play a significant role in elite revolutionary behavior.[14]

The role of emotions in the coming of the Terror has not been entirely ignored by scholars. The great historian Georges Lefebvre was well aware of their importance, and in recent years William Reddy and Sophie Wahnich have written thoughtful essays on the question.[15] However, the present study seeks to go beyond the concept of the undifferentiated "sentiment" proposed by most recent authors and to focus on the impact of specific emotions. Considerable attention will be given to the enthusiasm and fervor in the Revolution, to the intensity of conviction, to the "supernatural effects" of liberty and equality. But in our effort to understand the mentality of the Terror, particular emphasis will be placed on the emotion of fear and the specific contingencies that engendered such fear. Indeed, the argument will be made that fear was one of the central elements in the origins of Revolutionary violence: fear of invasion, fear of chaos and anarchy, fear of revenge. Moreover, as we shall discover, the psychology of the Revolution was increasingly characterized by a predominant fear of conspiracy, a belief that would be a major factor in the emergence of anger and hatred among the elites and in the imposition of state-sponsored violence and repression. By 1793 this "paranoid style of politics"—to use the term of Richard Hofstadter—was no longer an episodic reaction to individual cases of counterrevolutionary plots—for which demonstrable evidence had been uncovered—but an obsessional fear of a ubiquitous, monolithic "grand conspiracy." Virtually all of the difficulties encountered by the Revolutionaries would be attributed to the actions of a few omnipotent figures manipulating the strings behind a veil of secrecy.[16] In our effort to comprehend the violent events of the Revolution, we must seek to understand how it was that the Terrorists themselves felt terrorized.[17]

Any history that hopes to take into account both the rational and the emotional repertoires of Revolutionary behavior invariably confronts the problem of sources. The present study makes use of a wide range of manuscript and printed documents, including parliamentary debates, newspapers, and brochures. But of particular importance are the contemporary series of letters and diaries of some seventy or eighty individuals who experienced the events of the Revolution directly. The sustained use of correspondence in a study of this kind may strike the reader as surprising. In general, when historians look to personal testimonies, they are far more likely to draw on the memoirs or "histories" of contemporaries. The memoirs of Talleyrand, Alexandre Lameth, Bertrand Barère, Paul Barras, Marie-Jeanne Roland, and the marquis de Ferrières were called on repeatedly by nineteenth- and twentieth-century historians. Consisting of preconstructed narratives, already sorted and organized, such materials are relatively easy to access and integrate, and we will have occasion to consult a certain number.[18] Unfortunately, however, most memoirs were written twenty or thirty years after the events described, and all were subject to the transformative effects of memory. Almost all were also colored by the experience of the Terror and the Napoleonic period.[19]

Letters, by contrast, are more difficult to use. They typically wander over a wide range of topics, interspersing accounts of political events with personal observations of all kinds—family news, health problems, local gossip, or instructions concerning a farm or a business. Yet day-to-day accounts of this kind by thoughtful contemporaries, presenting observations and opinions without foreknowledge, can provide rich insight into the development and dynamic of the Revolution. They can be especially valuable for our understanding of the impact of emotions. The eighteenth century was, after all, a golden age of correspondence. Much more than in our own century of electronic media, letter writing between friends and loved ones was a serious enterprise, as individuals passed along in the form of an ongoing conversation the impressions and information they felt were most important.[20]

Of course, no two sets of letters are the same. Much depended on the specific relationship between individual writers and their correspondents, and unfortunately we usually have only one side of the "conversation." In general we have given preference to longer and sustained exchanges between close friends, colleagues, or relatives. Such letters are particularly useful, moreover, when they are read "in series," when one compares the reactions and impressions conveyed by several different witnesses who passed through the same experiences. Used in this manner, series of letters allow us to integrate a kind of "microhistory" into our macrohistorical account, where the microhistories in question are not of local regions or villages but of the experiences of specific individuals.

The sets of correspondence examined here represent a variety of social milieus, men and women, commoners and nobles, Parisians and provincials. They include deputies, magistrates, publishers, businessmen, retirees, wives of officials, and soldiers on their way to the front. With only a few exceptions—notably Georges Couthon, Pierre Vergniaud, and Gilbert Romme—the correspondents led relatively modest lives, largely forgotten by historians. Though they might well take passionate positions on specific events, they were ultimately observers rather than players. Indeed, relatively few personal letters are preserved for Robespierre, Danton, Barnave,

Saint-Just, Barère, Brissot, and many of the other major leaders. The impact of such figures must not be ignored, but in this case we must rely primarily on the excellent biographies of such individuals published over the years.[21]

Invariably our list of witnesses is especially rich for the city of Paris. Four Parisian correspondents, with letters dating from the late Old Regime through the Revolution, will appear particularly frequently. Adrien-Joseph Colson, the principal estate agent for a noble family living in the city, wrote two or three letters a week to a friend and business associate in the province of Berry in central France. From his upstairs apartment not far from the city hall, he provided a running commentary on the events and perspectives of his Right Bank neighborhood. Just across the Seine, the minor publisher and book seller Nicolas Ruault penned regular missives to his brother, a parish priest in Normandy. A great admirer of Voltaire, whose works he helped edit, Ruault self-consciously identified with the Enlightenment, and he provided lengthy analyses of developments in his radical Left Bank publishing district. Rosalie Jullien, wife of a future member of the National Convention, divided her residence between Paris—not far from Ruault's home—and her husband's family residence in the southeastern province of Dauphiné. Well educated and highly literate, she pursued an intense correspondence with her husband and her older son (both named Marc-Antoine) whenever the family was separated. Gilbert Romme, a mathematics teacher and an amateur scientist, maintained a lifelong correspondence with his childhood friend Gilbert Dubreul in Auvergne. After seven years as a private tutor in Saint-Petersburg, Romme returned to Paris in 1786, where he soon entered politics and served until his suicide in prison in 1795.[22]

Our Parisian contingent of witnesses is enlarged for the Revolutionary period itself by Nicolas-Céleste Guittard de Floriban, a retired landowner who kept a diary in his apartment, near the Place Saint-Sulpice and the celebrated Café Procope, which he frequented; by various members of the Mareux family—especially Toussaint and his daughter Adelaïde—who ran a theater on the Right Bank; and by Edmond Géraud, a student who wrote to his father in Bordeaux. An additional invaluable Parisian source comes from the writings of the prolific playwright and novelist who later sat in the Convention, Louis-Sébastien Mercier. While little of Mercier's correspondence remains, we will make extensive use of his remarkable and very personal "ethnographies" of Paris on the eve of the Revolution and after the Terror.[23] All of these individuals would strongly support the Revolution. Romme and Ruault would soon join the Jacobins, while Mercier and Géraud sympathized with the Girondins. Colson, Guittard, and Toussaint Mareux participated in neighborhood politics and, insofar as their age permitted, served in the national guard. Both Rosalie Jullien and Adelaïde Mareux frequented various political meetings and generally supported the radicals.

Unfortunately, substantial runs of correspondence from provincial France are more difficult to find. Several noble women—the baronne de Barbier-Schroffenberg from Alsace, Madame de Médel from Poitou, Madame de Lisleroy from near Lyon, and Madame Audouyn de Pompery from Brittany—wrote fascinating letters on the life of the provincial nobility, largely from a conservative perspective.[24] Both Pierre Vergniaud and Félix Faulcon left important epistolary records from their homes in Bordeaux and in Poitiers—until they left to become deputies in Paris. For Faulcon we also possess numerous responses from a network of friends and relatives in western France. Additional information on the provinces can be culled from the correspondence of a number of deputies in the national assemblies addressed to their families, friends, and constituents. Among our most loquacious letter writers in the first National Assembly were the three lawyers Jean-François Gaultier de Biauzat (from Auvergne), Théodore Vernier (from Franche-Comté), and Laurent-François Legendre (from Brittany) and the noble magistrate from Poitiers, Pierre-Marie Irland de Bazôges. For the period of the Legislative Assembly and the Convention, there is ample correspondence by the legal men Georges Couthon and Antoine Rabusson-Lamothe (both from Clermont-Ferrand) and Jacques Pinet (from Périgord), as well as by the Provençal physician François-Yves Roubaud; the port employee from Brest, Claude-Antoine Blad; the wealthy merchant from Nantes, Etienne Chaillon; and the farmer from Poitou, Pierre Dubreuil-Chambardel—to name only a few of the more important.

Finally, two additional sets of printed materials should be mentioned. First, private correspondence can be complemented by the periodic commentaries published in newspapers by individual journalists, some of whom sat in the Revolutionary assemblies. Of particular importance are the running accounts of Louis-Marie Prudhomme (in *Les Révolutions de Paris*), the marquis de Condorcet *(Chronique de Paris),* and Dominique-Joseph Garat *(Le Journal de Paris).* All three constitute analytical histories of the Revolution, written day by day (Condorcet and Garat) or week by week

(Prudhomme). Also of interest are the commentaries by Count Mirabeau (the *Journal de Provence*), by Jacques-Pierre Brissot *(Le patriote français),* and by Jacques Dulaure *(Le Thermomètre du jour).*[25] Second, we have drawn extensively on a body of secondary studies focusing on specific French regions or towns. While some of these works are relatively recent, others date from the early decades of the twentieth century in the heyday of "positivist" local history. Accounts of the Revolution in Poitou by the marquis de Roux, in Franche-Comté by Jean Girardot, in Bresse and Bugey by Eugène Dubois, in Upper Languedoc by Charles Jolivet, and in Quercy by Eugène Sol are all outstanding works of descriptive history. They reproduce contemporary letters and other manuscripts and are rich in narrative detail for our understanding of the Revolutionary experience as it unrolled in the provinces.[26]

As the reader will discover, the book is divided roughly into two major parts. The first part, Chapters 1 through 6, focuses on the origins of the Revolution and on a series of themes central to the development of the Revolutionary psychology that emerged during the first three years after 1789: the intensity of Revolutionary commitment, the breakdown of authority and legitimacy, the impact of counterrevolution, the spread of a climate of fear and mistrust, the emergence of toxic factionalism, and the influence of the political and emotional culture of the urban working classes. There can be no doubt that the outbreak of war with Austria and Prussia in the spring of 1792 marked a pivotal moment in the Revolution. It will be argued, however, that conditions amenable to a political culture of violence among the elites already existed before the declaration of war. In the second part of the book, Chapters 7 through 11, the study shifts from a more analytical mode to a more narrative mode. It explores in some detail how, given the Revolutionary psychology of 1792 and under the pressure of events, the specific institutions and practices of the Terror were developed and put into place. For the most part such institutions were created in Paris, and there is thus a somewhat greater emphasis in this part on developments in the capital. Since the book is primarily a study of the origins of the Terror and not of the Terror itself, the principal analysis ends in the autumn of 1793, with the solidification of the structures of the Terror and the trial and execution of the Girondins—the first political show trial of the Revolution. Chapter 12, which can be seen as an extended epilogue, recounts the year of the Great Terror, the Year II in the Revolutionary calendar, through the denouement of Thermidor and the death of Robespierre.

Although the origin of the Terror—like the fall of Rome or the outbreak of World War I—has long provided fertile ground for reductionist interpretations, one must avoid the alluring appeal of monocausal explanations. It is rare indeed that any historical phenomenon as complex and multifaceted as the Terror can be reduced to a single causative factor. This is not to say that one must fall back on a mere sequential narrative of events. The task of the historian is to isolate elements of explanation based on empirically verifiable contemporary evidence, with particular attention to how the situation metamorphosed over time. Hopefully, in this manner, through the identification of some half a dozen factors integral to the French Revolutionary process, the present study may facilitate comparisons with episodes of terror in other major revolutions in other times and in other places.[27]

IN CONCLUSION, I must admit a personal reticence toward condemning outright the men and women of the French Revolution for their acts of violence, even for their obvious moral crimes, without attempting to understand and contextualize why they did what they did. What was going on in their minds? How was it that essentially well-meaning, even high-minded, individuals came to commit evil acts? How could both the lamb and the tiger inhabit the same individuals? Without exonerating them, we have to ask whether we ourselves would have acted differently if we had been in their physical and emotional position. These are fundamental historical questions. And they are perhaps the most important questions posed for people living through perilous political times.

I

The Revolutionaries and
Their World in 1789

Could they have known? Did they even suspect—the great Revolutionary conflagration that would soon sweep over France and over much of the western world? The Old Regime testimonies of our future Revolutionaries suggest that they did not. Most had passed comfortable lives before 1789. While a few had been nobles or clergymen, the great majority were "Third Estate" commoners: lawyers or judges, doctors or government officials, merchants or manufacturers.[1] The majority were also townsmen, who firmly embraced the culture and pace of life of the eighteenth-century urban world. For some this meant the city of Paris itself, the immense metropolis on the river Seine with well over 600,000 people; or the smaller regional cities—like Lyon, Marseille, Bordeaux, or Nantes—with populations of around 100,000. The greatest number, however, resided in the smaller universes of provincial capitals and market towns dispersed across the kingdom: towns with only a few thousand people, serving the legal, administrative, and commercial needs of the surrounding countryside.

Few of our Revolutionaries-to-be were truly wealthy. A significant number were younger men just beginning their careers, still awaiting family inheritance and struggling to find their way in life. Pierre Vergniaud, the future Girondin leader, had taken several years to choose a profession, beginning in a Catholic seminary before switching to law. By 1789 he had discovered his talents as a plea lawyer in Bordeaux, but he still had to budget carefully to set up his law office and library and maintain the standard of dress requisite for attracting clients. Much the same could be said of Vergniaud's future political rival, Maximilien Robespierre. Raised by relatives in Arras

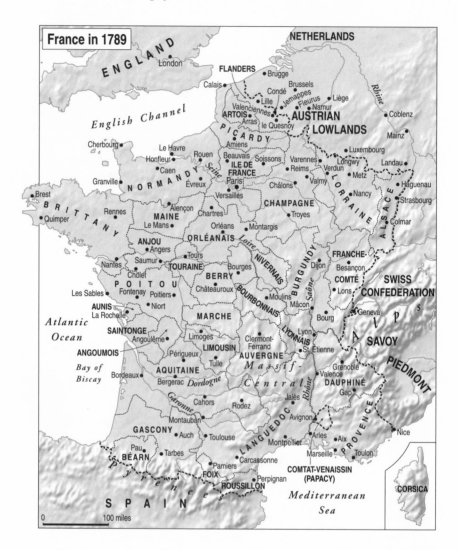

after his mother had died and his father had disappeared, he too was just establishing himself in a modest provincial law practice when the Revolution broke out. Robespierre's school friend, the future Jacobin journalist Camille Desmoulins, found it even more difficult to enter a profession because of a persistent stutter. He was forced to borrow heavily from his father, as he struggled to pursue a career as a writer in Paris. Indeed, several of the young men who had encountered particular frustrations or difficulties finding their way in life—Antoine Barnave, Lazare Carnot, Jean-Louis

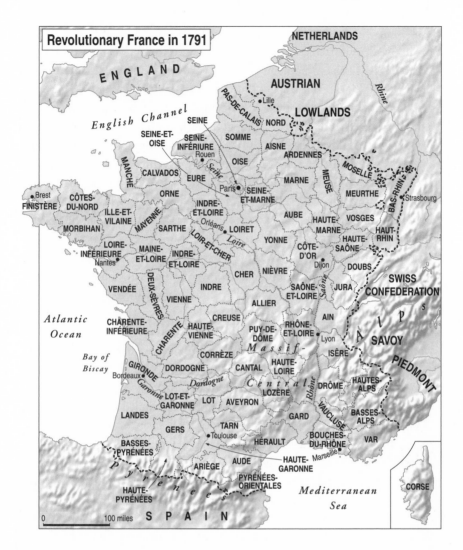

Prieur, Jean-Paul Marat, and Jacques Brissot, to name a few—would embrace the ideals of 1789 with particular fervor and would rapidly move toward a more radical version of Revolution.[2]

Yet economic realities alone cannot explain radical commitment. Most of the future Revolutionary elites were, in fact, already well established in 1789.[3] A few were merchants directly profiting from the great expansion in colonial trade that brought such wealth to eighteenth-century France. But even the nonmerchants, the majority, possessed lands, investments, and professional incomes that kept them abreast of inflation and helped them maintain a comfortable standard of living. The future Jacobins Bertrand Barère, Félix Faulcon, François-Marie Ménard de la Groye, Jean-François Gaultier de Biauzat, and Jacques Pinet—to name only a few—stood among the principal notables of their local communities, following professions similar to those of their fathers and grandfathers and sharing in the family's accumulated wealth. None, to be sure, was immune to the threats of disease and childbirth that struck with such unpredictable force, carrying away spouses and children and other loved ones in the prime of life. In general, however, they were sheltered from the periodic economic crises that brought suffering and anxiety to the great mass of the population. Even the least wealthy could participate in the consumer revolution at the end of the Old Regime that allowed their acquisition of stylish clothing and an ever-greater profusion of household furnishings. They invariably wore the powdered wigs, the knee-breeches, the silver-buckled shoes that were the markers of their elite social standing.

The future Revolutionary leaders were also bound together by their education. With rare exceptions they were among that exclusive group—only 1 or 2 percent of the population—who had followed the full cycle of instruction in the French secondary schools.[4] The humanist education, devised by the Society of Jesus in the sixteenth century, continued to prevail—even after the expulsion of the Jesuits in the 1760s. At the core of their studies was the reading and translation of the Latin classics, which boys were compelled to learn by heart and recapitulate during their six or seven years of courses. Immersion in the texts of Caesar, Cicero, Horace, Plutarch, and Tacitus was essential. The future Conventionnel, Louis-Sébastien Mercier, left a graphic description of his upbringing: "As soon as I began my studies," he wrote, "I was told stories of Romulus and his wolf, of the Capitol and the Tiber. The names of Brutus and Cato and Scipio pursued me in my sleep; the letters of Cicero were piled into my memory. . . . And it was only several years later that I came to realize I was actually French and a resident of Paris."[5]

While young women from families of such elites, the wives and daughters of the future Revolutionaries, would rarely advance so far, they too might receive substantial instruction in the classics through tutoring at home or in convent schools. Both Marie-Jeanne Roland and Rosalie Jullien, soon to be fervent supporters of the Jacobins, salted their correspondence with references to the Ancients. Indeed, the stories and quotations from the classics that had been "piled into" their memories would create a common vocabulary among all Revolutionaries, women and men, a reservoir of references that they could readily recognize and insert into their speeches and pamphlets. Of course, the classics, like the Bible, could be cited in support of widely contradictory positions. Such training could never provide the Revolutionary generation with a systematic ideology. But it is significant that in speeches and newspapers during the Revolution Cicero would be cited ten times more frequently than the contemporary philosopher Jean-Jacques Rousseau.[6]

And if they had all been immersed in the classics, a great many of the Revolutionary elite had also received training in the law. In most cases, this entailed a university degree in one of France's law faculties, followed by some form of apprenticeship in a law office or a royal court. A substantial proportion of the Revolutionaries was among the 1 percent of the population who had attended the university.[7] All of the future deputy lawyers and magistrates and most government officials had pursued such studies.[8] An attestation of legal studies represented a kind of status marker, even for individuals who later pursued careers in commerce or journalism or agriculture. A number of deputies in the first three Revolutionary assemblies had not only practiced law but also produced legal treatises. Of all the future deputies who published before the Revolution, those writing in the field of legal studies were perhaps the most distinguished. Armand-Gaston Camus, Merlin de Douai, Durand de Maillane, Jean-Denis Lanjuinais, Jacques Brissot, and Emmanuel Pastoret—all important Revolutionary leaders—had written nationally known legal texts. Others who had acquired considerable local or national reputations as trial lawyers included such future radicals as Vergniaud, Robespierre, Target, Guadet, Gensonné, Gaultier de Biauzat, and Vernier. Clearly, a legal turn of mind would be one of the most characteristic features of the culture of Revolutionary leadership.

Yet if the future Revolutionary leaders seemed bound together by similar economic, social, and educational backgrounds, to what extent did they self-consciously think and speak of themselves as members of a single group? To what extent did they feel some sense of cohesion within a greater imagined community of commoner elites? In point of fact, there was no generally agreed-upon expression of common identity. When pushed to make distinctions, they might refer to themselves as "respectable people" or "the right sort." Once the Revolutionary period had begun, they would increasingly identify with the "Third Estate," although many would be quick to specify "the *upper* Third," to distinguish themselves from the masses of the population. Sometimes they also called themselves "bourgeois." However, this term had multiple meanings in the eighteenth century. In some towns it signified any legally recognized citizen, enjoying municipal tax privileges and capable of participating in municipal elections. Once the Revolution began the expression "bourgeois" would rapidly change its meaning and become, for a time, an expression of opprobrium, tantamount to "counterrevolutionary." Yet prior to 1789 the term was also used more or less in the modern sense to designate a non-noble, nonclerical member of "the comfortable class" within a town or a city. The Parisian publishers Mercier and Nicolas Ruault frequently made use of the word and clearly identified with the city's bourgeoisie. Ruault would recount his delight in celebrating Epiphany at the home of a family of "honest bourgeois." Such Parisians, he modestly announced, "are the best people in France and consequently the best on earth." And he would clearly distinguish the bourgeois segment of society, to whom he belonged, from the city's artisan and working classes.[9]

A sociologist might well describe the future Revolutionary elites as belonging to the "middle class." In fact, such a term was never used in the eighteenth century and in certain respects it is misleading. Unlike the middle class of the contemporary world, the social group to which the leaders belonged was not in the "middle" of the general distribution of wealth in society. In a chart of the spread of incomes under the Old Regime, we would find them situated far to one side, with revenues well above the vast majority of the population. Numerically, moreover, they represented only a small proportion of the 28 million people living in France in 1789, perhaps some 10 percent of the urban inhabitants and an even smaller proportion of those living in the countryside.[10] In most towns the group of future leaders was so small that all would have known one another, sometimes as friends and relatives, sometimes as bitter rivals.

Yet in another sense our future Revolutionary leaders did indeed see themselves in the "middle." In reflecting on their place in the world, they invariably separated themselves from two other elements above and below them in society: the nobility, on the one hand, and the teeming masses of the common people, on the other.[11]

The Nobility

The nobility was ultimately a social caste, whose existence and privileges were defined by law and based, in theory, on the paternal bloodline.

Legally one either was or was not a noble, and individuals devoted considerable time and money documenting their genealogy as far back in time as possible. Yet in Old Regime France the nobility was not a closed caste. With enough money and the right connections it was possible for a commoner to enter its ranks, usually by purchasing a specific office that conferred noble status. Several hundred families had done just that over the last two centuries before the Revolution.[12] But in reality the desirability of such social advancement was diminished by the contempt and condescension with which the newly ennobled were treated by "aristocrats"— those whose families had been nobles for several centuries. Nothing was more typical of Old Regime society than the "cascading scorn" conveyed by the superior ranks in the status hierarchy toward their "inferiors." In any case, for the vast majority of our future Revolutionaries, the expense of obtaining a patent of nobility would have been utterly beyond their means.[13]

There were, in fact, many levels and gradations within the French nobility. They ranged in prestige and wealth from the great courtiers who frequented the king's entourage in Versailles—princes of the blood, peers of the realm, dukes, and counts—to the minor untitled nobles living in the countryside, sometimes in relatively humble conditions. To the end of the Old Regime, the majority of noblemen, regardless of wealth, saw themselves as members of a warrior class. Virtually every noble family attempted to send at least one son into the army or navy, where a significant number lost their lives in France's numerous wars during the eighteenth century. A smaller subgroup of families had acquired property in office as royal judges. These nobles of the "robe"—referring to the dress they wore in the courtroom—held politically influential positions in the Parlements, the dozen or so major appellate courts of the kingdom, or in other lower-level royal courts.

Careerwise, the French nobility held significant advantages over the commoners. Many of the most important positions in government and society were largely restricted to members of their caste. The bishops and abbots and other great churchmen, most officers in the military, the highest-level administrators in the bureaucracy (ministers and intendants), and most of the parlementary magistrates: all came exclusively from the nobility. The greatest advantages in the acquisition of such positions were usually given to those who could claim a noble pedigree over many generations, and who might thus be considered "aristocrats."

While the incomes of noble families differed substantially, the great majority were wealthier and often vastly more wealthy than the majority of commoner families. Their revenues came in part from their "seigneurial rights," a myriad of fees and dues—varying enormously from village to village—levied on the populations living within the boundaries of their *seigneuries*. Most nobles also derived substantial incomes from personal landholdings, which they often leased out to local farmers. And despite laws that forbade their participation in commercial activities, many profited from indirect involvement in the grain trade, in mines and manufacturing, or in colonial plantations and the sale of slaves. The wealthier nobles, no less than the middle class, were fully engaged in capitalist strategies for increasing their revenues. In addition they also benefited from a variety of tax privileges. While all nobles paid some royal taxes, they invariably escaped many of the most onerous burdens weighing on the mass of the population. Thus, despite considerable variations among individual families, the nobility as a whole was a distinctly wealthy and privileged class. Within the Estates General of 1789, the revenues of the average noble deputy were some ten to fifteen times greater than those of the average commoner in the Third Estate.[14]

Given their considerable wealth, prestige, and connections, the nobles played a key role in the patron-client system that remained characteristic of French society to the end of the Old Regime. At one time or another, virtually all of our future Revolutionaries would have found themselves, hat in hand, seeking the assistance of noble "protectors"—whether seigneurial lords, royal administrators, or aristocratic churchmen—to obtain a position or advance their careers in other ways. Félix Faulcon had relied heavily on various noble contacts to procure his position as a magistrate in Poitiers. Maximilien Robespierre obtained a scholarship to study in Paris through the assistance of a noble abbot. Both Gilbert Romme and Marc-Antoine Jullien had served for a time as tutors to the children of great aristocrats. And Pierre Vergniaud cultivated several noble patrons on whom he relied for assistance and in whose chateaus he sometimes spent vacation periods.[15]

To some extent, of course, the nobility of the Old Regime was linked to the future Revolutionary leadership through the elements of a common culture. Most male nobles had spent at least a few years studying the classics, either with tutors at home or through secondary schools. In the most prestigious such schools they might sit on the same benches with boys from the middle class. A certain segment of the nobility, those destined for careers in the royal courts, had also received training in the law. A few even prided themselves in their learning, whether as robe nobles or courtiers or churchmen or seigneurial lords, retired in their town houses or rural estates. They read widely, wrote essays in the scientific or Enlightenment tradition, and produced poetry or other literary works.[16] Based on the achievements of such individuals, historians have sometimes suggested that the aristocracy and the bourgeoisie formed a common "elite" at the end of the Old Regime—some would even say a single "class"—with a common culture and value system.[17]

Yet on the whole, noble culture differed substantially from that of the commoner Revolutionaries-to-be. A large proportion of noblemen began their military apprenticeship while they were still adolescents, and they were never able to finish the full cycle of secondary education or even consider university studies. Some were sent off to one of the French military schools for training. Others obtained commissions in the army or cavalry at an early age and were dispatched as "officers in a bib"—as the phrase went—at fourteen or thirteen or even younger. Subsequently a few of these individuals might attempt to remedy their lack of education through private reading or association with provincial academies or other learned societies. The vast majority, however, were anything but paragons of Enlightenment learning. On the eve of the Revolution several nobles commented on the inadequacies of their education and on that of their caste as a whole. The marquis de Lezay-Marnésia, who had made a career as an author and who was elected to the Estates General, lamented the situation of the sword nobles, "who are commonly neglected in childhood and who enter and leave the military without an education." Some would complain bitterly at the beginning of the Revolution that they did not possess the language skills and general knowledge to stand up to the Third Estate.[18]

In addition, one should not underestimate the impact of a military ethos on the noble order as a whole. Whether through socialization in their families or through long years in the army or navy, most noblemen embraced a value system based on hierarchy and a strong sense of personal honor, which they were always ready to defend if necessary. The majority had imbibed an ideology centered on "race" and "blood" and the undoubting assumption that they were biologically superior members of society—a persuasion that ran directly counter to the basic assumptions of the Enlightenment. This conviction was only further strengthened when they found their status under attack at the beginning of the Revolution.[19]

The distinctiveness of noble culture is further confirmed by the group's penchant for the ritualized violence of dueling. Despite a veneer of sophisticated gentility reputedly linked to a "civilizing process," aristocratic men continued to kill and maim one another on "the field of honor" with remarkable persistence to the very end of the Old Regime—a record described by one historian as the "brutalization" of the French aristocracy.[20] It was a practice that touched not only nobles in the military but also courtiers living in the presence of the king. According to Count Tilly, one of the best witnesses of court mores at the end of the Old Regime, "France is the country of dueling. . . . Nowhere else have I encountered this disastrous sensitivity, this unfortunate predisposition to believe oneself insulted and demand redress for affronts that are often in fact imaginary."[21] Anxious to put a stop to such activities, the government repeatedly issued prohibitions against dueling. Yet all such efforts were patently ineffective, and over 800 duels have been documented in the eighteenth century alone—a figure that is certainly far below the reality, since the duelists generally attempted to conceal their encounters from the authorities.[22]

To be sure, not all nobles embraced this distinctive value system. A small minority, including a fair sprinkling of court aristocrats—the marquis de Lafayette, the duke de La Rochefoucauld, the count de Mirabeau, the Lameth brothers—would initially throw in their lot with the Revolutionaries. A handful would persist with their Revolutionary support into the most radical phase of events, even accepting the suppression of the nobility and the monarchy.[23] Yet the great majority would acquiesce only grudgingly to the Revolutionary transformations. And a significant number of all nobles, both of the "sword" and of the "robe," would emigrate and embrace a militant counterrevolution. Here they would maintain their opposition to the Revolution with ferocious tenacity, a Revolution conceived as a direct affront to their honor as hereditary nobles. There should be no mystery, then, that the term "aristocrat" came rapidly to be associated with the enemies of the Revolution and of all that its supporters held dear.

The People

Unlike the nobility, that segment of Old Regime society "below" the future Revolutionary elites had no specific legal definition. The frontier between elites and nonelites was inevitably somewhat ambiguous and uncertain at the margins. As with the middle class of the Old Regime, a variety of designations were applied to the lower levels of society: "the rabble," "the mob," the "lower-third," or sometimes simply "the people."[24] Yet whatever the vocabulary used, the future Revolutionary leaders were well aware of the differences in economic conditions, standard of living, and culture separating them from the great mass of the common people. By far the largest segment lived in the countryside, the peasantry represented some 80 percent of the entire population, scattered across the kingdom in over 40,000 villages and hamlets. From one region of France to another there were enormous variations in the patterns of agriculture, in the types and distribution of dwellings, in the languages or dialects spoken, and in the cultural mores. While most of the Revolutionaries had at least some association with the peasantry, the occasions for contact were usually limited. The political elites were, after all, primarily town dwellers, and throughout the Revolution, they would encounter considerable difficulty in understanding the motives and behavior of the countrypeople.

By contrast, their interaction with the working classes in the towns and cities was invariably greater. To be sure, there was always some social segregation by neighborhood, in which generally wealthier and generally poorer inhabitants resided in separate districts. Yet in most of the larger towns, such segregation was partly vertical, with the more comfortable citizens inhabiting spacious apartments on the lower floors and the humble living directly above them in small rooms and garrets. Many Revolutionaries-to-be thus had ample opportunities for daily interchange in streets and stairways with artisans and shopkeepers, wagoners and porters, washerwomen and unskilled day laborers. They were also linked to the lower classes through the intermediaries of their domestic servants—who often constituted 10 percent or more of the urban population.

Yet whether they lived in the towns or the countryside, the great mass of working people stood out sharply from the future Revolutionary elites. Unlike the elites, they worked with their hands and the sweat of their brow—a distinction that had long been fundamental in the social imaginary of the Old Regime. While a few of the shop owners possessed incomes sufficient to provide for themselves even in the worst of times, most of the masses led uncertain lives, on the fringes of indigence. When conditions were bad, there was always the danger of falling into dire poverty. Indeed, the economic boom of the later eighteenth century that brought prosperity to much of the middle class caused considerable anxiety for the laboring people, whose salaries might not rise fast enough to match the ongoing inflation. Both before and after the Revolution began, the perspectives of the masses were invariably colored by the challenges of making ends meet and procuring food, clothing, and housing for themselves and their families—exigencies that were quite absent from the lives of the middle class.

Moreover, the great majority of the common people, especially outside Paris, were functionally illiterate. Even when they managed to sign their names on birth or marriage certificates, they would have found it all but impossible to read a newspaper or a Revolutionary tract. The situation was even more difficult for women of the popular classes, who were always less literate than men and who lived primarily in an oral culture. Communications were also restricted in that many of the lower classes—especially in the countryside—spoke languages or dialects distinct from the standard French used by the elites.

To further complicate relations, many men and women of the working classes had a clear propensity for the use of violence that shocked and disconcerted the future Revolutionaries. Throughout the eighteenth century there were thousands of "rebellions," large and small, of almost every variety.[25] Though the single greatest number—some two-fifths overall—involved protests against various forms of taxation, others expressed anger over insufficient food supplies, the arbitrary actions of royal officials or seigneurial lords, or problems related to work or religion. In fact, the number of such events seems to have increased significantly in the last thirty years of the Old Regime, the period in which most of the future Revolutionaries were entering school and beginning their careers. During these decades, some fifty instances of collective violence broke out every year in the towns alone.

Although disturbance of this sort arose in virtually every region of the kingdom, the greatest concentration took place in Paris itself and the countryside nearby, where hundreds occurred in the last decades before 1789. Here, as one historian has described it, there was a "continuous and pervasive agitation for every reason imaginable that produced a kind of tenacious harassment of all authority."[26] Mercier, who wrote some twelve volumes of observations on Parisian society at the end of the Old Regime, was convinced that violence in the French capital would have been even worse if it were not for the well-organized system of police and police spies.

If ever the repression were to ease up—as he wrote in 1783—he feared "there would be no limits to their disorder; . . . they would abandon themselves to the cruelest forms of violence and would be quite unable to stop."[27]

Not all the popular violence, however, was collective and "political" in nature. Violence was also exercised between and against individuals for a whole range of personal motives. Particularly among the male working classes, there was a clear inclination to resolve private conflicts through physical force. In most towns a remarkable number of fights or brawls or vendetta feuds broke out almost every night: clashes between individuals, between small groups of drinking friends, or among family members or guild journeymen.[28] There were endless confrontations in streets or courtyards or wine shops, sometimes but not always fueled by alcohol. Fights could arise over contested ownership, over women, over verbal insults (real or imagined), over a desire for revenge from long-standing scorn or mistreatment, and over the perceived need to defend one's honor. About two-thirds of the fifty or so fights described by the Parisian windowmaker Jacques-Louis Ménétra in his autobiography involved guild journeymen in various workplace feuds, while most of the remainder were over women. The majority involved fists, clubs, or various weapons picked up from the ground. But a surprising number of working-class men, both in the countryside and in the towns, managed to produce knives, swords, and sabers. There is even evidence of "a certain democratization" in the carrying of swords in Paris during the last decades of the Old Regime.[29] On occasion, violent encounters took the form of veritable prearranged duels in defense of one's "honor," fought in alleys or along the quays and assisted by seconds. In this sense the male culture of honor of the artisan classes was remarkably similar to that of the nobility.[30]

A certain number of the future Revolutionaries expressed sympathy for the plight of the masses under the Old Regime. Gilbert Romme meditated in the 1770s on the miserable situation of the French peasantry and the injustice of the seigneurial system. Robespierre, Pétion, and Gaultier de Biauzat did likewise in the late 1780s. And on occasion Mercier took the defense of the poor in Paris, deploring the "terrible inequality of fortune [that] gives rise to internal conflicts closely resembling a civil war."[31] Once the Revolution had begun, a portion of the most radical leadership would embrace the common people, especially those of Paris. Some would openly glorify them and project an almost mystical image of their essential goodness and political wisdom, even to the point of accepting their actions of collective violence, rationalized as necessary and unavoidable. For the most part, however, such expressions of sympathy were relatively rare before the Revolution. Most of the elites sensed an unbridgeable economic and cultural chasm between themselves and the masses, whom they ultimately had great difficulty understanding. Prior to 1789 Faulcon offered only a few disparaging remarks about the peasants' difficult life "to which they are born." Mercier underlined what he felt were the foolish credulity, irrational emotions, and excitability of the common people: "For them the imaginary world is the real." In the end, he concluded, "stupidity and political ignorance are characteristic of the masses of Paris."[32] Two of our other Parisian observers, Ruault and Adrien Colson, had little but scorn for the "rabble" of urban poor, who were unfavorably compared to "proper people" and "honest men."[33] In describing the situation in July 1789, Ruault would emphasize the stark differences between the "bourgeois" elements of Paris, to which he belonged, and "the people" of artisans and day laborers of whom he remained wary and suspicious.[34] Coming to grips with the beliefs and behavior of the common people—with their violence and their readiness to accept even the most unlikely rumors—was one of the most difficult challenges the Revolutionaries would face in the years after 1789.

Daring to Know

In some respects, the middle class from which the Revolutionary leadership arose had changed rather little over the previous century. Their training in the classics and the importance of their legal formation were not very different from the education received by their great-grandparents. So too their relationship with the nobility, on the one hand, and the masses of the common people, on the other, had elements of long-term continuity. It is clear, nevertheless, that in their outlook on life, in their attitude toward the world and their place in it, they differed dramatically from their predecessors of a hundred years earlier.

For there was optimism in the air. There was a growing passion to discover the world in all its complexity, coupled with an expanding self-assurance and confidence in the possibilities of changing at least some aspects of their daily existence. Many individuals began expanding their personal libraries and reading about a whole variety of subjects, well beyond the religious and devotional texts preferred by their grandparents. They subscribed to the information sheets and newspapers that were just beginning to be published in the major provincial cities as well as in Paris. They made rock collections or they surveyed and attempted to classify the local flora and fauna. They also participated in a whole variety of voluntary associations. There were local academies or literary societies and "museums." There were reading societies, first-generation public libraries where they had access to books and journals that they could not necessarily afford themselves. There were agricultural associations, where they could discuss the latest innovations in land usage and cultivation techniques. Many such associations had been initiated by royal administrators, and they also included members of the nobility and the clergy, but it was the elite commoners who dominated the meetings and formed the bulk of the membership.[35]

The more energetic and motivated members of their generation went beyond mere meetings and discussions and submitted their thoughts in published form. A myriad of books and tracts were appearing in print, ranging from science, geography, and economics to history, literature, and poetry. Some individuals, eager to share their ideas and perhaps hoping to make their mark in the literary world, participated in the numerous essay contests organized by learned academies around the kingdom—over 1,400 in the last four decades of the Old Regime alone. Although a great diversity of subjects were proposed each year, there was a clear trend toward more utilitarian questions, with a sharp rise in science, technology, and economics and a decline in literature, philosophy, and ethics.[36] And those who had neither the time nor the talent to publish books or write long essays might pen letters to the editors of local newspapers. Here too, many of their reflections entailed practical suggestions of rather mundane concern: how best to erect a lightning rod or improve street lighting or exterminate gophers. But sometimes they broached issues of broader significance in society, proposing reforms in education or poor relief or farming and manufacturing techniques.[37]

The curiosity and the reflections on improving daily life also emerged in the correspondence of our future Revolutionaries. In letters to his closest friend, Gilbert Romme described no less than 177 books he had read during his five years of study in Paris. Most dealt with his primary interests in science and medicine, but others ranged from history and geography to economics, literature, pedagogy, and religion.[38] So too Faulcon and his friends regularly exchanged letters describing the many books and essays they had read on a wide variety of subjects. Faulcon, along with Ruault, Romme, Vergniaud, and Colson, also followed as best they could the principal political happenings both in France and in other parts of the world. They passed along information on the succession of European monarchs, the events at court, and the endless wars in which they were involved.[39] Several of the correspondents were also fascinated by the latest experiments in science, and especially with the flights of hot-air balloons in both Paris and the provinces. Vergniaud wrote a poem about such an ascent in Bordeaux. Faulcon was entranced by "aerostatic machines," described to him in letters from one of his Parisian friends, and he wondered if people would soon be able to travel from Poitiers to Paris by air in a single day. All were exuberant with the symbolism of the balloons and the idea that man, through his own devices, had now found the means of rising into the heavens.[40]

On occasion the letter writers also reflected on reforms they hoped to see carried out in the future. Ruault discussed the various changes that might help increase France's population, notably through the liberalization of laws on illegitimate children. Jean Texier, one of Faulcon's closest confidants, mused on the "incoherence" of laws from one province to another and the need to bring about some kind of standardization. Faulcon himself sometimes reflected on the necessity of establishing equal civil rights for Protestants and on modifications of the legal system to make justice more affordable for the population.[41]

Yet there were also clear limits to their hopes for reform. After mulling over his suggestions for judicial changes, Faulcon was quick to conclude that transformations of this magnitude would probably never be possible in the real world: "What good are all these recriminations," he wrote, "since I have no means of destroying the abuses that exist. We must learn to tolerate what we cannot prevent." So too for Dominique-Joseph Garat—the future deputy and minister—dramatic changes were quite impossible; the most one could hope for was gradual reform. It is possible, he wrote, that "there once were countries and ages where the boldest truths directly presented to a sovereign people . . . could make a revolution as soon as they were known." But "for us it is only with time that truth can triumph over prejudice."[42]

The sources of the self-confidence, curiosity, and optimism at this particular moment in French history—commonly associated with the age of the Enlightenment—the passion for exploring the world of knowledge and for considering the possibilities of reform, are by no means obvious. Perhaps it was related to the great economic prosperity of the age, to the multidecade upturn that may well have imprinted a sentiment of optimism and that undoubtedly expanded the possibilities of leisure and facilitated the acquisition of books and periodicals. Perhaps it was also linked to the "scientific revolution" and to the long-term advances in general literacy. In any case there was a huge increase in the total number of journals, newspapers, and books of all kinds published in France over the course of the eighteenth century, an increase that clearly reflected the growing demand for such materials.[43]

In the various writings by future Revolutionary leaders, however, it is difficult to identify a coherent ideology or a single dominant intellectual influence. Over the years a number of historians have attempted to link the Revolution of 1789 with one or another of the literary trends in the eighteenth century, said to have exerted a preponderant influence on the Revolutionary generation. For some it was the impact of "the Enlightenment" in general that defined the thought of the Revolutionaries; for others it was the political theories of Jean-Jacques Rousseau, or the feelings promoted by the sentimental novel, or the power of Jansenist rhetoric, or even new trends in Catholic moral theology.[44]

The problem with all such approaches is that they usually entail basic assumptions about the reading experience of Old Regime elites, assumptions that would privilege the reception and internalization of only certain strands and themes of eighteenth-century thought, assumed to be inherently dominant and appealing. Such approaches greatly underestimate the complexity of the reading process, the manner by which eighteenth-century readers—indeed, readers in any period—selected and filtered the ideas they encountered in readings or lectures or discussions. It is easy to underestimate the major divide between reading and believing.[45] In fact the writings of the age were enormously diverse and often contradictory, both in their specific programs for change and in their basic philosophical and political assumptions. Some writers in the century emphasized a rational, scientific approach to knowledge, while others placed a premium on emotion and instinct; some advocated reform through royal or administrative fiat from above, while others extolled public opinion and popular will; some spent great energy castigating the orthodox Catholic Church or revealed religion in general, while others promoted a veritable "Catholic Enlightenment" that would reconcile the ideals of humanism and self-determination to the Christian message. Some wrote in a literary and philosophical vein, while others focused primarily on political economy. Some extolled the advent of "public opinion" as a new arbiter of programs and ideas, while others put in doubt the very possibility of a single identifiable "public."[46]

Indeed, the best-known individual writers identified with the French Enlightenment were by no means consistent in their assertions and suppositions over the course of their careers. Voltaire, Rousseau, and Diderot could assume dramatically different positions depending on the particular problems they were invoking and audiences they were addressing. To some extent their writings involved voyages of intellectual discovery, a willingness to follow certain strands of argument to their logical conclusions and then to reverse direction or tack a new course and explore other areas of inquiry. Moreover, based on the lists of books being published or marketed by booksellers and of those contained in the libraries of individual eighteenth-century elites, we know that the reading public was interested in an extraordinary range of subjects, of which the writings of the most famous Enlightenment philosophers made up only a small proportion of the total. Law and history, poetry and novels, geography and travel literature, natural history and scientific theory, not to mention theology and devotional texts—and a certain measure of pornography and court gossip—all played a part in the cultural consumption of eighteenth-century readers. In all probability—and as best we can tell—most such individuals read for their professional needs as well as for their pleasure and to satisfy an exuberant curiosity about the world in all its diversity, but with little effort or desire to constitute a new world view or a logically consistent program for reform.[47]

There is no way, of course, that we can reconstruct the innermost thoughts, the intellectual development of the complex individuals who would soon come to support the Revolution. Yet the Old Regime correspondence of several of our future Revolutionaries can provide some inkling of their range of interests and orientations and their manner of interacting with the culture of their age.[48] At one end of the spectrum, the Parisian bookseller and publisher—and future Jacobin—Nicolas Ruault clearly identified with certain strands of the "Enlightenment." He liked to present himself as worshipping in the "temple" of philosophy, whose principal priests were Voltaire, Diderot, D'Alembert, and Buffon. He collaborated in the publication of an early edition of Voltaire's correspondence, and he delighted in spicing the letters to his brother with Voltairian sarcasm and iconoclastic attacks on a wide range of contemporary institutions and social groups. He railed against "the infamous yoke" of the Catholic Church, and he readily attacked the nobility: "They are on our backs and crush us with their weight." On occasion he even attacked the reigning king, Louis XVI, and he was convinced that the king's lack of leadership and the queen's outrageous behavior—notably during the famous Diamond Necklace Affair, when she seemed to squander huge sums of money—had tarnished the reputation of both. In his personal political views, however, he obviously preferred the more elitist position of Voltaire to the democratic tendencies of Rousseau—whose name he never mentioned. Indeed, he reserved great praise for the regime of Louis XIV, and for the contemporary "Enlightened absolutism" of Frederick the Great of Prussia and Joseph II of Austria.

Ruault, however, wrote from his office on Rue de La Harpe in the heart of the Left Bank publishing district, soon to emerge as the most radical neighborhood in all of France. Other future Revolutionaries who have left testimonies from the Old Regime were generally far more diverse in their interests and less clearly linked to any specific cultural tradition. Neither Faulcon nor Romme nor Colson nor Vergniaud nor Rosalie Jullien ever made critical comments about the nobility. All were resigned to working through the existing system and relying on the levers of noble patronage on which they depended at one point or another in their lives. None conveyed sentiments critical of the monarchy, and all of them, including Ruault, were forever passing along news they had heard of marriages and pregnancies and births within the royal family, and of the movements of the king among his various palaces. Vergniaud, the future radical Republican, specifically referred to Louis XVI as a father figure. While both Colson and Faulcon mentioned the Diamond Necklace Affair, they described it as anonymous news, with no particular political meaning. It was in no way construed as "desacralizing" the image of the queen or the king.

While none of our letter writers seems to have been exceptionally pious, several of them continued to maintain ties with religion. Colson attended mass regularly well into the Revolution. Romme, who had passed through a Jansenist phase early in his life, persisted in taking religion seriously to the very end of the Old Regime. Rosalie Jullien is known to have read the Gospels with her husband Marc-Antoine, a future Jacobin supporter of the Terror. While Faulcon and Vergniaud were perhaps somewhat more detached, the latter had attended seminary earlier in his career, and Faulcon was apparently sincere when he asked his two sisters, both of them nuns, to pray for him.[49]

All of our witnesses, and no doubt all of the future Revolutionaries, were aware of the principal figures of the Enlightenment and were probably familiar, either directly or indirectly, with at least some of the works of Montesquieu, Voltaire, and Rousseau. Yet works of the canonical Enlightenment represented only a small portion of their reading. When they did mention the writings of Voltaire and Rousseau, their greatest praise was often for the more purely literary achievements of the two: for Voltaire's epic poems, for example, or for Rousseau's novel *La nouvelle Héloïse*. Vergniaud had only a handful of "philosophical" books in a library overwhelmingly dominated by legal and literary texts, a library that aptly reflected the two most important intellectual activities in life, his law practice and his poetry. We do not know the content of Faulcon's library, but when he was pushed to announce his preferred authors, he readily cited the seventeenth-century playwright Racine and the now obscure eighteenth-century author Thomas d'Hèle. Garat declared that his preferred writers were Montesquieu and Virgil. Romme and the Julliens were both enthusiastic followers of Rousseau's pedagogical theories set down in *Emile*. But Rosalie Jullien gave equal weight to several writers from antiquity and to the seventeenth-century authors Fénelon and La Fontaine, while Romme preferred books about science and generally disdained "mere literature." As Romme described his reading agenda on another occasion, "universality is my weakness. I throw myself body and soul into whatever interests me."[50]

Romme's words might have been written by almost any member of his generation. Each of the future Revolutionaries had his or her own particular focus of interests, both for professional and leisure-time activities. Yet all of them impress us by the breadth and range of their pursuit of knowledge, by their veritable passion for "universality." Most commonly it was a question of knowledge for its own sake, for the pure exhilaration of throwing oneself "body and soul" into learning and literature of all kinds and from all sources. Clearly some of these men and women were prepared not only to observe the world but to rethink it and to suggest possible changes for the better. Most of the proposed reforms, however, were relatively small, involving problems and aggravations in their day-to-day existence. Only very rarely did they entertain the possibility of more sweeping changes of institutions and practices. There can be no doubt that many of them had thought critically about the nobility and the injustice of noble privilege and tax advantages.[51] A great many individuals, who had come to believe that personal ability was a "meaningful distinction among men," had undoubtedly reflected on the need to open up positions in society to talent and not accord them only on the basis of birth.[52] But for the most part, such criticisms were put forth cautiously and with little hope for immediate change. It is clear that in the late eighteenth century critical thinking existed hand in hand with social deference.

If this was the experience of the Enlightenment, then it was a movement, a trend that is best understood not as an ideology but as an epistemology. It was an attitude, a new way of understanding how and what it means to know, the readiness and self-confidence to use one's own good sense, one's "reason" to think all things through critically. Such was the "Enlightenment" in its broadest sense, the Enlightenment as defined by the eighteenth-century philosopher Emmanuel Kant. The motto of the age, wrote Kant in a well-known essay, is best expressed by the Latin phrase *Sapere aude:* "Dare to know." It was this new attitude, rather than any specifically defined ideology or program, that would energize the men of 1789 when they were unexpectedly given the opportunity to make a Revolution.

Ambiguous Attitudes toward Violence

But would the experience of the Old Regime have in any way prepared the future Revolutionaries to promote or condone the policies of Terror? From one perspective the "middle-class" elites seem to have been distinctly less predisposed to violence than either the nobility or the working classes. They represented only a tiny percentage of those participating in duels or tavern fights and brawls. The very concept of "defending one's honor," so important for both nobles and urban artisans, seems to have had relatively little meaning for them.[53] Throughout the eighteenth century dueling was rarely practiced and almost universally condemned by the commoner elites. Mercier denounced "this senseless and barbaric practice" in which individuals "tear one another apart like wild animals over imaginary questions of honor."[54] In 1789 numerous "statements of grievances" of the urban elites specifically asked that dueling be outlawed. By contrast, none of the grievances lists written by the nobility was critical of such activities.[55] During the Revolution itself, almost all of the duels between deputies in the National Assembly would involve members of the Noble Estate, who insisted on interpreting statements of political disagreement as personal affronts. The prince de Poix challenged the count de Lambertye; the count de Puisaye fought the chevalier de Cazalès; the count de Lameth took on the duke de Caylus; and the marquis de La Tour Maubourg battled the vicount Mirabeau, to list only a few of the more dramatic examples. At one point in the early Revolution, the count de La Gallissonnière would even propose settling a political dispute between noble deputies by lining up an equal number of swordsmen from opposing sides and fighting it out on "the field of honor." The Third Estate deputies, in contrast, seemed generally surprised and bewildered by the very idea of a politics of honor.[56]

Most future Revolutionary leaders revealed little patience with collective violence in any form at the end of the Old Regime. To be sure, a certain number made an effort to understand the motives which pushed men and women from the popular classes into violent acts. Mercier proposed a thoughtful social and economic analysis to explain the incipient unrest in Paris in the 1780s. Both he and Ruault underscored the stark class differences between rich and poor and the problems of provisioning a city as large as Paris. Others might express sympathy for the poor in the countryside, pushed to revolt by unemployment or insufficient food supplies.[57] Yet even those who tried to explain the roots of violence had little sympathy for the violence itself. Colson strongly condemned "the violence by which we are threatened" and which, in his view, "grows only greater every day."[58] Virtually anyone who left a description of the Réveillon riots in Paris in April 1789—attacks against two notables thought to have made insensitive remarks about food supply for the poor—harshly denounced all those involved. The rioters were portrayed as "rabble," "mobs of rogues," "violent animals." None of the future Revolutionaries who mentioned the event in their correspondence conveyed any sympathy for the large number of Parisians killed during the harsh military repression that followed.[59]

Indeed, the attitude of the Revolutionaries toward the Parisian repression of April 1789 is revealing of their general position on punitive and exemplary justice. Much has been written about the attacks on capital punishment by certain eighteenth-century writers. Montesquieu, Voltaire, Helvétius, Rousseau, and the writers of the *Encyclopédie* had all strongly criticized capital punishment for cases of simple thievery and the tendency to punish crimes against property more harshly than crimes against persons.[60] Mercier was pained by "the frightful spectacle" of executions for petty theft: "I would be tempted to pardon the unfortunate wretch who, possessing only his courage and a pistol, would attack me out of hunger." Ruault was particularly outraged by the use of torture in the execution of such criminals.[61] And some writers went even further, opposing capital punishment for almost any crime, including murder. The influential Italian jurist Beccaria, whose writings were rapidly translated into French, was especially eloquent on this score. "The death of a citizen," he had written, "is neither useful nor necessary," and society would be more just and provide a better deterrent if life imprisonment were substituted for death.[62]

Yet it is important to note—and significant for attitudes during the coming Revolution—that even the strongest critics of the death penalty insisted on making an exception for the crime of treason. Beccaria, as Voltaire and Rousseau, clearly supported execution in cases involving "the security of the nation." Brissot, Marat, and Pastoret—all members of Revolutionary assemblies and authors of books that opposed capital punishment in general—agreed that death was justified for "those secret conspiracies that threaten the fatherland."[63] For the future Revolutionaries who had the time and inclination to read such literature—and the large proportion trained in the law undoubtedly did—the message was clear. The one crime that always deserved death was treason, an act that put in danger the very survival of the state.[64] This was precisely the crime for which a great many people—including Brissot himself—would be executed during the Terror.

Moreover, whatever the positions of eighteenth-century reformers, many influential legal scholars continued to advocate capital punishment—and even torture—to the very end of the Old Regime for a whole range of crimes. Daniel Jousse, perhaps the single most widely read jurist of the period, specifically condoned the use of "cruel executions for the prevention of certain of the most dangerous crimes."[65] During the last decade before the Revolution, the Parlement of Paris, the most powerful court of justice in the land, persisted in issuing dozens of death sentences every year. Such executions were usually by hanging, more rarely by decapitation or by one of the more brutal methods that constituted a veritable torture—such as breaking on the wheel or "quartering."[66]

At least some of our future Revolutionaries seemed to have no problem with executions. Throughout the eighteenth century, the fear of crime was a virtual obsession among many members of the elite. Colson referred repeatedly to the threats of theft and murder to law-abiding citizens in Paris. It was widely believed among such groups that public executions could serve as useful deterrents.[67] Occasionally, in fact, the word "terror" was used to describe the rationale for capital punishment. The eighteenth-century jurist Jean Lavie had supported the death penalty as a means of "terrorizing" criminals.[68] Close synonyms were also employed, delineating a veritable "pedagogy of fear," the need to inspire fright in the population in general, if crime were to be deterred. This was the principal justification for the theatrical nature of punishment. Sentences involving any kind of public chastisement—and there were hundreds of whippings and brandings in Paris each year in addition to executions—required the convicted individual to make a *parcours infamant* (passage of infamy) through the city in a two-wheeled horse cart. Dressed in a long white shirt, holding a torch, and bearing a sign specifying the crime committed, the individual was compelled to kneel at various points along the way and repeat a formal confession. Advance notices of such rituals were hawked throughout the city, and the executions could be witnessed by thousands of spectators, some of them shouting out commentaries or pleas for mercy—never with any effect—when an individual seemed especially repentant and undeserving of death.[69] In the larger cities public executions and the "passage of infamy" were common elements in Old Regime urban life, reinforcing the public sensitivity to both crime and punishment.

In attendance at such spectacles were not only large masses of the common people but also substantial contingents of the upper and middle classes, many of them paying for choice viewing sites from windows and rooftops. Mercier took note of "the polite society" present for such events along with the "populace," crowds that also included substantial numbers of women from all classes. While Colson claimed never to have attended such executions himself, he seemed to have no qualms against others doing so and often took note of friends who had been present.[70] Clearly, not all Revolutionaries-to-be approved of the theatricality of public executions. Yet a general belief in the necessity of capital punishment seems to have been widespread among the urban elites in 1789. In the statements of grievances sent to Versailles in 1789 there was not a single request for the total suppression of the death penalty—though some demanded a reduction in the number of crimes subject to execution.[71]

In May 1791 Robespierre and several of his allies would make impassioned pleas that the death penalty be abolished without exception. Yet the vast majority of deputies would reject Robespierre's motion. Even Mercier would argue that this was not the time to "relax the impact of terror" in every instance.[72] To be sure, the number of cases subject to the death penalty would be reduced and all forms of torture during the execution process would be abolished, soon to be replaced with the "quick and painless" decapitations of the guillotine. But capital punishment for murder, counterfeiting, and the elastic crime of "lèse-nation"—conspiracy against the Revolutionary regime—would all be maintained. Not insignificantly, the representatives would also refuse to abolish the *parcours infamants* preceding the execution.[73]

Moreover, if virtually all future Revolutionaries accepted the state-instituted violence of capital punishment for certain crimes, they were also prepared to accept within limits the international violence of war. To be sure, the attack on war and militarism had been a common theme in much Enlightenment literature.[74] Voltaire's indictment in the *Philosophical Dictionary* and his vicious satire in *Candide* are well known. Both Rousseau and Diderot in their later writings could be equally condemnatory against both war in general and the use of military violence to subject colonial peoples and promote slavery. "We spend three to four million pounds a year," wrote Mercier, "on wars that are insane and useless." Yet the pacifism of the philosophers had its limits. Voltaire could also write lengthy poems and historical studies praising the military prowess of Henry IV, the Maréchal de Richelieu, and Louis XIV. And virtually all writers recognized the possibility of "just wars" in cases of self-defense.[75]

In their correspondence our Revolutionaries-to-be seemed to have few difficulties with the fact of war in specific instances. Faulcon commented at length on the feasibility of a French military intervention in the Netherlands in 1787. "Without being an apologist for war, this curse of the human race," he wrote, "there are certain imperious circumstances where it cannot be avoided." Colson, as many of his contemporaries in Paris, eagerly followed the war in America, and he celebrated the Franco-American victory at Yorktown. And Ruault, the admirer and publisher of Voltaire, reserved his venom for Christian nations who fought and destroyed one another. Yet he had no difficulty in urging war against the Muslim Turks in order to "expel these barbarians from an Egypt they have debased and corrupted for a thousand years."[76] It is perhaps not surprising, then, that there would be so little opposition to a declaration of war against Austria in April 1792, a state castigated in Revolutionary rhetoric with much the same moral opprobrium dealt by Ruault to the Muslim Turks. The limited opposition that did arise—led by Robespierre and a few of his close associates—would be based not on a dislike of war in general, but on the issues of military preparedness and the dangers of internal conspiracy.

In the chapters that follow, the argument will be made that the Terror was not preordained in 1789, that the great augmentation of state-sponsored violence emerged rather out of the Revolutionary process itself. Yet it is also clear that on the eve of the Revolution the commoner elites held positions on violence that were patently ambiguous. They revealed little tolerance for popular rioting, and they were generally impatient with dueling by any class in society. Some also maintained a fashionable condemnation of war, at least when it occurred between European states. Yet they often showed no qualms against violent punishments to deter crime and "terrorize" criminals, to repress collective riots deemed irrational, or to halt conspiracy against the state. And war itself seemed to pose no problems in situations of self-defense or of true national interest.

2

The Spirit of '89

Few moments in modern history have been more dramatic and transformative than the year 1789 in France. Within the space of a few weeks during the spring and summer, a traditionally elected representative body that had not met for 175 years would unilaterally declare itself to be the sovereign voice of the nation, claim ultimate authority to decide all taxes, and announce its intention of drafting a constitution. Soon thereafter it would issue a decree that would fundamentally reshape French political and social structures and promulgate a Declaration of the Rights of Man and the Citizen that would serve as a model for democratic reform the world around. Such transformations, which scarcely anyone would have anticipated just two years earlier, generated emotions of joy and enthusiasm, a quasi-millenarian fervor that would bind patriots together with a new sense of unity and hold them in its sway for years to come. But almost from the beginning the Revolutionaries were also confronted with the presence of violence, violence that they would have great difficulty understanding or controlling. Almost from the beginning the joy and enthusiasm would exist hand in hand with fear and uncertainty.

The Pre-Revolution

The origin of the French Revolution is one of the most intensely debated questions in all of history, a question that absorbed the Revolutionary generation itself and that has continued to fascinate historians ever since.[1] It now seems clear that the direct impulse to the events of 1789 came not from an ideological struggle or a class struggle, but from a financial and fiscal crisis of the French monarchy, and that this crisis was above all the product of a geopolitical struggle in which that monarchy found itself engaged. Throughout much of the eighteenth century the great powers of Europe had been swept up in a series of ever-more-costly wars, many of them genuine world wars involving competition for territories both on the continent and in colonial lands around the planet. The last of these wars, fought between 1778 and 1783, saw France intervene in support of the American struggle for independence from Great Britain. Though the conflict began in North America, it soon found France allied with Spain, and Holland battling Britain in many other parts of the world.

Among the French the War of American Independence had been relatively popular. Several of our future Revolutionaries—Vergniaud, Romme, Colson, Ruault—conveyed in their letters their intense interest in the conflict. Colson commented on the fortunes of the French forces in numerous of his business notes, commonly referring to them as "we"—a clear sign of early sentiments of national identity. Significantly, however, none of our witnesses described the war in ideological terms or even used the word "revolution." They invariably viewed it in a European context, as France's opportunity for revenge against England after the beating it had taken in the earlier Seven Years War.[2] But the defeat of the British cost the French monarchy dearly. It had been necessary to dispatch some 6,000 troops across the Atlantic to fight side by side with the Americans, and to build a large new navy to take on the English fleet around the world. Such expenditures were financed through a series of massive loans that pushed the monarchy to the brink of bankruptcy.

The disastrous budgetary situation was complicated, moreover, by three additional factors. First, France's tax collection system, patched together over the centuries, was extremely heterogeneous and inefficient. There were numerous separate taxes, differing from region to region, and a whole segment of the fiscal machinery was privatized under the general tax farm, charged with collecting most of the indirect taxes. The system was further weakened by various class and provincial privileges, so that it relied inordinately on contributions from the least wealthy elements of society. During the last two wars, in particular, the monarchy became increasingly dependent on high-interest loans from various international financiers. This ramshackle apparatus stood in sharp contrast to the far more efficient, equitable, and transparent British fiscal system—a system that was at least partly responsible for England's naval and military successes during the century.[3] Second, the monarchy's efforts to raise or reform taxes were invariably opposed by the French sovereign courts or parlements. Throughout most of the eighteenth century the parlementary magistrates—of which those in Paris were the most influential—claimed the right to block the execution of royal decrees. Again and again, they would obstruct the monarchy's efforts to reform the tax system—reforms that would have increased the fiscal burden on the magistrates themselves. Third, the French state was plagued by a failure of leadership. Louis XVI, the last Bourbon king of the Old Regime, was not unintelligent, and at times he applied himself seriously to his tasks. But he was generally awkward in society and profoundly lacking in self-confidence. Early in his reign, he placed himself in the hands of two seasoned ministers, Count Maurepas and Count Vergennes. It was the latter who, as foreign minister, had engineered the victory over the British during the American Revolution. But both Maurepas and Vergennes had the bad grace to die during the 1780s. Thereafter, the king lurched from one group of ministers and advisers to another and from one set of policies to another. Confronted with the regime's dire financial situation, Louis would oscillate between hard-line and conciliatory approaches. In his more liberal moments, in an effort to outflank the opposition, he would support a series of remarkably radical, even "revolutionary" reforms. In this sense, the monarchy itself would play a central role in teaching the French the possibility of radical transformations.

The crisis reached a head at the end of 1786, when the finance minister, Charles-Alexandre de Calonne, presented the king with a general budget—the first comprehensive budget in French history—which substantiated the precarious condition of state finances. Calonne then proposed a program for sweeping reforms that would rationalize tax collection and make the process far more uniform. The most radical measure was to subject all citizens, including the nobility, to a tax levied equally in proportion to one's landholdings. The proposal also included the suppression of internal customs, free grain trade, and a system of elected provincial assemblies in which all citizens would take a role in local tax assessment. The problem, however, was to win approval for such measures from the parlements. Calonne's solution was to convene a special "Assembly of Notables" in early 1787—influential nobles, churchmen, and a few commoners—who were expected to examine and approve the reforms and thus strengthen the monarchy's position before the magistrates.[4] But in his effort to impress the Notables with the seriousness of the situation, Calonne took the unprecedented step of publicly announcing the normally secret details of state finance. Shocked and appalled by the extent of the deficit and reticent to give up their tax privileges without guarantees that the money would be spent responsibly, the Notables ultimately rejected many of the king's proposals. With the failure of his grand scheme Calonne was dismissed, and his successor struggled over the next year to negotiate a solution to the crisis. At first there was an attempt to return to the parlements. When this too failed, the king was persuaded in May 1788 to abolish many of the parlements altogether and replace them with a decentralized court system that could no longer block reforms. Yet this "coup d'état"—as opponents called it—collapsed after only a few weeks, when creditors ceased providing short-term loans, leaving the state's coffers entirely empty.[5] Finally, almost in desperation and after appointing yet another finance minister, the king was convinced that no major reforms would be possible unless they received the backing of an Estates General—the traditional representative body that was the closest institution France ever had to the English Parliament. Over the centuries the French monarchs had done everything possible to avoid such a meeting, only too aware of the growth of Parliament's authority across the Channel. But now, for the first time in 175 years, the Estates General was summoned to convene in the spring of 1789.

At first the politics of the crisis had played out at the highest levels of government in negotiation with France's leading aristocrats, churchmen, and magistrates. But as the political struggles grew ever more intense and as the financial crisis and the king's radical proposals became public knowledge, the broader population was progressively drawn into the affair.[6] Given the secrecy of the royal administration, most French citizens initially had no idea why the Assembly of Notables had been summoned. Adrien Colson realized the unprecedented nature of the event, but he was altogether uncertain of the objectives, the meeting date, or the composition of the "Notables," and virtually every letter to his friend in the provinces recounted the latest rumors—many of them false—concerning the Assembly. He culled such news from the meager information available in the newspapers or from stories circulating in the streets. Only gradually did it become evident that the government was in deep financial straits and that the monarchy was encountering unexpected and highly articulate opposition from the aristocracy. By spring Colson, along with Nicolas Ruault in Paris and Félix Faulcon and his correspondence network in Poitou, were devoting ever more space in their letters to the extraordinary struggle between the king and the Notables. In the course of the following year they began describing events not only as outside observers, but as concerned citizens with opinions of their own. Some supported the monarchy, others the parlements, though it was not uncommon for them to modify their opinions from week to week as the situation evolved. Soon broader elements of Paris also became involved. There were several demonstrations and processions through the streets in support of the parlement, led in particular by young law clerks, fearful of losing their jobs if the sovereign court was abolished.[7]

The politicization of the French public between 1787 and 1789—the "Pre-Revolution," as it is sometimes called—was further stimulated by the convocation of the provincial assemblies in many regions of the kingdom. The three "estates"—the Clergy, the Nobility, and the commoners of the Third Estate—all chose representatives through successive local and regional elections. The deputies thus selected were to collaborate with the intendants—the royal officials in charge of each province—in administering the province and levying taxes. All assembly votes would take place "by head"—rather than by corporate estate, as had usually been the case in the Estates General. It was a stunning innovation by a monarchy that had long claimed to rule by divine right through an authoritarian bureaucracy. It provided an apprenticeship in representative politics for many individuals who would soon sit as deputies in the Estates General.[8]

Moreover, once the Estates General had been summoned—in July 1788— the new finance minister, the Swiss banker Jacques Necker, took the remarkable step of seeking the opinion of French citizens on how the assembly should be organized. His circular letter to municipal governments throughout the realm stimulated an extraordinary mobilization of hundreds of town councils and improvised citizens' committees. Such groups not only debated the organization of the Estates but also discussed solutions for other perceived problems faced by the nation. Soon a critical question became the number of representatives that each estate would elect and the manner in which the deputies would vote: by individual (as in the provincial assemblies) or by corporate estate (as in the most recent Estates General of 1614). The nature of the vote seemed particularly important, since the First and Second Estates (the Clergy and the Nobility) were both expected to be controlled by the aristocracy, so that a vote by estate would place them in a position of dominance.

In certain regions, local citizens, calling themselves "patriots," went well beyond Necker's directives and began organizing their own assemblies at the provincial level. In Dauphiné, in southeastern France, commoners and liberal nobles were able to reach a compromise and work together in proposing a joint "regeneration" of the kingdom. In Brittany by contrast—on the opposite side of the kingdom—nobles and commoners literally came to blows, and the Third Estate concluded that no compromise was possible. During the same period in Paris a highly influential group of liberal aristocrats and a sprinkling of commoners began meeting—a "Committee of Thirty," as historians would dub them—to advocate a series of liberal reforms and attempt to influence the coming elections.[9]

The political awakening of the population was further intensified by the great flood of pamphlets published and circulating throughout the country. Stimulated by the exceptional events and by the king's apparent efforts to solicit their views—notably through the end of censorship—literate citizens everywhere began focusing their attention not only on finances but on a range of other problems besetting the state. They sorted through the great diversity of ideas that had emerged in the century and improvised new solutions to fit the circumstances, proposing their own plans for reform or offering commentaries on the plans of others. They applied themselves in much the same spirit of pragmatic reform—"daring to know"— that had moved citizens in previous years to propose solutions for poor relief or improved agriculture or street lighting.

A number of future Revolutionaries—like Faulcon, Gaultier de Biauzat, Robespierre, Jérôme Pétion, and Antoine Barnave—added their own contributions to the flurry of pamphlets. Many of their writings were not exceptionally radical, at least by the standards of the coming Revolution.[10] Yet almost all spoke of the necessity of expanding the influence of the Third Estate commoners. Increasingly, they also reflected on the need for some kind of written constitution and for filling government and church positions on the basis of talent rather than of ancestry. Many were also sharply critical of the aristocracy, even as they professed their praise and love for the king. Both Colson and Ruault, neither of whom penned pamphlets of their own, followed the debates with growing interest. Colson regularly stopped by the Palais Royal in central Paris to browse and sometimes to buy the latest publications, dozens of which were appearing on the shop stands every day.[11]

By late 1788 and 1789 a concerted opposition to such reform proposals was also beginning to emerge. Both the Parlement of Paris (in September 1788) and a second session of the Assembly of Notables (in December) supported an organization of the Estates General that would maintain a vote by order and the dominance of the aristocracy. Several nobles who had once supported liberal reform now reversed their positions and embraced a conservative backlash, frightened by the ever-more-radical positions of some members of the Third Estate. In late 1788 one such noble, Duval d'Eprémesnil, formed a reactionary "club" meeting in Paris, said to be frequented by a hundred or more nobles who actively promoted conservative candidates for the coming elections to the Estates General. This "Committee of a Hundred" was undoubtedly far more influential among the nobility of the nation than the liberal Committee of Thirty. Thus, by early 1789 a "patriot" party and an "aristocratic" party were already beginning to emerge, organized in sharp opposition to one another.[12]

The Creation of the National Assembly

The convocation of the Estates General finally got under way in March of 1789. In the end, the king and his council agreed that the number of deputies representing the Third Estate would indeed be "doubled," that they would equal the combined number of clerical and noble deputies.[13] Although the process was complex and differed substantially from region to region, it represented the broadest and most democratic election in European history. Within the Third Estate, any commoner who paid almost any amount of tax could take part. The elections were organized in several stages, so that those actually sent to the Estates General would have passed through three or even four successive electoral assemblies, an experience that served as further training in parliamentary procedures. In most cases, it was the best educated and most articulate members of the urban professional and commercial classes who ultimately won out. By contrast, the selection of noble deputies took place in a single stage and frequently led to the choice of the most prestigious aristocrats present. The successful use of fear tactics on the part of the conservatives greatly limited the number of liberal nobles dispatched to the Estates. As for the clerical deputies, most electoral assemblies were bitterly divided between the noble bishops and the commoner parish priests. But here too the electoral rules were remarkably democratic, so that some two-thirds of the clerical delegation to the Estates General would consist of simple parish clergymen.

At least as important as the election of deputies, however, was the provision that each assembly, at every stage in the process, should draw up a statement of grievances or *cahier de doléances*. The practice itself was not new and had been a part of the process in centuries past. But in the present circumstances, in the midst of the municipal mobilization and the pamphlet campaign, it encouraged citizens everywhere to take stock of their situation. There were public debates not only on the problems of state finances but on a whole array of social and economic issues that people encountered in their daily lives. Some assemblies relied heavily on "model *cahiers*," brochures circulated in the provinces to encourage people to transcend local issues and consider broader, more "liberal" proposals. In the end, especially among the Third Estate, the *cahiers* process generated soaring expectations, as people began dreaming that many of their hopes—some long held, others only just "discovered"—might actually be realized.

The Estates General formally began on May 4, as a thousand elected deputies from the Clergy, the Nobility, and the Third Estate paraded through the streets of Versailles, the royal capital some fifteen kilometers to the west of Paris. Not all of the representatives had yet arrived. Some—like those from the city of Paris—remained to be elected, and others were still making their way from distant corners of the kingdom and from far-flung French colonies around the world. But in the cultural language of eighteenth-century France, the ordered procession of the deputies present—most of them bedecked in the appropriate dress of their estate—symbolized the unity of France and the hope for a new order in which all elements of society might participate. Almost everyone who described the scene that day waxed poetic. "Perhaps nothing of its kind," wrote Ménard de la Groye, "has ever surpassed the magnificence of this imposing ceremony, admired by all the world as the most beautiful ever to have shown on the face of France."[14]

Few of those present could have predicted the events that would transpire during the tumultuous weeks that followed.[15] Indeed, historians sometimes wonder how the representatives of the Third Estate became so radical so rapidly. In part the representatives' views had already been profoundly transformed by two years of debates in pamphlets and in various provincial and electoral assemblies. It was out of this experience, no doubt, that the commoner deputies quickly adopted the strategy of refusing even to confirm their credentials or to organize their sessions until the representatives of all three orders agreed to sit in the same room and vote by head. They were also encouraged in such a position by the actions, or rather the inaction, of the king. Louis had still failed to make a decision on how the deputies were to vote, probably because his advisers were themselves in disagreement. There was also no clear conception as to what the Estates might and could accomplish. In theory, they remained a consultative body, conceived to support the tax reforms proposed by the government. After two years of debates, however, a great many Third Estate deputies had come to view the body as empowered to go far beyond the discussion of fiscal questions. If the king had stepped in early in the process and had given the deputies specific instructions, it is possible that the majority would have accepted some kind of negotiated compromise. Yet the king long refrained from intervening in any meaningful way, and the commoners came to the conclusion that the good monarch wanted them to debate the issues and reach conclusions on their own. Left to their own devices, many members of the Third drifted toward ever-more-radical positions.

This radicalization grew, moreover, through the very situation in which the Third Estate deputies found themselves. They were irritated with the deputies of the Nobility, not only because of their refusal to consider any form of compromise but also because of their haughty and contemptuous attitude whenever the commoners encountered them. This perception of arrogance only further crystallized the impatience of the Third Estate toward aristocrats and aristocratic privilege in general. The Third's attitude was also affected by the treatment they received from the general population among whom they lived. The people of Paris and of Versailles had been intensely politicized by the ongoing electoral assemblies, the public readings of pamphlets, and the informal debates unrolling throughout the city. Men and women ostentatiously supported the commoner deputies, embracing them in the streets, offering them flowers while they sat in cafés; cheering and urging them forward as they deliberated in their hall. With no armed forces at their disposal, relying only on the strength of their principles, the Third Estate readily accepted the people's support. All of their meetings were open to the public—in sharp contrast to the secret sessions of the Nobility and the Clergy. "Those voting," as one deputy wrote, "had to draw their energy and their purity from the opinions and attendance of the public."[16] It was a first instance of the elite's reliance on the popular classes, a trend that was to have a long and complex history during the Revolution.

The early days in Versailles also represented an intense intellectual experience for the Third Estate deputies. The initially chaotic meetings—with representatives milling about the hall or standing on chairs to give improvised speeches—gradually became more ordered. Despite their original opposition to any kind of organization, it soon became necessary to appoint a president and to assume some semblance of parliamentary procedure. By late May and early June, the Third entered into a series of passionate debates over the purpose of the Estates General and the objectives they should be seeking. Several of the deputies were gifted orators, and they began to share ideas, playing off one another, learning from one another, while the less articulate members listened with rapt attention. In their correspondence to friends and family, many individuals conveyed the power of the arguments they heard and the extent to which they were swayed toward more radical positions from one day to the next. Deputies described the meetings as a didactic experience, as a veritable "school of Revolution."[17]

As early as May 20 a small group of radicals in the Third Estate, led by the deputies from Brittany, proposed summoning the other two estates to join with them in a common meeting; if the others did not appear, it was argued, the Third should proceed on its own without them. At the time, the proposal was massively rejected in favor of continuing negotiations with the Nobility and Clergy in the hope of reaching a compromise. But in early June, after a month of inaction and faced with both growing popular pressure and the persistent intransigence of the Nobility, a majority of the Third was persuaded—partly through a speech by Abbé Sieyès—to return to the Breton proposal. A formal roll-call was read in the hall of the Third Estate on June 10, calling out the names of all of the deputies in all three estates. In fact, only three clergymen broke ranks and joined with the commoners for the roll-call. On June 17, following lengthy debates, the Third deputies unilaterally converted themselves into a sovereign "National Assembly." Equally dramatic, they declared that all former taxes were illegal—although they would be maintained temporarily until a new fiscal system could be put in place. The two declarations, both of which would have been unimaginable to the majority only a few weeks earlier, were now accepted with near universal assent. The representatives sealed their decision with an oath, vowing in the name of God, the king, and the nation to faithfully fulfill their functions as representatives of the nation. On June 19 a majority of the Clergy, dominated by the contingent of commoner parish clergymen, voted to leave their hall and sit jointly with the new National Assembly.

Reactionary nobles had long urged the monarch to take a hard line and coerce cooperation from the Third Estate. Faced with the unprecedented declarations of June 17 and the Clergy's decision of June 19, the conservatives were finally able to shake Louis into action. The king agreed to return in person and make a formal declaration to the "three estates." In the meantime, the hall of the National Assembly was locked, supposedly to rearrange the room for the king's appearance. On June 20, stunned and outraged at being closed out of their hall, and cheered on by the crowds following their every action, the deputies migrated down the street to an indoor tennis court. There they swore a second and far more sweeping oath, never to disband as an assembly, even if they were forced to meet elsewhere, until they had drawn up a new constitution and fulfilled their obligations to the nation.

In the "Royal Session" of June 23, Louis XVI adopted almost all of the positions of the conservative nobles, rejecting the existence of a "National Assembly," commanding a vote by order on most questions, forbidding the Estates from touching any of the rights and privileges of the Nobility without their consent, and threatening to dissolve the assembly if the Third rejected his commands. Although all of the deputies were then ordered to leave the meeting hall, the commoner deputies, by previous agreement, remained in their seats. Gilbert Romme, who was watching from the galleries, described the scene: "Sorrow and dejection, tempered by admirable courage, filled every heart and was painted on every face."[18] In a series of rousing speeches, several of the assembly's most powerful orators—Mirabeau, Barnave, Sieyès, Camus—now declared that not even the king could disband a National Assembly and that the deputies must remain true to their previous oaths. They then voted themselves parliamentary immunity: anyone attempting to arrest them or disperse them would be guilty of a capital offense. It was yet another dramatic revolutionary escalation.

We know from their private correspondence that a great many deputies were anxious and uncertain by this turn of events and by the apparent opposition of the king. Once outside their meeting hall and beyond the brave words of Mirabeau and the others, they were beset by doubts and fears. They liked to believe that Louis had been misled and badly advised and that he would eventually understand the "desires of the nation," but many wondered if they would not do better under the circumstances to accept the king's "compromise." Yet the new National Assembly received enthusiastic approval from a number of other sources. Everywhere they went, as

The Tennis Court Oath, June 20, 1789, by which deputies of the new National Assembly vowed to write a Constitution. This celebrated depiction by Jacques-Louis David well illustrates the spirit of '89 and the extraordinary fervor with which patriots supported the Revolutionary changes. The president Bailly stands on a table to administer the oath. One can distinguish the abbé Sieyès, sitting just beneath Bailly; Mirabeau (right foreground, in a dark coat, striding forward); Barnave (just behind Mirabeau); Robespierre (right of center, baring his breast with his two hands); Pétion in front of Robespierre with his back turned; Barère (sitting at left, writing his newspaper); and the trio of the Protestant Rabaut Saint-Etienne, the priest Grégoire, and the monk Dom Gerle (center foreground). Engraved by Jazet, © Coll. Musée de la Révolution française, Domaine de Vizille, MRF 1988.48.

delegations or as individuals, the deputies continued to be cheered and feted by the general population of Paris and Versailles. The clerical deputies who had voted to join with them on June 19 never relinquished their support and persisted in meeting with them in the Versailles church where they had taken refuge after their hall had been locked. And then, on June 25, forty-seven liberal nobles, following a night of soul searching, also abandoned their order and began sitting with the National Assembly. Many of them came from the greatest aristocratic families of the realm, and as they entered the hall, each was introduced separately and welcomed by an explosion of applause and emotion.

It was only on the afternoon of June 27, however, that all of the elected deputies from all three orders were finally convened together. Shifting his position once again, the king now ordered the dissident Nobility and Clergy to sit in the combined assembly. Louis persisted in referring to the deputies as the "Estates General." And many of the nobles and clergymen compelled to sit with the commoners seethed with unforgiving rage—some even leaving Versailles to demand the approval of their "constituencies" or to abandon the assembly altogether. But for the majority of the deputies and for most of the nation looking on, it seemed like a great victory. Jean-Sylvain Bailly, the president of the new National Assembly, called for a two-day adjournment, and the populations of Paris and the surrounding villages and towns gave themselves over to an enthusiastic celebration. For many observers, it seemed that the revolution was over—and indeed, a number of journalists and deputies now began for the first time to use the word "Revolution" to describe the events that had transpired. When the deputies returned they would elect a committee to begin formulating a constitution, a constitution that most believed could be drafted quite rapidly.

The Revolution, however, was far from over. The patriots liked to tell themselves that the king had reversed his position because he had finally understood the just demands of the nation. But in retrospect, there is evidence that the king was still under the influence of conservative advisers and that the decision of June 27 was only a ploy, allowing him to play for time while a military coup was organized. Within a week everyone was aware that large numbers of mercenary troops—most of them German-speaking—were being concentrated around Paris and Versailles. And then, on July 11, there was the frightening news that Jacques Necker and the other liberal members of the king's council had all been dismissed and replaced by archconservatives. Whatever the king and his advisers had in mind—and historians continue to debate Louis' motives—the revolutionary dynamic would now turn ineluctably toward violence.[19]

The Violence of '89

In fact, outbreaks of violence had beset the nation during much of the previous year. In the beginning the troubles could be traced to a series of meteorological accidents which directly coincided—through a strange course of fate—to the period of the Pre-Revolution. On July 13, 1788, just as the king was summoning the Estates General, a terrible series of storms swept across northern France. A combination of high winds and hail, a veritable "hurricane," as people described it, flattened much of the ripening wheat and left it rotting in the fields. In some areas the grain harvest was thought to have been reduced by a third or more, a disastrous situation in a society in which bread represented such a large proportion of the diet. Colson quickly realized the extent of the disaster and the potential effects for the political stability of the country: "We fear there may be riots," he wrote in early August, "over the impending rise in the price of bread." And he reported rumors that large numbers of troops were being brought into the Parisian area to protect against the anticipated unrest. By autumn the price of bread in Paris and in most of France was already rising rapidly.[20]

But the situation was made immensely worse by the harrowing winter of 1788–1789, which may well have been the coldest of the eighteenth century: "without example in human memory," as one woman in Alsace described it.[21] For some seven weeks, from late November through the second week in January, the cold was particularly intense. By the end of December three feet of snow lay on the ground in Champagne, the Loire River had three to four feet of ice, and rivers all over France—the Seine, the Saône, the Rhône—were frozen solid. Fruit trees split open from the cold, vineyards were badly damaged or killed, and wine bottles froze and exploded in people's cellars. The ice on the Seine not only blocked all transportation of grain for over forty days but halted the functioning of mills for grinding the grain already available. As Gilbert Romme traveled to Paris in December, he was reminded of the winters in northern Russia, which he had only just left. To make matters worse, fountains also froze in many of the cities, and it became difficult to obtain water for drinking and cooking. When a thaw finally began in late January, great blocks of floating ice ripped out mills and bridges and riverside factories and caused widespread flooding. In some areas the winter wheat was said to have been "totally destroyed." It was feared that the spring crops would germinate later than usual, postponing the normal harvest and causing further upward pressure on bread prices.[22]

Amateur scholars scoured the archives to find records of worse winters at any time in French history. Thousands died of the cold or the induced hunger: "the most horrible famine that men have ever seen," as a canon in Troyes described it. Sickness born of the cold was pervasive in Paris: "Everywhere," wrote Colson, "we hear the sad symphony of coughing."[23]

But at least as bad as the real famine was the fear of impending famine. Rumors spread of wealthy merchants or bakers hoarding grain to capitalize on the disaster and push up their profits. By midwinter, as prices continued to rise, grain revolts began breaking out in towns and rural areas almost everywhere. In Berry, Lemaigre reported a constant fear of violence incited by bread prices. In Rouen, crowds had "declared war" on bakers whose shops were openly raided. Spreading through fear, spreading through rumors of hoarding, spreading through neighboring examples, hundreds of food riots, large and small, exploded across the country. Sometimes the rioters turned against specific groups in society—the nobles or the clergy, for example. But for the most part, the uprisings were focused on the problem of food, of finding sufficient quantities of grain and of compelling merchants and bakers to sell it at a "fair price." One historian has described the rioting that winter and spring as constituting the greatest wave of subsistence violence in the eighteenth century and perhaps in all French history.[24]

Everywhere people worried about the large numbers of poor and hungry roaming the countryside looking for something to eat. Robber bands or "brigands" were said to be circulating in rural areas, preying on the countrypeople through theft and extortion. There were stories—some no doubt true, some not—of ragged strangers announcing that a peasant's barn or grain supply might suddenly catch fire if the beggars were not fed or given money. "We're assaulted here from every direction by brigands," wrote Lemaigre in central France in December 1788. By April and May there were small-scale panics in some parts of the country, with rumors spreading of bands of "brigands" on the move, stealing and burning and raping as they went. In the face of such unrest the royal government created a system of exceptional courts without appeal, conceived to streamline the prosecution of rioters, courts that would prefigure in some respects the Revolutionary Tribunals of 1792 to 1794.[25]

From April through June there was a relative lull in the rioting.[26] The election of the Estates General and the drafting of local statements of grievances brought even many of the most humble citizens into the political process, and everywhere people were waiting with high expectations for the results of the assembly in Versailles. But as meetings of the Estates General dragged on without results, and as grain prices peaked at the highest levels of the century, the increasingly volatile mixture of anticipation and fear set everyone's nerves on edge. In July and August rebellions and panics would explode throughout the kingdom, bringing waves of violence even worse than in the spring, unlike anything in France since the seventeenth century.

For the political elites of the nation gathered in Versailles, the most immediate and threatening acts of violence were those occurring in Paris itself. The city had been relatively quiet in the years immediately preceding the Revolution, and there had been no major collective uprisings since 1775. Yet no population was more directly attuned to political events than the Parisians. Long years of religious turmoil between Jansenists and anti-Jansenists and decades of well-publicized struggles between the Parlement of Paris and the monarchy had left the citizens of the city suspicious of authority and in some cases prepared to criticize the king himself. All observers agreed, moreover, on the Parisians' propensity for violence, especially among males of the artisan and working classes.[27]

Within weeks after the "hurricane" of July 1788, small grain riots had broken out in parts of Paris—much as Colson had feared—although the massing of the military in and around the city seems to have cowed the population through the spring of the following year. But an event arising out of the elections for the Estates General in Paris—organized over a month later than in the rest of the country—produced a major revolt at the end of April 1789. The errant words of two of the electors, misinterpreted and misrepresented through the city's rumor mill—and supposedly mocking the subsistence problems of the common people—brought hundreds of men and women into the streets in the always restless Saint-Antoine neighborhood on the eastern edge of Paris. The attack on the house of the elector Réveillon led to the deaths of several soldiers and of dozens—and perhaps hundreds—of the rioters themselves, killed at the time or in the harsh repression that followed.[28]

Throughout the months of May and June the citizens of Paris closely followed the debates in Versailles and experienced much the same fluctuations of emotions as the deputies themselves. With the massing of mercenary troops around Paris in the first weeks of July and the rumors of an impending attack against both the National Assembly and the city, and with the continuing increases in the price of bread, anxieties became almost unbearable. In nearly every letter, Colson reported frightening rumors, with stories that bread would soon entirely run out and that civil war could begin any day.[29]

On the morning of July 12 the news of the dismissal of Necker and of the formation of an archconservative ministry sparked widespread turmoil in the city. Parisians feared for the future of the new National Assembly, but they were perhaps even more frightened by the threat of armed invasions of their neighborhoods. Anticipating an attack, men barricaded their streets at night and women dug up paving stones and carried them to the rooftops, so they could bombard enemy soldiers if they should appear. Roving bands of people, some of them led by radical elites, attacked military contingents in the city. They also launched a variety of uncoordinated attacks on customs stations and against various individuals and convents thought to be hoarding grain. On several occasions royal troops sent to halt the uprisings mutinied and came to the support of the people they were ordered to repress, "remaining deaf to the orders of their commander," as Romme described it. Finally, after a day of seething violence, "bourgeois" leaders, who had continued to meet in the city's electoral assemblies, took steps to halt the descent into chaos. Pushing aside the Old Regime officials whom they no longer trusted, they took control of the Parisian government, effecting a veritable municipal revolution. At the same time they began reorganizing and greatly expanding the city's "bourgeois" militia, creating a citizens' guard to keep order in the streets.[30]

Then, on the afternoon of July 14, semiorganized groups of Parisians found themselves in open battle against the Bastille, the medieval fortress with its eight massive stone towers near the eastern edge of the city. The action began as a peaceful appeal by citizens for arms and ammunition to defend themselves. But the nervous soldiers manning the fortress opened fire on the people in the courtyard below. Soon several hundred artisans, shopkeepers, and minor officials, armed with makeshift weapons, entered into a full-scale firefight. At a critical moment the people were assisted by a group of professional soldiers who arrived on the scene, some of whom positioned a cannon in front of the inner drawbridge. In this situation, the commander of the fortress decided to surrender.[31]

The fall of the Bastille did not, however, lead to an end of the violence. Close to a hundred Parisians had been killed at the foot of the fortress in what seemed for all the world like an ambush, and there were widespread cries for revenge.[32] The commander and several of the defending soldiers were killed, along with the former political leader of the city—the *prévôt des marchands*. Colson, who lived nearby, was convinced of the treachery of the soldiers who had defended the Bastille, and he readily justified the killings. In any case, the heads of several victims were paraded through

Attack on the Bastille, July 14, 1789. French citizens and patriotic soldiers attack the drawbridge of the Bastille from the inner courtyard, as they are fired on from above by defenders on the ramparts. Over a hundred people were killed. Jean-François Jainet, © Coll. Musée de la Révolution française, Domaine de Vizille, MRF 1988.117.

the streets on the end of pikes—the razor-sharp pole-like weapons originally devised for a defense against cavalry. Other suspicious enemies, as well as suspected looters, received similar treatment. Romme summarized the events: "Any individual who was suspected was immediately led away to the city hall and, if he was found guilty, executed. Armed pillage was punished on the spot with a bullet through the head."[33] There was also a growing mistrust of all nobles in Paris, nobles widely suspected of having plotted an attack against the National Assembly and Paris. They were forbidden to leave the city, and many retreated in terror to their residences. The rumors of ambush, the popular demands for just revenge, the merging of fear and anger were patterns of behavior to be repeated on a number of occasions in the coming years.

All these events were followed with growing anxiety by the deputies in Versailles some twenty kilometers from the city. No one was certain of the objectives of the crowds or the extent to which the violence could be contained by the new municipal leaders. Yet everything seemed to change on the morning of July 15, when the king, accompanied only by his two brothers and a small contingent of troops, suddenly appeared in the deputies' hall. Equally uncertain of the events in Paris and unnerved by the growing number of mutinies among royal troops, Louis now announced his acceptance of the "National Assembly," with whom he vowed to work for the salvation of the nation. Necker was recalled to his post as minister, and two days later the king traveled into Paris to be welcomed by its citizens with thundering ovations. Within the Assembly itself, those noble deputies who had boycotted the meetings after June 27 declared that they too were ready to cooperate. With such a turn of events, most of the patriot elites came to condone the violence of July 14 as a regrettable necessity, imagining that the Parisians had been motivated solely by the desire to save the National Assembly.

The problem was that the violence persisted, even after the king had embraced the Revolution. Particularly mystifying to the patriot deputies was the popular torture and murder on July 22 of the royal official Foulon and his son-in-law, the intendant of Paris, Berthier de Sauvigny—both rumored to have been involved in grain-hoarding schemes. Those who witnessed the event on the square adjoining the city hall were appalled by the "atrocious and barbarous acts," the "unimaginable refinements of cruelty"—during which both men were decapitated and Foulon's heart was cut out and carried into the council chambers.[34] The radical journalist Prudhomme, who had previously glorified the events of July with breathless enthusiasm, now struggled to understand and explain the continuing violence. In the wake of the "tumult of revolutions," he wrote, "the national character has disappeared, and a normally kind and amiable people has become ferocious and barbarous." And he appealed to his fellow citizens: "Frenchmen . . . your hatred is dreadful and appalling. . . . Your executions are an outrage to humanity and make nature itself shudder."[35]

Yet even as the patriots struggled to confront the violence in Paris, chaos and anarchy seemed to be spreading across the whole of France.[36] People in the provinces had initially received only confused and fragmented accounts of the attack on the Bastille, an attack that seemed threatening and terrifying. Wild rumors began spreading of possible harm done to the king and queen, and of brigands and bandits being chased from Paris and heading for the countryside. Romme himself—and no doubt other Parisians as well—contributed to the rumors when he announced to his friends in central France that armed vagabonds had been expelled by the Parisian national guard and were scattering across the countryside, spreading terror to many other regions.[37] In Paris and in a few other towns of northern France, rumors also spread that great bands of "brigands"—bands who in fact never existed—were being paid by the nobility to destroy the ripening grain crops—all as part of an aristocratic conspiracy to destroy the Revolution and punish the people. In most of the kingdom, however, it was the overwhelming fear of the collapse of authority and of roving bandits attacking homes and villages—*not* of an aristocratic conspiracy—that set off one of the most extraordinary mass panics in history, known to contemporaries and to historians since as the "Great Fear."

There had been talk for months of the threat of criminal bands, and sometimes during the spring of 1789 stories of approaching "brigands" had sparked local alarms. But in late July and August a series of chain-reaction panics, moving from village to village, from town to town, swirled and crisscrossed over hundreds of kilometers, ultimately affecting nearly three-fourths of the kingdom. One wave of fear, descending from the north, even entered Paris itself, with rumors coursing through neighborhoods of marauding brigands attacking the northern suburbs of Saint-Denis and the Champs-Elysées. In some instances the terror led to the hysterical flight of men, women, and children into nearby woods or caves or to the nearest town. There were numerous reports of miscarriages among pregnant women, traumatized by the rumors. But in other cases, local people did their best to organize a defense, arming themselves with whatever they could find, throwing up impromptu barricades, or even marching out to confront the imagined attackers. Particularly in the towns, citizens sought to establish local militias for their protection. Often they also took steps to replace or reorganize their municipal governments, deemed incompetent or unpatriotic. There was thus a wave of "municipal revolutions," sometimes in direct imitation of the events in Paris, and more or less violent depending on local personalities and circumstances. But in most cases, all social groups in the community initially drew together in an attempt to stop the spreading chaos, with the new urban leaders and militia officers chosen from local nobles and clergymen as well as from commoners.

Yet not all regions of the kingdom knew such social solidarity. In addition to the chain-reaction panics, seven smaller zones were touched by violent peasant uprisings, uprisings that were sometimes linked to the Great Fear but that usually developed independently. In parts of lower Normandy, Hainaut, Alsace, Franche-Comté, Mâconnais, Dauphiné, and Vivarais, thousands of rural people, impelled by a diversity of local grievances, rose up in rebellion. The target of choice was usually the nobility, and dozens of chateaus were attacked and sometimes burned, as the countrypeople sought to punish hated individual lords or even to destroy the seigneurial system altogether. In some cases uprisings were instigated by rumors that the king himself had ordered the people to attack the nobility. But the insurgents could also threaten any or all of those groups who had oppressed them in the past. Local clergy, tax collectors, royal administrators, municipal officers, Jews, owners of small factories, or middle-class landlords and money lenders: all might find themselves under attack, depending on the local region and the social situation.[38]

Exhilaration and Anxiety

The deputies of the National Assembly—as municipal leaders throughout the country—agonized over how they might bring a halt to the violence and anarchy spreading across the kingdom. Just as people in the provinces were often misinformed and confused by the events in Paris, so too the patriot leaders in Versailles had great difficulty discovering what was actually taking place in the countryside. From the beginning there was a tendency to conflate the panic of the Great Fear with the peasant rebellions, so that many concluded the whole nation was in a state of insurrection. The great debates in late July and early August over how to end the chaos—whether through repression or appeasement or some combination of both—deeply divided the deputies and led to the emergence of a first major factional divide among the patriots. In the end, the view that conciliation was the best means of bringing peace to the nation was a major factor in the spectacular decrees voted on the evening of August 4.

Already at the beginning of August a certain number of radicals had begun discussing the possibility of reducing or abolishing some of the more onerous seigneurial dues and obligations.[39] During the night of August 3 a plan was developed by members of the so-called Breton Club, the informal group of liberal deputies from various provinces meeting with the delegation from Brittany. A liberal noble would step before the Assembly and offer to renounce the seigneurial dues owed to him personally.

Three other commoner deputies would then promote the idea and paint the evils of the seigneurial system in general. But once the maneuver had been executed in the evening session of August 4, the whole Assembly seemed swept away by an "electric whirlwind" of generosity—as Mirabeau put it. Numerous deputies rushed forward to propose additional suppressions of a whole range of Old Regime institutions. Not only all of the seigneurial dues but seigneurial courts, the lords' hunting rights, the salt tax and other excise taxes, venality of office, the royal administrative system, the clerical tithes, and plurality of benefices were all swept away. Perhaps equally important were the renunciations of provincial and municipal privileges of all kinds, with the assumption that every French citizen would henceforth share in the same equal rights. Moved by fear, moved by generosity, moved by a sentiment of national fraternity—moved no doubt by all at once—nobles, clergymen, and commoners, both radicals and conservatives, participated in this hecatomb of Old Regime institutions and privileges.[40] Toward two o'clock in the morning, at the end of the epic session, sixteen articles of renunciations were drawn up and accepted by acclamation.

In fact, many of the most dramatic "suppressions" would be implemented only during a transitional period of more than a year. And despite the deputies' declaration that they had "abolished feudalism," a number of the seigneurial rights would still be considered as "property," and the peasants would be required to purchase their freedom at a substantial cost. Yet the thrill and inspiration of the moment cannot be underestimated. The journalist Prudhomme painted the scene in Paris, when people first heard word of the August 4 decrees. Everywhere, on all the major streets and bridges, groups of citizens began gathering and talking and shouting out the news to passersby. "The exhilaration of joy spread quickly to every heart. We congratulated one another. And in our enthusiasm, we christened our deputies 'the Fathers of the Country.' It seemed as though a new day was breaking over France. . . . Everywhere there were feelings of fraternity, sweet fraternity." When Gaultier de Biauzat tried to write home, he found he was "at a loss to express to you the grandeur and the beauty" of what had just transpired. He wished, he said, that he had the powers of a poet.[41]

Just two weeks later the National Assembly took up the issue of a general declaration of rights within the new regime. The debates were far more arduous and contentious, however, than on August 4, and they would drag on for almost a week. While the majority of deputies agreed on many of the fundamental "rights of man," a number of nobles and clergymen were convinced they must add a "declaration of duties," and an amendment to that effect was defeated by only a slim margin. The representatives also wrangled at length over the precise wording of several of the articles. The most controversial concerned religious toleration, whether Catholicism should be considered the official state religion, and whether Protestants and Jews should be treated as equals. In the end, the whole question was left ambiguous—"none should be troubled because of their opinions, even religious"—in a decision that pleased neither liberals nor conservatives. At the time several of the formulations were considered to be temporary compromises to be reconsidered at a later date, when the Assembly was not preoccupied with so many other pressing issues. Nevertheless, the "Declaration of the Rights of Man and the Citizen" rapidly came to be treated as a second foundation document of the Revolution, honored with reverence by all good patriots.

In their scholarly analysis of causes and effects, of personalities and alliances, of movements and countermovements, historians writing about 1789 sometimes overlook the extraordinary emotional experience of those who lived through such events. Whether they directly participated in the Assembly or followed its achievements at second hand, contemporaries were exuberant with joy and amazement. Letters written during the summer of 1789 were filled with a kaleidoscope of impressions, scraps of images and memories jotted down pell-mell, as observers struggled to understand and describe their emotions. "Future generations," wrote Dr. Campmas, "will find it difficult to believe the events of this year." They were in awe that they achieved so much so rapidly, and numerous witnesses drew on the metaphor of eons of time compressed into days. The month of July, as one observer put it, "contained the events of an entire century." Dominique Garat was quite overwhelmed. "It was scarcely two years ago," he said, "that we first began hearing those extraordinary and moving words, 'individual liberty,' 'national liberty,' 'constitution.' And during those two years, so many events have pressed one upon another, so many revolutionary new insights have emerged among us, that one might say whole ages have gone by."[42]

The Night of August 4 and the Declaration of Rights seemed all the more amazing in that hardly anyone had anticipated them. To be sure, during

the previous century virtually all of the individual elements of those decrees had been proposed by one writer or another, at one time or another.
But before that summer few of the future Revolutionaries had even imagined that the totality of such changes was a real possibility. The declarations of the National Assembly went far beyond the demands of the great
majority of the French population, as expressed in their statements of grievances just five months earlier. Brissot wrote of "this totally unexpected
event"; Prudhomme of "this unforeseen blessing." For Ruault, it was as if
they suddenly awoke to find that "woodcutters had brought down an entire forest in a few hours." As Garat remembered it several years later, it
was only in the summer of 1789 that "I began to hope . . . that ideas, which
up until then had seemed only the stuff of dreams, could actually be realized on earth."[43]

Many were convinced that the transformations they were witnessing
could have been effected only by divine intervention. "All that has transpired," wrote the deputy Théodore Vernier in August, "is clearly the effect
of Providence."[44] When news of the recent decrees arrived in the provinces, local leaders ordered special church ceremonies in which the clergy
intoned the *Te Deum,* the traditional liturgy of thanksgiving offered up to
Heaven. Elsewhere there were collective oathtaking ceremonies, with citizens, men and women, making a solemn religious pledge to adhere to all
the National Assembly's decrees. The waves of oathtaking not only reinforced the new bonds of citizenship uniting the population but also served
as a powerful symbol of the transfer of sovereignty to the community as a
whole.[45]

Numerous witnesses returned repeatedly in their letters to the image of
a new age and a new man to emerge from the extraordinary events of that
summer. "Now everything will change," wrote Ruault in late July, "morals,
opinions, laws, customs, administration. Soon we will all be new men."
Romme elaborated at length on the novelty of the new conception of the
state. While virtually all other governments were based on "force, ambition, and ignorance," the French "want to create a regime founded on reason
and justice, as the sole guarantees of liberty and the natural rights of man."
And he described how the events of the Revolution had come to totally
dominate their lives: "It so utterly captures our attention and absorbs our
time, that any other activity has become almost impossible."[46] There was
no better example of the transformative power of emotion in a time of revolution, pushing events forward further and faster than anyone could have

imagined only a few months earlier. For a great many people, the experience that summer and the ensuing commitment to the new system of political values had all the impact and power of a religious conversion, with much the same intensity of commitment as in the Protestant Reformation 250 years earlier.

In the generosity of the moment, many Revolutionaries urged patience and tolerance for those fellow citizens—the nobles and the upper clergy in particular—who were obviously having difficulty accepting the new system of values, the ethos of liberty and equality that was integral to the "new man." Both Jacques Brissot and the marquis de Lafayette promoted clemency for all those who had previously opposed the Revolution. In the Assembly patriot deputies supported reconciliation and fraternity, and many were hopeful that with time, the recalcitrant nobles could be convinced to "renounce the prejudices of their education." Throughout the month of July they encouraged the noble and clerical deputies to participate in Assembly debates. As one gentleman recalled, "for the time being the orators of the Third Estate yielded up the rostrum; the nobles, they said, should be allowed to speak their mind." Similar policies might also be advocated by provincial leaders. Antoine-Claire Thibaudeau underscored the speech of a local patriot in Poitiers: "Citizen nobles, your minds have temporarily gone astray, but your hearts have not. You will lose nothing in the Revolution."[47]

Yet the patience and forbearance of the patriot Revolutionaries were not unlimited. There were bounds beyond which negotiation and compromise would always be unacceptable. Having once tasted the new system of liberty and equality, they could no longer abide the return to an authoritarian government or a hierarchical society based on birth. If they rapidly grew impatient and intolerant with the opposition, their intolerance came from their fervent belief that the values in question were necessary for the new society they had come to envision and that patriots must be prepared to do whatever necessary to save the Revolution and preserve those gains. This was the spirit in which French men and women everywhere would soon begin swearing an oath to "Live free or die!"

Indeed, throughout 1789 and throughout much of the Revolution the exuberant enthusiasm for change and the hopes for the future were always bound together with fear and anxiety: fear of the chaos generated by Revolution, fear of the potential for revenge by those whose special rank and privileges had been stripped away by the sweeping transformations.

The uneasiness and anxiety for the future had already been evident on the eve of the Estates General. In March of 1789 Colson had shared his apprehensions with his friend in Berry: "France," he wrote, "is faced with a future that could be either extraordinarily fortunate or extraordinarily unfortunate. Not in the last ten centuries has there been such a crisis, a crisis that before the end of the year will either raise the nation to the summit of power and grandeur, or reduce her to utter calamity and destruction."[48]

As the summer progressed and as the waves of panic and violence touched nearly every province of the country, the anxiety and volatility became even more intense. By August it was evident to almost everyone that the absolute monarchy had crumbled and that the nation was faced with a veritable interregnum until new political and administrative structures could be established in the place of the old. Ruault returned to this theme again and again, despite all his enthusiasm for the political changes and the "new man" that he hoped would emerge: "The most difficult is having simultaneously to tear down and rebuild on the same terrain; during the interval one must live in the street or under a tent. This is what happens with the collapse of all power and all royal authority." In late August Rosalie Jullien poured out her anxiety to her husband, who was away on business in southern France: "We are pushed about by so many currents, we are agitated by such diverse passions . . . that it is like whirlwinds rushing and colliding in a violent storm."[49] The crisis of power and authority, the fear of incipient anarchy were to continue for many long months and lead to a whole range of problems for the Revolution and the Revolutionaries.

The October Days

During the months of August and September the tensions and threats of violence only slowly abated. Although the peak of the turmoil had occurred in July, the reverberations of the Great Fear and the peasant uprisings continued to unsettle the countryside well into the autumn, with several mini-panics and new sightings of "brigands" recorded in various parts of the kingdom.[50] In early August Colson's colleague in Berry, the local agent for the noble family they both served, was threatened by the peasants and had to be placed in protective custody. In September there were reports of continued rioting in Châteauroux, Vierzon, and Orléans. And there was seemingly unending agitation in Paris itself, as a series of bread riots and labor protests broke out. Members of the Revolutionary municipal government were threatened, and rumors circulated of a plan to lynch Lafayette, the commander of the new national guard. There were newspaper stories of bands of aristocrats pouring into the city, some said to be plotting to kidnap the king and launch a counterrevolution. Fears of grain shortages were also rising once again. Colson, Ruault, Jullien, and many of the National Assembly deputies in Versailles all commented on the difficulties of finding bread. One had to line up at the bakery by four o'clock in the morning in order to obtain a loaf. The bread sold was of such poor quality that many complained it was making them ill, and the city was forced to mobilize the national guard to protect the bakers. In mid-September, Colson participated in a special forty-hour prayer session in his parish church, beseeching God for a return of peace and prosperity to the city and the kingdom.[51]

In the midst of such concerns, a crucial debate was unrolling in the National Assembly over the powers to be given to the king in the new Constitution.[52] Led by Joseph Mounier and many of his colleagues from the province of Dauphiné, a group of moderates began advocating strong royal authority to hold the nation together, a government in which the king would hold an absolute veto over any laws voted by the legislature. The coalition—known to historians as the "Monarchiens"—developed the most highly organized political block in the Assembly, with regular evening meetings to determine strategy and maintain voting discipline. Soon the group had attracted a following among the more moderate members of the clergy and nobility, and an alliance with certain reactionary nobles who sought to exploit the democratic process to defeat the radicals at their own game. The lengthy debate between those who urged an absolute veto and those who advocated no veto at all finally ended in the compromise of a "suspensive veto." Yet such an arrangement potentially allowed the king to block laws for up to six years, leaving many deputies angry and disgruntled. The whole issue was even more disconcerting for the "Left" of the Assembly in that Louis had still never formally accepted the August 4 decrees or the Declaration of Rights.[53]

The factional confrontations in the Assembly were yet another cause of the continued unrest in Paris. Throughout August and September crowds gathered daily at the Palais Royal in central Paris, where they were harangued by various self-appointed speakers standing on tables to make themselves heard. Attacks were leveled not only against the aristocrats but against the Monarchiens as well, with some demanding a purge of all those deputies supporting a royal veto. At the end of August, the radicals in the Palais Royal even attempted a march on Versailles to convey their views to the king and the Assembly—although the movement was quickly blocked by Lafayette and units of the national guard.

However, the idea of such a march continued to be discussed by the Parisians. Passions were aggravated with reports of a reception in the king's palace, in which aristocratic officers in the presence of the queen had insulted the Revolutionary symbol of the "cocarde"—the tricolor target-like badge now worn by all patriots. On the morning of October 5, upset by the recent events in Versailles and tired of standing in bread lines, several hundred Parisian women began mobilizing. Colson saw them walking through the street below his window, laughing and mocking the men who watched them pass by, men who readily teased them in return. Mercier too underscored the carnival-like atmosphere: "It would be difficult to imagine the exuberance, the turbulence, the comic exhilaration . . . the cries, the noise, the picture of an ancient saturnalia." But the women displayed anger and violence as well as wit. Many of them were ostentatiously armed with simple weapons, knives or small swords. Their first objective was the city hall, where they apparently went looking for arms and where they threatened to lynch a clergyman whom they found standing nearby.[54] Then, accompanied by a smaller number of men, they set out on the long route through the city and westward across the countryside toward the royal chateau, slogging through an increasingly heavy downpour. As they made their way they recruited other women, some joining with enthusiasm, others through coercion. They finally arrived in Versailles toward nightfall and burst into the National Assembly, soaked and bedraggled.[55] Although the women's principal demand was for bread, they clearly had a sense of the political situation and insulted and threatened several of the Monarchien deputies. The situation became more dangerous with the arrival of thousands of men, national guardsmen led by Lafayette, as well as other unorganized bands of Parisians.

Eventually the Assembly leadership took a delegation of women to see the king, who met them in the palace and promised to consider their demands for bread. But early the next morning the crowds of women and men, who had spent the night outside in the rain, grew unruly once again. Several palace guards were attacked and killed, and hundreds of people broke into the palace itself. The king and queen escaped unharmed. But Louis was terrified for the safety of his family, and he now agreed not only

Market women leave Paris en route to Versailles, October 5, 1789. One woman is astride a cannon pulled by other women, some carrying pikes. Another stands up above the cannon and urges other women to follow them. They are accompanied by a few men, though the main force of national guardsmen would follow only later. Jean-François Jainet, © Coll. Musée de la Révolution française, Domaine de Vizille, MRF 1984.661.

to do what he could to increase the bread supply but to accept all the August decrees and the initial articles of the Constitution. Equally significant, he promised to move his residence to the Tuileries Palace, the western wing of the Louvre in central Paris. Within a week the National Assembly would follow the monarch and set themselves up in an indoor riding stadium a few hundred meters from the Tuileries. Henceforth both the king and the Assembly would reside in the midst of the most intensely politicized city in all of France.

The October Days left a powerful impression on everyone who lived through them. A great many deputies and middle-class Parisians were deeply shaken. It was often their first direct contact with the violence of the crowds, and the experience was nothing less than traumatic. One clerical deputy suffered a nervous breakdown and was incapacitated for weeks. Others felt profoundly disillusioned with the actions of "the people," whom they once thought they knew and who now seemed foreign and incomprehensible. Rosalie Jullien found the episode enormously upsetting: "I am overwhelmed with sadness," she wrote to her husband, "and remain at home, without personal fears but only with prayers to heaven for the stability of the state."[56]

Yet other Revolutionary elites—almost all of them future radicals—were ready to see the people's violence as a regrettable necessity. The deputy Goupilleau expressed satisfaction with this "second revolution," the capitulation of the king, and the humiliation of the aristocracy. The journalist Brissot also emphasized the positive results of the event. In order not to "diminish the joy of this memorable day," he wrote, "they must cover the recent bloody incidents with a patriotic veil." Others went out of their way to attribute the violence to the people's misery. Romme went even further. He was increasingly convinced, he wrote to his friend, that violence itself had a role in the transformation of France and that rational argument might not always suffice. If they were ever to convert the whole population to the blessings of the Revolution, "reason will perhaps need to be accompanied with terror."[57]

It had been an extraordinary, exuberant, and tumultuous year. For the majority of the townspeople the great declarations of August, abolishing feudalism and announcing the Rights of Man, would remain engraved in their memories as they were engraved on the tablets of town halls and club rooms throughout France. To the end of his life the Paris windowmaker Jacques Ménétra would never forget the events of that summer, which "were to lead us to freedom and give us laws worthy of a great people," a time when all "men saw themselves as brothers."[58] For a great many men and women the very concept of identity seemed to have mutated in 1789. The transformed sense of self, of the new links among individuals and between individuals and the state was integral to the image of the "new man" that was so pervasive in the writings of the period. It was an image evoking a sense of brotherhood and nationhood that was part and parcel of the "spirit of '89." Among our Revolutionary witnesses, the very tone and character of the correspondence seemed to change during the year. Colson's business notes became ever more politicized, his comments on current events, previously consisting of only a few lines, now consuming entire letters. So too Ruault's Voltairian sarcasm and bemused detachment were replaced by a far more serious and passionate style. Faulcon was self-conscious about similar changes in his prose: "I can neither feel in my heart nor express with my pen that happy cheerfulness with which I formally seasoned my writings." In the present situation, "It is impossible for a well-intentioned man not to paint the situation in somber colors."[59]

For the year 1789 had a darker side. It was impossible to have lived through those months without retaining a deep sense of uncertainty—intermixed at times with anxiety and suspicion. If 1789 was extolled as a year of liberty, it could also be described as "a terrible year."[60] It had begun with the most frightful winter anyone could remember. Thereafter there had been hundreds of grain riots and thousands of deaths through starvation, followed by a summer of violence and chaos in Paris and the provinces and a terrifying panic that touched much of the country—the "year of the Fear," as people still remembered it in the mid-nineteenth century.[61] The events of those months prefigured and foreshadowed many of the problems that would plague the Revolution for years to come: the rapidly evolving power vacuum, the emergence of a counterrevolution in sharp opposition to the new ideals, the rise of factional divisions among the patriots, and the periodic explosions of popular violence.

3

The Breakdown of Authority

O VER THE following year the new National Assembly, the "Constituent" Assembly as it now called itself, set out with great energy to write a constitution and create a new regime from the wreckage of the old. The deputies who made up that body were, in many respects, a remarkable group of individuals. A certain number emerged as exceptional orators, capable of influencing the whole assembly through the power of their logic and their rhetoric. There was the impassioned speaker, writer, and journalist, Count Mirabeau; the young lawyer from Grenoble, Antoine Barnave, only twenty-eight years old; the veteran of the American Revolution, Alexandre Lameth, scion of one of the great noble families of France; the golden-voiced Protestant pastor, Jean-Paul Rabaut Saint-Etienne; and the two staunch defenders of the common man, Jérôme Pétion and Maximilien Robespierre. But a great many others—whose names are remembered today only by specialists—were at least as influential, working long hours behind the scenes in committee meetings or on the floor of the legislature.

The deputies had not only to terminate all those institutions abolished on the Night of August 4 but also to create entirely new administrative, tax, and judicial systems, along with new civil and penal codes, while simultaneously pursuing sweeping reforms of the military, the police, and the clergy. Moreover, the reforming vision of the patriot deputies continued to expand, with a number of new Revolutionary moments: the projected nationalization of church property in November 1789, the emancipation of the Protestants in December, the suppression of monastic orders in February 1790, and the abolition of the nobility in June of that year. The task was all the more daunting in that decisions involved such an exceptionally large and often unwieldy body of legislators—close to 1,200 men, compared to the 558 members of the contemporary House of Commons or the mere 106 in the U.S. House of Representatives.[1]

Throughout this period it was the hope of virtually all of the patriots that they might work hand in hand with the king. The monarch was widely perceived as the vital center, essential for the unity of the new nation. It was a view that had found popular expression in the statements of grievances in March 1789 and that continued to be expounded in letters received by the Assembly from citizens throughout the kingdom.[2] A monarchy was, after all, the only system the French had ever known, and for the present hardly anyone considered the possibility of a nation without a king. Among the Assembly's earliest constitutional decisions—in September 1789—was that France should remain a hereditary monarchy in the male line. Even the firebrand Jean-Paul Marat would continue to praise the king through the end of the year.[3]

In retrospect, however, we know that the king was profoundly unhappy with the Revolution as it developed after June 1789, and especially after the October Days, so traumatic and unsettling for Louis and his entourage. In a secret letter to his cousin, the king of Spain, written soon after the October events, he formally repudiated all those acts passed by the Assembly since the fall of the Bastille, acts that he felt had been extorted through intimidation; and he embraced a traditional image of authoritarian kingship. His efforts to bring about necessary reform had, in his view, been perverted by a small conspiracy of radicals, unrepresentative of the French population as a whole. Thereafter, he seems to have followed a *politique du pire,* assuming that the Revolution would soon fall apart through an accumulation of unworkable laws.[4] Yet the patriots had no inkling of Louis' inner sentiments. They preferred to believe that the king was essentially well meaning and that he had now reconciled himself to the Revolution.

The Edge of Anarchy

As the constitutional framework for the new central government began to take shape in Paris, however, the nation was swept by a crisis of authority unlike anything the French had experienced in their lifetime. In the thinking of the National Assembly, most of the structures of the Old Regime were to be maintained, to carry on business as usual until a new set of institutions could be created to take their place. But after all that had happened during the first summer of the Revolution, business as usual was scarcely a viable option, and many of those institutions were soon on the verge of collapse. The intendancy system, the linchpin of administration under the absolute monarchy, had already been seriously weakened in the two years before the Revolution, especially when the intendants had been forced to share power with the provincial assemblies.[5] But it was the brutal murder of the intendant of Paris, Berthier de Sauvigny, in July 1789 that struck terror in the hearts of all royal administrators. In the weeks that followed, numerous intendants resigned or abandoned their posts, along with their local agents, the subdelegates. "All the intendants," reported Nicolas Ruault, "are deserting their posts, abandoning their offices, and fleeing as rapidly as possible." Even those who stayed on until they were formally dismissed in the summer of 1790 had essentially lost all their authority, and did little more than pass along decrees from the National Assembly.[6]

The intendants, moreover, were not the only royal officials to experience the loss of their legitimacy. Tax collectors, police commissioners, and those in charge of the grain supply fled for their lives or lay low throughout the summer and sometimes long afterward.[7] The judiciary was also deeply affected. The decrees of August 4 had abolished the seigneurial courts, the most important form of justice at the parish level, and though the seigneurial judges were supposed to continue functioning until they were replaced, they were widely ignored and disobeyed. Even the highest courts of the land, the parlements, were reduced to a shadow of their former selves. In Paris, the parlementary magistrates ceased all activity during the mid-July crisis and never again convened as a full body. The National Assembly ordered them to remain permanently "on vacation" after the summer recess and thereafter their functions were assumed by a small vacation chamber or by the local Châtelet court in Paris. Judges in the lower royal courts, accused of having favored the privileged orders under the Old Regime, were now widely scorned or ignored. Many of them simply ceased making judgments, especially since there was often no reliable police to enforce their decisions. They were also wary of vigilante actions by crowds of people— like those who had murdered officials in Paris. In November 1789 the minister of justice, Champion de Cicé, noted the difficulties encountered by any judge who attempted to rule against popular sentiments: "It would be altogether cruel to compel them to maintain a function that would put their lives in danger."[8]

The National Assembly itself was only too well aware of the breakdown of authority penetrating much of the kingdom. Mirabeau lamented the present situation in which all recognized authority, he felt, had ceased to exist. "There is no longer a king," wrote Adrien Duquesnoy, "nor a parlement, nor an army, nor a police; . . . All rights and all duties are ignored; . . . Anarchy is increasing and will continue to increase."[9] In such a state of affairs, and in their urgent effort to hold the country together, the Assembly and the royal ministers were forced to improvise. They communicated as best they could with the intermediary commissions of the provincial assemblies or with whatever remnants of the Old Regime bureaucracy were still in operation. They also worked through individual deputies, who were encouraged to send decrees and declarations directly to the local electoral assemblies or correspondence committees with whom they had remained in contact.[10] It soon became clear, however, that the only administrative bodies still consistently functioning with some measure of legitimacy were the town governments.

To be sure, municipal politics throughout the realm often remained turbulent and unsettled. The "municipal revolution" that had begun in Paris in July continued to spread, as local citizens attempted to modify or oust the Old Regime oligarchies that had controlled their towns for generations. Faced with the need to defend themselves from the imagined "brigands" during the Great Fear and from the growing chaos in the countryside, groups all over France set up emergency committees to take charge of local affairs. Such transformations frequently began in the provincial capitals and then spread by example to the smaller towns. Sometimes through violent revolts, more often through various forms of persuasion and coercion, the former municipal leaders were forced to stand aside or associate themselves with the patriots or at least substantially change their ways and embrace the Revolutionary values of liberty and democracy. Sometimes the new "permanent committees" set up in the towns were the direct heirs of the improvised patriot groups first formed in 1788, prior to the convocation of the Estates General.[11]

In almost every case, the first act of the reformed town government was to declare its allegiance to the National Assembly. Throughout the last months of 1789 the Assembly was flooded with hundreds of letters of adherence. Formal statements of loyalty were frequently reinforced by collective oaths sworn by the whole population—men, women, and children—in dramatic ceremonies organized in the town square or before the city hall. Imitating the oaths of the deputies in June 1789 or adhering to the decrees of August 4, citizens everywhere raised their hands and vowed to be faithful to "the nation, the law, and the king."[12] The enormous reserves of devotion and enthusiasm for the National Assembly displayed by the townspeople would be of immeasurable value in holding the nation together during the dangerous interregnum that followed the summer of '89.

In the short term, however, this "municipalization" of the Revolution also had its drawbacks. Even as they proclaimed their allegiance to the Constituent Assembly, some of the towns began acting as veritable minirepublics, eager to assert their independence after years of domination by the Old Regime bureaucracy. Several proceeded unilaterally to raise their own taxes, arrest suspects, and issue "ordinances" or "proclamations"—normally the prerogative of a sovereign body—all in the name of "public security" and popular sovereignty. Faced with the chaos of the surrounding countryside, they also created paramilitary "national guard" forces, mobilized to intervene against rural and urban uprisings and to ensure supplies of grain for their citizenry.[13]

The deputies in Paris realized the dangers of such a situation, and they placed a high priority on creating a new administrative system that would tie the nation together. After lengthy debates in the fall and winter of 1789–1790, they established a four-level hierarchy of departments, districts, cantons, and municipalities, in descending order.[14] To see to the judicial needs of the new regime, they also created a network of tribunals at the district and departmental—and eventually national—levels. Both the tribunals and the administrative bodies were to be elected by the local population. In defining the electorate, however, the majority of the Assembly made the fateful decision of limiting suffrage and the pool of potential officeholders to "active citizens," those men who paid a certain minimum amount of taxes. The creation of this two-tiered system of "active" and "passive" citizens would be vigorously opposed by a small group of deputies, led by Pétion and Robespierre. The demand for universal male suffrage would soon become one of the major bones of contention between radicals and moderates in the Assembly.

In February 1790 formal elections were organized to replace the provisional municipal governments. It was a signal moment in the Revolution in that democratic elections were now instituted not only in the towns but in thousands of villages throughout the realm that had not previously been touched by such changes. Even though the electorate was limited to "active citizens," it was a major step in instructing the population in the workings of democracy and self-government. The creation of the upper levels of the administration, however, took substantially longer. Unlike the municipalities, there were no institutional predecessors for the districts and departments. Special commissioners were appointed to oversee the process of setting up lists of eligible voters, organizing elections, and mediating the struggles that frequently arose between competing towns and regions within the new departments.[15] It was well into the summer of 1790 before the new officials were in place. The law courts created by the Constituent Assembly required even more time before they began operation. Many were elected only in late 1790 or 1791, and they often began functioning several weeks or months after the Old Regime courts had been disbanded.

Once the system was up and running, those elected to office demonstrated great dedication to their duties. The vast majority firmly believed in the ideals of the Revolution, and they did their best to implement the Assembly's decrees. But it was no easy task to read and understand the reams of new laws arriving almost daily. Such laws dealt with everything from the tax system, elections, and the sale of church property to restructuring municipal and parish boundaries, organizing the national guard, and supervising compensation for Old Regime offices abolished by the Revolution. For administrators who took their jobs seriously—and almost all of them did—the demands on their time and energy were immense.[16]

The local leadership had also to contend with an array of internal power struggles. The new administrations had not been implanted in a vacuum. They were invariably affected by local political rivalries and animosities, some dating to the Old Regime, others to the yearlong interregnum when communities and individuals had acquired a taste for self-determination. Given the considerable authority that had been granted them, the new administrative elites ruffled the feathers of other local dignitaries, especially those who had lost their former power. Certain regions were plagued by successive resignations of officials, who were frustrated with the impossibility of obtaining compliance and who sometimes feared for their own safety.[17]

In theory, the lines of authority within the new system were quite clear: emanating downward from the royal ministers through the department, district, and municipal bureaucracies. But in reality it was extremely difficult to enforce laws and directives sent from one level to the next, and there would be numerous examples of recalcitrance, passive resistance, or open disobedience to instructions arriving from above. In some instances—especially in the more controversial questions such as church reform or the prosecution of emigrants—local authorities might drag their feet or devise policies of their own for political or ideological reasons.[18] The situation could be made worse, moreover, by the coexistence of different levels of the bureaucracy in the same locale. In over eighty cases all three sets of officials—department, district, and municipal—were located in the same town, facing each other from offices across the central square or within the same building, each with its own somewhat different agenda and constituency. Numerous complaints flowed into Paris, lamenting the difficulties and insubordination generated by such rivalries.[19]

Following the conclusions of the nineteenth-century writer Alexis de Tocqueville, historians and social scientists have often emphasized the continuities between Old Regime absolutism, on the one hand, and the strong centralizing tendencies of the later Revolution and the Napoleonic era, on the other. But it is a mistake to overlook the intervening years from 1789 through 1793, when the Revolution was characterized by intense decentralization.[20] There can be no doubt that such a state of affairs made it extremely difficult to know who was in charge in a given place in a given moment, and it would thus help promote an atmosphere of uncertainty and mistrust.[21]

The Dynamics of Democracy

Yet the breakdown of authority was not only a question of institutions. It also arose from the evolving attitudes of the Revolutionaries themselves. The values of liberty and democracy came rapidly to penetrate the whole society, and they led to a questioning of authority, to a delegitimization of traditional power relations at almost every level. Many years later the windowmaker Ménétra recalled the thrill of excitement that he and his friends had experienced in Paris during those first heady days of the Revolution, when "the word 'liberty' repeated so frequently had an almost supernatural effect enflaming every patriot."[22]

The initial decrees of the National Assembly and its Declaration of the Rights of Man had elevated the concepts of freedom and self-determination to the status of fundamental principles. Such ideas were further inculcated through the remarkable electoral culture created by the Assembly. Soon a substantial proportion of the citizenry was empowered with the right to choose not only their deputies and local administrators but also their court magistrates, justices of the peace, parish priests, and bishops. As one historian has described it, "The elective principle became the battering-ram of the new regime against the old. . . . Henceforth, no institution was safe from the sanction of public consent."[23] In fact, the concepts of liberty and public consent were so fundamentally untested that no one was quite certain of their limits. Mirabeau was quick to size up the potential danger: "Once all the old boundaries have been erased," he observed, "it will take a certain time before new limits can be known and respected."[24]

The ambiguous impact of the new culture of liberty was epitomized by the extraordinary development of newspapers. Under the Old Regime periodical publications had been limited in numbers—especially by comparison with the English press—and submitted to tight government control. Though a few newspapers, imported from outside the French state, might escape such censorship, a substantial portion of the reading public continued to rely on official or semiofficial government papers like the *Journal de Paris* or the *Mercure de France* or the various local newssheets printed in the provinces. It was only in July 1789 that newspaper censorship finally collapsed. Thereafter, there was a remarkable explosion of publications, as ambitious writers and publishers rushed to capitalize on the new freedom and make a name for themselves. Some 30 new papers appeared in Paris alone during July, 28 more in August, and by the end of the year no less than 140 titles had come out—59 of them published as dailies. Soon dozens more were appearing in provincial towns. As editors sought to carve out niches for themselves in a climate of vigorous competition, there was a rapid experimentation with subject matter, styles, and approaches to journalism. Some papers provided scrupulous accounts of the "facts," including careful digests of debates in the National Assembly with few or no editorial comments. Others were published in a didactic mode to explain the new laws as they were promulgated and to educate various elements of the citizenry to the meaning of democracy—urban workers, for example, or women, or peasants.[25]

However, the period also witnessed the appearance of an intensely partisan press, with journalists—and sometimes individual deputies in the Assembly—defending specific factions or positions across the political spectrum from radical egalitarian democracy to reactionary aristocracy.[26] Since censorship had disappeared and libel laws were scarcely enforced, editors might fill their columns with exaggeration, rumor, and violent attacks against their rivals. For the journalist Mercier, such extremes were unfortunate, but they could best be limited by the "market," as the public simply ceased purchasing newspapers known to contain lies. Yet Ruault, who had long supported freedom of the press, grew impatient with the lack of balance and the false accusations: "All these journalists, some fanatically supporting, others fanatically opposing our Revolution, are swept up in the fury of a publishing volcano. One can only pity both their hatred and their enthusiasm."[27]

The "supernatural effect" of liberty was also central to the great surge of protests by workers for higher wages and better working conditions. There was, to be sure, a long tradition of journeymen organizations within the guild system of the Old Regime. Yet the late summer of 1789 and the months that followed saw a proliferation of meetings, marches, and strikes. At the end of August Adrien Colson was amazed by the number of Parisian workers who wished to create separate associations and elect officers to demand higher pay and shorter hours.[28] Over the following weeks journeymen tailors and wigmakers, blacksmiths and cobblers, coal heavers, carters, carpenters, and typesetters all demanded the right to organize collectively to improve their situations. Even groups with little tradition of association under the Old Regime were uniting to make demands: clerks in the courthouse, for example, and groups of domestic servants from all over the city.[29] Significantly, such activities often went hand in hand with demonstrations of political support for the new regime. In January 1790 the coal heavers marched in procession, three by three, to the Paris city hall to declare their endorsement of the newly elected municipal government. Soon thereafter, the porters in the central market did much the same. Most such workers were quick to adapt the rhetoric of the Revolution to their own economic struggles. Thus, the journeymen typesetters demanded to be "freed from the chains of despotism" imposed by the masters. They also set about establishing a representative government, with their own version of a legislative assembly consisting of delegates from each print shop. Colson was particularly surprised when in 1791 workers began demanding full political equality, no matter what their incomes, "on the pretext that all men have been declared equal before law and nature."[30]

A similar questioning of authority permeated the French military, as soldiers and sailors and low-ranking officers—all of them commoners by birth—leveled attacks against their aristocratic commanding officers. The potential for insubordination was already in evidence in the summer of 1789 when hundreds of soldiers had refused orders to use force against the crowds of patriots in Paris. The soldiers' sympathy for the cause of the Revolution and their open rejection of orders from their superiors had been a central factor in the success of the early Revolution. Yet episodes of insubordination continued well into 1791, reflecting the soldiers' long-standing grievances against their meager pay and the draconian discipline under which they suffered. Protest was undoubtedly influenced as well by the efforts of civilian patriots, suspicious of the motives of the noble officers who dominated the command structure of the military. Patriotic societies invited soldiers garrisoned in their towns to attend club meetings. Soon pro-Revolutionary committees were established within military units, militating for better pay and living conditions. According to one young soldier, Joseph Noël, officers were accused of keeping them in a state of "slavery."[31]

Between August 1789 and October 1791 there were nearly fifty instances of revolt or insubordination of soldiers against their commanders, most of them occurring in frontier garrisons or seaports.[32] Although many of these protests were relatively minor, a few led to major confrontations and violence. By far the most dramatic occurred in the northeastern town of Nancy in August 1790, when several hundred soldiers mutinied, accusing their commander of dishonesty with company funds. Heavy cavalry and artillery were sent in brutally to repress the insubordination. In the fighting that ensued, over two hundred individuals were killed, some thirty were hanged in reprisal, and over eighty soldiers from the Swiss mercenary regiment of Châteauvieux were sent off to the galleys as prisoners. The majority of the National Assembly, now increasingly worried by the threat of war and unsettled by the widespread military indiscipline, fully approved the harsh repression. But many Parisian radicals protested, and the Nancy Affair became a *cause célèbre* dividing radicals and moderates among the Revolutionary elites.[33]

The most massive rejection of traditional authority, however, occurred in the countryside. Beginning in the spring of 1789 and continuing in sporadic waves through 1793, peasants in virtually every corner of France took part in a variety of protests aimed at all those institutions and social groups that had dominated them under the Old Regime. Most such protests took the form of passive resistance and noncompliance, but there were also uprisings that spread across several provinces. While the explosion of riots in the spring of 1789 had been motivated primarily by rising grain prices and the fear of famine, after the summer of that year, peasants frequently focused on the seigneurial system. The "abolition of feudalism" by the National Assembly on the Night of August 4 had only temporarily calmed the situation and soon aroused at least as many problems as it solved.[34] The legislators determined that most feudal dues were a form of property, so that peasants would be expected to purchase their freedom from such "property rights" through moneyed compensation. Yet almost everywhere the countrypeople interpreted the "abolition" of August as immediate and definitive and simply ceased all payments. In careful studies in Poitou, Franche-Comté, Bresse, Vivarais, and Quercy historians have been hard pressed to find a single community initiating the "purchase" stipulated by the decrees. Once the laws were clarified in early 1790, some lords launched suits through the courts to force payment from their former "vassals." But the rural communities responded with a combination of countersuits, passive resistance, and threats of violence—or real violence—toward anyone trying to collect the dues. In many cases, the noncompliance was supported by local officials and national guard units.[35]

Moreover, the rural insubordination went well beyond the seigneurial dues. Throughout the kingdom, people began entering and exploiting the private forests and other uncultivated lands of the nobles and clergy—as well as the royal forests of the king. There were hundreds of complaints of countrypeople cutting wood, killing animals, picking fruit, or netting fish in various private lands, both for their own use and for sale in the towns— activities that the National Assembly and its committees seemed unable to halt. Already in July 1789 a police official in Soissons had noted the sudden appearance of large game animals—deer and boar—in the local butcher shops. The royal forests of Chantilly were devastated by poachers throughout the first years of the Revolution. There were also reports of trees being surreptitiously cut down at night along roadways or in public squares. Those attempting to halt such activities—gamekeepers or rural police—were threatened and mistreated. In one case peasants even tried to force their lord to refund poaching fines that he had imposed on them before the Revolution.[36]

As they rejected the seigneurial dues, a great many countrypeople—and some city dwellers as well—rapidly ceased paying their taxes. The National Assembly's first formal act on June 17, 1789 had been to declare all Old Regime taxes illegal, since they had not been accepted by the nation. Though the deputies immediately stipulated that the taxes must continue to be paid until they could be replaced by a more equitable system, a great many people—through wishful thinking or feigned ignorance—preferred to imagine that all taxes had been abolished outright. Soon it was virtually impossible to collect any form of public assessment. State income taxes, sales taxes, excise taxes, municipal duties, and tithes for the church all dried up. If they bothered to justify themselves, the peasants pointed to the crop failures of the previous year, to the economic downturn caused by the disruption of commerce, to the substantial contributions now paid by the privileged classes and which, it was argued, ought to suffice. This refusal of all taxation was strongly opposed by both the National Assembly and the local elites. Town leaders were concerned not only with the fiscal viability of the Revolution but with municipal finances that relied on entrance dues, market fees, and other local levies. They issued "ordinances" demanding compliance, and they mobilized the national guard in an attempt to enforce collection. But at least through early 1791, when the nation finally abolished the Old Regime taxes and converted to the new system, the crisis persisted, and collectors took their lives in their hands if they tried to demand payment.[37]

The rural resistance might also take the form of violent rebellion. In the summer of 1789 such rebellions had been limited to seven specific areas. However, successive incidents of peasant uprisings would continue to break out well into 1792 and ultimately touch almost every region of the country. Although the crisis in grain production was largely resolved in the Paris basin by November, other provinces were hit by later crop failures, made all the worse by the widespread popular opposition to the transport of grain from one region to another. Many of the riots targeted wagons or river barges filled with grain for interregional shipment. But food was not the only cause of rebellion. Other insurrections involved taxes and tax collectors, Protestant-Catholic rivalries, feuds between national guard units, or attacks on the tithes—especially after the National Assembly "abolished" these clerical taxes on the Night of August 4 but continued to require transitional payments through the end of 1790.[38]

There was also a marked upsurge in violence directed against seigneurial lords. A first great wave swept across the southwest in late 1789 and early 1790, as the fall harvest came in and as many lords attempted to force continued payment of their dues in money or in kind. Violence spread by contagion across the regions of Limousin, Quercy, Aquitaine, and Rouergue—provinces largely untouched by such uprisings the previous summer. Asserting that the National Assembly had suppressed such dues, peasants attacked both noble chateaus and their occupants. But there were probably even more assaults against the symbols of feudalism, such as chateau weathervanes or church pews owned by nobles. At times the violence seemed to resemble a charivari, the traditional raucous rite of community disapproval, with peasants adopting an exuberant celebratory mode as they tore down weathercocks or made bonfires of the lords' benches pulled out of the churches.[39] The violence against individuals was probably greatest where nobles banded together in an attempt to protect their property, sometimes leading to small-scale civil wars. Yet as in the earlier insurrections, the countrypeople could lump together several different grievances, so that depending on the social dynamics of a given community, they might also direct their anger at clergymen, state officials, wealthy townsmen, or Protestants. In Alsace there were violent attacks against Jews, whose homes were looted after the occupants were forced to flee for their lives.[40] In one village of central France, rioting peasants forced their curé to draw up a list of grievances, like a new *cahier de doléance,* with a whole series of demands: the right to hunt and gather wood on the noble's private lands, improved rights for sharecroppers, an immediate lowering of the tithes, and the right to inspect the grain stores of local notables to ensure against grain hoarding.[41]

Faced with the incessant violence and threats of violence, the urban elites did their best to control the situation. They mobilized the local national guards or the Old Regime police and courts. But on occasion the guardsmen sympathized with the rebels and refused to act, and the courts were themselves threatened or ignored. The townsmen could do little more than watch and hope for the best or appeal to the National Assembly. "In the midst of the anarchy which is devastating the countryside and of so many other obstacles," pleaded the leaders of Besançon in late 1789, "how can a municipal government ever hope to fulfill its functions?" Ruault summed up his own fears: "With this single word of 'liberty,' one can burn down a house or a chateau or a town and wreak destruction throughout the countryside."[42]

The Fracturing of Authority

As the Revolution progressed, the situation became even more complicated with the emergence of several parallel powers, organizations that competed with the official structures created by the National Assembly and sometimes with the Assembly itself. Three such powers would pose particular problems for the Revolutionary authorities: the national guards, the sections of Paris, and the popular societies.

National guard units had first been created by the town governments, as they struggled to maintain order in the chaotic conditions of the summer of 1789. Once the crisis had been overcome, the new guardsmen spent much of their time in drill practice, marching about in fine martial regalia, accompanied by flags, music, and drums, and providing ceremonial enhancements for diverse patriotic events.[43] Almost everywhere, they were dominated by young men of the middle classes, since they alone had the leisure to train and the resources to purchase uniforms. Indeed, the National Assembly decree of June 1790, which sought to standardize the great variety of improvised militias formed over the previous year, specified that only "active citizens" could participate. Units were organized by neighborhood, and sometimes by age cohort, with adolescent boys and senior citizens forming their own companies.[44] At first relatively few of the guardsmen possessed firearms. Most marched about with sabers or antique hunting pieces or diverse agricultural tools. But in moments of danger, muskets were distributed from government armories, muskets that were rarely returned to the authorities afterward, so that many companies were able to accumulate significant stores of arms. By 1791 the small town of Varennes and most of the surrounding communities had stockpiled substantial supplies of weaponry, following a series of rumored foreign invasions. In this way town leaders would mount a surprisingly impressive show of force when the king was captured as he attempted to flee through the region in June of that year.[45]

Over time many national guard companies were increasingly radicalized. Not all citizens had the inclination and the staying power to continue regular participation, so that units commonly came to be dominated by those most fervently committed to the spirit of '89. With their immense faith in the patriotic cause and their possession of arms, they became the self-appointed shock troops of the Revolution. With or without the support of the town governments to which they were theoretically subordinated, they aggressively kept watch over the former privileged classes and the other real or perceived enemies of the Revolution. The National Assembly's committee on research received numerous complaints from town governments against guardsmen who refused to obey their orders. In some cases, it was a question of individual rivalries, with power struggles born in the Old Regime now playing out in the competition between municipal leaders and commanders of the national guards. In Brittany several units undertook unilateral incursions into the countryside to attack rural nobles and suspect clergymen. In Quercy they initiated a series of assaults against chateaus, until they were successfully halted by the town authorities. In Languedoc companies of guardsmen were often divided along confessional lines, in which more radical Protestant companies faced off against pro-Catholic units, rivalries that sometimes exploded into violent confrontations. Already in November 1789 the minister of justice would complain against the unruliness of the guardsmen: "I do not have the means of disciplining the national guards, nor of commanding them to follow the law, nor of opposing them with enough force to control them."[46]

In Paris the evolution of the national guards was somewhat different. As elsewhere in the kingdom, the Parisian guardsmen were initially volunteers from the middle class. Both the lawyer Colson and the editor Ruault would offer their services several times a week. Yet given the deputies' desire to maintain law and order in the city where they themselves resided, the National Assembly would be particularly concerned to maintain control over local companies. The institution's first commander, the marquis de Lafayette, was himself a deputy, and he could generally be counted on to cooperate closely with the Assembly. In addition to the volunteers, Lafayette also recruited a number of paid professional soldiers, who long remained loyal to him personally. From the fall of 1789 through 1790 the young commander kept them busy putting down riots and investigating suspected counterrevolutionary activity throughout the city.[47]

Over time, however, the democratic impulse affected the Parisian citizens' militia, as it touched so many other institutions. The guardsmen were allowed to elect their own officers, so that politics might be a factor in the choice of leadership. Several such officers were enmeshed in neighborhood activities, and they encouraged their battalions to become more radical and independent. In late 1790 and 1791 some district battalions began acting on their own or refusing orders from the central command. Their insubordination would be especially dramatic on April 18, 1791, when guardsmen prevented Louis XVI and his family from leaving the Tuileries Palace, despite the direct orders of Lafayette.[48]

Another Parisian institution would reveal even greater independence from the beginning of the Revolution: the sixty neighborhood district assemblies.[49] Created as primary electoral bodies for the Estates General, they refused to disband after the elections had taken place, and they rapidly established themselves as the principal organs of grassroots democracy in the capital. During the interregnum of 1789 and 1790 they asserted control over a range of neighborhood functions, including the provisioning of food, the operation of markets and fountains, and the administration of charity. They also directed the surveillance of suspects and counterrevolutionaries, and they were soon competing with the municipal government and with Lafayette himself for control of the national guard battalions that had been organized by district.[50]

Certain district leaders evolved a theory of popular sovereignty that went further than anywhere in France in promoting the concept of direct democracy. During debate on the royal veto in September 1789, several districts took strong political positions, and two demanded that no decision be made by the National Assembly until the issue had first been discussed by the districts.[51] Some neighborhood leaders attacked the very idea of "passive" citizenship and supported universal male suffrage and the participation of all men in the national guard. In the spring of 1790 they attempted to create a separate, more democratic central committee, in direct competition with the official Paris government.[52] Finally, in May the National Assembly attempted to put a stop to such unruliness by entirely reorganizing the neighborhood institutions. The sixty districts were dismantled and replaced by forty-eight "sections" that were henceforth to convene only for voting purposes. National guard units remained organized by the older districts, making it difficult for the sections to control them. In some cases, there seem even to have been efforts at gerrymandering, to break up centers of radicalism and combine them with more moderate neighborhoods. Yet in the administrative magma that persisted in the spring of 1790, the spirit of neighborhood independence was rapidly reborn in the sections. Sectional assemblies were soon acting very much like the defunct districts, meeting regularly—not just for electoral purposes—and adopting strong political positions.[53] Though they no longer controlled the national guard, they could still mobilize large collective demonstrations and petition the National Assembly to make their opinions known on specific issues. By the summer of 1791 the sections had become a power to be reckoned with by all future revolutionary governments.

Many of the same men who participated in the national guards would also create associations of like-minded individuals dedicated to supporting the National Assembly and the new constitution. Some of these associations were only very loosely organized, like the groups meeting in cafés in Paris or other large cities. The Parisian Guittard de Floriban described himself as a "member" of the Café Procope in Paris, where he met regularly to discuss political questions and sometimes to draw up petitions or send delegations to meet with deputies.[54] Far more influential were the popular patriotic societies or "clubs," as they were commonly called. Some of the clubs could be linked to Old Regime associations like Masonic lodges or reading societies or the political groups that had mobilized in the towns in the fall of 1788. The earliest such societies were created independently in late 1789 in a number of the larger French cities. By the end of the year some twenty were meeting in Bordeaux, Lyon, Dijon, Lille, Nancy, and several other major towns. But the most influential by far was the "Society of Friends of the Constitution" organized in Paris about the same time. The "Jacobin Club"—so called because it met in the disaffected convent of Saint-Jacques—was created by a coalition of progressive deputies from the National Assembly itself, so that it rapidly acquired a semiofficial status as the voice of the Left in the Assembly. Among the most important leaders were Barnave, the Lameth brothers (Alexandre and Charles), Pétion, and Robespierre, although it initially included a wide variety of deputies from all three former estates.[55]

Soon the Paris Jacobins had inspired the creation of similar patriotic societies in the provinces, most of which formally affiliated with the mother society and entered into regular correspondence with it. Over 300 such groups had formed by the end of 1790, and some 800 by June of 1791—including at least one in every department in the country.[56] But while the Parisian Jacobins remained the most prestigious of the clubs, it was never as dominant in the early years of the Revolution as it would later become. The records of the provincial societies reveal that they exchanged letters and speeches with numerous other clubs in the kingdom, creating a dense and relatively decentralized network for the communication of thoughts and ideas. Bordeaux, Toulouse, Marseille, Poitiers, and a number of other regional capitals were major poles of attraction, their deliberations serving as examples for clubs in nearby smaller towns.[57]

Like the national guard units with whom they were often allied, the clubs were dominated by the urban elites. Membership dues remained relatively high, and only the more comfortable elements of society had the leisure to participate regularly in meetings. Yet as a mark of their democratic commitment, they opened their discussions to the general public, and all citizens, including women, were invited to observe the proceedings, sitting in the galleries or in other spaces outside the debating floor. In Bordeaux a certain number of nonmembers described themselves as "the regulars of the galleries." Artisans, shopkeepers, or soldiers for the most part, they seem to have attended quite regularly and to have provided the background register of cheers and hisses to accompany the Jacobin debates.[58] The central purpose of the clubs, as the members saw it, was to support the constitution being drafted by the National Assembly, and prior to the summer of 1791 they almost never took positions against that Assembly. In addition, most societies assumed an educational role, subscribing to an array of newspapers—made available to the membership—and reading and discussing the most important decrees. Many worked to propagate the new ideas in the countryside, distributing simplified accounts of the laws and assuring the translation of texts into local languages and dialects. In this manner, they assisted the population in the apprenticeship to democracy and to Revolution. Like the national guards, however, they also assumed a surveillance role, rooting out and condemning suspected plots and other counterrevolutionary activities. By January 1791 all Paris Jacobins were obliged to swear an oath, vowing to denounce conspiracies wherever they might be found. The clubs thus embodied the dual psychological sentiments felt by the Revolutionary elites in general: the passionate hope for the creation of a new society, coupled with the anxiety that those who had the most to lose were secretly organizing to destroy the Revolution.[59]

Over time the popular societies, like the national guards, tended to embrace more radical positions. The Paris Jacobins had initially enrolled a broad range of patriot deputies, including moderates like Lafayette and Talleyrand. But by mid-1790 they were admitting numerous nondeputies, many of them substantially more zealous and impatient with moderation. As the sessions became increasingly spirited and raucous and as the speakers adopted progressively more democratic positions, most of the moderate deputies resigned or simply ceased attending. A similar trend toward radicalization could be observed in many of the affiliated provincial societies.[60]

The year 1790 also saw the formation of a number of more moderate clubs. Perhaps the most notable was the Society of 1789, created in Paris by a group of eminent intellectuals and influential deputies, men such as Lafayette, Mirabeau, the abbé Sieyès, and the philosopher Condorcet.[61] Further to the right was the "Monarchist Society," formed in late 1790 and self-consciously positioning itself in opposition to the Jacobins. By mid-1791 some fifty conservative clubs of one sort or another had been created around the country, modeled on the Paris monarchists and adopting names such as "Friends of the King," or "Friends of Peace." While supporting the constitution in general, they sought a more elitist approach to politics and the strengthening of the powers of the king. However, the majority of such associations were soon forced to disband, after they were attacked by popular demonstrations or by the local authorities who suspected them of counterrevolutionary tendencies.[62]

Other clubs even more to the left than the Jacobins were also created in Paris. The society of the "Friends of Truth," growing out of an earlier semi-secretive *Cercle social,* initially met in the Palais Royal on the Right Bank and drew together many radical intellectuals of the city.[63] Even more influential was the Society of the Friends of the Rights of Man, usually known as the "Cordeliers Club." Heir to the assembly of the Cordeliers district, abolished in 1790, it brought together many of the most radical journalists and political figures in the city. Several of its members would later play leading roles in the National Convention and the Terror: Georges Danton, Camille Desmoulins, Jean-Paul Marat, François Robert, Louis-Stanislas Fréron, Philippe Fabre d'Eglantine, and Pierre-Gaspard Chaumette, among others. Unlike the Jacobins, none of the Cordeliers leadership sat in the National Assembly, so that the group was not initially linked to the legislative establishment. Since they originally formed in opposition to a decree of the National Assembly dismantling the districts, they never shared the deferential attitude toward the Assembly long maintained by the Jacobins. They saw their central vocation to be the full application of the Declaration of the Rights of Man and the Citizen. If all men were equal before the law, all men should have the right to vote, not just those who had property and paid greater taxes. In this sense, the constitution being drafted by the Assembly was deeply flawed. In general, they saw themselves as the defenders of the lower classes: opposing extensive powers for the king, encouraging the politicization of soldiers and sailors, and supporting free-peoples of color. But they were closely akin to the Jacobins in their suspicions of the former privileged and their preoccupation with the possibilities of hidden conspiracies.[64] Indeed, the symbol of the club was a large eye of watchfulness.

As the Jacobins developed a system of affiliated clubs throughout France, the Cordeliers helped create a network of some thirty like-minded "fraternal societies" in various neighborhoods of Paris. The lower classes were encouraged to participate, and one of the clubs even called itself "the fraternal society of the indigent." Equally important, the network favored the participation of women. The Cordeliers themselves welcomed female attendance and occasionally permitted speeches by women. The "Fraternal Society of the Two Sexes," which was strongly supported by the Cordelier François Robert and his journalist wife, Louise Kéralio, allowed women virtually equal membership, including the right to speak and serve as club officers.[65]

Soon clubs attended exclusively by women also began forming. At least sixty such societies were created throughout the kingdom, some with well over a hundred members. The English agent William Miles reported that everywhere in the streets of the city "the women assemble and discuss political questions."[66] Though Rosalie Jullien had been frightened by the turmoil and chaos of 1789, she soon acquired a taste for the new democratic culture and was sitting in the galleries of the Constituent Assembly and the meetings of her section. She also attended sessions of the Jacobin Club, along with 200 or 300 other women, some of them arriving three hours before the meeting in order to have a seat.[67] She followed with growing excitement the great street demonstrations of 1791 and 1792—often with her young son in tow—and by the summer of 1792 she was totally enthralled with politics: "State affairs," she wrote, "are the affairs of my heart. I think, I dream, I feel only them."[68]

Many women were now forging new careers for themselves as Revolutionary journalists or writers. Indeed, the period would see a sharp increase in the number of female authors publishing books, articles, and pamphlets.[69] Among the most radical, Olympe de Gouges, a playwright and novelist before 1789, applied the logic of liberty and equality to the plight of women in a *Declaration of the Rights of Woman and the Citizen*. She spoke out forcefully against "the perpetual tyranny" exercised by men over the female sex, declaring that "women are born and remain free and equal to men" and that they should have the right to vote and be given access to "all honors, positions, and public offices, according to their abilities."[70] Other writers, notably the marquis de Condorcet, questioned whether women were really inferior by nature, as Western culture had so long assumed, or whether they were simply disadvantaged by a lack of equal education. To be sure, only a tiny minority of educated women demanded complete political equality and female suffrage, and the majority assumed the continuation of some kind of hierarchical gendered relationship. Yet there were growing demands for equal inheritance, equal property rights, and the equal control of children for wives and mothers. It was another indication of the contagion of liberty and equality and of the questioning of authority among every element of society.

The vibrant activity of the "parallel powers"—popular societies, sectional assemblies, and national guard battalions—was one of the most characteristic features of the period. Such groups were at once a fount of energy and support for the Revolution, and a potential source of disunity and disaggregation. As the rhetoric of the Jacobin Club evolved in a more radical direction and as membership in the Cordeliers Club and the fraternal societies of men and women grew, the majority in the National Assembly became increasingly uneasy. Soon the surveillance role of the clubs was being extended to the laws passed by the Assembly itself, laws that were sometimes characterized as profoundly wrongheaded, if not counterrevolutionary.[71] Such suspicions would be transformed into open opposition at the time of the king's attempted flight in June 1791.

The Limits of Fraternity

Despite the anxiety and uncertainty experienced by wide segments of French society during the first year of the Revolution, the late spring and early summer of 1790 were marked by a growing strand of optimism. There was an infectious hope that once the new administration had been established, replacing the moribund system of the Old Regime, the chaos would subside, the Revolution might be completed, and the ideals of liberty and equality, part and parcel of the spirit of '89, could be peacefully enjoyed by all.

In February of 1790 the Revolution seemingly received a great boost when Louis XVI appeared before the National Assembly and pledged his support to the new regime, urging the deputies to assist him in reestablishing unity and order in the realm. Although the speech was probably written by the minister Necker and in no way reflected the king's inner ambivalence, the deputies and the population as a whole were convinced that Louis had embraced the new regime, and they were ecstatic. For Colson the king's appearance signaled a new alliance between the monarch and the nation. The following Sunday his parish priest even read the king's speech at the pulpit, and the whole congregation broke into applause and shouts of "Long live the King!" "I rejoice in the public joy," wrote Ruault, "in the hope that we may all now live together as friends, that all hatreds will be extinguished in a general reign of peace." The event also sparked another wave of solemn oathtaking: first in the Constituent Assembly itself—the third such oath the deputies had sworn since June 17—and then throughout the capital and across the nation.[72] In the midst of the general euphoria, the king and his family were allowed to leave Paris for the first time since the October Days and to spend the Easter season in the royal chateau of Saint-Cloud just west of the city.

The surge of optimism and good feelings was also marked by a "Federation" movement sweeping across the nation. Most historians describing this trend have focused on the great festival in Paris on July 14, 1790, the first anniversary of the fall of the Bastille. But in fact the earliest such movements can be traced to the autumn of 1789 and a series of grassroots organizations to promote unity in the provinces. In the wake of the Great Fear and the collapse of the royal bureaucracy and police, a number of towns and small regions began improvising local alliances to preserve law and order and insure the grain supply. The majority of such alliances seemed to have developed in eastern and southern France at a considerable distance from Paris. Communities in Franche-Comté, Vivarais, Burgundy, Upper Gascony, and many other areas banded together and coordinated the activities of their local militias in an attempt to bring peace and security to the surrounding countryside. In the foothills of the Pyrenees, for example, in late September 1789 the small town of Lavaur drew up a "contract of unity" with twenty-four other municipalities in the region to organize joint operations against acts of violence which "plunge the country into fear and distress." At almost the same moment, the municipal authorities of Millau and Villefranche in the Massif-Central created a "confederation" to confront "the dire effects of rampant anarchy, this scourge of public order." References were made not only to various forms of sedition but also to the failure of individuals to pay their taxes. In the following months similar movements were afoot in many other regions of the nation, from Brittany to the Rhône Valley.[73]

As time went on, there was an evolution in the motives and spirit of such federations. Emphasis was placed not only on maintaining law and order but also on expressions of fraternity and a common devotion to the fatherland and the Revolution in general. Guardsmen joined together in Besançon in November, in Valence in January, in Anjou and Brittany in February. In the latter case speakers declared that henceforth they "were neither

Bretons nor Angevins but French!" By the spring federation ceremonies were being held in almost every corner of the kingdom.[74] Flags deployed and drums beating, local militias converged for grand military reviews before the various municipal authorities. Religion frequently played a central role, with a formal blessing of flags and masses sung within a church or at an improvised outdoor altar. There were patriotic speeches, artillery salutes, and solemn oaths by guardsmen with swords extended. Some spoke of their hope that "the French would henceforth have but a single soul." They swore to protect the rights of man, to maintain law and order, to promote the free circulation of grain, and to fight the enemies of the fatherland if necessary. Thereafter, everyone in attendance, including women and children, repeated the oath. The whole might be sealed with neighborly handshakes and the "civic and fraternal kissing of cheeks," followed by banquets, street theater, fireworks, and public balls lasting well into the night. Throughout southern France celebrations often ended in the joyous dance of a farandole, with guardsmen, officials, soldiers, priests, and much of the population, women and men, linking hands and snaking their way through the town to the sound of drums and diverse folk instruments.[75]

The deputies of the National Assembly and the Paris municipal leaders had closely followed the ceremonies unrolling in the provinces. The enthusiasm for acts of fraternal union swept through the Assembly itself on June 19, 1790, the eve of the first anniversary of the Tennis Court Oath. In a dramatic night session, compared by many to the Night of August 4, the deputies voted to abolish altogether the hereditary nobility in France. For the patriot majority, including a number of liberal nobles who had long supported the Revolution, the new decree fulfilled the promise of the Declaration of the Rights of Man, marking a final step in the creation of a true commonwealth of equality and fraternity.[76] The following evening patriots from Paris and Versailles organized a great banquet in the park of the Bois de Boulogne to celebrate their support for Revolutionary fraternity and the freedom of all peoples and nations. In the spirit of unity, toasts were even drunk to the conservative deputies in the National Assembly, the "blacks," and to the "conversion of the aristocrats." It was a vision of fraternity that was truly universal and inclusive.[77]

The monumental Festival in Paris on July 14 was conceived as the ultimate national expression of the diverse provincial federation movements over the previous months. National guardsmen from towns in all eighty-three departments were invited to the capital to participate. Salaried workers

Federation Ball, July 18, 1790. After the great Federation ceremony on the Champ de Mars (July 14), festivities continued for almost a week. Here men and women dance, drink, and rejoice around a great obelisk of Persian lanterns built on the Champs-Elysées. A few priests and nuns are also visible. Jean-Louis Prieur, engraved by Pierre-Gabriel Berthault, © Coll. Musée de la Révolution française, Domaine de Vizille, MRF 1986.59.41.

and unpaid volunteers labored for weeks to construct a great earthwork stadium on the parade grounds of the Champ de Mars just to the west of Paris, a collective effort that seemed the very symbol of fraternity. Colson was unusually eloquent in describing the scene: the teams of dock workers, coal heavers, apprentice wigmakers, schoolboys, "swarms of clergymen," nuns from the Hôtel-Dieu, and a great many women from every element of society, pushing wheelbarrows and shoveling dirt "with as much energy and enthusiasm as the men." "There was a general feeling of happiness, joy, and satisfaction."[78] Much the same enthusiasm was felt by the guardsmen themselves, marching into Paris from all over France to take part in the celebration. Contemporary travelers described the hundreds of young men crowding the roads en route to the capital. A great many had never journeyed outside their home towns or villages, and the trip itself—sometimes involving several hundred kilometers on foot—seemed a kind of pilgrimage, a first physical encounter with the nation that was henceforth to shape a new sense of identity.[79]

Some deputies and municipal officials had worried that counterrevolutionary forces might profit from the festival to launch a coup. Horses and carriages were banned from the streets that day, and men were forbidden from carrying canes or clubs.[80] But in fact the ceremony went off without a hitch. Despite the blustery weather and the periodic downpours, several hundred thousand people cheered with abandon as officials, soldiers, guardsmen, and the king himself took oaths of allegiance to the new Constitution. Events were punctuated throughout the day with the jaunty and optimistic song that had only recently appeared in the city: "Ça ira! Ça ira!"—"It will be ok, it will all work out."[81] And the Federation in Paris coincided with similar celebrations in towns and villages throughout the nation held at the same hour, accompanied by weeklong festivities of all kinds. The creative innovations by local officials seemed endless: outdoor masses at altars to the fatherland; concerts of bands and bells and batteries; flags, fireworks, and illuminations with torches and candles throughout the night; women in white dresses with tricolor scarfs and little boys in national guard uniforms marching in serried ranks; newborns baptized for the occasion with names like "Liberté" or "Mars-Victoire."[82]

For a great many French, there was the ardent hope that the Festival of Federation would bring an end to the Revolution; that the new regime supported by the king and soon to be embodied in a Constitution would at long last restore the kingdom to calm and stability. Contemporaries returned to the vision of a new age in which all humankind would become happier and better off, in which the king, the Catholic religion, and the former privileged would each have a place.

Within a few weeks, however, the mood of harmony and good feelings would rapidly dissipate. As summer merged into fall, the rancorous partisan politics that had characterized debates in the National Assembly from its earliest weeks would intensify. Too many critical issues remained unresolved: the national debt and the new forms of currency, the organization of the church, the indiscipline of the military, the continuing refusal of the peasantry to pay taxes and seigneurial dues.[83] Though the administrative power vacuum disappeared with the installation of a new bureaucracy, the crisis of legitimacy remained: the problem of reestablishing civic discipline and setting the bounds of freedom and autonomy. Even in their more exuberant moments of enthusiasm for fraternity, the French continued to grapple with the simultaneous fears of external threats and internal conspiracy.

Many of the conservative nobles and clergymen in the National Assembly and in the society at large had been anything but enthusiastic about a Festival of Federation that seemed to signal the king's acceptance of the patriot agenda. Colson was saddened that so many Parisian nobles, including the marquise for whom he worked, had refused to take part and were leaving the city because they did not want even to see the Federation. It was patently obvious that aristocrats such as these had not been excluded from the nation. They were excluding themselves.[84]

And in the first six months of 1791 three new sources of uncertainty would enormously complicate the task of the National Assembly and intensify a growing culture of suspicion and mistrust: an incipient religious schism; an expanding wave of noble emigration; and above all, an attempt by the monarch himself, Louis XVI, to abandon the constitutional monarchy created in his name.

4

The Menace of Counterrevolution

THROUGH the end of 1790 and through much of 1791 the National Assembly continued its efforts to draw up a constitution. Yet as the Old Regime crumbled and as the spirit of democracy and decentralization penetrated the whole nation, the deputies were confronted with an array of problems and responsibilities they had never anticipated: from peasant uprisings and national guard rivalries to worker unrest and revolts in the military. After 1790 they had also to face a series of insurrections in the French colonies of both free people of color and slaves, insurrections that many attributed to the Revolutionary emphasis on liberty. In Paris itself the representatives found themselves increasingly under pressure from the sections and the various clubs and fraternal societies. A major debate in the Assembly could bring thousands of men and women into the streets: surrounding the hall, packing the audience galleries, and shouting out their opinions in the midst of the speechmaking. But most troubling of all, patriots throughout the nation were assailed by multiform movements of opposition that sought to block or destroy all their attempted reforms. It is impossible to understand the Revolutionary elites during this period without taking into account the very real forces of counterrevolution that opposed them.

No doubt every major revolution engenders resistance from those whose social and political positions are threatened or whose values are put into question. In the case of the French Revolution such opposition can be traced to the earliest transformations of 1789. Although a certain number of Old Regime aristocrats—like Lafayette or Mirabeau or the Lameth brothers—

continued to support the Revolution, the majority was fundamentally opposed and often openly hostile. They adhered for the most part to a value system radically different from that of the emerging Revolutionary culture. Through their family upbringing and life experiences, most nobles continued to believe in an inegalitarian and hierarchical society that was ultimately "racist" in its conception.

To be sure, one would be hard-pressed to identify a unified counterrevolutionary position in 1789. Like the Revolutionaries themselves, those opposing the new regime would only gradually develop a coherent ideology, an ideology drawn from a variety of eighteenth-century themes and ideas, pieced together after the fact to justify their actions. Like the patriots, they too sometimes took elements from the Enlightenment. They sprinkled their texts with the watchwords of "reason," "nature," and "happiness"—arguing that the changes pushed by the radicals were eminently irrational and would only lead to chaos. They too appealed to the writings of Rousseau, though they often adopted the more moralistic strands of that complex and sometimes contradictory thinker. Yet the opponents of the Revolution were also influenced by the "counter-Enlightenment" of the later eighteenth century. For decades a host of influential Catholic apologists—supported by the Sorbonne, the Parlement, and the Clergy of France—had hammered away at the ideas of the best-known philosophers of the Enlightenment. A particularly virulent attack—destined for a long life in the counterrevolution—was leveled by the ex-Jesuit abbé Barruel and other writers associated with the conservative review, *L'année littéraire*. Throughout the 1770s and 1780s the group alleged the existence of a conspiracy of philosophers, Protestants, and Free Masons, working in secret to overthrow the monarchy and destroy the church. In addition, the conservative aristocracy may well have been inspired by the "troubadour literature" of the Old Regime: histories, novels, and poetry—largely ignored by scholars today—that lionized the knights of the Middle Ages. Many pictured themselves as brave and honorable warriors, pledged in a crusade to win back the holy land of France for their king and their God.[1]

The rare statements of grievances of the period, written by individual noblemen in March 1789, revealed a group that was on the whole profoundly conservative, opposed to almost any change in the social system, and often unwilling to give up their tax privileges. Even the more broadly conceived collective grievances, drawn up by groups of nobles to be sent to Versailles and sometimes influenced by the articulate minority of liberals, were substantially more conservative than those of the commoners, especially in their views on society.[2] Indeed, during the last months of the Pre-Revolution the opposition had been solidified, especially under the influence of Duval d'Eprémesnil's "committee" in Paris. Once the meetings had begun in Versailles, the conservative stalwarts won over even more of the Second Estate by playing on the threat to all noble privilege if the patriots were allowed to have their way. In the end only about one in six of the noble deputies had supported the patriot position in June 1789.[3]

From the beginning of the Revolution a sharp difference in attitudes was already clear in the rhetoric of the debates. While the patriots were enthralled with innovation and the "new man," the nobles placed a premium on tradition and antiquity. If the Revolutionaries proposed a Declaration of Rights, the aristocrats insisted on a "declaration of duties."[4] It soon became evident, moreover, that many of those opposing the Revolution would defend their position with all the conviction and moral fervor of the revolutionaries themselves. While the patriots swore an oath to "live free or die," their opponents made it clear that they too were ready to die rather than to accept the overturn of the Old Regime and the values it represented.

The Paths of Aristocratic Opposition

Within days after the fall of the Bastille a first group of dissident nobles began trooping across the frontiers.[5] Many of them followed the king's youngest brother, the count of Artois, to the kingdom of Piedmont-Sardinia in northwestern Italy, ruled at the time by the count's father-in-law. By September the young prince had established the first counterrevolutionary committee with the explicit intention of overthrowing the Revolutionary government. For the next fifteen months the group attempted to foment a variety of insurrections. They imagined—with an almost total incomprehension of the nature and extent of the Revolution—that all the recent changes had been imposed by a tiny minority, and that with only a small effort on their part the population would rush to join them and welcome the return of the Old Regime. They soon concocted a variety of conspiracies, linking themselves with dissidents in the southeastern regions of Languedoc and Provence and the city of Lyon. Most of their plans also included the "liberation" of the king from Paris. A first botched plot at the end of 1789—probably supported by the king's second brother, the count of Provence—led to the arrest and execution of one of their accomplices, the marquis de Favras. A more ambitious plan, set for December 1790, would have freed the king and launched a general insurrection throughout the kingdom. But this too was uncovered by the Revolutionary police and resulted in numerous arrests.

The efforts of these early "emigrants" were long hampered by internal squabbles between Artois and the other great aristocrats who had joined him. Soon the prince also had a falling out with his father-in-law, who was not anxious to bring down the wrath of France on his own small state. In January 1791 the small band of reactionaries was forced to leave Italy and travel northward, finally finding refuge in the German Rhineland. Here the group would receive more competent leadership from Charles-Alexandre de Calonne, the former finance minister, who soon became the prince's de facto prime minister. With considerable political savvy, Calonne began negotiations with various of the major European powers in an attempt to win support for a general invasion of France. The emigrants also set out to create their own counterrevolutionary army—or in fact, three separate armies, since the diverse emigrant factions continued to quarrel among themselves.

With the advantage of hindsight, most of the early counterrevolutionary movements originating outside France seem remarkably inept and at times ridiculous. Yet the Revolutionaries themselves could never be certain how extensive and effective such plots might be. After all, great aristocrats had dominated French society for centuries, and it was logical to think that they might continue to control the situation as they had in the past. The Constituent Assembly soon had solid evidence of the various attempted uprisings. As word of the conspiracies leaked out to the public and as they were taken up and debated by the deputies, fears were inevitably aroused in Paris and elsewhere in the country. Rumors of such activities would help engender periodic panics spreading through the streets of the capital.[6]

Both the Assembly and the population were also affected by opponents to the Revolution present and directly visible inside France itself: conservative groups working openly to oppose, modify, or bring down the new regime. Three organs of internal opposition were particularly evident to patriots in Paris: the reactionary deputies within the National Assembly, the reactionary newspapers, and the diverse conservative clubs. Although there was always a fine line between conservatism and counterrevolution, many participants in these three groups moved rapidly toward open and intransigent opposition to everything the Revolution stood for.

For the majority of the formerly privileged deputies in the National Assembly—the nobles and "upper" clergy of bishops and other aristocratic clergymen—the summer of 1789 had been altogether traumatic.[7] The forced union of the three estates, the destruction of the seigneurial system and the tithes on August 4, the rise of popular violence—much of it aimed directly at them—had all been profoundly threatening and upsetting. A substantial number of noble deputies had even left the Assembly in July and August, some going home to consult with their constituencies, others making plans to leave the country.[8] In the short term most such deputies reconciled themselves to many of the changes. After all, they had been ordered to participate in the National Assembly by the king himself. They were also comforted by the Assembly's decision that their seigneurial "property" would be respected until it was reimbursed by their former "vassals." For a time, they opted to accept the new rules of the game and work within the system—with the possibility of slowing and perhaps reversing the Revolution. Many were also swept up in the struggle to obtain advantages in the new administrative system for the towns they represented, notably in the choice of capitals for the departments and districts. Toward the end of 1789 the staunchly conservative noble, Irland de Bazôges, expressed his hope that "in the new order of things I can still be called to serve in public life."[9]

The conservative and reactionary deputies also began organizing politically.[10] In alliance with the more moderate "Monarchiens," the Right managed to win several votes in the Assembly, and during the autumn of 1789 they were sometimes able to dominate the choice of the presidents and secretaries in the Assembly's bimonthly elections. The central issue that held the various factions of conservatives together may well have been the fate of the clergy and the church. While the aristocrats undoubtedly included a certain number of deists and religious scoffers, as a group they remained close to traditional Catholic orthodoxy, and they soon developed a close alliance with the majority of clerical deputies in the Assembly. If we can believe Baron de Gauville, it was the debate on the question of religious toleration in the Declaration of Rights that first united the group and led them to sit together on the right side of the hall.[11] Indeed, the coalition soon became known derogatorily as "the blacks"—in part no doubt because of the substantial number of black-robed clergymen who sat in their midst. When the Assembly moved to Paris after the October Days, the reactionary deputies began meeting regularly to debate strategy in the convent of the Grands Augustins on the left bank of the Seine. Several exceptionally talented orators emerged to defend their position, including Abbé Maury, the chevalier de Cazalès, Reynaud de Montlosier, and the marquis de Foucauld de Lardimalie. Maury, in particular, was ostentatious and flamboyant in his opposition, taunting and baiting the patriots, challenging virtually every Revolutionary measure, and prophesying that the whole experiment would soon collapse in ruin.

By early 1790 one deputy described the intensely polarized Assembly as consisting of "two armies ready for combat," continually confronting one another in rhetorical clashes.[12] One of the most dramatic and tumultuous debates occurred in mid-April 1790, once again over the issue of religion. Compromise votes the previous November and December had approved the principle of selling a portion of church land to pay the state debts that were threatening to overwhelm the Revolution. But the details of the sale had been left purposely vague—and many assumed that only the lands of the regular clergy would be affected. Now, however, the patriot leadership demanded the auctioning off of virtually all ecclesiastical property. Many clerical deputies felt deeply betrayed, believing they had been promised the preservation of church lands. In the midst of the debate one patriot clergyman, hoping to calm the fears of the conservatives, proposed that Catholicism be officially declared the state religion. But the patriot majority rejected the motion, arguing that it was incompatible with the principle of religious freedom. The "blacks" exploded in indignation, and with their hands raised to heaven they took an impassioned oath to sacrifice their lives for the defense of the Catholic Church.[13] Some 300 of them met in the neighboring Capuchin convent to draw up a formal protest, repudiating the legitimacy of the Assembly's majority vote and sending thousands of pamphlets throughout the kingdom condemning the decision. Although most patriot groups in the provinces rejected the pamphlet, it helped inflame Catholic-Protestant tensions in certain regions of southern France.[14] For the patriots the maneuver seemed clear proof that the conservative minority sought to incite violent opposition against the Revolution.

The incident of April 1790 marked a first turning point in attitudes for many nobles in the Assembly. Irland was outraged by the decision, and he increasingly concluded that political cooperation with the Assembly was impossible: "What a strange abuse of eloquence, reasoning, and language!" he wrote, referring to what seemed to him a blatant attack on the Catholic faith. "No people on earth has ever done the like."[15] Even more upsetting for nobles like Irland was the Assembly's decision the following June 19 to abolish the hereditary nobility altogether. Whatever the enthusiasm of the moment among the patriots, there can be no doubt that a certain spirit of revenge also played a role in the decision: revenge against the Right's rejection of majority rule in April, revenge for their steadfast opposition to almost all Revolutionary measures, revenge for the long years of noble condescension under the Old Regime. "So we have revenge at last," wrote one commoner deputy, "for all the humiliations we had to endure from these arrogant little counts." Nicolas Ruault described the reaction in Paris: "The people rejoice over the decree abolishing the nobility . . . , because they were tired of seeing the nobles with all their insolence and arrogance." "This spirit of vengeance," he added, "is not the most desirable."[16] The patience and compromise displayed by the patriots the previous summer now seemed largely to have disappeared.

Predictably a great many of the nobles were beside themselves with fury. Individuals who had never before spoken in the Assembly came forward with passionate protests. Noble status, they declared, was a question of blood and of "race." It was an absurdity and an affront to their honor that the Assembly should claim to abolish their God-given prerogatives and superiority. Foucauld de Lardimalie protested "with all his soul" a decree that "overturns and destroys everything and will create a chaos of people mixed together from every condition." For the count d'Escars, "There is no power on earth that can prevent me from leaving my title of nobility to my descendants, a title that was given only by God."[17] Over the following month hundreds of protests poured into the conservative press from nobles throughout the kingdom, denouncing and rejecting the decree. Though most members of the former Second Estate had ultimately been convinced to abandon their seigneurial rights—for which, in theory, they were to be reimbursed—they drew the line at the "honor" of their noble status. A great many ceased attending the meetings or abandoned the Assembly altogether, choosing to emigrate rather than to remain in a kingdom controlled by the Revolutionaries.[18]

But while the voice of opposition was increasingly silenced in the National Assembly after the summer of 1790, it was vigorously maintained to the very end of the monarchy in the conservative press.[19] Like the patriot newspapers, the eight to ten Parisian periodicals on the Right represented a wide variety of styles, formats, and political stances. There was the more staid and moderate *Mercure de France,* close to the Monarchiens in the Assembly; and the brilliantly satirical *Actes des apôtres,* composed by a team of conservatives, many of them deputies in the Assembly. There was also an assortment of far more vitriolic sheets: the *Gazette de Paris* by Farmian du Rozoi; the *Ami du roi* of the Abbé Royou, the self-conscious heir of the *Année littéraire* of the Old Regime; and Gautier de Syonnet's *Journal de la cour et de la ville,* widely known as "the petit Gautier." They were written by a curious variety of editors. Several had emerged from the same milieu of Old Regime "Grub Street" authors that spawned the patriot journalists. Most of them had initially supported the Revolution. But whether through genuine conviction or because they sensed a lucrative niche opening up for opposition newspapers, they rapidly moved to the right after the October Days. In 1791 the opposition papers taken as a whole could boast some 100,000 subscriptions in Paris and the provinces and a substantially larger total number of readers. As best we can tell, the readership was dominated by the former privileged classes, nobles and clergy, perhaps a fifth of whom were women.

By early 1790 the conservative journalists were describing the Revolution as an unmitigated disaster. Endless accounts were given of the destruction of time-honored institutions, of massacres and mayhem, of the perpetration of intolerance and cruelty—despite all the patriot rhetoric about reason and logic. In fact, the very ideas of liberty and equality were folly, since "inequality is inherent in the world" and "subordination is the basic link, the very soul of society."[20] Left to their own devices the common people were vicious animals. If France was to be saved, it was essential to return full authority to the king and to recognize the impossibility of the people ruling themselves. For the editors of the *Ami du roi* and several other journalists, the Revolution had nothing to do with popular sovereignty. Returning to the pre-Revolutionary predictions of Abbé Barruel, they announced that all that had transpired was the work of a small minority of philosophers, Protestants, and Free Masons. Soon such newspapers not only attacked the Revolution but actively promoted its overthrow. They urged the other European powers to invade France and oust the "Jacobites"—as they commonly termed the Friends of the Constitution—and they strongly encouraged nobles to emigrate and join the counterrevolutionary armies. The image of the chivalrous knights of old was called upon repeatedly to justify the struggle: they were "crusaders setting forth to conquer the holy land of their fathers," as the *Gazette de Paris* put it. And there were endless references to the celebrated warriors of the past, like Du Guesclin or Bayard or Turenne.[21] On several occasions the Parisian crowds attacked the publishing offices and roughed up the editors of papers that so castigated the Revolution. For the most part, however, a liberal commitment to freedom of the press prevailed and the conservative newspapers were allowed to continue publishing to the very end of the monarchy in August 1792.

The most fanatical of the conservative journalists easily matched such patriot extremists as Marat and Fréron in the violence of their rhetoric, the brutality of their attacks on individuals, and their calls for revenge and blood. "One must have the courage to repeat the fact," wrote the *Petit Gautier,* "that France can only be regenerated through a bath of blood. You must seize the iron sword of destiny that presides over all empires and revolutions."[22] Like certain of the patriot extremists, they characterized their opponents as bloodthirsty "monsters" preparing a new Saint-Bartholomew's Day—referring to the massacre of Protestants in Paris in the late sixteenth century. The patriot and the counterrevolutionary journalists clearly read their opponents' papers.[23] They played off one another, sparred with one another, as both sides developed a Manichaean logic that demonized and dehumanized their opponents. The increasingly intense verbal violence flaunted in the extremist press served to prefigure the physical violence that would soon explode throughout the country. In any case, the Rightist press played a major role in sensitizing the patriots to the presence and the danger of counterrevolutionary threats. "Aristocratic, royalist, and anti-patriotic brochures are more numerous and more violent than ever," wrote Ruault in early 1790. "Civil war is in people's minds. May God keep it from going any further!"[24]

As for the conservative clubs, most were not strictly speaking counterrevolutionary. Thus, the Parisian "Constitutional Monarchy Club," as its name implied, advocated granting greater authority to the king within a constitutional structure. Yet the patriots were immediately suspicious, especially when it became clear that membership was dominated by the former privileged orders and when the club began giving charity to the poor in what seemed an obvious ploy to win popular support. The deputy Legendre worried that "beneath the mask of an acceptable title, a horde of aristocrats are meeting."[25] Many of the Parisian common people clearly agreed, and soon thereafter a crowd invaded the club and forced it to close.

Yet conservatives of various stamps continued to meet less publicly in cafés, at the homes of individuals, or in the "salons" of Duval d'Eprémesnil, Madame d'Escars, or the chevalier de Bouville. Bouville, in fact, was one of the principal organizers of the so-called *salon français*, which soon became resolutely counterrevolutionary. It seems to have come into existence in the spring of 1790 and to have been attended by deputies who had supported the failed resolution to declare Catholicism the state religion. But like the Jacobins, the group soon saw the participation of numerous nondeputies—up to 600, according to one report. In addition to organizing a series of formal protests against the decrees of the National Assembly, coordinated primarily by Bouville, the salon seems early to have been in correspondence with the count of Artois and the emigrants in Germany. The group was probably involved in an early conspiracy to remove the king from Paris and, perhaps, in the abortive uprising in the southeast at the end of 1790. It may also have been the rallying point for the flood of young nobles who rushed to the Tuileries Palace on February 28, 1791, when rumors spread that the king's life was in danger. A few months later, following the emigration of most of its members, the salon français largely ceased its meetings. Thereafter, the small group that remained in Paris provided the nucleus for one of the earliest spy networks in France. It secretly sent information on the Revolution—usually of dubious value—to the count d'Antraigues in Italy, who forwarded it to various foreign powers. Led by Pierre-Jacques Lemaître, a former Jansenist with considerable experience in clandestine activities under the Old Regime, the network would be uncovered by the police only after the Terror in 1795.[26]

The Religious Catalyst

The religious policies of the Revolution incited opposition not only among the conservative deputies but also among elements of the larger population. The refusal to declare Catholicism the state religion, the decrees granting equal rights to Protestants and Jews, and the election of a Protestant pastor (Rabaut Saint-Etienne) as president of the National Assembly could all arouse protests. In provinces like Languedoc and Alsace, with large non-Catholic minorities, many Catholics were convinced that the followers of Luther and Calvin had seized control of the Assembly. During the spring of 1790 such fears led to violent religious troubles in the southern towns of Montauban and Nîmes. The Nîmes conflict, in particular, resulted in the death of some 300 Catholic supporters. In August of that year 20,000 Catholic national guardsmen met on the plateau of Jalès in northern Languedoc, largely in reaction to the Nîmes disaster. The meeting was modeled on the recent federation movements among the patriots. But participants replaced

Confrontation between Catholics and Protestants in Montauban, May 10, 1790. A Catholic mob, supposedly led by the clergy (on the left) killed several members of the Protestant-dominated national guard in this southern town before the national guard of Bordeaux (on the right) arrived to rescue them. B. Espinasse, engraved by J. B. Simonet, © Coll. Musée de la Révolution française, Domaine de Vizille, MRF 1990.46.3.

the patriot tricolor badges with red crosses on their hats, and rather than a show of unity and reconciliation, there was a strong undercurrent of hatred and revenge. In the weeks that followed, several of the leaders of the Jalès federation established ties with the count of Artois and the emigrant army.[27]

About the same time a rather different set of religious and political forces led to open civil war in the small enclave of papal territory near the mouth of the Rhône River. A conflict between pro-French sympathizers in Avignon and supporters of the Pope in the surrounding towns was complicated by a bitter factional struggle within Avignon itself, pitting Catholic moderates and anticlerical radicals. In October 1791 over sixty Catholic citizens would be brutally murdered by radical extremists and thrown into the tower of La Glacière in the Palace of the Popes. The "Massacre of La Glacière" would become a major scandal, debated and denounced in the National Assembly and throughout France.[28]

Religious tensions were thus already high in certain provinces when the National Assembly decreed the reorganization of the Catholic Church, known as the "Civil Constitution of the Clergy" (passed on July 12, 1790). Although the deputies insisted that they had no intention of touching the Catholic religion itself, their transformation of the ecclesiastical structures was remarkably radical. Having already abolished the regular clergy and announced the sale of most church land, they now eliminated the positions of all clergymen not directly administering the sacraments—such as canons, chaplains, and nonresident benefice holders—who were sent into retirement with small pensions. Bishops and parish clergymen were converted into "civil servants," henceforth to be paid by the state and elected by the lay population, rather than being picked by the Catholic hierarchy. The boundaries of all dioceses were redrawn to correspond with the civil administrative departments—thus eliminating over fifty bishoprics and their bishops; the revenues of the bishops were greatly reduced, and in the future they would be chosen from among the parish clergy rather than from great aristocratic families, as in the past. Equally radical, the deputies simply announced the new law to the Pope in Rome, without requesting his ratification or blessing.[29] Not since the Reformation of the sixteenth century had a European state unilaterally effected such sweeping changes in the church.

The whole situation was rendered even more complicated at the end of 1790 when the Assembly voted that all "ecclesiastical civil servants" must swear an oath of allegiance to the new Constitution, including the Civil Constitution of the Clergy. A small minority of clergymen had begun denouncing certain elements of the reforms, and the deputies had grown increasingly impatient. "It is difficult to feel forgiveness for [these priests]," wrote Theodore Vernier, who in his youth had considered joining the clergy. "There are times when we can be indulgent, but now it is time to find out, once and for all, if the Nation is to be respected."[30] In fact, the legislation passed in late November was specifically intended for the bishops, widely believed to be the primary source of opposition. It was almost as an after-thought that the deputies also included the parish clergy, assuming that the vast majority would readily comply. Any priest who refused to pronounce the required formula "purely and simply" without restrictions of any kind was to be dismissed from his post.

In the early weeks of 1791 clergymen all over France were compelled to stand at their altar, raise their hand, and swear a solemn, religious oath. The political leadership was not surprised when all but two of the bishops serving in France refused to acquiesce. They were stunned, however, when almost half of the 50,000 parish clergymen also refused. In fact, the parish priests and their assistants were deeply divided over the Civil Constitution and its meaning for the church. A great many enthusiastically embraced the Revolutionary legislation, convinced that the new laws would initiate reforms necessary for the spiritual renewal of Catholicism. Others, how-ever, felt that they could not accept such an oath without restricting it to civil questions alone. The state must respect their independence in spiri-tual matters and their allegiance to the Holy Father in Rome. The deci-sion was even more complicated because of the pressure exerted on priests by the laity. In some regions the oath ceremony was transformed into a kind of general referendum for or against all of the religious policies of the Revolution, policies that might be perceived very differently depending on the local religious culture. This active involvement of the parishioners may help explain the remarkable regional variation in oathtaking. Thus, in the heavily Protestant regions of Languedoc and Alsace, where many Catho-lics were convinced that the Revolutionaries were trying to force them to become Calvinists or Lutherans, people might riot against any clergymen who attempted to take the oath. Likewise around much of the periphery of the kingdom—from Brittany, Normandy, Anjou, and western Poitou through the northern border provinces of Lorraine, Franche-Comté, and portions of the Pyrenees—the clergy was often encouraged to refuse the oath. The first popular protests against the Revolution in the department of Vendée—site of a massive counterrevolutionary uprising in 1793—can be dated to the implementation of the oath in the region. By contrast, throughout the greater Parisian Basin and in a large swathe of provinces in central, southwestern, and southeastern France, both priests and parishioners generally supported the oath. In these regions the local population might even do violence to clergymen who rejected the new legislation.[31]

The patriot leaders in Paris, however, had little understanding of the complexities of the oathtaking process, of the pressures from parishioners, or of the subtleties of theological reasoning. For them the oath was essentially a political, not a religious, act, and they were baffled by the actions of the "refractory" clergy who rejected it. Throughout the first six months of 1791, no other topic so dominated the correspondence of the deputies who wrote home to their families and friends. In nearly every letter Gaultier de Biauzat expounded at length on the religious crisis. He agonized over the fact that so many priests in his home province of Auvergne—some of them his friends—had failed to comply. He marshaled all possible arguments in favor of the Civil Constitution; he tried to imagine the "effects of fear" or the "scrupulousness of conscience" that might have led to such refusals; and he hoped against hope that clergymen would soon change their minds and acknowledge the benefits of the new legislation. François-Joseph Bouchette was not the only deputy forced to confront opposition to the oath in his own family. His sister would continually scold him for his "impiety" in supporting the Civil Constitution.[32]

Many provincial administrators were at least as impatient with the refractories as were the legislators. To them the basic fact seemed obvious: the refractory priests had rejected the Constitution and, by that very act, had embraced a counterrevolutionary position. The situation was only made worse by those parish clergymen—a minority no doubt—who vigorously contested their impending eviction from their parishes for failure to swear an unrestricted oath. They attacked the "constitutional" priests, sent in to replace them, as sacrilegious intruders whose sacraments would be inefficacious and who would place the souls of their parishioners in peril of damnation. It was feared they might also make use of the pulpit and the confessional to castigate the patriots and denounce the Revolution in general. Especially in those areas where a large proportion of parish clergymen rejected the oath, local administrators were angry and fearful that the clergy was undermining their authority and the legitimacy of the new regime.

They became obsessed with the possible links between refractories and counterrevolutionaries. They knew that a number of bishops had fled the country and were in relation with the emigrant princes across the Rhine and that they were smuggling in pastoral letters repudiating the Civil Constitution and the newly elected constitutional bishops. They also saw the reactionary press calling for a crusade against the Revolution in order to save the "true religion."

At first, in the name of religious freedom, the majority of the National Assembly had supported a policy of toleration. The refractories should be left alone and even allowed to perform the sacraments, as long as they stayed out of politics and did not disturb the peace. But many local authorities rejected such a position from the leadership in Paris who, in their view, had no experience with the reality of the problem. The refractories were viewed as the secret source of all unrest and opposition in the rural areas. "In alarming the consciences of timid and scrupulous people," wrote the leaders of the department of Aisne, "they are creating a faction that will soon outweigh that of good citizens."[33] In many departments blanket directives were issued requiring all refractories to leave their former parishes or move to a town where the national guard could keep an eye on them. In a few cases they were even imprisoned. By 1792 no less than twenty-eight departments had issued such directives, all of them technically illegal. Especially in western France, Alsace-Lorraine, and the Massif-Central, the ecclesiastical crisis created an ever-greater polarization between patriot townsmen and the strongly orthodox rural populations.[34] The schism that was created within the Catholic Church was to last for over a decade and was to have momentous effects on popular attitudes toward the whole Revolution.

Emigrants and Emigration

As the clergy confronted the crisis of the Civil Constitution and the oath, the French nobility also found itself facing a series of agonizing dilemmas. The vast majority—perhaps a hundred thousand individuals—still lived in rural chateaus or provincial townhouses scattered across the kingdom, and like their commoner neighbors, they initially struggled to understand what was happening in Versailles and in Paris. Based on the contemporary correspondence that has survived, many were overwhelmed by the Revolutionary events. They felt besieged, as their basic assumptions about society came under attack and as they saw themselves the target of suspicion and hatred. During the summer of 1789, Marie-Alexandrine de Lisleroy, residing in her country house in northern Languedoc, was beset with anxiety. The uprisings of the local peasantry and the people's sudden refusal to pay their seigneurial dues "led me to sleepless nights, and to days of weeping, sighing, and praying. I was overwhelmed with dark and frightful suspicions." They felt a mixture of consternation and humiliation at having to appease their new "masters," men who frequently came from the "dregs of society." "It is only the nobles," lamented the baroness de Barbier in Alsace, "who are forced to smile and be silent and submit to everything demanded of them, if they want to avoid being massacred as 'aristocrats'"— and all this in the face of a village council composed of a tailor, a butcher, a carpenter, and two peasants, who delighted in lording it over them.[35]

Many noble families opted to lie low as best they could, retired in their country houses or urban residences and consoling themselves with religion.[36] But for a great many younger gentlemen resignation was not an option. Spurred on by conservative newspapers, incited by conversations with fellow officers in the regiments where many of them served, prodded by letters from nobles who had already left for foreign lands, they began thinking increasingly of emigration and armed struggle. They were, after all, soldiers trained to fight, and the overthrow of the evil that was Revolution seemed a goal that was eminently worth fighting for. At the end of 1790, the British ambassador Earl Gower was amazed by the number of nobles he encountered in Paris who "express openly in public their hopes of a speedy counter-revolution." Soon the reactionary *Gazette de Paris* was publishing the "sacred list" of officers who had vowed to "offer their swords" to fight for the liberation of France.[37]

The emigration of the French nobility occurred in waves. A first cluster of departures had begun in the summer of 1789, when Artois and other members of the court aristocracy had fled across the borders. A second surge followed the National Assembly's suppression of the nobility in June 1790, a decree that for many nobles marked a major break with the Revolution. But the largest movement emerged in the summer and autumn of 1791. In June of that year the entire corps of officers, almost all of whom were nobles, was compelled to take an oath of allegiance to the Constitution, not unlike that imposed on the clergy a few months earlier. Many officers were already deeply unhappy with the Revolution. For months they had been struggling with the indiscipline of their troops, troops who were joining

Revolutionary clubs in ever-increasing numbers and who sometimes entered into open revolt against their commanders. And just as they were pondering their decision on the oath, they learned that the king himself had attempted to flee Paris and France. Taken together, the oath requirement and the king's flight generated a large new wave of emigration.[38]

For those currently serving in the military, the departure from France was relatively simple. A great many were stationed near the frontiers, and only a short ride was necessary to bring them onto foreign soil. The majority were relatively young and unmarried and thus had fewer family commitments to hold them back. According to one estimate, some three-fourths of all army officers had abandoned their posts by the end of 1791. At about the same time an equal proportion of naval officers in the port of Brest had failed to appear for service.[39] Yet noblemen residing in the interior of the kingdom also felt great pressure to emigrate. "Those officers who remained in France," remembered the marquise de La Tour du Pin, "received letters from those who had emigrated, reproaching them for their cowardice and their disloyalty to the royal family." The image of the brave and loyal knight, fulfilling his chivalrous destiny to defend the king and protect the church, increasingly appeared in every letter, in every conversation among the gentlemen of France. Many years later Antoine-Claire Thibaudeau vividly recalled the nobles he had encountered leaving Poitou in 1791: "They imagined themselves 'paladins' of old, flying away on the wings of honor, bragging they would soon return like thunder and lightning and force the patriots to come to their senses."[40]

But for the older generations of the nobility, for those who had never been in the army or who had long since retired and had wives and families, the decision could be wrenching. The Barbier family in Alsace, like the majority of more modest noble families, ultimately decided that emigration was economically impossible. The baronne explained to her son, who was already living in Austrian territories, that all they possessed was their landed property, and that if they left their home, they would lose everything and would have nothing left to live on. "We have no choice but to abandon ourselves to Providence and await with confidence the instructions He may give us." But many gentlemen felt compelled to leave, regardless of their economic and family situations. Madame de Médel described the situation near Poitiers where her fifty-year-old husband, a former officer, struggled to decide what to do: "In spite of themselves even sensible men have been swept up in this frenzy. No one is left. They have all gone off, with much regret and without any money. Three-fourths of them are depressed to leave behind their wives, their children, and their estates." Médel's husband eventually succumbed to the pressure, and he would still be away fighting for the counterrevolution when she died in 1799.[41]

By the end of 1791 at least 10,000 emigrants had left. They came from virtually every corner of France. Ironically, many regions of the country that had been little touched by the refractory clergy were now confronted with the departure of a significant segment of the local aristocracy.[42] Deputies of the National Assembly and its successor, the Legislative Assembly, regularly saw large numbers passing through Paris on their way to the frontiers. By late 1791 over half of the nobles who had sat in the first Assembly had also begun leaving the country, most of them joining the counterrevolutionary armies forming across the Rhine.[43] Irland de Bâzoges, the noble magistrate who had never served in the army and had scarcely handled a firearm, left to enlist as a simple soldier.[44] The population in general and the patriot leadership in particular were intensely aware of such emigration and of the dangers it posed. A great many of the nobles made no effort to hide their intentions as they packed up and left their provincial residences and streamed through the capital en route to Germany.[45] Such behavior provided direct and visible evidence of the numbers of the former dominant class who were now heading off to swell the ranks of the forces waiting to invade the nation and destroy the Revolution. It also helped raise suspicion against those nobles who remained behind, any of whom might well be in correspondence with the enemies abroad and plotting internal uprisings.

The King's Flight and the "Terror" of 1791

It was in the midst of the growing tension over the refractory clergy and the emigrant nobles that the extraordinary news swept across France: the king, Louis XVI, had disappeared and was presumed to have fled to foreign lands. On the morning of June 21, 1791 he and his entire family were found missing from their rooms at the Tuileries Palace.

The king had been deeply troubled by the Revolution, and he was unable to reconcile himself to his loss of the power and prerogatives of the Old Regime. If we can believe the memoirs of one of his ministers, he merely made a pretense of cooperation with the patriots, while waiting for the new regime to collapse in anarchy from its own unworkable schemes.[46] Yet his royal consort, the Austrian princess Marie-Antoinette, was far less passive in the face of events. As early as 1789 she urged the king to leave Paris, and by late 1790 she and her "friend" and probable lover—the Swedish count Axel von Fersen—were making detailed plans for the king to escape to Austrian territory. Though the king himself long opposed the plan, fearing for the safety of his family and always finding it difficult to make major decisions, he finally came around to the idea in the spring of 1791. He was deeply unhappy with the Civil Constitution of the Clergy, which his advisers had convinced him to approve. And he was indignant over the events of April 18 of that year, when he and his family had been prevented by crowds of Parisians from leaving for an Easter sojourn at the palace of Saint Cloud— crowds who were angered that Louis was taking communion with a refractory priest and who feared that the outing was an excuse for a permanent departure. As so many of the counterrevolutionaries, Louis had convinced himself that a small clique of radical Jacobins in Paris had seized control of the country and that if he could only reach the provinces, the vast majority of the nation would welcome his return to leadership.

At first the great escape, which began in the night of June 20–21, went remarkably well. The goal was to travel secretly to the northeastern frontier, there to be welcomed and protected by a contingent of troops under the command of the marquis de Bouillé. If necessary, they would receive support from the Austrian army, positioned just across the frontier. With the help of Fersen, the king, the queen, and their two children—along with a small group of servants—succeeded in slipping out of the palace and escaping unnoticed from the ever-suspicious city of Paris. By dawn they were rolling across the plains of Champagne in a caravan of two carriages and two guards on horseback, disguised as a train of Russian nobles. Though the king was recognized on several occasions, the witnesses were too shocked and uncertain to act, and the party was allowed to continue its journey. For a variety of reasons, however, the travelers fell several hours behind schedule and a detachment of troops, sent by General Bouillé to meet the royal party, concluded that the king was not coming and retreated from the scene.

Toward eight o'clock that evening, as they crossed the small town of Sainte-Menehould on the edge of Lorraine, the royal couple was recognized once again, this time by a manager of the relay stables named Drouet who had once served as a cavalryman in Versailles. After the party had moved on, Drouet convinced the town council to act, and he and a friend gal-

The king's flight halted by the national guard in Varennes, June 21, 1791. The royal carriage had just emerged from the archway in the center of town when it was blocked by a cart filled with furniture, positioned by Drouet and local guardsmen. One can just see the king in the carriage window. After his capture, the king and his family were forced to return to Paris. J. Bulthuis, engraved by Daniel Vrijdag, © Coll. Musée de la Révolution française, Domaine de Vizille, MRF L 1985.848.59.

loped across country to overtake the caravan. In the small town of Varennes the two men were able to rouse a group of patriots and national guardsmen, and the king and his family were forced to halt. There ensued a long night of negotiations between Louis and the Varennes town fathers. But with pressure from the crowds in the streets and with the arrival of a courier from the National Assembly, the royal family was forced to turn around and begin a slow, humiliating trip back to Paris, escorted by hundreds of national guardsmen. The return of the carriage into the capital was watched by tens of thousands of Parisians, lining the streets in sullen silence, refusing even to remove their hats in an obvious insult to the king.

Over the next three weeks, with the king and queen now held virtual prisoners in the royal palace, the deputies of the National Assembly struggled to find a solution to the crisis. They no longer believed that the king had been "kidnapped," as some had initially suggested. But they were frightened by the consequences of trying or punishing the monarch and appalled by the prospect of rewriting a Constitution on which they had labored for almost two years. Ultimately, the majority convinced themselves that Louis had once again been misled by his advisers. In mid-July they voted to continue drafting the Constitution as planned and present it to the king. If he agreed to sign it and abide by it, they would return him to power. Otherwise a regency would be established until the king's young son, educated by pro-Revolutionary tutors, could assume the throne.

In the face of this decision, a number of monarchists and conservatives argued that the Assembly had gone too far and outstripped its authority; that a king had the right to travel wherever he wished and that confining him to the Tuileries after his return was an outrage to his sacred person. The reactionary press lambasted the Assembly, and one paper even launched a campaign for volunteers to serve as "hostages" for the royal couple, allowing them to escape their house arrest. In short order hundreds of men and women, overwhelmingly members of the former nobility, wrote passionate letters vowing to sacrifice themselves for the freedom of Louis and Marie-Antoinette.[47]

Yet the great majority of French patriots had been profoundly shocked by the attempted escape. The Assembly was flooded with anguished letters from citizens throughout the kingdom, recounting their surprise and their consternation. Madame de Pompery, who rarely concerned herself with politics, described the reaction in her hometown in Brittany: "Here, as everywhere, we are deeply affected by the terrible news shaking the whole of France. Everyone is caught up in 'what if' and 'why?' and 'how?' Since the alarm is so widespread, even those normally little interested in politics are worried and distressed, thinking of their absent friends and losing sleep at night."[48] During the interval of almost a month—with the king suspended from power and the Constituent pondering the decision it should take—everywhere in the country popular societies, town councils, district and department assemblies, and improvised citizens' committees began debating the situation on their own. Patriots had been especially angered by the personal message the king had left behind when he fled, a message in which he repudiated almost all the Revolutionary decrees that he had previously signed and sworn to uphold. Many citizens were convinced that if the king's flight had been successful, it would have been followed by a foreign invasion to crush the Revolution. Everywhere he was treated with extraordinarily harsh language and brutal caricatures—portrayed as a pig, a fool, a drunkard. In hundreds of letters addressed to the Constituent he was described as a traitor and a liar who had perjured his sacred oath to support the Constitution. Many announced that they would follow the decision of the Assembly whatever that decision might be, and a surprising number declared they were prepared to see Louis removed from the throne. A few even recommended that the monarchy be suppressed altogether and a republic created. Gaultier de Biauzat admitted receiving a large number of letters from towns and clubs in his province of Auvergne, demanding "that the nation treat the king as a criminal guilty of treason."[49]

The most dramatic and well-organized reaction against the monarchy was orchestrated in Paris.[50] Within days of the king's flight the Cordeliers Club and the various fraternal societies had organized a series of protest marches across the city, with thousands of Parisian men and women linking arms and shouting out slogans promoting the dethroning of the king and the creation of a republic. Soon the movement had attracted the support of a number of journalists, from Jacques Brissot, Louise Kéralio, and Jean-Paul Marat to the ex-marquis de Condorcet, all of whom vigorously supported the republican position. Dismayed by the Constituent's refusal even to read their petitions and by its decision to reinstate Louis if he signed the Constitution, the protesters planned a monumental petition-signing event for July 17 on the Champ de Mars. Tens of thousands of Parisians came out on that warm Sunday afternoon, some to sign the demand for a "new organization of executive authority" and some simply to watch the proceedings. But the majority in the National Assembly, feeling that their authority had been flaunted and that republicans and unruly crowds were pushing an insurrection, now lost all patience. Mayor Bailly and the Parisian city council were pressured by the Assembly to declare martial law. When a large contingent of national guardsmen was sent to the Champ de Mars to halt the ceremony, people began pelting them with stones. And the guardsmen, whether through anger or fear, opened fire on the crowd and then charged with fixed bayonets and with cavalry on horseback. Dozens—and perhaps hundreds—of citizens were shot or stabbed or trampled in the panic that ensued. Tragically the killings occurred on the very spot where the great festival of brotherhood had taken place just one year earlier.

For the first time the patriot majority in the National Assembly had passed the threshold of state-sponsored violence. They had strongly urged the Paris militia to crush the movement. Thereafter, throughout July and much of August, the deputies pursued a policy of repression which has sometimes been portrayed as a trial run for the Terror.[51] The Assembly's surveillance committee continued to track down participants in the counterrevolutionary conspiracy that had nearly succeeded in separating the king from the Revolution. But it was equally preoccupied with the "republicans" who had directly defied the authority of the Assembly. Martial law was maintained and numerous individuals were arrested in Paris, many of them held in prison without indictments. National guardsmen and plainclothes police spies circulated in the city with orders to halt all demonstrations or street gatherings. Surveillance of the press was reinstituted for the first time since early 1789, and a number of key journalists from both the conservative and the radical republican press were arrested or forced into hiding—Du Rozoi, as well as Marat, Desmoulins, and Kéralio. Many of the more moderate deputies hoped to end once and for all the persistent popular turmoil that had reigned in Paris for months and to break the strength of those parallel powers—the sections and the clubs—that had put in question their policies.

While much of the repression in Paris was directly supervised by the committees of the National Assembly, similar or even harsher measures were pursued independently in the provinces by various administrative bodies. Unknown strangers found traveling through France, individuals rumored to have used seditious language, anyone who even looked "suspicious": all might be arrested and imprisoned without trial. Mail written by or addressed to suspect persons was illegally opened and searched for evidence of evildoing. But it was the refractory clergy and the nobility who were subjected to the greatest scrutiny. For weeks local authorities had felt harassed by the activities of the nonjuring priests, and the news of the king's flight had set off a new surge of noble emigration. National guardsmen and police agents were sent to raid chateaus and religious houses all over the country, looking for unsavory activities. Refractory priests were rounded up, whether or not they had caused disturbances. On occasion all nobles in a given area were confined to their homes or required to reside in specific towns. A letter from the town council of Limoges was typical of dozens addressed to the National Assembly during this period. Officials complained of the large number of former officers and royal bodyguards crossing their town en route to Paris—many of them carrying letters from emigrant princes across the Rhine urging them to join up or suffer the "brand of infamy." In general, the officials announced, "Our aristocrats and refractory priests show the greatest audacity and are counting on the success of the counterrevolution."[52]

The crisis of Varennes also led to a terrible schism within the Jacobin Club. Already in the spring of 1791 a majority of the Jacobin deputies had been recoiling from their earlier radical positions and pushing for an end to the Revolution. As the onetime radical Basquiat de Mugriet put it in late May, "a time for moderation has begun. Despotism has been entirely overcome. We now must establish the edifice of liberty on a foundation of unity and peace among all citizens."[53] In the days after the king's flight, the violent language of many of the nondeputies in the Jacobin Club, spoken out against the king and in favor of a republic, had outraged the more moderate majority of the Constituents. On July 16, led by the so-called triumvirate of Barnave, Duport, and Alexandre Lameth—the onetime Young Turks of the Jacobin movement, now the advocates of moderation—almost all of the deputies walked out of the meeting and formed a rival "friends of the Constitution" across the street in the buildings of the former Feuillant monastery. Only a handful of deputies—including Pétion, Robespierre, Abbé Grégoire, and four or five others—refused to leave the original club. Thereafter each of the two groups claimed to be the true embodiment of the original society.[54]

Over the coming weeks the Jacobins, led by Pétion, attempted several overtures for a compromise with the "Feuillants." Sister clubs in the provinces, appalled by the split, wrote fervent appeals for reunification. Eventually some sixty of the Constituent deputies returned to the original mother society. But the schism proved irreparable, and it rapidly became the source of extraordinary bitterness between the two rival groups. Basquiat railed against his former colleagues who had remained in the Jacobins and who, in his opinion, thought more of popularity with the masses than of the good of the nation. It was essential that all true patriots abandon "a society where exaggeration had replaced patriotism, where . . . a few Friends of the Constitution, under the pretense of seeking popular support, sought to plunge us into the most frightful anarchy." Bouchette even accused them of being paid agents of a foreign power, bent on destroying the Revolution: "It is said that money from abroad is being used to promote republicanism. . . . The goal is to launch a civil war." Those remaining in the Jacobins, for their part, were outraged by the "tyranny" and repression of the Feuillant majority in the Assembly. Surely it was more than a coincidence that they had seceded on the very eve of the brutal massacre of patriots on the Champ de Mars, a massacre promoted by a Feuillant majority in the Assembly. Patriots who once thought of themselves as brothers, moved by the common goal of creating a better world, now accused one another of treachery and betrayal.[55] The terrible schism within the Jacobins in the wake of Varennes would have an enormous impact on factional divisions among the patriots in the years to come.

In the midst of the crisis and the split of the radicals, the National Assembly forged ahead. With most of the conservative deputies boycotting the meetings and with the radicals in disarray, the Feuillants made a supreme effort to complete the Constitution, hoping that the king would sign the document and that the Revolution could be ended and calm restored to the country. In early September, exhausted by their efforts and by their long confrontation with opposition on both their right and their left, the deputies declared that the final version had been finished, and the document was presented to the king. After reading and considering the Constitution for over a week, Louis announced he would accept it. On September 14 he went to the Assembly hall to affix his signature and pronounce an oath of adherence. With the king's support, the Assembly then decreed a general amnesty in favor of all prisoners arrested for political reasons. Everywhere the prisons were emptied of counterrevolutionary and pro-Republican prisoners alike. From all over France patriot elites wrote letters to the Constituent, affirming their allegiance to the new regime.[56]

But even though the Revolution was declared to be "over," deep suspicions persisted. In the minds of a great many citizens, the refractories and the emigrants remained as great a danger as ever. Even if the patriots hoped with all their heart that the king had mended his ways, they were beset with doubts. Had Louis not already ignored and perjured three or four previous oaths? Could one really be confident that he would honor his latest signature? René Levasseur described the atmosphere in the autumn of 1791: "People still spoke . . . of general reconciliation, of union, of fraternity. But everything had changed. Unity was on their lips, but dissension was in their hearts."[57] Such were the prevailing anxieties as the National Assembly formally disbanded and the newly elected Legislative Assembly began its sessions on the first day of October.

5

Between Hope and Fear

FROM THE very beginning, in their efforts to transform the nation, the Revolutionaries had placed a premium on reason and on the rational reconstruction of French society and institutions on the basis of liberty and equality. And their organizational achievements, many of which would have a long-term impact on France and on much of western Europe, should not be underestimated. Yet a time of Revolution is very different from normal times. The experience of the years after 1789 invariably aroused a range of emotions, emotions that would often have a profound influence on the actions and perceptions of the elites. Before we turn to the second phase of the Revolution, the era of the Legislative Assembly, it is important to take stock of the evolving mindset of French men and women during this first period.

The creation of a National Assembly, the fall of the Bastille, and the Revolutionary decrees of August 1789 had sparked an intense thrill of excitement and joy among a large number of French citizens. Changes that few had ever imagined possible in their lifetime had engendered a surge of near millenarian hopes for a world transformed, in which a "new man" might take control of his destiny and forge a society based on reason, equality, and universal brotherhood. Although this Revolutionary faith was initially centered in Paris and in the major towns of the kingdom, over the following years it even penetrated the rural villages, where the great mass of the population lived. It spread through the impact of popular elections by which active citizens everywhere were invited to choose their officials and magistrates. It spread through participation in citizens' militias, where even relatively humble men who paid sufficient taxes might be elected officers. It spread through the efforts of Revolutionary clubs to educate the population and to organize oathtaking ceremonies, festivals, and fraternal banquets in which the new democratic ethos was hailed and performed in the presence of the whole community.[1] It is easy to forget how stirring was the mantra of "liberty, equality, fraternity" as experienced by the men and women of the Revolution. For it embodied a system of values, a whole new basis for society that the Revolutionaries believed would change the world forever.

Yet even before the Estates General had met, hope and enthusiasm had gone hand in hand with fear and uncertainty. From the spring of 1789 Adrien Colson, Nicolas Ruault, and Félix Faulcon had all conveyed their concerns that attempts to enact major reforms might lead to chaos and anarchy, to "utter calamity and destruction," as Colson had put it. Such anxiety had increased tenfold during the harrowing summer of 1789, with the waves of panic and violence and the emergence of a power vacuum in which many Old Regime institutions had collapsed and lost their legitimacy before a new system could be created to take their place. Almost from the beginning, moreover, patriots had been beset with fear that the transformations were too good to be true, that those who had dominated society under the Old Regime would do everything in their power to turn back the clock and reverse the achievements of 1789. The reality of the threat seemed confirmed, moreover, by the emerging movement of counterrevolution, led by a warrior class that was prepared to defend to the death an aristocratic and inegalitarian system, sanctioned in their view by both nature and religion. This complex mixture of contradictory emotions, the feelings of both fervor and fear, optimism and pessimism was much in evidence in the correspondence of the period. "You have seen," wrote the Breton lawyer Jean-Pierre Boullé, "how tormented I am by doubt. I am devoured by anxiety, . . . between hope and fear." The small-town barrister from central France, Antoine Durand, described many of the same feelings: the "striking contrast between good and evil, anguish and hope, joy and sadness, which so rapidly follow upon one another."[2]

To be sure, throughout the Revolution the relative balance between the two emotional penchants could fluctuate in the face of changing events. For a time, in the spring and summer of 1790, the Revolutionaries had felt a wave of confidence that once the transition had been achieved, once the Constitution had been instituted and the new administration had begun functioning, everything would fall into place and the new age of liberty would be permanently established. There had been just such a surge of self-confidence during the federation celebrations spreading across the nation and culminating with the monumental ceremony in Paris on the first anniversary of the fall of the Bastille. The rituals of collective oathtaking at the core of these festivals produced powerful feelings of unity and common purpose which contemporaries described in the most glowing terms.

However, the effects of such celebrations rarely endured more than a few weeks before the Revolutionaries found themselves facing a new array of dangers. The spring of 1791 had been particularly unsettling in this regard. The menace of the emigrant armies gathering in Germany and ostentatiously announcing their imminent return to power was invariably disturbing. Perhaps even more distressing were the perceived counterrevolutionaries living in their midst, notably the tens of thousands of nobles still residing in the countryside and the large numbers of parish clergymen who had rejected the constitutional oath. Until such priests could be replaced, it was feared, the whole rural population might be turned against the Revolution.

By late 1791 the feelings of anxiety had even penetrated the dreams of some of our witnesses. In October of that year Guittard de Floriban, who rarely mentioned his inner emotions, confided to his diary a terrifying nightmare in which he fell off a high wall into a great basin of water. "Dear God," he cried out, "have pity on my soul!" A few months later Rosalie Jullien recounted a dream in which she was walking in the pale moonlight within a strange landscape when she too fell into a deep abyss.[3] This climate of uncertainty, generated in large measure by the very nature of the Revolutionary process, would be intensified by the effects of two other phenomena that increasingly influenced the population: rumor and denunciation.

Rumor in Revolution

Rumor, of course, is a phenomenon common to every society and to every age. In classical antiquity Virgil even treated it as a kind of female demigod, insidiously disrupting society with "facts and falsehoods mingled."[4] In the more innocuous form of gossip, accounts of the private lives of neighbors or persons of note might pass as a form of entertainment. Louis-Sébastien Mercier described such activities in Old Regime Paris, in which individuals "eager to feed themselves on the latest gossip . . . forget their families and the dinner hour, and give themselves over to the singular passion for exchanging nonsense in the middle of the street." Colson frequently confided to his friend in the countryside an assortment of unsubstantiated hearsay pulsing through the city, some of it true, some of it not. There were reports that the king's sister, Madame Elizabeth, was about to join a convent; that a royal sister-in-law was pregnant; that the queen herself was with child. Much of this information was picked up by Colson from various individuals he encountered in his daily activities: the wine merchant across the street, or a cook he knew who worked in Versailles, or the unmarried daughter of his downstairs landlord. Other, more scurrilous accounts of the great might circulate through the city in manuscript notes or printed scandal sheets, some of them distinctly pornographic in nature.[5]

But rumors could also involve much more serious concerns. Social scientists have demonstrated that people are particularly susceptible to rumor in times of uncertainty, ambiguity, and perceived danger and where there is a general lack of trust in the institutions conveying information.[6] In this sense, rumors have been described as an alternative form of news, "improvised news," produced as a community struggles to ascertain the reality of its situation and to develop appropriate responses. Rumors were almost certainly amplified under the Old Regime by the extreme secrecy of the royal government and by the tight censorship of the press, which made reliable information frustratingly difficult to come by. In fact, we often forget how few of the decisions of monarchs and ministers were actually made public to contemporaries.

In periods of high tension, the city of Paris and other urban centers could vibrate with improvised news concerning the price of bread and the causes of its increase, or the threat of war, or the actions of the police. Rumors could reverberate from street to street and from window to window with extraordinary rapidity, following complex networks of conversations exchanged or overheard at a fountain or in a bread line or across a courtyard. Peddlers, water carriers, bakers, and household servants were said to be particularly active in passing along such accounts. Any one individual might easily hear several different, even contradictory, versions, for rumors rarely moved in a simple linear chain. As the stories were repeated and discussed in multiple exchanges, they were typically modified and metamorphosed. Such modifications might occur in part through misunderstandings in moments of tension and in part as individuals sought to justify their own terror by exaggerating the extent of a perceived danger—implying that their fear came not from personal weakness or cowardice, but from a truly frightful situation.[7] Modifications might also entail simplifications that made the message easier to remember and convey but that also edited away nuance and inflated oppositions, rendering an account that glorified heroes and denigrated villains into simplified, black-and-white roles. Such accounts were also commonly affected by previously held attitudes concerning those persons and groups touched by the rumors. Individuals might subtly modify stories in such a way as to justify and confirm preexisting resentment toward long-standing antagonists. One might readily believe the worst and even embroider a more exaggerated account, when a rumor involved nobles or priests whom one had long disliked for other reasons. As the historian Marc Bloch put it, "We are easily led to believe what we need to believe."[8] Moreover, rumors not only disseminated interpretive versions of the "news"; they could also communicate moods and feelings. The emotions of anger or fear or general anxiety could move through the streets hand in hand with the stories of secret grain hoarding or of outrages exacted by the police.[9]

With the advent of the Revolution, both the nature and the intensity of rumors were substantially altered. Stories circulating in the countryside concerning events in the capital in July 1789 had played a major role in the chain-reaction panic of the Great Fear that spread across much of France. In Paris itself, to judge from the correspondence of our witnesses, the rumor networks continued to function as under the Old Regime, but they became far more politicized. Rumors closely linked to Revolutionary events often replaced the social gossip and anecdotes of the earlier letters. The "improvised news" proliferated through an array of new centers for the exchange of speculative information. The sectional assemblies, the national guard meetings, and the neighborhood clubs were all constantly attuned to the latest stories circulating in the city. Rumors were further amplified through the flood of often contradictory assertions in the hundreds of uncensored newspaper and pamphlet publications which had suddenly become available. Confronted with this profusion of writings and with little previous experience in evaluating a free press, many literate citizens could only treat the print media as another source of rumor.

The confusion provoked by the mass of papers and pamphlets was increased, moreover, by the activities of newspaper hawkers. Commonly illiterate themselves, the paper peddlers poured through the streets every morning and afternoon, filling the air with shouts of impromptu "head-lines," conceived as much to attract sales as to convey the actual content of their merchandise. The deputy François Roubaud described the spectacle: "the endless roar of several thousand bellowing voices from seven in the morning until noon and from five to midnight, announcing a major de-cree, a great victory, a frightful plot of the aristocrats and the priests, an insurrection in such and such a town, always with the names and the facts completely distorted." As time went on, some of the newspaper editors them-selves felt compelled by the competition to develop short, pithy first-page articles that could attract more sales and could be adapted by the paper sellers. In any case, Mercier was appalled by the effects of the rumors and falsehoods propagated in the city: "Simple proposals are transformed into formal decrees, and a whole neighborhood argues endlessly or is seized with fright over something that never took place. Though the common people have been misled a thousand times by such false announcements, they con-tinue nevertheless to believe them."[10]

The power of rumor was especially tenacious among the Parisian pop-ular classes, a great many of whom were functionally illiterate and who partook primarily of an oral culture. The educated classes, on the other hand, maintained a more ambiguous position toward the stories circulating in the streets. Colson was often quite condescending in his description of such sources. He derided the rumors that were obviously untrue, even ri-diculous, and he added snide remarks about the credulity of the common people. "The news," he wrote, "is mixed with fables, which greatly affect its veracity."[11] On occasion he even attempted to verify a particularly trou-bling rumor, as when word of a riot near the city hall sent him scurrying over to see for himself (the news turned out to be totally unfounded). But if anxiety and the need for action were intense enough, and if a rumor was repeated often enough—for repetition could increase credibility—certain unproved rumors might even be accepted by those who were normally more skeptical of word-of-mouth reports. Thus, when the subject was especially important for him and when no other information was available, Colson did sometimes take rumors into consideration and give them credence. So too Rosalie Jullien reported to her husband even some of the more unlikely "news" she had heard through her apartment window, shouted out by a neighbor in the street for everyone to hear. As Dominique Garat explained, living as he did "with so many people thinking and behaving on the basis of suspicions, it was sometimes impossible not to have suspicions myself."[12]

Over time rumors seemed to reverberate through Paris with ever-greater intensity. The British spy William Miles commented on the extraordinary number circulating in the city in the spring of 1791, some based on possible events, others quite unbelievable: "All these tales," he wrote, "absurd as some of the fabrications are, pass for authentic, and serve no less to bewilder than to inflame the public mind." For Mirabeau it was not just a question of "absurdities" among the "vulgar," but of rumors that might cut across cultural divides and touch the whole of society—especially in this time of upheaval: "In periods of calamity nothing is more striking to an observer than the widespread tendency to believe and to exaggerate the most appalling news. It would seem that logic no longer consists of calculating degrees of probability, but of giving credence to even the most unlikely rumors. . . . We then resemble children, for whom the most frightening tales are always the most eagerly followed."[13]

The number and nature of the rumors circulating in Paris and in other parts of the country can of course never be known. Since such stories were normally passed by word of mouth—over the "grapevine," as it were—they are invariably difficult to document. Yet we learn bits and pieces of the more unsettling rumors filtering through the streets from accounts in newspapers and the correspondence and diaries of our various witnesses. Clearly the Great Fear of July was by no means the last major rumor to affect Paris. Soon after the October Days, a surge of panic coursed through the city that gangs of thieves were planning to attack private homes during the night: "This abominable plot," wrote Colson, "has caused alarm throughout Paris; a great many women, in particular, have fallen ill from terrible fright." On October 10, under public pressure, the town fathers ordered the whole city illuminated during the night. All inhabitants were told to place candles or lanterns in their windows, so that the police and the national guard could more easily survey the streets.[14] An even more chilling story began sweeping through neighborhoods in early December—conveyed to Colson through a conversation with his landlord and from the words of a newspaper hawker outside his window. Thieves and murderers were said to be plotting to break out of the Paris prisons and attack good citizens. Someone was said to be marking the houses of the city with white and red crosses, indicating those who were to be robbed and those who were to be both robbed and killed—apparently reviving memories of the Saint-Bartholomew's Day Massacre in the sixteenth century. Soon thereafter rumors raged that hundreds of aristocrats had acquired national guard uniforms and were planning an attack on Christmas Day to kill all the patriot leaders. Anxiety was so great that officials once again ordered an illumination of the city during Christmas night. Colson ultimately rejected the Christmas plot as ridiculous and un-proven and revived his mocking condemnation of popular credulity. Yet the usually more skeptical Ruault seems to have believed it, crediting the city's salvation only to the timely actions of the municipal government and the mobilization of the national guard.[15]

Such rumors were probably influenced in part by the widespread belief—among both the elites and the masses—that the chaotic conditions and power vacuum of the early Revolution were allowing criminals to prolif-erate. Colson returned again and again over the first two years of the Rev-olution to what he perceived as a veritable crime wave.[16] Whether the per-ceived increase in theft and murder was real or not is difficult to confirm, but much of Paris clearly believed it was real. The rumor and reality of thefts and acts of violence even led to a series of lamppost lynchings by vigilante groups in certain neighborhoods. Between May 1790 and February 1792 no less than thirteen lynchings or attempted lynchings are known to have taken place in Parisian neighborhoods.[17]

In the wake of the king's attempted flight in June 1791, the rumor mill became even more intense, bewildering, and disconcerting. Another wave of stories swept through Paris that criminals were about to escape from the prisons and attack the Revolutionaries. At the same time there were new chain-reaction panics in the provinces, with rumors sweeping across much of northern France that the Austrian army was on the march, burning and killing as it went. As the story spread westward from village to village and from town to town—eventually reaching the outskirts of Paris—the imagined invasion grew from a few hundred to tens of thousands of sol-diers.[18] Increasingly, as we shall see, all such rumors were dominated by the deeply unsettling stories of counterrevolutionary conspiracy.

The Dialectics of Denunciation

Beyond the suspicions generated by the circulation of rumors, fear and mis-trust were reinforced during the first years of the Revolution through the expanding practice of denunciation. From the earliest months denuncia-tion was actively promoted by patriot elites as a salutary act, necessary and unavoidable if the gains of 1789 were to be preserved. Given the extraordi-nary scope and novelty of the transformations the Revolutionaries sought to bring about, their feelings of vulnerability were perhaps all but inevitable. As early as July 1789 a journalist calling himself *Le dénonciateur national* had warned his readers against the machinations of the aristocracy and the possible betrayal of political leaders in general, all of whom were assumed to be subject to corruption. In such a situation it was essential for all citizens to "keep their eyes focused on everyone and everything."[19] The elites were perhaps also influenced by their studies in secondary school and the denunciatory texts of the Latin orators Cato and Cicero, which they had all been compelled to memorize. There were endless references in pamphlets and speeches to Cicero's preservation of the Roman republic by rooting out the conspiracy of Catalina. It was largely on the basis of such texts that Camille Desmoulins proclaimed a "declaration of the rights of the accuser," affirming the fundamental prerogative and duty of every citizen in a democracy to search out the enemies of the state. If the ideals of the Revolution were to survive and the threats of counterrevolution beaten back, citizens must be constantly on the watch against the adversaries of liberty, whoever they might be: "In the present circumstances, it is important to favor denunciation." It was in much the same spirit that Mirabeau had praised the positive value of such acts: "Under a despot," he wrote in the autumn of 1789, "an act of denunciation would be repulsive. But in the midst of the perils that surround us, it must be considered as the most important of our new virtues, as the protector of our nascent liberty."[20]

Yet the manner in which this new virtue was to be utilized, the form and function of denunciation in actual practice, was at first somewhat uncertain. Many Revolutionaries hoped that it would be sufficient to sensitize citizens to the dangers they faced and that the disapproval of the community, as determined by the "tribunal of public opinion," would intimidate all real or potential counterrevolutionaries.[21] Several of the most talented newspaper editors of the period developed denunciation as a central component of their journalism. They styled themselves as watchdogs of the Revolution and continually urged their readers to be vigilant. Jacques Brissot set the tone in July 1789 through the epigram published at the top of each issue of his *Patriote français:* "A free newspaper is the vigilant sentinel of the people." The champion of the denunciatory art, however, was undoubtedly "the people's friend" Jean-Paul Marat. From the first appearance of his newspaper, accusation became a fundamental element of his stock in trade. "I am the eye of the people," he wrote in September 1789. "Will you forever be children, will you never see the truth, and must the friend of the people continually remove the scales from your eyes?" He encouraged citizens to address denunciations directly to him, so he could publish them in his paper. And when he strongly suspected the shady activities of one or another official, he might even compose a "letter to the editor" himself.[22]

Of course, patriots were also aware that unscrupulous individuals might make false accusations out of a desire for personal gain or revenge. It was for this reason that all denunciations were supposed to be made openly and in public, with denouncers signing their names to written statements. If an accuser was mistaken or motivated by personal animosity, the accused would have no difficulty—so the argument went—in defending himself before the jury of public opinion, and the truth would come out.[23] Indeed, the need to make denunciations openly was one of the most powerful arguments for complete freedom of the press. In August 1790 Gaultier de Biauzat admitted that at times "such freedom has led to libel and calumny." But in the present situation, with the Revolution still struggling to consolidate itself, such exaggerations had to be tolerated: "After its long servitude, liberty now reasserts itself with enormous energy, and sometimes, at first, oversteps the bounds."[24]

Not all patriots, to be sure, shared in the enthusiasm for such accusatory practices. The radical newspaper, the *Révolutions de Paris,* cautioned that an excess of denunciations could destroy all confidence among citizens, lead to exaggerated suspicions, and provide a means of vengeance and intrigue for those acting primarily from unsavory personal motives. If the denunciations continued unchecked, no one would want to serve in public office. Several of the Constituent deputies, like the Breton Legendre, complained of the endless denunciations. Colson quickly grew tired of Marat's jeremiads. He even wondered whether the Friend of the People was not being paid by the aristocrats to promote fear and confusion among citizens and whether his paper should not be renamed "the enemy of the people."[25]

Yet there was also an economic logic to the inclusion of ample denunciations in the newspapers. The editors were faced with heavy competition, and there could be no doubt that denunciation made excellent copy and provided drama for the hawkers in the streets. The journalists were well aware of the anxieties already widespread among their readers and of the suspicions of conspiracy propagated by rumors. Moreover, the newspapers were not the sole organs of denunciation during the early years of the Revolution. Accusatory practices were reinforced by the activities of many of the patriotic clubs. If one were truly a friend of the Constitution, one must not only support the propagation and understanding of its ideals but also do everything in one's power to foil those who sought to undermine or destroy it. Many popular societies included a commitment to surveillance and denunciation in their foundation charters, as a fundamental obligation of membership. Thus, in Marseille, each new member took a pledge "to defend with my fortune and my blood every citizen who has the courage to denounce traitors to the fatherland and enemies of liberty." "Never avert your eyes," they were warned; "spy upon the public conduct and even the private lives of officials in order that they cannot prevaricate in their sacred functions." Some provincial Jacobins, like those in Toulon, wore tricolor badges with an eye painted over, as a sign of vigilance.[26] In this they followed a practice initiated by the Cordeliers in Paris, who prominently affixed the eye of surveillance to all of their publications and who urged their affiliates throughout the city to be forever watchful of the former privileged and of the possibilities of hidden conspiracies.[27]

The Paris Jacobins made no mention of denunciations in their original charter of February 1790. But by the spring of 1791 they were following the lead of certain provincial clubs in requiring an oath to "denounce all traitors of the fatherland, even at the risk of our lives and our fortunes."[28] In late 1791 they addressed a circular letter to their network throughout the country, requesting reports on any suspicious activities taking place locally. "We invite you, brothers and friends," they wrote, "to give us as soon as possible accurate and precise information on the condition of your department . . . and generally on everything concerning public tranquility and security." Thereafter, at the beginning of almost every session, the secretary read the correspondence arriving from the provinces denouncing various groups or individuals.[29]

That the efforts of the popular societies and the newspapers were having an effect is well documented for the city of Bordeaux, the great Atlantic port in southwestern France.[30] In the spring of 1791 the Bordeaux Friends of the Constitution followed the Paris Jacobins in requiring all its members to swear a "second oath" to be on the lookout for the enemies of the nation and to formally denounce any they discovered. Over the next two years the club received over 200 letters of accusation from both members and nonmembers against a host of perceived evildoers. Inevitably, many of the denunciations were aimed at the nobility and the refractory clergy and their purported local supporters. These two groups were commonly presented as enemies of the Revolution by definition, and they aroused particular suspicion when stories circulated that they were holding secret meetings—meetings which no patriot had actually witnessed but in which counterrevolutionary plotting was assumed to have taken place.

Yet the great majority of the accusations before the Bordeaux club—some three out of four—were aimed not at nobles or clergymen but at other commoners, neighbors, and colleagues in the community. Citizens were attacked for a variety of misdeeds, from anti-Revolutionary sympathies to administrative malfeasance. There were strong condemnations against all those who had joined the rival conservative club, "Friends of the Law." Even after the club was forced to shut down, patriots continued to identify and pursue all those who had attended the meetings and who were never forgiven for this sin of their past political options. Other citizens were called down for various forms of inegalitarian actions or words. Individuals were criticized for a failure to use the address of "citizen" rather than "Monsieur," or for speaking in "a haughty tone" or for being "accustomed to seeing themselves as a superior beings." One commoner notable, sarcastically described as a "puny hero," was chastened for taking on airs and ostentatiously riding about town on a white horse. It was a dramatic demonstration of the obsession with equality that rapidly penetrated the whole patriot community.

As time went on, a growing number of the accusations were aimed at other members of the club itself. Brother Jacobins were blamed for various forms of misconduct during the meetings, or in their roles as officials, or for using unacceptable language, or for "hiding behind the mask of patriotism." Sometimes such accusations were clearly coded to target "incorrect" political orientations. Especially during the Legislative Assembly and the Convention, one finds the first clear evidence of factional rivalries within the club and a tendency to support one or the other of the two major factions in the Convention, the Girondins or the Montagnards. It is not insignificant—and it is an ominous harbinger of the future—that by the fall of 1792 the Bordeaux Jacobins had essentially ceased denouncing clergymen and nobles and had turned to denouncing one another.

Denunciations in the eminently public forum of the Bordeaux Friends of the Constitution invariably left an effect on the whole community. There were protests that anyone with public responsibilities was now being spied upon and accused for even the most petty actions. "Will there never be a limit to their accusations, their indictments, their denunciations?" wrote one club member who found himself attacked. Individuals who were so accused before their fellow citizens—particularly those who supported the Revolution and who saw themselves as good patriots—felt profoundly distressed and humiliated. They penned passion-filled replies, denying the accusations outright or contending that it was all a case of mistaken identity or of a misunderstanding of their words or actions. They recounted their past service to the Revolution, and they concluded with a series of oaths—to hate the enemies of the fatherland, to defend the Revolution—often the same oaths sworn by those who had just denounced them. Some also complained about the unfortunate consequences of such accusatory practices on the morale of the community. The denunciations, as one writer put it, "invariably cause trouble not only in my family, but in the whole neighborhood where I live."

Throughout the kingdom by 1791, the image of the insidious enemies of the Revolution wearing the "mask of patriotism" to hide their true intentions became a leitmotif in the culture of denunciation. Marat had introduced the phrase as early as November 1789, and Brissot would return to the conundrum repeatedly throughout his Revolutionary career: "I have greater fear of [a conspirator] with a mask than with a dagger in his hand."[31] The problem, as the Revolutionaries frequently argued, was that those plotting in secret rarely left evidence of their true motives. "It seems a general principle," wrote Prudhomme, "that conspiracy can never be proven by written evidence; only an imbecile would leave a written trail of his actions. Without such evidence, one can only look to personal observations and the implication of events, and observations and events can constitute proof for anyone ready to make the connections."[32] Several journalists even offered primers on the techniques for distinguishing genuine patriotism from the cynical machinations of secret counterrevolutionaries. As Jacques Dulaure explained to his readers, "charlatans of patriotism" could often be spotted "by their pretentious exuberance, by their feigned exaggeration, by their eagerness to propose measures that could jeopardize liberty, by their grand pronouncements, protests, and excessive ardor."[33]

Beyond the "tribunal of public opinion" the Revolutionaries would also establish a variety of surveillance institutions, conceived to evaluate the flood of denunciations and subject the guilty to serious disciplinary measures. As early as July 28, 1789, in the midst of the chaotic first summer of the Revolution, the National Assembly had created a special Committee on Research to confront and investigate accusations of counterrevolutionary activities. A few months later, the municipality of Paris established its own research committee and opened a register in which local citizens could formally inscribe their denunciations. Brissot, who was himself a member of the municipal committee, was delighted with the measure: "Paris is the eye of France," he affirmed. "There is not a single citizen who does not watch out for the intrigues of our enemies."[34]

Over the two years of its existence, the Constituent Assembly's Committee on Research received hundreds of denunciations from around the country of suspicious activities, real or imagined. They were sent in by a variety of administrators, popular societies, national guard officials, and individuals.[35] Many of the newly elected administrators gave top priority to rooting out conspiracy. The first formal address of the department directory of Oise in July 1790 was an appeal for vigilance toward the secret forces opposing the regime: "It is not through open opposition but through insidious suggestions that they work to overthrow the edifice of your happiness. . . . Watch out for their treacherous insinuations."[36] With the rising tide of noble emigration and, perhaps above all, with the emergence of the refractory clergy as a cause of concern, a flood of complaints poured into the Constituent committee. Thus in June 1791 the directory of Aisne reported on their independent inquiry into dangerous individuals living within the department. The administrators had convoked special meetings in the districts so that citizens could denounce local suspects and propose means for thwarting the schemes of the enemies of the Constitution.[37] Significantly, some administrators were even prepared to take into consideration anonymous denunciations that had not been signed. In dangerous times such as these, they argued, could one really maintain such scrupulous technicalities? As one citizen from La Rochelle put it, "We know that anonymous reports can be despicable, yet nothing is despicable when it is a question of saving the state."[38]

Ultimately, the new legislation on criminal law and police surveillance would be patently vague on the issue of anonymous denunciations. The law would formally legitimize and even require civic denunciations: "Anyone who has witnessed an attack against liberty, against another person, or against public security . . . must immediately report it to the local police." A similar requirement would soon be incorporated in the new penal code, and all public officials would eventually be compelled to take an oath to denounce conspiracies. Such accusations would normally have to be signed. But even if the denouncer chose to remain anonymous, the police were authorized to investigate whenever they thought it was warranted by the potential danger of the situation.[39] In the end, "saving the state" must always take precedence.

Yet for the most part, the various administrators and their committees could only investigate accusations and recommend judicial action to the courts. Prior to 1791 such referrals led to relatively few actual convictions.[40] There was a growing belief among patriots that the judges, many of them holdovers from the Old Regime reelected in 1790, were refusing to convict or even to try dangerous suspects. Both the clubs and the radical newspapers complained that local magistrates were not taking their denunciations seriously and were dismissing "criminals," supposedly because of insufficient proof. Soon suspicions were running high that the judges themselves were dangerous counterrevolutionaries and that there was a "triple coalition of the new tribunals, the former clergy, and the nobility."[41]

In Bordeaux, as throughout the kingdom, the logic of repeated accusations against perceived conspirators could have a devastating cumulative effect. Fearful of being denounced themselves, many individuals became all the more energetic in denouncing their neighbors. Jacques Ménétra would be beside himself with fury and frustration when he was attacked by one of his neighbors in Paris. "I would never have believed," he wrote, "that, after living fifty-seven years without making a single enemy, a man who had called himself my friend would denounce me." Mercier considered denunciation to have been one of the most disastrous practices of the Revolution: "It gave rise to resentment, hatred, treachery, and jealousy; and even the bonds of family were affected."[42] Whether through genuine suspicion or cynical tactical maneuvers, factional leaders were increasingly prepared to accuse their rivals as conspirators, false patriots, acting treacherously to undermine the Revolution.[43] The pervasiveness of fear and rumor, undergirded with the emerging accusatory culture of denunciations, had the potential for creating a kind of "everyday terror" where everyone spied on everyone else: a vicious circle of grassroots suspicion that, in some respects, preceded and prefigured the institutional Terror of 1793–1794.[44]

Conspiracy Obsessions

One measure of the effects of anxiety, rumor, and denunciation on the psychology of the Revolutionary leadership is the growth from the summer of 1789 among many individuals of a veritable obsession with conspiracy: a consuming suspicion of the activities of secret perpetrators willfully seeking to do harm to individual patriots or to the Revolutionary community in general.[45] When and in what manner a "paranoid style of politics" first came to influence the Revolutionary elites has been the subject of much debate.[46] There can be no doubt that a susceptibility to conspiracy interpretations was already widespread among the masses of the common people under the Old Regime. Throughout much of history, a pervasive explanation of undesirable events assumed the willed interventions of individual beings, sometimes human, sometimes supernatural. In the eighteenth century the belief that a wide assortment of villains might conspire to keep bread from the people in order to threaten or punish them—the so-called famine plot persuasion—was a common feature of popular collective mentality.[47] In a world where people's lives were so dominated by the undisclosed actions of the powers that be—whether royal, seigneurial, or ecclesiastical— such a belief was not necessarily irrational, for most conspiracy beliefs were based on a combination of observable facts and leaps of imagination. They placed the onus of misfortune not on one's own actions or on the workings of blind chance—which might have seemed singularly frightening and repulsive—but on the willed actions of others. They entailed assumptions about the single-minded efficaciousness of evildoers that was, as one anthropologist has phrased it, "far more coherent than the real world."[48]

The educated population as well was never entirely immune to such modes of explanation. At the end of the Old Regime a number of writers— including Voltaire and a great many Jansenists—were convinced of the nefarious conspiracies of the Jesuits. So too the ex-Jesuit abbé Barruel had claimed the existence of an unholy conspiracy to destroy religion and the monarchy.[49] Yet beliefs of this kind were seemingly the exception among eighteenth-century French authors. The vast majority never used the word "conspiracy" at all, and those who did referred primarily to events in the historical past. Montesquieu declared that conspiracies were far more unlikely in his contemporary world than in Greek and Roman times. Diderot derided the popular tendency to explain the high price of bread in terms of plots: "People know that wheat must be cheap, because they earn little and are very hungry. But they do not know, and will never know, how difficult it is to reconcile the vicissitudes of the harvest with the need for grain." Indeed, by the later eighteenth century new models for the analysis of political and economic events were becoming available to the educated classes, models that did not require the willed maneuvers of individuals. Mechanistic explanations of the world, born of scientific reasoning and a belief in natural causes, had a profound impact on elite views of causation. Applying such perspectives to human affairs, eighteenth-century thinkers made important advances in identifying more abstract political and economic processes at work in the world.[50]

Among our future Revolutionaries, the language of conspiracy had been rare or nonexistent in their Old Regime correspondence. Of thirty-two future Third Estate deputies who wrote pamphlets during the Pre-Revolutionary period, only one—Maximilien Robespierre—gave any indication of a "paranoid style" of analysis.[51] Most such writings were marked rather by a tone of optimism and goodwill. While they might be highly critical of the nobles, they were hopeful that the aristocracy could surmount its "prejudices" and be won over to the patriot cause through reason and persuasion. Much the same tone was to be found in the statements of grievances drawn up by the urban elites in early 1789. Although there were numerous demands for ministerial accountability and public knowledge of government finances, conspiratorial notions and language were largely absent.[52]

The summer of 1789, however, had brought a rapid expansion of conspiracy fears among both the elites and the masses. As with the spread of rumors, the spread of conspiracy explanations is frequently associated with times of upheaval, tension, and uncertainty. In a state of crisis, it is easier to cope with anxiety—and it is perhaps more generally comforting—if a specific group or individual can be held responsible.[53] But such fears had also been impelled by the evidence of very real conspiracies in July 1789—the massing of mercenary troops around Paris, the dismissal of Necker and his replacement by a group of archconservatives. It was precisely in the last days of June and the first days of July that many of our witnesses first began mentioning the possibility of conspiracy. It was only then that Colson passed along reports to his friend of plots to overthrow the National Assembly and attack the city. During the same period Gilbert Romme and François Ménard de la Groye first became preoccupied with the prospect of conspiracy, and Nicolas Ruault wrote several pages to his brother on the presumed conspiracy of the royal court against Paris and the Assembly. For the journalist Prudhomme, publishing in August, "each day reveals new crimes and unveils portions of the horrible plot of which we would all have been victims." It was in direct reaction to such fears that the National Assembly had created its investigative Committee on Research. "Plots are being hatched against the state, announced Adrien Duport in arguing for the Committee's creation. "No one can have any doubts."[54]

Over the following months waves of conspiracy fears had continued periodically to sweep through the popular classes in Paris.[55] As with all such rumors, the elites maintained an ambiguous position.[56] Within the National Assembly, concerns with plots and conspiracy were largely episodic, in response to real and proven instances of counterrevolutionary activities—the gathering of Catholic national guardsmen at Jalès in August 1790, for example, or the conspiracy of Lyon in December of that year. Other accusations appeared at intervals through the winter and spring of 1790–1791—linked to the growing barrage of threats from the emigrants and, above all, to the popular unrest generated by the Civil Constitution of the Clergy. Yet most of the deputies whose correspondence has been preserved for this period were cautious in their reaction to such interpretations. Many were lawyers or magistrates by profession, well trained in the use of evidence and wary of accusations without proof. They took pains to distinguish rumors of plots based on unverifiable hearsay, from those for which they believed irrefutable confirmation existed. In the spring of 1790 Gaultier reflected on the recent predictions of plots about to break that had never in fact materialized: "I have never really placed any credence in them, and you have seen that [such beliefs] were totally unfounded."[57]

The views of the Revolutionary elites would be profoundly affected, however, by the experience of the king's flight to Varennes. Once the deputies had come across the monarch's handwritten statement, denouncing much of the Revolution and affirming that his previous cooperation had been insincere, there could be no doubt that Louis had left on his own accord.[58] As the Assembly's various investigative committees delved into the affair, interviewing dozens of witnesses and reading confiscated documents in the royal household, it became patently clear that a comprehensive conspiracy had been afoot for months, involving numerous participants in Paris, in the army, and among the emigrants in Germany, entailing, as well, a pattern of blatant deception and perjury on the part of the king himself—who had sworn a solemn oath to uphold the Constitution. Though many rumors of impending flight had circulated in Paris over the two previous years, and though a handful of journalists, like Marat, had predicted such a conspiracy, the Assembly leadership and most of the elites had dismissed such suggestions as irresponsible ranting.[59] But in June 1791 all of the seemingly paranoid predictions had come true. Never, since the Revolution began, had there been more extensive and conclusive proof of the reality of a grand and coordinated conspiracy at the highest levels.

It was to be the first of a series of terrible betrayals of the Revolution by individuals whom the French had previously admired. And many of the elites felt deeply deceived and mortified that they had been fooled and unprepared. Such were the sentiments of the deputy Marc-Alexis Vadier, the rigid Jacobin who only a few weeks earlier had assured his constituency that predictions of the king's flight were certainly untrue, and who now felt angered and humiliated to have been so blind. Such also was the case of the Breton deputy Legendre, who had long cautioned skepticism toward theories of conspiracy but who now was convinced that plots were being hatched everywhere, that enemies were "extremely numerous in the capital," and that "the first attacks would soon take place within its walls."[60] Soon letters were pouring into the Assembly from the provinces—from administrative directors, popular societies, and diverse citizens' groups—harshly condemning the "treachery" of the king and his presumed conspiratorial links with emigrants and foreign powers. The experience of Varennes would be a major factor in the inflation of conspiracy fears among the deputies of the Legislative Assembly who took power at the beginning of October and in the growing belief that a vast "grand conspiracy" existed, uniting all of the Revolutionaries' enemies both outside and inside the nation.

The Demonization of the Other

Even as the Legislative Assembly began meeting, the great majority of the Revolutionary elites still believed fervently in the values of liberty and equality central to the spirit of '89. They continued to partake in communal banquets, in festivals of brotherhood, in collective oaths of unity and commitment. They would persist in doing so throughout the Revolution—even in the midst of the Terror of 1793–1794. Yet the mood of self-confidence and equanimity that had characterized the leadership in June 1789, the boundless hopes for the rapid creation of a new society, had been substantially eroded and deflated during the first two years of the Revolution.

Rumor, denunciation, and a growing obsession with conspiracy, all propelled by the uncertainty and anxiety intrinsic to a time of revolution, were both cause and consequence of a subtle transformation in the psychology of the Revolutionary elites. The emergence of collective anger and hatred in a society is always a complex process, involving many entangled emotions. In historical situations the arousal of hate is commonly associated with sentiments of betrayal, with the rejection of values and beliefs one holds most dear, and with real or imagined threats. In both individuals and groups, hate is often tightly interwoven with fear and to the stories one contrives to tell others and tell to oneself to justify and envelop one's fears. Such conclusions, proposed by the social psychologists, were long anticipated by William Shakespeare: "In time we hate that which we often fear."[61]

There was no better example of this transformation among the Revolutionaries than the growing tendency to demonize the opposition. Already by 1790 the forbearance of many patriots toward the "prejudices" of the nobility had largely disappeared. The adversaries of the Revolution were increasingly portrayed as not only wrong but evil. Rosalie Jullien's impatience and anger toward the aristocracy were palpable in the spring of 1790. "The aristocrats are posing so many obstacles, using so many ruses, planning so many horrors, that the friends of humanity, truth, and justice can only view them with indignation and anger. . . . All the devils of Milton are but angels compared to the devils of the aristocracy." Two months before Varennes, the deputy Fricaud announced that all aristocrats were "monsters": "Oh, how I now hate more than anyone else the aristocrats of our country." The Jacobins of Marseille would describe the "race" of the nobility as inherently vicious: they were "vampires" "with the claws of a harpy, the tongue of a bloodsucker, the heart of a vulture, and the cruelty of a tiger."[62] By early 1791 many Revolutionaries had come to attribute to the nobility a kind of original sin that could never be removed.

Much the same rhetoric was soon being mobilized, moreover, against the refractory clergy. The deputy Pierre-François Lepoutre, who had regularly practiced his Catholic faith under the Old Regime and who had once shown great sympathy for the clergy, now concluded that the refractories were "the greatest enemies we have within the state. They are more to fear than any of our external enemies." Gaultier called them "unjust and evil." The Legislative deputy Vincent Corbel de Squirio seemed to believe rumors of "the atrocious crimes, murders, and poisoning perpetrated by the refractory priests. These perverse men continue to outrage Heaven and earth in the name of a religion of peace and of love."[63]

It was part and parcel of the tragedy of the period that the counterrevolutionary press soon began expressing much the same hatred and using much the same demonizing rhetoric to characterize the patriots. One conservative newspaper readily proclaimed that the Jacobins were "brigands who thirsted only after gold and power and who preached violence to drunken brutes." The *Gazette de Paris* urged "all the sovereigns of Europe to hasten as rapidly as possible to exterminate" the revolutionary "virus." Later the same paper would make reference to the "monsters" of the revolution, these "murderous men who thirst after blood" and who, it was argued, were preparing a new Saint-Bartholomew's Day Massacre of the priests and the nobles.[64]

To be sure, this penchant for demonization, like the conspiracy obsession, did not affect all individuals with equal intensity. Some leaders seem to have been far more susceptible than others. And such beliefs tended to fluctuate over time, partly in reaction to specific events. Prior to 1791 the demonization primarily involved attacks between patriots and aristocrats, revolutionaries and counterrevolutionaries. But in the course of the new Legislative Assembly a Manichaean language would increasingly be utilized by patriots to refer to rival factions of other Revolutionaries. Indeed, the inflationary hatred and verbal violence of the first years of the Revolution, born from a culture of fear, rumor, and denunciation, as well as from a genuine menace of counterrevolution, would anticipate and help foster the psychology of the Terror.

6

The Factionalization of France

AFTER the trauma and violence of the summer of 1791, the majority of the French undoubtedly hoped for a return of calm and the end of upheaval and revolution. Those whose thoughts have been preserved in letters or diaries were elated by the ceremonies in Paris that September, marking the king's acceptance of the new Constitution. Colson described "the boisterous joy" and the resounding cries of "Long live the king!" when Louis took his oath of allegiance before the Assembly. Guittard was dazzled by the festivities and nighttime illuminations ordered in celebration of the event. Hundreds of Persian lanterns were hung in the trees of the Tuileries Gardens, the Champs-Elysées, and the major boulevards. When the deputies of the new Legislative Assembly arrived to take their seats on October 1, most believed that their assumption of power would mark the beginning of a stable constitutional government. "Paris wants no more revolution," announced the Breton delegates who had just arrived in the city. A representative from Clermont-Ferrand was equally hopeful that the advent of the Constitution would bring a reign of "union and harmony among all citizens."[1]

Yet the Constitution in question would survive scarcely ten months before a second and far bloodier revolution would bring down the regime and set France on a radical course toward the creation of a republic. A fundamental problem for the settlement of 1791 was clearly the monarch himself. Louis XVI had solemnly sworn to accept the new government and his role as executive authority, with powers not unlike those of the recently created American president. But in fact, both Louis and his queen con-

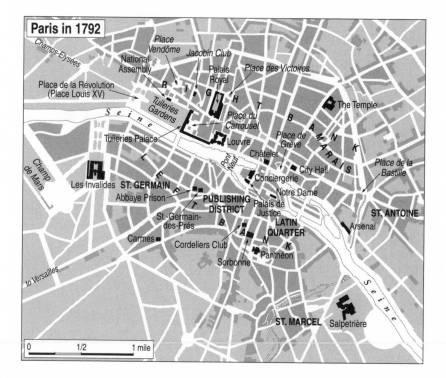

Paris in 1792

Champs-Elysées
Place Vendôme
Jacobin Club
National Assembly
Palais Royal
Place des Victoires
Place de la Révolution (Place Louis XV)
R I G H T
Tuileries Gardens
B A N K
The Temple
Seine
Place du Carrousel
Tuileries Palace
Louvre
Place de Grève
Pont Neuf
L E F T
Châtelet
City Hall
M A R A I S
Place de la Bastille
Champ de Mars
Les Invalides ST. GERMAIN
Concergerie
Abbaye Prison
Notre Dame
PUBLISHING DISTRICT
Palais de Justice
B A N K
St.-Germain-des-Prés
LATIN QUARTER
ST. ANTOINE
Arsenal
Carmes
Cordeliers Club
Panthéon
Sorbonne
to Versailles
ST. MARCEL Salpetrière
Seine

0   1/2   1 mile

tinued to play a double game. They would secretly encourage the intervention of other European states to end a regime that the king had never genuinely accepted and to restore most of his former prerogatives and those of his "loyal nobility." The failure of the king to embrace the Constitution and to accept limitations on his power would be the fatal flaw in the whole experiment in constitutional monarchy.

The presence of an unreliable monarch, however, was not the only crisis the legislators would have to face. The deputies would find themselves threatened not only by counterrevolution but by the rise of a movement of radical militancy in Paris. Soon they were also confronted with waves of popular violence in the provinces and with a massive slave uprising in their wealthiest colony in the Americas. The following spring they would greatly compound their difficulties by pushing the country into war. Instability, suspicion, and war would be central to the emergence of a culture of intense factionalism within the Assembly and among revolutionary elites throughout the nation.

Faction and Unrest in the Provinces

During the fall and winter of 1791–1792 all of the forces of disorder that had arisen in the early Revolution seemed only to intensify. Many of these problems arose from the tenacious logic of the Revolution itself. The "supernatural effect" of liberty, the difficulty of setting the bounds of democracy, the tendency to question authority: all continued apace during the era of the second National Assembly, disrupting attempts to impose order and civic discipline. Citizens persisted in avoiding their taxes and seigneurial dues; workers demonstrated for higher wages; rural people pursued their assaults on public and private forests; soldiers remained recalcitrant to the authority of their officers. Surveying the scene in February, the deputy Roubaud would lament that "all the departments swarm with malcontents; all the cities are overwhelmed with sedition; everywhere the authorities are ignored; the laws are violated." "It would seem that we are pushed forward by fearsome blind fate."[2]

While much of this "anarchy" was nonviolent, there was also a renewed surge of riots and insurrections, reaching a peak in the spring of 1792, a period that approached the summer of 1789 in the frequency and fury of the outbreaks. An exceptionally hot summer had produced drought in central and southwestern France and raised fears of famine.[3] Equally serious for the grain supply were the effects of the National Assembly's own policies. The free trade supported by the deputies aroused anxiety among the popular classes, who feared that the export of grain would create local shortages. Although the Legislature eventually halted shipments across national frontiers, it did nothing to block sales from region to region, as grain merchants angled for maximum profits.[4] The situation was compounded, moreover, by the instability of the Revolution's new currency, the *assignats*. The French had long been suspicious of paper money, and with the fear of impending war in early 1792, the value began dropping rapidly. In Paris many people did everything possible to rid themselves of the bills, further depressing their value. As Colson explained, "the general anxiety over the uncertain future of the *assignats* makes everyone eager to use them to buy all kinds of property and pay off their debts." The resulting inflation disrupted local economies and brought considerable hardship to the lower classes, particularly those in the towns.[5]

As in 1789 the larger insurrections targeted a variety of individuals suspected of manipulating markets or secretly hoarding grain: wealthy landowners, government officials, even rich peasants and clergymen. But now, far more than in 1789, the countrypeople went after the seigneurial lords. There was growing anger that nobles could lay claim to "feudal dues" until they were reimbursed by the peasantry and that they could even launch suits against villagers who refused to pay. The dues seemed particularly galling after the National Assembly ostentatiously abolished the nobility in June 1790. The nobility became the single most common target of collective violence in the first half of 1792, as waves of attacks on chateaus spread over large segments of the country.[6]

The popular violence was all the more upsetting for the patriots in that they were also faced with continuing counterrevolutionary activity. During the autumn, reports came in from across the country of noblemen heading for the frontiers, some of them openly announcing their plans to join the emigrant armies.[7] The Parisians were acutely aware of the large numbers of aristocrats passing through the capital en route to Austrian or German territories—"our Don Quixote's of the counterrevolution," as the deputy Claude Le Coz scornfully called them. Ruault claimed that thousands had passed through the city in October and November, some of them stopping at the Tuileries Palace to salute the royal couple before leaving. There were also reports of posters appearing mysteriously on walls, promising the rapid return of the emigrants to execute the Revolutionary leaders and put an end to their "rebellion."[8] Although Ruault believed this was all empty boasting, many Parisians grew anxious. There was in fact solid evidence of conspiracies between the emigrants abroad and nobles living in the interior. The Assembly had uncovered plans for an uprising in western France, the so-called coalition of Poitou led by the baron de Lézardière.[9] Faced with such discoveries and with the swell of emigration, the deputy from Cahors, Pierre Ramel, tried to maintain a brave front, declaring that it was just as well that so many unworthy citizens were leaving. Nevertheless, he admitted that "these fanciful ideas of counterrevolution . . . upset the French people and deprive them of the contentment that the new Constitution should normally have given them."[10]

Patriots were even more concerned, however, with the perceived threat of the refractory clergy. By the autumn of 1791 most of the nonjuring curés had been replaced by clergymen willing to take the oath of allegiance to the Constitution. Yet there were certain regions where oath rejections had been so widespread that it was difficult to find replacements and where refractories had to be maintained at their posts to ensure the administration of the sacraments. Even those nonjurors who had been ejected from their positions were allowed by the laws on religious freedom to remain in their parishes and celebrate "refractory" masses in nearby chapels or convents.

Local patriots remained deeply suspicious of such "anticonstitutional" activities. Even if the priests in question avoided politics in their sermons and public pronouncements, no one could be certain of what they were saying in private conversations or in the intimacy of the confessional or in catechism lessons to the children. In the department of Var, administrators concluded that all refractories "detest the constitution and are working secretly to increase the number of its enemies."[11] Patriotic clubs and national guard units did everything in their power to mobilize opposition to such clergymen. But as parishioners themselves split in their positions on the ecclesiastical oath, violence broke out in towns and villages between those supporting and those opposing the nonjurors. Religious conflict was the third most common cause of violence in 1791 and 1792—after antiseigneurial revolts and subsistence riots.[12]

In the midst of this turmoil, another rather different problem was evolving in a great many regions of France: the bitter factional rivalries among the patriot elites themselves. Competition between such groups had long been part of political life in towns and villages. Depending on the case, divisions might be based on clashes between families or neighborhoods or religious affiliations (where Protestants or Jansenists were present), or on confrontations among local associational groups—such as different confraternities, guilds, or Masonic lodges. Sometimes such feuds had persisted through several generations.[13] After the Revolution began, the politicization of the towns and the lack of institutional clarity could both reactivate older conflicts and produce a range of new ones. Every community was, in fact, a microcosm with its own specific history and factional dynamics.[14] The wave of municipal revolutions during the second half of 1789 could create enduring animosities, as former power brokers who had been pushed aside refused to accept their fate and resented the upstarts who had forced them from office. Sometimes those fomenting municipal revolutions had sought alliances with more humble individuals such as artisans and peasants, so that conflicts between the ins and the outs acquired a social dimension.[15]

The situation had been further complicated with the creation of competing department, district, and municipal authorities. In many regions there was a tendency for the department directories to be more cautious and conservative and committed to following the letter of the law. The district and municipal leaders, by contrast, might evolve more radical positions, impatient with the perceived leniency of the National Assembly and of their immediate superiors. The reasons for this dichotomy are not entirely clear. Perhaps it arose because lower-level officials found themselves more frequently in the trenches, directly confronting refractory clergy and recalcitrant nobles.[16] The municipal administrators might also include citizens somewhat lower in the social hierarchy than those in the departments.[17] In any case, political divisions between departments, on the one hand, and districts and towns, on the other, was a pattern emerging throughout the nation. The Jacobin deputy Michel Azéma urged the leaders of his own department not to follow the "aristocratic" policies of other such administrators but to rely on the views of the municipal governments and the clubs.[18] The situation was summarized by Legendre in mid-1791: "The unfortunate division between the different levels of public administration has become the greatest obstacle to the return of calm and tranquility."[19]

Whatever their origins within local politics, many rival factions soon lined up behind specific national "parties." Numerous towns had seen the creation of several distinct popular societies, each representing a different neighborhood or social milieu.[20] The conflict could become particularly intense if one of the clubs positioned itself in opposition to policies promoted by the Paris Jacobins. Inspired by the conservative "Club monarchique" in Paris, they might advocate a strengthened monarchy and a regime of law and order that would enforce greater discipline among the popular classes. Such dissident societies were often led by precisely those individuals who had earlier been ousted from power.[21]

By 1791 confrontations among rival popular societies could develop into veritable "club wars." Brawls broke out in Dijon, Limoges, Auch, and several other towns in Languedoc. The department directors in Toulon described their frustrations after a violent clash between clubs in the central square led to injuries and deaths on both sides: "Anarchy is increasing from day to day. . . . The authorities must struggle against both the enemies of the Revolution and those who would urge sedition."[22] In the small town of Pamiers in the foothills of the Pyrenees, two competing "parties" that had arisen out of the municipal revolution of 1789—between the winners and the losers—rapidly formed rival clubs and linked themselves to more radical or more moderate groups in the National Assembly. Soon the Jacobin deputy Vadier, a native of Pamiers, was actively intervening in local politics to favor those who had overthrown the Old Regime oligarchy.[23]

Following the schism between the Jacobins and the Feuillants in July 1791, the two rival Parisian clubs sent repeated correspondence to the provincial societies, each claiming that they alone represented the true embodiment of the Friends of the Constitution. When the two warring societies refused to unite, club members everywhere felt compelled to choose sides. In the end the majority opted for the Jacobins, but the Feuillant position, with its emphasis on a strong monarchy and its distrust of the masses, attracted the more moderate and conservative elements of many local communities.[24]

As citizens gathered in electoral assemblies at the end of the summer to select deputies for the new Legislature, the division between the two societies was very much in the air. To be sure, participants were eager to announce their detachment from all factions and their determination to remain independent. Some of the elections seem to have been relatively calm and free of factional struggles.[25] But a number of others were intensely politicized, with significant clashes between local groups linking themselves directly or indirectly to the two major parties in Paris. In Dijon and in Tulle virtually the whole delegations were chosen from the Jacobin clubs. Troyes, Toulon, and Châteauroux, by contrast, saw a general dominance of the Feuillants. In the department of Gard several deputies from the National Assembly intervened to ensure the dominance of the Feuillants in the election.[26] In Pamiers the long struggle in which Vadier had involved himself ended in triumph for the Jacobins and the choice of one of their own for the new Assembly.[27] The divisions and mistrust born in part of provincial turmoil and local politics would measurably influence the Legislative Assembly when it convened on October 1.

Factions in the Legislative Assembly

The 742 deputies who assumed their seats in the new Assembly were substantially different from those who had preceded them. A law passed the previous May had formally disallowed individuals from being reelected.[28] The new representatives were younger, with an average age of only about forty-one years when they assumed power, compared to forty-seven for those in the Constituent Assembly. They were also more likely to have originated in small towns and villages, and only 5 percent lived in Paris, compared to 18 percent among the former deputies.[29] Some historians have argued that political immaturity and a general lack of experience on the part of the

Legislators was partly responsible for the relatively brief survival of the Assembly. Yet if none of the deputies had held positions at the national level, the great majority had considerable experience in local politics. Nearly four-fifths had previously been elected as administrators or magistrates in departments, districts, or municipalities.[30] The most striking difference, however, was in their social composition. Slightly over half of the deputies to the first National Assembly had come from the privileged orders of the clergy or nobility. But with the Constitution of 1791, in which separate "estates" had ceased to exist, only about 10 percent of the deputies were priests or former nobles.[31] Of the nobles none had been court aristocrats or Old Regime bishops; most came from families only recently ennobled. The clergymen, for their part, were all oathtakers and supporters of the new regime. Overall the new representatives were vastly more homogeneous and, by the very nature of the electoral process, fully committed to the success of the Revolution.

It is ironic, then, that the Legislative Assembly would soon be sharply torn into factional alignments that were at least as divisive and antagonistic as the patriots and aristocrats had been under the first National Assembly. After only a few days, members were self-consciously arranging themselves on the left, on the right, or in the center of the assembly hall, thus perpetuating the pattern first set in 1789.[32] The precise number who adhered to either of the two rival "parties"—the Jacobins or the Feuillants—is difficult to know. Especially during the first weeks, there was a certain fluidity, with a number of deputies moving from one faction to the other. About 130 are known to have signed up with the Jacobins of Paris at the beginning of October, but the list is incomplete. By the winter of 1791–92 somewhat over 200 were either members or strong sympathizers regularly voting with the group.[33] For their part, the Feuillants seem not formally to have congregated as a club at the beginning of the Legislative. By November, representatives on the right had sufficiently organized themselves to vote as a bloc for a single candidate as president of the Assembly.[34] It was only in early December, however, that the Feuillants reconstituted themselves and began public meetings—perhaps in response to the aggressive Jacobin leadership during the autumn.[35] Thereafter, some 260 deputies generally voted with this club. Although they were forced to cease public activities a few weeks later—when radical militants invaded their hall and disrupted the meeting—many continued to meet privately, and they remained more or less united through the fall of the monarchy in August 1792.[36]

The relative strength of the two coalitions in the Legislative ebbed and flowed over time. By December, the Feuillant adherents almost certainly outnumbered those regularly supporting the Jacobins. To be sure, the Left was able to attract enough support from the nonaligned center to prevail in several important debates during the winter and spring. Yet they continued to feel threatened. One measure of the relative strength of the two factions was the bimonthly election of the assembly's president. From October to February, the Jacobins were able to win several elections. But from mid-March through the beginning of August Feuillants or Feuillant sympathizers consistently won the presidency on close votes.[37] The young radical Claude Basire would complain that the Feuillants were now "those who decide the presidents." In February Prudhomme concluded "that the cause of the people is being betrayed by a large faction in the National Assembly, a faction that grows more numerous every day."[38]

By early 1792 the atmosphere in the Assembly was often extraordinarily contentious and polarized. Rabusson-Lamothe described the daily scene in one of his letters home: "They insult one another, they accuse one another with a violence that approaches frenzy." For Roubaud the hall represented "a strange Bacchanalia" which "often comes close to leaving dead on the floor." There were even reports that some deputies attended the sessions armed with pistols in their coats.[39] In such an environment, the great majority of deputies—whether or not they formally adhered to a club—began lining up and voting with one or the other of the two rival parties.[40] Enormous pressure was exerted on the ostensibly nonaligned to declare which side they were on. Delegates denounced one another with such fury that "citizens who prefer to avoid both sides, are ultimately compelled to choose one or the other."[41] In the summer of 1792 the near parity between the two alignments would create a virtual deadlock in the midst of a national crisis, a situation that would seriously reduce the authority of the Legislative.

The origins of such passionate rivalries remains one of the more mysterious aspects of the Revolution. There were, to be sure, certain differences in the general attitudes toward society of the two alignments, especially in their views on the political role to be given to the masses. The Jacobins emphasized the principle of popular sovereignty and were usually far more sympathetic with the plight of the common people, whom they imbued at times with a kind of innate political wisdom. "The people are everything," wrote Azéma. "We are the people. We can be nothing except by the people and for the people."[42] The Feuillants, by contrast, were generally wary of the masses and of the threat of popular uprisings to the stability of the nation. Again and again they accused their rivals of pandering to the common people, of promoting anarchy and thus destabilizing the government. In letters to his mother, the deputy Louis-Michel Demée repeatedly attacked the Jacobins, who promoted, in his view, "the spirit of chaos and anarchy" and who would give power to "cannibals" for whom "liberty consists in doing whatever they want."[43] The Jacobins, for the most part, placed greater emphasis on the rights of the community and the *salut public,* while the Feuillants stressed the prerogatives of individuals and the Rights of Man. The first were prepared to bend or set aside certain laws, when it seemed necessary for the survival of the state, while the second insisted on a strict construction of the existing laws no matter what the circumstances. Indeed, the Feuillants prided themselves as defenders of the Constitution and the constitutional monarchy, which they claimed the Jacobins were trying to undermine. As the club's manifesto proclaimed: "the Constitution, the whole Constitution, nothing but the Constitution."[44]

Yet differences in attitudes toward law and society were actually less stark than the major ideological divide separating patriots and "aristocrats" under the first National Assembly. By the time the new representatives had taken their seats, the prospects of republicanism, once the major bone of contention between the two parties, had substantially faded. The Jacobins' deputies, no less than the Feuillants, had sworn an oath to defend the Constitution and the constitutional monarchy it established. The Jacobin Gilbert Romme made the seriousness of this commitment clear in a November letter to his friend Dubreul: "Submission to the laws and the preservation of the Constitution: henceforth those must be the goals that guide all our actions." Even the Jacobin leader, Jacques Brissot, announced that republicanism was now only a dream.[45] Both of the alignments claimed a deep antipathy for the institutions and social structures of the Old Regime and the privileges of the nobility, and both remained nervous and uncertain about the reliability of the king.[46] Despite their many tumultuous debates on specific issues and strategies, they were in notable agreement on a number of the most important questions. Votes were close to unanimous on the repression of emigrants and refractory priests and on the rights of free people of color, as well as on the issue of war.[47] For the Feuillants and the Jacobins—as later for the Girondins and the Montagnards—ideology was far from being the sole source, or even the most important source of factional affiliation.

In some cases previous political experience helped shape factional allegiance, experience rooted in a variety of local struggles and only indirectly related to issues of national politics. We have seen how local rivalries—some in existence before the Revolution, some pitting the "ins" and the "outs" following the municipal revolutions—could play a role in the emergence of political affiliations. In this respect, it is significant that the distinction between more conservative department officials and more radical district and town officials often carried over into the Legislative Assembly. In comparing the collective biographies of Jacobin and Feuillant deputies, one finds almost exactly the same average age and social breakdown.[48] Yet the Feuillants were more likely to have held posts at the department level, while the Jacobins had often been based in the districts or municipalities.[49] Many Legislative deputies began their tenure with factional associations already clearly formed from their provincial experience. Both Georges Couthon and Gilbert Romme arrived from Auvergne with a strong Jacobin allegiance and immediately began attending the mother club in Paris. Even before they had taken their seats, the two had categorized their future colleagues, largely on the basis of their known positions and affiliations, into "those who follow true principles," on the one hand, and "the weak, the imbeciles, and those in the hands of the ministers," on the other. They readily described the latter as their "enemies."[50]

Once debates had begun, individual personalities could also play a role in the formation of factional alignments. On the Feuillant side, the most effective leadership in the early weeks of the Legislative came from several ex-deputies who had remained in Paris. The "triumvirate" of Antoine Barnave, Adrien Duport, and Charles and Alexandre Lameth, all central figures in the Feuillant party during the summer of 1791, continued to do everything in their power to shape the policies of both the king and the Assembly and to thwart the ambitions of the Jacobins. Their leadership was often affected, however, by disagreements with their longtime rival Lafayette. Until the fall of the monarchy in August 1792, Lafayette was probably the single most respected figure among deputies on the right. As for the deputies themselves, Viénot-Vaublanc, Mathieu Dumas, and Ramond de Carbonnières all emerged as capable speakers—though none could be described as charismatic. Overall the Feuillants as a group would speak substantially less frequently than their Jacobin rivals.[51]

Among the Jacobins the single most prominent deputy was undoubtedly Jacques Brissot. After a difficult career as a writer and sometime philosopher—with prolonged travels in England, Switzerland, and America—Brissot had discovered his calling as a Revolutionary journalist and an active participant in Parisian politics. Throughout his life he had delighted in gathering around him a circle of close acquaintances.[52] The earliest "Brissotin" party consisted of just such a group of talented friends who had known Brissot previously or who had gravitated to his circle after their arrival in the Legislative and who took the habit of meeting several mornings a week before the Assembly convened.[53] Among the most prominent were Pierre Vergniaud, Armand Gensonné, Elie Guadet, Jean-François Ducos, and the former marquis de Condorcet. Since all but Condorcet hailed from the department of Gironde in the Bordeaux region, the group was often known to contemporaries as the "Girondins." Within this coterie and among the Jacobins in general, Brissot exercised something resembling personal charisma. Various observers commented on the power of his optimism and his "earnestness" but also on his intense self-confidence in the policies he promoted, his impatience with those who opposed him, and his "love of glory." Marie-Jeanne Roland, who with her husband often welcomed Brissot and his friends to their home, found him "excessively confident" and "naturally calm." For Etienne Dumont, the Calvinist pastor who also knew him well, he was the "leader" of the faction: "Brissot was continually writing, moving about, convening meetings, directing all the maneuvers."[54]

The initial objectives of Brissot and his friends in the autumn of 1791 remain obscure. At first the group revealed no distinctive ideological differences from the Jacobins in general. Nor, in all likelihood, did they seek to overthrow the monarchy. If they did have a central strategy, it was perhaps above all to obtain political power—rationalized in their minds as the best way to save the nation. There would be numerous examples of modifications or contradictions in their positions and goals between 1791 and 1793, as they maneuvered to influence other deputies.[55] Dumont claimed to have been profoundly shocked when Brissot described his Machiavellian maneuvers to bring several of his friends into the royal ministry in the spring of 1792.[56] But for a time, through the spring of 1792, Brissot and the Girondins were remarkably successful in winning over the Jacobin deputies through the power of their rhetoric and the force of their personalities.

Yet there was another ingredient in factional formation under the Legislative, an ingredient that would soon render such factions particularly contentious and toxic: the veritable metastasis of fear and suspicion that spread among all political classes following the summer of 1791.[57] Although under the previous Assembly such fears had been largely episodic, there was a rapid inflation of conspiratorial fears among the new corps of deputies. More than ever plots were conceived as part of a monolithic "grand conspiracy," where internal conspirators, external conspirators, and conspirators in the court itself were all thought to be working together, with one or a few master operators pulling the strings. References to such overarching plots appeared ever more frequently in both the speeches and the private letters of the Legislators. For Gilbert Romme, almost everything that went wrong in the Revolution could be traced to a single source. The fanatical actions of the refractories, the rising price of grain, the decline in the value of the *assignats,* the waves of riots and unrest in the countryside, even the factional splits in the Assembly itself: all were caused by "a handful of individuals who secretly pull the strings and who have penetrated everywhere, even into the patriotic societies and the National Assembly." In Claude Basire's view, "we are surrounded by conspirators. Everywhere plots are being prepared and we must continually denounce specific incidents that are, in fact, linked to the grand conspiracy, whose existence no one can doubt."[58] If such views were perhaps initially most widespread among Jacobins—like Romme and Basire—they were increasingly embraced by many Feuillants and other moderate Legislators as well. Thus, the centrist deputy Codet became convinced that "the league of internal conspirators is constantly kept in motion by the external league." By March 1792 the Feuillant sympathizers Roubaud and Aubert-Dubayet were likewise persuaded of the dangers of general conspiracy.[59]

The culture of suspicion that rapidly penetrated the perceptions of the deputies also affected the manner by which rival groups in the Legislative viewed one another. The harsh crackdown against radicals and republicans in Paris in July–August 1791, engineered by the dominant Feuillant faction in the National Assembly—and especially the bloody Champ de Mars massacre—had left a legacy of anger and mistrust among the Jacobins. The obvious links to the royal court of several of the Feuillant leaders only intensified their apprehensions. By the fall of 1791 many Jacobins concluded that their opponents were traitors deeply enmeshed in conspiracy: a "ministerial party," as they were derisively called, in league with the circle of treacherous ministers around the king—and especially the queen—often referred to as the "Austrian Committee." The Jacobin Pierre-Joseph Cambon reported that the Feuillants "are continually intriguing against the National Assembly"; Guillaume Causse was convinced that "there were numerous aristocrats in disguise" among the Feuillants.[60] But deputies on the right claimed to see similar perfidy on the part of the Jacobins. The Feuillants had grown deeply suspicious of the Jacobins' earlier flirtation with republicanism and their apparent attempts to mobilize the masses to attain their goal. Théodore Lameth, the younger brother of Alexandre and Charles, asserted that the faction around Brissot "was paid off by English money and led by vile men in league with the dregs of the nation."[61]

During the winter and spring of 1792, however, the factional lines in the Legislative would be substantially complicated by a division within the Jacobins themselves. Central to the schism was the personal confrontation between two of the "party's" most influential leaders, Brissot and Robespierre. Both men were possessed with an exceptionally strong sense of self-esteem and self-confidence, and both tended to view themselves as the central figures of the radical Revolution. Robespierre, the former deputy who had recently been elected to the Paris criminal tribunal, was greatly admired by the Jacobins for the strength of his convictions and his talent for conceptualizing them in his speeches. René Levasseur, who sat with him on the benches of the Convention, described him many years later: "Sober, chaste, with few personal needs, he had no desire for economic gain and his only ambition was to acquire a reputation as the best and most honest citizen." But Dominique Garat, who also knew him well, stressed his pride, his susceptibility, and his near paranoid suspicions.[62] The confrontation between Robespierre and Brissot began in December 1791 over whether or not the country should go to war, a possibility that Brissot supported passionately but that Robespierre came rapidly to oppose. The exchange in the Jacobin Club was relatively civil at first, until Brissot and the Girondins began a series of direct attacks against Robespierre, claiming that they, and not he, best understood and were supported by the people. Robespierre, who had long identified with the common man and who viewed himself as the voice of the people, was indignant and outraged. Thereafter the rivalry became extraordinarily personal and bitter, involving the friends and allies of the two men in a series of brutal attacks by both sides.[63]

In the short term Brissot and his supporters succeeded in crushing the antiwar position within the Assembly, and they did their best to humiliate Robespierre in the Jacobin Club. But Robespierre continued to maintain a strong following in the Club, and over time, especially as the war went

Maximilien Robespierre, leader of the Montagnard faction of the Jacobins. Bibliothèque nationale de France.

badly, he would win the support of a minority in the Legislative as well.[64] Already by the spring of 1792 his followers there were coming to be known as "the Mountain" or "the Montagnards"—from their habit of sitting on the highest seats at the left end of the hall. And as Feuillants and Jacobins exchanged accusations of treason, Brissotins and Montagnards were doing much the same. Both Brissot and his friend Guadet insinuated that Robespierre was insidiously pushing pacifism in order to undermine war preparations and thus favor the Austrians.[65] Robespierre was soon making a similar allegation against the Girondins, accusing them of having sold out

Jacques-Pierre Brissot, leader of the "Brissotins" or Girondin faction. Bibliothèque nationale de France.

to the Austrian Committee and of being "counterrevolutionaries." About the same time his friend Camille Desmoulins would publish a broadside attack in his pamphlet "Brissot Unmasked."[66] The Montagnards' mistrust became all the greater when four of the friends and protégés of the Girondins were brought into the ministry in March 1792. By the spring of 1792 contemporaries widely reported the existence of not two but three warring factions in the Assembly, vying with one another in an oscillating and unstable set of revolving relationships: the Feuillants, the Girondins, and the Montagnard Jacobins.

It is not impossible, of course, that political posturing and demagoguery played a role in the accusations between factions. Yet if we can believe the observations of Dumont, by March of 1792 the Girondins were totally swept up in the culture of suspicion. When the Genevan pastor met with the group that spring, "they talked only of the conspiracies of the emigrants and the 'Austrian committee,' and of the treachery of the court."[67] The terrible factionalism reminded Dominique Garat of the stories he knew so well in his studies of ancient history: "Parties that hoped to destroy one another, accused each other of trying to destroy the state." "In the beginning such allegations were perhaps only suspicions born of hatred or harsh insults arising from all-consuming anger; but in the end they became a profound conviction." The deputies' personal correspondence conveys the intensity of the fears of treachery and conspiracy, conspiracy both external and internal to France, and inside the Assembly itself.[68] Their vision of events was rapidly penetrated by the same Manichaean imaginary touching so much of French society, in which factional rivals were not simply misguided or dull minded, but treacherous and morally tainted.

Whatever the origins of factionalism in the Revolutionary assemblies, once deputies came emotionally to identify with a given "party," their allegiance rapidly crystallized and took on a life of its own. Factional confrontations assumed the character of a struggle for power and for survival. For Cambon, writing in October 1791, the principal objective of both the Feuillant and the Jacobin clubs was to destroy their opponent. Each side seemed to define itself as much by what it opposed in the factional "other" as by what it actually supported.[69] Elements of both revenge and fear of revenge came into play. The anger and hatred long focused on aristocrats and the refractory clergy were now directed at the opposing faction, as competing groups came to vilify and demonize their antagonists.[70] Representatives on the left used emotionally charged epithets from the first National Assembly, stigmatizing their Feuillant rivals as "blacks" or "ministerials." The Jacobins Malassis and Cavellier would complain of "our Maury's, our Cazalès', our Malouet's"—referring to three of the most eloquent defenders of the Right in the previous Assembly. "For," they added, "we too have such men."[71] The demonization of rival factions was amplified, moreover, by extremist journalism on both the right and the left, in which there was a rapid inflation of rhetoric and violent, very personal recriminations directed against opponents.

In any political situation, the formation of factions is a complex process, involving the entangled interaction of class, ideology, personal charisma, rhetorical and journalistic simplification, and contingent circumstances. In a time of revolution, however, additional factors emerge that can enormously magnify and polarize such rivalries. The intensity of commitment of the protagonists, the emergence of real counterrevolutionary opposition, the power vacuum produced during the process of transition: all combined to create an atmosphere of uncertainty, a psychology of profound apprehension and doubt that permeated the whole political culture. The gnawing apprehension after Varennes that the king's affirmations of loyalty could not be trusted only compounded the climate of incertitude.[72] It was perhaps above all the profound and deep-seated fear of conspiracy, arising above all from the revolutionary process itself, that led to the moralization of factional options, to the dehumanizing and demonization of one's opponents, and ultimately to that toxic form of factionalism that would eventually be prepared to embrace violence and the physical elimination of one's political rivals.

The Mobilization of Militant Paris

In the meantime the political climate of the city in which the deputies lived and worked was being rapidly transformed by the growth of radical militancy. As a movement, political radicalism had originated in the popular societies of the early Revolution: the Cordeliers Club, the various neighborhood "fraternal societies," and the Jacobin Club—after schisms had led to the departure of the moderates. Many of the leading members of the Cordeliers, in particular, were writers or journalists who had lived a marginal existence before 1789 but who now seemed to find themselves in the Revolution.[73] Several were destined for prominent careers in the Convention or in radical Parisian politics. Yet numerous other publishers and intellectuals on the Left Bank—including Nicolas Ruault—frequented the club, along with a contingent of local merchants and shop owners.[74] Currents of radicalism also flourished in many of the neighborhood districts and their successors, the sections. Until the summer of 1792, however, the leadership of the sections was restricted by law to "active citizens," and they were dominated by members of the liberal professions, "bourgeois" living off their investments, merchants, and relatively wealthy artisans and shopkeepers—most of whom owned their own businesses and employed many salaried journeymen.[75]

Nevertheless, since late 1790 the educated elites who frequented such circles had enlisted support from the broader masses of the population. Such efforts were driven in part by their belief that true democracy must include all male members of society. They were also aware of the need for greater numbers to bolster their movement and outweigh the moderate middle class who generally dominated the political process. These more humble recruits were initially referred to simply as "the people." But soon they came to be called the *sans-culottes,* those who generally wore the working man's long trousers rather than the more stylish knee-breeches. Originally, the sans-culottes were clearly conceived as a social category. Rosalie Jullien was careful to distinguish such individuals, whom she often described as being "in rags," from the wealthier and more comfortable "bourgeoisie" of which she considered herself a member. In fact, "in rags" was partly a manner of speech. There can be no doubt, however, that a great many of the men and women whom she watched parading in the street beneath her window wore the simple dress of the working people.[76] Nevertheless, the meaning of the word "sans-culottes" would evolve over time, and eventually came also to include all of the radical militants who closely identified with "the people." In this sense, the term did not refer to an economic class but to an essentially new sociopolitical alliance created by the Revolution—a "popular front," as Georges Lefebvre would call it, unlike anything that had existed under the Old Regime.[77]

The politicization of the common people of Paris was a complex process, a process that is particularly difficult to follow since so few such individuals left letters or diaries documenting their lives.[78] They had, of course, already played a major role in the events of 1789. But their participation at that time may have been motivated less by a desire to support the new National Assembly than by a fear of famine and of an attack by mercenary troops. A greater self-conscious political awareness came in part through their recruitment into neighborhood fraternal societies—largely created by elite militants for this purpose—or through attendance in sectional clubs which existed parallel to the official sectional meetings.[79] They were also influenced by the great mass of newspapers and pamphlets circulating in Paris. Although the majority could not read well enough to have direct access to such materials, they listened to others read them aloud in cabarets and cafés—of which there were several hundred in the city.[80] Or they debated with one of the self-appointed neighborhood speakers, "these street-corner orators," as Mercier called them, "who speak among themselves of radical motions [in the Assembly] or of uncovering insidious plots." A good deal of information or misinformation was also imparted by the newspaper hawkers, shouting out improvised headlines to better sell their merchandise.[81]

Over time the coalition of Parisian militants developed a program for change, an ideology of sorts that was in many respects a synthesis of the goals of the working classes and the radical middle class. Central to the Cordeliers' vision was the expansion of the ideals of 1789 and the creation of a full democracy that would sweep away the concept of "passive citizens" and grant to every male in society the right to vote and hold office. Some even advocated a direct democracy, where all citizens would have the right to ratify all measures passed by their representatives. After the crisis of Varennes, a great many militants had been converted to republicanism, in which the ultimate "sovereign," the people as a whole, would reign. Most embraced an idealized vision of "the people" and especially of the people of Paris. Perhaps such a vision was influenced in part by the writings of Jean-Jacques Rousseau. Yet it also arose out of the very experience of the recent events. The people of Paris, so it was maintained, had been the constant defenders of the Revolution. It was they who had been its salvation in July 1789 and again in October. For the deputy Pierre Soubrany, the people represented "the essential portion of the population, those who feed us, furnish all our needs, and constitute the true strength of the nation." Jean-Louis Prudhomme turned almost mystical in his praise of an idealized common man: "The people, like God Himself, see everything and are always present. . . . The people never die; they can sometimes be misled, or enchained, or lulled to sleep; they are not invulnerable; but they are immortal." Jullien was not alone in citing the old Roman adage, "The voice of the people is the voice of God."[82]

Yet these idealistic conceptions were mixed in the militants' register with more mundane demands emanating from the people themselves. The sansculottes had their own lives and itineraries, and to some extent their political culture evolved independently from that of the radical elites with whom they were allied. They were at least as concerned about the price of bread as they were about an expansion of democracy. It was essential to halt all grain hoarding and the manipulation of prices, to stabilize the value of the paper money, and perhaps to impose fixed prices that would bring a halt to the terrible inflation that eroded their standard of living and caused them such anxiety. In addition, the Parisian masses partook of a political culture in which the desire for revenge and retribution and a readiness to resort to violence were deeply embedded. They were always closely attuned to the hundreds of rumors—some astute, some absurd—swirling through the city.[83] Hoarders and counterfeiters and economic manipulators should be discovered and executed. The same fate must be meted out to political conspirators, who were assumed to be numerous and dangerous. And if the courts did not act quickly enough, the people were prepared to step in and do the job themselves. While initially many of the elite militants would probably have preferred peaceful methods, their lower-class allies would be ready and able to resort to violence—or at least to the threat of violence—in order to obtain their goals, intimidate their enemies, and foil their plots. The ethos of the militant/sans-culotte alliance was constructed of a fluctuating symbiosis of idealism, fear, anger, and a penchant for revenge.

During the winter and spring of 1792 the Parisian militants and their sans-culotte associates adopted a whole set of symbols that helped bind them together. The idea of the red Phrygian liberty cap or *bonnet rouge* originated in the educated middle class, adopted from the head covering said to have been worn by freed slaves in ancient Rome. Brissot first supported the concept in his newspaper in February 1792. On March 15 several members of the Jacobin Club arrived wearing the cap, and within days over half of the membership followed suit. They were soon imitated by spectators attending the Legislative Assembly. Actors in a major Paris theater did likewise at the end of a performance of *The Death of Caesar* and then dramatically placed the cap on the bust of Voltaire in the theater's foyer. To be sure, not all of the elites took to the idea. Robespierre disapproved of it, and Ruault found it "sullen" and refused to wear it. The elderly Guittard de Floriban thought it all seemed like a "masquerade": "It looks so bizarre that we find it ridiculous." In the end, Mayor Pétion and the Jacobin leadership decided to discourage it, arguing that the tricolor targetlike badge (the *cocarde*) was a sufficient mark of one's patriotism. But even as many of the elites left their liberty cap at home, it was adopted with great enthusiasm by the popular classes, and soon it had replaced "the absurd three-cornered hat"—as Prudhomme called it—as the requisite headpiece for the sans-culottes.[84]

It is not entirely clear when the first liberty trees appeared in Paris. The earliest examples may well have appeared in the provinces. But during the spring and summer of 1792 various popular planting ceremonies were organized about the city. Typically the trees were surmounted by a red liberty cap and decorated with tricolor ribbons and signs such as "Liberty or death" or "Union makes strength." According to the deputy Malassis, in a letter of June 1792, "Parisians have been busy over the last week planting liberty trees on every street." His colleague Corbel du Squirio described a petition from a national guard unit on the Left Bank to plant such a tree at the door of the Legislative Assembly itself, to be surmounted by a *bonnet rouge*. "Come and attend the apotheosis of the liberty cap," urged the spokesman, "whose splendor outshines even a crown." Corbel saw such actions as symbolic of the new spirit of patriotism sweeping through the population.[85]

More ominous and far from merely symbolic was the movement to arm the Parisians as an additional line of defense before the prospects of war. With muskets in short supply, the weapon of choice became the pike, the pole with a sharp hook-like blade at the end, devised by the Swiss for the wars of an earlier age.[86] It was once more Brissot who emerged as the prime promoter—drawing inspiration from the citizen soldiers of Greece and Rome. The idea was of considerable political significance in that it was a means of arming "passive citizens," previously forbidden to participate in the national guard. With both the city and the Assembly fraught with obsessive fears of plots, the pike was billed as the ideal instrument for intimidating internal opponents and counterrevolutionaries. A number of the militants referred to the pikes' potential for "terrorizing" their enemies. Couthon wrote of the "salutary terror" they would generate, acting like "the scarecrows that peasants place among their crops to keep away undesirable animals." Soon several of the sections of Paris were independently ordering the manufacture of pikes. Urged on by a group of patriotic women, the fraternal societies even took up a collection to subsidize their production throughout the city.[87]

Although the militants and their supporters might wield pikes to "terrorize" their enemies, their efforts were also pursued through nonviolent methods. One particularly creative practice developed early in the Revolution was the fraternal banquet. Hundreds or even thousands of men, women, and children were invited to join in a potluck picnic—"simple and frugal, but altogether fraternal"—organized out of doors in streets or parks or public squares. Bands played, militant leaders delivered speeches, and toasts were offered to various patriotic causes. One such banquet in April 1792 saw speeches by Danton, Mayor Pétion, and several other radical leaders. The crowds present drank toasts to liberty, to the National Assembly, and to the patriotic societies, as well as to the fall of tyrants and the end of the slave trade.[88]

The militants might also make their views known through direct physical intervention in or near the Assembly hall. The deputies had long been anxious to promote an image of public transparency and had opened up a portion of the balconies to spectators on a first-come, first-served basis. By the spring of 1792 the "galleries" seem always to have been packed with militants, vociferously supporting the positions of the most radical deputies. When major debates were announced, the crowds could be far more numerous than the galleries could hold, and hundreds or even thousands might congregate outside, shouting out their demands in chorus as the deputies arrived to take their seats. In January 1792, soon after the king had vetoed the decrees on emigrants and refractory priests, a great crowd could be heard outside crying, "No veto, no sanction!" Even larger masses of people showed up for the debates on the declaration of war and for a much-anticipated speech by Brissot in late May announcing a counterrevolutionary plot. The Feuillant leader Viénot de Vaublanc remembered one such occasion when "not only were the galleries of the Assembly filled to overflowing, but the courtyards, the avenues, and the corridors of the hall were entirely blocked. Many spectators were even to be seen sitting or standing on the window ledges."[89]

How such activities were organized is not altogether clear, though it seems likely that both the sections and the clubs played an important role. There can be no doubt, however, that these two groups were instrumental in the great street demonstrations that so impressed Parisians of the period.[90] Building on a tradition of religious processions, such demonstrations could involve thousands of people arriving from all over the city, with both middle-class radicals and sans-culottes converging on the Assembly. Men, women, and adolescents marched together arm-in-arm, grouped by neighborhood or profession. They shouted slogans, sang Revolutionary songs to the rhythm of drums, and proclaimed their views with banners or diverse symbolic paraphernalia—models of the Bastille, copies of the Declaration of Rights, pikes topped with liberty caps. Once they arrived at the Assembly, delegations were sent inside with petitions to be read before the deputies. In a few dramatic instances the demonstrators were allowed to continue their parade through the hall itself—along with their songs and banners and symbolic decor.

Demonstrations and petitions of this kind had been central to the protest movement in Paris following the king's flight. After the massacre of the Champ de Mars and the period of repression that followed, there had been a long lull in such activities.[91] However, in the winter and spring of 1792, perhaps in response to the king's vetoes, the crowds had come to life once again. In April of that year a massive demonstration was held to celebrate the amnesty of forty Swiss soldiers who had mutinied in Nancy a year and a half earlier and had then been sentenced to hard labor. For the militants, the soldiers had been the victims of "despotism" for daring to disagree with their aristocratic commander—none other than Count Bouillé, who had later played a central role in the king's flight. The entry of the liberated Swiss into Paris was celebrated by public picnics, dances, parades in the streets, and a boisterous procession through the Assembly with all the symbolic décor that had come to be associated with the sans-culottes. Most of the festival seems to have been organized by the Jacobins and the more militant sections, who took charge of choreographing the pageant and helped subsidize the construction of decorated carts and wagons in the midst of the parade.[92] For contemporaries who took part, the political import of the event was clear. It was vigorously opposed, moreover, by the Feuillants, who did everything in their power to block the crowd's entry into the Assembly.[93] For no one could now doubt that the radical militants and their sans-culotte supporters fully embraced the Jacobins in the Assembly and opposed the Feuillants. They had become major players in the politics of Paris, and their influence would only increase in the months to come, especially after the French found themselves at war.

The Whirlwinds of War

At the beginning of the Legislative Assembly, with the Constitution written and the Revolution "completed," many deputies imagined that they would devote themselves primarily to the positive reforms and civic improvements that the previous Assembly had left untouched or had been unable to achieve: reorganizing the education system, for example, or completing a civil justice code, or working to improve agriculture. But in fact the representatives would direct their energies primarily toward defending the new regime from the various forces thought to threaten its existence. The preoccupation with such threats was not unrelated to the recent experience of the deputies themselves, who as former administrators and magistrates in the provinces had directly faced the problems posed by refractory priests and nobles of dubious loyalty. Extensive debates in October and November led to tough legislation against both the emigrants and the nonjuring clergy—decrees vetoed by the king, much to the deputies' frustration. The assembly also created a powerful new surveillance committee and a special High Court to search out and punish conspirators. Soon, however, the deputies found themselves absorbed above all else with threats from abroad and the possibility of going to war.

For the first year of the Revolution, the French had scarcely concerned themselves with foreign affairs, wrapped up as they were in the extraordinary project of transforming their government and remaking society. Colson offered a rare comment on the question at the end of 1789 in a letter to his friend in Berry: "For me the word 'war' is altogether foreign. We never even think of other lands and other countries outside Paris and France."[94] The Revolutionaries had been shaken out of their national self-absorption only in May 1790, when a diplomatic crisis between Britain and Spain—over an obscure region off the Pacific coast of North America—incited the government to mobilize a portion of the French fleet in support of its Spanish ally. Unsettled by the news, the National Assembly had launched a major debate on the rights of the king and the legislature in making war and peace. The debate also produced a remarkable declaration that the French nation would never initiate an offensive war.[95]

After the crisis of 1790 had faded without incident, some of the deputies occasionally reflected in their correspondence on the prospect of war.[96] It was the event of Varennes, however, that made war a very present possibility. The National Assembly leadership convened an emergency council of military leaders. Volunteer national guardsmen were hurried off to support the regular army, and several deputies were sent to the frontiers to inspect the troops and the defensive fortifications. Even before the arrival of the representatives from Paris, local citizens' committees, sometimes in a state of near panic, began mobilizing guardsmen and shoring up the city walls. In the end, the war that everyone expected never came.[97] But the experience of this dress rehearsal had an exhilarating effect on the Revolutionaries. They felt a great surge of national pride and self-confidence, and they were convinced that if the need arose in the future, they were prepared for a military confrontation.[98]

When the Legislative deputies assumed their seats in October, the immediate prospects of foreign intervention seemed substantially diminished. "The outbreak of a war with the neighboring powers," wrote the Breton deputy Bagot, "becomes more unlikely every day."[99] The dramatic reversal of opinion over the next few months is by no means easy to explain. For Jean Jaurès it was one of the great enigmas of the period: "How did it happen that in the autumn of 1791 the Revolution suddenly discovered within itself the soul of a warrior?"[100] In part, the drift toward war arose as a logical consequence of the debates over the threat of emigrant nobles and refractory priests. The Legislators were outraged that two small states in the German territories across the Rhine, seemingly supported by Austria, were harboring the king's renegade brothers and the armies they were raising to invade France and overthrow the Revolution. It was at this time that Brissot and his allies intensified their denunciations of an insidious "Austrian Committee," said to include many of the present and former ministers and the Austrian-born queen herself. In his first major speech Brissot raised the possibility of an attack on the German states if they refused to expel the emigrants. By the end of November Couthon, who had long downplayed the prospect of war, began to envision it as a serious possibility.[101]

The penchant for war was also nourished by the rise of an intense, often chauvinistic nationalism. French nationalism had not originated with the Revolution.[102] But strong sentiments of French identity had expanded rapidly since 1789, marked by waves of enthusiastic oaths of allegiance to the nation and by the great celebrations of national unity on the first two anniversaries of the fall of the Bastille. Such feelings were underscored by a variety of symbolic representations, from liberty trees and the new tricolor flag to the emergence of Revolutionary songs like "Ça ira." Many citizens made it perfectly clear that they considered France to be the model, the exemplar for the future of all mankind—the "first in the universe," as they delighted in saying in their exuberant imagery. "The whole world," wrote Colson, "must now cast its eyes on us, and we can only cast our eyes on ourselves." "Oh you the French!" proclaimed Prudhomme, "what an extraordinary people you are, unlike any other in all of history!"[103] The effect of such nationalism on the deputies themselves was illustrated by the passionate oathtaking ceremony of October 4, 1791. At the beginning of the session they had all risen spontaneously with their hands raised to Heaven and shouted out the "sacred commitment" to "live free or die"—the catch phrase that had spread so rapidly in the weeks after Varennes. The enthusiastic cries lasted for over five minutes and were echoed by similar affirmations from the audience in the galleries.[104]

Soon war with the German states was being justified not only on the basis of self-defense but as a necessary affirmation of French national honor: "as the result of a sense of dignity that must never be lost by a great nation," as the deputy Tardiveau explained it in a letter to his constituency.[105] By the end of the year, Brissot and the Girondins, who increasingly made war the cornerstone of their political ambitions, had considerably expanded their vision. Adopting the argument of many of the foreign immigrants living in Paris—notably the Prussian patriot Anacharsis Cloots—they began demanding a war against Austria itself, and envisioning such a conflict as a great moral commitment to spread the achievements of the Revolution to all the "enslaved peoples" of Europe. "To war, to war! Such is the cry of all patriots," wrote Brissot in mid-December, increasingly carried away by his own rhetoric. "The moment has come for a new crusade . . . a crusade of universal liberty."[106]

The Girondin rhetoric reached a climax in mid-January 1792, with impassioned orations by one speaker after another. In a particularly dramatic speech on January 14 the Bordeaux lawyer Guadet vowed that the nation would defend to the death the French Constitution against all the enemies of Europe. As he spoke these words, all of the deputies were swept by a wave of enthusiasm. For a time, at least, factional animosities were set aside and all rose with raised arms, shouting out together, "Yes, we do so swear!"—an oath vigorously repeated by the spectators in the hall. Colson, who seems to have been present, thought the event was even more dramatic than the Tennis Court oath two and a half years earlier.[107] Four days later Pierre Vergniaud, another Bordeaux barrister, delivered a rousing indictment of the Austrians and a plea for war: "To arms! To arms! The honor and the salvation of the nation demand it. To arms! To arms!" Even the philosopher-journalist Condorcet, who had once supported theories of perpetual peace, now joined the fray, justifying war in the name of the greater good of bringing liberty to all humanity.[108]

In the midst of this frenzy in France, Austria and Prussia were also becoming more receptive to the possibility of war. For the first two years of the Revolution, the leaders of both states had been perfectly content to see their great rival to the west caught up in political upheaval, while they pursued a long war against Turkey, with the prospects of a further partition of Poland.[109] But in August 1791 peace had at last been signed between Austrians, Russians, and Turks. Following the Varennes debacle, both the emigrants and the French royal family put ever-greater pressure on the Austrian emperor Leopold II to intervene in France. The European monarchies were increasingly impatient with the Revolution's contention that political legitimacy should be based on popular sovereignty. This had been the grounds for France's unilateral annexation of Avignon and the Comtat Venaissin, which had long belonged to the Pope. In August 1791 Leopold and his foreign minister Kaunitz arranged a rapprochement with their long-time rivals the Prussians and issued the so-called Pilnitz Declaration. The joint pronouncement promised a European intervention to "restore the King of France [to] complete liberty and to consolidate the bases of monarchical government."[110] In fact, the declaration may have been intended primarily as a threat to cow the Revolutionaries into maintaining a strong monarchy and releasing Louis and Marie-Antoinette—Leopold's sister—from their palace captivity in the weeks after Varennes. The irony was that the Austrians would wrongly assume that their threat had worked, that their declaration was responsible for the return of the king to power in September 1791, and that similar intimidation might be used in the future to "manage" the Revolutionary leadership.[111] Over the coming months such attempts at coercion would play directly into the hands of the French war party. By late winter an exchange of threats and counterthreats between France and Austria succeeded only in inflaming the deputies' sense of patriotism and offended honor. Moreover, most of the Legislators had great difficulty comprehending the subtle expressions and maneuvers of traditional international diplomacy: "this treacherous diplomacy," as Pierre Ramel put it, which "seeks to envelop all decisions in an impenetrable fog."[112]

The road toward war was facilitated in France when both the king and most of the Feuillant leadership joined the bandwagon, each assuming that a war would be to their own advantage. Though Barnave would ultimately oppose it, Lameth, Duport, and Lafayette all came out in favor and most of the deputies on the right followed suit.[113] A great thrill of excitement swept through the Assembly and the galleries when the king announced that the army would be commanded by generals Lafayette and Rochambeau, two heroes of the war in America. "A free France," wrote Rubat, "will not fear any enemies. You cannot imagine how much this decision, taken jointly by the Assembly and the king, infused the people of Paris with energy and confidence."[114] Step by step nearly all elements of the political nation were rallying in support of war. Only Robespierre and a handful of his closest associates continued to oppose it. To his mind the threat of internal conspiracy was far greater than any external threats: "The source of the evil," he announced, "is not in Coblenz"—the principal base of the emigrants—"it is among you, it is in your midst."[115]

But the Girondins and their allies only mocked Robespierre and responded with a heady mixture of rationales for war, now portrayed as the remedy for all the problems, fears, and uncertainties faced by the nation. War would bring defeat, once and for all, to the emigrants and an end to their arrogant threats; it would teach a lesson to all foreign powers—especially the Austrians—who imagined they could meddle in France's internal affairs; it would defend before the world the honor of Revolutionary France; it would bring assistance to enslaved peoples everywhere who were struggling for their liberty; it would put a stop to the endless internal turmoil by rallying all French around the fatherland, inspiring citizens everywhere to obey the law, to pay their taxes, to accept the *assignats*. War would also force into the open all the internal conspirators who were thought to be threatening the nation and who were generating such agonizing mistrust among the Revolutionaries. "This state of uncertainty, of rumors, of foreboding," declared Vergniaud, "is far more frightening and terrible, it seems to me, than an actual state of war."[116] By the end of 1791 Couthon, the Jacobin who had once been so skeptical of war, had entirely changed his mind: "War has now become our only option: for our national interest, for our honor, for our glory." The Feuillant sympathizer Rabusson-Lamothe largely concurred: "We will only overcome internal disorder and establish peace in the kingdom, if we reassert our preponderance among the nations of Europe."[117]

On January 25 the Assembly voted an ultimatum that if the emperor did not renounce all treaties directed against France and its Constitution within three weeks, the nation would declare war. In fact, the diplomatic process prolonged the negotiations for another two months, much to the chagrin of the deputies, convinced that it was all a new trick on the part of the ministers to prevent the war they so ardently desired.[118] The Girondins won a major victory in March, however, when they convinced the king to appoint several of their close friends and allies—Roland, Clavière, Servan, and Dumouriez—to various ministries. The prospects for a conflict were further increased by the death of Emperor Leopold and the succession of his much less cautious son, Francis. On April 20, 1792 Louis XVI came to the National Assembly himself and formally requested a declaration of war against Austria. Only seven of the Legislators opposed it.[119]

All sides in the conflict predicted a rapid victory. The emigrants and the German officer corps were utterly dismissive of the Revolutionary riffraff and the "army of lawyers," and they predicted a parade into Paris.[120] The Revolutionaries, for their part, projected the image of an overpowering people's army, fighting to defend its liberty and its constitution. Some called up memories of the ancient Greeks overcoming the mighty Persian empire.[121] "The success of the war," wrote Jacques Pinet to his constituency in Bergerac, "cannot be doubted." Couthon shared his anticipation of victory with friends in Clermont-Ferrand. The efforts of all the "crowned heads" of Europe to attack the French nation, he argued, will only make their tyranny more detestable among their own people. The French, he believed, had ample funds in their coffers and were in possession of a "powerful army in both numbers and quality." "Twenty-five million men whose will is strong," declared Isnard, "can only be victorious."[122]

In fact, the war that was launched that spring would persist in one form or another for almost a quarter of a century. And it would be difficult to overestimate its immense impact on France and on Europe. Suspicion, mistrust, and fear were already very much present throughout the nation before the declaration of April 20. But they would be enormously inflated by the seemingly endless and grueling war that followed.

7

Fall of the Monarchy

By the late spring of 1792 the atmosphere in Paris and in many provincial towns across the nation had changed dramatically from that of just three years earlier. An erosion of the bonds of authority at all levels of society, coupled with the aggressive threats of counterrevolution from across the Rhine and from reactionary newspapers within France itself, had produced feelings of nervousness and mistrust and a growing obsession with conspiracy. The fervent belief in the possibility of change, the spirit of '89, was still very much present. But there was now a growing demand to push the Revolution further, to expand the blessings of liberty and equality to include the entire male population. The emergence of radical militancy in Paris, closely allied with elements of the working classes, had injected politics with a new stridency and anger, a willingness to resort to violence if necessary to ensure change and punish enemies. At the same time the patriot faithful, once so strongly united, had divided into warring factions, seemingly distrusting one another as much as they distrusted those who promoted counterrevolution. All such trends, trends that had emerged from the very process of the Revolution itself, would be enormously intensified through the outbreak of war and through a series of terrible betrayals by individuals whom patriots once thought they could trust.

Whether or not the Revolution had now crossed an irreversible threshold could be debated endlessly. Yet from the summer of 1792, the train of events, as traced in the following chapters, seemed to rush forward with all the inexorable force of a classical tragedy, toward the harrowing regime of the Terror.

The May Panic and the Events of June 20

It was with a mixture of excitement, anticipation, and apprehension that the people of Paris had followed the final debates on war in the Assembly and the formal declaration of hostilities in April. Over the following weeks, dozens of groups and individuals appeared in the Assembly to offer their support, both moral and monetary. Contingents of merchants, artisans, apprentices, women, and even schoolboys arrived with small patriotic contributions for the soldiers at the front. Guardsmen and common citizens from several Parisian sections trooped en masse through the hall to affirm their backing.[1] The appearance of some 6,000 men and women from the Gobelins section in the Left Bank working-class suburb of Saint-Marcel made an especially strong impression. They carried pikes, pitchforks, or tridents as they passed in front of the president's table, and the room was filled with the cries of "Long live the Nation and death to tyrants."[2]

Yet the French war effort soon went badly, or more precisely, it went nowhere at all. The Girondin-backed foreign minister Charles-François Dumouriez had attempted to isolate Austria by courting alliances with various other European states. But in the end he had failed miserably. The Prussians signed a treaty with Austria, and the two powers made plans for a joint invasion of France. The widely predicted popular uprisings in Belgium in favor of the French never materialized. The timid entry of the French army into the Austrian Lowlands was easily halted when inexperienced French troops abandoned the field after the first shots were fired. Some of them then proceeded to murder two of their aristocratic commanders who were accused of treason. Thereafter, the French generals refused to take the offensive. Rochambeau resigned, and Lafayette, deeply disturbed by the rise of radicalism in Paris, began secret negotiations for a truce with the Austrians, preparing the possibility of turning his army against Paris.[3]

For the political leadership the miserable performance of the army in the first weeks of the war was profoundly shocking. "It would be difficult to describe," wrote Rabusson-Lamothe, "how much the National Assembly and the public in the capital have been affected." All the old anxieties about conspiracy and the threat of internal enemies striking from within reemerged with a vengeance. Rumors of all kinds swept through the city: that the king was about to flee again and that the crown had already been sent to Germany, that a palace official was seen burning papers, that the king's private guard included a number of refractory priests in disguise, that plans were afoot to kill the Revolutionary leaders.[4] Everyone began seeing suspicious strangers prowling about the city. Radical journalists predicted a new Saint-Bartholomew's Day Massacre of the patriots. Once again Rosalie Jullien was overcome with that terrible confusion of emotions she had known in the summer of 1789: "the horror, the pity, the admiration, the joy, the pleasure, the grief . . . and the terrible dangers." She and many of her neighbors were frightened to leave their apartments, and she pleaded with her husband to return from the south: "I'm dying with anxiety."[5]

In the midst of this seeming disaster, with all their expectations of a rapid victory crushed, the political factions in the Legislative Assembly turned on one another. Though the war enthusiasm had briefly generated a measure of peace between the Feuillants and the Jacobins, suspicion and hatred between the two groups now escalated. Moreover, the Jacobins themselves were more divided than ever, with Girondins and Montagnards castigating each other as traitors and conspirators. "The present moment," wrote Jacques Pinet, "is a time of crisis for the Friends of the Constitution . . . who are afflicted with an unfortunate division among its members."[6]

Brissot and the Girondins were compelled to face the apparent failure of their war policy.[7] In such a situation it was only too tempting to embrace the rumors that the war effort had been sabotaged by conspiracy from within. On the morning of May 23 Brissot and his friend Gensonné delivered successive speeches to the Legislators. They claimed the existence of a colossal plot to destroy the Assembly and the Revolution itself. The whole was said to be masterminded by the Austrians and by the "Austrian Committee" surrounding the king—said to include the Austrian-born queen and several current and former ministers. Brissot recognized that there was only indirect evidence for such a plot. But after all, it was the essence of conspiracies to be secret and impenetrable and leave no written records. The plotters had hidden their activities behind a mask of pro-Revolutionary pronouncements, and if one waited to uncover "legal proof," it might be too late.[8]

The speeches caused a sensation among both the deputies and the Parisians, partly because the Girondins, in their *fuite en avant*, seemed to confirm what everyone already believed. Jullien, who had listened from the galleries, announced that only a "crass imbecile" could doubt the evidence of this "barbarous plot" in the circle of the king. Even many of Brissot's

Feuillant rivals believed they must take the accusations seriously. "Both sides," wrote Rabusson-Lamothe, "now speak only of machinations and plots." That night tens of thousands of Parisians who had been closely following the Assembly surrounded the Tuileries Palace to prevent the king from attempting another flight.[9]

During the next several days the Parisians and the deputies worked themselves into a veritable panic. On May 28 the Assembly voted to go into permanent session, with at least some individuals remaining at their seats around the clock to confront the anticipated coup. The whole of Paris was "illuminated" for several nights in succession, with citizens ordered to burn candles in their windows to make it easier to spot the villains who were thought to be readying their attack. The normally phlegmatic Ruault was overcome with anxiety over the "present chaos of ideas and opinions" in Paris and the Assembly. "One hears shouts everywhere that the king is betraying us, that the generals are betraying us, that we should have confidence in no one." As he described it to his brother, he only wished he could be a thousand leagues from Paris.[10]

The Left in the Assembly now took advantage of the crisis to push forward a whole series of new laws of major portent for the future.[11] A decree was passed dissolving the king's personal guards, widely believed to have been involved in the plot. The result was to give even greater power to units of the Parisian national guard—many of them under direct or indirect control of the sections—a major victory for the radicals.[12] The deputies also approved a proposal by the Minister of War to summon 20,000 volunteers from national guard units around the country to help protect the city. Finally, they voted a new decree against the refractory clergy, thought to be deeply entangled in the grand conspiracy and the source of much of the popular unrest in the country. Any priest denounced by twenty active citizens in a given canton was to be deported from the country. Even the Feuillant sympathizer Louis-Michel Demée had lost all patience with the refractories, who "exude only hatred, fury, and vengeance"[13]

The king was ultimately convinced by his advisers to accept the law disbanding the royal bodyguard (though he secretly continued paying their salaries). However, he quickly vetoed the laws that would bring volunteers to Paris and that would increase repression against the nonjurors. In many parts of France, however, administrators simply ignored the royal vetoes and dispatched guardsmen to Paris, acting as though the Assembly's decrees alone set the laws of the land. Some departments also instituted measures against the refractories never authorized by the monarch.[14] Gilbert Romme encouraged such "illegal" procedures in his home constituency. "An exact fidelity to the law," he wrote, "would be inappropriate in the present situation."[15] Clearly, in many parts of the country the king was entirely losing his legitimacy. The perceived needs of national salvation and the preservation of the Revolution were given precedence over the royal will.

After several of the Girondin ministers had also protested the vetoes, the king responded on June 12 by dismissing them and replacing them all with more manageable—and conservative—ministers. The appointment of the Girondin "patriot" ministers the previous March had been greeted with enormous enthusiasm by most of the patriots. Their removal would produce a crisis of major proportions. Some compared Louis' conduct with his dismissal of Necker in July 1789, and many were convinced of the nefarious influence of the queen. By mid-June the tension and anger of a great many Parisians were palpable. Colson described them as "extremely agitated," and Roubaud sensed "a terrible ferment" throughout the city. For the radicals, at least, there could be no doubt that the king and his court were at the heart of the problem. The king, according to Ruault, "has lost all respect, all believability."[16]

On June 16 various section leaders proposed a major demonstration before the Legislative Assembly and the Tuileries Palace to vent their anger and pressure the king to remove his vetoes and recall the Girondin ministers. A final planning session was held on the evening of June 19 at the home of Santerre, the national guard leader of the radical Saint-Antoine neighborhood. Mayor Pétion was informed of the plan, but he was uncertain what to do, and in the end contradictory orders were sent out to national guard units across the city as to how they should react.[17]

The demonstration was launched late on the morning of June 20, as large numbers of armed and unarmed citizens, including a considerable contingent of women, began moving westward from Saint-Antoine and northward from the Saint-Marcel neighborhood on the Left Bank. Joining forces in central Paris they picked up additional groups of demonstrators as they crossed other sections. Both Ruault and Jullien were outside watching the great mass of people—Ruault estimated 25,000—marching through the narrow streets of the Right Bank and into the Place Vendôme just north of the Assembly. When a delegation from the demonstration was allowed to speak to the deputies, the speaker read a remarkably strong indictment against the king. He denounced Louis' vetoes, his dismissal of the ministers, and the complete inaction of the French armies at the front. He invoked the Declaration of the Rights of Man granting citizens the right to resist oppression. The French people had now awoken, he said, and they would not allow themselves to be betrayed by "executive authority." The actions of the king must be investigated by the Assembly, and if the monarch has failed in his duties to the nation, then "he no longer exists for the French people."[18]

After a bitter debate between the Left and the Right, the demonstrators were allowed to walk in procession through the Assembly. About one in the afternoon, with some of the Feuillants leaving the hall in disgust, the extraordinary parade began. A small military orchestra was set up in the stands to intone Revolutionary songs, and thousands of guardsmen and other male and female citizens entered the building and marched before the deputies, dressed in the uniforms or costumes of their professions, "all mixed together in the spirit of equality and fraternal union."[19] The demonstrators carried an amazing array of weapons—muskets, pikes, sabers, pistols, swords—but also flags and banners and other symbolic decor, including a tablet containing the Rights of Man and, by one account, a calf's heart stuck on a pike with the sign "heart of the aristocrats." As they passed the Feuillant side of the hall, some of the marchers shook their fists and shouted out condemnations.[20]

The leaders of the demonstration had always planned to march on to the nearby Tuileries, but it is unclear how many had the preconceived idea of entering the heavily guarded palace itself. Roederer, a representative of the Department of Paris, had warned the Assembly that the marchers might try to confront the king directly.[21] At any rate, the demonstrators halted before the palace gates, and as Ruault watched, some of the leaders entered into discussion with the national guardsmen assigned to protect the entrance.[22] Whether or not they had received orders to do so, the guards soon stepped aside and the huge crowd surged through one of the doors and up the stairs into the palace, muskets and pikes at the ready, with one group even dragging along a pair of cannons. They found Louis in a room surrounded by a small group of nobles, but nothing could halt the pressure of the huge crowd, and the king was soon pushed back into a window emplacement. Apparently he was never physically threatened: the old mystique of the French kingship still seemed to hold sway. But the demonstrators angrily taunted him and confronted him for his policies, demanding that he revoke his vetoes. They asked him whether he supported France in the current war, whether he was truly king of the French or merely king of the emigrant armies across the Rhine. Someone pushed forward a red liberty cap on the end of a bayonet, and the king awkwardly pulled it over his head. Another presented him with a bottle, and Louis willingly toasted the nation. But he remained remarkably placid and steadfastly refused to discuss his policies, announcing that this was not the occasion. Somewhat later shouts arose that the people must be allowed to see the queen, and two doors were battered down until she agreed to appear, holding the young heir to the throne by the hand.[23]

In the meantime, word of the break-in reached those deputies who were still gathered nearby. They rushed back to their hall, reconvened the meeting, and sent a succession of delegations in an attempt to mediate. After some two hours, the king's calm behavior and the deputies' efforts to harangue the crowds seemed to appease the demonstrators, and they began filtering out. By eight or nine o'clock that evening all had gone home and the palace was quiet.

The dramatic events of June 20 and the confrontation between the king and the Paris militants stirred an enormous controversy throughout the nation. Over the next several weeks hundreds of letters flowed into the Legislative Assembly, arguing for and against the people's entry into the Tuileries Palace and, by extension, for and against the king himself. Although many variations existed, there was a tendency for the north of France and the region around Paris to sympathize with the king, while the south and especially the southeast more commonly supported the popular demonstration and harshly criticized Louis. But this de facto referendum also intensified local factional divisions, with the department leaders more likely to pronounce themselves firmly royalist, while the districts, municipalities, and clubs attacked the monarch.[24] Indeed, Paris itself was becoming increasingly polarized. Although the militant sections continued to justify their actions, the department of Paris launched a campaign against the radicals, and some 20,000 Parisian residents signed a statement condemning the "outrage" committed toward the royal family. Guittard was appalled by the potential danger of the incident: "It would take no more than a spark to set Paris ablaze in civil war."[25]

Not surprisingly, the Legislative Assembly divided sharply along factional lines. For a Montagnard like Georges Couthon, the demonstration had been nothing more than a legitimate and peaceful expression of popular opinion, in which citizens "went to visit the king" to let him know their views and then "peacefully retired, cheerfully singing the charming tune of 'Ça ira.'" But the Feuillant sympathizer Roubaud had a rather different view: "The National Assembly has been defied, royal dignity debased, the hereditary representative of the nation outraged, his palace attacked . . . and the law was everywhere ignored and challenged by a horde of brigands."[26]

The event of June 20 seemed only to accentuate the split in the Assembly. The deputies on the left, especially the radical Montagnards, were now largely in agreement with the militant sections of Paris. The king, this "present-day Pygmalion," as Jacques Pinet called him, was committing treason by impeding the war effort and secretly supporting the emigrants and the foreign armies. If the Revolution were to survive, Louis would have to be removed. It was now necessary to look to the spirit of the law and not the letter and to support "the constitutionally unconstitutional actions of the people."[27] They were persuaded, moreover, that many of the Feuillants, in their perpetual support for the king and his ministers, were themselves traitors. With opponents such as these, compromise was out of the question. Pinet quoted La Fontaine: "Trying to make an evil man honest is like trying to change a snake into a dove."[28] At the same time the event of June 20 seemed to provide the Right with a new surge of energy and to attract greater support from deputies who had previously remained uncommitted. For Rabusson-Lamothe, the greatest danger to the state was not from the king, but from the radicals whose unconstitutional extremism would "compromise and dissolve the state," destroy the economy, and bring general anarchy to the country. Roubaud was both indignant and terrified by the maneuvers of the radicals and convinced that it was they who were orchestrating the Parisian militants.[29]

In the midst of this polarization and the mutual demonization of the Left and the Right, the Girondins found themselves in an unenviable position. They had been thrown off guard by the dismissal of their allies in the ministry, and they struggled to establish a new position. In general they supported the Left, and there was even a short-lived reconciliation between Brissot and Robespierre. But they still hoped against hope that the king might be brought around and return them to power. In letters to his family Vergniaud confided his belief that it was still a question of a good king badly advised, and he admitted his growing uneasiness about the activities of the militants in Paris. Popular outrage against the king's vetoes was understandable, and yet "such sentiments could accelerate developments and escape the control of the constituted authorities and the rule of law."[30] It was in this context that he, Guadet, and Gensonné penned a secret letter to Louis, announcing they would do all in their power to protect him if he would bring back the Girondin ministers dismissed on June 12.[31]

The political divisions were further intensified at the end of June when General Lafayette suddenly "crossed the Rubicon" and appeared in the Legislative, leaving his army at the front. In a short but concise speech he demanded the prosecution of the perpetrators of June 20, the destruction of the Jacobins—this "sect," as he called them—and the restoration of authority to the king. He also announced that his soldiers supported him in these demands, a veiled threat of military action if the Legislative failed to comply.[32] The Feuillants were exhilarated by the speech, and the general was greeted with rousing cheers as he crossed the hall and took a seat among the Right. But the Left was furious and, in many cases, deeply disillusioned. Pinet could only express his bitterness and sadness: "I believed him to be the ardent and zealous defender of liberty. But I had to face the reality, and I now feel horror and hatred in my heart, since I see him as a traitor who, in the guise of patriotism, is cleverly leading us into an abyss."[33]

Later that day and throughout the night Lafayette attempted to mobilize the Paris national guard, which he had once led, for an attack against the Jacobins. But everything had changed since the days when he was revered by all the Parisians. Whatever the support he enjoyed among the conservatives, he met only suspicion from the guardsmen. And the king and especially the queen—who would forever detest him—refused to accept his plans for deliverance. He was forced to abandon his efforts and return to his army the next day. It was a terrible moment for the radical Revolutionaries, already prone to suspicion of hidden plots. It now seemed evident that Lafayette himself was part of the grand conspiracy everyone had feared, in league with the Austrian Committee. If even those you had most trusted could betray you, where would it all end? How was one ever to know the true from the false Revolutionary, hiding behind the mask of patriotism?[34]

The Marseillais

Although the Legislators found it increasingly difficult to reach a consensus on a great many issues—and especially on how to deal with the king—they were in general agreement that the war was going badly. The Prussians had now entered the conflict, and there was the imminent prospect of their opening up a second front in northeastern France. On July 11 the Assembly voted almost unanimously to declare that France was in imminent peril (the *"patrie en danger"*). The vote was followed by a moment of unusual silence, as everyone took stock of the gravity of the situation.[35] Ten days later the declaration of the "fatherland in peril" was formally read by heralds in all the public places of Paris, and a warning cannon was fired over the Seine every hour throughout the day. Recruitment stations were set up throughout Paris, and large numbers of young men rushed forward to volunteer for the army. Guittard de Floriban, who was himself too elderly to fight, watched in amazement as nationalist fervor swept through the city: "It's like a frenzy," he wrote. "The patriotic zeal is overwhelming, the likes of which have never been seen since the world began. . . . All the young men show extraordinary enthusiasm as they sign up."[36]

Yet it was clear that Paris alone could never stand up to the combined armies of Austria and Prussia. The Girondin war minister Servan had foreseen this problem when he had urged legislation summoning volunteers from national guard units all over the nation, the "Fédérés," as they were now called. At first, following the king's veto of the proposal, the new Feuillant minister of the interior had attempted to block the departure of the provincial guardsmen. But after June 20, the king seemed to reverse his position—perhaps in response to the Parisians' "visit" to his palace or perhaps because he hoped to have influence over the guardsmen who were already on their way. On July 2 the Legislative voted a new decree asking volunteer national guards to come to Paris for the July 14 celebration, the third since the fall of the Bastille. They would then move on to a camp near Soissons, northeast of Paris, to help prepare a line of defense for the capital. This time the king accepted the decree.[37]

By July 14 several hundred guardsmen had already arrived in the city. Pinet proudly accompanied to the Assembly the contingent from his own town of Bergerac—a contingent he had encouraged even before the king reversed his position: "these brave young men, the courageous defenders of the nation."[38] After their participation in the great patriotic festival, the provincial guardsmen were supposed to move on to Soissons. But it is clear that a substantial portion of them did not do so. Both the clubs and the section leaders urged them to remain. Robespierre had appealed to the Fédérés in a speech on July 11. They were in Paris, he said, to defend not only the "fatherland in peril" but also the "fatherland betrayed." Pinet likewise encouraged the guardsmen from his home town to stay on, asking his friends in Bergerac to take up a collection to help defray their expenses.[39]

By the end of July over 5,000 young guardsmen had arrived in Paris, and a great many of them announced they planned to remain there. They came from Angers and Rennes, and Nantes in western France; from Besançon and Dijon in the east; from Lyon, Montpellier, and Toulon to the southeast; and from Bordeaux, La Rochelle, and Angoulême in the southwest. They arrived with a myriad of accents and uniforms. Some from the Midi sported long, drooping moustaches, which initially struck the Parisians as bizarre but which soon became the symbol of the soldiers of the Revolution.[40] Almost everywhere over the previous three years the guardsmen had been radicalized. Closely allied with the local Jacobin clubs, of whom a great many were members, they had come to see themselves as the agents of the Revolution in the provinces and they had frequently been involved in repressive activities against perceived local counterrevolutionaries. Now they were eager to answer the call of the National Assembly and help rid the fatherland of all of its foreign and internal enemies. Once in Paris, the majority closely allied themselves with the militants and sans-culottes. A Fédéré central committee began meeting nightly, with representatives from all the provincial contingents, along with leaders of the Jacobins, the Cordeliers, and several of the sections. The central committee rapidly became the focal point for the organization of an armed insurrection to compel the king to resign his throne.[41]

Though the Fédérés came from almost everywhere in France, two of the largest contingents arrived from the farthest extremities of the nation. On July 26, 4 to 500 Bretons marched in from the port city of Brest, with several hundred more expected from the province in the coming days.[42] Four days later an even larger body of citizen soldiers arrived from Marseille and Provence in the far southeast—"armed to the teeth," as Pinet put it—and accompanied with artillery. Though most of the national guards were dominated by the middle class, the "Marseillais" were primarily workers and artisans.[43] They had been anticipated for weeks by the militants in Paris, especially after their radical patriotic declaration had been printed and sent ahead, and their entry into the city made a particularly memorable impression on the Parisians. As they marched through the Saint-Antoine quarter and into the Place de la Bastille, they were singing the "Song of the Army of the Rhine," composed several weeks earlier in Strasbourg and rapidly renamed "La Marseillaise." It was stirring and intensely patriotic but also ferocious, warning the world that they would soon soak the land with the blood of their enemies—traitors, slaves, and conspiring kings.[44]

The King Must Be Removed

The young volunteers from Marseille and Brest were full of energy and radical enthusiasm, and both groups soon made it amply clear that they had no intention of continuing on to the front until the problem of the king had been resolved. Within days, they had sent a petition of their own to the Assembly demanding the dethroning of the reigning monarch: "The very name of 'Louis XVI' now means 'treason' to us."[45] By the beginning of August, the Marseillais and the other citizen soldiers arriving in the city from around the country had become a factor to be reckoned with by the Parisians, the Legislative Assembly, and the monarchy.

Throughout late July and early August section after section in Paris joined with the Fédérés in demanding the deposition of the king. Other similar petitions were said to be "flooding into the Assembly" from the provinces, primarily from local Jacobin clubs but sometimes also from district or municipal administrators. On August 3 Mayor Pétion arrived with a collective petition from forty of the forty-eight sections of Paris calling for the king's removal. The demand was justified with a complete "history" of Louis' supposedly treacherous actions during the Revolution and of the many oaths he had taken and then broken. Despite all the "benefits" that the nation had granted him, the king's conduct consisted only of "perjury, treason, and conspiracy against the people." They had pardoned him for his flight to Varennes in 1791, "but to pardon is not to forget." And now, in their view, it was clear that the king was "the first link in the chain of counterrevolution" that was leading the Revolution to ruin.[46]

As Pétion spoke before the Assembly, the Parisians were just learning of the so-called Brunswick Manifesto, sent to the king several days earlier and now made public. Written in the name of the Prussian commander by one of the emigrant nobles, the statement sought to intimidate the Parisians with the threat of "delivering the city of Paris to an exemplary and ever memorable vengeance" if the Tuileries Palace were attacked or if the royal family received the least insult or violence. Yet this curious document seems only to have further infuriated the Parisian radicals. Ruault snarled at its "insolence," which he maintained "only increases our courage." In the Saint-Marcel neighborhood, a copy of the Manifesto was burned in a public square.[47]

On August 6 a great demonstration of Parisians, organized by the central committee of the Fédérés and by various of the sections, marched in procession across the city, chanting and singing as they made their way to the Champ de Mars. Here thousands of people filled fifty-five pages with their signatures on a petition—at the very spot where the national guard had fired on a petition gathering ceremony one year earlier. This time the only national guardsmen present supported the petition, the combined program of the militants and the sans-culottes. There were thirteen demands altogether, including the removal of the king, the calling of a new constitutional convention, universal male suffrage, severe measures against grain hoarders and monopolizers, a return of the patriot ministers, the replacement of the "suspect" departmental directories who continued to support royalism, and the indictment of Lafayette. A special delegation then delivered the gigantic petition to the Legislative Assembly.[48]

The Assembly, however, remained as divided as ever and was unable to take a position. Beginning in late July the various petitions demanding the king's removal were sent to a committee for consideration, and the deputies regularly promised to take up the issue. But the proposed debate was continually postponed. While the Montagnards strongly supported the removal of the king and the Feuillants strongly opposed it, the Girondins and the moderates who held the swing votes were mired in indecision.[49] Ruault, who strongly objected to the Assembly's delay tactics, understood nevertheless the deputies' predicament. Even if the king were removed, there was wide confusion as to what to do next. Should they leave him in France as a simple citizen, or escort him to the frontier, or imprison him? And should they then create a republic or turn over power to his heir? If they maintained the monarchy, who would serve as regent until Louis' young son attained his majority?[50]

Under increasing pressure from the militants, the Assembly finally pledged to discuss the question of the king's removal on August 9. But when the day arrived, Condorcet, who reported for the Legislative's steering committee, only presented a learned analysis of the Constitution and the difficult issues that remained to be answered. In the end the question was returned to the committee and the decision was put off once again. In the meantime, a debate on the behavior of General Lafayette had come to a head. The Left had long argued that he should be indicted for having abandoned his troops in the midst of the war and having threatened the deputies if they did not follow his recommendations. But on August 8, with the Feuillants passionately defending their hero and the moderates fearful of removing a general during a campaign, the Assembly gave Lafayette a vote of confidence, 406 to 226. For a great many Parisian militants, the deputies' decision neither to debate the king nor to prosecute Lafayette was the last straw. "We are outraged against the National Assembly," wrote Colson, "for having declared Lafayette innocent, when the public so firmly believes he is a traitor."[51]

In the midst of the continual agitation and attacks against Louis, the supporters of the monarchy were by no means inactive. Both Lafayette and the former duke of La Rochefoucauld-Liancourt proposed detailed plans for moving the king into the provinces.[52] But the queen was revolted at the idea of placing her family in the hands of either Liancourt or Lafayette, both of whom had supported the Revolution in 1789. In any case, Louis ultimately rejected all such proposals, arguing—correctly no doubt—that they would lead to civil war.[53]

In the end, the monarchy fell back on a purely defensive strategy, shoring up the fortifications of the Tuileries Palace and bringing in more troops to man them.[54] Such preparations were all the more difficult in that the Legislative, suspicious of the threat of counterrevolution, had largely dismantled the armed forces directly available to the king. The royal bodyguard had been disbanded in May, and most of the regular troops once garrisoned in Paris been had sent to the front. As a replacement, the ministers summoned several hundred gendarmes police and Parisian national guardsmen, many of the latter from the more conservative sections of western Paris. The king also had at his disposal close to a thousand Swiss guards—attached to the protection of the monarchy since the sixteenth century—and some two or three hundred volunteer nobles, many of them former members of the royal bodyguard. In all, by early August some 4,000 men had been concentrated in and around the palace. As events would prove, the loyalty to the king of the gendarmes and the guardsmen was altogether uncertain.[55] But the intentions of the king were by no means obvious to the Parisians. On the night of August 9, the leader of the Saint-Marcel national guard battalion, Charles Alexandre, made a clandestine tour of the palace, and he found it bristling with activity. If the confrontation were to turn into an armed combat, it was not at all clear to him who would have the upper hand.[56]

Faced with such a situation, many of the militants agonized over how the king's removal was to be accomplished. They had long been hopeful that such a transformation could be effected peacefully, through the expression of popular will in petitions and through the actions of the Legislative Assembly. Even the Marseillais, in their addresses to the Assembly, had urged the use of nonviolent means. France must be delivered from "the evil of kings," they had written, "not by a violent insurrection, but through a peaceful demonstration of the national will."[57] Yet how could they not listen to the rumors in the streets, fueled by newspaper accounts, that the Tuileries Palace was planning a massacre against the patriots? Was it not clear that the king had turned his palace into an armed camp from which such an attack might easily be launched? Was there any choice but to conspire themselves, if France were to be saved from the conspiracies of the court? Rosalie Jullien had clearly come to such a conclusion: "The king's treason is so disastrous for the success and glory of the nation, that we are faced with the cruel necessity of either destroying it or of meekly accepting the chains that are prepared for us."[58]

Assault on the Tuileries Palace

Throughout the month of July 1792 a significant transformation of the sections of Paris was taking place, sometimes through Legislative decree, sometimes through the initiative of the militants themselves. It was during this period that the sections acquired the right to meet in regular daily assemblies—a measure granted by the Assembly as a war provision for maintaining tight surveillance in the city. They also obtained ever-greater control over the national guard battalions based in their circumscriptions. By the end of the month they had established a centralized bureau to coordinate policy among all of the sections. Equally important, many sections were eliminating on their own initiative the division between active and passive citizens, inviting the whole population—sometimes including women and adolescents—to attend and vote in the neighborhood assemblies.[59]

The Parisian sections were thus acquiring ever-greater leverage in their demand that Louis XVI be removed from the throne. With the Assembly's procrastination in debating the king's fate and with its absolution of Lafayette, the militants concluded that they would have to remove the monarch themselves. This would be accomplished by the combined forces of the Paris national guards and the Fédérés from the provinces: hopefully through coercion and negotiation, but by force if necessary, in a general insurrection.

On the evening of August 9, 1792, a carefully planned and widely announced mobilization of Paris began. All of the sections were convened and met throughout the night, and most of them sent elected "commissioners" to the city hall to coordinate decisions. Just before midnight the bells in the Cordeliers church began sounding the "tocsin," the rapid, insistent tolling that traditionally indicated danger. Soon the bells in many other churches across the city followed suit and picked up the rhythm. By midnight everyone was awake. Rosalie Jullien described the scene in a breathless late-night letter to her husband: "The tocsin is ringing, the call to arms has sounded, and fear and apprehension are spreading through all Paris." The streets were full of citizens, with many women trembling at their windows. "Some 800,000 people are given over to an anguish and terror that is only increased by the black veil of night." National guard battalions rushed into formation and prepared for action. Ruault was up all night guarding a bridge with his detachment—although he was replaced at dawn and would not participate in the day's events.[60]

Around five in the morning, just as the day was beginning to break, the militants captured the royal arsenal in eastern Paris, and more arms were distributed to the guardsmen and Fédérés. Toward seven in the morning, the section commissioners who had been meeting in the city hall, just next door to the legally constituted municipal council, announced that they were taking over and creating a new "Insurrectional Commune." When protests were raised by the "legal" counselors—most of whom were Feuillant sympathizers—they were told that "when the people enter into a state of insurrection, they take back all power for themselves." Soon thereafter the royalist commander of the Paris national guard, who had been preparing the defense of the Tuileries Palace, was brought before the Commune and arrested. As he was being escorted to prison, he was shot through the head by an unknown individual on the steps of the city hall: a violent act that was to initiate a day of violent revolution.[61]

Even as the insurgents were seizing control of the arsenal and the city hall, radical guardsmen and pikesmen and provincial Fédérés were on the march from their various neighborhoods, converging on the Place du Carrousel on the east side of the Tuileries Palace.[62] There they were to wait for over three hours as the insurgents attempted to negotiate with the various troops who barred their way. If we can believe Alexandre, who led the guardsmen of Saint-Marcel and the Fédérés troops from Brittany, no one talked of an attack. The goal was to disarm the palace and ensure that the king was peacefully removed from power. And at first the insurgents seemed to be successful. Little by little most of the national guardsmen and gendarmes guarding the courtyard and the entrance to the palace were convinced to abandon their posts and come over to the side of the "people." Then some of the Swiss were also won over and began to leave their formations. Invariably, these developments caused great consternation inside the Tuileries. Although the king and the queen considered remaining in the palace, a representative from the department of Paris convinced Louis that the cause was hopeless and that he would do better to take his family to the safety of the Legislative Assembly. At about eight-thirty that morning, the royal family and the king's ministers left by the west side of the palace and walked a short distance across the gardens to the Assembly, where they took refuge.

Shortly after the royal family's departure the bulk of the Swiss guards and the nobleman volunteers inside the palace opened fire on the insurgents. The decision came in part as the Swiss officers saw discipline breaking down among their own men, and the "deserters" may have been among the first shot. But thereafter the outside courtyard became a killing field, with dozens of Parisians and Fédérés cut down in a withering cross fire arriving from several directions at once.[63] The royal forces quickly swept clear the Tuileries courtyards and the adjoining Place du Carrousel, killing or wounding more of the insurgents and seizing several of their cannons. As the survivors fled, word of the "ambush" spread rapidly through the city. The story only confirmed the widespread belief of a counterrevolutionary conspiracy hatched in the palace, and the militants and sans-culottes were livid with anger and a desire for revenge.

At first the Swiss seemed to be winning the day, but then a large new contingent of insurgents arrived from eastern Paris led by Santerre, newly named commander of the national guard by the Insurrectional Commune. The guardsmen from the Saint-Antoine district had been slower to organize, but now they advanced through the streets in three separate columns. Colson peeked out his window and saw one of the columns passing by: "a furious multitude armed with pikes and other weapons," heading for the palace.[64] Falling on the Swiss from three sides at once, they quickly forced them back into the Tuileries. There followed a brutal hand-to-hand combat

Storming of the Tuileries Palace, August 10, 1792. The fédéré troops from Marseille and Brest, along with Paris national guardsmen and other citizens, are attacking the palace from the Place du Carrousel with muskets and pikes. Swiss guards can be seen in the background rushing into the palace while shots are fired at the insurgents from the windows. Charles Monnet, engraved by D. Vrijdag, © Coll. Musée de la Révolution française, Domaine de Vizille, MRF L 1985.848.82.

with sabers and bayonets, as the Parisians and the Fédérés forced their way into the palace and up the stairs by sheer force of numbers, with numerous attackers and defenders killed or wounded. A substantial number of the noble volunteers were captured and sent to prison. But the Swiss guards in their bright red uniforms became the target of choice, as the people sought revenge for the ambush and killing of their comrades. Some of the Swiss were able to break out to the west and flee across the Tuileries Gardens. A portion of them burst into the Assembly hall and were protected by the deputies with great difficulty until they could be escorted to prison. But another contingent fled to what is today the Place de la Concorde, and there they were surrounded by the Parisians, and all were killed. Enraged with fury, the guardsmen and Fédérés tracked the remaining Swiss stragglers throughout the city. Those who were unable to shed their uniforms and hide were also killed.

The terrible civil war in the heart of Paris had lasted little more than two hours. Yet over a thousand people had died—the greatest hecatomb in the city since the sixteenth century. The largest toll was among the Swiss guards, of whom some 600 had been killed. But another hundred or so of the noble volunteers had also succumbed, and close to 400 insurgents were killed or wounded. The young volunteers from Marseille and Brittany caught in the cross fire of the courtyard represented the single largest number of patriot casualties. Other victims came from nearly every quarter of Paris and from many different provinces of France.[65]

As the shots died away and the smoke cleared, Parisian civilians began venturing out. They found the palace in shambles and both it and the surrounding streets "littered with bodies." By then fire had broken out within the Tuileries, and Parisian firemen would still be struggling to contain it at three the next morning. The medical student Edmond Géraud had difficulty walking in the area without stepping on corpses.[66] All over the city, women and men rushed to see if their loved ones had returned. Rosalie Jullien ventured out with her son and saw women who "threw themselves into the arms of their husbands in the middle of the street." Alexandre, leading his battalion back to Saint-Marcel, described similar "truly heart-rending" scenes, including his own father in tears embracing him as he reached their house. "Thus," he wrote, "we returned to our homes, which many of us thought we might never see again, and we rested from the exhaustion of that terrible day."[67]

It had indeed been a terrible, brutal affair, and the Parisian elites who lived through it were beset with a complex mixture of emotions as they sought to explain and justify the violence. Almost forty years later, Victoire Monnard still remembered trembling in her room, watching through the window as the Parisians captured and cut down one of the Tuileries defenders fleeing through the streets. Yet as Alexandre explained, the insurgents were convinced that if they had lost, they would not have been treated any better by their adversaries. And everyone returned again and again to the treacherous attack on the patriots in the courtyard. Adelaïde Mareux, daughter of a theater owner in the Marais, wrote a feverish letter recounting her personal outrage when the Swiss suddenly fired on the Marseillais and the other national guardsmen: "Everyone was overcome with rage against these monsters." Pinet described the "abominable treachery" of the royal forces in luring the people into the palace and then opening fire. It was after this act that "the fury of the people was aroused."[68] And nearly all of the radicals were convinced that the battle of the Tuileries had saved Paris from a far worse fate being plotted by the king and the court: "this abominable court that was weighed down in blood," as the Parisian notary and future deputy Bancal des Issarts described it. Bancal went on to lament the number of young men without any training in combat who had laid down their lives and were butchered by the professional soldiers in the Tuileries. For many Revolutionaries the real massacre was not that of the Swiss guard but of the patriots, the "Saint Lawrence's Day Massacre," they called it—referring to the calendar saint for August 10. Bancal shuddered to think how close they had come to losing everything. He could only conclude that "an admirable Providence is watching over the French, ensuring the preservation of liberty and the triumph of equality."[69]

8

The First Terror

Virtually no one doubted the meaning of the events of August 10. Both those who had directly participated in the attack on the Tuileries Palace and those who had only observed from afar understood clearly that this violent episode marked an authentic "second revolution." In its first formal declaration the Paris Insurrectional Commune proclaimed that the people had "recovered their rights for the second time." Both Adrien Colson and Nicolas Ruault soon began referring to "the new revolution," which had "nullified that of 1789."[1] Everyone knew, moreover, that Louis XVI had been overthrown. Within days, the king and his family were escorted under massive guard to the medieval fortress of the Temple in northern Paris, where they were treated as state prisoners. In a letter to his constituency the Breton deputy Jean-Baptiste Digaultray emphasized that "Louis the Last"—as he called him—would never again return to his palace or rule in France. Ruault mused on how the Sun King Louis XIV might have reacted if he had known the monarchy would be overthrown less than a century after his death.[2]

For most French men and women, the interregnum between the fall of the monarchy on August 10 and the first meeting of the Convention on September 20 could be both exhilarating and immensely frightening and unsettling. The complex intermingling of hope and anxiety, of optimism and fear that had characterized much of the Revolution was again very much in evidence. Whatever their disgust with the behavior of the king and their acceptance of his overthrow, a great many individuals felt tense and uncertain as to what the future held in store. In a country that for well over a thousand years had always known a monarchy, the very idea of living without a king was sobering and disturbing. Ruault, a longtime member of the Parisian Jacobins, admitted his apprehension to his brother: "Nothing is more dangerous for a people than a change in the regime and the government, especially for the French who are so accustomed to a monarch." Charles-Alexis Alexandre, who had played an important role in the storming of the Tuileries, also claimed to have had misgivings: "Whatever my political opinions and my support for the Revolution, I had been raised under a monarchy, and its fall left me with a feeling of amazement, of pity, and of fear."[3]

Such fears would be intensified over the coming weeks, a period in which France arguably came closer to anarchy, to the breakdown of law and order and the spread of uncontrolled violence, than at any other time in the Revolution, a breakdown that would culminate in a series of terrible prison massacres in early September. Though much of the violence would be popular and spontaneous, it would often receive substantial sympathy from elements of the elite population. It was a period that has been aptly described as "the First Terror."[4]

The Interregnum

For the deputies of the Legislative Assembly, August 10 had been as unsettling as for the Parisians in general. After the king and his family had taken shelter in their hall, they found themselves reduced to the status of observers who could only wait and listen with trepidation as the battle raged in the palace a few hundred meters away. Jacques Pinet described the scene in a breathless letter: "Bullets whistled by our ears, crossed the hall and fell at our feet." They were entirely in doubt as to which side was winning, and for a time they feared that their lives might be in danger. When a group of Swiss guards burst into the hall—in fact simply looking for shelter—"we all rushed onto the floor, crying 'Long live the nation,' and swore to uphold liberty and equality or to die at our post." The deputies were calmed only when it was clear toward the end of the morning that the Parisians had won the day and when a delegation of insurgents arrived in the hall and demanded the removal of the king—who was still sitting with his family just behind the Assembly president. Soon thereafter, on a motion by Vergniaud, the Assembly voted to suspend the king and to convoke a Constitutional Convention to determine the fate of the nation.[5] The Girondin

A pro-Montagnard image of the people entering the Legislative Assembly on August 10, 1792. After successfully capturing the Tuileries Palace, delegates from the insurgents enter the Assembly hall and demand that the king be dethroned. They point at the king and queen (visible behind the grille). The king seems to look away in fright, burying his head in the queen's bosom while she scowls at the crowd, still wearing her very high aristocratic coiffure. The crowds seem also to point accusingly at the president, Pierre Vergniaud, a leader of the Girondin-dominated Assembly. The Assembly would only "suspend" the king, much to the dissatisfaction of the people. Only the Montagnard deputies, on the left, cheer the people. The people have also placed on the floor the treasure they had found in the palace and have refused to loot. François Gérard, engraved by E. Rosotte, © Coll. Musée de la Révolution française, Domaine de Vizille, MRF 2004.19.14.

support for a suspension, rather than for the permanent removal of the king, as the people had demanded, would be sharply attacked by the Parisian militants.

In the end, the fall of the monarchy would greatly simplify the political situation within the Assembly, effectively empowering the Jacobins, and above all the Girondin faction of the Jacobins, to take control. Many of the most conservative deputies had already been threatened and harassed by the crowds.[6] With the violence of August 10 itself, the great majority of the Feuillants either ceased attending the Assembly altogether or refused to take part in debates. Through the end of the Legislative, a rump of only around 300 of the 745 deputies seems to have been present and voting. "Fear," wrote Jean-Marie Rivoallan, "kept a great many deputies away or in hiding." A Breton visitor passing through Paris in early September noted, "The patriot side of the hall is always more full than the opposite side. Those on the Right seem to take no part in the deliberations."[7]

To be sure, a certain number of the former Feuillants moved toward a rapprochement with their Jacobin colleagues, some through fear and coercion, others after much soul-searching and a genuine change of heart. They had been badly shaken when they learned that General Lafayette, the longtime hero of the Right, had deserted his army and gone over to the Austrians. Others began reevaluating their position when a cache of secret ministerial documents seized by the insurgents was opened and made public. The documents appeared to present evidence that the king, as Pinet put it, "was the leader and the very soul of all the schemes of our enemies." He had not only continued to use public funds to pay his former bodyguards now living in Germany, but he had received secret correspondence from his emigrant brothers, and he had subsidized counterrevolutionary newspapers and pamphlets, many of which were found preserved in the ministerial files.[8] Aubert-Dubayet, who had generally leaned toward the Feuillants in the past, claimed that "all the documents found in the palace in the office of the king's intendant, reinforced our belief in the treason of the court." "The scales have fallen from my eyes," wrote Rabusson-Lamothe, "and to my great surprise, I have come to recognize that all kings are incorrigible."[9]

Brissot and the group of friends in his entourage now utterly dominated both the Assembly and the central government.[10] Since the king had been suspended and imprisoned, the Legislative established a separate Executive Council of ministers to take over the day-to-day tasks of governing the country. The previous royal ministers were unceremoniously removed and replaced with six individuals chosen by majority vote in the Assembly. At least four of the six were clearly allied with the Girondins, including the powerful minister of the interior, Jean-Marie Roland.[11] But apparently as a gesture of goodwill to the Paris militants, the deputies also elected as minister of justice the Cordeliers Georges Danton. In fact, the energetic and determined Danton soon emerged as the single most effective leader of the government, so that the Executive Council sometimes assumed a certain distance from the Assembly.[12] In the Assembly itself, with the Left now entirely in control, a host of new laws was pushed through, laws that would constitute a veritable second surge of democracy. On the afternoon of August 10 the Legislative formally summoned a new Constitutional Convention to entirely rethink the organization of government and the nature of executive power. That election and all future elections were to be based on universal male suffrage and the suppression of the very idea of "passive" citizenship. Over the following days and weeks most of the remaining seigneurial rights were abolished outright without compensation; communal property was nationalized and declared susceptible to redistribution; and the property of emigrant nobles—and all other emigrants—was to be seized and sold in small lots.

In addition a whole series of measures were aimed at the church and the clergy. All ecclesiastics, not just those in charge of parishes, would now be required to take an oath of allegiance to a regime of "liberty and equality," and any who refused would be immediately deported or—if they were aged or infirm—placed in detention. Most of the remaining church property was put up for sale, and all religious houses were emptied and closed. Even the "constitutional" clergy, those who had taken the oath and supported the Revolution, would be forbidden to wear clerical garb in public and would lose their right to register births, marriages, and deaths—a task henceforth assumed by the municipal administration. Equally dramatic was the introduction of a remarkably liberal divorce law, unprecedented in eighteenth-century Christendom, a law that even allowed couples to dissolve their marriage on grounds of incompatibility.[13] Some of these measures had already been discussed and partially passed before August 10, but it was only the end of the veto that made such rapid advances possible. The deputies were able to move forward "in giant strides," as Pinet put it, "now that the people have taken charge. We must profit from the situation and complete the revolution" that the previous Assembly had only begun.[14]

Yet even as the Assembly moved forward with a sweeping array of reforms, it found its leadership challenged as never before by the various parallel powers long present in Paris but now more active and influential than ever. The logic of popular sovereignty and unbounded democracy had always posed problems for effective government. During this new interregnum, however, until the new Convention could take power—an interregnum even more chaotic than that of 1789–1790—the climate of suspicion and mistrust pushed the city and the country to the edge of anarchy. The Insurrectional Commune, the Jacobins Club, and the individual Parisian sections would all challenge the authority of the National Assembly, so that in the end no one was quite certain who was governing the country.

The single most powerful rival to the Legislative Assembly was clearly the new Paris insurrectional government, the Commune. The mayor, Jérôme Pétion, and most of the major municipal officials had maintained their positions. For a time, however, Pétion was not allowed to leave the mayoral residence, and all real power passed to the General Council of the Commune, which met in permanent session throughout the period. For the most part, this body was dominated by the same alliance of radical militants and sans-culotte shopkeepers and artisans that had directed the overthrow of the king. Many of the leaders were veterans of the Cordeliers Club and closely linked to the Montagnards: men like Hébert, Chaumette, Collot d'Herbois, Fabre d'Eglantine, and Billaud-Varennes. But the single most influential member was undoubtedly Robespierre, who joined the Commune on August 12 after several months without an official position. No one had greater prestige among the radicals, and no one possessed more consummate skill as a politician.[15]

From the outset relations between the Commune and the Legislative Assembly were fraught and uneasy. In the eyes of a great many militants, the Assembly had already failed in its most important responsibilities. It was the militants and their sans-culotte and Fédérés allies who had taken the initiative in overthrowing the monarchy. Even though the rump now in control of the Assembly claimed to support the achievements of August 10, the Commune leaders, perhaps most notably Robespierre, remained deeply mistrustful. They were angry that the Assembly had only suspended the king and had not dethroned him outright.[16] They were unhappy that the Legislative did so little to organize judicial vengeance against the surviving royalists and Swiss Guards, responsible for the "ambush" of the insurgents on August 10. During one session of the Assembly, a representative of the Commune openly lectured the deputies: "It was, after all, the people who saved themselves through their own efforts. Remember this truth: when a schoolboy becomes bigger than his teacher, so much the worse for the teacher!" Rosalie Jullien said much the same in a letter to her husband: "The representatives were saved by those they represent. . . . Public opinion has now become the enlightened tyrant of the capital."[17]

During the first days of its existence, the Commune exercised a veritable dictatorship over the city, with aspirations for control over the nation as well. Its surveillance committee was extremely active in tracking down and arresting real or presumed opposition forces—nobles, refractory priests, and miscellaneous "royalists"—both within the city and in the surrounding suburbs. The Commune even began sending out independent delegates to the provinces, sometimes in direct competition with representatives from the Legislative Assembly and the Executive Council. Some were sent to neighboring departments to requisition food for the city and look for counterrevolutionaries. Others were dispatched much farther afield to promote patriotism, recruit troops, and requisition arms and supplies for the war effort.[18]

The situation in Paris was even more complicated in that the Commune never fully controlled the forty-eight neighborhood sections of the city that it supposedly represented.[19] The end of passive citizenship, giving all adult males the right to participate, made the sections all the more volatile and unpredictable. Frequently, the sections remained dominated by elites who had the commitment and the leisure time to serve on the governing committees. Yet specific debates could bring much greater participation, so that the positions of individual sections could change dramatically from day to day. The sections had also been allowed to create their own surveillance committees and police commissioners. The committees busied themselves arresting suspects, closing down newspapers deemed royalist, and censoring plays performed in neighborhood theaters.[20] They were also in charge of issuing passports, and even foreign ambassadors sometimes found it impossible to leave the city, because their sections refused to give them permission.[21] Depending on local politics, however, there could be substantial differences from section to section as to the policies pursued and the specific individuals who were arrested or declared suspect. In addition the sections eventually succeeded in taking command of the local national guard units. However, the guardsmen were in the midst of a major transition, and many battalions remained in turmoil throughout the interregnum. At the time of the September Massacres, the guard units that might have intervened were still poorly organized, badly armed, and of uncertain reliability.[22]

Political instability in the capital, born of competing parallel powers, was intensified by the revival of the factional divisions between Girondins and Montagnards. During the royalist backlash that followed June 20, the two groups had developed an uneasy modus vivendi. Yet Robespierre probably never abandoned his earlier belief that Brissot and his friends were secretly attached to the monarchy and linked to the foreign powers. His suspicions were only confirmed by the Girondins' inconsistencies on the question of the king during July and by the remarkably impolitic proposal from the Brissotin journalist Jean-Louis Carra that the Prussian general, the duke of Brunswick, be made king of France and welcomed to Paris along with his army.[23] But it was above all the institutional rivalry between the Girondin-dominated Assembly and the Montagnard-leaning Commune that antagonized suspicions and hatred between the two factions. Jullien summed up the situation: "Robespierre is at the head of the Commune and Brissot is the leader of the senate: the perfect conditions for a war!"[24] Pétion, who was deeply divided between Brissot, whom he had known since childhood, and Robespierre, who had been his close friend and ally since 1789, wrote an impassioned letter to Robespierre: "While we may differ on a number of minor points, we are not enemies. . . . No, we will never sit in opposing parties; we will always share the same political ideals." But the leader of the Mountain would only criticize Pétion for having "too much confidence" in the Girondins, and soon the break between the two former friends was irreparable, and Pétion would openly ally himself with the Brissotins.[25]

In any case, few among the Girondins shared Pétion's spirit of reconciliation. In early September, in the midst of the prison massacres, the Commune's surveillance committee searched Brissot's apartment and even issued an arrest warrant for both Brissot and Roland.[26] The Brissotins convinced themselves thereafter that Robespierre had intended to have them murdered in the massacres, and that he and the Commune were the real traitors allied with foreign enemies. Their supporters spoke of the faction of Marat and Robespierre who were fomenting chaos to bring down the Revolution. It was a "plan of destruction and counterrevolution, promoted by the paid agents of the emigrants, the Prussians, the Austrians."[27]

The breakdown of authority that had grown in France since the beginning of the Revolution seemed to reach a new stage in the late summer of 1792. The English chargé d'affaires described the situation succinctly: "The people are all armed and the government is extremely feeble." Ruault too was appalled, despite his Jacobin sympathies: "It is complete anarchy, anarchy unlike anything ever before seen in ancient or modern times."[28]

Vengeance and Fear in Paris

Ruault's concerns were hardly misplaced. Even if open violence in Paris ceased for a time after August 10, the tension and fear remained palpable. On several occasions shots were heard in the middle of the night or church bells rang out, although no one was quite sure what the reason might be. The Commune and the sections remained in permanent sessions. They continued to require nighttime illumination of the city, and they periodically closed and reclosed the city gates.[29] The reasons for such tensions were complex and were related in part to the continuing dispersal and ambiguity of authority. But they were also linked to the powerful presence of anger among the Parisians. Demands for vengeance had risen in a great chorus immediately after the battle for the Tuileries on August 10. The journalist Jacques Hébert claimed that 4,000 houses in the city had been marked for attack if the royalists had won.[30] For the vast majority of Parisians of all classes, there could be no doubt: the royalist nobles and the Swiss guards had treacherously lured the people into the Tuileries courtyard and then opened fire, killing or wounding dozens of their friends, neighbors, and relatives.

Hatred of the monarchy was exhibited in widespread attacks against the symbolic representations of the king. On the Place Royale, the Place Vendôme, the Place des Victoires, and elsewhere throughout the city all the statues of the kings of France were pulled down, and those in bronze were sent to the foundry to be turned into cannons and cannonballs. Even the images of Clovis in the church of Sainte Geneviève, of Philippe le Bel in Notre Dame, and of the traditionally beloved Henry IV on the Pont-Neuf were desecrated and hauled away. All were subjected to the "death warrants"—as Pinet put it—issued by the crowds. In the Assembly itself the portrait of Louis XVI was replaced with the Declaration of the Rights of Man, while the Jacobins substituted a statue of Brutus.[31] Moreover, the symbolic vengeance extended not only to the royalty but to the royalists as well. Busts and images of several of the onetime heroes of the Constitutional Monarchy—Lafayette, Bailly, Necker—were also the objects of popular wrath.[32] Lists were published of those who had supported the Feuillant candidates in past elections or who had signed promonarchical petitions after June 20. There were movements in several sections to have all such "suspects" declared inadmissible for holding office or even to have them arrested and prosecuted. Ruault, who strongly sympathized with the republican cause, wondered nevertheless where it all might lead: "If we sen-

Memorial service for the patriots killed in the attack on the Tuileries, August 26, 1792. In the Tuileries Gardens, behind the palace, men, women, and national guardsmen mourn the citizens killed on August 10 when the palace was captured. All were convinced that the insurgents had been ambushed in the courtyard, and this and numerous similar ceremonies helped keep alive the hatred and desire for revenge. Charles Monnet, engraved by Helman, © Coll. Musée de la Révolution française, Domaine de Vizille, MRF 1984.66.

tence to death all those who once supported the king . . . how many scaffolds will we have to build!"[33]

The desire for retribution was vigorously promoted by many of the radical journalists. Marat demanded the death penalty for all officers of the Swiss guards: "What folly to call for a trial. It has already taken place!"[34] The spirit of revenge was kept alive by a series of memorial services celebrated throughout the month for those citizens killed on August 10. Funeral processions, memorial masses, and outdoor speeches took place in nearly every section, with officials reading the lists of neighbors who had died or been wounded in the fighting. Theaters gave special performances to raise money for widows and orphans.[35] On August 26 a giant citywide remembrance celebration was organized. A long procession of officials, military and national guard units, drum batteries, and a full orchestra made its way along the streets of the Right Bank from the city hall to the Tuileries Palace. It ended in the Tuileries Gardens with the dedication of a monumental obelisk in Egyptian style on which the names of all the dead were inscribed.[36]

Periods of accrued tension had always produced a proliferation of rumors, and August 1792 was no exception. Stories spread rapidly of an array of conspiracies about to explode: of 400 nobles, escaped from the Tuileries on August 10, hiding out underground and waiting to strike; of huge caches of weapons concealed beneath the Pantheon and the Palais Royal in preparation for a counterrevolution; of armed men threatening to attack the Jacobins; of evildoers placing pieces of glass in the cities' flour supply.[37] While the leaders of the Commune had their doubts about some of the more bizarre rumors, they clearly shared the view that conspiracies against the Revolution were rampant. In their first proclamation on August 10 they had vowed to investigate "this chain of treason that has placed liberty in peril." Four days later they set up a municipal surveillance committee that took the initiative in tracking down real or presumed opposition forces—nobles, refractory priests, and miscellaneous "royalists." The Commune encouraged the creation of similar surveillance organs in each of the Paris sections, and all of these committees opened registers where citizens could make denunciations of the plots assumed to be widespread in the city. By early September the central surveillance committee was dominated by several Cordeliers radicals, including the journalists Marat and Fréron, whose reputations had been built in large measure through their denunciation of conspiracy.[38]

Arrest warrants were issued against former royalist ministers, royalist journalists, and royalist deputies in the Constituent Assembly like Antoine Barnave. A wide range of suspect nobles, from the Prince du Poix to the aging Madame du Barry—Louis XV's onetime mistress—were also brought in. Even before the official decree by the Legislative Assembly ordering the deportation of priests who refused an oath of allegiance, the Commune and the sections began systematically arresting all refractories. "Every night," wrote Pinet, "numerous suspects are carried off to one of the prisons, which are now overflowing with inmates."[39] In fact, Pinet greatly exaggerated the reality: we know from careful studies that the total population of the prisons acquired only a few hundred new inmates during the month of August and that the cells were far from full.[40] Yet contemporaries were convinced they were packed to overflowing.

The fear of conspiracy and the desire for revenge convinced many people that the regular criminal tribunals were moving too slowly in handling the mass of evildoers thought to be piling up in the prisons.[41] There were continual threats that the people were prepared to take justice into their own hands. On August 15 Robespierre spoke in the Assembly in the name of the Commune: "The people are resting," he announced, "but they are not asleep. They demand the punishment of the guilty." It was in the face of such pressure that the deputies agreed on August 17 to create a new "Tribunal d'exception." Conceived to try political cases without appeal and with jury members elected by the sections, the "Tribunal of August 17" would serve as a model for the Revolutionary Tribunals of 1793–1794. All those found guilty would be immediately executed at the guillotine, the recently devised machine for decapitations set up on one of the major squares of the city.[42]

Yet the new Tribunal moved more slowly and deliberately than many Parisians would have desired. Among the first executed were a royalist journalist, the director of the king's budget, and three convicted counterfeiters. But several others were acquitted and set free. Many citizens were soon convinced that this Tribunal, like the previous ones, was procrastinating and not doing its job. "Since August 10," wrote Adelaïde Mareux, "only three people have been guillotined and the people are outraged. We seem to be sold out by every side!" By the time Mademoiselle Mareux wrote in early September, crowds would already be breaking into the prisons and taking charge of the "executions" themselves.[43]

Violence in the Provinces

At first no one in Paris was certain how the assault on the Tuileries and the arrest of the king would be greeted in the provinces.[44] As early as August 10 the deputies began flooding the departments with addresses, decrees, and letters in an effort to garner support. A centerpiece of this propaganda was the publication of the documents seized in the palace suggesting the king's treachery and double-dealing. Individual deputies also worked to persuade their constituencies, justifying the overthrow of the monarchy and extolling the positive outcome of August 10 in both saving the Revolution and transforming the nation. "The counterrevolution was a certainty," explained Sylvain Codet, "if vigorous action had not been taken to rapidly halt the internal and external conspiracies."[45]

Clearly, the greatest potential danger for Paris and the Assembly was posed by the various French armies positioned on the frontiers. The defiance of General Lafayette and his attempt to influence his soldiers to march on the capital after August 10 had been the source of enormous anguish. The Legislative Assembly quickly dispatched several teams of deputies, many of them officers themselves, to explain and justify the new political situation to the soldiers. Although several generals resigned, two of the most able, Custine and Biron, both announced their acceptance of the overthrow of the king. Moreover, Lafayette's army and most of his lower-level officer corps refused to follow their commander. In fact, the soldiers had been closely following the events in Paris through newspapers distributed by the local Jacobins. According to the young recruit from Nancy, Joseph Noël, news of August 10 "spread joy and elation among all our volunteers. They believe that 'ça ira,' that everything will work out. All shout out, 'No more kings, no more kings!'" When one of Lafayette's officers had attempted to win them over, he was insulted and greeted with cries of "Long live the Jacobins! Down with the Feuillants!" It was in the face of such opposition that the general and his principal lieutenants had opted to cross the frontier and turn themselves over to the Austrians.[46]

As for the civil authorities, a number of department directories initially questioned or even rejected the removal of the king. The most dramatic case was the department of Ardennes on the northeastern frontier, where Lafayette had his headquarters and was able to convince the local leadership to disavow the events of August 10. However, the Assembly quickly sent commissioners to the departments, as they had done to the armies, and the administrators in the Ardennes and in a half dozen other departments were summarily arrested or suspended. In most of the country the arrival of representatives from the capital, along with pressure from the popular societies, convinced the local leadership to accept the fait accompli in Paris.[47] By the end of August the deputies were receiving hundreds of formal adhesions to their authority—though some departments were much slower than others. "Letters of approval," wrote Jullien, "arrive in large numbers to the National Assembly. From every direction the major towns, the generals, the army all exclaim 'liberty and equality!'"[48]

In many regions, however, the power vacuum during the interregnum brought much the same breakdown of authority as in Paris itself. With control of the central government altogether uncertain and with conflicting instructions emanating from the Legislative Assembly and the Commune, there was ample room for the intensification of power struggles among local factions. In the weeks and months after August 10 the Pyrenean department of Ariège passed through the most unsettling period of the entire Revolution. Various levels of the bureaucracy gave contradictory orders. The departmental directory was said to have lost the confidence of much of the population, and at the end of August it was formally disavowed by the electoral assembly. Tribunals were ignored, peasants refused to enroll in the military, taxes went unpaid, and bands of pillagers roamed the countryside.[49]

The period also saw a continuation in the provinces of vigilante attacks and killings against suspected conspirators or counterrevolutionaries that had already begun in June and July.[50] In regional towns, the apparent vacuum of power in the capital and the lack of reliable information about the war would lead citizens of all classes to give credence to rumors and could generate fear and mistrust just as in Paris. Stories of the secret stockpiling of arms, suspicions of collusion with foreign enemies, careless words pronounced or thought to have been pronounced in public: all could trigger rumors and even massacres. From the fall of the Tuileries to the convocation of the Convention at least ninety-three individuals were killed in forty-two separate incidents. Such killings took place in thirty-two of the eighty-three departments but were especially concentrated in a zone around Paris, and in towns of the Rhône Valley, the Mediterranean, and the region south and east of Bordeaux. The victims might include nobles, administrators, or various other citizens accused of an array of evil deeds. Yet the group most commonly attacked—over a third of all those killed—was the refractory clergy, widely believed to be the principal source of counterrevolutionary activities in the interior. Most of those assaulted had already been suspected in recent months for a variety of pernicious activities, and now in a period of widespread fear it was all the easier to demonize them. Some were killed with extreme brutality, and decapitated heads and body parts were carried about town—just as in the most violent uprisings of the seventeenth century. A few of the provincial killings were probably inspired by events in Paris. This was undoubtedly the case of the forty-four prisoners being moved from a jail in Orléans, who were murdered in Versailles on September 9, only a few days after the September Massacres. Other vigilante actions in the departments, however, continued through September and even October.

A certain number of chain-reaction panics also occurred—not unlike the much larger "fears" of July 1789 and June 1791. In the midst of the foreign invasion on the northeastern front, rumors spread that Prussian or Austrian troops were about to arrive and were pillaging and killing their way across the country. No matter how improbable the stories—and some arose in villages hundreds of miles from the front—the rumors could spark widespread turmoil.[51] A more direct effect of the war came from groups of armed volunteers circulating in France during August and September. Certain regions near the capital were terrorized by national guard units sent into the countryside by Parisian sections to look for conspirators and hidden stores of arms and food—actions that would anticipate, in certain respects, the "revolutionary armies" of 1793. Some of these actions were of short duration and directed at very specific targets. On August 15 a detachment of Parisian guardsmen and Fédérés troops rushed to the country house of the seminary of Saint-Sulpice, rumored to be storing arms.[52] Far more serious was the incursion between August 15 and 20 of some 200 armed Parisians of dubious intent into the department of Oise, northwest of the city. The men announced that they had come to inspect the chateaus of the region, to confiscate weapons, to look for suspects, and to destroy any Old Regime symbols still in view. Later they seem also to have raided a hospital and made off both with a quantity of silver and with two of the resident nuns. Although the nuns were later released, the silver was apparently never recovered.[53]

In other regions of France volunteers on their way to the war were involved in various forms of violence. Virtually all were strongly patriotic young men. Many belonged to local popular societies and national guard units, while others, too youthful to have been members, had passionately followed and supported the activities of their elders. One witness described their passage through western France: "There was a procession of young men on their way to the army, shouting out 'Long live liberty,'" and swearing "eternal hatred for the Bourbon kings, and demanding death for traitors."[54] Well-armed and filled with intense Revolutionary convictions, they shared the same suspicions that pervaded the rest of the society. They could thus easily be convinced by the rumors or denunciations of counterrevolutionaries that they heard in the course of their journeys. Having volunteered to preserve the Revolution by fighting its enemies on the frontier—to "live free or die"—they might well be persuaded to begin their mission by bringing death to "conspirators" in the interior. Almost half of the vigilante killings in the provinces during the interregnum are known to have involved volunteer soldiers about to leave their hometowns or en route to the front.[55]

One such group of volunteers from western France came across the duke of La Rochefoucauld in the town of Gisors, as he was being escorted back to Paris after having been arrested near his country estate. The onetime friend of Franklin and Jefferson and of several of the eighteenth-century philosophers, the duke had played an important role in support of the early Revolution. But as president of the department of Paris, he had earned a reputation for conservative monarchism. When the volunteers discovered who he was and heard the inevitably exaggerated stories of his misdeeds before August 10, they pulled him away and killed him.[56]

The Invasion of France

Invariably the violence both in the provinces and in Paris was influenced by the foreign invasion and the disappointing performance of French troops in the war. By the middle of August France had been locked for four months in a frustrating stalemate with the Austrian army along its northern frontier. But the entry of Prussia into the conflict and the creation of a second front in northeastern France would totally transform the character of the conflict. Heir to the triumphant forces of Frederick the Great, the Prussian army was reputed to be the most capable and efficient in Europe. The Prussian commanders were brimming with confidence and generally assumed that the invasion would lead to a rout of the French, whose forces contained numerous raw recruits and whose officer corps had been decimated by emigration and resignations. Many of the Prussians predicted a military parade into Paris, much like their expedition five years earlier—also led by the duke of Brunswick—that had crushed a revolution in the Netherlands.[57] Foreign observers in Paris at the time largely agreed. English diplomats wrote of "the impossibility of [France's] resisting the combined forces of the Emperor and the King of Prussia." It was "a great and formidable army commanded by the ablest general in the world."[58]

To be sure, the invasion force also had potential weaknesses. Despite their reputation, the Prussians had not fought a major war for almost twenty years, and much of their officer corps was relatively elderly. The army was accompanied by their young king, Frederick William II, who would sometimes pull rank on Brunswick and intervene in the campaign in a less-than-helpful manner. Moreover, the Prussians sent a substantially smaller force into France than they might have done. This decision arose in part from their assumption that a mediocre French army could be easily overcome. But both Prussia and Austria were also preoccupied with the situation in the east and the possibility of another partition of Poland. For this reason, they chose to retain substantial segments of their armies in central Europe. In the end, about 42,000 Prussian troops would cross the frontier into France, complemented by some 29,000 Austrian, 5,500 Hessian, and 4,500 emigrant troops. The sheer size of the French army—over twice as large as the invading coalition—would give it a potentially significant advantage.[59]

Nevertheless, the initial phase of the invasion seemed to substantiate all the predictions of a rapid French collapse. By mid-July 1792 the Prussians had assembled their forces and had begun to move southward at a relatively leisurely pace—very much in the tradition of eighteenth-century warfare—to allow the positioning of a secure supply line. Their first engagement with the French came in mid-August, when they entered Lorraine and arrived before the frontier town of Longwy, just south of Luxembourg. Longwy was one of the fortresses in the defensive line built by Vauban in the age of Louis XIV to protect France from invasion. Whether or not the French garrison there could have sustained a lengthy siege is open to debate, but in fact the city capitulated on August 23, after an artillery bombardment of only three days. The Prussians then advanced farther south to the great citadel of Verdun, the keystone of France's northeastern defenses. Here too the Prussian victory was rapid and stunning. Once again a three-day artillery attack was sufficient to force a capitulation. The surrender was supported by many local citizens, fearful of the destruction to their town that a long siege might bring. It was also facilitated by the suicide—or perhaps murder—of the garrison's commander, who had previously vowed never to submit.[60]

For the French, this rapid breakthrough on the frontier produced a jolt of consternation and fear. Until late August the Parisians had been largely preoccupied with the internal crisis, the overthrow of Louis XVI, and the effort to win the support of the rest of the nation. They had convinced themselves that the citizen soldiers of the Revolution would soon triumph over the "slave armies" of Austria and Prussia and that the military stalemate on the northern frontier had been caused by the treachery of the king and the generals. Now with the disastrous news arriving from Lorraine, they concluded that the treachery went much deeper. Who could say whether the present military commanders, like Lafayette before them, might not be collaborating with the enemy? Who could say that the foreign invaders were not working closely with secret conspirators in the capital itself? In much of the correspondence emanating from Paris during this period, the fear of internal conspiracy sapping the war effort became an all-consuming obsession. In a long letter the deputy Digaultray agonized over the fall of Longwy and the widespread rumors that fifth column forces had sapped the city's resistance from inside the walls. Guittard summarized in his diary the feelings of his fellow citizens now that the way seemed open for the Prussians to march on Paris: "Never since the Revolution began has Paris been in such a crisis as that in which we find ourselves today. . . . The enemy is practically at our gates. Our fate will doubtless be decided in the battles to be fought in the coming month."[61] The panic was only accentuated by the actions of the authorities themselves. In a general circular distributed on August 27 the minister Roland wrote that "all necessary measures are acceptable. When it is a question of saving the fatherland in the face of such danger, no efforts should be spared!" A few days later he lamented, "We are betrayed on every side!"[62]

The fear of conspiracy and betrayal in Paris pushed the authorities to organize a massive search throughout the city, pursued around the clock between August 29 and 31. With gates locked tight, the streets kept illuminated throughout the night, and all citizens ordered to remain in their homes, national guardsmen and city commissioners went from house to house, looking for hidden arms and secret conspirators waiting to strike. The results of the search were relatively disappointing. Officials were able to round up several hundred guns and muskets—most of them hunting pieces or useless antiques—and an additional eighty or so refractory priests were arrested. But the operation itself only further agitated and terrified the population. "The rumor of fear is spreading," confided Guittard in his diary. "It raises an alarm throughout Paris." Rosalie Jullien was beside herself with anguish. As the guardsmen pursued their rounds, their drums reverberated so insistently, she wrote, "that it sounded like rain beating down in the streets." Agitated by the tumult outside, no one was able to sleep. "All the women remain at their windows," looking out for the enemies whose imminent arrival everyone was now predicting. There was also a great increase in the number of denunciations. "Still more traitors, still more treason," continued Jullien. It was a situation that "puts us a hair's breadth from disaster."[63]

Such was the atmosphere on the eve of what was to be the single most terrible outbreak of urban popular violence in the entire Revolution: the massacre of inmates in the Paris prisons at the beginning of September.

Five Days in September

The fear of prisons and of the prisoners they housed had a long history in Paris, going back to the very beginning of the Revolution—and no doubt to the Old Regime. Several state and municipal prisons existed in the very heart of the city, an immediate presence that inevitably gave rise to speculations as to who was detained within and whether the inmates might attempt an escape.[64] Since the fall of 1789 persistent stories of inmates about to break out and fall upon the patriots had circulated in the city. A spate of such rumors had spread in late 1789 and 1790 and again at the time of the king's attempted flight in June 1791.[65] Even more frightening were the stories circulating that the prisoners had somehow managed to arm themselves. A series of fires set by those in La Force Prison in January 1792 led to wide speculation that some of them were planning an armed escape and that they would then attack good citizens. "We fear," wrote Guittard at the time, "that the brigands might set fire to all of Paris."[66]

By the spring of 1792 the prisons were thus already viewed as sites in which counterrevolutionary forces were lurking and from which paid "brigands" might break out and turn against the Revolution and the Revolutionaries. As early as June 20, petitioners from the sections had threatened to break into the prisons and execute the prisoners if the courts were not compelled do their job.[67] With the events of August 10 and the widespread arrests of "suspects"—nobles, the surviving Swiss guards, and miscellaneous refractory priests—the fear of the prisons was mixed in the minds of many Parisians with the desire for revenge against the perpetrators of the "Saint Lawrence's Day Massacre." The two sets of rumors that had long festered in the city, conspiracy rumors and prison rumors, now seemed to transmute and coalesce. Word spread wildly that an impending prison breakout would be coordinated with the foreign invasion, and that the noble and clerical prisoners would pay common criminals to fall upon the unprotected families of the patriots who were leaving to fight at the front.

The Commune of Paris may have helped intensify the rumors when it ordered section leaders to visit the prisons and post "a list of all the enemies of the Revolution" held inside so that local citizens would know precisely the danger they faced.[68] Codet was aware of the threats and was deeply troubled: "There is a great mass of conspirators in the prisons," he wrote on August 19, "and within a week or so many heads will fall." Rosalie Jullien had also heard of the prison conspiracies and the possibility of preventive vigilante action: "The number of criminals there terrifies me." And she meditated ominously, "We must be barbarous for the sake of humanity and cut off an arm to save the body."[69] Clearly the fear and anxiety had become so great and the logic of the threat so powerful that even large numbers of the political and social elites, who in other times and other situations might well have been skeptical, now came to embrace the rumors of a prison conspiracy.

On September 2, with the fall of Longwy already confirmed and the imminent surrender of Verdun predicted, the Commune ordered posters nailed up throughout the city: "To arms! The enemy is at our gates!" The municipal leadership then sent representatives to all of the sections to discuss emergency measures that would have to be taken. In addition to fortifying the city walls and promoting military enrollments, many of the sections probably discussed the need to halt the "prison conspiracy" that everyone believed to be a reality. Thus, in the Poissonnière section in central Paris, citizens resolved that they must "exercise a prompt justice on the spot against all the conspirators and evil doers in the prisons," a resolution that was immediately copied and sent to all the other sections.[70]

It was later that same day that the killings began. With the cannons on the Seine bridges firing their warnings of danger and the church bells sounding throughout the city, crowds fell upon a group of prisoners being transferred to the Abbaye prison near Saint-Germain-des-Prés, and all of them were put to death.[71] People then proceeded to break into the Abbaye prison itself and later into the nearby Carme prison, systematically executing the inmates, both the "counterrevolutionary" nobles, refractory priests, and Swiss, and the common criminals, viewed as "brigands" soon to be paid to do the dirty work against the Parisians. Over the following days, from September 2 to 6, most of the other prisons of Paris were assaulted: the Concièrgerie, the Salpetrière, the Châtelet, the Bernardins, Saint-Firmin, the two La Force prisons, and the hospital-prison of Bicêtre, just south of the city. Over this period some 1,100 to 1,400 individuals were killed.

Faced with the outbreak of such massive violence, the fractured power structure in the city reacted in generally ineffective ways. The Legislative Assembly sent two successive delegations of deputies in an attempt to halt the vigilantes. But both proved totally useless, and the deputies themselves were threatened by the crowds. The representatives also issued a vaguely worded proclamation urging calm and unity. In reality, however, the Assembly was overwhelmingly preoccupied with the war and the effort to halt the invasion, and it ultimately devoted only limited energy to the problem of urban violence.[72] The Paris national guard, in the midst of transition and in disarray, did virtually nothing. Indeed, many of its members almost certainly participated in or at least supported the massacres.[73] On September 3, the Commune's surveillance committee—of which both Marat and Fréron were members—issued a printed circular describing the popular executions as "acts of justice that seem indispensable for halting through terror the legions of traitors hidden inside the walls." The committee then expressed their hope that "the whole nation will hasten to adopt similar methods so necessary for public security."[74] To be sure, neither the Commune nor the surveillance committee directly initiated the massacres. Yet it is clear that their members, as so many other elites, had come fully to believe the prison conspiracy rumor and to accept the necessity of eliminating the threat. Their implicit support may well have contributed to the continuation of the massacres after the first two days.

Many Commune members did, however, worry that the crowds might kill all of the prisoners indiscriminately. They thus sent delegates to the prisons, not to halt the executions outright but to organize improvised tribunals and judges to ensure a proper triage between the "innocent" and the "guilty." In several cases, Commune representatives remained present during the "trials" or even served as judges.[75] Those prisoners who had been incarcerated as debtors or for family quarrels or for minor civil infractions were usually freed, as were most of the women. All those released were cheered and embraced by the crowds outside. Those considered to be "counterrevolutionaries" (all the refractory priests, the Swiss guards, and most of the nobles) and those guilty of theft or counterfeiting or murder—the feared "brigands"—were pushed out the door to be executed in adjoining courtyards or streets by volunteer executioners wielding swords or axes or pikes or clubs.[76]

We will never know for certain who actually performed the killings: the "septembriseurs," as they came to be called. But a great many were undoubtedly Paris national guardsmen and Fédéré troops from the provinces, who had remained in the city since their arrival in Paris in July or early August. The British spy George Monro, who observed the massacres firsthand, claimed that all the killers he saw were "either Marseillais, Brestois, or the National Guards of Paris." For the most part, these were the same men from Paris, Provence, and Brittany who had risked their lives three weeks earlier in the storming of the Tuileries Palace and who would soon leave to fight the invading armies. As the Revolutionary leader Fabre d'Eglantine put it, "it was the men of August 10 who broke into the prisons."[77] In the minds of such men the Massacres of September were probably both an act of revenge and a service to the city, ensuring the safety of its citizens on the eve of their departure. Ruault told of meeting some of the septembriseurs in the midst of the carnage who bragged of the number they had killed during the day.[78]

Whoever did the killing, it seems certain that in the anxiety of the moment, a large segment of the Parisian elites either supported the massacres or accepted them as a necessary evil. Virtually none of the Paris newspapers entirely condemned them—whether radical or moderate, Girondin or Montagnard or independent. For the relatively moderate *Courrier français,* "the people made it their duty to purge the city of all the criminals, so as not to fear a prison breakout that would fall on the women and children." Those in the prisons "had done so much harm to us," wrote the Montagnard Audouin in the *Journal universel,* "they had so long conspired, that they were sacrificed in these days of vengeance with the swords of the people." The Girondin sympathizer Gorsas called the events "terrible but necessary."[79]

In their contemporary correspondence a wide sweep of Revolutionaries from various political positions came to similar conclusions. For the Montagnard sympathizer Pierre Dubreuil-Chambardel, "the whole wicked race of the refractory clergy has received the fate their deeds deserve. There is reason to believe that the nation will soon be purged of all these monsters." The Feuillant Pierre Ramel was also ready to accept the event: "It is unfortunate for the virtuous individuals who may also have been the victims. But the people are to be pitied and not to be blamed." "It is sad to be forced to such extreme measures," wrote the elderly Guittard, "but as they say, it is better to kill the devil before he kills you." In a long letter to her husband, Rosalie Jullien agonized over the events she had heard described, but ultimately concluded they were an "atrocious necessity" that could not be avoided: "The people, terrible in their fury, are avenging the crimes of three years of vile treason," and now "France has been saved."[80]

To be sure, there were exceptions, individuals who condemned the killings from the very beginning. "Oh the crime! Oh the shame!" wrote Ruault to his brother. "It is the extreme of horror and political infamy! All the prisoners have been massacred these last few days, in cold blood, without pity, without remorse." The young Montagnard Claude Basire was equally outraged and horrified: "It takes courage to remain in politics and to keep one's composure when faced with such terrible crises and calamities." Significantly, however, both Ruault and Basire—unlike most of our other witnesses—had directly observed the massacres. Basire was one of the delegates sent to the Abbaye prison by the Legislative in the futile effort to halt the killings, and Ruault had twice pushed his way through the blood and bodies at the same prison to beg mercy for a neighbor who was imprisoned and waiting to be "judged."[81]

Yet exceptions such as these do not invalidate the general conclusion that in the emotion of the moment, a broad cross-section of Parisian citizenry of diverse factions and political persuasions was convinced by the rumors of an impending prison breakout, and that they accepted the killings as either a positive good or an unfortunate necessity.[82] It was only in the weeks and months that followed, as the rumors of imminent conspiracies and the situation that promoted such rumors abated, that a great many Parisians came to look at the massacres in a new light and express their shock and horror over what had happened.[83] In this sense, the Massacres of September were not isolated acts of violence by the enraged lower classes but a phenomenon initially supported by a broad consensus of much of the Parisian population.

By SEPTEMBER 6 the wave of mass killings had largely run its course. Most of the prisons of the city now stood empty, with all of the prisoners either released or executed. Toward the end of the massacres the Commune did in fact step in. Faced with the extent of the bloodshed and the piles of corpses accumulating in the streets, many members of the General Council seemed to experience a change of heart. Efforts were made to send in armed forces to secure the one or two prisons that had not yet been breached.[84]

Yet the end of the massacres by no means brought an end to the atmosphere of tension and fear in France. Throughout the month of September all kinds of rumors continued to swirl through Paris: stories that the enemy army was nearing the city gates, that new aristocratic conspiracies were about to break, that another wave of massacres was in the offing. "Every passion imaginable," wrote Pinet, "is now appearing and coming into play." Adelaïde Mareux feared widespread looting: "We are in a state of terrible consternation. We are regularly threatened and we fear that the all the shops might soon be pillaged." In the midst of the chaos, a particularly audacious group of thieves managed to break into one of the royal depositories and walk off with the crown jewels—including what would later be known as the "Hope Diamond." Many Parisians were convinced that gangs of criminals were profiting from the situation to launch a renewed crime wave in the city.[85]

Conditions had become so frightening that many wealthier families began fleeing Paris. With rumors that all the former nobles would soon be massacred like the refractory clergy, the family who employed Colson—and who had consistently supported the Revolution—agonized over the possibility of withdrawing from the city for their own safety. The roads out of the capital were gorged with men and women rushing to find refuge in the provinces, often crossing paths with the volunteers marching in the opposite direction. One traveler en route to Orléans reported that "he had encountered nothing but a series of large and small carriages, carrying away crowds of people from Paris, in whose eyes one could read an inexpressible fear." Others, however, seem to have concluded that the countryside was even more dangerous than Paris. Roubaud—the former Feuillant deputy—decided that the roads were too insecure to return to his family in Provence: "If we are to be swallowed up by death, it might as well be in our own apartment rather than somewhere on the open highway." But he shared with his brother his anxiety for the future. "Profound unrest on one side, somber terror on the other, widespread mistrust everywhere: this is the situation in which we find ourselves in Paris."[86]

Yet as the summer turned to autumn and the frightful month of September drew to a close, there were clear indications that the violence was tapering off and that the First Terror was coming to an end. Overall the number of riots and insurgencies in the countryside declined during the last months of the year. So too the waves of provincial massacres, many in the wake of the events in Paris, diminished and all but disappeared. In Paris itself there were far fewer street demonstrations and riots than there had been in the heat of the summer, and none now involved physical violence.[87]

"Paris has become a bit calmer," wrote Dubreuil in November. By December the Mareux family found the situation had stabilized enough to open their theater once again.[88]

The reasons for the end of the First Terror are invariably complex. In the countryside the near complete suppression of seigneurial rights was no doubt a major faction in appeasing the population. Tensions were also relieved as the large numbers of young volunteers, who had often wreaked such havoc in Paris and the provinces, found their way to the front and were integrated into the regular army. But two other developments were to be especially important in the ebbing of the violence: first, the extraordinary reversal of the military situation, ending the immediate threat to France; second, the assumption of power by the new National Convention and its concrete efforts to restore order.

9

The Convention and the Trial of the King

T RAVELING through Paris in early September 1792, a patriot from Brittany commented on the curious mixture of emotions he found in the city: "Every day," he wrote, "presents an extraordinarily varied scene. The most intense joy, the most somber sadness, with happiness and grief following upon one another in rapid succession."[1] It was yet another sign of the contradictions and incongruities of the Revolution that the suspicion and brutality of that summer went hand in hand with the most intense patriotic enthusiasm and readiness for self-sacrifice. Many observers urged their fellow citizens to "cover with a veil" the terrible violence of September, a seeming callousness that can be understood only in the context of the panic fear of internal conspiracy in the face of the invading Prussians. Louis-Jérôme Gohier made his views clear in a letter of September 3: "These events [the massacres] must not preoccupy us now; the state of the nation and the peril it is facing must be the sole object of our concern." For his colleague, Vincent Corbel, "the National Assembly can be nothing at present but one great military committee, focusing exclusively on the national defense."[2]

The months of August and September saw masses of volunteers from all over the nation streaming toward the front. Pierre Gillet, en route from Nantes to the National Convention, found the roads covered with them: an "incredible multitude of young men marching forward endlessly."[3] And as the soldiers-to-be passed through Paris, the population of the capital rallied with immense energy. The same church bells and cannons on the bridges of the Seine that had moved people to invade the prisons now spurred them to organize for war. Recruitment stands were set up throughout the city.

Enrollment of volunteers in Paris, summer of 1792. This is a nineteenth-century rendition of young men rushing to sign up for the military with the announcement in July that "the fatherland is in peril." A woman grieves the departure of her husband or lover. Raised enrollment stands were set up throughout the city, this one in the Palais Royal. Witnesses described the extraordinary enthusiasm with which volunteers joined up. Marin Lavigne, © Coll. Musée de la Révolution française, Domaine de Vizille, MRF 1985.522.

Apprentices, journeymen, even some married men rushed to join the ranks, though most such individuals had never carried a gun in their lives. Colson watched as two detachments of newly minted soldiers marched below his window: "We have never seen such intense and widespread enthusiasm." Although most of the men still had no uniforms, they carried their muskets and sabers with pride, "crying out 'Long live the nation,' as they marched away in a mood of excitement and joy." Contingents of troops were invited almost daily to march through the National Assembly, where they cheered and shouted out patriotic slogans to the deputies.[4] Several young men sent letters home, describing the scene as they moved in a column out Saint-Martin's gate and headed for the front, surrounded by crowds of women and men accompanying them with cheers and tears and patriotic songs. Again and again they proclaimed their patriotism to their parents: "Death would be a hundred times preferable to slavery," wrote one; "we will brave any danger in our zeal to serve the nation," wrote another.[5]

Those Parisians not young enough to serve in the army were mustered for an improvised home guard, organized by section. Adrien Colson heard a crier beneath his window summoning all able-bodied men under age sixty to sign up for service. Even Guittard de Floriban, who was close to seventy, dutifully enrolled and marched off with his neighbors to the Luxembourg Gardens. They paraded through the streets three abreast, for a formal inspection and roll call. Many of these senior recruits were put to work shoring up the walls and other defenses of the city. At the same time contributions of money and blankets and clothing for the troops poured into the Assembly and the war office. Church grillworks were pulled down to be converted into pikes. Coffins were disinterred to provide lead for musket shot. Horses were requisitioned throughout the city to haul the artillery and provide for the cavalry. Some wealthy citizens found themselves forced to walk home when the horses pulling their carriages were abruptly unhitched and taken away for the armies of the fatherland.[6]

Valmy and the Reversal of Fortunes

But all the patriotic fervor would be of little avail if the invading Prussians could not be stopped. Once the forces of the Duke of Brunswick had breached the frontier citadels of Longwy and Verdun, they set their sights on Paris and began moving slowly and methodically westward.[7] With the desertion of General Lafayette to the Austrians, the difficult task of defending France's northwestern frontier fell to Charles-François Dumouriez, veteran of the Seven Years War and minister of foreign affairs under the short-lived Girondin government of the previous spring. The Prussians scoffed at this fifty-three-year-old "political" general who was said never to have distinguished himself in any campaign. Some French troops as well had serious misgivings: "So here we are," wrote one soldier, "with a new general who is altogether singular, and perhaps a bit mad."[8] And initially such appraisals seemed only too justified. In the first weeks of September, Dumouriez attempted to improvise a defense along the hills of the Argonne Forest, the last significant natural barrier between the Prussians and Paris. But in what was perhaps the most inspired maneuver of the campaign, Brunswick lured the bulk of Dumouriez's forces with a clever feint at the central pass of Grandpré, while a sizable contingent of his army pushed through the Argonne farther to the north and outflanked the French. Although Dumouriez was able to regroup his troops to the south, they now found themselves in an almost untenable position, facing northwest with their backs to the Argonne and the Prussians between them and Paris. Fortunately, at the last moment, Dumouriez's army was reinforced by some 27,000 professional troops pulling back from the eastern frontier, led by General Kellermann. It was they, rather than the raw volunteers under Dumouriez, who would engage the Prussians in the epic artillery duel at Valmy on September 20, 1792.

Despite an eleven-hour cannon barrage and several attempted Prussian infantry advances, the French held their ground, partly through the advantage of their more elevated position, partly through Kellerman's patriotic leadership. Though it was hardly as massive and deadly an affair as later Revolutionary battles, the daylong exchange between two of the world's best artilleries—with over a hundred cannons firing thousands of rounds—had a powerful effect on those who were present. As described by the writer Goethe, who was present on the Prussian side, "the earth literally trembled," with "the thunder of the cannons, the howling, whistling, and crashing of the balls through the air."[9] During the night that followed, the French shored up their lines for what they assumed would be a renewed attack. The next day, however, saw only a few minor cavalry skirmishes, for the Prussians had already suffered a major psychological defeat. On the eve of the battle, according to Goethe, the Prussians had assumed the French would crumble as soon as they were subjected to a serious bombardment—just as had occurred at Longwy and Verdun—and that they might then easily "devour" them on the battlefield. But after numerous failures to make any inroads, "the greatest consternation was diffused amidst the [Prussian] army. . . . Everyone went about solitarily, no one looked at his neighbor, or if it did happen, it was to curse or to swear."[10]

For over a week the invaders maintained their position, but their plight became increasingly tenuous. Weeks of rain had turned the countryside into a quagmire and had brought the Prussians' long supply train across northern France to a virtual halt. Both troops and horses were incapacitated by hunger and disease. Realizing that time was on his side, Dumouriez initiated negotiations across the lines, playing on Prussian hopes that he might be won over to the counterrevolution. At the same time he continued to bring in more troops and concentrate them in a great arc around the enemy forces. Finally, after ten days of inactivity and with his situation ever more precarious, Brunswick ordered a general retreat toward Germany.[11] But now, with his soldiers wracked by hunger and disease and fearful of a French attack on their rear, the vaunted Prussian discipline collapsed, and the army fell into panic and disorder. Goethe described the chaos of wagons, carriages, emigrant coaches, dying horses, and sick and dying men. Gabriel Noël, a recruit from Nancy, felt a certain pity, as he marched with his company in pursuit of the Germans and viewed the bodies of soldiers and women camp followers, lying in ditches and in nearby woods, often stripped of their clothing. "In a word, their army is in the most deplorable condition."[12]

The encounter at Valmy has sometimes been described as the "Marathon of the French Revolution."[13] Although the large number of new recruits from Paris and the provinces played virtually no role in the battle itself, they provided an immense resource of energy and dedication, as the French armies began advancing on all fronts. Soldiers felt a sense of exhilaration when they liberated Verdun and Longwy in October, and watched the Prussians straggle back across the frontier. "It seems," wrote Denis Belot to his father, "as though the French army has been electrified with a new courage that will make all despots tremble. Oh liberty! Oh equality! Oh my country! What a wonderful transformation!"[14]

Over the following weeks the armies of the Republic moved forward in a series of campaigns that were nothing short of spectacular. They crossed the Rhine and advanced rapidly northward to capture Mainz and Frankfurt. They moved into the bishopric of Porrentruy within the Swiss Confederation and eventually entered Geneva. Farther south, they attacked

Savoy—which had joined the coalition with Austria and Prussia—and swept across the French speaking regions, seizing all lands to the crest of the Alps, as well as the county of Nice along the Mediterranean.[15]

Perhaps the most stunning advance was the three-week conquest of the Austrian Lowlands in what is today Belgium. Dumouriez hailed from France's northern frontier, and he had long dreamed of capturing this region. During much-heralded appearances at the Convention and the Jacobin Club in mid-October, he promised, "with a kind of flamboyant self-assurance," that he would soon march into Brussels.[16] And in early November, with the Prussian army out of action, he launched a northward invasion of four separate French armies. The smaller Austrian force chose to make its stand just south of Mons at the village of Jemappes. Far more volunteer French troops were involved than at Valmy, and many sang the "Marseillaise" and the "Carmagnole" as they attacked with muskets, bayonets, and knives. When they seemed to falter, Dumouriez and the duke de Chartres (the future king Louis-Philippe) personally intervened to urge them forward and win the day. Thereafter, the French moved rapidly to capture Brussels. By the end of November they entered Namur, Liège, and Antwerp to the very frontier of the Dutch Republic. As the Revolutionary armies swept forward, the large French emigrant population who had taken refuge in Brussels fled in panic.[17]

Throughout France the patriots were ecstatic. "It was with tears in my eyes," wrote the Breton deputy Claude Blad, "that I heard the account [of the battle of Jemappes]. The spirit of liberty was hovering above our army." "How wonderful is our situation now!" exclaimed Boyer-Fonfrède. "What an extraordinary era France is living through!" Dumouriez became a national hero. Louis Louchet, deputy from Rodez, gave him unbounded praise for both his military talents and his devotion to the Republic. Edmond Géraud was amazed that the general had been able to keep his promise to march into Brussels by November 15.[18] Across the nation patriotic festivals were organized for all the recent victories. In Cahors in south central France both Valmy and Jemappes were celebrated by local administrators, national guardsmen, and the general citizenry, joining together to sing the "hymn of the Marseillais" and hear a *Te Deum* in the cathedral. Châlons-sur-Marne commemorated both the final evacuation of French territory by the Prussians and the success of the French armies in Switzerland. October 14 saw a festival in Paris at the Place de la Révolution (the present day Place de la Concorde) honoring the capture of Nice and Savoy. It was organized around a large goddess of liberty holding a pike—replacing the equestrian statue of Louis XV that once dominated the square. Soon after the fall of Belgium, soldiers brought back a giant Hapsburg eagle pulled down from the belfry of Tournai, parading it "in chains" through the streets of the capital in a ceremony reminiscent of the victory marches of ancient Rome.[19]

It was a stunning reversal of fortune. The soldiers of the Revolution had gone far beyond the conquests of Louis XIV, advancing farther than any French armies since the time of Charlemagne, a thousand years earlier. By November the Revolutionaries were reviving the theory of France's "natural frontiers," bounded only by the Rhine and the Alps.[20] Invariably, the string of victories had an enormous impact on the outlook of the patriots. Nicolas Ruault, who had long agonized over the viability of a republic in France, now convinced himself of "what a great people can accomplish once they have abolished a throne that only blocked their momentum." The former Legislator François Roubaud seemed entirely to have forgotten his earlier pessimism. "We could hardly be more delighted," he wrote of the victory in Nice—across the river from his hometown of Grasse; "all opposition collapsed before our triumphant armies." Jacques Pinet was also exuberant: "The despots had no idea what would happen when a free people went to war."[21]

In the short term, many of the patriots felt a sense of exaltation and invincibility, a veritable hubris that would color their actions and decisions for months to come. All the Girondins' exuberant predictions of the previous spring seemed to have been realized. They were also more convinced than ever that the earlier failures of their armies, fighting in the name of liberty, must have been caused by treachery. If ever those armies should falter in the future, it could only be through new acts of conspiracy contrived by the enemies of the Revolution.

The National Convention and the War

The French were given a further sense of confidence and security with the assumption of power by the National Convention. Summoned by the Legislative Assembly in the aftermath of August 10, the Convention was empowered to draft a new constitution that would resolve the contradiction of a constitutional monarchy that had lost its monarch. It was thus conceived as a second "constituent" assembly, the organ of popular sovereignty, with unlimited powers to remake the nation. The choice of its members was determined in rapidly improvised elections, unrolling throughout the country in late August and early September. As one year earlier, the voting was organized in two stages, with ballots cast first in primary and then in secondary assemblies. With passive citizenship abolished nearly all male citizens over twenty-one years of age could now take part. Yet despite the much larger electorate, participation seems to have been relatively low. Strong supporters of the monarchy were often absent, either through self-exclusion or through intimidation by radicals. Many citizens may also have been deterred by the ongoing invasion and the anxiety it created.[22]

In their biographic profile—age, social origins, residence—the newly elected deputies differed little, for the most part, from those in the Legislative. Substantially fewer, however, were chosen from the department administrators. The radicals clearly remained suspicious of the royalism of such officials, and they apparently influenced the electorate to shun them. Since this time there was no exclusionary rule, over a third of the new representatives had served in previous assemblies—83 in the first National Assembly and 194 in the Legislative.[23] Both Robespierre and Brissot would reappear, along with a substantial number of their most articulate supporters. Also of note was the election of no less than seventeen Parisian journalists, all of them radicals and many of them soon to become major players in debates—including Marat, Desmoulins, Fréron, Carra, and Gorsas.[24] Overall, it was a remarkable group of individuals, men with well-developed ideas on a range of questions and with a considerable store of political experience at both the local and national levels. They would constitute one of the most celebrated—or infamous, depending on one's point of view—assemblies in European history.

On September 20 the still-incomplete corps of new deputies assembled in the Tuileries Palace, just as the French were battling the Prussians some 200 kilometers to the east. The next day toward one o'clock in the afternoon they filed across the Tuileries Gardens to the assembly hall and formally replaced the Legislative Assembly.[25] That very afternoon, as their first major decree, they unanimously voted the abolition of the monarchy and the creation of the first French Republic. It was an act long anticipated by many of the radicals. In the previous Assembly the Girondins had carefully avoided such a move—much to the ire of the Parisian militants—specifying only that the current king had been "suspended." Now, however, the whole Convention roared its approval, with shouts of "Long live the nation" that continued for several minutes. "It seemed," wrote Pinet, "like the hall might collapse from the thundering applause."[26]

Thereafter and over the next several months, the Convention set to work writing a Constitution and confronting the extraordinary challenges raised by the radical transformation of the political situation and the continuing difficulties of fighting a war. The deputies quickly established a constitutional committee, though in deference to the "sovereignty of the people" they committed themselves to submitting the final document to ratification by the whole population. At the same time they created a range of other committees, most of them modeled on those in the two previous assemblies—for finance, commerce, agriculture, education, and other purposes. They also took steps to halt the chaos of the First Terror and restore law and order in Paris and the provinces. The very existence of a Convention elected, in theory, by universal male suffrage gave the Assembly a legitimacy that had been sadly lacking for the lame-duck Legislative after August 10. The deputies moved rapidly to reassure the population by declaring that "all persons and property are placed under the safeguard of the nation."[27] Over the coming weeks, they would suppress martial law, end censorship, dismantle the Revolutionary Tribunal of August 17, and create a special commission to investigate the Paris prisons and determine if those interred had been fairly treated. They also passed a series of measures to limit the authority of the Insurrectional Commune of Paris. Indeed, once the Convention had begun its meetings, the Commune could no longer present itself as the central political body holding the nation together. The deputies reined in the power of the Commune's surveillance committee—which had played a significant role in the massacres. They compelled the Commune's leaders to present their accounts and justify their demands for continuing state subsidies. In late November new elections were organized in the city, and the Insurrectional Commune of August 10 was dissolved and replaced.[28] During the same period the Provisional Executive Council, overseeing the day-to-day functioning of the government, took measures to strengthen control over the army and the departments. The minister of the interior Roland worked overtime, distributing propaganda to promote the new regime. He also commissioned a number of personal agents to militate for the Republic.[29]

Yet all such measures, conceived to end the chaos of the previous summer, could hardly have succeeded without the victories of the French armies.

During the first two weeks of the Convention, until it was clear that the Prussians were actually in retreat, the deputies wrote tense letters to their constituents, urging them not to lose heart and to continue the fight even if Paris were captured. Thereafter they described with growing excitement the string of successes. By the second week in October Jeanbon-Saint-André, the Protestant pastor from Montauban, described the Prussian army, "the successors to Frederick the Great," fleeing "like a flock of sheep, frightened by their shepherd's crook."[30] It now seemed obvious to them that the only thing blocking the French victories six months earlier had been the actions of a treacherous king and his court. Once the monarchy had been abolished, everything had become possible. "The end of the monarchy," wrote Riffard de Saint-Martin, "seems to have marked the end of all our difficulties."[31] By late September the Convention had consecrated the "Marseillaise" as the de facto national anthem, and the deputies sang it lustily at the end of every session: "To arms, citizens! Form up your battalions. March on, march on! Until our furrows are soaked with their impure blood."[32]

As the French armies continued to advance on every front, the Convention also found itself compelled to develop policies to deal with the newly occupied territories. The debate began when French-speaking representatives from the newly "liberated" Nice and Savoy arrived in the Convention to demand annexation to the Republic. Some of the deputies had their doubts, recalling the Revolution's previous commitment never to engage in a war of conquest. But what should they do when another people specifically appealed to join the French nation? There was, moreover, the precedent of the former papal enclave of Avignon, annexed to France in September 1791 after local patriots had asked to become part of France. In the end, following a stirring speech by the Convention president Grégoire, the deputies voted nearly unanimously to create a new department of "Mont-Blanc" that would incorporate most of the French-speaking portions of Savoy. "We have gained a province of new brothers," wrote Bancal, "returned to their freedom through our principles and our arms."[33] The decision reinforced the Revolution's definition of international sovereignty, where frontiers were no longer determined by treaties among dynastic states but by popular vote.

The debate on Savoy and Nice, coupled with the news of the conquest of Belgium, fired a renewed vision of a world revolution and a universal republic where kings would cease to exist. The Revolution's destiny to liberate all the peoples of Europe, declared the previous January by Brissot and the Girondins, now seemed within reach. "There is the wonderful possibility," wrote the deputy Philippe Lebas, "of destroying tyranny throughout the whole of Europe."[34] In a revealing letter to Dumouriez, Brissot declared that the French must no longer even think of negotiating treaties or acting like ministers of the Old Regime: "How can their petty schemes compare to the uprisings of the whole planet and the momentous revolutions that we are now called upon to lead." By next year, he predicted, the French would march into Berlin. The journalist Prudhomme summarized the Convention's understanding of the logic of the war: "The war in which we are engaged is a sacred war, . . . unlike anything in the past. . . . You are not being compelled to fight. You leave rather with full knowledge and you know why you fight. You do so on your own behalf."[35]

The Revolutionary hubris seemed to have no bounds. There was talk of "liberating" Poland, Naples, and Spain. If this meant taking on the whole of Europe, so be it. Recent events had demonstrated that a free people could easily overcome the best armies on the Continent and "incite terror in all tyrannical governments." Vergniaud pushed his eloquence to new heights, as he dreamed of a war to end war: "Men have died in the recent fighting. But it is so that none will ever die again. I swear to you in the name of the universal fraternity which you are creating, that each battle will be a step towards peace, humanity, and happiness for all peoples."[36]

The effort to define a new attitude toward war and toward the rest of Europe reached a head in mid-December and was embodied above all in a speech by Pierre-Jacques Cambon. The Protestant cloth merchant from Nîmes readily adopted the rhetoric of a "revolutionary war." But as a leading member of the committee on finance and a watchdog for fiscal responsibility, he also saw no harm in combining a war of liberation with a "profitable war." The countries in question would obviously be prepared to pay taxes to France for a campaign that had liberated them. France would also be justified in introducing the *assignats* into the new territories to help strengthen its own national currency. Debated in a moment of exaltation and supreme self-confidence, Cambon's proposal received nearly universal support from the deputies of the Convention. In Pinet's view it was "a wonderful and truly revolutionary decree, that would be the equal of several armies." It would also make a European-wide war all but inevitable.[37]

Girondins and Montagnards

On the eve of the Convention, some observers were still hopeful that a new beginning was possible, that the factional divides of the previous assembly could now be overcome. "No more parties," wrote Prudhomme in early September. "Now we are all united. A much desired and necessary harmony will guide our efforts."[38] Yet within days after the Convention had convened, Girondin and Montagnard deputies were attacking one another with at least as much ferocity as that shown by Feuillants and Jacobins in the Legislative Assembly. During the first months, the struggle probably involved only a relatively small minority of the deputies. As late as January 1793 Vinet described the confrontation as consisting of two groups of about "fifty individuals at each end of the hall."[39] A substantial majority would remain nonaligned and sit in the center or "Plain" of the Assembly. Yet many of those linked to the two factions were among the Convention's most vigorous speakers, and their mutual animosity would profoundly affect the atmosphere of the whole body.

At the core of Girondin leadership in the Convention were the men who had dominated the Legislative Assembly in the last days of its existence: Brissot and the trio of lawyers from Bordeaux, Vergniaud, Gensonné, and Guadet. They were now joined by the passionate young orator from Marseille, Charles Barbaroux, and by two ex-deputies who had once been Robespierre's closest collaborators: Jérôme Pétion and François Buzot.[40] Also central to the group was the minister of the interior, Jean-Marie Roland. The apartment of Roland and his wife, Marie-Jeanne, became one of the principal meeting places for the Girondins.[41] In addition, they could rely on a corps of deputy-journalists—Carra, Gorsas, Louvet, and Dulaure—who, along with Brissot himself, helped maintain a positive image for the faction in the Parisian press. Rosalie Jullien, whose husband would be a staunch Montagnard, was saddened by the loss of so many individuals whom they had once considered their friends. She was especially distressed by the departure of "the good Pétion," the onetime leader of the Jacobin deputies and mayor of Paris. "How could such good individuals," she lamented, "have become so vile?"[42]

The leadership of the Mountain was dominated above all by a corps of radicals from Paris, most of them veterans of the Insurrectional Commune and the Cordeliers Club: Danton, Marat, Desmoulins, Collot d'Herbois, Billaud-Varenne, and of course Robespierre. The Parisians would also attract the support of a small number of provincial deputies, such as Claude Basire from Dijon, Philippe Lebas from Artois, and the fiery Jeanbon-Saint-André. After the first few weeks, they would be joined by the partially paralyzed lawyer from Clermont-Ferrand, Georges Couthon, and the icy Artois orator, Antoine de Saint-Just—the youngest member of the Convention. As during the Legislative, the group sat at one end of the hall, where the rows of seats rose somewhat higher, directly facing their Girondin opponents at the opposite end.[43] Though some of the Montagnards were close associates and even friends, their central meeting place was not a private "salon"—as with the Girondins—but the public arena of the Jacobin Club. Since the Jacobins could no longer define themselves as friends of a Constitution that had been repudiated, they adopted the name of the Friends of Liberty and Equality. By October 1792 many of the members had returned to wearing the red "liberty cap," ostentatiously linking themselves to the Paris working people.[44]

As with the earlier Jacobin/Feuillant split, it is often difficult to know why given individuals aligned themselves with one side or the other—or for that matter, why the majority sought to avoid all such alignments. In their ages and professions the adherents of the two factions were remarkably similar.[45] Perhaps the most striking variation was in their geographic origins. The Montagnards came from virtually every corner of the country, with at least one supporter from all but four departments. The Girondins, by contrast, were absent from twenty-eight departments and were especially prominent in regions near the Atlantic and Mediterranean coasts and the periphery of France, at a considerable distance from Paris. Overall, however, they were not particularly concentrated in the major commercial cities, as has sometimes been suggested. Virtually the same proportion in the two factions came from larger and from smaller towns.

In their ideological assumptions, the factions were often in close accord. All had endorsed the abolition of the monarchy on September 21—despite the Girondins' reluctance to do so under the Legislative. Both groups claimed to support the general principle of popular sovereignty, the repression of emigrant nobles and refractory priests, and a continued commitment to the war.[46] If there was one issue that separated the two alignments under the Convention—as under the Legislative—it was their attitude toward the Parisian masses. Influenced in part by the Jacobin Club and by their constituency of Parisian militants, the Mountain continued to glorify the people. Pinet would specifically define the Montagnards as those "who refuse to compromise when it is a question of the rights of a people who have invested them with their confidence."[47] By contrast, Brissot and his colleagues, whatever their onetime support for the masses of Paris, now seemed to exhibit a near physical revulsion toward them. The Montagnards were seen as pandering to the mobs, and castigated as "anarchists," "disorganizers," and "the men of September." Pétion summoned up the image of hordes of ignorant barbarians: "The present struggle," he proclaimed, "is between light and darkness, between ignorance and knowledge." Brissot would accuse his opponents of advocating a complete leveling of society.[48] Over time, through the very dynamics of the factional struggle, the Girondins seemed to position themselves against everything the Mountain supported—just as the Feuillants once defined themselves in large measure by their opposition to the Jacobins.

Two days after the Convention's first meeting, a dozen Girondin sympathizers initiated what could only have been a carefully coordinated frontal attack on their opponents.[49] The principal issue was the September Massacres, for which the Mountain and the members of the Paris Commune were said to have been responsible. Though in the midst of the massacres many of Brissot's friends had also supported, or at least acquiesced to, the killings, they now claimed to have been outraged. The change of heart may well have been motivated by Brissot and Roland, who would never forgive the Commune for issuing arrest warrants against them in early September—in what they believed was an attempt to have them murdered. In speech after speech—by Vergniaud, Brissot, Barbaroux, Buzot, Lasource, Lanjuinais, and others—the Girondins condemned the killings and claimed that Robespierre, along with Marat and Danton, had instigated them in the hope of using the Parisian mobs to eliminate their rivals and make themselves dictators. There were also insinuations that the Mountain leadership was secretly allied with foreign governments. Led by Barbaroux, the Girondins demanded a new march on Paris by volunteers from the provinces, not this time in support of the Parisians and the overthrow of the monarchy—as during the previous summer—but to protect the Convention from the threat of Parisian violence. As the debates developed, Brissot and his supporters pushed for the appointment of a special investigation committee, which they hoped would have Robespierre, Danton, and Marat arrested and expelled from the Convention.

At first the leadership of the Mountain seemed unprepared for the onslaught. Robespierre and Danton parried the attacks as best they could, rejecting as ridiculous the supposed plans for a dictatorship and denying any complicity in the massacres. Several of their allies—Tallien, Fabre d'Eglantine, Basire, and Billaud-Varenne—all came to their defense. Danton even took care to disassociate himself from Marat: "I fear that the subterranean depths in which he has lived so long have embittered his soul."[50]

Although there was no clear victor in September, the terrible feud was pursued over the following weeks. Throughout the autumn both Roland and Brissot took their case directly to the nation. Brissot through various publications and Roland in his role as minister of the interior directed to the provinces numerous attacks against their adversaries.[51] The Girondins also made good on their threats to summon national guardsmen from the departments. Soon a second generation of "Fédérés" troops began arriving from Provence and Brittany—without the Convention's sanction. By late October a contingent of Marseillais was marching through the streets of Paris, shouting "Long live Roland" and demanding the heads of Robespierre, Marat, and Danton.[52] The Jacobins countered by ousting many of the Girondin leaders from their society—although most had ceased attending the meetings the previous summer.[53] The Mountain would soon refer to their rivals as "the Right" or "the blacks," the terms first applied to the "aristocrats" in the Constituent Assembly and later to the Feuillants during the Legislative.[54]

Whatever the initial reasons for the feud, those on both sides increasingly demonized their opponents. Jean-Baptiste Louvet's attack against Robespierre on the floor of the Convention was particularly dramatic: "There exist only two parties in France," he proclaimed in late October. "The first [the Girondins] is composed of philosophers; the second [the Mountain] of thieves, robbers, and murderers." In speeches and in letters home deputies easily fell into similar moralizing language. The Girondin sympathizer Corbel wrote of the "the cruel and most dangerously seditious men" who were "monsters in society."[55] But the Montagnards could mobilize much the same rhetoric. Robespierre frequently matched Louvet in his Manichaean logic: "Only two parties exist in the Republic," he would announce to his constituency: "the party of good citizens and the party of evil citizens, those who represent the French people and those who think only of their ambition and personal gain." The Montagnard Pinet accused the Girondins of wearing "the mask of patriotism to cover their aristocracy."[56] And both sides argued—and apparently believed—that their rivals were traitors, secretly plotting with foreign enemies.[57] Given the depths of their mistrust and their hatred, neither side was prepared even to consider a compromise. Barbaroux made this clear in rejecting all thought of mediation, announcing "that it was impossible for vice to work together with virtue." When Pinet's constituency urged him to attempt reconciliation, he responded in much the same manner: "Vice and virtue can never be allies, . . . for the evil man never changes."[58]

Although most of the deputies avoided direct involvement in the factional squabbles, the majority seems initially to have sympathized with the Girondins' accusations against their rivals.[59] It was thus not surprising that Brissot and his friends initially dominated the elections of the Convention's officers, the president and the six secretaries. Six of the seven chosen on September 20 were clearly associated with the Girondin inner circle. Thereafter, through mid-January 1793, Girondins were chosen to twenty-eight positions, compared to only ten for those who would come to identify with the Mountain. The key constitutional committee, chosen by the deputies in early October, also contained a solid majority of Girondins.[60]

Yet while the Girondins were broadly supported by a large number of deputies throughout October and November, they were never able to convince the Convention that the leaders of the Mountain should be expelled and arrested. Robespierre's carefully worded speech in early November seemed to assuage the majority. Many would undoubtedly have shared the lament of an unnamed deputy: "Now that the royalty no longer exists and that the success of our armies signals the conquest of the world in the name of liberty, by what terrible fate has the sanctuary of the laws been transformed into an arena of gladiators?"[61] A certain number grew tired of the Girondins' constant railing against the Mountain with unproven accusations, when there were so many other important problems to solve. Several of the deputies who had once been persuaded by the condemnation of Robespierre and Marat now came to support the Mountain. Even Durand de Maillane, who often sympathized with the Girondins, found that their endless, unsubstantiated attacks did more harm than good: "To treat [the Montagnards] as guilty but without proving it, was only to antagonize them and to gain nothing."[62]

The Girondins felt increasingly frustrated at their inability to deliver a death blow against those they proclaimed to be the root of all evil. In late November, in a letter to Dumouriez, Brissot complained bitterly of the situation. Despite his desire to devote himself entirely to the revolutions "of the whole planet," he was compelled to wallow in factional infighting against the Montagnards: "We are languishing here, forced to follow step for step these miserable anarchists."[63] Perhaps the Girondins' very frustration over their failure to win the factional struggle can help explain their erratic maneuvers during the trial of the king, a trial that would dominate the Assembly during much of December and January.

To Try a King

Throughout the first months of the Convention Louis XVI and his family had remained imprisoned in the Temple, the great medieval fortress originally built by the Knights Templar. Though the king, the queen, and their two children remained under heavy guard, they were generally well treated and allowed to maintain a team of servants and cooks to see to their needs. Over time, however, as rumors spread in Paris of a plot to free the king, the internment became substantially more rigorous. Louis was moved to smaller quarters and separated from the queen, and most of his attendants were sent away. The king spent much of his time reading and tutoring geography to his young son, whom he still hoped would one day replace him.[64]

During the early weeks of the Convention, the deputies seemed largely to ignore the problem of the king. The Girondins were far more concerned with the perceived threat of the Montagnards and the Parisian militants, and all of the representatives remained preoccupied with the war.[65] It was only in mid-October that the Convention formally commissioned its legislative committee to examine the king's situation and develop a proposal. On November 7 Jean-Baptiste Mailhe, a doctor of jurisprudence from Toulouse, delivered an eloquent and learned report for the committee. The king must be tried by the Convention, he argued, for Louis was clearly guilty of treason and of the brutal repression of the people on August 10. The "law of nature" overrode the "inviolability" granted to the king by the Constitution of 1791. But, significantly, Mailhe also linked such a judgment to the international situation. The success of the French armies would soon transform the whole of Europe and bring the destruction of all kings. The Convention's treatment of their own former king "must serve as an example for all nations."[66]

A week later, based on this report, the deputies began a lengthy debate on the modalities of such a trial, a debate remarkable for the variety of opinions expressed and the arguments mobilized.[67] The former Constitution, the existing laws, various versions of "natural law," the expressed or imagined will of the people: all were broached and developed in a myriad of ways. There were also comparisons with the seventeenth-century trial of the English king Charles I. Several deputies, like Jacques Pinet, linked Louis' trial and punishment to France's general struggle against European despots: "The preservation of liberty for all people," he wrote to his constituency, "depends on the punishment of Louis XVI. It is a final blow against despotism, and this blow will overturn every throne."[68] Only a small group—many of them Girondin sympathizers—continued to claim that the king was "inviolable" and could not be tried at all. An equally small minority of Montagnards—notably Robespierre and Saint-Just—argued that the king had already been found guilty by the people and did not need to be judged. Far more common was the argument that the law must be applied equally to all men, including a king—as based on the Declaration of the Rights of Man. Other deputies appealed to a stipulated "contract" between the monarch and the people, which Louis was said to have broken. Still others followed Mailhe in invoking "natural law," which was deemed anterior and superior to the "relative" law enforced by normal judicial institutions. Following this logic, the king was declared to be a criminal to humanity who did not deserve a normal legal process. It is difficult to say whether such language had been picked up by deputies during their legal studies, or from listening to earlier speeches about the war and the sins of foreign tyrants, or from the rhetoric used by Mailhe in his report. In any case, the concept of natural law, understood and received in a variety of ways, could clearly serve as an excellent rationale for overriding the inviolability clause of the Constitution.[69]

In the midst of the debates, the minister Roland announced the dramatic discovery and opening of the king's secret safe in the Tuileries Palace. The safe produced proof that the great Mirabeau, long lionized by the Revolution, had been paid by the king to advise him on how best to manipulate the National Assembly. Thus, another Revolutionary hero—like Lafayette a few months earlier—was revealed to have been a secret conspirator. As soon as they learned the news, the Jacobins removed Mirabeau's bust from their meeting hall, and his ashes were disinterred from the Pantheon. "That's the way it is!" penned Guittard in his diary. "At first we passionately support a man and praise him to the sky, and then we end up by despising him." The discovery seemed further to reinforce the fear that even the most fervent revolutionaries might be traitors in disguise.[70]

Yet the contents of the safe were also damaging to the reputation of the king. While there was no "smoking gun" of openly treasonous activities, the papers gave ample indication that Louis had favored the counterrevolution and the emigrants and that he hoped to see the Old Regime Church reestablished. Together with materials uncovered after the storming of the Tuileries, the evidence seemed to obliterate the image of a well-meaning king misled by advisers. "Now you can see," wrote Claude-Antoine Blad in a letter to his constituency, "that our good king was more vicious than stupid."[71]

As the new evidence was revealed, as the deputies shared their opinions in the Convention, as they reiterated the popular view of Louis' perfidy on August 10, the language used to characterize the king in letters and speeches became extraordinarily harsh. Louis was described as a "traitor" who called the Prussians and Austrians into their lands and partook in intrigue and seduction. He was "a ferocious beast" who must never be exempt from judgment, a "tyrant whose barbarous hands are covered with the blood of the children of the fatherland."[72] The word "monster," in particular, returned like a leitmotif in their descriptions of the monarch, appearing at least sixty times in the 102 speeches published by the deputies in early December.[73]

In the end the overwhelming majority of the representatives voted to put the king on trial before the Convention, which now empowered itself to serve as both grand jury and collective judge—even though such a procedure was forbidden by the criminal code of 1791.[74] On December 10, 1792 a formal indictment was read by Robert Lindet, a deputy from Normandy and future member of the Committee of Public Safety. It was a long litany of the king's purported conspiracy and treason against the French people. It also included a total reinterpretation of the recent past, damning all of Louis' actions from 1789 to the present.

The next day, December 11, Louis himself was summoned to the Convention to face the charges. It was the first time in almost four months that he had been allowed to leave the Temple, and a massive show of force was positioned along the route taken by the king's carriage on its way to the Convention. Entering the assembly hall, he was told to stand at the "barre"—the platform where outsiders were permitted to address the body. Directly across from him were the assembly's president and a statue of Brutus, the hero who had led an uprising against the last Roman king.[75] To almost everyone's surprise, Louis never questioned the Convention's right to try him. He responded briefly but forthrightly to all of the articles of indictment as they were read out to him. And he denied all guilt. Many of the actions he was accused of, he said, occurred before there was a Constitution and when he still had complete royal power. Others were carried out by ministers and were not his responsibility. He claimed to have no knowledge of the hidden safe, and his vetoes of key laws passed by the Legislative were entirely within his Constitutional right.

There can be no doubt that Louis' appearance at the Convention made an impact on a number of the deputies. Despite all their previous condemnations, many now felt a certain sympathy for the king. The Girondin Blad, who had earlier announced he would vote for death, admitted, "I could not keep myself from feeling a certain involuntary pity." For the staunch Jacobin Monestier, "Louis Capet appeared and stood at the barre in the most modest clothing, with a calm and serene expression . . . revealing neither irritation nor fear nor hope." Couthon, by contrast, steeled himself not to be taken in by the king's show of cooperation. He was indignant when Louis refused even to recognize his own signature on documents that were presented to him. The ex-deputy Roubaud, who could only follow the proceedings in the newspapers, was struck by how low the mighty had fallen: "If kings still exist a hundred years from now, this terrible event will reveal to them, in letters of blood, what they might well become."[76]

It was a measure of the sympathy aroused by the king that the Convention voted overwhelmingly to grant Louis' request for legal counsel—despite the opposition of a small group of Montagnards.[77] Three eminent Old Regime jurists—Malesherbes, Tronchet, and Desèze—agreed to take the case and were given two weeks to build a defense. When the trial was resumed on December 26, the defense devised by the legal team differed very little from the king's improvised responses on December 11. The king, they argued in a two-hour oration, was inviolable by the Constitution of 1791; the trial procedure was unfair since it did not conform to the criminal code; the Convention had no right to judge the king's motives, only his acts, and in their view nothing he had actually done was illegal. After the lawyers had finished speaking, the king briefly addressed the Convention for a second time. Again he fervently rejected the accusations, proclaiming his love for "my people" and denying that he was in any way responsible for the shedding of French blood.[78]

Once the lawyers had made their best effort, the weight of a final judgment fell on the deputies. But their decision would not be soon in coming.

Trial of Louis XVI, interrogated by the Convention, December 26, 1792. The former king stands at the "barre" (on the right) for his second appearance in the Assembly. He reads his defense surrounded by his legal team and facing the president, Jacques Defermon. The deputies of the center (the Plain) and the spectators in the galleries above are clearly visible. Miller, engraved by D. Vrijdag, © Coll. Musée de la Révolution française, Domaine de Vizille, MRF L 1985.848.101.

Throughout the pretrial debates and the period between the king's two appearances, acrimonious confrontations between Girondins and Montagnards had erupted periodically. Now, however, the factional hatreds and accusations became more intense than ever. At the end of December the Girondins abruptly adopted a proposal that the king's fate be determined by an "appeal to the people," a national referendum in which all male citizens would be asked to confirm or reject the Convention's decisions. Presumably Brissot and his friends hoped thus to portray themselves as the true supporters of popular sovereignty, and in this way to retake the initiative from the Mountain. Ironically, Brissot himself had long opposed the idea, arguing as recently as October that an appeal to the people would only lead to chaos and anarchy.[79] On December 27, in a move that must have been coordinated in advance, a trio of Girondins—Salle, Serre, and Barbaroux—supported the proposal. Thereafter, on successive days many of the faction's most talented orators—Brissot, Vergniaud, Gensonné, Pétion, Rabaut Saint-Etienne, and Carra—all followed suit. A referendum was necessary, in part, they argued, in order to block the Montagnards, who wanted the king's death so that they could take power themselves—men who had been bought, as Louvet claimed, by "a great many English guineas."[80]

In response, the Montagnards mobilized some of their own best speakers. Saint-Just, Robespierre, Jeanbon-Saint-André, Joseph Lequinio, and Dubois-Crancé all rose to speak in opposition. They too took the occasion to attack their rivals, described as a "criminal faction," a "cabal" of "treacherous enemies of the people," who were hypocritically proposing a measure that could prolong the trial for months and might ultimately save the guilty king. Many potential voters in the countryside, they argued, were illiterate, and it would be impossible for them to be well informed and see all the evidence. Throwing the trial open to a popular vote would delegitimize the Convention and stir up chaos and perhaps civil war. The debate ended with a brilliantly argued speech by Bertrand Barère, the former Constituent and journalist who had long kept his distance from the Mountain but who now fully embraced their opposition to a referendum.[81]

From all accounts by late December the factional confrontation had become remarkably brutal and violent. "Our sessions are extremely stormy," wrote the deputy Gaultier, who tried to remain unaligned. "There are no maneuvers that agitators in the various parties have not used in their attempt to mislead us and gain their ends." At one point the Girondins became so outraged against their rivals that Barbaroux, Louvet, and several dozen of their colleagues rose from their seats and charged down the middle of the hall to confront the Mountain at the other end—with pistols in their pockets, according to one report. Pierre Dubreuil described another scuffle in January in a letter to his son: "You can judge the confusion and the lack of good faith when, at the end of the session, dozens of voices shouted at the top of their lungs 'Ah, you damnable rogues, you should all be murdered!' "[82]

Then, in early January it was revealed that three of the Girondin leaders—Gensonné, Guadet, and Vergniaud—had secretly corresponded with the king on the eve of August 10—an accusation confirmed by the court painter Boze, who had served as intermediary. The three men in question admitted the facts, maintaining that they had acted only to save the fatherland in the midst of a dire military situation. However, coming scarcely a month after the revelations of Mirabeau's double dealing, the effect was devastating. The disclosure seemed to underline the Girondins' meager faith in the courage of the French national forces. It also strengthened the charge that members of the faction were closet royalists. The Montagnards recalled how the Girondins had changed their position on the king the previous summer and had only voted his suspension on August 10. Some wondered if Brissot and his friends were not trying once again to save Louis.[83]

The debates on the king's fate that so divided the Convention were also followed closely by virtually all social groups in the capital. The young Greek student Constantine Stamaty was amazed by the intensity with which views were expressed: "The trial of Louis XVI has captured everyone's attention. All citizens are freely expressing their opinion on this affair: some vote loudly for his condemnation; others, who are less severe, are inclined to see him banished." The theater owner Toussaint Mareux gave much the same analysis, although he believed that the majority of his friends and neighbors hoped the king's life would be spared.[84] The Parisian militants, however, continued to demand revenge against the king for the "massacre" of the patriots on August 10. On December 30 delegates from eighteen of the Paris sections petitioned the Convention for a prompt execution of the "tyrant." They were accompanied by several of those wounded in the August insurrection who had difficulty walking and by a group of women carrying pieces of bloodstained clothing worn by friends and loved ones killed that day in the courtyard of the Tuileries.[85]

Finally, on January 15, after endless shouting and posturing and mutual accusations between the two factions, the members of the Convention began formal voting. Although the opinions of many of the deputies were known through their speeches or pamphlets, no one was certain of the outcome. "The majority," wrote Dubreuil, "has still not revealed how they will vote; they keep their opinions to themselves."[86] There would be four separate votes over a five-day period, each with a formal roll-call, continuing day and night, almost without a break. In the end, despite the passionate pleas of the king and his lawyers, the deputies were overwhelmingly persuaded that Louis had committed treason. He was found guilty by a vote of 693 to 0 (with 26 others counted as abstentions). The second vote, on whether the Convention's decision on the king should be ratified by an appeal to the people, seemed far more uncertain. Some members of the Mountain were convinced that their opponents would win.[87] But ultimately a strong majority of 425 to 286—including virtually all of the Montagnards—rejected the appeal. Pinet was overjoyed that the Mountain had been supported by so many good republicans: "Tears of joy flowed from my eyes." For the Girondins, who had given the measure their overwhelming support, it was a crushing defeat, an unmitigated disaster.[88]

With the appeal to the people rejected, the deputies then turned to the king's punishment. In a marathon session lasting over twenty-four hours, every deputy went to the tribune, one by one, and pronounced his opinion and his vote. A few wandered on interminably as they attempted to justify their decisions for their colleagues and for themselves. Some merely pronounced the vote itself: "Death!" for example. But most spoke at least a few additional words to explain their position.[89] There were now only rare references to the king as a "monster," nor were there any assessments of the king as an "outlaw" within a framework of "natural law."[90] Most decisions were justified on the basis of carefully reasoned arguments, in which deputies reiterated their view that the king was guilty but in which they argued various possible punishments thought to be most appropriate. For some the decision was simple and clear-cut. In Louchet's view, the king was a "perjurer, a traitor, and an assassin of the French nation," and by the principle of equality proclaimed in the Declaration of Rights, he merited the punishment specified by the law. Others, while acknowledging his guilt, argued that it would be impolitic to execute him; that it would be better to imprison or exile him, and thus perhaps influence certain of the foreign powers to remain neutral in the war. Bordas from the Limousin concluded that any decision on the king "could not be a judicial act, but must of necessity be a political remedy, a measure strongly linked to national security." Others, however, like Blad, felt that such a strategy was hopeless, since the Great Powers would fight not to save the king, but to save the monarchy.[91]

A substantial number stressed the painful nature of the decision they were forced to make. Jean Debry recounted his "anxiety" over the quandary: "I agonized over the truth of the matter, and even as I stepped to the speaker's platform, I was still weighing the motives for my vote." Lebas also stressed, in a letter to his father, how difficult the choice had been: "My health was completely upset by the long deliberations of that terrible week." For Mercier "the consideration of this question gave me a fever for two days, as I passed through my mind several volumes of reflections. I became completely ill."[92]

When the vote had finally concluded on the evening of January 17, the tally was exceedingly close. Of the 721 who participated, 361 had voted purely and simply for death—a majority of one. Yet the decision was somewhat stronger if one also included—as the Convention ultimately did—those who voted for death, while urging the deputies to consider giving the king a reprieve. On the following day a number of Girondins, in an apparent last-ditch effort to save the king, took up the call for a reprieve and pushed through a fourth roll-call vote. But when the tally was reached at three o'clock in the morning on January 20, this motion too was rejected. It had only succeeded in further identifying the Girondins with support for the king.[93]

And so on the morning of January 21 "Louis Capet," as he was now called, was taken from the Temple to the vast Place de la Révolution, where an estimated 80,000 to 100,000 people had pushed their way in to watch the event.[94] A cold winter's rain was falling intermittently as the coach pulled up before the guillotine, toward the west side of the square. The king remained a few minutes with his confessor and then stepped out bravely toward the platform. He lost his composure, however, when the executioners took hold of him roughly to remove his coat, cut his hair, and tie his hands behind his back. Once atop the stairs, he began struggling with the executioners and managed briefly to break loose and attempted to speak to the crowd. But the leadership ordered the drum battery to resume, and his last words were heard only by those closest to him: "People, I die an innocent man. I pardon those who have decided my death. I pray God that my blood will not come down upon France." As he was pulled down onto the cutting block, frustrated and no doubt terrified by his fate, "he uttered a frightful scream, that was stifled only with the fall of the blade."[95]

At first the crowd remained stunned and silent, but soon great cries arose of "Long live the nation! Long live the Republic." One observer noted a contingent of schoolboys waving their hats in the air. The head executioner exercised his traditional prerogative of selling off locks of the victim's hair, while other enterprising salesmen peddled "cakes and pâté around the decapitated body." As he watched the extraordinary spectacle, Mercier could not help remembering Louis' coronation some seventeen years earlier, when he had been "hailed by the cheers of thousands and adored almost as a god, whose every word and gesture was taken as a command." "So now we have the end of this tragedy," wrote Stamaty. "What will be the result? Only God can say." Colson also remained anxious for the future. Yet he had no doubts that the story of the execution "would reverberate to the far corners of the earth and through the end of time."[96]

A Point of No Return?

In his annual New Year's message to his brother, Roubaud reflected back on the year 1792: "What year has ever lasted so long and been so filled with events as that which has just come to an end? What year will so go down in history? And now that it is finally over, should we cheer or lament?"[97]

Roubaud did not specify the events of the year that stood out most in his mind. But he must have reflected back on the previous summer, so filled with violence and terror. He must also have considered the first four months of the new National Convention. The abolition of the monarchy and the creation of a Republic were signal moments in the history of France, achievements that would have been scarcely conceivable just three years earlier. The weeks that followed had seen a remarkable series of victories over the combined forces of Prussia and Austria, with sweeping advances by the Republican armies through Germany, Belgium, Switzerland, and Savoy. The sudden turn of events had thrilled virtually all the patriots—including Roubaud himself—regardless of their political positions. It had led to an almost millenarian vision of the imminent liberation of the whole of Europe and the demise of kings and "tyrants" everywhere. It had also influenced their perception of their own king and the rhetoric deployed in describing him. It confirmed their suspicions that it was Louis' treachery that had previously prevented the French forces from advancing. It had thus been a significant factor—though not the only factor—in the decision aggressively to pursue the judgment of "Louis Capet."

The condemnation and execution of the king soon after the new year began was not the first case of capital punishment imposed by the government for a political crime. Several "counterrevolutionaries" had been guillotined in the summer of 1792 during the First Terror. But the killing of a king had a vastly greater symbolic import and emotional impact. The French monarch had long been a quasi-mythical figure. Even if most elites in the eighteenth century no longer believed he had supernatural powers, he had maintained the image of a father figure, an image that may even have been strengthened during the early Revolution—at least until the fiasco of his flight to Varennes.[98]

Many Conventionnels undoubtedly hoped—in the words of Jean Debry—"that the tomb of the tyrant will be that of our hatreds, that the death of the king will bring the death of all factions." But the execution of January 21 seemed only to exacerbate those animosities and make them more toxic. If one could justify the killing of a father-king, could one not justify the killing of almost anyone of whose evil intentions one had become convinced? The regicide of 1793 was "a traumatic and unprecedented shock," an event that would help obliterate the previously conceived threshold of political violence and extend the boundaries of what was morally acceptable and thinkable.[99] With the king eliminated, the conspiracy obsession would now focus more than ever before on potential enemies among the patriots themselves. Indeed, there was a certain truth in Mercier's observation: "It was because they had cut off the head of Louis XVI that they were emboldened to cut off those of their colleagues." The king's execution did not lead directly to the Terror. But a case can be made that when the Terror did come, his execution would be a major factor in its becoming a "killing Terror": not just the repression, imprisonment, or banishment of one's enemies, but their extermination.[100]

As fate would have it, another act of violence the day before the king's execution would further intensify the factional hatreds. On the evening of January 20 the deputy Le Peletier de Saint-Fargeau was paying his restaurant bill in the "Garden of Equality"—the former Palais Royal—when he was attacked by six men and stabbed in the chest with a saber. He died early the next morning, just seven hours before the king.[101] Although he came from one of the great Parisian families of the robe nobility, Le Peletier had transformed himself into a staunch Montagnard who had voted for the king's death. It was his reputation as a turncoat within the nobility that had drawn the ire of his royalist assailants. Deputies had long expressed fears that their lives might be in danger. The Girondins complained repeatedly of being threatened by people in the streets. The Montagnard deputies Robespierre, Drouet, and Chabot all claimed to have received death threats.[102] Now there was proof that no one's life was safe.

For a brief moment, the funeral for a fallen colleague seemed to bring the Convention together. Organized by the great painter Jacques-Louis David "in the style of the Ancients," it was the grandest ceremony that Guittard had ever witnessed. He was amazed to see the body carried through the streets in Roman fashion, face upward on a plank, the upper torso unclothed, so that the bloody wound "three fingers wide" was clearly visible. The burial was followed with speeches by Revolutionary officials and hymns intoned by several celebrated singers, all producing "a profoundly mournful and religious sight." At the end of the ceremony virtually the entire corps of deputies swore an oath "to extinguish all personal animosities and come together to save the fatherland." "May God will," wrote Couthon, "that we will not have sworn in vain."[103]

Yet the show of unity during Le Peletier's funeral was short-lived and superficial. Several Montagnards openly blamed the rival faction for the murder of their comrade. Amar would even mock the Girondins' fears of threats to their lives: "Now we see for which side the daggers were prepared." "The infamous cabal," wrote Lebas, "who tried to save Louis and bring back slavery" had openly incited the murder of Le Peletier by calling him outrageous names. But now, he predicted, "the reign of such rogues is over."[104]

10

The Crisis of '93

T HEY HAD tried and executed a king. They had buried one of their own, murdered by a counterrevolutionary only a few steps from their meeting hall. Now, in the weeks and months that followed, the members of the National Convention would endeavor to return to their original function of writing a new, republican constitution. In fact, however, the elimination of the "tyrant" would raise a host of new problems and passions within the Assembly and within the country, so that much of the year 1793 would remain extraordinarily troubled and turbulent.

Like the deputies of the first National Assembly the Conventionnels would go well beyond their role as a "constituent" body. They would craft new legislation to reorganize the army and the navy, to transform education, and to reform taxation and public welfare, and they would find themselves continually intervening in "executive" functions. In theory the day-to-day activities of the government were directed by a provisional executive council appointed by the Convention. But the ministers who sat on that council were frequently suspected of not working for the best interests of the nation or of being too closely linked to one of the two rival factions. The deputies felt compelled to watch and supervise their actions, so that the ministers were frequently subordinated to the relevant Convention committees. At the beginning of the year the Assembly had also improvised an umbrella "Committee of General Defense" to direct all aspects of the war.

In their service to the nation the deputies were compelled not only to attend daily sessions—which sometimes lasted twelve hours or more—but also to sit on committees, compose reports, pursue correspondence with their constituencies, and occasionally to journey out on missions to the provinces. Few could afford to hire secretaries or to bring their families to Paris. They complained of being "crushed with work," of leading an "exhausting life," of staying up half the night in the Convention and then going home to face the "necessary reading" of new bills and newspapers and of "letters sent to us from all over."[1]

There was also evidence of a subtle evolution in the culture of the deputies, expressive of the new democratic ideals and—at least for some of the representatives—of a self-conscious identification with the popular classes. Many had now taken to changing their mode of clothing. Brissot had long preached the importance of a greater simplicity in dress, of a repudiation of the luxurious standards of the Old Regime aristocracy, which had once been the arbiter of taste and fashion. "If a simplicity of style is a characteristic of the free man," he had written, "a simplicity of manners and especially of dress is even more so." Over the months since 1789, powdered wigs, knee breeches, silver-buckled shoes, and elegant vests had all been abandoned by many of the Revolutionaries, to be replaced by the long leather boots and rough coats they might have worn while hunting or tromping about in the fields. To be sure, not all of the radicals adopted the sartorial transformation, and Robespierre continued to wear his wig and knee breeches to the end of his life. But in a letter to his wife in late 1792 Pierre Campmas described the apparel of the Montagnard colleagues with whom he sat: "We now all look like beggars. Boots and threadbare clothing, such is our stylish costume." A certain number had also begun wearing the red "liberty cap," which had made a dramatic comeback in the Jacobin Club the previous October and which was now the head covering of choice for the common people.[2]

Another mark of the times was the increasing use of the familiar "tu" [you] pronoun when addressing one another—rather than the "vous" form, habitually used in polite society under the Old Regime. The concept had first been proposed in 1790 by leftist intellectuals—notably Louise Kéralio—but it seems to have become general practice in the Jacobin Club only after the overthrow of the monarchy. By the end of 1792 many of the sections began requiring the "tu" form, in the name of general equality, and Robespierre had adopted this mode of expression with many of his friends. The usage seems first to have made its appearance on the floor of the Convention in the context of insults. In February the deputy Thomas used the familiar form to rebuke Marat for one of his outbursts: "Shut up, you imbecile!" In May the Montagnard Philibert Simond would even address—and insult—the Girondin president of the Convention in this manner. By the fall of that year virtually all of our letter writers began using "tu" with their correspondents, and it was even adopted in the formal directives of Revolutionary ministers.[3]

The overall tone of the Convention, however, continued to be set by the terrible feud between Girondins and Montagnards. Though some deputies had hoped that the conclusion of the king's trial would bring an end to political divisions, in fact, the rivalries seemed only to intensify in the months that followed. The two parties, wrote Nicolas Ruault to his brother, "hate each other as bitterly as they hate the royalists." If you are a "Jacobin of longstanding"—as he considered himself to be—you dared not even speak in the presence of a Girondin, "without inciting a bitter reaction. What a frightful situation!"[4]

To Conquer the World

For a time, in the immediate aftermath of the king's execution, the Montagnards seemed in the ascendancy. They had been particularly successful in linking their rivals to royalism—since so many of the Girondins had opposed Louis' death—and they were now able to win the support of many in the nonaligned Plain.[5] Significantly, between early February and early April they prevailed in four of the five elections for president and almost all of those for secretary—in sharp contrast to the Girondins' domination before the king's trial.[6] From January through early April the Mountain was also able to win many of the most important debates in the Convention. They handily beat back a Girondin effort to reopen the question of the September Massacres—a scarcely veiled indictment of the Montagnard leadership. Theirs was the dominant voice in the reform and democratization of the military, and in February they succeeded in tabling a draft constitution written by the Girondin-dominated constitutional committee—a draft that they pictured as elitist and inaccessible to the general population.[7] A number of observers at the time commented on the Mountain's triumphs in the Assembly. "They are attracting so many votes from those in the Plain," wrote Jullien, "that I no longer fear obtaining a solid majority."[8]

The one issue on which the Girondins still exerted leadership during this period was the expansion of the war. It was, after all, a call for war that had brought them to prominence in 1792. As they found themselves on the defensive on domestic questions, they vigorously promoted a formal declaration of hostilities against England and Holland. To be sure, the evolution of the international situation had made conflict with Britain all but inevitable. The British government had been deeply disturbed by the abolition of the monarchy and by the spectacular military successes that brought the French to the frontier of Holland. In December 1792 they began calling up sailors and preparing their navy for military action.[9]

It was in response to this situation that Brissot's faction reactivated the war rhetoric they had used with such effect a year earlier and that they had flaunted again after the French victories in the fall. In early January the Girondin supporter Armand Kersaint, a veteran naval captain who had fought in the American Revolution, delivered a lengthy address castigating the British and their supposed neutrality. "In a war of kings against men," he proclaimed, "everyone is either a friend or an enemy." There could be nothing in between. And then he developed an extraordinary vision of the conquests France would achieve once they had settled with the English and their Dutch allies. They would move to liberate all the colonies held by the two powers: "Asia and America are calling us." And why not also bring the Revolution to Portugal and Brazil? On January 12 Brissot himself expounded a similar message. In money, ships, and men the French had a clear advantage over Britain, which was now, he claimed, "the mere shadow of a great power," deeply in debt from its previous wars. War with England would also provide the occasion to bring the blessings of freedom to India.[10]

The final impulse for war came when the execution of Louis XVI prompted the British court to expel the French envoy in London. Armed with this "insult" to the French nation, the Girondins stepped forward to demand a formal declaration of war. On February 1 Brissot and two of his friends all pressed the issue. When someone tried to raise another question, Louvet shouted out: "War, war, the only subject is war!" Brissot rehearsed much the same logic and rhetoric as in 1792: it was not for France alone that they must now do battle with England and Holland, but for the liberation of all Europe from the hands of tyrants. Yet if the principal initiative for the expansion of the war came from the Girondins, it was backed by all deputies from all factions, and the declaration passed unanimously. Several of the Montagnards followed up with strong prowar affirmations.[11]

Whatever the initial causes of the conflict in the minds of the deputies, few seemed to doubt that France would soon triumph over the whole of Europe. Throughout the weeks of February and early March, in letters both to patriotic societies and to family and personal friends, they predicted the rapid and overwhelming victory of the armies of the Republic. There was a remarkable optimism, a veritable exaltation among Girondins, Montagnards, and members of the Plain alike. "I cannot doubt," wrote the Montagnard stalwart Georges Couthon, "that if we firmly desire it, we can liberate Europe in six months and purge the earth of all tyrants." Brissot's friend Bancal fully agreed and predicted the coming conflict would be a war to end wars: "the last that will ever bring grief to Europe." The young merchant from the Gironde, Boyer-Fonfrède, recognized the challenges that lay ahead, but he was convinced of ultimate victory: "An end to repose, an end to peace, an end to all feeble fears. We reject any thought of compromise. We will save the nation," he concluded, "as long as we never look back."[12]

It was in this same mood of unbounded confidence that the deputies now began annexing almost all of the territories previously occupied by their victorious armies. In each case they did so only after the local citizenry—or at least a portion of that citizenry—formally requested annexation. Yet by the first week of March Belgium, Nice, the Right Bank of the Rhine, some areas of Switzerland, and the formerly independent enclave of Salm in Loraine had all been slated for incorporation into France.[13] Jacques Pinet was ecstatic: henceforth the French and the Belgians "are all one. There will be no more distinctions between them, and these two nations will form but a single people of brothers and of friends." Monestier was already thinking about the name they would give to a new French department in Belgium, deciding that "Plaines du Nord" would be most suitable.[14] It was in this same mood of undoubting confidence that on March 7 the Convention unanimously declared war on Spain: "One more enemy for France," declared Barère, "will bring one more triumph for liberty."[15]

Of course, a war to be pursued against the whole of Europe along all of France's frontiers and on the high seas would obviously demand more troops and perhaps a reorganized army and navy. The deputies were well aware, moreover, that many of the volunteers of 1792 had only enrolled for a limited period and had now left the front and returned home. Yet they felt optimistic that most such men would take up arms once again as soon as they realized the nation's need for new sacrifices. In mid-February the former army officer Dubois-Crancé elaborated a comprehensive plan for a reorganized military. After careful calculations he determined that France would need some 300,000 additional soldiers for a multifront war. A decree was passed establishing quotas for each department, to be apportioned among the individual towns and villages. All those individuals holding public functions or involved in war production were excused, a provision that potentially exempted much of the middle class. The Convention avoided instituting conscription—which, as Pinet explained, "is not appropriate for a free people"—but the ultimate determination of the mode of recruitment was left to local authorities.[16]

In general, they assumed that new troops could be raised without difficulty. They took note of France's large population, with a greater supply of young men than any other nation of Europe, and they recalled the enthusiasm of the summer of 1792, when national guardsmen and other volunteers from towns all around France had rushed to join up and confront the Prussians. "We are hopeful," confided Claude-Antoine Blad to his friends in Brest, "that the cry of the 'fatherland in peril' will bring to our aid far more defenders than we have asked for." Prudhomme strongly agreed: if they were to resist the whole of Europe leagued against them, they would need several hundred thousand more men. "We will have them," he wrote. "They will soon march off." For the volunteers would know that they were fighting for all the patriots of Europe.[17]

But could young Frenchmen summon up the same enthusiasm to fight for all the patriots of Europe as they had when their homeland had been invaded and when Paris was in imminent danger of falling? Moreover, many of the most fervent young patriots—townsmen for the most part—were already serving in the armies. If the recruitment were to be successful, there must be a considerable number of new enlistees from the lower and lower-middle classes and, above all, from the mass of the peasantry. And as the Convention would discover to its distress, a great many Frenchmen, and especially a great many peasants, were not at all ready to fight.

The *Enragés* and the Feminist Moment

As the deputies of the National Convention set their sights on conquering the world, the political culture of militant Paris continued to evolve, partly through interaction with the Convention, partly through its own internal dynamics. Radical militants from the middle-class elites—meeting in the Cordeliers Club and the Jacobin Club and the sectional committees of the city—continued to play a major leadership role, as they had since the beginning of the Revolution. With the advent of universal male suffrage, however, they were joined by ever-greater numbers from the popular classes. The period saw the arrival of a new generation of street-savvy militants, all jostling for power and influence. Those individuals from the working classes gifted with oratorical skills and organizational abilities and possessed with the ambition to lead were soon competing with one another for prominence on a stage of political activism never before open to them. As they encountered one another in cafés and street-corner debates, as they contended in the meetings of the sections and the national guard, there was an inflation of rhetoric, of coarse invectives and mutual defamation, appealing to the fears and animosities of the social groups over whom they sought ascendancy.[18]

In the competition for power and political prestige, some local leaders pushed policies that were ever more radical.[19] There were demands for the tight control of food prices and the creation of an imposed "maximum" on basic consumer commodities. There was talk of heavily taxing or even seizing the goods and property of the rich and redistributing them to the poor. There was also a tendency to promote violence as a solution for a range of political and economic difficulties, stimulating and agitating the culture of suspicion through attacks on an array of potential conspirators and evildoers. In this, they played on the penchant for violence so prevalent among lower-middle-class males before the Revolution. The most extreme came to be called and to call themselves the *enragés* (the "furious"). They proudly donned the red "liberty cap," and a substantial number now began sprouting moustaches, rarely seen in France at the end of the Old Regime, as an additional sign of virile militancy. During the popular insurrection at the beginning of June, deputies would refer to "the men with moustaches" who were controlling the exits to the Convention hall. However, the group never held a single coherent position, and they commonly competed with one another as much as with those who were less radical.

As the enragés and sans-culottes became ever more prominent in neighborhood politics, many middle-class militant radicals came also to adopt their clothing and their rough-and-ready language and accents. The journalist and municipal official Jacques Hébert, entirely middle class in his origins, won his reputation by appropriating the crude and colorful lower-class vernacular for his newspaper, supposedly written by the stove maker "Father Duchesne." By the middle of 1793 many of the most radical deputies in the Convention also adopted the designation of sans-culottes and began tilting toward the popular classes in their dress and language and their use of the familiar "tu."

Since at least 1791, the radicals had idealized "the people," viewing them as the heart and soul of the Revolution. Now they began emphasizing the corollary: that a great many rich were "egoists," more preoccupied with their personal wealth than with the public good and the salvation of the nation, and perhaps attracted to various insidious conspiracies. The "rich bourgeois" were increasingly lumped together with the refractory priests and the aristocrats in the rogues' gallery of enemies of the Revolution. "Egotism, self-interest, and corruption," wrote Rosalie Jullien, "the three monsters common to aristocrats, priests, and the rich, have always preyed upon the poor people."[20] The sans-culotte leader François Hanriot—the son of a peasant from the outskirts of Paris who had risen to prominence through his role in the national guard—put it bluntly in a speech before his section: "The rich have made the laws for long enough. Now it's time for the poor to make them, so that equality will reign between rich and poor."[21]

Throughout the first months of 1793, Parisian militants continued their efforts to exert pressure on the Convention—as they had earlier attempted to influence debates in the Legislative Assembly—with demonstrations in the streets and near the assembly hall, with petitions by the sections read before the deputies, with occasional marches through the hall itself, whenever they could obtain the representatives' permission. The recent changes in the organization of the national guard gave the Parisians even greater potential influence. Since the late summer of 1792, guard units had been made to coincide with the sections and were effectively placed under the control of the section leaders.[22] Thus, in the various mass demonstrations of the sections before the Convention in the spring and summer of 1793, many of the men would come armed with pikes and muskets. At the end of May and the beginning of June the Parisians would impose their will on the Convention in part through the direct threat of armed intervention.

The first months of 1793 also saw an ever-more-active participation of women.[23] To be sure, women had closely followed and participated in Revolutionary events from the very beginning. But now a significant number from both the middle and the popular classes were asserting their right to take part in national politics on a continuous basis. In part, this mobilization was linked to the ever-increasing price of grain and to women's traditional role as guardians of the food supply. They would be the primary participants in a wave of Parisian riots in February 1793, protesting the high cost not only of bread but of other commodities considered essential to their lives, including coffee, sugar, candles, and—for the large numbers of washerwomen—soap and soda. According to Guittard, the women had first attempted to work through the political system, presenting their grievances to their sections and to the Convention. It was only after no one listened to them that they announced they were ready to act on their own. Between February 25 and 27 the women, soon joined by large numbers of men, confronted bakers and grocers throughout the city, threatening them with lynchings unless they lowered their prices. Sometimes they simply seized goods, leaving behind a payment they thought was fair. Far more women may well have been involved in the riots of February 1793 than in the march on Versailles in October 1789.[24]

Another major impetus for women's politicization was the growing number of Parisian families whose male breadwinners had left to fight on the frontiers. Women had been led to believe that when their husbands and brothers went off to war, the Convention would help provide for their families. When this did not happen, groups of women mobilized to insist on their "rights," often demanding a tax on the rich to subsidize their family economy. Some women also used the departure of so many men as a justification for their own greater role in politics. They announced that henceforth there was to be a division of labor. They would concentrate on internal enemies, while the men took charge of fighting the foreign enemies. By the spring many had become active in their sectional meetings, regularly demanding the arrest of the Girondins and other "conspirators" in their midst.[25]

In early May some of the most militant among them formed a new society of "Revolutionary Republican Women." Women had long been attending male clubs—usually sitting in the balconies—and had even formed clubs of their own. But the new society was substantially more radical than those that had preceded it. The members closely linked themselves to the enragés and the Cordeliers Club, and they adopted many of their most radical proposals. They also demanded the creation of an armed company of women to serve in the national guard. Soon they could be seen marching through the streets of Paris, shouting slogans and carrying banners marked with the eye of vigilance, a few even dressed as Amazons. Guittard was amazed to see a group of some 200 to 300, parading through the city and its suburbs, "beating a drum and carrying a sort of flag," some wearing "helmets like soldiers or the police." Soon he reported that women were regularly taking part in local politics. When his section marched to the Convention to present a petition, there were so many women that they could walk three by three, arms linked, with a woman between every two men.[26]

The remarkable integration of women into the sectional life of the city invariably led to an expanded vision of their place in the new political culture and in society in general. How many of them knew of the "Declaration of the Rights of Women" by Olympe de Gouge would be difficult to say. De Gouge was in fact a known royalist, who would not have been appreciated by the "Republican Women," and Rosalie Jullien never mentioned her. Yet comments in Jullien's correspondence help us assess the evolving political consciousness of some middle-class women. In 1792 Jullien had remained only an observer of events, reporting on the insurrection of August 10 from her window or as she walked through the streets with her youngest son. Only occasionally had she attended the National Assembly or the Jacobin Club. By the spring of 1793, however, she had become a "regular" in the Convention galleries, watching, taking notes for her older son who was away in the provinces, and cheering or shouting out comments on the proceedings she witnessed.

In the beginning she had come primarily to support her Montagnard husband, who had just been elected to the Convention, attending from her "desire to see and be near my deputy [her husband], . . . my love for the public good being joined with my love for him."[27] Yet over time her presence came to mean something more. On one occasion, an offhand comment over the dinner table by her husband's colleague Bertrand Barère compelled her to join in the conversation. Barère had asserted that the women of Paris loved neither the Revolution nor the Republic. But Rosalie quickly responded that "all the women I know are patriots and republicans. They support the Revolution, even if they don't care for all its noise and confusion." Barère's mistake was in thinking only of aristocratic women. In fact, she declared, "I am much happier with all that comes from my sex than with all that comes from yours. You men possess everything and you are too proud of your advantages; while we women, the sensible and loving portion of humanity and the soul of all societies, are often forgotten." There were already many women, she believed, who were true Spartans and Romans, and who were better able to attain republican virtues than the men.[28]

Jullien's active presence in the Convention underlines another element in the evolution of Parisian politics during the period: the ever-more-vocal intervention in the debates of the audience, women and men, sitting in the balcony galleries. The Convention's formal rules of September 1792 forbade any commentaries from the public, and at first the deputies had made a concerted effort to keep the spectators quiet, imposing a policy that was generally maintained into early 1793. When the audience openly cheered Brissot's speech on February 1, calling for a declaration of war, it was still considered unusual. One deputy shouted out at the time, "The galleries should be praised in this instance for breaking the rules." The next day they were again allowed to cheer when Nice was officially annexed to France.[29] Thereafter, the spectators were generally given free rein to express their views, particularly during the weeks when the Montagnards dominated the presidency. For it soon became clear that the vast majority of those in attendance favored the Mountain.

The Girondins angrily protested the "tyranny" of the galleries. According to Blad, during the Convention's mid-April roll-call on a proposed indictment of Marat, every individual who voted in favor was covered with hisses and even threatened by the galleries.[30] There was some hope on the part of Brissot and his friends that the larger hall into which the Convention moved in early May—erected in the Tuileries Palace where the king had once lived—would change the situation. The balconies were now farther away and more clearly delimited by columns. There was also an attempt to reserve the balconies closest to the speaker for visitors from the departments, who were thought to support the Girondins and who were provided with special admission passes. Jullien sized up the situation on the first day, when she saw large numbers of "aristocrats" surrounding her in one of the new balconies. If the rules were enforced, she thought, "the smaller galleries would soon be the lair of counterrevolutionaries and the lackeys of the Brissotins." However, members of the Revolutionary Republican Women soon positioned themselves at the doors to the galleries and refused entry to anyone presenting a pass, arguing that such a procedure was opposed to the principle of equality. A few days later, when a young man with a pass somehow worked his way inside, the women raised such a ruckus that debates in the Convention were interrupted until the individual was escorted out.[31]

In the face of Girondin attacks on the galleries, Jullien made a passionate defense of their role in the Revolution: those in attendance did nothing more than "to applaud the orators who support the people and indicate their indignation against their adversaries." In this, moreover, they were simply following "the example set by the legislators themselves, who express their approval and disapproval in the same manner." Indeed, she argued, the galleries were generally calmer and less agitated than the "senate." In her view, the galleries had now become an essential part of the political process: "a reef against which all the plots of our enemies are shattered." "They are made up of the purest and finest patriots of the Republic."[32]

Initially, the new recruitment law of February had elicited strong support from the Parisian militants and popular classes. There were reports that the majority of the sections provided far more than their quotas, some even more than double the contingent specified in the law. And once again, as in the summer of '92, battalions of young men paraded boisterously through the hall of the Convention, cheering and singing patriotic songs, before heading for the front.[33] The popular classes were angered, however, that many middle- and upper-class men refused to volunteer. Some among the working classes announced that they would not leave unless all social groups were called upon, or at least until heavy taxes were levied on the wealthy to help pay for the war effort. The rich, reported Jullien, have no desire to leave for the war and "the brave sans-culottes don't want to leave without them." By April and May the issue began to create fissures among the sections, exacerbating a division between moderates and radicals that the Girondins would do their best to exploit. Ruault told his brother of groups of well-dressed individuals who assembled in large numbers on the Champs-Elysées "not to enlist but to make motions and protest." There were even rumors that some of the individuals in question had shouted "down with the Republic." Such a reaction only confirmed Jullien's suspicions that the upper classes were closet counterrevolutionaries.[34] The divisions in Paris between rich and poor within the various sections of the city would continue throughout the summer.

The Barbarism of Civil War

If the recruitment issue was the cause of dissension in Paris, it would soon engender full-scale insurrection in many of the provinces. By 1793 local politics had probably become even more complex and diverse than in any previous period of the Revolution. The tendency toward decentralization had been reinforced by the factional splits in the Convention that saw deputies questioning the policies and even the loyalty of their colleagues and aggressively condemning their rivals in letters home. There were many instances of departments elaborating or expanding or rejecting laws passed by the Convention, of districts refusing to obey orders from the departments, of small towns and villages rejecting or ignoring directives from both. Administrators at every level could drag their feet and put off as long as possible the implementation of decrees that they knew were unpopular. Yet there were endless variations in the patterns of rivalries from department to department, from town to town, so that it is extraordinarily difficult to generalize.

During the first months of the Convention, turmoil in the provinces was generated by a variety of problems. A new cycle of food riots broke out in the autumn in many parts of France, notably in Maine, Normandy, Touraine, and portions of the south.[35] Religious disturbance also persisted through early 1793, notably in regions with large numbers of refractory parish priests. The nonjurors had sometimes been allowed to remain at their posts well into 1792. Yet with the deportation law of August 1792, they were forced out or arrested almost everywhere, much to the unhappiness of the countrypeople.[36] The situation was particularly tense in much of western France, where the countryside was often massively refractory but where town elites were ferociously anticlerical. Feelings were inflamed when town administrators dispatched national guards into the villages, arresting refractory priests and badly treating the villagers who supported them.[37] By early 1793 an administrator of the district of Les Sables-d'Olonne in the department of Vendée was despondent over the evolution of the situation: "The great majority of the people," he wrote, "is entirely corrupted by fanaticism. They complain that for them the Revolution has been a long series of injustices."[38]

The Convention's decree of February, calling for 300,000 new recruits, would ignite one of the most violent waves of insurrections in the countryside since 1789.[39] By 1793 the most politically committed young men, the great majority coming from the towns, had already left for the army, and a substantial proportion of the militants remaining were serving in positions that gave them immunity from serving. Moreover, in setting local quotas, the law took into account past recruitment history, so that departments that had previously shown the least enthusiasm were now asked for the largest contingents. Paris itself and a number of the larger towns easily met their quotas through volunteers.[40] But elsewhere, in rural regions far from Paris and far from the front, new volunteers were extremely rare. In numerous villages not a single young man stepped forward. Local leaders were forced to use various forms of persuasion and coercion, from drawing lots to holding votes on who should be designated to go. Unfortunately, as Blad surmised, it was only too easy for people to link the current recruitment decree to the hated conscription laws of the Old Regime. At the beginning of March the Convention was already aware of the disappointing response, which often appeared "desperately slow."[41]

In the eyes of many rural citizens, the decrees of the Revolution had taken away their priests, killed their king, and passed a variety of laws that scarcely diminished or even raised their taxes, laws that had often been enforced by rough and arrogant urban national guardsmen arriving from the towns. Now the Convention wanted to send them off to die for such a Revolution, in a war that was hundreds of kilometers from their homes—while many of those who had started and supported the war remained in their towns to count the taxes and administer. As one rebel leader would explain, "the conscription law brought an explosion of indignation among people already long unhappy with the wrongs they had suffered under the Revolution."[42]

Soon there were reports of riots in almost every corner of the country: in Alsace and Lorraine, in Franche-Comté, in Burgundy, in Auvergne, in Languedoc, and even in a number of generally patriotic towns like Grenoble, Bordeaux, Angoulême, Orléans, and Toulouse. The opposition was sometimes accompanied by acts of defiance, shouting slogans against the Republic or cutting down liberty trees.[43] While most of these protests were short-lived and quickly repressed by national guardsmen from the towns, a veritable insurrection arose across a large swathe of provinces in western France, both north and south of the Loire River. The uprisings began everywhere at about the same time, in the second week of March, just as recruitment laws were beginning to be applied. Soon panic-stricken reports were pouring into the Convention from towns besieged by countrypeople in Brittany, Normandy, Anjou, Maine, and western Poitou. Numerous towns, including the great port cities of Brest and Nantes, were entirely cut off and lost all contact with Paris. Stunned deputies on mission in the Breton capital of Rennes reported that "nearly the entire countryside is marching [against us] in battle formation, led by talented leaders."[44]

The ultimate cause of the massive uprisings in the west has been the subject of endless debate. It is clear that a certain number of local nobles and returning emigrants had been active in the area for over a year, hopeful of fomenting just such an uprising. Several of those who would soon lead the peasant armies in the region had been present in the Tuileries Palace, attempting to save the king on August 10.[45] But in most cases, it was the countrypeople themselves who took the initiative in recruiting nobles to lead them. Many of the peasants in question were sharecroppers whose rents had actually been raised by the Revolution. The new tax laws allowed landowners to raise such rents, since they no longer had to pay the tithes and seigneurial dues and the value of the rental property, they argued, had now increased.[46]

The central factor, however, uniting virtually all of the rebels in the west, was anger and indignation over the Revolution's religious policies. Throughout the region the overwhelming proportion of the parish clergy had refused the oath of loyalty to the Constitution. There can be no doubt that many local curés, like Yves-Michel Marchais of La Chapelle-du-Genêt, had dealt harshly with the Revolution in their sermons and in the confessional and that they continued to venerate the "late king of blessed and beloved memory." Most such priests abhorred violence and would never have preached open rebellion.[47] However, much of western France was characterized by a rather different religious tradition among the laity. A relatively recent revitalization movement seems to have created a particularly intense religious culture. The rich pilgrimage and processional tradition in the region was placed under attack when Revolutionary authorities closed down rural chapels. Curé Marchais was surprised by the vigorous popular insistence on pilgrimages early in the Revolution. The expulsion of the large numbers of refractory clergymen in the area only further stoked popular anger. In any case, observers reported that religion was the rallying cry in 1793 almost everywhere: "We want our priests back! We are free. We do not want to go to war, but if we must die, let them kill us in our own homes and fields."[48] Many rebels in the west had clearly been influenced by the ideals of 1789. They were quick to claim the right of self-determination and to view their uprising as a form of revolution. "Your so-called republican government," wrote a leader of the Vendée insurrection, "adopted the principle that sovereignty resides essentially in the people. Well! This sovereign people desires a king and the free exercise of their religion. This has always been their will, and you have despised it. They have all risen up to forcefully oppose tyranny."[49]

Many of the rebels in the west were thus motivated by a veritable rage against the Revolution and the Revolutionaries. The majority of the towns under siege were able to fend off attacks by the countrypeople. But those that did fall could be subjected to fierce reprisals, even massacres, especially if the patriots had defended themselves and had killed some of the rebels in a firefight. Dozens and sometimes hundreds of patriots were killed in the small towns of Montaigu, Mortagne, Machecoul, and elsewhere. Revolutionary administrators, judges, Constitutional priests, and patriot national guardsmen could all be cut down where they were captured or killed afterward in makeshift prisons. Curé François Chevallier, from a small Breton parish on the edge of the Vendée, was saddened by the violence of his parishioners—even though he had supported their cause and would serve as a chaplain to their armies. It was in the small town of Machecoul, he wrote in his memoirs, "that the horrors began and were perpetuated, a carnage that one could scarcely have imagined." He had been appalled to hear his own villagers declare "that it was essential and indispensable for peace that no patriot should be left in France." "The people," he concluded, "throwing off their chains and their silence, fell upon the patriots with unbelievable fury."[50]

Thus from the beginning—even before the Convention had learned of the events—the insurrections in the west led to a brutal civil war between the patriot "Blues"—overwhelmingly urban—and the insurgent "Whites"— massively from the countryside: between fervent supporters on both sides, fighting to the death with terrible ferocity.[51] Patriot officials sent vivid descriptions of struggling for their lives and for what they believed, as they were besieged by peasant armies equally motivated by their own passionate convictions. The fears and hatreds were fueled on both sides, moreover, by rapidly spreading rumors. Some Republicans, terrified by the overwhelming numbers they faced and aware of the massacres already committed by the rebels, fled in panic to the larger towns, where they sometimes exaggerated the atrocities to explain and justify their fright.[52]

Soon patriot national guardsmen and other volunteers from all the surrounding regions—Limousin, eastern Poitou, Bordeaux, Tours—were marching toward the west, coming to the aid of their beleaguered brothers but also fearful that the rebels might decide to move against their own towns. And from the beginning, the patriots were prepared to reply in kind to the violence of the insurgents. "Citizens," declared the local Republican military commanders in March, "you have allowed yourselves to be led astray by your priests and your nobles. . . . We regret that we must now shed your blood; but if you persist, we will exterminate you to the last individual."⁵³ As early as March 13, the besieged city of Nantes created a revolutionary tribunal on its own initiative to try captured rebels, for which no quarter was to be given. In the end, the insurgent countrypeople—including hundreds of women and children—would be killed in far greater numbers than the patriots. But the weighing and comparing of mutual atrocities can in no way diminish the horrors perpetrated inexorably by both sides in the tragic civil war that ensued. As Curé Chevallier described it, Frenchmen on both sides, "turning their fury and rage against one another . . . ultimately forgot that they were human beings."⁵⁴

In the end the patriots succeeded in repressing the March recruitment riots in most of the west north of the Loire. Even in Brittany, which initially seemed to have the worst uprisings of any province, Revolutionary officials and national guardsmen were able to defeat the rebels and execute many of their leaders.⁵⁵ But south of the Loire, in the region soon known as the "Vendée"—in Western Poitou, southern Brittany, and Anjou—the Republicans were anything but successful. It was a zone with a sparser distribution of towns—compared to the areas north of the Loire—and thus with substantially smaller contingents of patriot national guardsmen. Perhaps more important, there were far fewer regular troops stationed in the region.⁵⁶ Rapidly organized by local nobles with military skill and by one or two exceptional commoners, the Vendée armies were soon winning victory after victory: marching into battle with banners depicting religious symbols of the cross and the sacred heart; or ambushing Republican armies marching between hedgerows—hedges filled with stones and trees that were more like walls. Thereafter and for the next several years, the Vendée rebellion became the symbol for the Republicans of all that was most fearful and most hateful in the internal counterrevolution.

The March Crisis and the Structuring of the Terror

The civil wars in the provinces, the turmoil and radical critiques of the Parisian enragés, and the dramatic reversals on the war front would be the backdrop for a crisis and near panic in the Convention in the course of March and April. The crisis would see the rapid creation of a whole range of repressive institutions in reaction to the threats. It would also reinforce the terrible recriminations and suspicions among the Revolutionaries themselves. The disastrous news received by the deputies during this period would so crowd together that it is often difficult to determine who in Paris knew what and when and the extent to which specific events or rather the general fear and uncertainty influenced the decisions taken. But there can be no doubt that the clustering of unanticipated events directly threatening the very survival of the Revolution from without and within—just at a moment when the political leadership had been so optimistic—led directly to the improvisation of measures that would form the basis for the regime of the Terror.

It was on the war front in the north that the series of disasters began. The spectacular French sweep across Belgium the previous November had been a central factor stimulating dreams for the expansion of the Revolution. From this base, Revolutionaries hoped to move on into Holland and then, perhaps, across all of Germany. In retrospect the situation in Belgium was already far from reassuring at the end of 1792, even though the Convention, in the euphoria of the moment, gave it little attention. General Dumouriez had moved rapidly to impose Revolutionary institutions on the former Austrian Lowlands, and was reinforced in his efforts by the return of homegrown Belgian revolutionaries who had fled their country in 1788. The attempted sale of church land and the confiscation of sacred vessels for the French war coffers had rapidly disenchanted many Catholics and clergymen, and riots had broken out in Belgian cities during the winter. The French army had also experienced serious difficulties in its provisioning: partly since the system inherited from the Old Regime was so cumbersome, partly since the army had moved forward so rapidly. Perhaps most serious, a segment of the French forces had melted away during the winter, as volunteers, led to believe that they had only enrolled for the fall campaign, now began returning home. The return of so many volunteers had been a major reason for the recruitment laws of February.[57]

Just as the French were invading Holland in what they expected to be a rapid victory, news began seeping back to Paris of a new offensive by the Austrians. On March 1 France's defensive right flank near Aix-la-Chapelle was assaulted in a massive counterattack, and it was soon in danger of collapsing. Much to his anger, Dumouriez was ordered to pull back from Holland and attempt to rally his troops. He was then defeated in a close battle near Neerwinden, and the French army found itself reeling back toward its own frontier. To make the situation worse, the Austrian offensive was coordinated with a Prussian attack on the Republican army in Germany, and here too the French were forced into full retreat.[58]

At first the deputies seemed to ignore the reports. They had great difficulty in setting aside their vision of the inevitable triumph of the forces of liberty. Blad described the initial news from the north as a "small setback" that would soon be overcome. The Convention blithely proceeded to declare war on Spain, even as ever more disturbing dispatches were arriving from Belgium.[59] Only after the deputies Danton and Delacroix had returned from the front on March 8 and presented a report was the Convention confronted with the full gravity of the situation. Pinet was stunned. "The disorder and fear in Belgium," he wrote, "is extreme. It is with great sorrow that we heard the disastrous account." And scarcely two weeks later came word of the calamitous defeat at Neerwinden and the French evacuation of Belgium. The predicament seemed all the more painful in that the Convention had only just annexed its northern neighbor. The argument was made that it was the territory of France itself that had now been overrun. "We must have revenge!" cried Fonfrède. "Revenge for the attack that our brothers have suffered. We must take back Liège which belongs to us, and Aix-la-Chapelle, which is ours."[60]

But almost simultaneously with news of the Neerwinden defeat, reports began arriving of the recruitment riots in the provinces. During the terrible weeks of late March, the Convention was bombarded daily with letters concerning both the war disasters and the internal insurrections. Speeches proposing emergency measures to shore up the northern frontier were interrupted by letters from the provinces with desperate calls for aid against insurrections that were seemingly breaking out everywhere at once. Panic-stricken correspondence poured in from towns all over Brittany, all said to be besieged by "brigands."[61] Those deputies who came from the affected departments were particularly distressed, and several wrote desperate letters to loved ones in the area. Etienne Chaillon, who lived in a small town to the west of Nantes, learned only after several days of anxiety that his oldest daughter had succeeded in escaping with his other children across the Loire River to Paimboeuf. But Paimboeuf had also been besieged for a time, and the daughter reported rumors she had heard of terrible massacres and pillaging throughout the area. "By now all my furniture and personal effects have probably been lost," he wrote. But at least "my children are out of danger." And since it was at first impossible to assess the extent of the uprisings, many other deputies with friends and loved ones near the affected region were also beset by apprehension. When

Dubrueil heard that rebels had taken Parthenay, he immediately feared for his own family living just south of the insurrection zone. Campmas even worried that the uprisings might spread as far as the Massif Central, several hundred kilometers away, and he urged his family to flee to Albi.[62]

Indeed, from March through May 1793 no single issue more preoccupied the deputies in their letters home than the internal counterrevolutions. They were horrified when one of their colleagues on mission in Orléans, Léonard Bourdon, was beaten and nearly killed in an antirecruitment riot.[63] And virtually without exception, they were convinced that it was all a coordinated plot. Surely it was not simply a coincidence that the internal uprisings occurred just when the Austrians and Prussians were attacking in the north. How else could one explain that the recruitment riots seemed to have all broken out at once? To a man they were persuaded of the role of the nobles and the refractory clergy in leading the revolts. What other explanation was there for the revolt of a peasantry who, they believed, had gained so much from the Revolution? Both Girondin and Montagnard deputies were in agreement: the recruitment issue "was merely a pretext to disguise this great plot." "The internal and external enemies undoubtedly combined to hatch a conspiracy against liberty and the Convention."[64]

Coming on the heels of these multiple disasters and perhaps even more shattering was the betrayal at the end of March of the Revolution's commander in chief on the northern front, Dumouriez. Although some Parisian militants had already put in doubt the general's loyalty, both Girondins and Montagnards had rejected such accusations out of hand. "The whole Convention," wrote Pinet on March 13, "was indignant."[65] Concern was aroused, however, when Dumouriez sent a blistering attack against the Jacobins and the Convention itself, blaming them for not sufficiently supporting the army and for all the war reversals. Eventually, after the French defeat at Neerwinden, the Convention felt compelled to send four deputies and the Minister of Defense to confront the general. By now, however, Dumouriez had made a pact with the Austrian army, and when the commissioners arrived, he had them all arrested—and shipped off to an Austrian prison, where they would remain for several years. He then announced his plan to turn the French army around, march on Paris, dismiss the Convention, and place Louis XVI's young son on the throne.[66]

In fact, the Republican soldiers, intensely patriotic volunteers always suspicious of their officers, would reject Dumouriez's orders, and the general would be forced to flee across the lines—much as Lafayette had done just six months earlier. But the effect on the Revolutionaries was devastating. After the betrayal of Louis XVI in his failed flight to Varennes; after the once-idolized Lafayette had attempted to betray the nation; after the discovery that the great Mirabeau had been playing a double game, the treason of a general in whom they had placed so much trust seemed an overwhelming calamity. Deputies from every faction wrote back heartfelt letters to their friends and constituencies. Blad could scarcely believe that "the conqueror of Valmy and of Jemappe, whom the Republic had only recently honored for his triumphs, was only a vile rogue." Pinet was mortified that he had allowed himself to be so deceived and had not penetrated this new conspiracy. Where would the treachery stop? Whom could they ever trust? It was proof positive that they were surrounded by traitors.[67]

Until it was clear that the soldiers had refused to follow their general, a near panic swept through the streets of Paris. Soon, however, the fear turned to anger and a desire for revenge. "People are furious," wrote Colson, "against the black treason, so deep and cleverly covered up, carried out in league with our enemies." The gates of the city were closed, surveillance committees sat around the clock, and many individuals were ordered arrested during domiciliary visits. Rumors swirled of plots to murder the deputies, producing an atmosphere not unlike that experienced by the Legislative Assembly the previous May. The Convention went into permanent session, with some representatives remaining in the hall around the clock. For Prudhomme, the danger had never seemed so great. Though he had recently been suspicious of the crowds, there now seemed no choice but to fall back on "the people": "Brave sans-culottes! You are now the only ones we can truly count on."[68]

In this climate of anguish and uncertainty, as everything seemed progressively to collapse around them, the Convention cobbled together a series of emergency measures, improvised and modified as each new disaster emerged. In the second week of March, the first task was to reinforce the army on the northern front and accelerate military recruitment. Since the crisis of Varennes, the assemblies had occasionally sent a few of their members on various ad hoc missions. But now the deputies resolved systematically to dispatch commissioners—soon dubbed "representatives on mission to the people"—to all of the departments in order to promote recruitment. A few weeks later a second wave of commissioners was sent out to oversee the various armies. With the explosion of recruitment riots—sometimes before, sometimes after the representatives arrived in the provinces—they

The representative on mission, Jean-Baptiste Milhaud, in a painting by the school of Jacques-Louis David. Milhaud, an ex-military man and Montagnard deputy, proudly wears the uniform designed by David, with a tricolored hat band, feathers, and sash across his chest. Note also the moustache and long, unpowdered hair, typical of the militant Revolutionaries. © Coll. Musée de la Révolution française, Domaine de Vizille, MRF D 1991.14.

were granted powers to repress the "brigands," as well as to raise local armies and requisition war supplies. Soon they had acquired all but dictatorial control over local administrators, including the authority to purge officials "for reasons of public security." Dressed in dramatic Republican "uniforms" conceived by the artist-deputy Jacques-Louis David, they came rapidly to wield much the same authority over local decisions as the royal intendants of the Old Regime.[69]

The overwhelming majority of the first cohort of representatives on mission consisted of Montagnards. The choice was apparently made by the Convention secretaries—the majority of whom were themselves Montagnards. Whatever the reason, however, there can be no doubt that the new team of *missionaires* carried with them the impatience and readiness for aggressive action and repression that characterized the Montagnard movement as a whole. In the coming months, they would play a key role in overcoming the long-standing trend toward decentralization and in initiating Terrorist policies in the provinces. Yet it is also clear that the departure of so many deputies from the Left would temporarily change the balance of power within the assembly, much to the pleasure of the Girondins.[70]

During the same period, the Convention also found itself increasingly preoccupied with organizing repression against all the internal enemies seemingly aligned against the Revolution. From the outset, the people of Paris had a major influence on such policies. On the night of March 8–9 the Assembly had sent out teams of deputies to meet with the forty-eight sections of Paris, to declare that the *patrie* was once again in danger, and to promote the need for more volunteers to bolster the Belgian front. In almost every case numerous young men quickly came forward—more than enough to fill the sections' quotas. Many of the individuals in question, however, expressed fears of leaving their families behind when the threat of conspiracy was ever present in the city. After a series of marathon debates, the Convention finally decided—at four-thirty in the morning on March 11—to establish a special Revolutionary Tribunal that would try cases without appeal, much like the tribunal created the previous August 17 and later dismantled. The deputies remembered only too vividly the assault on the Parisian prisons in September as an earlier contingent of volunteers was about to leave for the front. It was in this context that Danton made his oft-cited remark, "Let us profit from the mistakes of our predecessors. We must be terrible, so that the people will not have to be."[71]

Many Girondins had initially opposed the Revolutionary Tribunal. But with news of the recruitment insurrections virtually all of the deputies readily supported an even stronger series of repressive laws. On March 18 Barère delivered a dramatic speech in the name of the Committee of General Security. He spoke of the war reversals, of the attack on Leonard Bourdon, of the recruitment riots, and of what many thought had been an attempted social uprising of the *enragés*. He then demanded a series of repressive decrees. Prosecution in the newly created Revolutionary Tribunals must be made more efficient. Those leading "counterrevolutionary" actions or opposing recruitment must be sent before a military commission and executed within twenty-four hours. All foreigners who could not justify their presence must be expelled. The rich must be taxed to pay for the national defense and all property of emigrants must be sold. There should also be a death penalty for anyone promoting the seizure of private property—an obvious reference to the attacks on Parisian shops in late February. At one point when Barère called for the death penalty, the whole Convention— first the Montagnards but then all of the deputies—began shouting out, "Death! Death! Death!"[72]

Most of Barère's proposals were immediately accepted by all factions without discussion, with details to be elaborated over the next few days. The Montagnard Louchet was pleased that even the moderates in the Convention, who had "now opened their eyes to the deep chasm before us," had voted with the majority.[73] On March 21 with fears riding high against all foreigners, many of them presumed to be foreign agents, the Convention voted that all must carry passports and be kept under close observation, a vote supported once again by all parties in the Convention. Special surveillance committees were to be created in each municipality to take charge of this task. Rapidly thereafter—first in Paris and soon in cities and towns throughout the country—the new committees assumed surveillance functions over all kinds of political misconduct, promoting denunciations of suspicious activities, and sending "suspects" before the Revolutionary Tribunals. Such committees served to institutionalize the improvised practice of denunciations before municipal governments and popular societies that already existed in towns like Bordeaux.[74]

The terrible revelation of Dumouriez's betrayal, coming on top of all the previous deceptions, stimulated yet another wave of anguished decrees. Almost immediately, the two factions began accusing one another of implication in the general's "conspiracy." After a series of mutual recriminations,

A surveillance committee during the Terror. An upper-class couple is brought
before the committee, whose members all seem to be sans-culottes, wearing the red
Republican caps. A few are armed with pikes or muskets. Several point accusingly
at the man and woman. The sign on the door indicates that while in the room
everyone is expected to use the familiar "tu" form of address, used by all good
Revolutionaries. The busts of the martyrs Le Peletier and Marat are on the wall
at the right. Fragonard fils, engraved by Pierre-Gabriel Berthault, © Coll. Musée de
la Révolution française, Domaine de Vizille, MRF L 1984.253.2.36.

both sides accepted the fateful decision of abandoning parliamentary immunity. The decree of April 1, eliminating the deputies' exemption from
prosecution first voted in June 1789, would have untold consequences for
the future, facilitating periodic purges of the Convention carried out over
the next two years.[75]

In early April the Convention created yet another institution destined
for a powerful presence during the period of the Terror. A number of proposals had been made over the previous weeks to consolidate leadership
in a single Convention committee, but all had initially been blocked by
the Girondins, decrying the dangers of dictatorship.[76] With Dumouriez's

desertion, however, and with national defense seemingly on the verge of collapse, it seemed essential to create a "vigorous government," as Gillet described it. On April 6, with the support of the Girondins and the Plain as well as the Mountain, the Convention established a Committee of Public Safety as a centralized "executive" authority holding extensive power over all of the ministries. First nine and then twelve deputies would sit on the Committee, which was to meet in secret without the presence of outsiders—unlike the much larger Committee of General Defense. The first such committee was largely dominated by more moderate Montagnards, including the powerful personality of Georges Danton, who assumed much the same leadership position as during the previous August and September. In the months that followed the membership would be modified several times, as the Committee of Public Safety eventually acquired nearly absolute power to prosecute the war and pursue repression.[77]

The Purge of June 2

Even as the new Committee of Public Safety and the representatives on mission began centralizing authority, the two factions in the Convention went after one another with ever-intensifying hatred and fury. Many members of the Mountain were convinced that their Girondin rivals had been linked to the treachery of Dumouriez, that they were closet royalists in league with foreign enemies. They recalled how Dumouriez had long maintained a close correspondence with Brissot and his friends. On the very day that Dumouriez's treachery was confirmed, Robespierre formally denounced Brissot and the other Girondin leaders for all their actions since Valmy, demanding that they be chased from the Assembly. He maintained, nevertheless, that the purge must be pursued "legally" through a vote in the Convention itself.[78] The Girondins in turn were quick to accuse the Mountain of treachery. Birotteau implied as much when he demanded the end of parliamentary immunity, and Vergniaud was far more direct in a dramatic verbal duel with Robespierre on April 13, claiming the Montagnards hoped to seize power by placing their erstwhile ally, the duke d'Orléans, on the throne.[79]

For a time, through the months of April and May, the balance of power in the Convention seemed to tilt in favor of the Girondins. With a large number of Montagnards on mission in the provinces, Brissot and his supporters were able to turn the tables on their rivals in the biweekly elections, winning three presidencies in a row and all but one of the secretaries.[80]

Louchet complained to his constituency that the Mountain was now in the minority through the "absence of our colleagues sent into the departments."[81] The Brissotins began regularly taunting the Mountain that the provinces would soon dispatch volunteers to put the "anarchists" in their place. "All the departments," proclaimed Guadet in a speech on May 12, "will send into oblivion this handful of traitors and anarchists, who are far more to be feared than the emigrant armies or the rebels of the Vendée."[82] Convinced of their support in the departments and with a new majority in the Convention, they also went on the offensive in the Paris sections, attempting to rally what they believed to be a moderate "silent majority" in the city. And to some extent, especially in the wealthier sections of western Paris, they were successful.[83] In mid-May Brissot himself made his position clear in his newspaper. He accused the Mountain of every sin possible, including a plan to murder the opposition and make themselves dictators. Some individuals, he said, had asked him to be conciliatory. "Never! Never!" he replied. "What kind of truce would be possible between proud republicans devoted to liberty and treacherous royalists resolved on tyranny! Between virtue and crime, there can be only implacable war, eternal war!" And he left no doubt that their goal was to crush and eliminate the Mountain: "You can be sure," he wrote, "that we are ready."[84]

In mid-April, armed with a relative majority and a new sense of confidence, the Girondins were able to indict Marat for recent articles he had published and which, it was argued, had incited the people to riot. The Brissotins were thus the first to take advantage of the removal of parliamentary immunity, sending the Montagnard firebrand before the Paris Revolutionary Tribunal.[85] In this case, however, their plan backfired. After hiding out for several days, Marat turned himself over to the Tribunal, and the court quickly exonerated him. His supporters carried him back to the Convention in triumph, adorning him with a victory crown of laurel.[86]

In the end, neither the Girondins nor the Montagnards were able to eliminate their rivals through "legal means." The endless vituperations of the two factions against one another only succeeded in eroding the authority of the deputies.[87] It was in this situation, with the very legitimacy of the Convention in question, that groups of Parisian militants and sans-culotte leaders stepped into the vacuum and began pushing for a purge. There was no doubt which side they supported. During the debates on the king in January, there had already been talk in the city of eliminating from the Convention all those who had opposed Louis' execution. With the debacle in Belgium and the Dumouriez betrayal, the more radical sections began presenting regular petitions urging the removal of the Girondins, often indicating the specific individuals—twenty-two names were commonly given—whom they felt should be expelled and arrested.[88] Groups of women strongly supported such demands: marching with the men as they demonstrated before the Convention, marching by themselves to present their own petitions, packing the balconies to cheer on the Montagnards and shout down their rivals. Some petitions make it clear that they were prepared to act alone if the Convention could not come together.[89]

Faced with this barrage of denunciations, the Girondins attempted a counterattack. They claimed to have found evidence of a conspiracy to destroy the Convention, and on May 18 they convinced the majority to create a commission of twelve deputies to lead an inquiry. Whether the Montagnards took part in the vote is uncertain, but in any case the elected body consisted entirely of Girondins. The "Commission of Twelve" immediately set about investigating and attacking the Parisian radicals. It seized the minutes of the Commune of Paris and of several of the sections, and it arrested some of the key radicals, including Hébert and a number of other militant leaders, all of whom were interred in the Abbaye prison. When demonstrators protested, many of them were arrested as well, including a few women.[90]

The Parisian sections now focused all their efforts on obtaining the suppression of the Commission and the liberation of the prisoners, using the Commission's activities as one more justification for the expulsion of the Girondins. The Convention, however, continued unable to act, abolishing the Commission in a night session on May 27, when most of the Girondins were absent, and then reinstating it the next day when they had returned in force. At one point the Girondin Isnard, recently elected president of the Assembly, openly taunted and threatened the petitioners. Confident that the great majority of French citizens supported his party, he predicted that the city would soon be overwhelmed by forces arriving from the departments. If an attack were made on any of the deputies, "I declare to you, in the name of the whole of France, that Paris will be annihilated. Soon men will walk on the banks of the Seine and wonder if the city ever existed."[91] But the Girondin rhetoric only further inflamed the situation. Even the normally detached Ruault was furious. The Girondins "are mad," he wrote. "Like the prophet Isnard, they speak of destroying Paris." It was if they were doing everything in their power to "force the people into an insurrection against the Convention."[92]

The insurrection feared by Ruault was not long in coming. As in August 1792, the initiative now passed to the militants in Paris. Leadership was assumed by an improvised central committee of delegates from the sections, which began meeting in the former bishop's palace next to Notre Dame—a hall where the Constituent Assembly had once briefly met. Not all the sections were represented—only thirty of the forty-eight were present on May 30. But numerous nondelegates also took part, including a substantial number of women and at least one deputy, Marat, with an estimated 500 people squeezing onto the floor and another 100 cheering from the balcony. Leadership was concentrated in a "Central Revolutionary Committee," eventually consisting of twenty-five men. They were an extraordinary mixture of individuals, from an ex-noble to several simple artisans, but generally weighted toward the lower middle classes, well below the social level of the Conventionnels. Their central demand was that the Convention be compelled to abolish the Commission of Twelve and expel the designated twenty-two Girondin leaders. A few of the most violent enragés urged the disbanding of the entire Convention and the "Septemberization"—the immediate execution—of the Girondins, all of whom were assumed to be traitors.[93]

For almost a week, from late May to the beginning of June, Paris remained in a state of near continuous agitation. Day after day, tens of thousands of men and women marched on the Convention and encircled it, while thousands more packed the surrounding streets or crowded their way into the galleries. Some of the demonstrations seem to have been led by women.[94] On the night of May 30–31 the Central Revolutionary Committee formally declared an insurrection. The tocsin began ringing at two o'clock in the morning, guardsmen were called to arms, the city gates were locked, and warning cannons were fired over the Seine. The newly appointed commander of the Parisian national guard, Hanriot, seized control of the arsenal and broke into a meeting of the Commune of Paris, who assured him that it would lend its support.[95] Rumors flooded through the city, so that common citizens were uncertain of what was happening. Watching from his apartment, Guittard was terrified: "My legs so trembled that I could no longer stand."[96]

In the turmoil and confusion, and with a minority of the sections still opposed, the national guard and the crowds converged on the Convention in the late afternoon of May 31. The petitioners once again asked for the arrest of the Girondin leaders, along with a number of other popular demands, such as fixing a maximum price on bread. After much rancorous debate—accompanied by a boisterous chorus in the balconies—and with many of the Girondins apparently absent, the Convention finally voted to abolish the Commission of Twelve. All the other demands, however, were sent to the Committee of Public Safety for consideration. With this, the crowds and the armed guardsmen were convinced to return home.

For most of those on the Central Revolutionary Committee, May 31 was a failure, a fiasco. The Convention had been allowed to pass only "half measures," while the treacherous Girondins had been left in place. Throughout the day of June 1 there were tumultuous meetings and recriminations in the sections and at the bishop's palace. In the Convention itself many deputies never left the hall, sitting in permanent session, "overwhelmed with exhaustion," as Blad tried to explain, "and with my thoughts swarming in such rapid succession that I have difficulty conveying them to you."[97]

On the night of June 1–2 the Revolutionary Committee ordered Hanriot to return to the Convention with his armed guardsmen and not to leave this time until the Girondins were arrested. Thereafter, the commander seems carefully to have organized his forces so that contingents from sections that might still support the Girondins were assigned well away from the meeting hall. When he and his troops converged on the Assembly, it was a Sunday morning, and the crowds of men and women were even larger than two days earlier, including a contingent from the club of Republican Women ostentatiously bearing arms. Many of the Girondins were once again absent, and those who did appear were said to have carried pistols.[98]

The session of the Convention began with more bad news from the Vendée, further raising tensions and underlining the need to act.[99] A delegation from the Commune of Paris, sent by the central committee, arrived soon thereafter. This time, unlike May 31, they did not petition the Convention; they delivered an ultimatum: "The people are tired of seeing their demands forever postponed. . . . Save them now, or we declare to you that they will save themselves." Almost all of the deputies—even those in the Mountain—were outraged by the threatening language of this and the other petitions presented, and some feared the crowds might consist of counterrevolutionaries. Ultimately the Committee of Public Safety came up with what it hoped would be a compromise. Those deputies under fire who were present were asked voluntarily to "suspend their powers." Several immediately did so, but two of them indignantly refused. At this point in the midst of another stalemate, the deputies became aware that guardsmen were barring the doors and preventing them from leaving the hall. The Montagnards Delacroix and Basire both complained of being pushed and roughed up when they tried briefly to leave. When the moderate Boissy d'Anglas attempted to go out, people were said to have ripped his clothes and pointed bayonets at his chest. Even the Council of Ministers, meeting nearby, was surrounded and prevented from leaving. Danton roared that "the majesty of the nation is outraged." When the Convention formally demanded that the doors be opened and that all armed men leave the area, Hanriot supposedly replied, "I don't give a damn about your Assembly!"[100]

Then, in an extraordinarily dramatic moment, Barère convinced the Convention to leave its hall and directly confront the crowd.[101] The reasons for this decision are uncertain and differ among the witnesses—whether to compel the crowds to end the deputies' imprisonment or simply to find out what they wanted and to ensure that they were not counterrevolutionaries. As the deputies began filing out, women in the galleries shouted that they must not leave, but only a handful of Montagnards (including Robespierre, Marat, and Chabot) seem to have remained inside. According to the deputy Dulaure, his colleagues walked together pell-mell, with all of the factions mixed with one another. This time, when the whole Convention confronted the guards, they were allowed to exit the hall. But after a few paces, they were blocked from crossing a fixed perimeter, even though they marched in procession all around the building—first toward the Louvre, then toward the Seine, and then toward the Tuileries Gardens. At one point, if we can believe the Girondin sympathizer Saladin, they directly confronted Hanriot himself. When the commander asked Hérault de Séchelles—the Montagnard who had temporarily assumed the role of president—if he would agree to arrest the Girondins, Hérault refused to do anything under duress. "In that case," Hanriot was said to have answered, "I will not be responsible for what happens." And he ordered his gunners and his infantry to prepare their arms, and at least some of the guardsmen were said to have aimed their muskets at the deputies.[102] Colson, however, who had marched that morning with his section and was stationed outside, gave a rather different account. They all stood calm and serene, he said, surrounded by large numbers of women; and though they strongly opposed the "counterrevolutionary" deputies, they felt only brotherhood for the Conventionnels in general, some of whom shouted out, "Long live our brave Parisians!"[103]

In any case, when they returned to their hall, the great majority of the deputies felt cowed and humiliated. Armed men returned once again to block the doors. There now seemed to be little choice in the matter, and after a relatively brief debate, it was decreed that twenty-nine Girondin deputies—including those who had been on the Commission of Twelve—along with two ministers who had generally supported them would all be arrested. Although the original motion would have sent them to the Abbaye prison, it was ultimately decided only to place them under temporary house arrest. Those who had earlier offered to resign would be left unguarded, as long as they promised not to leave Paris. How many actually voted this measure is unclear. According to Dulaure, "a great many members took no part in this deliberation"[104] Yet for the time being, the leaders of the insurrection seemed mollified, and the guardsmen and the crowds outside began leaving the Assembly and making their way home to their neighborhoods.

"Their Blood Too Must Flow"

The events unrolling in Paris that winter and spring of 1793 would mark a major turning point in the coming of the Terror. For a time, after the king's death, the deputies had felt a great sense of confidence, an extraordinary hubris that the Revolution was about to sweep over the whole of Europe. But the visions of victory had soon been dissolved through a series of unprecedented threats to the Republic, of crises that clustered together, that piled one upon another.

With historical hindsight, it is easy to conclude that it was largely the Revolutionaries' fault, that it was madness to expand the war and take on all of Europe, that they should have realized the allies would launch a counterattack against their armies, that those armies were greatly depleted in numbers and poorly provisioned, and that much of the rural population would be unwilling to abandon their fields for a distant war. But the reality is that most of them anticipated nothing of the sort. And faced with so many threats, the deputies became extraordinarily nervous and volatile, sometimes on the verge of panic. For well over a year they had spoken endlessly, had been haunted by the menace of a "grand conspiracy." It now seemed patently clear that the external and internal assaults were all of a piece, all working together to destroy the Revolution. Virtually every deputy who left contemporary testimonies—whether of the Mountain or the Gironde or the Plain—was convinced such a conspiracy existed. They were particularly angered by the internal insurrections in the provinces, the stab in the back, just as the *patrie* was being invaded. But they were also beset by suspicions that some of those in their midst, including members of the Convention who fashioned themselves as patriots, might well be secret conspirators, like Lafayette and Mirabeau and Dumouriez. The deputy Mercier, writer and sometime philosopher, understood the situation only too well. "Few men," he wrote, "are able to maintain their integrity, when everything around them is threatening and shaking and collapsing. . . . They are pushed along and carried away without ever realizing it; they are swept up in the passions of others."[105]

It was in this atmosphere of passions and mistrust, as they attempted to respond to the dangers they faced, that the deputies cobbled together almost all of the basic institutions that came to constitute the Terror. There was never a systematic plan, and they would continue to improvise and invent over the coming months, as they progressively implemented and strengthened those institutions, some of which were at first only sketched. Although the new structures would soon work to the advantage of the Mountain, both major factions in the Convention helped create them. Almost all of the institutions in question had precedents contrived in earlier crises. The Revolutionary Tribunal, the representatives on mission, the surveillance committees, the Committee of Public Safety—all had been prefigured after the flight to Varennes or in the weeks following August 10, sometimes in national decrees, sometimes through the improvisations of local administrations. To be sure, the removal of parliamentary immunity and the subsequent purge of the deputies were unprecedented. But the Girondins themselves had implicitly demanded such a purge since they first sought to oust the Montagnard leaders in the autumn of 1792.

Yet the crisis of '93 had a profound effect not only on the institutions of the Terror but also on what might be termed the "mindset" of the Terror. Again and again, deputies from every faction drove home the idea that when the Revolution itself was in danger of destruction, all means were justified to preserve it. Georges Couthon, the Montagnard leader, was explicit in early May: "Measures that would be political crimes under a peaceful and well-established government, now become indispensable." The Girondin sympathizer Edme-Michel Petit made much the same argument: "When faced with dire necessity, we have had to set aside the laws. . . . Such is the terrible compromise we must make in order to preserve our Revolution." For the farmer-deputy Dubreuil, who now usually sat with the Plain, "the Convention can no longer rely on half-measures, but those required by circumstances. Only thus will the fatherland be saved and our cowardly enemies struck down and defeated."[106]

Most were convinced, moreover, that "dire necessity" required the ultimate penalty; that if they did not "strike down" their enemies, those enemies would certainly do the same to them and crush the Revolution; that the terror they were implicitly summoning was to be one of executions and death.[107] This evolution in attitudes could be charted by the growing prominence in the patriot vocabulary of the word "exterminate." The term seems first to have received wide currency among the deputies in reference to the war and to the foreign kings who must be eliminated once and for all. "Let us wage war," Monestier had written. "It is our duty to exterminate all tyrants." It had subsequently been adopted in debates on the fate of their own tyrant, Louis XVI. In the spring of 1793 extermination had become a common prescription for counterrevolutionaries on the home front. "The brigands in the provinces and the Austrian mercenaries will soon be exterminated," wrote the Girondin Boyer-Fonfrède. "Let us all unite, friends and brothers, and fight and exterminate all our enemies once and for all," concurred the Girondin sympathizer Corbel. Lazare Carnot, the Montagnard officer who would soon lead French armies to victory, suggested much the same: "We can never hope for a genuine peace with our enemies, neither with those inside nor those outside the nation. Either we pulverize them or we will be crushed by them; any weakness will be fatal."[108]

Toward the end of March, Louis-Marie Prudhomme published an extraordinary call for repression in his widely circulated newspaper, *Révolutions de Paris*. Though Prudhomme had long been a fervent supporter of the Revolution, he had urged moderation in recent months and would be briefly arrested on June 2—unjustly no doubt—as a Girondin sympathizer. A few years later he would harshly attack the whole regime of the Terror. But now, in the midst of the disasters of that spring, he lost all patience: "They want our blood," he repeated again and again, like a litany, as he enumerated the enemies aligned against them. The aristocrats, the treacherous priests, the faithless ministers, the suspect foreigners living among them—"they all want our blood." He reserved particular venom for the "monsters" in the Vendée, who "have cut to pieces the faithful magistrates and administrators of the people, and the few good priests." "Well then," he continued, "since it's blood they want, then let blood flow." And "let it be the blood," of all those who had betrayed them, including perhaps a certain number of the deputies: "You too must tremble, treacherous representatives!" For all these enemies of the Revolution, he concluded, "now their blood too must flow."[109]

II

Revolution and Terror
until Victory

Despite the dramatic measures taken by the Convention in the spring of 1793, the situation of the Revolution remained grim and uncertain throughout much of the summer. On the various war fronts—in Belgium, the Alps, the Pyrenees, and Germany across the Rhine—the Republican forces struggled to hold their own and were frequently pushed back inside their own frontiers. Fortunately for the French, the Prussians and Austrians were at least as concerned with competition in central Europe as with the war in the west. They were also mindful of the disaster at Valmy the previous autumn and determined this time to advance more slowly and methodically. Yet the loss in July of the French fortresses of Condé and Valenciennes and the surrender of Mainz—long a center of German support for the French Revolution—were particularly harsh blows with a profound impact on Revolutionary politics. By August the Austrians were scarcely 175 kilometers from Paris and their cavalry had penetrated even closer.

During the same period, moreover, the peasant insurgents in the Vendée went from victory to victory. In June they swept out of their backcountry hamlets and villages and began capturing towns in the lowlands of the Loire Valley. Saumur, Loudun, Chinon, and Angers all fell. They even laid siege to the great Atlantic port of Nantes, fighting their way to the very center of the city until a desperate defense by the patriot townsmen finally halted the attack. Thereafter the Republicans attempted numerous counterattacks and won a few small victories, but their own disorganization and the intense motivation of their opponents left them nowhere nearer defeating the insurrection. Indeed, observers in Paris remained far more preoccupied with the internal threat than with the wars on the frontiers. "We are living through grim times," wrote Pierre Dubreuil in early June. "The civil war seems to be devouring and destroying everything."[1]

With the economy dislocated by war and inflation, the common people of Paris continued to suffer from shortages. Fears of insufficient grain led citizens to line up at the bakeries long before daybreak and sometimes throughout the night. In late June washerwomen raided barges arriving on the Seine to compel the sale of soap at prices they could afford. The situation was aggravated by the continuing cold war between the various sections of the city, pitting radical militants who supported the Montagnards and the purge of June 2 against the more moderate sections who persisted in their sympathy for the Girondins. And always there were rumors pulsing and vibrating through the city, rumors of new conspiracies, of new aristocratic plots to block the grain supply or to kill the patriots.[2]

Suspicions were only intensified by the long months of turmoil within the Convention. The unrelenting factional rivalries had eroded the legitimacy of that body and raised questions as to who, if anyone, was actually in control of the government. The June 2 intervention of the Parisian militants to compel the arrest of twenty-nine Girondin deputies would arouse outrage throughout much of the country. It was a central factor in a rebellion against the Convention of several of the Republic's largest cities, a rebellion that would threaten the very survival of the Revolution and play a major role in the advent of the Terror.

The Crisis of "Federalism"

The so-called federalist revolts of the summer of 1793 were rooted as much in local conflicts as in national politics. Although the specific confrontations varied from city to city, they frequently involved factional rivalries that had first emerged in 1789 or even earlier. Typically, more moderate factions presented themselves as the defender of property, while more radical faction claimed to champion the poor. But there was rarely a clear class confrontation. If the radicals failed to provide for the needs of the working classes, those classes might well change sides and throw their support to the moderates. It was soon apparent, moreover, that all factions were prepared to resort to violent repression in order to eliminate their rivals and that they would have no qualms against the use of "terror" whenever they felt it served their ends.[3]

However, tensions in the cities were never entirely detached from events in Paris. From the earliest weeks of the Convention the Girondins had done all in their power to influence provincial politics. Brissot and several of his friends had attempted to summon departmental "armies" to Paris to protect themselves and to counter the Parisian militants and sans-culottes. Throughout the first half of 1793, and especially after the Paris sections began demanding their expulsion, they sent a barrage of letters to their constituencies, warning them of the threat to the Revolution from the "anarchists" in the capital. Barbaroux, Salle, Boyer-Fonfrède, Grangeneuve, and Gensonné had all written home urging preparation for action against the capital. Vergniaud, who had rarely been in contact with his constituency in the past, penned a particularly passionate letter in early May: "Men of the Gironde, rise up! Strike with terror those who are leading us to civil war."[4] Such letters were reinforced through the incessant rhetoric of the Girondin newspapers, several of which (by Brissot, Gorsas, and Carra, in particular) circulated widely in the provinces. By late May a number of cities were already contemplating a break with the Convention. In Marseille the moderates had pushed the Jacobins from power and forced the Convention's representatives on mission to flee the city. On May 27 an uprising broke out in Lyon, violently overthrowing the municipal regime of the Montagnard sympathizer Chalier. At almost the same time the town of Bourg-en-Bresse, northeast of Lyon, declared itself in insurrection, and the Norman town of Caen called for a departmental army to march on Paris.[5]

In the midst of this already tense situation, news of the June 2 purge incited widespread consternation, deeply dividing the provincial elites. Some two-fifths of the department directories soon sent letters adhering to the June 2 decrees. The strongest support for the Convention came from regions along the frontiers, where France was at war, or from those adjoining the zone of the Vendée insurrection: precisely those areas most dependent on a united front to ensure their defense. Yet well over half of the departments addressed protests, expressing their anger that twenty-nine duly elected members of the Convention had been removed and arrested through the influence of the Paris "anarchists." Emergency assemblies were convoked in which local officials debated the situation. Many invoked the principle of popular sovereignty to buttress their opposition. The Convention, it was argued, no longer represented the nation as a whole, but only the opinion of a minority in the capital.[6]

In reality most of the protesting departments soon backed down. The Montagnards mobilized all their energy to win over the provincial leadership, urging them not to cause disunity in a time of war, committing themselves to drafting a new Constitution as rapidly as possible and promising amnesty to those who withdrew their opposition. The representatives on mission, already present in the departments, were also influential in goading and coercing local officials. Almost everywhere, moreover, the elites were themselves deeply divided. Many lower-level administrators in the districts and smaller towns rejected the protests of their superiors. Faced with such opposition, many departmental officials had second thoughts and reversed their position.[7]

Yet a dozen or so departments, most of them dominated by cities with long-simmering opposition to the Montagnards, steadfastly refused to back down, even in the face of civil war. In Marseille, Lyon, Toulon, Nîmes, Bordeaux, Caen, and several departments surrounding these cities, officials formally disavowed the Convention. Proposals were made to establish a new Convention, perhaps in Bourges near the center of France. Committees of public safety were established to begin raising armies for a march on Paris, to restore the arrested deputies, and to punish the Parisian militants who thought they could lord it over the whole nation. Local Jacobin clubs were closed, and Montagnard sympathizers were imprisoned and sometimes executed. In some cases, representatives on mission were also arrested.[8]

Soon the rebellious cities were exchanging correspondence and delegates to urge each other on and buoy up enthusiasm. In this way they convinced themselves that the whole of France was ready to rise up and that departmental armies would be welcomed as liberators by the vast majority of Parisians. Bordeaux, the home base of the Girondin delegation, sent out eighteen delegates to circulate through the Republic and proselytize for their cause. One of their representatives even appeared in Paris and announced that the Montagnards and the militants were all royalists, that they were planning to establish a new king and make Robespierre their prime minister.[9]

Initially the most dangerous insurrection seemed to be in the west, with opposition centered in the town of Caen, scarcely 200 kilometers from Paris. Here local officials were reinforced by a bevy of Girondin leaders who had escaped from house arrest in the capital to pursue their fight in the provinces. Buzot, Pétion, Barbaroux, Lanjuinais, Gorsas, and a half dozen others helped establish a "Central Committee of Resistance to Oppression." For a time they were also promised support from nearby departments in Maine and Brittany, as well as in Normandy. Small contingents of national guardsmen from these regions converged on Caen, and led by a general from the Old Regime nobility, some 2,000 men set off for Paris at the end of June.[10] In the meantime both Marseille and Lyon began raising local armies. Forces from Lyon succeeded in linking up with several neighboring departments and in controlling a swathe of territory to guarantee food supplies for the city. The departmental army of Marseille did likewise, and by early July it was marching north along the Rhône River, collecting contingents from Nîmes, and making plans to link up with Lyon. Bordeaux announced that it too would soon raise an army and march northward.[11]

For the Parisians, this "federalist revolt"—as they now began calling it—and the threat of an attack against Paris by provincial armies seemed ominous and terrifying. They well remembered the arrival of another provincial army, the Marseillais of August 1792, and the role it had played in overthrowing the monarchy. They could scarcely forget the threats of the Girondin Isnard that provincial forces would soon totally destroy Paris.[12]

Yet the rebellion also had serious weaknesses. The areas controlled by the federalist rebels were beset by internal divisions, with many lower-level officials in nearby districts and municipalities refusing to lend their support and with currents of opposition within the insurrectional cities themselves. Despite their grandiose schemes to send armed forces against Paris, the rebels confronted many of the same problems encountered by the Convention itself in its attempts to recruit soldiers. The middle-class leadership was unable to convince the working classes and the peasantry to leave their homes and enlist in a fight against Paris. They also had problems finding funds to clothe and equip such armies. Ultimately the major centers of insurrection were never able to link up. The Rhône corridor between Marseille and Lyon was blocked by the smaller town of Valence and the surrounding department of Drôme, a zone that remained sympathetic to the Montagnards and that was soon reinforced by Republican forces pulling back from the Italian frontier. Bordeaux and Caen remained even more isolated and were soon surrounded by departments that repudiated their earlier promises of opposition and threw in their lot with the Convention.[13]

In the end, all of the federalist movements in western France soon collapsed. Most officials in this region were far more concerned with stopping the Vendée rebels than with supporting factional squabbles among the urban elites. The small army from Caen was surprised and routed by a band of Parisian national guardsmen rapidly thrown together by the Convention to confront the danger. Bordeaux managed to recruit only 400 men, who marched scarcely fifty kilometers out of the city before they lost courage and returned home.[14] It was the insurrection in the southeast that proved the most serious. Rebels in Lyon, Marseille, and Toulon would all organize serious military campaigns to resist the forces of the Convention. As the three cities felt themselves increasingly threatened, they allied themselves with a range of opponents to the Montagnards, including royalists and counterrevolutionaries. The Marseillais would even attempt an alliance with the enemy English, though Republican troops would capture the city before such an alliance could take effect. Toulon, however, successfully invited in the British to take control of the port and protect the local rebellion.[15] Occurring at a time when the Convention was confronting foreign armies on all of its frontiers, Toulon's betrayal to the enemy and the loss of the great Mediterranean port would be a brutal shock and arouse demands for revenge among the Parisians and the Montagnards. They soon convinced themselves that all the federalists must be linked in conspiracy with the European "tyrants" and the "brigands" of the Vendée.

The Montagnards Take Charge

As whole regions of France rose in rebellion, the Convention and its designated leaders in the Committee of Public Safety struggled to hold the nation together. The events of June 2 had not removed all the Girondin sympathizers from the Assembly. Within three weeks some seventy-five deputies signed a formal protest against the arrest of their colleagues. The two youngest deputies from Bordeaux, Boyer-Fonfrède and Ducos, had managed to escape the purge of their friends, and for a time they provided a certain opposition leadership. Most of the Girondin supporters, however, either boycotted the debates or ceased attending altogether. For some six weeks Claude-Antoine Blad, who had signed the protest, abruptly halted the correspondence with his home city of Brest that he had pursued so regularly over the previous months. The Mountain even attempted to compel participation by calling a formal roll call on June 15 and threatening to expel any deputy who failed to show up. Most of the Girondin sympathizers did appear for the day, but when their names were called out, they responded with phrases like "present but oppressed" or "present in the midst of tyranny." During a celebration on July 8 honoring the new Constitution, the left side of the hall, according to Jullien, was entirely filled, while the right remained all but empty.[16]

With most of the remaining Girondins having abandoned the fight, the 300-odd Montagnard deputies were now largely able to dominate the Convention. For over a year thereafter every elected presidents of that body would be Montagnards. Throughout the summer many of the major figures of the faction would succeed one another as president. On July 25 all eight of the deputies receiving any votes were Montagnards. During the same period, virtually all of the elected secretaries came from the same faction. At no other time in any of the assemblies since 1789 had one faction so utterly dominated the leadership.[17]

Initially, however, the majority of the Montagnards was far from being vindictive. Whatever their continued suspicion and mistrust of the Girondins, most were deeply distressed at having been coerced on June 2 by the threats of the crowds. They were also aware of the need to maintain the support of the majority of the nonaligned deputies and they feared the reaction of the province. Led by the more moderate wing of the Montagnards— including Danton, Barère, and Hérault de Séchelles—the Committee of Public Safety seemed to distance itself from the actions of the Paris militants on June 2. Four days after the event Barère delivered a major report in the name of the Committee. A distinguished lawyer and journalist from southern France and veteran of the first National Assembly, Barère was praised by contemporaries for his Gascon charm, amiability, and wit.[18] But over the previous year he had emerged as one of the Convention's most forceful and influential orators, and he now became the principal speaker of the Committee. His report of June 6 seemed strongly to encourage compromise. Though he began with a note of praise for the efforts of the Parisians to end the factional chaos in the Assembly, he suggested that they had overreacted. There was now the danger that the Convention would lose its legitimacy among the departments. "What will happen," he asked, "if the National Assembly is no longer obeyed by anyone?" He then proposed a series of measures to prevent future coercion of the Convention by the militants and sans-culottes, including the suppression of the Central Revolutionary Committee that had organized the recent insurrection. He went on to insist that the June 2 arrest of the Girondins was only temporary. And he added the remarkable proposal that deputies should volunteer as hostages to live in various of the provincial cities until the Girondins could be fairly judged and perhaps returned to their seats. Danton, Couthon, and Barère himself all announced their readiness to volunteer.[19]

In fact, the hostage proposal came to nothing, when it was repudiated by Fonfrède, speaking for the remaining Girondins.[20] Yet throughout most of June the majority of the Montagnard leaders remained conciliatory toward the arrested deputies. Each was guarded in his residence by a single gendarme, and all were allowed to receive guests and to move about the city at will. Many continued to gather together in the evenings, as they had done in the past. According to Riffard de Saint-Martin, sixty to seventy Girondin sympathizers went daily to visit the arrested leaders. When Garat stopped by the apartments of Gensonné and Vergniaud in mid-June, he found them surrounded by visitors. The Convention even voted the continued payment of the Girondins' salaries, as though they were still officially deputies.[21]

The lenient position toward the Girondins was paralleled, moreover, by the Committee's efforts to negotiate with the recalcitrant departments. Through the first weeks of summer, the federalist rebellion was clearly viewed in a very different light from the Vendée insurrection. Georges Couthon, a member of the Committee since late May, underscored their efforts to reach an amiable reconciliation. Most of those who had protested against the Convention, he argued, had been misled. He was hopeful that the whole affair was "a lover's quarrel which will soon be resolved." "I desire only union, fraternity, and cooperation." Even Saint-Just would offer to travel to Normandy with the minister Garat in an effort to work out a settlement.[22]

As an additional means of luring the recalcitrant departments back into the fold, the Montagnards began rapidly drafting a new Constitution, the task that was, after all, the original reason for the existence of the Convention. As Dubreuil described it, such an act would be "the single best remedy we can apply to all the difficulties we face."[23] Written primarily by Hérault and Couthon and quickly approved by the Montagnard majority, the new "constitutional act" adopted many of the principles proposed by the Girondins the previous February. But it was drafted in more straightforward prose—without Condorcet's lengthy philosophical reflections. Shorn of all articles relating to the monarchy and including almost nothing on local institutions, it was only about a third as long as the Constitution of 1791.[24] The Declaration of Rights, by contrast, was substantially longer, including several new articles on the social responsibilities of the Republican government: a commitment to public education for all citizens, a promise of public assistance for those in need, and the abolition of the slave trade. Unlike its predecessor, the new Constitution would be submitted to a referendum among all male citizens, voting in their primary assemblies.

Whatever the Constitution's value for winning over the departments, it may well have influenced many of the representatives linked to the "Plain" who had long wavered between the two warring parties. Louis-Jacques Taveau, who sat with the Plain, urged his friends in Honfleur to accept the new Constitution and rally to the Convention. It was time, he wrote, to "throw a veil over all the wrongs that have been done" by both sides in the past and "to silence the passions of the two parties." "Let us rally and all pull together, and fight only the tyrants and the rebels who support them." So too Pierre Vinet, the deputy from Saintonge who had often found fault with both Montagnards and Girondins, reminded his constituents that "eight consecutive months had passed without the Convention achieving any important progress." And now, "whatever one might say, [the Convention] is still the only center of unity," if they were ever to survive against their enemies inside and outside France. The purged deputy Barbaroux would be particularly bitter that so many of those in the center of the Assembly "recognize the existence of the Convention and continue deliberating with the Mountain."[25] Some 130 deputies who had not systematically voted with the Mountain over the previous months would agree to sit on Convention committees or serve as representatives on mission.[26]

Yet the mood of reconciliation among the majority in the Convention—and which had probably never been accepted by all members of the Mountain—rapidly dissipated in late June and July, as attitudes toward both the Girondins and the federalists progressively hardened. It was easy to be conciliatory when department officials backed away from their "errors" and formally adhered to the decrees of the Convention. But when they refused to negotiate and, even worse, when they began arresting the Convention's representatives and launching a "terror" against the local Montagnards, a great many deputies lost patience. The dramatic execution in the central square of Lyon of the Jacobin true believer Joseph Chalier would have a particularly strong impact on both the Convention and the Parisian militants.

The Girondins greatly hurt their case, moreover, when they began taking advantage of the Convention's lenient policies and fleeing into the provinces. By the end of June all but nine of the original twenty-nine deputies expelled from the Convention had escaped from Paris, along with at least ten other Girondin sympathizers who had not been arrested. Only two of the principal leaders of the faction, Vergniaud and Gensonné, would refuse to leave.[27] To make matters worse, almost all of the escapees would openly support the provincial insurrections. No fewer than seventeen converged on Caen, where they championed the march on Paris by the departmental army from Calvados. Two others, Birotteau and Chasset, traveled to Lyon and strongly supported the insurrection there.[28] As news spread of the Girondins' flight and their alliance with the rebels, many patriots expressed their anger. Dubreuil, who had been deeply unhappy with the events of June 2, was outraged by the Girondins' "cowardly" flight, which could lead to many regions' being torn apart by war. And for the first time he recommended their punishment: "All these monsters who are destroying the nation will receive a just penalty for their crimes."[29]

But no single event more envenomed attitudes toward both the federalists and the Girondins than the assassination of Jean-Paul Marat in his bath in the early evening of July 13. The assassin, Charlotte Corday, was just twenty-four years old, the daughter of a minor noble family, residing with her aunt in Caen. Her ultimate motives may never be known. Though she had been raised in a convent, she did not seem particularly pious and would reject the last rites of the church on the eve of her death. It is clear from her testimony, however, that she had avidly followed the Revolution through newspapers and pamphlets and that unlike the rest of her family—several of whom joined the emigrant army—she generally supported the patriots. She was enormously impressed when over a dozen of the most famous Girondin leaders—thirteen of whom she would list by name during her trial—suddenly appeared in Caen and took up residence across the street from her apartment. The assassination plan was not their idea, but it must have been inspired in part when she met them and talked with them. Soon thereafter she traveled to Paris on her own, apparently believing the Girondin army from Caen would soon enter the capital, and resolved to help the cause by killing one of their most execrated enemies. After claiming she had a message for Marat, she pulled a dagger from her bosom and thrust it into his chest just above the heart. He died almost immediately in a great pool of blood.[30]

News of the murder swept through Paris with extraordinary speed. Soon great crowds had massed before Marat's apartment, and it was only with difficulty that officials prevented the people from lynching Corday. As Ruault

Assassination of Marat by Charlotte Corday, July 13, 1793. Corday is surrounded by neighborhood people and is in danger of being lynched as others lift the dead Marat from his bath. The murder weapon has been dropped on the floor. The original caption reads, "Since they could not corrupt me, they assassinated me." Brion de la Tour, © Coll. Musée de la Révolution française, Domaine de Vizille, MRF 1984.195.

described it, the event made "an extremely violent impression on those among the sans-culottes," and many of the Paris sections went into emergency session.[31] The Convention was officially informed the next morning, with the deputy Chabot brandishing the knife used in the act. Though most of the Montagnards had long kept their distance from the violent and unpredictable rhetoric of Marat, the murder of one of their own, after the earlier killing of Le Peletier and the near assassination of Bourdon, sent a ripple of fear through the assembly hall. The event seemed to provide conclusive proof that their very lives were threatened by conspiracies afoot in Paris. "Yet another patriot," wrote Pinet, "has fallen under the knife of the royalists."[32]

A dramatic funeral for the Ami du Peuple three days later further impressed upon the city and the representatives the horror of the act.

Organized by the artist Jacques-Louis David, one of Marat's closest friends, the evening procession wound through the streets by torchlight. Guittard watched the long, somber cortege as it passed near his home. He would then attend a second ceremony two weeks later to place Marat's heart in the Luxembourg gardens.[33] Everywhere in France the bust of Marat would be placed side by side with that of Le Peletier, permanent reminders of the danger of assassination for any devoted Republican.

For most of the deputies and for the people of Paris, there could be no doubt that the murder was directly ordered by the Girondins who had escaped to Normandy. It appeared inconceivable to the male leadership that a woman could plan and perform such an act on her own. Suspicions seemed confirmed when it was discovered that before the murder Corday had visited the Girondin sympathizer Deperret and had given him a letter from Buzot in Caen. Rumors spread that the assassination was part of a vast plot to murder the leading Montagnards and liberate Marie-Antoinette. Vengeance became the order of the day. One pamphlet published a long list of those who should be executed in retribution for the murder. Jacques Hébert demanded that Old Regime torture be returned, since the guillotine was too mild a punishment for a "monster" like Corday. For Couthon, speaking in the Convention on July 14, it could be "mathematically proven" that "this monster to whom nature had given the form of a woman" had been sent by Buzot, Barbaroux, Salle, and the other fugitive conspirators in Caen. It was all part of "a royalist plot, there can be no doubt," and it could also be linked to the rebellion in the Vendée. The next day the radical Montagnard Billaud-Varenne launched an extraordinary two-hour tirade against all of the Girondins. The murder of Marat was only the most recent act in the long history of the faction's conspiracies, which he linked directly to actions by the Right in the Constituent and Legislative assemblies and to the betrayals of Lafayette, Dumouriez, and the federalists. He demanded that all the purged deputies be tried for their life.[34] Those still waiting under house arrest were now moved to prison. Two weeks later they were declared to be the accomplices of those who had fled and who were condemned in absentia as traitors and outlaws.[35]

By late July any thought of conciliation with the federalists was also slipping away. Anger over the murder of Marat was accentuated by the French losses of Condé, Valenciennes, and Mainz and by a growing conviction of the treason committed by their military commanders. Only a few days before Valenciennes had fallen, Lazare Carnot had inspected the fortress there and was convinced that it could sustain a long siege.[36] Fears arose once again of a "grand conspiracy" of those who opposed the Convention for any reason. Pinet wrote home of "this system of treason to which all our generals belong." "Oh my dear compatriots," lamented Couthon, "how can men be such scoundrels? When I arrived in Paris, I thought I was versed in the science of the human heart, but now I see that I was in this sense a mere child."[37]

On July 10 the Convention voted to "retire" from the Committee of Public Safety those deputies who had been most vigorous in urging reconciliation with the federalists and the Girondins. Danton, Delacroix, and Cambon were all asked to step down, and the radical Montagnard Pierre-Louis Prieur, from the department of Marne, was elected in their stead.[38] Even more significant was the election to the Committee two weeks later of Robespierre. Since the spring of 1793 no one had more consistently proclaimed the existence of a grand conspiracy linked to the Girondins and the need to take all necessary measures to repress it. He seems never to have accepted the conciliatory policies of his Montagnard associates. In personal notes, jotted down about this time, he left no doubt about his attitude toward both the Girondins and the federalists. The only means of ending the civil war was "to punish all the traitors and conspirators, especially the guilty deputies and administrators, and to make terrible examples of the scoundrels who have outraged liberty and spilled patriot blood." The minister Garat was present at the Committee's meetings in late July, and he claimed to have watched as Robespierre cowed the other deputies with his powerful logic and stern self-confidence: "They all remained silent in the face of his words and his principles." From that point on, as Barère remembered it, "a policy of intransigence became the order of the day," a policy that he himself had now clearly come to embrace.[39]

On August 1 Barère delivered another speech in the name of the Committee, a speech that differed dramatically in its policies and its tone from the one he had given just two months earlier. After a long enumeration of the threats and plots faced by the Republic, he asked for much harsher treatment of both the Girondins—now described as "arrogant and conspiring"—and the various rebels in the provinces. Members of the Committee itself were to be sent to the frontiers to oversee the war effort and scrutinize the activities of their generals. All foreigners whose countries were at war with France were to be arrested, and a series of ferocious measures were to be taken to liquidate the Vendée insurrection, which had now come to symbolize all that was most treacherous in the internal rebellions. The

Committee recommended the total destruction of the rebellious areas, "to exterminate this rebel race, destroy their homes, set fire to their forests, and cut down their harvests." All property of the Vendée rebels was to be confiscated and used to indemnify patriots living in the area whose property might also be destroyed. Only women, children, and the elderly were in theory to be spared.[40]

The Committee and the Convention also abandoned all patience with the insurrectional cities who continued to resist. On August 4 a Republican army was ordered to march against Lyon, an army that would arrive at the city walls three days later and begin the first stage of a long and terrible siege. At the same time a second army began advancing toward Marseille, battling its way south until it finally entered the city on August 25. The military operations would be the prelude to a harsh repression against all those who had joined with the rebels or who were suspected of having shown them sympathy.

Terror the Order of the Day

Civil war against the federalist cities and the Vendée rebels was not the only element driving the Convention's leaders toward greater intransigence and repression. They also faced powerful pressures from radical militants in Paris and, especially during the month of August, from provincial militants as well. Whether the wave of rumors in Paris was greater that summer than at other times during the Revolution is difficult to say. Yet terrifying tales of plots were constantly announced in the streets or in bread lines or by newspaper hawkers. There were stories of emigrants hiding out in houses of prostitution, of Roland returned to the city and up to no good, of English carriages slipping through the city at night, of priests disguised as women planning to kill the patriots. In early September Chaumette, the leading official of the Commune, underlined the fears: "Every day we learn of new treason, new crimes, every day we discover the emergence of new plots." Parisians were "tired of seeing their fate continually floating and uncertain." The ongoing problems of subsistence, the fear of grain shortages leading to endless bread lines, only amplified the old anxieties of an insidious "famine plot."[41] Occasionally the population awoke to find walls plastered with posters thrown up by federalist sympathizers, threatening the city with retribution. On July 24 and 25 the national guard had been mobilized to counter a rumored counterrevolutionary plot in the "Palace of Equality"—the former Palais Royal. Indeed, Barère delivered his August 1 speech in the midst of yet another panic in the city. On popular demand, the Convention ordered the city gates closed, although the act itself may have further increased the rumors and the general uncertainty. Couthon feared an imminent outbreak of violence and perhaps a new assault on the prisons, said to be packed with aristocrats: "The people are indignant; I fear that in their desire for justice they may become terrible."[42]

The fear and suspicion, the "floating and uncertain" mood in the city, invariably affected the political life of Paris as well, although the situation remained tangled and complex. Throughout the angry months of July and August several radical militants presented themselves as the successors of the murdered Marat. Both Jacques Roux and Jean-Théophile Leclerc launched newspapers with titles formerly used by Marat. Each attempted to outdo his rival in the inflation of rhetoric, the violence of proposals, and the denunciation of conspirators. Not to be outdone, Jacques Hébert also entered the race, as his *Père Duchesne* moved progressively closer to the extremist positions of the enragés.[43]

Many of the female militants also assumed an ever-more-aggressive stance. The Revolutionary Republican Women would play a prominent role in the funeral procession for Marat, carrying aloft the bloody shirt in which he had died and even lugging his bathtub through the streets. On the day following the funeral a group of women came before the Convention and vowed to raise their children on the "gospel" of Marat. Thereafter, in street demonstrations and in appearances before the sections and the Convention, they persisted in the role defined for themselves the previous spring as prime opponents of the "enemies within," while the men were away fighting on the front or in the Vendée. Led by such militants as Claire Lacombe and Pauline Léon, the Revolutionary Republican Women moved progressively closer to the enragés, and they earned great praise from both Leclerc and Roux. "It is you who will ring the tocsin of liberty," wrote Leclerc, who readily adopted the women to his cause and eventually married Léon.[44]

A portion of the Convention clearly responded to the feminist surge. In June women were given the right to vote in their villages on the division of communal property, a remarkable decree granting them for the first time a measure of suffrage. In late August there was a brief but passionate debate on the rights of women over communal property within marriage. Although some of the deputies were strongly opposed to any such measure, others—including Danton, Desmoulins, and Couthon—energetically supported an expansion of women's rights. "The marital authority" of husbands, declared Desmoulins, "is a creation of despotic governments."[45]

Rosalie Jullien was never as radical as Lacombe or Léon. Nevertheless, she proudly described herself as one of "the truly republican mothers," all of whom displayed "firm resolution and virile pride." And during the summer of 1793 she experienced what was perhaps her most intense political engagement. She continued her daily attendance in the Convention, sitting in a special section for spectators just below those of the Mountain. When her husband fell ill, she set herself the role of substitute deputy, taking careful notes on the debates and attending daily in order to report back to him. About the same time she even produced a pamphlet, which she sent off to their home department of Drôme, extolling the wisdom of the Convention and castigating the federalists of the southeast. She entered the publishing arena with certain misgivings, admitting self-doubts to her son that "the notoriety that comes from authorship could be a taint to my modesty and is perhaps not appropriate for a respectable woman." Nevertheless, she wondered aloud whether her idol Jean-Jacques Rousseau might not think differently of women, if only he had lived to see the Revolution: "Circumstances have so changed, that even the good Jean-Jacques himself might change his opinions."[46]

In any case, in their competition for the leadership of the far Left, Hébert, Roux, Leclerc, and many of the Revolutionary women pushed forward a veritable program for a politics of terror. All traitors, all those even suspected of unpatriotic opinions, must be tracked down, arrested, and punished. There was growing agreement that merchants and the rich were often as dangerous as priests and aristocrats and that they too must be closely watched. The Revolutionary Tribunal needed to be greatly expanded and compelled to pursue counterrevolutionaries far more vigorously. The death penalty must be instituted for a whole range of crimes, but most notably for hoarding and speculation in the grain supply. The paramilitary "revolutionary army," promised by the Convention the previous June, must be implemented, both to bring in grain from the country and to round up suspects hiding in rural parishes. In pamphlets and speeches the enragés extremists, men and women, regularly attacked the Convention, the Committee of Public Safety, and Robespierre himself. Soon after Marat's assassination, a certain Godinot published a brochure that was not untypical: "It is now more than time that we act with full severity. . . . Do not say 'liberty or death,'' but 'death to all those who stand in our way.' No more pity. Our only choice is to act with the same merciless ferocity as they do." There was even talk of a new general uprising to exterminate all traitors, seemingly on the model of the September Massacres.[47]

Throughout the months of July and early August, male citizens everywhere in the country were given an unusual opportunity to participate directly in the construction of the new Republic. Following the decree of June 27, the Convention sent out copies of its proposed "Constitutional Act" to every municipality in France. There it was to be discussed and voted on in primary assemblies within each of the approximately 4,800 primary cantons, the subdivisions of the districts. Similar arrangements were made for men serving at the front and in the navy. After a vote on the text of the Constitution, each assembly was to choose a delegate to deliver the results to Paris and there to participate in a great celebration on August 10 marking the first anniversary of the overthrow of the monarchy. In this way the Convention fulfilled its promise of the previous September to call a referendum on the new Constitution. The process was also conceived as a means of drawing away support from the federalist insurrection, by coopting the lower-level cantons against the generally more conservative departments. It would be the first truly direct election in the Revolution—eliminating all secondary assemblies—and the first such referendum in European history.[48]

In fact, by 1793 many of the small towns of France had experienced trends toward radicalization, not unlike those in the larger cities, and a great many of the cantonal assemblies were dominated by the most militant local Revolutionaries. A few even allowed female participation in the discussions and the voting and vigorously supported the expansion of rights for women. To be sure, not all of the cantons could be convoked in time for the August 10 deadline. In about 10 percent—mostly in insurrectional zones of the Vendée and the region near Toulon—the assemblies were never organized. Remarkably, however, a great many took place in cantons near federalist cities in open rebellion against the Convention. Substantially more men voted that summer than in the primary elections for the Convention a year earlier. While almost all of the cantons ultimately accepted the Constitution, some were critical of certain aspects and a few proposed modifications and amendments.[49]

Often the cantonal assemblies were immediately followed by celebrations in honor of the new Constitution.[50] In Paris whole neighborhoods marched to the Convention, women and men walking arm in arm, to present the final tallies of votes. From her seat in the gallery, Jullien described the scene as 2,000 to 3,000 individuals, citizens of all ages, arrived from each section, singing Revolutionary songs and sometimes accompanied by bands. Many carried signs or various symbolic objects (a liberty tree or a tablet of the Rights of Man or a bust of the slain Peletier). Individual sections might underscore those special groups living in their neighborhoods: deaf-mutes or the blind from local institutions, wounded veterans from the Invalides hospital, boys from neighborhood schools (sometimes dressed as soldiers). "I watch the whole universe parade before me," wrote Jullien, "as in a religious service in honor of the new divinities of liberty and equality."[51]

By early August the delegates from all over France began converging on the city: an estimated 8,000, with some cantons and sections sending more than one delegate and others from popular societies attending on their own initiative. With tensions still high from the recent military defeats and the continuing rebellions in the Vendée and the southeast, the Parisians were initially anxious that it might be the occasion for a counterrevolutionary coup. Clubs and sections in the city mobilized to indoctrinate the new arrivals. Orders were sent out that delegates must be housed only in the homes of good patriots and that all residents must place tricolor banners on their houses reading, "The Republic One and Indivisible" or "Fraternity, Equality, and Liberty, or Death!"[52]

The ratification ceremony, organized by David, began with a great procession of the cantonal delegates and other officials across the city, stopping as in the Stations of the Cross at several celebrated Revolutionary spaces—like the Place de la Bastille or the Tuileries Palace—before ending at the altar of the fatherland on the Champ de Mars. The itinerary even included a special stop in honor of the women who had marched to Versailles in October 1789. Female veterans of the march were seated on a cannon, appearing, according to Pinet, as if they were "inspired by the god of combat." After the president of the Convention had presented them with crowns of victory, the women boldly announced, "We accept these crowns, and at the end of the Convention we will place them on your heads, as long as we find you worthy."[53] After the ceremony was completed and ratification lists had been collated, the Constitution was found to have been accepted by over 90 percent of all those voting.

Four days later Barère, speaking for the Committee of Public Safety, addressed a group of delegates invited to attend the Convention. He formally instructed them to return home and there to "propagate the salutary principles of the unity and indivisibility of the Republic, to root out the seeds of royalism, and to watch out for the plots of the federalists." A number of the delegates would soon be mobilized as "national agents," the direct contacts between the Committee and the districts.[54] In fact, like the national guardsmen of the summer of 1792, many would stay on for a time in Paris, meeting regularly as a group, electing a central committee to represent them, and firmly embracing many of the positions of the radical militants and sans-culottes.[55]

The cantonal delegates played a significant role, along with the clubs and sections of Paris, in promoting another Revolutionary development of the period: the total mobilization for war. If only the entire French society could be recruited, they proposed—men and women, young and old, each with their assigned tasks—surely the Republic could at last overwhelm all the enemies who threatened them. The idea seems first to have been proposed in one of the Paris sections at the end of July. But it was quickly adopted by the club of cantonal delegates, who proposed it to the Convention.[56] Following these recommendations, and with strong support from the sections and the Commune, the deputies voted the celebrated decree of the *levée en masse* on August 23. The basic text seems to have been drawn up by the two military engineers recently brought into the Committee of Public Safety, Lazare Carnot and Claude-Antoine Prieur (from the department of Côte-d'Or). But it was articulated by Barère in epic language. "From this moment," he declared, and "until our enemies are expelled from the territory of the Republic, all French are permanently enlisted for service to the armies." Young men would fight, married men would forge arms and transport food; children would shred rags for bandages; old men would be carried to the public squares where they would deliver patriotic speeches. As for women, "who must at last take their place and follow their true Revolutionary destiny, they will set aside futile work; and their delicate hands will stitch uniforms, make tents, and serve in hospitals." Although the full organization of such an enterprise would take months, by the beginning of September France was already embarked on the first great effort of "total war."[57]

But for both the Paris radicals and the cantonal delegates who remained in the city, it seemed clear that mass mobilization for war could never be effective without a parallel intensification of repression to root out the enemies whom they all believed were lurking within. The old fear resurfaced once again: if so many men marched away to the front, who could preserve the women and children from the threat of plots and conspiracy? Jacques Hébert regularly demanded a range of repressive measures to crush all opposition, attacking both the Convention and the Committee of Public Safety for being too soft. In mid-August the provincial delegates who had remained in Paris began promoting a "law of suspects," requiring the arrest, rapid trial, and execution of all perceived enemies. Claude Royer, a radical "red priest" and leader of a committee of delegates from Burgundy, put it succinctly: "You must be terrible, if you are to save our liberty." And in the Jacobin Club at the very end of August he introduced a phrase that soon became a watchword for radicals in both Paris and the Convention: "Terror must be made the order of the day."[58]

The Committee Turns to Terror

Throughout the summer the Committee of Public Safety had veered toward a policy of greater repression, partly in reaction to rebellion in the provinces, partly through pressure from the Parisian militants and provincial delegates. In their relation to the militants, the deputies were clearly torn. They remembered only too vividly the humiliation of June 2, when crowds from the city had dictated their actions. Yet the Montagnards still held the people of Paris in great respect and felt compelled to listen to their demands. The quandary was pressed on them once again in the first days of September, when they were confronted with another popular intervention into Convention politics, compelling the leadership to embrace an array of radical demands and to invigorate the repressive institutions created the previous spring.

Rumors in Paris of impending food shortages seem to have increased in the late summer. Between August 21 and September 4 noisy demonstrations in the streets and threats against bakers broke out almost every day.[59] The frustration and anger in the city were intensified on September 2 when news arrived in Paris that Toulon had welcomed in the British navy and had agreed to accept the son of Louis XVI as the new king of France. There seemed to be no end to the treachery and conspiracy.[60] Two days later many workers in the city began leaving their jobs, urged on by militants from the sections. They converged on the city hall, where they drew up a petition demanding more measures to increase the bread supply and to root out traitors and suspects. The municipal leaders Chaumette and Hébert gave dramatic speeches in support of such proposals. Hébert demanded not only a price freeze on basic necessities but the immediate organization of a Revolutionary Army, a corps created in theory the previous spring but never actually implemented. The paramilitary "army" would circulate in the countryside, both to compel the peasants to sell their grain and to arrest "suspects" who might be found there. The petitioners then decided that they would march on the Convention the next day to present their grievances. That evening the Jacobin Club gave its support to the march, despite Robespierre's plea to let the Convention and the Committee of Public Safety, on which he sat, handle the crisis.[61]

The great demonstration set off from the city hall a bit after noon on September 5, led by key members of the Paris Commune and the clubs, and including the vociferous presence of the Revolutionary Republican Women.[62] Only about two-thirds of the sections were represented, with many of the more moderate neighborhoods refusing to cooperate. Arriving at the Convention about an hour later, they were given permission to enter the hall, and "an enormous number of citizens" filed in to a roar of applause from the galleries and from many of the Montagnard deputies. As they had sometimes done in the past, a whole segment of the crowd took up seats on the largely empty benches of the right side of the hall, demonstrating symbolically that they too intended to take part in the process. Hundreds of other men and women crowded onto the floor of the assembly, singing patriotic songs and shouting, "Long live the Republic!" Some also carried signs proclaiming, "War on tyrants and aristocrats!" or "War on grain hoarders!"

The rhetoric of petitioners was more violent than ever. Chaumette demanded the immediate arrest of unspecified "suspects" and the surveillance of the rich, these "new lords" who purchased the property of "their former masters" and who speculated on the people's misery, just as the aristocrats once did. It was time, announced a speaker for the Jacobins—adopting the phrase of the abbé Royer—"to make terror the order of the day." The violent rhetoric reached a climax in a speech by the Conventionnel Jean-Baptiste Drouet, the onetime stable master who had led the arrest of Louis XVI at Varennes in 1791. All pity for the enemies of the Revolution, he declared, must be ended. Anyone suspected of evil intentions must be arrested, and if ever the liberty of the nation were placed in peril, they must be massacred without mercy. We must "be brigands!" he cried out, in the defense of liberty. The obvious suggestion for a renewal of the September

Massacres drew immediate disapproval from many of the deputies. Thuriot, who still sat on the Committee of Public Safety, countered with a passionate speech of his own: "Revolutions are not made to commit crime, but to bring the triumph of virtue."

Yet the pressure to intensify the repression was enormous. The Committee of Public Safety—like the Convention itself—struggled throughout the day to find an adequate response. At one point the crowds even burst into the Committee's normally closed meeting to make their opinions known. Finally, toward the end of the day, Barère stepped up once again to deliver a message from the intimidated Committee members. His speech, improvised under the influence of the crowds, was scattered and rambling. He began with rhetoric clearly intended to please the militants, including a repetition of the Jacobin phrase, "Let us make terror the order of the day!" He then declared that the Revolutionary Tribunal must be used to crush not only royalists but moderates as well. Yet he too repudiated Drouet, making it clear that justice and repression must be pursued through the institutional authority of the tribunals. In the end, his immediate proposals were relatively meager, demanding only that a Revolutionary Army be implemented and that unattached soldiers in the streets of Paris be rounded up—a demand that no one had actually made. Nevertheless, he issued a solemn promise that the Committee would soon develop other proposals in response to the demands made in the Convention that day.[63]

Once again Barère managed to mollify the crowds, who now seemed satisfied and exited the hall. Yet the Committee of Public Safety continued its meeting long into the night in what could only have been an agonizing session. We will never know the details of their discussions. Not all of the members seem to have been in agreement, and there may have been an open confrontation between Robespierre and Thuriot.[64] But the majority of the Committee may well have made a series of fundamental decisions about the direction of the Revolution. All of those present undoubtedly sympathized with the plight of the people. At the same time all, including Robespierre, were deeply unhappy with the eruption of the crowds into the Convention and the Committee. They were suspicious that the people might be misled by secret conspirators, including perhaps some of the militant leaders themselves. And they were convinced that if they were to lead a successful war against both internal and external enemies, they could not tolerate the chaos and the threats from the streets. It is unclear whether they established a comprehensive plan of action. Nevertheless, they almost certainly considered strategies for acquiescing to militant demands while simultaneously acting to prevent popular disruptions in the future. The minister Garat, who often sat with the Committee in the past, described its general dilemma and the tightrope it was compelled to cross: "When one lacks the power to enforce one's authority, one can only be successful if one acts with great caution." And more succinctly, "before attempting to govern, one must have a government." Robespierre had much the same thought in mind when he jotted down in his private notes the absolute necessity of creating a functional, centralized government—"a single will" (a *volonté une*)—that could save the Revolution.[65]

As a first step toward placating the militants, the Committee members resolved to invite the Convention radicals Collot d'Herbois and Billaud-Varenne to join them in the Committee. They thus coopted two of their harshest critics, both of whom had strongly supported the demands of the militants on September 5.[66] At the same time they moved rapidly to attack the most vulnerable of the militant leaders. There could be no question at this point of directly confronting Hébert—who remained a member of the Paris Commune and who had the support of Collot and Billaud. But they obtained the arrest of two of the enragé leaders, Jacques Roux and Jean-François Varlet, while largely muzzling Leclerc through intimidation. A few weeks later, they moved to shut down the club of Revolutionary Republican Women, who were so closely allied with the enragés.[67] There was also an effort by the leadership to rein in the activities of the Paris sections. On a motion by Danton, the Convention voted to end the "permanent" sessions of the sections that had existed for over a year and to limit them to two meetings per week.[68] To be sure, the poorest male citizens were now to be paid if they attended such meetings—ostensibly to make them more democratic—and neighborhood popular societies, along with the Jacobin and Cordeliers clubs, would continue to be active. Yet direct popular interventions into the Convention would largely cease, and there was a dramatic decline after September in the number of collective demonstrations by the radical militants and sans-culottes.[69]

Nevertheless, the Committee could no longer ignore the demands of the September 5 petitioners and Barère's promise to increase the prosecution of "suspects." Over the following weeks the Committee would expand and invigorate the institutions created in the panic atmosphere of March and April and promote a vastly more efficient state-supported organization of repression. Although the proposal that "terror be made the order of the day" was never formally decreed, for all practical purposes the phrase now came to characterize state policy, and it would be repeated dozens of times in the Convention over the following months.[70]

On September 9 the Convention created the Revolutionary Army that the Parisian militants had so long clamored for, implementing a law that had been on the books since June 2 but that had never been executed.[71] By the autumn a paid paramilitary force of dedicated militants was roaming the countryside, compelling the peasantry to sell their grain and turn over anyone who appeared suspicious. Commonly recruited from the lower classes of Parisian society, the well-armed and poorly disciplined irregulars would have a terrifying effect on the rural people and would soon actively promote an attack on the church and the Christian religion. At the same time, by sending hundreds of such men out into the countryside, the Committee and the Montagnard leadership succeeded in removing temporarily some of the city's most active—and disruptive—militants.[72]

Equally important, however, in the institutionalization of the Terror was the infamous "law of suspects," passed by the Convention with very little debate on September 17. The intention of the law was supposedly to give a more precise definition to the concept of "suspect." In fact, however, the text included a series of elastic clauses, targeting all those who "have shown themselves to be the partisans of tyranny or federalism or are enemies of liberty" or who could not produce evidence of *civisme*—a term signifying "public spiritedness" but whose meaning was never itself clearly defined.[73] In any case, the actual designation of suspects was entirely in the hands of the local surveillance committees, which assumed the role often played earlier in the Revolution by the popular societies. Such committees would be all the more threatening, moreover, in that virtually no appeal was possible against their decisions and that they were now to be purged and to consist only of the most radical patriots. The previous June Barère had attacked the activities of such surveillance committees for their violations of the Declaration of Rights. But since then the Committee of Public Safety had clearly changed its position. As Collot d'Herbois explained it, "the rights of man were not made for counterrevolutionaries, but only for the sansculottes." Jullien readily admitted to her son that arrests were sometimes made in error. She described the case of a friend who had been jailed, she believed, merely because he originated in the rebellious city of Lyon: "The anger is such as to make it a crime even to come from Lyon." But she seemed ultimately resigned to the situation. Such "arrests sometimes cause problems and concern for everyone. But they are so necessary for the security of the state that even those who are innocent victims cannot complain if they are truly republican."[74] In any case, the number of prisoners in Paris now increased rapidly, nearly doubling between late August and late October.[75]

The investigation and trial of all these new prisoners was the central concern of the Revolutionary Tribunal. Since its creation the previous March, there had been numerous complaints from the radicals that the court was too slow and too lenient.[76] In the wake of September 5, however, the Tribunal was substantially enlarged, with the recruitment of a considerable number of new judges and jurors and the creation of four separate sections, so that multiple cases could be tried at the same time. An increasing proportion of magistrates and jury members originated from among the Parisian radicals, with a strong contingent of artisans and small tradesmen. Indeed, the period from September through the end of the year would see a sharp augmentation in both the number of cases tried and the number and proportion of individuals condemned to death. In late September the Tribunal was also given its own prison, the adjoining Conciergerie, where all those assigned to the court's jurisdiction were held before their trials and while awaiting execution.[77]

All of these measures, initiated by the Committee of Public Safety, were ratified by the majority of the Convention. To be sure, some of the Montagnards complained about the obvious swing toward such a policy of Terror. On September 25 Thuriot, who had been increasingly at odds with Robespierre and who had just resigned from the Committee in protest, made a passionate plea that the repression be moderated. "We must halt this raging torrent," he declared, "that is leading us to barbarism." But both Barère and Robespierre defended the policies of the Committee and implicitly took Thuriot to task. Anyone who attacked the Committee, declared Robespierre ominously, "is an enemy of the nation. . . . He is an ally of the tyrants who wage war against us." Then, in a dramatic act, Robespierre proposed that he and the entire Committee should resign. But the Convention refused even to consider such a proposal and declared that the Committee had "their full confidence."[78]

For the next ten months the twelve men who sat on the Committee of Public Safety in mid-September would be maintained continuously in their positions by the Convention, and throughout the fall the Committee continued to consolidate its power. On September 13 it was given the authority to nominate the membership of all Convention committees. By October it had also obtained the right to direct the specific inquiries of the Revolutionary Tribunal. In the meantime, the Committee of General Security, in charge of the repressive activities of the Convention, was packed with radical Montagnards, who would henceforth work closely with the Committee of Public Safety.[79]

Even more important was a decree of October 10 that formally endowed the Committee of Public Safety with executive and governmental authority. Such a measure had been proposed by Danton over two months earlier, but it had been rejected at the time by several of the members themselves, including Robespierre and Barère.[80] Now Saint-Just was able to obtain just such an expansion of its powers. He spoke to the Convention of the problems of the war and the economy, although he placed his greatest emphasis on the internal situation, and notably on the treachery, self-interest, and "moderation" of a great many government officials. "The enemies of the Republic," he proclaimed, "are within the government itself." They must pursue a far harsher repression, to cleanse the state of the conspiracies that infest it and to "govern with the sword those who cannot be governed through justice." He then demanded that the Committee be recognized as the executive authority of France and that the Constitution be set aside for the duration of the war: "The provisional government of France must be revolutionary until victory is achieved."[81]

The attitudes of the deputies toward this array of repressive and centralizing measures is difficult to assess. Most were no longer willing to share their thoughts with friends in letters that might well be opened by surveillance committees or the police. Yet a great many in both the Plain and the Mountain probably felt they had no choice but to grant full powers to the Committee, if all the enemies who threatened the Republic were ever to be defeated. In a letter to her son, Jullien described the plight of her deputy husband, a staunch supporter of the Mountain and of Robespierre. He continued to suffer, she said, both physically and morally from the terrible situation in which the Revolutionaries found themselves. "Our enemies," she exclaimed, "have compelled the legislators to take measures that diminish their humanity, even though they are ultimately dictated by wisdom." Pierre Dubreuil also divulged his discouragement in a letter to his son on their farm in Poitou. He admitted that he was exhausted and that he had hoped the Convention would soon complete its tasks, so that he could return home. But in the course of September he had changed his mind. All the "true patriots" were now telling him that he must stay the course: "You have saved the fatherland," they told him. "But it is still in danger. Your mission is not yet completed. You must remain at your post." He only hoped that Heaven would soon grant the nation the peace and tranquility it so badly needed.[82]

The Death of the Girondins

One of the most difficult problems that the Convention and the Committee of Public Safety had to face concerned the fate of the Girondins. Since June 2 Parisian militants had pushed for their trial and punishment. No one would do so more vigorously than Jacques Hébert, who never forgot the personal humiliation of being arrested and interrogated the previous May by the Girondin-controlled Commission of Twelve.[83] The Montagnard leadership, however, had long put off a decision. They had initially treated the house arrest of the twenty-nine deputies as a temporary expedient. In early July Saint-Just, designated by the Committee of Public Safety to sift through the evidence, had recommended trying only a few of the leaders, describing most of those in question as "misguided" men who deserved amnesty. According to Rosalie Jullien, who often saw Barère and other members of the Committee, the leaders had too many other difficult problems to confront. "The trial of these fine gentlemen," she wrote in late June, "would only open the door to quarrel and discord."[84]

It was only after so many of the Girondins had escaped and joined up with the federalists that the position of the leadership toughened. When Brissot was captured in Moulins and brought back to Paris, the Convention had immediately sent him to prison, and with the killing of Marat the remainder of those still in Paris were subjected to similar treatment. Over the summer other Girondin sympathizers were arrested as well: one who had helped Pétion escape, another who had been on mission in the provinces, and two who had been visited by Charlotte Corday shortly before she had assassinated Marat. On July 28 all those who had fled were formally declared "traitors" and thus subject to immediate execution.[85] It was under this decree that the Girondin journalist Gorsas was judged when he was caught slipping back into Paris to visit his mistress. On October 7 he became the first deputy of any Revolutionary assembly to be executed.[86]

Throughout this period the Convention remained under intense pressure to bring all of the Girondins to justice. Barère seemed to have promised such a trial in his September 5 speech. Yet Hébert continued his attacks in his newspaper, and there were numerous petitions demanding a trial presented to the assembly by the sections and the Jacobin Club. The militants had argued since the previous spring that the Girondins were traitors and conspirators, and now they demanded immediate retribution: "that Brissot and his accomplices receive without delay the punishment justified by their crimes."[87]

Finally on October 3 Jean-Pierre Amar, a member of the Committee of General Security, presented a long formal indictment of the Girondin deputies. The list was now expanded from twenty-nine to forty-one—though only twenty-one were actually present in Paris—and it included the two young Girondins Boyer-Fonfrède and Ducos, who still sat in the Convention.[88] The Committee had undertaken extensive research into the past activities of the accused, poring over their speeches and publications and the correspondence seized in their homes or opened at the post office. A whole panoply of evil deeds was developed to tarnish the reputations of specific individuals and of the "faction" in general. Much was made of Carra's strange proposal in July 1792 that the duke of Brunswick be made king; of the secret letters to the monarch written about the same time by Vergniaud and Gensonné; of Brissot's known links to Dumouriez; and of Isnard's threat to have Paris destroyed. But the central accusation was that the Girondins had incited and directly participated in the federalist uprisings and that they could be linked to the assassination of Marat and perhaps even to the Vendée rebellion and to the British prime minister Pitt. Amar admitted that the group had sometimes seemed to disagree on certain specific issues. But this, he argued, was only "better to hide their criminal association," and there could be no doubt that "they acted together to bring ruin upon the nation."[89]

The indictment of the Girondin leadership had not been unanticipated and had been announced the previous night in the Jacobin Club. Far more unexpected was Amar's demand that seventy-five other Girondin sympathizers be arrested. The expanded list included all those deputies who had signed protests against the June 2 decrees, protests that had never been published but had been found in the pocket of the deputy Deperret when he was arrested in July. As Amar began speaking, the doors of the hall were locked, and all those on the list were immediately pulled from their seats and transferred to prison. Claude-Antoine Blad, whose name was on the list and who was arrested that day, seems to have been taken totally by surprise. Louis-Sébastien Mercier was likewise taken away and incarcerated. Several Montagnards demanded that these men also be placed on trial, but Robespierre intervened on their behalf, and all were interred in La Force Prison, where they would remain for over a year.[90]

The Girondins' trial before the Revolutionary Tribunal began on October 24 and continued for seven days. Sitting in judgment were five magistrates and a jury of fourteen men, all of them radical militants and the majority from Paris itself. An estimated 1,200 spectators, including Rosalie Jullien, followed the proceedings from the rear of the chamber or in the balconies.[91] The crowd was no doubt attracted by the presence of several of the major leaders of the faction, including Brissot, Vergniaud, Gensonné, Lasource, Fonfrède, Ducos, and Carra. But the remainder were relatively less known, and some were very much on the margins of the group—"small fry," as Jullien called them. It was the first time a large group of diverse individuals was "bundled" together, a procedure that was to characterize several of the major political trials over the coming year.[92] As in the trial of the king in January, the Girondins were permitted to have a defense attorney—apparently named by the court—and were allowed to testify in their own defense. However, they were not allowed to see the evidence against them in advance, and they were never able to call witnesses in their defense—only prosecution witnesses were heard. A great deal of hearsay or secondhand testimony was entered into evidence, despite the vigorous protests of the defendants. The prosecution was led by the able and sinuous Antoine Fouquier-Tinville, but at times the magistrates and the jurors also spoke up and aggressively attacked the accused.[93]

The chief witnesses for the prosecution were all leading militants: Chaumette, Dobsen, Léonard Bourdon, and above all Hébert himself. In many respects, Hébert served as a second prosecuting attorney, attacking the defendants incessantly with extraordinary energy and anger. But Brissot, Gensonné, and especially Vergniaud had been among the most effective orators of the Convention. At one point Vergniaud summoned all his soaring eloquence to respond to the accusations of Hébert. He recalled his long dedication to the Revolution, insisting that all his actions must be placed in the context of past events and that they were motivated only by love of the Republic. Listening to the speeches, Jullien admitted that she was tempted to sympathize with the accused: "My heart suffered, for austere justice does not exclude tender humanity and pity."[94]

The relentless Fouquier-Tinville quickly countered by producing Verg-niaud's letter to his constituency, the "Men of the Gironde!" appeal of the previous May, which seemed to call for an insurrection against Paris and the Montagnards.[95] Yet both Fouquier and Hébert realized the danger of their being bested in the courtroom and of losing the support of public opinion. Frustrated and increasingly uneasy, Hébert demanded in his news-paper and in the Jacobin Club that the trial be curtailed. The court mag-istrates also appealed directly to the Convention. If they were compelled to follow the letter of the law, they argued, all of the accused might give endless rebuttals and the trial could go on forever. In their view, however, the outcome was already clear: "The proof of their crimes is evident; all of us maintain the firm conviction that they are guilty." The Jacobins also petitioned the deputies. In order that "these monsters may perish" and that "the terror remain the order of the day," they must end the trial and con-vict the accused. In the face of such pressure, Robespierre and Barère pro-posed a "compromise" that the trial could be concluded as soon as the jury affirmed that their conscience was sufficiently enlightened.[96]

The next day, October 30, the jury initially insisted that they still did not have enough evidence, and so the testimony continued for several more hours. But after a long afternoon adjournment—and most likely after a certain amount of persuasion by the magistrates and the prosecutor—the jury announced they were ready to deliberate. A contemporary observer described the moment when the jury returned about ten o'clock that night, after three hours of deliberations and after the accused had been led back into the court: "The torchlit room and the advanced hour of the night, with both the judges and the audience exhausted by the long session: all gave the scene a somber, imposing, and terrible appearance."[97] But the scene was even more terrible when the jurymen announced their verdict. All twenty-one defendants were found guilty of conspiracy against the unity and in-divisibility of the Republic. One of the jurors then read an explanation of the decision. There was ample evidence, he declared, that the accused had long acted together through secret conclaves at night and had conspired to encourage treasonous uprisings in the provinces, including plans for an armed march against the city of Paris. Such behavior had brought the Re-public to the edge of disaster. It was hoped that the example of the severe treatment dealt to them would frighten other deputies who might be tempted to imitate their behavior. Jullien, who was also present, seemed similarly

Brissot and the Girondins sentenced to death by the Revolutionary Tribunal, October 30, 1793. The sentence has just been read and the condemned deputies gesticulate in protest while the audience also reacts. The Declaration of the Rights of Man is behind the judges. Perhaps one of the women in the scene is Rosalie Jullien. Bibliothèque nationale de France.

convinced: "During the seven days that this great affair was considered by the tribunal, all the defendants spoke vigorously and at length, but the prosecution witnesses clearly revealed the falsity of all their explanations."[98]

The head judge then issued his sentence. By virtue of the law on "crimes against the unity of the republic"—a law passed unanimously by the Convention the previous December—all twenty-one would be sent the next day to the guillotine.[99] The Girondins seemed stunned and unprepared for such a sentence. "Terror was painted on all their faces," wrote Jullien. "Brissot dropped his head. Vergniaud raised his arms and seemed to appeal to the people. Gensonné tried to challenge the sentence, but he was told there was nothing more to say." Others cried out, "I am innocent!" or even "Long live the Republic!" Suddenly they all spontaneously rose to protest and the whole room fell into turmoil, with everyone shouting at once. Then the convicted deputies were gathered up by the police and carried away to their cells. One of the twenty-one remained behind, however. Dufriche-Valazé, in whose apartment the Girondins had so frequently met, lay inert on his bench, having stabbed himself through the heart.[100]

On the following day, October 31, the twenty men still alive were placed in four carts and submitted to a "passage of infamy," not unlike that of the Old Regime, a slow drive in a cart from the prison of the Conciergerie up the Seine to the Place de la Révolution. All had read stories of the Romans who bravely went to their deaths, and most were determined to do so themselves. The two youngest, Fonfrède and Ducos, were said to have sung patriotic songs. Some, like the men from Bordeaux, had been close friends since well before the Revolution, and according to witnesses, they all embraced one another at the foot of the scaffold. They then lined up, climbed the platform, and faced their death one after another. Until that day, it was the greatest number ever devoured at one time by the great machine.

According to a police observer present to record the event, many people began leaving after the sixth execution, "with somber faces and a look of great consternation." When the last head had fallen, there were the inevitable shouts of "Long live the Republic! Long live the Nation!" But after that, he wrote, "few people spoke to one another."[101] Many of those executed would have been well known and easily identifiable to the crowds. Only recently they had ranked among the most influential and powerful men in France. For many of those present, their demise could only have been sobering, if not terrifying.

12

The Year II and the Great Terror

E VEN BEFORE the Girondins went to their death, contemporaries were becoming much more cautious as to what they set down in writing. Many ceased correspondence altogether. For those who continued, the transparency of their thoughts and opinions was frequently clouded by fear and self-censorship. Some burned everything they had previously written or received, or tore out and destroyed whole sections of their diaries.[1] Adrien Colson confined his messages strictly to business. The elderly Guittard de Floriban continued his journal, but he generally recounted only the "facts," the events that he read in the newspaper or that he observed from his window or during his walks near Saint-Sulpice. For a time Rosalie Jullien remained more forthright, since her letters were sent in a special pouch to her son, the personal agent of Robespierre. Yet by February 1794 she felt compelled to add a note to anyone opening her letter, begging them not to block a message from a mother to her son. Thereafter, she and many of the other observers whose letters are preserved became much more ideological and stilted in their expression. Of all our witnesses, perhaps only Nicolas Ruault persisted in writing candid letters. But they were sent far less frequently and only when he could confide them to a private messenger whom he trusted. Otherwise, as he noted to his brother, he would be compelled for reasons of personal safety to conform to the dominant politics and language.[2]

From Radical Reform to Dechristianization

To be sure, throughout the "Year II"—from September 1793 to September 1794, following the new Revolutionary calendar—the spirit of '89, the idealism and fervor for the improvement of humanity never disappeared. In some respects they became even stronger. The period was marked by a series of measures that sought to create a more just and egalitarian society. The Declaration of Rights voted by the Convention in June 1793 had committed the Republic to universal education and public assistance for all those in need. In December of that year the deputies decreed that every commune should have a primary school with teachers paid by the state. The following February they voted a budget of ten million livres for aid to the indigent, the aged, the infirm, and unmarried women with young children, even those born out of wedlock. "Illegitimate" children were henceforth to be considered equal before the law to all other children—a remarkable innovation considering the prejudices of the age. Additional measures were aimed at promoting agriculture and transportation—partly no doubt to assist the war effort but also to improve conditions for the general population.[3] The attempted division of communal property and the so-called Ventôse decrees in late February and early March represented preliminary attempts at land redistribution. Pushed through the Convention by Saint-Just, such laws would have distributed among the poor the property seized from those condemned by the Revolutionary Tribunal.[4] Perhaps even more extraordinary was the decree on February 4, 1794 abolishing slavery throughout the French colonies. France became the first great power in modern times to pass such a law. Indeed, the end of slavery was the occasion for a major popular celebration in Paris, attended by thousands of men and women, including a number of Africans living in the city. Even Guittard—who had lost all his investments in the Caribbean after the slave uprisings there—was surprisingly enthusiastic: "So now all the slaves are free and on their own." And in honor of "this memorable day of emancipation," he drew a little sketch in his diary of a black man and black woman holding hands.[5]

The Convention had also pursued a series of remarkable changes for women. Decrees instituting rights for wives within the family—over family property and the control of children—had substantially improved their condition compared to the Old Regime. With the advent of divorce, thousands of French women would turn to the courts to escape unhappy marriages.[6] However, the Convention had also moved to restrict their political rights. In September and October 1793 the radical club of Revolutionary Republican Women, dominated by middle-class members, was involved in a series of bitter quarrels with the working-class women in Paris. Those in the central marketplace, in particular, were enraged by the club's efforts to force them to wear the red Republican caps, and other specified elements of dress. In October the market women urged the Convention to abolish the club. The deputies, who were already impatient with the club's links to the enragés, took the occasion to abolish not only this society but all female popular societies. Some of the deputies accompanied their speeches with misogynist rhetoric about the need for wives and daughters to confine themselves to their homes. But if they were no longer allowed to create their own clubs, they were by no means ready to return to their housework. They were still allowed to sit in the galleries of male clubs, and a great many continued to do so and to attend and petition the Convention and the neighborhood sections. Rosalie Jullien followed politics as passionately as before—at least until the fall of Robespierre in July 1794.[7]

In reality many of the Convention's social decrees, including those on education and land redistribution, were implemented only haltingly, if at all. The war and the terrible factional politics inside France often made it impossible for the Montagnards to carry through such reforms before they fell from power. Yet some such efforts were realized by individual representatives on mission acting on their own initiative. Thus Gilbert Romme, assigned to several departments in the southwest, attempted to use his all-encompassing powers at the local level not only to support the war and repress counterrevolution but also to promote greater equality and "fair shares for all." He worked to ensure food provisions for all classes—the "bread of equality"—to promote education and agriculture, and to expand assistance for the sick and the poor. He and many other such representatives shared the dream of "a society reconciled with itself," a *grande famille* in which children from all classes would receive an equal education and in which the gap between rich and poor would be diminished.[8] Even if the efforts of Romme and other idealists among the representatives on mission failed or were short-lived; even when so many of the egalitarian decrees of the Convention, including women's rights and the abolition of slavery, were swept away by later regimes; the attempts would serve as a powerful legacy for future generations of men and women, inspiring dreams throughout the nineteenth and twentieth centuries of a more equal and humane society.

Unfortunately, however, during the Year II such dreams did not always include the virtues of tolerance. From early in the Revolution many patriots had shown impatience toward those unprepared to embrace their vision of the "new man." By 1793 a whole segment of the most radical militants were attacking not only the counterrevolutionaries, but anyone whose attachment to the Revolution was deemed insufficiently energetic. Moderation and passivity could be treated as crimes. Those who did not support their views in every respect must be against them. The intolerance of the militants was particularly salient in their attack on the church and the clergy.[9] Nothing better illustrates the extraordinary distance traveled since 1789 by the most militant Revolutionaries than their rapidly evolving views on religion. With the progress of the Revolution and the overthrow of all the old authorities, was it not time, they asked, to declare the reign of reason and to cast aside the superstition of the saints and the Trinity and the magical hocus-pocus of the Catholic liturgy? Was it not now clear that all religion was a sham, concocted by the clergy to maintain their positions of power and influence in society?

There can be no doubt that the great majority of the population—even among the working classes of Paris—had continued to support Catholicism through the early years of the Revolution. When leaders of the Paris Commune tried to forbid the midnight mass on Christmas Eve 1792 and the Corpus Christi procession in May 1793, much of the population ignored the interdictions and pursued these popular religious celebrations as before.[10] By the autumn of 1793, however, with the radical militants increasingly influential in the Convention and in control of the Commune and the sections, many felt the time had come to entirely expunge "superstition" from the Republic. In September the representative on mission Joseph Fouché began forcibly closing down churches in two departments of central France, expelling the clergy, and aggressively promoting atheism. Similar initiatives were soon followed by representatives in other regions of the country, and by the end of the winter there were hardly any parishes in all of France where clergymen were still saying mass. The Constitutional priests, most of whom had strongly supported the Revolution and the Republic, were told they were no longer needed, and they were forced to resign and retire. Whether through fear or conviction, several thousand also burned their letters of priesthood and repudiated their former profession. Hundreds of them then proceeded to take wives.

In Paris the movement of "dechristianization" arrived with a vengeance in October and November of that year. A new Revolutionary calendar, conceived in part by Gilbert Romme, was formally adopted in October and implemented in late November. Time was henceforth to be measured not from the birth of Christ, but from the birth of the Republic on September

21, 1792. The twelve months of the year were renamed with more rational denominations describing the seasons. Thus, November 25, 1793, now became 5 Frimaire (the chilly month) of the Year II of the Republic. Even more dramatic was the replacement of the seven-day week by the ten-day "decade," so that the day of rest would no longer be on every seventh Sunday but on every tenth "decadi." To further emphasize the radical break, the militants set about changing the names of places—of towns, streets, and physical features—effacing all reference to the saints or the Virgin or anything that smacked of the Christian religion, just as they had earlier removed references to royalty.[11]

At first Guittard's parish of Saint-Sulpice in Paris attempted to celebrate Catholic mass on both the decadi—to pray for the success of the French armies—and on the former "Sundays." But then the Commune, led by its *procureur* Chaumette, began enforcing the closing of all churches and strongly encouraging the end of all masses.[12] The last service in his parish was held on October 15. For a time, there was an effort to continue saying mass in private chapels, but this too was discouraged and soon perceived as dangerous. Guittard entered into his diary in unusual detail a description of the new state of affairs. The reliquary of Sainte Geneviève and all of the chalices of Saint-Sulpice were carried away to be melted down in the mint. Three priests from the parish came to his section, accompanied by their new wives, and ostentatiously burned their ordination letters. Theology, they declared, was only petty nonsense and, in fact, "they had never believed a word of what they had preached, which had only served to deceive the people." Local militants built a bonfire of sacred books and vestments, and "a philosopher gave a speech announcing that there was no more religion and no more God, and that everything was a question of Nature." At about the same time the bishop of Paris and nearly all other clergymen sitting in the Convention removed their crucifixes and renounced the priesthood. Celebrations in the ex-cathedral of Notre Dame were held in honor of a statue of liberty and a "goddess of reason." Soon thereafter sans-culotte militants began knocking off the heads of the long rows of Gothic saints carved on the building's exterior. "This," wrote Guittard, "is the new religion, or rather cult, established now in all the churches of Paris."[13]

Although Guittard described these events without commentary, we know from ensuing entries that he was extremely upset. Several months later, he expressed his satisfaction when both Chaumette and the former bishop of Paris were sent to the guillotine. It was they who had said that "that there was no God and that man had no soul." "But God uncovered the schemes of these wretches."[14] And Guittard was not the only Jacobin supporter angered by the antireligious culture being imposed by the militants through coercion and terror. Nicolas Ruault was convinced—like Voltaire whom he so admired—that the common people needed religion. He worried about the effects in the provinces of "the repression of priests and the destruction of all churches and of religion." And he was appalled by the bacchanalian antics of some of the younger militants in the streets near his apartment: "A hundred scoundrels marched in a carnival-like procession, dressed in priestly vestments, leading a donkey draped in clerical garb." He was also saddened by the destruction of the tombs of the French kings in the basilica of Saint-Denis just north of Paris. "What sad times," he wrote, "when both the living and the dead are so persecuted."[15]

Rosalie Jullien, who leaned toward a more Rousseauist vision of religion, shared Ruault's unhappiness with the events unrolling in her city, events that had taken her quite by surprise. Everyone, she wrote, was "struck with an electric shock." "It was a revolutionary flood that was impossible to halt in Paris. Like the members of the Convention we are all quite stunned." Yet to some extent she was torn. For the attacks on religion seemed to represent the will of the people—or at least those who now dominated the sections—the people whom she had so long trusted and revered. Perhaps, after all, the essence of Christianity was to be found in its ethical system. Like Jacques Hébert, she wondered if Jesus should not be viewed as "the best of the sans-culottes."[16]

For the time being, the private opinions of Guittard, Jullien, and Ruault could have no effect on the situation. But Robespierre was also angered by the atheism that the new movement seemed to promote. Like Jullien, he had long been attached to Rousseau's more spiritual interpretation of religion, and he openly condemned dechristianization in the Convention. In his view, it was all part of a foreign plot to sow dissension among peaceful Catholics who desired to practice their faith. He then pushed through a decree reaffirming continued religious tolerance, as guaranteed by the Declarations of Rights of 1789 and 1793.[17]

In the short term, Robespierre's efforts met with only mixed success. However, after he had consolidated his political influence in the spring of 1794, he would be largely responsible for the crackdown on the nonbeliever Chaumette and the defrocked bishop of Paris. He took the lead in promoting a more "deist" religious cult of the "Supreme Being" that openly

Festival of the Supreme Being, June 8, 1794. Contingents of national guardsmen, women, and children march in front of the "Mountain" designed by David in the Champ de Mars, where the altar of the fatherland previously stood. A cart holds a woman dressed as the goddess of liberty. Robespierre delivered a speech that day from somewhere on the mountain. © Coll. Musée de la Révolution française, Domaine de Vizille, MRF 1984.734.

repudiated atheism. In early June, he officiated at a magnificent ceremony in the heart of the city in honor of the new cult. The artist-deputy Jacques-Louis David had a symbolic mountain erected in the Champ de Mars, where the altar of the fatherland once stood—"an artificial mountain that was charming, picturesque, and magnificent," as Jullien described it. An estimated 400,000 women and men came out for the occasion. Robespierre, who was president of the Convention at the time, stood on a platform, gave an appropriate speech, and then dramatically set fire to an effigy of the "monster of atheism." Afterward everyone was invited to sing hymns in honor of the Supreme Being.[18]

Ruault, Jullien, and Guittard all seemed sincerely enthusiastic about the great June festival and prepared to accept this more moderate, deist form of dechristianization. But others were far more critical. On the extreme left, radicals like Billaud and Collot, both members of the Committee of Public Safety, would probably have preferred to be rid of religion altogether. They were enormously irritated by the role of "pontiff" that Robespierre seemed to assume during the ceremonies and of all his self-righteous talk about "virtue." On the other hand, in large areas of France, the whole movement of dechristianization, the violence done to deeply held beliefs, was experienced as perhaps the harshest and most unconscionable of all the acts of the Year II. To be sure, a few of the more fervent patriots in the towns were prepared to accept and enforce such measures and to embrace the new Revolutionary culture—whether in the form of a cult of Reason or a cult of the Supreme Being. Yet a great many others in all social classes, including those who had embraced the Constitutional Church, were horrified and indignant by the closing of their parishes and the removal of their priests. Who would now administer the last rites to loved ones and offer prayers for their passage through the afterlife? This "cultural revolution," pushed through by a minority of urban militants, seemed to place their very souls in jeopardy.

Winning the Wars

If the Revolutionaries of the Year II proved relatively ineffective in transforming French cultural beliefs, they would be far more successful in their epic struggle against the great powers of Europe. By the fall of 1793 hundreds of thousands of young Frenchmen were demonstrating their readiness to fight for the new regime. Some, to be sure, had been drafted into the military with little choice in the matter. Desertion would continue to pose a problem for French commanders, and in certain regions of the country peasants would persist in their protests against conscription.[19] Yet the French armies could never have succeeded if large numbers of soldiers had not been deeply committed to the Revolutionary goal to "live free or die." Many had previously participated in the national guard units and popular societies of their hometowns. Others, adolescents too young to join such organizations, had enthusiastically watched and listened from afar, sometimes forming separate youth clubs or national guard companies.[20] When offered the opportunity, a great many had rushed to volunteer, and by early 1794 the French forces had grown to some 750,000 soldiers. Once at the front, the new recruits would continue to be influenced by propaganda from clubs in the towns where they were billeted and from radical newspapers—like the *Père Duchesne*—freely distributed by the war ministry. Not a few would march into battle singing the "Marseillaise" or the "Chant du départ": "Now the Republic calls on us. We can only triumph or perish. All French must learn to live for it. For it all French can also die."[21]

During the summer of 1793, despite all the patriotic fervor, the Revolution had once again seemed on the verge of collapse before the combined forces of the European coalition. The counteroffensive begun in March 1793 had continued through late August, pushing forward slowly on all fronts, and the French often found themselves backed up into their own territory. As late as January 1794 dozens of towns and villages within France's borders were still occupied by foreign armies, including the northern fortresses of Valenciennes, Condé, Le Quesnoy, and Haguenau, captured by Austrian or Prussian armies.[22]

Yet slowly at first, in September and October, and then with growing success at the beginning of winter, the armies of the Republic began reversing the momentum and taking the offensive once again. As in the past, success came in part from a failure of coordination among the great powers. The Prussians sent much of their army into eastern Europe to ensure a second partition of Poland. The British made it clear they were far more interested in achieving control of English Channel ports than of pursuing joint attacks with the Austrians. The key to success for the French resurgence, however, was the extraordinary mass mobilization within the Republic itself, promoted by Parisian and provincial radicals in August and now embraced by the Convention and the Committee of Public Safety. By the end of 1793 the appeal for a "total war" to save the Revolution was beginning to work its magic. Ever greater numbers of Frenchmen were arriving on the frontiers, and much of the economy was now being mobilized to funnel armaments and supplies to the troops.[23]

The Committee of Public Safety devoted all its waking hours to organizing the war effort, with several members acting as de facto ministers with virtually unlimited powers. Lazare Carnot oversaw the general organization and strategy of the army; Claude-Antoine Prieur took charge of munitions and armaments; Robert Lindet looked after food supplies; Jeanbon-Saint-André, the onetime sea captain, supervised the reorganization of the navy. On several occasions, Carnot, Prieur, and Saint-Just traveled to the front themselves, collaborating with other deputies on mission to the armies and sometimes directly participating in operations on the field. During the same period, deputies from the Convention, assigned systematically to all regions of France, were actively involved in recruiting soldiers and requisitioning horses, saddles, food supplies, and metal for muskets and cannons. They did all in their power to cultivate popular support, overseeing local clubs and newspapers and promoting popular festivals to nurture patriotism.[24]

To a certain extent, war itself was being revolutionized by the French, as they experimented with new strategies to match the sharply modified composition of their armies. For the most part the soldiers of the Republic no longer needed the strict drilling and ordered movements in rows and columns, necessary to keep the conscript armies of the Old Regime marching into battle. Rather than advancing ponderously through a series of careful maneuvers and sieges, the politically motivated young Frenchmen were sometimes sent in mass attacks against one point in the enemy lines, rushing forward with abandon to "terrorize" their opponents.[25] They largely abandoned the goal of winning over opposing soldiers to the cause of the Revolution. They spoke rather of giving no quarter to the "slave armies" who opposed them. "We will no longer fight like Don Quixote," wrote Etienne Chaillon, the Breton deputy who sat with the Plain. "Our new approach is to bring fear and terror to all those who oppose us." At one point, the Convention even decreed that no English prisoners would be taken—though officers in the field seem never to have taken such extreme measures seriously.[26]

One of the most difficult problems for the leadership was to find competent commanders to lead the French armies, especially after so many officers had fled the country. The betrayals of Lafayette and Dumouriez had left the Convention deeply suspicious of aristocratic generals, even those who ostensibly embraced the Republic. To lose a skirmish or to advance too slowly could be grounds for arrest, and even quite capable commanders were sometimes sent to the guillotine. Yet slowly, through a process of trial and error and the survival of the most talented—and always under the watchful eyes of deputies from the Convention determined never again to be betrayed—a new generation of able young generals devoted to the Revolution was placed in the field. Most of them were from commoner families or from the lowest levels of the nobility—men who would have had no hope of winning a command under the Old Regime. A few years later, many of these new officers would become marshals in the Napoleonic armies and lead French troops across the whole of Europe.[27]

In Paris and in cities and small towns throughout France, an impressive string of victories in December 1793 incited enormous enthusiasm. Spurred on with ruthless pressure by Saint-Just, the Austrian forces were pushed out of French territory in the northeastern province of Alsace. There was even more excitement when the British were finally expelled from the great Mediterranean port of Toulon. The treason of the Toulon leaders, turning the city over to the enemy fleet, had been the very symbol of internal conspiracy. But after a long siege, the young lieutenant Bonaparte, just twenty-four years old, had succeeded in capturing the heights above the city, and the French artillery began bombarding the fleet and forcing a rapid departure of the enemy. When news of the victory arrived in Paris, everyone hurried outside to tell their friends and neighbors and anyone else they encountered in the streets: "We all rushed to shake hands and embrace. Wherever patriots met, they congratulated one another and shared in the common joy." Some of them, like Jullien, hurried to the Convention to express their general jubilation.[28]

At almost the same time, news arrived of a series of major victories over the peasant insurgents in western France. The previous October some 30,000 armed men from the Vendée, followed by at least as many women and children, had dramatically left their homeland, crossed the Loire River, and headed north toward Normandy, apparently in the hope of reaching the coast and linking up with a British fleet and a portion of the emigrant army. At first they continued to defeat all who tried to block their way. But they were ultimately unable to capture the port of Granville or locate the British navy. Disillusioned and with no aid in sight, they attempted to return south and regain their homes. This time, however, they were confronted and badly handled on several occasions by Republican armies. When they reached the Loire just west of Nantes, they were unable to find sufficient boats for the crossing, and they were cornered and crushed in battle. Thousands of those who were not killed were captured and executed in the ruthless repression that followed. An estimated three-fourths of all those who had made the trek northward never returned to their farms.[29]

In January the French armies went into winter quarters. But in the spring the soldiers of the Republic began advancing once again. Following a key victory in June over the Austrians at Fleurus, French troops swept across Belgium, and soon they had reentered Antwerp and arrived on the frontier of Holland. In the south and southeast they also made substantial gains against the Spanish and the Savoyards. In every letter Chaillon offered his friend the "keys" to another city, as he put it: to Charleroi, Mons, Bruges, Brussels, and Namur in Belgium; to Landau in Germany. "They are no longer mere victories," he concluded. "They are wonders to behold." Vadier wrote of "victory at a gallop. Brussels is now ours and the Austrians are in full flight. The retreat of our enemies is the order of the day."[30]

Throughout the country, the French victories were marked by a series of joyous celebrations. A great festival was organized in Paris at the end of December to honor all of the recent successes and especially the fall of Toulon. Guittard stood on a bridge in the cold winter wind, as representatives of each of the fourteen French armies paraded past on foot or on horseback, followed by a marching band, decorated wagons filled with wounded veterans, and contingents from the Convention, the Commune, and all the clubs of the city. There was also a wagon with a statue of liberty surrounded by a hundred sans-culottes wearing red Republican hats, all moving from the Tuileries Gardens to the Champ de Mars. The men were attended by groups of young women in white dresses, shivering a bit, holding up laurel branches, the symbol of victory. Guittard drew another little sketch in his diary with the men and horses and flags marching across the page.[31]

In June and July the victories in Belgium gave rise to new celebrations in the capital, some of which attracted hundreds of thousands of people. For one such ceremony, the deputy Jean-Baptiste Marragon came out with his wife and three children to watch the nighttime illuminations in the Tuileries Gardens and listen to music provided by the opera. "It is impossible," he wrote, "to convey the delicious sensation I felt and shared with all those around me."[32] There was also a series of commemorative picnics, especially after the victory at Fleurus, with neighborhoods setting up tables in the streets and joining together in "fraternal" meals. In mid-June the Jullien family joined with a hundred other neighbors for an evening repast outside their apartment: "Poor and rich were all mixed together and they got on in such a friendly and fraternal fashion that we have never had a more agreeable meal." They toasted the health of the Republic and the Convention, and then Jullien's usually grave husband stood up and led the singing of the Marseillaise. Similar group picnics marked the Bastille celebration of 1794. Once again, they were potluck affairs, with everyone contributing what they could. On the Place Saint-Sulpice, as Guittard described it, "we offered toasts to everyone who passed by, even when we did not know them. We sang, we laughed, we danced." Everything was eaten on the same plates, and some even used their fingers, since not every citizen had a fork. "We ate as if we were one large family."[33]

A Revolution Devouring Its Children

Yet as was the case throughout much of the Revolution, the sentiments of enthusiasm and brotherhood were always intermixed with feelings of uncertainty and mistrust, an anxiety that was far more intense during the Year II than at any time since 1789. Even during the exuberant celebrations of June and July 1794 there were nagging suspicions that some of those sharing in the picnics might be secret conspirators, who had merely assumed the mask of patriotism. Jullien asked just this question: Were there not revelers who simply feigned their support, while concealing "the devil" inside? And Guittard would intermingle descriptions of patriotic festivals, for which he obviously felt real emotion, with lists of the hundreds of "conspirators" now going to their deaths at the guillotine.[34]

For if the Year II of the Revolution was marked by spectacular military victories, by an advance of the ideals of social justice, and by moments of deeply felt sentiments of brotherhood, it was also a period of oppressive fear and suspicion and of ever-greater numbers of executions. And it was above all the "Terror" of these months that would dominate the memories of the men and women who lived through them and the histories written by future generations. The fever of the Terror was fueled by the experience of past betrayals of those they had once respected, by contradictory class demands, and by the ever-present fear of traitors in their midst. It would lead not only to repression against an array of enemies or perceived enemies of the Revolution but also to a veritable politics of self-destruction within the ruling faction itself. While many of the leaders undoubtedly believed the accusations of treason directed against former friends and colleagues, the political rhetoric would increasingly tilt toward the posturing and demagoguery of opposing egos, a struggle for power and survival and sometimes for revenge, in which the stakes literally concerned life or death, and in which cynical manipulation might sometimes take the place of patriotism and statesmanship.

In the weeks after September 5, 1793, the executive Committee of Public Safety had fully embraced the concept of making "terror the order of the day." In this it worked in close partnership with the Committee of General Security, the central authority overseeing arrests and repression. Decrees by the Convention in October and in December had invested the first of these Committees with all the powers of a Revolutionary war government: direction over ministers and diplomats; the right to appoint and dismiss generals; and broad powers over the representatives on mission in the departments. The two great Committees would also supervise a network of surveillance committees and revolutionary tribunals, conceived to root out hidden conspiracy and punish those who had openly rebelled against the Republic.

Though no one individual ever dominated the French Revolution—as was sometimes the case in twentieth-century revolutions—the remarkable yet deeply flawed personality of Robespierre was clearly a central figure in the political drama of the Terror. Historians will forever argue over Robespierre's motives. No doubt he was sincere in his dream of promoting political "virtue" within the Revolution, of the selfless, almost puritanical dedication of all citizens to the fatherland and to the "social contract" that bound them together. It was a theme he developed in two major speeches in the Convention on December 25, 1793 and on February 5, 1794—described by one historian as among "the most notable utterance in the history of democracy." It is by no means clear, however, that all leaders of the period embraced this severe moralistic conception of the Revolution or the specific emphasis on virtue.[35] In any case, Robespierre would oscillate in his politics from week to week, in part as he attempted to hold together the alliance of diverse positions in the Committee. At times, and it should not be underestimated, he sought to moderate some of the worst elements of the Terror. On several occasions he personally intervened in favor of the seventy-five deputies arrested the previous October as Girondin sympathizers and whom the radical militants sought to execute. Yet he also deeply believed in the existence of "grand conspiracy," in the "elusive, numberless, invisible swarms of foreign spies" which so many had feared since at least the autumn of 1791.[36] His nagging obsession with pervasive plots seemed to expand over time, as he was beset with exhaustion and sickness and as he struggled to confront the imagined—and sometimes real— attempts on his life. There can be no doubt that he was an important player but by no means the only player in the acceleration of political executions in Paris during the spring and early summer of 1794.[37]

In its initial stages much of the repression of the Terror was directed toward those who had openly engaged in civil war against the Convention. Although the defeat of the federalists proved relatively rapid in many regions of the country—in Normandy, in Bordeaux, in Marseille—the rebellions in Lyon and Toulon were overcome only after long and costly sieges. In both cities individuals professing royalism had openly joined in the uprisings, and the repression would be pursued with particular vigor and brutality. Executions would be exacted not only as a form of exemplary justice, to intimidate future counterrevolutionaries, but also from a desire for revenge—revenge for the patriots killed during the sieges, revenge for the conspiracy perpetrated with France's foreign enemies in an attempt to bring down the Republic—or so it was widely believed. In the aftermath of civil war, few were prepared for reconciliation. In Lyon alone, close to 1,900 individuals would be executed—some cut down in a field outside the city, with grapeshot fired by artillery.[38]

The Republican leaders revealed themselves to be even more harsh in the terrible civil war in western France. Here too they were outraged that so many patriots had been massacred and that the counterrevolution had been closely coordinated, they believed, with the Austrian counteroffensive in March 1793. The Revolutionaries, who almost all originated in towns and cities, never understood and often felt great scorn for the Vendée peasants, assumed to be ignorant, benighted, and manipulated by their priests. Even the relatively moderate Chaillon, who sat in the Plain of the Convention, was beside himself with fury toward the "brigands" of the west. As was the case with many other deputies from this region, his family lived near the area under attack, and he agonized over their safety. Virtually every letter to his friend in Nantes contained the latest details of the civil war and stories of the killings of patriots by the rebels. "What!" he exclaimed in November 1793, "there are still brigands and still citizens being massacred by these scoundrels! You must act, my friend: strike while the iron is hot and finish exterminating the miserable remains of the brigands, so that not one is left standing on the soil of liberty."[39] Only the frightful effects of the civil war and the demonization of the Vendée rebels—who themselves had demonized the patriots—can explain the massive killings of those caught armed or even suspected of sympathy. Although estimates vary, it is likely that some 250,000 to 300,000 people were killed in the west, either in military combat or during the repression that followed, including perhaps 100,000 on the Republican side and a substantially larger number of Vendéen soldiers and civilians. The infamous Jean-Baptiste Carrier, deputy on mission in Nantes, was himself responsible for perhaps 10,000 of these deaths, through firing squads or the mass drownings of prisoners in the Loire—prisoners who included not only suspected insurgents but also priests and nuns who had rejected the Revolution.[40]

However, the patriot leader would not only execute counterrevolution-aries, they had also begun executing one another. Virtually everyone in the eighteenth century—both before and during the Revolution—had supported capital punishment for treason against the state. Since some of the Girondins had openly supported the federalist insurrection against the Republic, it could be argued that by the laws of the land they deserved the death penalty. Yet, as we have seen, the trial itself had not followed the laws of the land. Under great pressure from the Paris militants to reach a guilty verdict, the court had treated the accused not as individuals, but as a bundled "faction" whose guilt was known in advance. In the ten months following the trial, the Revolutionaries continued to track down other Girondins and their sympathizers who had supported the various federalist uprisings and who had now been declared "outlaws," subject to immediate execution. In mid-November Marie-Jeanne Roland, in whose home so many of the faction had congregated, was sent to the guillotine. As soon as he learned of his wife's death, the former minister Roland com-mitted suicide. In December, the Protestant pastor Rabaut Saint-Etienne was found hiding in Paris and immediately dispatched. Several months later Guadet, Salle, Birotteau, and Barbaroux were caught near Bordeaux and guillotined in the city, while Pétion and Buzot killed themselves in a field as they were about to be captured. Condorcet long hid out near the capital, where he wrote his remarkably optimistic book on the inevitable progress of humanity, *The Sketch of the Progress of the Human Mind*. But when he too was captured in March 1794, he apparently took poison and died in his cell. By the end of the Terror, nearly two-thirds of the sixty or so closest to the Girondin leadership had been killed or had taken their own lives. Most of the others either fled to foreign lands or were held for long months in Parisian prisons.[41]

During the same period, the two Committees and the Revolutionary Tribunal also went after many of the earlier leaders of the Revolution. The deputies of the first National Assembly received especially harsh treatment for having supported a constitutional monarchy in 1791. Large numbers were arrested as suspects, and several were executed during the Year II, often with far less real evidence of "treason" than that produced against the Girondins. Barnave, Bailly, and Philippe d'Orléans all fell in the hecatomb of November 1793 that also saw the execution of the former queen Marie-Antoinette. Le Chapelier, Thouret, and d'Eprémesnil went to their deaths together the following April—despite their starkly differing political positions. Three of the leading generals in the first National Assembly, Custine, Biron, and Beauharnais, were also eliminated, though they had continued to support the Republic. In all some eighty-eight members of the Constituent Assembly were executed, died in prison, committed suicide, or were murdered.[42]

In the course of the winter and spring of 1794, the terrible politics of self-destruction spread even further, as the once solid Montagnard faction began to break apart and turn on itself. By early 1794 the leadership was torn by opposing softline and hardline groups. On the one hand were those sometimes known as "the indulgents," led by Georges Danton and Camille Desmoulins. Both had played prominent roles in the construction of the Terror, but both were increasingly unhappy with the large numbers of arrests and executions. Desmoulins was horrified when the twenty Girondins were sent to their deaths, convinced that his own earlier publications had contributed to the demise of Brissot. Danton, always more conciliatory by nature, seems to have been especially upset when several of his friends in the Convention were arrested for accusations of corruption. In any case, Desmoulins, one of most brilliant journalists of the period, began a new newspaper in early December, the *Vieux Cordeliers,* which mobilized sarcasm and ridicule to attack the politics of the Terror and, increasingly, the actions of the two great committees.[43]

At the other extreme Jacques Hébert and his followers were demanding even greater repression. Through his influential newspaper, *Père Duchesne,* he positioned himself as spokesman for the Parisian masses, playing in particular on their difficult economic situation, exacerbated by the effects of the war and the continued inflation of France's paper money. In the face of such difficulties, Hébert pushed for more vigorous activities by the Revolutionary Army and implacable repression against grain hoarders, merchants who avoided the Maximum, and all the agents of foreign powers said to be manipulating the situation. He and his supporters were also strong advocates of dechristianization.[44]

By early 1794 the two loosely organized alignments, the Dantonists and the Hébertists, were not only accusing each other of treason but also attacking the Committee of Public Safety. The Committee itself did not take kindly to such attacks. It was jealous of its power and authority and impatient with those who opposed its policies, arguing that centralization was imperative if the Republic was to defeat its enemies. Both of Robespierre's celebrated speeches on the goals of the Revolution and the Terror also contained harsh warnings against the two factions, announcing that if the war was to be successfully pursued, the Revolution could not tolerate the extremes of either "moderation" or "excess."

The situation of the Hébertists reached a crisis in early March, when Hébert directly attacked the Committee in a meeting of the Cordeliers Club and then called for a "sacred insurrection." In fact, an attempted march on the Commune to stimulate an uprising was joined by only two of the forty-eight sections of Paris, and the whole project failed. Now, however, the two committees had strong justification to move against the Hébertists, whose attacks and continual disruption no longer seemed tolerable. Hébert and a group of his supporters were arrested in the night of March 13 to 14, following an attack against them in the Convention by Saint-Just. Another show trial was rapidly organized, bundling together a number of Hébertists and Cordelier leaders, along with several unsavory but essentially unrelated individuals—much as had been done with the Girondins. All but two were found guilty of conspiracy with foreign powers and executed on March 24. If we can believe Guittard, the death of the Hébertists aroused little emotion and was widely approved by the majority of Parisians. He apparently saw the executions himself, along with an estimated 300,000 others, filling the Place de la Révolution and the Tuileries Gardens. After the prisoners had been guillotined, all of the spectators cried "Long live the Republic" and applauded, some throwing their hats in the air "in a sign of joy."[45]

Why the two Committees then moved against Danton and his supporters is much less clear. Robespierre had long attempted to defend his friends Danton and Desmoulins. He had even spoken out in the Jacobin Club in early January to prevent Desmoulins, his former schoolmate, from being ousted. But when Desmoulins took Robespierre to task and even seemed to rebuff his support and when Danton became ever more critical of the Committee—demanding that power be returned to the Convention and that the Constitution of 1793 be implemented—Robespierre began marking his distance. He was perhaps even eager to demonstrate that political purity was more important than past friendship.[46] In the end, nearly everyone present in the Committee on the night of March 29 signed the arrest warrant for Danton, Desmoulins, and several of their allies.[47] Once again the arrest was effectively a death sentence. There was yet another show trial with Danton and his friends cynically tried together with a heterogeneous cluster of other men. As Vergniaud had done the previous October, Danton defended himself with extraordinary skill and passion. But when it appeared his rhetoric might be successful, the trial was rapidly curtailed, and all were summarily condemned and executed.

Nothing could have brought a greater chill to the Convention and to the whole of Paris than the death of Danton. Witnesses who had praised the purging of the Hébertists now merely mentioned the event or remained sullenly silent in their correspondence.[48] Although a few of the Montagnards suggested that all conspiracy had now been overcome and that the Revolution could feel secure, the executions in Paris would continue and even accelerate. In their pervasive fear that conspiracy and counterrevolution could be lurking anywhere, the two Committees and the Revolutionary Tribunal seemed to embark on a veritable witch hunt. Ruault, who had once supported the Jacobins and the Montagnards, was horrified by the situation. The Revolution "devours its own children; it kills its brothers; it gnaws at its intestines; it has become the cruelest and most horrible of monsters."[49]

At the height of the Terror at least 300,000 suspects had been arrested, awaiting trial in prison or guarded in their homes. They were indicted for a whole array of crimes, though by far the most common concerned various forms of "sedition."[50] We will never know the precise death toll. One careful count of all those executed through the judicial process yielded a total of just under 17,000. But such figures do not include executions without trial or deaths during incarceration—and given the miserable conditions in many of the prisons, a substantial number succumbed before they could appear before a tribunal. A total of at least 40,000 deaths seems not unlikely. All classes, moreover, were touched by the executions: over a fourth of the victims were peasants, and nearly a third were artisans or workers. Only 8.5 percent were nobles and 6.5 percent were clergymen.[51] Many of the individuals in question had almost certainly been captured in acts of open insurrection. By far the largest number of executions were in departments touched by the Vendée and Federalist rebellions. The death toll reached its peak for the nation as a whole toward the end of 1793, just as the major uprisings had collapsed or were on the defensive and as the terrible repression had begun taking effect. But elsewhere the impact of the Terror depended in part on the attitudes of local representatives on mission. All of them supported surveillance committees, and they sometimes established local revolutionary tribunals. Yet many were far less aggressive than others. The severity of the Terror from one region to another also de-

Nine emigrants are guillotined after they had returned to France. All had been captured carrying arms and all were under thirty years of age. The first has already been decapitated; the others wait their turn in line. This guillotine was set up on the Place de Grève, in front of the city hall, commonly the sight of executions under the Old Regime. Bibliothèque nationale de France.

pended on the particular patterns of local factional rivalries and the relative extent of cooperation or of hatred and mistrust. Six departments registered no deaths at all, and well over a third had fewer than ten.[52]

In Paris itself, however, the maximum number of executions took place in the spring and early summer of 1794—just as they were declining in the provinces. Of critical importance in this turn of events was the so-called Prairial Law (June 10, 1794), streamlining trial procedures in the Revolutionary Tribunal of the capital. Robespierre closely collaborated on the law, though it was ultimately written by Couthon. Couthon made his goal quite clear: "It is not intended to make a few examples, but to exterminate the implacable satellites of tyranny."[53] The most novel portion of the decree was the set of remarkably elastic clauses defining those to be considered as the "satellites of tyranny": anyone who attacked the Convention, betrayed the Republic, interfered with provisioning, sheltered conspirators, spoke ill of patriotism, misled the people, spread false news, outraged morality, abused public office, or worked against the liberty, unity, and security of the state. Henceforth suspects would be allowed no defense attorney, there would be no preliminary hearings, and the only possible verdict would be acquittal or death.[54]

The reasons for ratcheting up the Terror in Paris, just as it was declining in the provinces and as the armies of the Republic were becoming so successful, is by no means obvious. Some Revolutionaries seemed to believe that it was the repression itself that had brought military success and that if they were now to ease up, there was the danger of new treachery sabotaging their victories, just as had occurred in March 1793.[55] However, the passage of the Prairial Law can also be linked to a wave of fear that swept through the Convention—not unlike the panics of May 1792 and March 1793. The fear was initially prompted by the attempted assassinations on May 20 of both Collot and Robespierre by a man and a young woman. Throughout this period anonymous pamphlets and posters threatening assassination of the Revolutionary leadership continued to appear in the streets. The possibility seemed very real that the conspirators who had murdered Le Peletier and Marat might now set their sights on Robespierre and other members of the Committee of Public Safety. Robespierre himself seems to have become utterly obsessed with the threat of his being murdered. Chaillon argued at length that Pitt had made assassinations "the order of the day."[56] About the same time, new rumors spread of an impending prison breakout, with criminals to be paid to fall upon the patriots—much like the stories circulating at the time of the September Massacres. Indeed, the executions prompted by the Prairial Law began when the Committee of General Security ordered the emptying of several prisons and the execution of most of the prisoners. As in September 1792 many ordinary criminals, assumed to be brigands in the pay of the conspirators, were also put to death.[57]

To some extent the Prairial Law simply regulated practices already in use by the Paris Revolutionary Tribunal. For months, judges and juries had been sending groups of individuals to their death with relatively little attention to "due process." Yet the new law clearly led to a huge increase in the number of executions in Paris, and to what is commonly called the "Great Terror." Over the next seven weeks in June and July the Tribunal would condemn more people in Paris than during the previous fourteen months combined.[58] The acquittal rate, which recently stood at some 50 percent, now fell to only 20 percent of all those tried. Whole categories of individuals were sent to the guillotine, not apparently on the basis of any specific crimes committed but because of the positions they held under the Old Regime. All of the former directors of the general tax farm who could be located; numerous members of the former Parlement of Paris; men and women from the greatest noble families of Paris: all were decimated in a manner of weeks. The proportion of nobles among those guillotined rose from about 8 to 20 percent.[59] There were so many executions that in mid-June municipal leaders moved the guillotine to the eastern edge of the city, allowing a more efficient cleanup of the blood and the bodies.

In the claustrophobic atmosphere of suspicion, mistrust, and fear of assassination in which they lived, some of the leaders no doubt believed the accusations of conspiracy leveled against such individuals. One can only conclude, however, that at this point the executions were driven, at least in part, by hatred and a desire for revenge for wrongs perpetrated by the ruling class under the Old Regime and by the emigrants during the Revolution. Rosalie Jullien, who was close to the Robespierrists during this period, would use much the same rhetoric she had used at the time of the September Massacres. She seemed to have difficulty controlling her growing anger, railing against "the black evil of the aristocrats, the bloody fanaticism of priests, the atrocious pride of the nobles. . . . All those who oppose the public good are, in my eyes, enemies and monsters."[60]

Ruault, however, saw the situation very differently. He still believed that during the winter and spring the Committee of Public Safety had accomplished "many marvelous achievements" in assembling fourteen armies to battle the whole of Europe. "But today it has become atrocious through a multiplication of horrors and executions that are totally unnecessary." Since the Prairial Law, he continued, six to seven cartloads of people per day could be seen lumbering through Paris on their way to the scaffold. Who could believe that men like the Enlightened minister Malesherbes or the scientist Lavoisier or the Constituent leader Thouret were "partisans of slavery and tyranny"? Like so many of the others—magistrates, tax collectors, aristocrats—they were "noble, wealthy, enlightened. And so they were put to death." He then related the harrowing experience of walking home from an errand and suddenly encountering one of the carts carrying his old friend Anisson Duperron, the onetime director of the royal press. Ruault was so shaken that he fell back against a wall and began weeping. It was clear to him that large segments of the population would see friends, neighbors, and relatives carried away in this manner. The worst of it, he feared, was that they would never forgive the leadership for such acts, and that they might now turn against the entire Revolution.[61]

Thermidor

By the early summer a dark cloud of fear had descended over the Convention and over much of the population of Paris. Freedom of speech, freedom of the press, freedom of religion had all been essentially removed. Police spies were known to be wandering the city listening for suspicious language. Errant words or phrases could also be denounced to a section's surveillance committee by neighbors or citizen bystanders. Though they normally hid their feelings, the deputies occasionally conveyed glimpses of the uncertainty in which they lived. "We now find ourselves," wrote the Montagnard Pierre Campmas in spring 1794, "in such a crisis of anxiety, that it is impossible to describe." When someone asked him for a favor, he confessed that if he were to try to help, if he were to make himself known in any way, "within twenty-four hours I would perhaps no longer exist." His basic position, as he expressed it laconically, was that "I know nothing, I cannot do anything; I must do nothing." Ruault expressed much the same anxiety: "Death hovers over everyone's head." "None of us can be certain of avoiding it, since it strikes anywhere and everywhere."[62]

The precise nature of the political struggles and maneuvering during this period will probably never be known for certain. In the weeks after Danton's death a number of deputies in the Convention, who felt themselves in danger, began meeting and secretly discussing possible plans of action against Robespierre, perceived—correctly or incorrectly—as the single most dangerous threat to their survival. Some had been close friends or allies of Danton. Others had been attacked by Robespierre for being too harsh or too soft while serving as representatives on mission. Among those sensing a sword hanging over their heads were such influential Montagnard deputies as Fréron, Dubois-Crancé, Fouché, Carrier, Barras, and Tallien. It is likely, moreover, that Robespierre was kept abreast of at least some of their "plotting" through increasingly close ties with the police.[63]

But it was not fear alone that brought an end to the regime of the Terror. Critical was the growing division between the two great Committees themselves.[64] Members of the Committee of General Security were angered that the other great Committee was encroaching on their responsibilities and treating them as subordinates. Rifts were also opening up within the Committee of Public Safety: over the prosecution of the war and over accusations that Robespierre, Couthon, and Saint-Just were acting like a triumvirate, trying to dominate the others. The radicals Collot and Billaud, for their part, were impatient with Robespierre's support for the cult of the Supreme Being and with all his tiresome speeches about "virtue." Toward the end of June, Robespierre fell into a terrible quarrel with several other members of the Committee, storming out of the room and not returning for over a month. He claimed to be sick and exhausted, but there is also evidence of something close to a "mental collapse." He seemed to be losing the fine political skills he had once held. He was increasingly convinced that he alone understood the meaning of "virtue" and the route the Revolution must take, that he alone perceived the full extent of the conspiracies eating at the heart of the Republic. But though he kept aloof from the Committee, he still attended the Jacobins, where he maintained an admiring following.[65]

In late July he made the fateful decision of breaking with the two Committees and taking his case directly to the Convention. On the eighth day of the Revolutionary month of Thermidor (July 26, 1794), he returned for the first time in over six weeks and delivered a long, rambling speech. Much of it consisted of very personal complaints of the attacks to which he claimed to have been subjected. He reasserted his belief in a polarized world, consisting entirely of good and evil citizens. And he announced the existence of more conspirators who must be punished, some of whom were to be found in the Convention and in the two Committees themselves. At first, no one protested. But then Cambon, the Protestant deputy from Montpellier who was one of the few individuals actually named in the verbal assault, stepped forward to defend himself. With great courage, and perhaps feeling he had nothing to lose, he openly attacked Robespierre. Other deputies were more cautious, but they demanded that Robespierre name all those he was accusing. He responded that he would name them only when it was necessary. In the end, the Convention voted to send the speech to be considered by the two Committees, to the very men whom he had just indicted. It was an implicit slap at Robespierre.[66]

That night Robespierre repeated his speech in the Jacobin Club. Furious over the treatment he had received from the deputies, he made it clear that he was prepared to support an insurrection against the Convention if necessary. He alluded to a new purge of the Assembly, to be led once again by Hanriot and the national guard, as on June 2, 1793. When Collot and Billaud tried to protest, they were accused of being "conspirators" and were manhandled out the door with their clothing badly torn. They were even mocked by one of the Revolutionary judges present: "I'll look for you tomorrow in the Tribunal."[67]

With so many deputies and committee members convinced that their lives were in imminent danger, furious maneuvers took place throughout the night to block Robespierre in the Convention and bring an end to his influence. In the two Committees, which met until five in the morning in Robespierre's continuing absence, Collot and Billaud stormed with rage at their treatment in the Jacobins. A dozen or so deputies were said to have met in the Tuileries Gardens with Jean-Lambert Tallien, the young Montagnard deputy from Paris, in order to plan strategy. The next morning, Sunday, July 27 (9 Thermidor), several of the conspirators worked to win over the more moderate deputies of the Plain, stationing themselves in the foyer of the Convention to quietly ask for their support as they entered the hall.[68] Both Saint-Just and Robespierre were slated to speak that day. But Tallien interrupted Saint-Just after he had read just three sentences, and he went on the attack. When Robespierre tried to respond to this and other accusations, Collot, the president of the assembly, refused to give him the chair. After a period of tumult and with Robespierre accusing the whole Convention of being "assassins," Louis Louchet, the former priest and admirer of Danton, demanded that Robespierre be arrested. A chorus of "Tyrant, tyrant" arose from the assembly. Robespierre, Couthon, and Saint-

9 Thermidor Year II in the Convention (July 27, 1794). A nineteenth-century Romantic painting that conveys, nevertheless, the emotion of this tumultuous event. Robespierre with his powdered wig is in the center foreground, surrounded by Saint-Just (in the dark hat), Lebas, Augustine Robespierre, and the handicapped Couthon, sitting in a chair below. The speaker, Tallien, holds a dagger, which he threatens to use against Robespierre if "the tyrant" is not arrested. The president, Collot d'Herbois (high to the left), shows no pity for his former colleague on the Committee of Public Safety. Pierre-Raymond-Jacques Montvoisin, © Coll. Musée de la Révolution française, Domaine de Vizille, MRF D 1991.1.

Just were all ordered to prison. Robespierre's brother and his young friend Philippe Lebas both demanded to share their fate, and the five deputies were carried away by the gendarmes. Before they adjourned, the deputies took another of those passionate oaths that had characterized the Revolution from the beginning, vowing to save the fatherland or to die at their posts.[69]

Initially the five men arrested were escorted to five separate prisons.[70] But the Paris Commune, dominated by those loyal to Robespierre, ordered the prisoners released and moved to the city hall, and by midnight all had arrived there and had taken refuge near the city's general assembly. The Commune declared an insurrection against the Convention, much as

Robespierre had promised the previous night. Hanriot was sent to place cannons around the Convention hall, and an order went out to all the sections of Paris to march to the defense of Robespierre. This time, however, the deputies were far more aggressive than they had been on June 2. Meeting in permanent session throughout the night, they ordered Hanriot to be arrested, and decreed that all five deputies and anyone who supported the insurrection were "outlaws," subject to immediate execution. They also sent their own representatives to all of the sections to countermand the order of the Commune.

For members of the Convention and for all Parisian citizens, the night of July 27–28 was exceedingly tense and uncertain. "If I ever thought I would die," wrote Durand de Maillane, "it would have been in this moment." The tocsin bells began ringing, the city gates were closed once again, and "everyone," as Guittard described it, "was in a state of terrible fear and anguish." All the neighborhood sections went into emergency session, and soon representatives of the two competing authorities arrived to seek their support. Some seven or eight deputies on horseback appeared in Guittard's section, dressed "in full ceremony" in their tricolor sashes, escorted by men with cannons and by gendarmes carrying torches. They announced that Paris was in great danger, and commanded the sections to send armed men *not* to the city hall, but to the Convention to protect the deputies and the Revolution. "It was even more frightening, since it all took place at night, and everyone was afraid of being murdered."[71]

In the end only a few thousand men marched to the defense of Robespierre, while most of the guardsmen and most of the population came ultimately to support the Convention. Why this was the case is not entirely certain. Perhaps a large number of the most radical younger patriots had now left the city to fight in the war. Many of those who remained were deeply unhappy with the economic policies of Robespierre and the Committee of Public Safety. The price freeze of the "maximum" had never worked well. Almost everything except bread was in short supply and available only at higher prices through the black market. The freeze on wages, however, had worked only too well, and many workers were angry, and some had attempted to go on strike. Those who had recently participated in the fraternal picnics to celebrate the great victories in the war may well have wondered why so many sacrifices were still necessary and why so many people continued to be executed.[72]

Perhaps if Robespierre and his allies had acted decisively to direct the insurrection, events might have unfolded differently. The deputy Jean Dyzèz was convinced that if they had indeed done so, "we would all have been lost."[73] But the renegade deputies remained strangely hesitant and undecided. Robespierre had always been concerned not to appear as a dictator, and in the end he did nothing either to encourage the Commune or to rally the guardsmen who had gathered outside to support him. He simply allowed events to take their course. By one or two o'clock in the morning, the men outside, without any clear leadership from Robespierre and with the Convention ordering them to desist, began shouldering their muskets, leading away their cannons, and returning to their neighborhoods. Soon thereafter, two groups of guardsmen loyal to the Convention, led by Léonard Bourdon and Paul Barras—a former military noble—broke into the now-undefended city hall.[74] In the melee that ensued, Robespierre's younger brother leaped out a window and was badly injured, while Couthon was pushed down the stairway in his wheelchair and was also hurt. Robespierre and Lebas were shot. Whether or not the two had fired on themselves is still debated, but the result was that Lebas lay dead and that Maximilien's jaw and teeth were shattered and he writhed in pain on the floor.

The next afternoon, the two Robespierre brothers, Saint-Just, and Couthon were all taken before the Revolutionary Tribunal. Since the four had been declared outlaws by the Convention, all were condemned—along with Hanriot, the mayor of Paris, and sixteen other supporters in the Commune. As they now took their turn in the "the passage of infamy," carried by cart down the Rue Saint-Honoré, they were insulted by the people, as Guittard described it. Arrived at the Place de la Révolution, only Saint-Just of the four remaining deputies was able to climb the stairs of the scaffold unassisted. Robespierre screamed in pain as the bandages holding his fractured jaw were ripped away by the executioner. Ruault, who was present and who had little love for Robespierre, remarked nevertheless that he showed great courage in his final moments. Despite his suffering, "his eyes were bright and aware."[75] In his brief political career he had at times displayed remarkable vision for a brave new world of democracy, social justice, and civic virtue. Yet he had never been able to overcome his debilitating suspicions and his self-absorption, and he had been one of the major instigators—though hardly the only one—of the Great Terror. Now his physical agony and his mental anguish were quickly ended.

CONCLUSION

Becoming a Terrorist

THE DEATH of Robespierre and his closest associates did not end the executions of Thermidor. Over a period of three days, no fewer than 87 of the 140 members of the Paris Commune were also sent to the guillotine, including 71 on July 29, 1794, the largest number ever delivered up to the great machine in a single day. They included many small artisans and shopkeepers—shoemakers, cabinet makers, wigmakers—but also merchants, manufacturers, and lawyers: the mixture of popular sans-culottes and elite militants who had long represented the most radical segment of the city. All were said to have supported insurrection against the Convention and were thus declared "outlaws," subject to death after a mere confirmation of identity. Guittard de Floriban sketched in his diary a long line of men, their hands tied behind their backs, waiting before the scaffold.[1]

Thereafter, the lists of the condemned, so carefully inscribed by Guittard over the previous months, abruptly ceased. At first the remaining members of the Committee of Public Safety—those who had participated in the purge of their colleagues—urged the Convention to maintain the policies of the Terror and to avoid all backsliding.[2] Yet a sea change now swept through the Assembly. The more moderate deputies of the Plain had always constituted the majority, though they had been persuaded that strong central control was necessary to fight the enemies of the Republic and they had been cowed by threats of arrest and fear of the Parisian crowds. However, after the conspirators of Thermidor appealed for their support to overthrow Robespierre and with French armies advancing on every front, they effectively took control of the Convention and led a reaction against the regime of the Terror. Many of the Montagnard stalwarts, having narrowly escaped death themselves and sensing the way the wind was blowing, defected to the center. Already on 11 Thermidor (July 29) the Convention acted to reduce the authority of the Committee of Public Safety, decreeing that its membership would be renewed regularly, with one-fourth of the incumbents exiting each month. Those members just executed were replaced by two former supporters of Danton and a moderate who had voted for a reprieve of the king in January 1793.[3] By the beginning of September Barère and the two radical extremists Collot d'Herbois and Billaud-Varenne were rotated out. Governing powers were distributed among twelve executive committees, with the Committee of Public Safety maintaining control over war and diplomacy but losing its authority in internal affairs. The second major committee—of General Security—was purged of those sympathetic to Robespierre, and it too found its powers greatly diminished.

Over the following month many other institutions that had held France in the grip of Terror were eliminated or dramatically transformed. The Revolutionary Tribunal was reorganized and declawed. The head judge and several of the jury members had died with Robespierre, and the chief prosecutor, Fouquier-Tinville, was arrested. The surveillance committees were greatly reduced in number and lost much of their independence of action. The draconian Prairial Law was repealed. Henceforth, all those arrested had to be informed of the accusations against them, and they could be found guilty only if counterrevolutionary acts could be demonstrated, not on the basis of assumed intentions. Slowly at first and then more rapidly, hundreds of prisoners were released. Terror ceased to be the order of the day.

Members of the Convention and other French citizens, who had all but stopped writing during the Terror or who had carefully censored their letters, now took up their pens once again to describe the events of Thermidor and the weeks that followed. Almost without exception they assailed the tyranny of the Committee and the great number of executions, directing their ire above all at Robespierre, widely described as the "monster" who had directed it all. Many Montagnards, who had been deeply complicit in the policies of the Terror, were quick to adopt similar rhetoric, demonizing the "tyrant" and a few of his associates as the scapegoats.[4] Although the brutal representative on mission Carrier and the prosecutor Fouquier-Tinville were executed, others who had been virtually as ruthless escaped with their lives and continued their careers for many years to come.[5]

Yet no one who had lived through the period 1793–1794 could remain untouched. Especially during the terrible weeks of June and July 1794, Paris had been permeated with the sight and smell of death. Nicolas Ruault had been overwhelmed, shaken to tears as he watched those he knew were not guilty being carted through the streets to the guillotine. Dominique Garat, who had endured house arrest for months, awaiting convocation by the Revolutionary Tribunal, poured out his feelings in a "memoir" published soon after Thermidor. He expressed feelings of guilt when he reflected on his own survival, while so many of his friends and colleagues had been executed: "Luck and chance seemed to become . . . the blind divinities ruling over human destiny." Throughout the period he had been obsessed with the possibility of his imminent demise: "It is impossible to have seen Death descending on so many innocent heads throughout an entire year, without contemplating your own trip to the foot of the scaffold and what you would feel in your soul when faced with the end of life."[6]

Garat, like Ruault and Louis-Sébastien Mercier and so many other contemporaries, agonized over the course of recent events. How had things gone so terribly awry? Why had a significant portion of the Revolutionary elites—who had only just proclaimed the advent of tolerance, equal justice, and human rights—come to embrace a political culture of state violence? "How was it," as Mercier put it, citing the old adage, "that pure gold was changed into base lead?"[7] To be sure, a great many of the executions throughout the Republic were linked to the civil wars and armed insurrection against the state—acts of treason that virtually all agreed were deserving of capital punishment.[8] Yet even if one accepted such rationales, they could not justify the substantial number of "innocent heads" decapitated or of individuals sent before firing squads without anything approaching a fair trial.

With the hindsight of history, it seems clear that the appearance of a terrorist mindset cannot be explained in a one-dimensional manner—neither through Old Regime culture, nor through the influence of a few individuals, nor through circumstances alone. The Terror arose rather through a concatenation of developments emerging out of the very process of the Revolution itself. In the beginning, no doubt, was the intense emotion, enthusiasm and commitment with which an important segment of French society embraced the new Revolutionary values that emerged after 1787 and that were embodied in the major declarations of the summer of

1789. In our own day and age it is easy to forget how novel, how stunning, how unexpected such achievements were. Unlike many revolutions of late-modern history, the events in France were not based on a preexisting, well-defined ideology. They did not represent a simple appropriation of one strand or another of the philosophy of the Enlightenment. The writers and thinkers of the eighteenth century had produced an extraordinarily complex and often contradictory assemblage of ideas, on the basis of which one might have supported any number of programs for change or justifications for the status quo. Perhaps the most important effect of the age of Enlightenment was the self-confidence it instilled, the profoundly humanistic faith in the ability of individuals to use their own good sense, their "reason" to solve problems of all kinds. The Revolutionary period was itself extremely creative. It was only after the collapse of the Old Regime had provided the patriots with the possibility of reforming the state and society—a process that had begun in 1787 but that would reach a crescendo two years later—it was only then that the Revolutionaries improvised and cobbled together an "ideology" of sorts, based on a new synthesis of bits and pieces of earlier ideas and emphasizing above all democratic self-determination, civil liberties, and equality and an end to privilege. The enthusiasm for such achievements was immense, leading to a wave of fervent oaths sworn by men and women everywhere in support of the new regime and to a near-millenarian vision of the creation of a "new man," a veritable change in self-identity. It was exemplified as well by the growth of an intense nationalism that portrayed the French as the chosen leaders of the brave new world they envisioned.

At first many patriots promoted reconciliation for those who had difficulty grasping and accepting such transformations—notably among large elements of the nobility. However, the Revolutionaries would never accept a return to the Old Regime, to an absolute monarchy and a society based on birth. Their patience was not without limits. The very intensity of their commitment could easily lead to intolerance toward those who refused to adopt their vision for the future, or even worse, those who attempted aggressively to undermine it. Such intolerance arose not from a rhetorical snare in the discourse of the Enlightenment, or from the influence of Rousseau, or from an abstract reference to "virtue"—as has sometimes been argued. It came rather from the deep conviction that their conception of a society transformed was eminently fair and just and worth defending against all who would attempt to turn back the clock.

It was soon evident, moreover, that a substantial number of powerful individuals did indeed oppose the Revolution. Despite the presence of a small group of "liberal" nobles who embraced the ideals of 1789, the overwhelming majority was deeply unhappy and hostile to the new regime. As professional soldiers, many were prepared to fight and die in order to crush that regime, acting with much the same passion as those who sought to preserve it. Such opposition was apparent in the rhetoric of the "aristocratic" party within the National Assembly and in the rabid reactionary prose of the far right newspapers. It was also visible in the movement of emigration, in which thousands of nobles left the country, a great many to join armies in Germany openly committed to overthrowing the Revolution.

The situation was further complicated when the efforts of the National Assembly to reform the Catholic Church led almost half the parish clergy in France to refuse an oath of allegiance to the new Constitution. The Revolutionaries, who rarely understood the theological subtleties involved, were convinced that the "refractory" clergy had joined the counterrevolution. It was not difficult to imagine such individuals allying themselves with the nobles still residing in France and creating a fifth column closely linked to the emigrants abroad. Whatever the presence of real counterrevolutionary conspiracies—and such movements did indeed exist—it was not surprising that the patriots became obsessively preoccupied with the threat from two groups who had dominated French politics and society for centuries. With the massive uprisings of peasants in western France in the spring of 1793, motivated in large measure by opposition to the religious reforms, and with the insurgents' massacre of local patriots, the fury of the Revolutionaries knew no bounds. The Vendée rebels, in particular, were viewed as vile conspirators in the nation's midst, attacking them from behind just as France was being invaded by foreign armies. Ultimately, throughout the period, the Revolutionaries would be even more obsessed with internal enemies than with those assailing them from the outside.

The atmosphere of suspicion and mistrust was intensified, moreover, by a widespread breakdown of authority within the country. The rapid collapse of a great many Old Regime institutions after the Revolution began, as administrators and magistrates fled for their lives or were ignored by the population, produced a veritable power vacuum that would persist well into 1791. During this interregnum a series of "parallel powers" were improvised—municipal national guards, patriotic societies, neighborhood sections—most of which continued to function even after new bureaucratic and judiciary structures were implemented by the Revolution. At the same time the logic of liberty and popular sovereignty led to a questioning of traditional hierarchies throughout the society. Guild workers, soldiers, women's groups, large segments of the peasant population, slaves in the Caribbean—all began demanding freedom from "tyranny" and the right to self-determination.

The decentralization and social turbulence would help foment power struggles among competing elites in towns and provinces—between the ins and the outs and between various levels of the new bureaucracy. The situation was even more disconcerting after the Convention executed the king, with all the powerful patricidal symbolism that such an action entailed. There was a growing uncertainty as to who was ultimately in control and who might be manipulating the situation for personal advantage or on behalf of the enemies of the Revolution. The centrifugal tendencies reached a climax in the summer of 1793, when a number of major cities in the west and the south launched open insurrections against the central government. The reasons for these "federalist" revolts were complex, but the Revolutionaries in Paris were soon convinced that they were coordinated with the ongoing foreign invasion and the counterrevolutionary movement in the Vendée.

The void of authority, coupled with the promotion of democracy, also contributed to the growing influence of the Parisian popular classes. Throughout the period working men and women would reveal enormous stores of enthusiasm for the ideals of the Revolution and the determination to fight and die for the preservation of those ideals. Yet the artisans, shopkeepers, and workers of the capital were also prone to violence and to a culture of vendetta and revenge—whether as cabaret scuffles, interguild brawls, or semiformal duels. The demand for revenge was clearly in evidence amid the popular uprisings of July 1789, with the killings of various public officials, actions that so shocked the majority of the elites at the time. The popular classes would obtain increased influence through their de facto alliance with a minority of radical militants, both men and women, emerging from the elites. Such militants came rapidly to idolize the masses of the "sans-culottes," as they came to be called. They were extolled as the soul of the movement of liberty and equality, who had risen up on several occasions to save the Revolution. They were thus to be honored and respected, even in their acts of violence—acts that were justified, it was argued, by the centuries of repression under which they had lived. The militants played an important role in politicizing the popular classes, and thereafter the two groups evolved together, influenced the perspectives of one another, and exercised an ever-greater impact on national politics. They developed a whole repertoire of nonviolent strategies: petitions to the deputies, vocal pressure exerted from the Assembly's galleries, and great demonstrations pursued in the streets of Paris or through the Assembly hall itself. However, the penchant for violence and hatred, and the demands for retribution never disappeared among the sans-culottes and they soon influenced the radical militants as well. They reached a peak after the August 10 insurrection against the king, when several hundred Revolutionaries were killed in what was perceived by contemporaries as an ambush. Their anger and desire for revenge, mixed with pervasive rumors and currents of fear—fear of the invading Prussian army, fear of hidden conspirators—were essential ingredients in the terrible prison massacres of September 1792, killings that were accepted as necessary by a surprising proportion of the middle class. Indeed, in the atmosphere of tension and anxiety of that year and the two years that followed, there was often a partial merging of the emotional communities of the masses and the elites. In any case, the alliance between the Parisian militants and the sans-culottes would exercise a considerable influence on the repressive policies of the Convention and the Committee of Public Safety at the beginning of the Year II.

The fervent desire to preserve the new Revolutionary values, the presence of an active counterrevolution, the effects of the breakdown of authority, and the influence of the alliance of militants and sans-culottes were all linked inextricably to the emergence of a culture of fear and mistrust. Indeed, from the very beginning the powerful emotions of joy and enthusiasm engendered by the Revolution's extraordinary achievements were mixed with feelings of anxiety. The anxiety arose in part from the very nature of the Revolutionary situation, from the constant upheavals and uncertainty, and from the apprehension that those who had lost power and privilege would surely retaliate and seek to regain their positions. Fears were further inflated through the aggressive practice of denunciation and through the effects of rumor—rumor which in situations of menacing uncertainty could easily cross between the popular masses and the middle-class elites. The fear and suspicion were validated, moreover, by a series of high-profile betrayals. The duplicity of Louis XVI, of Lafayette, of Mirabeau, and of Dumouriez provided overwhelming evidence that even those whom one most trusted as supporters of the Revolution might actually be conspirators hiding behind a "mask of patriotism." Radicals felt shamed and mortified that they had been blind to such conspiracy in the past, and they vowed never to let it happen again. The direct physical threat to the Revolutionaries was brought home, by the assassinations in 1793 of Le Peletier and Marat and by the abortive assaults in 1794 against Collot d'Herbois and Robespierre.

Yet already by the winter of 1791–1792, even before France had gone to war, the pervasive atmosphere of fear and suspicion had produced a veritable obsession with plots among many Revolutionaries, the assumption that a "grand conspiracy" of internal and external opponents was responsible for virtually all of the troubles encountered by the Revolution. Once the war had begun, the conspiracy obsession engendered a string of panics in Paris, with rumors raging of imminent counterrevolutionary coups, rumors that spread both upward and downward between the popular masses and the political elites: in May 1792, in March 1793, and in June 1794. The crisis and panic of the spring of 1793 led to a series of improvisations that would constitute the institutional structure of the Terror. Panic fear among the leadership a year later would be an important factor in the Prairial Law and the Great Terror of the summer of 1794.

The culture of fear and mistrust was closely linked, moreover, to the emergence of intense factionalism. Political divisions arose in part out of local rivalries projected onto the national stage, in part over differences in policy—especially concerning the role to be given to the masses in the political process—and in part through competition between rival charismatic leaders. Whatever their origins, however, the factions quickly took on lives of their own, with adherents largely defining themselves in opposition to the factional other: patriots against aristocrats, Jacobins against Feuillants, Montagnards against Girondins. Not all Revolutionaries embraced such factions. Indeed the majority of the deputies attempted to remain nonaligned. But in the emotional climate after 1791, those who did so adhere readily demonized their opponents and persuaded themselves that they were dangerous traitors and conspirators. Toxic factionalism, born of fear, mistrust, and a struggle for survival, was a major element in the terrible politics of self-destruction in 1793 and 1794.

The Revolution, however, was not a linear process. The regime of the Terror emerged in fits and starts, through the interplay of individuals, factions, and events, in which fears fed by the fortunes of war and counterrevolution, by reasoned reflection and complex emotions all played a part. Already in the wake of the king's flight in June 1791 and following the attack on the Tuileries Palace in August 1792, the leadership had experimented with a variety of repressive measures, many of which anticipated the Year II. Yet even after creating the basic institutions of the Terror during the panic of March 1793, the Montagnard leaders hesitated to make full use of them. At first the Revolutionary Tribunal carefully followed the law and there were relatively few executions. Following the arrest of the Girondins on June 2, many members of the Mountain attempted to mitigate the situation, angered at having been coerced by the armed crowds and fearful of the reaction of the provinces to the purge of their deputies. Even such future Terrorists as Couthon, Barère, and Saint-Just initially treated the detentions as "temporary measures," just as they promoted reconciliation with the insurgent federalists. The full commitment of the Committee of Public Safety to state-sponsored violence emerged only in September: after the assassination of Marat, after the continuing violent resistance of the federalists and the Vendéans, after the entry of Robespierre into the Committee, and after a return of armed militants into the Convention.

Circumstances, then, had a powerful impact on the coming of the Terror. Yet circumstances alone would have been insufficient without a prior transformation of the psychology and mentalité of the Revolutionaries, a transformation with a tragic inner logic that was integral to the process of the French Revolution—and that is perhaps after all integral to the phenomenon of revolution itself. Of course, every revolution has its own specific contexts in time and in space, its own rhythms, its own mixture of historical contingency and individual decisions and emotions. Yet all major revolutions[9]—so many of which have included periods of terror—involve intense convictions that the society must and can be changed, convictions that easily breed impatience and intolerance with opposition. All revolutions engender counterrevolutionary opposition among those whose interests and values are threatened. All revolutions, during the inevitable process of transition, tend to produce power vacuums and create situations in which every authority is put into question, in which—as Mirabeau expressed it—"all the old boundaries have been erased." All revolutions can be pushed in unanticipated directions through the influence of the popular masses. And it may well be that all major revolutions are beset by periods of conspiracy obsession, of intense suspicion and lack of trust, of agonizing uncertainty as to who are one's friends and who are one's enemies, who are the true revolutionaries and who are the wolves in sheep's clothing, hiding behind the mask of revolutionary commitment.

THE EVENTS of Thermidor, with the purge and execution of Robespierre, did not bring a halt to Revolutionary violence. Indeed, ending a revolution can be at least as difficult as initiating one.[10] By the autumn of 1794 there were few members of the politically active elites in Paris and the provinces who had not been affected by one or another of the purges, who had not spent time as suspects in prison or under house arrest. Even as the radical Montagnard Terror was swept away, a "white terror" broke out in many parts of the Republic, with those who had lost family and friends in the Year II, those who had themselves been threatened and humiliated now turning the tables and seeking retribution in a "vicious cycle of vengeance and re-vengeance."[11] Hundreds of Jacobins and Montagnards were imprisoned or murdered. In December 1794 the surviving Girondin deputies were released from prison or came out of hiding, and they helped push the post-Thermidorian Convention even further to the right. After a final attempted insurrection by the sans-culottes in May 1795, the army would be returned to Paris and repression against the radicals would be accentuated. A number of deputies on the left were purged, and several were guillotined or committed suicide in prison—including Gilbert Romme, who refused to renounce the idealistic goals of the radical Jacobins. The various regimes that followed—the Directory, the Consulate, the Empire—would all resort on occasion to violent repression and arbitrary executions as they struggled to reimpose stability on a nation torn by factional striffe and civil war. The long shadow of the Revolution, the conflicting legacies of social reform and repressive reaction, of republicanism and authoritarianism, of utopian dreams and conservative fears would continue to divide the nation well into the nineteenth and twentieth centuries.

Abbreviations

AC	Archives communales de
ACSS	*Actes du . . . Congrès national des sociétés savantes*
AD	Archives départementales de
AE	Archives de l'évêché de
AHR	*American Historical Review*
AHRF	*Annales historiques de la Révolution française*
AM	Archives municipales de
AN	Archives nationales
Annales.E.S.C.	*Annales. Economies. Sociétés. Civilisations*
AP	*Archives parlementaires de 1787 à 1860, recueil complet des débats législatifs et politiques des chambres françaises. Première série (1787–1799),* edited by Jérôme Mavidal, Emile Laurent, et al., 82 vols. (Paris, 1867–1913)
AR	*Annales révolutionnaires*
BHVP	Bibliothèque historique de la ville de Paris
BM	Bibliothèque municipale de
Buchez and Roux	Philippe-Joseph-Benjamin Buchez and Abbé Pierre-Célestin Roux, *Histoire parlementaire de la Révolution française, ou journal des assemblées nationales depuis 1789 jusqu'en 1815,* 40 vols. (Paris, 1834–1838)
FHS	*French Historical Studies*
FRCMPC	*The French Revolution and the Creation of Modern Political Culture,* edited by Keith Michael Baker and Colin Lucas, 4 vols. (Oxford, 1987–1994)
JMH	*Journal of Modern History*
RF	*Révolution française*
RH	*Révue historique*
RHMC	*Révue d'histoire moderne et contemporaine*
Schmidt	*Tableaux de la Révolution française, publiés sur les papiers inédits du département et de la police secrète de Paris,* edited by Wilhelm Adolf Schmidt, 3 vols. (Leipzig, 1867–1870)

Notes

Introduction

1. Dieuleveult, "La mort des Conventionnels," 158–160, provides statistics based primarily on Kuscinski, *Dictionnaire des Conventionnels*.

2. Garat, *Mémoires sur la Révolution,* vi.

3. See, notably, Aulard, *L'histoire politique de la Révolution française;* Mathiez, *La Révolution française;* Lefebvre, *Le gouvernement révolutionnaire;* Soboul, *Histoire de la Révolution française;* and Vovelle, *La Révolution française.*

4. Hampson, *Prelude to Terror,* 42.

5. Ibid., 5–7, 42. See also Schama, *Citizens,* xv; and Furet and Ozouf, *A Critical Dictionary.* Note that the ideas of François Furet evolved substantially over time. For another attempted ideological explanation, see Israel, *Revolutionary Ideas.*

6. Mayer, *Furies;* Andress, *Terror;* Martin, *Violence et Révolution;* Sutherland, *Murder in Aubagne;* Edelstein, *Terror of Natural Right;* Linton, *Choosing Terror.* Among other important studies published recently that touch on the Terror, see Gueniffey, *La politique de la Terreur;* Gross, *Fair Shares for All;* Biard, *Missionnaires de la République;* Simonin, *Le déshonneur dans la République;* Walton, *Policing Public Opinion;* Baczko, *Politiques de la Révolution française;* Cowens, *To Speak for the People;* Jourdan, "Discours de la Terreur"; and Israel, *Revolutionary Ideas.* Recent years have also seen the publication of a number of important biographies touching on the period of the Terror, e.g., by Bossut on Chaumette; Biard on Collot d'Herbois; Lemny on Carra; Leuwers on Merlin de Douai; Sydenham on Léonard Bourdon; and McPhee on Robespierre. See the Bibliography for complete references.

7. While the Revolutionaries themselves frequently used the word "terror," the phrase "the Terror" and the words "terrorist" and "terrorism" appeared only after the event of Thermidor (July 1794) and the death of Robespierre.

8. The quote is from Baczko, "Terror before the Terror," 30.

9. Tackett, *Becoming a Revolutionary*. See also Tackett, *When the King Took Flight*.

10. Cited in Mathiot, *Pour vaincre*, 255.

11. Hunt, *Politics*, 176, and in general, 153–176. See also Garrioch, *Bourgeoisie*, esp. 172–174; and, for the dominance of elites among department and district administrators, Edelstein, *Birth of Electoral Democracy*, 243, 245, and 278.

12. Brinton, *Jacobins*; Rose, *Making of the Sans-Culottes*, 91–92. See also Burstin, *L'invention du sans-culotte*.

13. Garrioch, *Bourgeoisie*, 2–3.

14. Rosenwein, *Emotional Communities*, "Introduction." See also, e.g., Shula Sommers in Stearns and Stearns, *Emotion and Social Change*, 24–25. On rumor, see Chap. 5 in this book.

15. Lefebvre, *Great Fear of 1789*; Reddy, *Navigation of Feeling*; Wahnich, "De l'économie émotive de la Terreur."

16. Hofstadter, *Paranoid Style in American Politics*; also Tackett, "Conspiracy Obsession in a Time of Revolution."

17. See, e.g., Baczko, "Les peurs de la Terreur"; also Burstin, *L'invention du sans-culotte*, 208.

18. Of particular value here have been the memoirs of Pierre-Toussaint Durand de Maillane, Dominique-Joseph Garat, and René Levasseur. See the Bibliography for references.

19. Compare, e.g., the memoirs of Jacques Pinet or the marquis de Ferrières with their contemporary correspondence.

20. See Tackett, "Etude sérielle de la psychologie révolutionnaire."

21. Robespierre maintained an extensive correspondence with numerous individuals, but much of it was probably destroyed later in the Revolution, when it was dangerous to possess his letters: McPhee, *Robespierre*, 80–81. The same may have occurred with several of the other leaders who fell into disfavor. Of particular value have been the biographies of Ellery on Brissot; Gershoy on Barère; Hampson on Danton; Reinhard on Lazare Carnot; McPhee on Robespierre; and Reynolds on the Roland couple. See the Bibliography for details.

22. For the specific sources for these and the following individuals, see the Bibliography. On Jullien, in particular, see the excellent biography by L. Parker, *Writing the Revolution*. I thank Philippe Bourdin for his assistance with the correspondence of Romme.

23. See esp. Bonnet, *Louis-Sébastien Mercier*.

24. For other testimonies by nobles, most of them opposed to the Revolution, see Vaissière, *Lettres d'"Aristocrates."*

25. All but Prudhomme were also deputies at various times. Garat, who later served as minister (1792–1793), also published a remarkable memoir, written during the Revolution itself. Some of Mirabeau's articles may actually have been composed by his team of collaborators.

26. The principal local studies used are those of Arnaud on the department of Ariège; Baumont on Oise; Boivin-Champeaux on Eure; Boutier, *Campagne en émoi,* on Corrèze; Brégail on Gers; Bruneau on Cher and Indre-et-Loire; Corgne on the district of Pontivy; Deries on the district of Saint-Lô; Dorigny on Autun and its region; Dubois on Ain; Forrest on the region of Aquitaine; Fleury on the district of Mamers; Girardot on Haute-Saône; Godechot on the region of the "Midi-Toulousain"; Hanson on Caen and Limoges; Hunt on Troyes and Reims; Jessenne on Artois; Jolivet on Ardèche; Labroue on Dordogne; Pommeret on Côtes-du-Nord; Poupé on Var; Roux on Vienne; Sol on Quercy; Sutherland, *Murder in Aubagne,* on towns in Lower Provence; and Wahl on Lyon. This is a sample drawn from the immense body of local studies on the Revolution. See the Bibliography for details.

27. Note that in referring to "major revolutions," I am thinking primarily of those involving significant political, social, and cultural transformations—such as the twentieth-century revolutions in Russia, China, Cuba, Iran, etc.—all of which passed through periods of "terror" and violence. Among revolutions that social scientists are wont to compare, the eighteenth-century American experience was clearly rather different, much closer to a war of independence than to a social revolution. A comparison between it and the French Revolution has only limited value.

1. The Revolutionaries and Their World in 1789

1. On the social origins of the "new political class" of the Revolution, see especially Hunt, *Politics, Culture, and Class,* chap. 5. Only a small percentage of the future Revolutionaries were nobles or clergymen and thus not from the elite of the "Third Estate."

2. See, e.g., Vergniaud, *Vergniaud, manuscrits, lettres,* 1:1–10; McPhee, *Robespierre,* chaps. 1–4; Desmoulins, *Correspondance,* passim; Ellery, *Brissot de Warville,* chaps. 1–4; Reinhard, *Carnot,* 293–295. See also Darnton, "High Enlightenment."

3. On the collective biography of the future members of the first National Assembly, see Tackett, *Becoming,* chap. 1.

4. Roche, *France in the Enlightenment,* 430; Chartier, Compère, and Julia, *L'éducation en France.*

5. Mercier, *Tableau de Paris,* 1:254–256.

6. H. Parker, *Cult of Antiquity,* 18–19, 28.

7. Roche, *France in the Enlightenment,* 431.

8. At least two-thirds of the Third Estate in 1789 had most likely received legal training, along with over half of the membership of the Legislative Assembly and National Convention: Tackett, *Becoming,* 36–37; Baguenier-Desormeaux, "Origines sociales, géographiques," 165–166, 188–189.

9. Ruault, *Gazette d'un Parisien,* 37, 154 (letters of Jan. 10, 1784 and July 16, 1789). See also Mercier, *Tableau de Paris,* 1:256. Cf. the somewhat different perspective of Maza, *Myth of the French Bourgeoisie.*

10. Roche, *France in the Enlightenment,* 434.

11. See also Darnton, "A Bourgeois Puts His World in Order," in *The Great Cat Massacre,* 107–143.

12. Bien, "La réaction aristocratique."

13. At least fifty-eight members of the Third Estate in 1789 held titles of nobility, though all but a handful had been recently ennobled: Tackett, *Becoming,* 44.

14. Ibid., 40–41. See also Kwass, *Privilege and the Politics of Taxation.*

15. Tackett, "Paths to Revolution," 541–542. See also Turley, "Channels of Influence."

16. Tackett, *Becoming,* 54–65.

17. On the idea of a "convergent elite," see, e.g., Applewhite, *Political Alignment,* 11; Doyle, *The Ancien Régime,* 25–26; and Bien, "La réaction aristocratique."

18. Lezay-Marnésia, *Le bonheur,* 46–47. See also Chaussinand-Nogaret, *La noblesse au XVIIIe siècle,* 109; and Tackett, *Becoming,* 34–35.

19. See Chap. 4 in this book and Petitfils, "Les origines de la pensée contre-révolutionnaire" in Tulard, *La Contre-Révolution,* 16–32.

20. Serna, "L'encre et le sang," in Brioist et al., *Croiser le fer,* 306.

21. Cited by Serna, "L'encre et le sang," 308. See also Nicolas Ruault's description of a duel between two court women: Ruault, *Gazette d'un Parisien,* 401 (letter of Jan. 23, 1772).

22. Serna, "L'encre et le sang," 365, 410.

23. See, e.g., Serna, *Antonelle.*

24. For this and the following paragraphs, see esp. Roche, *France in the Enlightenment,* 322–332; and *People of Paris,* chap. 2.

25. For this and the following paragraph, see esp. Nicolas, *La rébellion française,* esp. chap. 1.

26. Farge, *La vie fragile,* 292.

27. Mercier, *Tableau de Paris,* 6:18.

28. See esp. Farge, *La vie fragile,* 292; Brennan, *Public Drinking and Popular Culture,* chap. 1; Garrioch, *Neighbourhood and Community,* esp. 33 and 48; Roche, *Ménétra,* 319. On interguild violence, see Kaplan, *La fin des corporations,* 294–295. On rural fights and feuds, see esp. Le Goff and Sutherland, "Revolution and the Rural Community," 96–119.

29. Farge and Zysberg, "Les théâtres de la violence," 1008; Roche, *Ménétra,* 319. It is not impossible that Ménétra exaggerated the number of fights in which he was involved, but his stories undoubtedly reflected an aspect of the lives of Parisian male artisans.

30. Serna, "L'encre et le sang," 311–313, and 364. By Roche's count, 6 of the 50 violent encounters related by Ménétra ended in formal duels: *Ménétra,* 319.

31. Galante Garrone, *Romme,* chap. 2; Tackett, *Becoming,* 105; Mercier, *Tableau de Paris,* 1:41–42.

32. Mercier, *Tableau de Paris,* 2:297–303; and *Paris le jour, Paris la nuit,* 125.

33. Faulcon, *Correspondance,* 1:159 (letter of May 13, 1783); Colson, "Correspondance," letter of May 3, 1789; Ruault, *Gazette d'un Parisien,* 34 and 96–97 (letters of Dec. 21, 1783 and Aug. 25, 1787).

34. Ruault, *Gazette d'un Parisien,* 153–154 (letter of July 16, 1789).

35. See, Quéniart, *Culture et société urbaines;* and Roche, *Le siècle des lumières en province,* passim; and Roche, *France in the Enlightenment,* esp. chap. 13.

36. Roche, *Le siècle des lumières en Province,* 1:324–355 and graph on 2:295; and Caradonna, "Prendre part au siècle des Lumières"; and Caradonna, *The Enlightenment in Practice.*

37. On letters to the editor, see, e.g., Andrews, "Between *Auteurs* et *Abonnés.*"

38. Erhard, "Un étudiant riomois à Paris," 1:58, 68, and 99–105.

39. Tackett, "Paths to Revolution."

40. Colson, "Correspondance," letter of June 20, 1786; Faulcon, *Correspondance,* 1:180 (letter of Jan. 9, 1784) and 1:200 (letter from Leroux, Aug. 10, 1784); Vergniaud, *Vergniaud, manuscrits, lettres,* 1:90 (letter of Dec. 20, 1783). Also Darnton, *Mesmerism,* 18–22.

41. Ruault, *Gazette d'un Parisien,* 19 (letter of Mar. 11, 1783); Faulcon, *Correspondance,* 1:93–94 (undated journal entry of mid-1781), 1:173 (letter of Nov. 12, 1783), and 1:257 (letter of Jan. 20, 1787).

42. Faulcon, *Correspondance,* 1:93–94 (journal entry of mid-1781); and 1:217 (letter of Apr. 28, 1785); Garat, *Eloge de Bernard de Fontenelle,* 82.

43. See, e.g., Quéniart, *Culture et société;* Furet, *Livre et société,* 1:3–32; Censer, *The French Press in the Age of Enlightenment.*

44. See, e.g., Furet, *Interpreting the French Revolution;* Baker, *Inventing the French Revolution;* Van Kley, *Religious Origins;* Reddy, *Navigation of Feeling,* esp. chaps 5 and 6.

45. Roche, *France in the Enlightenment,* 283.

46. Tackett, *Becoming,* 63–65 and 74–76. See Mercier's sarcastic treatment of "l'esprit public," which everyone claimed to know but which existed in scores of different versions, depending on one's point of view: Mercier, *Tableau de Paris,* 6:185; and *Le nouveau Paris,* 2:50.

47. See e.g., Furet, *Livre et société;* Quéniart, *Culture et société;* Hasegawa, "Constitution des bibliothèques privées de Poitiers"; Darnton, "A Bourgeois Puts His World in Order" in *The Great Cat Massacre,* 107–143; and Berlanstein, *Barristers of Toulouse,* 96–100.

48. For much of this and the following paragraphs see Tackett, "Paths to Revolution."

49. On Jullien see "Correspondance," esp. letters of Sept. 29 and Oct. 30, 1785. Faulcon also wrote that he hoped one day to meet his Protestant ancestors in Heaven: *Correspondance,* 1:305 (letter of Dec. 20, 1787).

50. Tackett, "Paths to Revolution." Of the 227 books in Vergniaud's library at the beginning of the Revolution, about 40 percent were law texts and 30 percent were works of literature: Vergniaud, "Bibliothèque de Vergniaud." See also Garat, *Mémoires,* 210. On the Julliens, see Rosalie's letter of July 16, 1787 in Jullien, "Correspondance"; on Romme's "universality," see Julia, "Gilbert Romme, gouverneur," 225.

51. See, e.g., Mercier, *Tableau de Paris,* 8:161–163; and Ruault, *Gazette d'un Parisien,* 18 (letter of Feb. 26, 1783).

52. Berlanstein, *Barristers of Toulouse,* 119.

53. In one sample of duelists found in eighteenth-century Parisian judicial records in the eighteenth century, only 1 of the 105 whose professions were known might be linked to the middle class—a "huissier," a minor court official. Most of the rest were nobles, soldiers, artisans, or shopkeepers: Serna, "L'encre et le sang," 362–363. See also Brennan, *Public Drinking and Popular Culture,* 32–36.

54. Serna, "L'encre et le sang," chap. 8; Mercier, *Tableau de Paris,* 1:294.

55. Cuénin, *Le duel sous l'ancien régime,* 293–294. No fewer than 56 of some 210 "general" *cahiers de doléances* of the Third Estate—those statements of grievances drawn up primarily by urban elites to be sent to Versailles—were critical of dueling.

56. Serna, "Le duel durant la Révolution"; and Tackett, *Becoming,* 137–138. Cf. the somewhat different perspective on the culture of honor in Walton, *Policing Public Opinion.* See also Smith, *Nobility Reimagined.*

57. Mercier, *Tableau de Paris,* 1:69–71; Ruault, *Gazette d'un Parisien,* 22–23 (letter of June 8, 1783); Faulcon, *Correspondance,* 1:225 (letter by Texier, Aug. 4, 1785) and 2:2–4 (letter by Leroux, Jan. 8, 1789). See also Andress, " 'A Ferocious and Misled Multitude.' "

58. Colson, "Correspondance," letter of Jan. 25, 1780. See also Faulcon, *Correspondance,* 2:4 (letter of Leroux of Jan. 8, 1789).

59. Colson, "Correspondance," letter of May 3, 1789; Boullé, AD Morbihan, 163 (letter of May 1, 1789); Tackett, *Becoming,* 166.

60. See notably Porret, " 'Effrayer le crime par la terreur,' " 60–62; Savey-Casard, *La peine de mort,* 56–63; Muller, "Magistrats français," 105; and Cossy, "Progrès et violence dans l'oeuvre de Voltaire," in Cossy and Dawson, *Progrès et violence,* 188.

61. Mercier, *Tableau de Paris,* 3:267; Ruault, *Gazette d'un Parisien,* 73 (letter of July 22, 1786).

62. Savey-Casard, *La peine de mort,* 60. Beccaria's principal work had been translated into French in 1766.

63. Faulcon, *Correspondance,* 1:80 (letter of Dec. 24, 1780); Farge, *La vie fragile,* 211–212; Desjardins, *Les cahiers des Etats Généraux,* 48–50; Imbert, "La peine de mort," 519; Savey-Casard, *La peine de mort,* 58–60, 62. On Marat, see Simonin, *Le déshonneur dans la République,* 236.

64. Savey-Casard, *La peine de mort,* 58–62.

65. A similar position was taken by the influential Muyart de Vouglans. See Porret, "'Effrayer le crime par la terreur,'" 56–57; and Muller, "Magistrats français," 80–81.

66. In the 1780s the Parlement of Paris issued death sentences in some 4 to 8 percent of all judgments meted out: Muller, "Magistrats français," 88–90.

67. Colson, "Correspondance," letters, e.g., of Oct. 12, 1783 and Apr. 4, 1786. See also Porret, "'Effrayer le crime par la terreur,'" 48 and 54.

68. Porret, "'Effrayer le crime par la terreur,'" 56–57. See also the Old Regime legal scholar François Serpillon: "Le principal objet de la Justice n'est pas seulement de punir les criminels, c'est de donner au public . . . des exemples qui soient capables de donner de la terreur à ceux qui les ont vu commettre . . .": cited in Bastien, *L'exécution publique,* 127.

69. See, e.g., Porret, "'Effrayer le crime par la terreur,'" 60–62; Farge, *La vie fragile,* 207; Bée, "Le spectacle de l'exécution," 858–859; Bastien, *L'exécution publique,* esp. chap. 3.

70. Colson, "Correspondance," letter of Oct. 12, 1783; Farge, *La vie fragile,* 207–215; Imbert, "La peine de mort," 509; Andrews, "Between *Auteurs* et *Abonnés,*" 386–388; Bée, "Le spectacle de l'exécution," esp. 846–847. Siméon-Prosper Hardy mentioned in his "Journal" some 180 executions between 1765 and 1789: Bastien, *L'exécution publique,* 132. See also Roche in *Ménétra,* 320.

71. Figures taken from the database on *cahiers* demands constructed by Gilbert Shapiro and John Markoff at the University of Pittsburgh. See also Desjardins, *Les cahiers des Etats Généraux,* 52–53.

72. See Savey-Casard, *La peine de mort,* 70–75.

73. *AP,* 26:618–623, 637–650, 685–689 (May 30–June 1, 1791). The deputy Custine moved that the "spectacle" of executions be ended and that in the future they take place in private: "qu'elle ne soit point aggravé par cet appareil effrayant qui la rend plus terrible à celui qui doit l'éprouver." But this motion was rejected: ibid., 687–688.

74. Here and for the following paragraphs, see Dawson, "Progrès et violence dans l'oeuvre de Voltaire," in Cossy and Dawson, *Progrès et violence,* 201–203; Roosevelt, *Reading Rousseau,* 53–54; and Srinivas Aravamudan, "Progress through Violence or Progress from Violence?" in Cossy and Dawson, *Progrès et violence,* 266, 271.

75. Mercier, *Tableau de Paris,* 3:258, 263; Cossy and Dawson, *Progrès et violence,* esp. 187–204 and 259–280.

76. Faulcon, *Correspondance,* 1:305 (letter of Dec. 20, 1787); Colson, "Correspondance," esp. letters of Aug. 8 and Dec. 21, 1779, May 23 and Sept. 3, 1780, and July 3 and Nov. 27, 1781; Ruault, *Gazette d'un Parisien,* 18 (letter of Feb. 26, 1783), 47 (letter of Dec. 1, 1784), and 104 (letter of Mar. 8, 1788).

2. The Spirit of '89

1. See, e.g., Doyle, *Origins of the French Revolution;* Kaiser and Van Kley, *From Deficit to Deluge;* and Campbell, *Origins of the French Revolution.*

2. Colson, "Correspondance," e.g., letters of Oct. 15, 1780 and Jan. 5, 1783; Vergniaud, *Vergniaud, manuscrits, lettres, et papiers,* 1:35 (letter of Jan. 13, 1781); Erhard, "Un étudiant riomois [Romme] à Paris," 52; and Ruault, *Gazette d'un Parisien,* 33 and 84 (letters of Dec. 21, 1783 and July 8, 1787). Cf. also Dzimbowski, *Un nouveau patriotisme français;* and Bell, *Cult of the Nation.*

3. Bosher, *French Finances, 1770–1795;* Brewer, *Sinews of Power;* Bozenga, in Kaiser and Van Kley, *From Deficit to Deluge,* 37–66; and Félix, in Campbell, *Origins of the French Revolution,* 35–62.

4. For this and the following, see esp. Egret, *French Prerevolution;* Gruder, *Notables and the Nation;* and Hardman, *Overture to Revolution.*

5. Le Goff, "Le financement de la participation française à la guerre d'indépendance et ses conséquences"; and additional analysis kindly shown to me by T.J.A. Le Goff.

6. For this paragraph, see esp. Tackett, "Paths to Revolution."

7. See Egret, *French Prerevolution;* and Alpaugh, *Non-violence and the French Revolution,* chap. 1.

8. Renouvin, *Les assemblées provinciales;* and Tackett, *Becoming,* 81–82.

9. Tackett, *Becoming,* 82–90; and Wick, *A Conspiracy of Well-Intentioned Men.*

10. The abbé Sieyès' celebrated tract, *What Is the Third Estate,* may have been less influential when it first came out. The deputy Maupetit had read it in February, but it was only in June that he realized its importance for the ongoing events: Maupetit, "Lettres," 18 (1902), 157–160 (letter of June 13, 1789). Gilbert Romme also mentioned reading Sieyès in February, but his annotated copy of the work was a third edition, suggesting that he only read it carefully several weeks later: Romme, "Lettres," copy of letter of Feb. 26, 1789; and Romme, "Correspondance," Museo del Risorgimento, dos. 70 (both kindly shown to me by Philippe Bourdin).

11. Colson, "Correspondance," undated letter of Feb. 1789; Ruault, *Gazette d'un Parisien,* 120 (letter of Oct. 3, 1788).

12. See Tackett, *Becoming,* 90–94.

13. For this and the following paragraphs see ibid., 94–99 and chap. 4.

14. Ménard de La Groye, *Correspondance,* letter of May 5. See also Gaultier de Biauzat, in Mège, 2:26 (letter of May 4, 1789).

15. For the following paragraphs, see Tackett, *Becoming,* esp. chap. 4.

16. Maillot, AC Toul, letter of May 7, 1789.

17. Ménard, *Correspondance,* letter of Dec. 22, 1789. See also Gaultier, in Mège, 2:44 (letter of May 9); Boullé, in Macé, 15 (1889), 116 (letter of Sept. 8, misdated Sept. 28 in publication); and Rabaut, 116–117.

18. Romme, "Lettres," June 23, 1789.

19. On the possible motives of the king, see, e.g., Caron, "La tentative de contrerévolution"; and Price, *Road from Versailles,* esp. 75–84.

20. Colson, "Correspondance," letter of Aug. 10; Jacob, "La Grande Peur," 127.

21. Barbier-Schroffenberg, "Extrait de la correspondance," 15 (1966), 71 (letter of Mar. 30, 1789).

22. Colson, "Correspondance," letters of Dec. 14, 1788 and Jan. 1789, passim; Romme, "Correspondance," letter of Dec. 21, 1788; Faulcon, *Correspondance,* 2:4 (letter of Jan. 8, 1789); Mareux, *Une famille de la bourgeoisie,* 69 (letter of Jan. 12, 1789); *Journal de Paris,* issues of Dec. 23, 1788, Jan. 6, 24, 25, and Feb. 2, 1789; Chaudron, *La grande peur,* 53; Dubois, *Histoire de la Révolution,* 1:51–52; Armoogum-Ninat, "La Grande Peur de 1789," 122–123.

23. Colson, "Correspondance," letter of Dec. 7, 1788. See also the various letters to the editor in the *Journal de Paris* in late 1788 and early 1789; and Chaudron, *La grande peur,* 60.

24. Colson, "Correspondance," letters of April 7 and 14, 1789; Faulcon, *Correspondance,* 2:4 (letter by Leroux in Rouen of Jan. 8, 1789); Markoff, *Abolition of Feudalism,* 242–249.

25. Colson, "Correspondance," letters of Dec. 2 and 14, 1788. Information on the summary, justice of 1789 kindly given me by Ted W. Margadant.

26. Markoff, *Abolition of Feudalism,* 270. There were still numerous "insurrectionary events" during this period, but the numbers leveled off after March and before the "spike" of July–August, the highest level during the entire Revolution.

27. See Chap. 1 in this book, and Farge, *Subversive Words* and *La vie fragile,* esp. 292–308; Brennan, *Public Drinking and Popular Culture,* chap. 1; and Garrioch, *Neighbourhood and Community,* esp. 33 and 48.

28. Rudé, *Crowd in the French Revolution,* 34–44. See also Colson, "Correspondance," letter of May 3, 1789; Boullé, in Macé, 163 (letter of May 1); and Tackett, *Becoming,* 166.

29. Colson, "Correspondance," e.g., letter of July 5, 1789.

30. Romme, "Lettres," letter of June 27, 1789; and letter to Dubreul, July 18. See also Ruault, *Gazette d'un Parisien,* 153–155 (letter of July 16). Ruault frequently used the word "bourgeois" in describing the municipal revolution and the formation of a citizens' militia. See also Godechot, *Taking of the Bastille,* chaps. 8 and 9; and Alpaugh, "Politics of Escalation."

31. Romme, in Galante Garrone, *Gilbert Romme,* 524 (letter of July 18, 1789); and Colson, "Correspondance," letter of July 19.

32. Godechot, *Taking of the Bastille,* 229 and 244–245.

33. Romme, in Galante Garonne, *Gilbert Romme,* 524 (letter of July 18, 1789); Colson, "Correspondance," letter of July 19; and Godechot, *Taking of the Bastille,* 243–244.

34. Visme, "Journal des Etats-Généraux," entry of July 22, 1789; Faulcon, *Correspondance,* 91 and 104 (diary entry of July 22 and letter of July 28).

35. *Révolutions de Paris,* issue of July 26, 1789.

36. For this paragraph see esp. Lefebvre, *Great Fear;* Tackett, "Collective Panics"; and "La grande peur de 1789."

37. Romme, in Galante Garonne, *Gilbert Romme,* 526 (letter of July 23, 1789). Cf. Lepoutre, *Député-paysan et fermière,* 71 (letter of July 30).

38. Tackett, articles cited in note 36.

39. For this paragraph, see Kessel, *La nuit du 4 août;* Tackett, *Becoming,* 169–175; and Fitzsimmons, *Night the Old Regime Ended.*

40. *Courrier de Provence,* no. 24 (Aug. 7, 1789). Legendre described the Night of August 4 as "une espèce d'ivresse": AM Brest 2 D 16–18, letter of Aug. 5.

41. *Révolutions de Paris,* issue of Aug. 9, 1789; Gaultier, in Mège, 2:224 (letter of Aug. 4).

42. Jean-François Campmas, BM Albi, letter of July 18; Delandine, *Mémorial historique,* 3: 271 (July 31); Garat, *Mémoires,* 211. See also Boullé, in Macé, 14 (1889), 114 (letter of July 21).

43. Brissot, *Patriote français,* issue of Aug. 6, 1789; Prudhomme, *Révolutions de Paris,* issue of Aug. 9; Ruault, *Gazette d'un Parisien,* 163 (letter of Aug. 8); Garat, *Mémoires,* 211. Compare the statements of Pierre-Philippe Gudin: "Ce grand spectacle que la France vient de donner au monde a produit des changements qu'on croyait tellement impossible, que personne n'eût osé les imaginer dans un roman: on les eût pris pour les rêves d'un malade": cited in Barny, *Jean-Jacques Rousseau dans la Révolution,* 15; and of the future Jacobin radical Jérôme Pétion: "Le Français est étonné de la situation présente, il est parvenu sans, pour ainsi dire, y songer": *Avis aux Français,* 226. On the comparison between the *cahiers de doléance* and the achievements of the Night of August 4, see Taylor, "Revolutionary and Non-Revolutionary Content in the *Cahiers.*"

44. Vernier, "Lettres," letter of Aug. 6, 1789. See also Maupetit, "Lettres," 19 (1901), 219 (letter of Aug. 5).

45. E.g., the letters written from around the kingdom in early August 1789: AN, C 91; also the letter to Romme from Dubreul in Riom, July 16, cited in Galante Garrone, *Gilbert Romme,* 174. On the broader meaning of popular oathtaking, see, e.g., Simonin, *Le déshonneur dans la République,* 213–214.

46. Ruault, *Gazette d'un Parisien,* 161, letter of July 30, 1789; Romme, cited in Galante Garrone, *Gilbert Romme,* 529 (letter of Sept. 8). See also the speech by Clermont-Tonnerre, Sept. 9: *AP,* 8:603. Garat cited in *Courrier de Provence,* number 21, July 31; Desmoulins cited in de Baecque, "L'homme nouveau est arrivé," 177. And, in general, de Baecque, *Le corps,* 172–183.

47. Shapiro, *Revolutionary Justice,* 20; Toulongeon, *Histoire de la France,* 1:111; and A. C. Thibaudeau, *Biographie, Mémoires,* 133. See also Duquesnoy, *Journal,* 1:138 (entry of June 28, 1789).

48. Colson, "Correspondance," letter of Mar. 17, 1789. See also Romme, "Lettres," letter of June 23.

49. Ruault, *Gazette d'un Parisien,* 163 (letter of Aug. 19, 1789); Romme in Galante Garrone, *Gilbert Romme,* 524 (letter of July 18); Jullien, "Correspondance," letter of Aug. 27.

50. Lefebvre, *Great Fear,* 198–199.

51. Ruault, *Gazette d'un Parisien,* 166–167 (letters of Aug. 25 and Sept. 3, 1789); Colson, "Correspondance," letters of Aug. 11, 18, 23, 27, and 30, and Sept. 6, 9, and 14; *Révolutions de Paris,* issue of Sept. 6; Jullien, "Correspondance," letter of Sept. 1; Buchez and Roux, *Histoire parlementaire,* 3:14 (entry for Sept. 2). See also, e.g., letters of the deputies Jean-François Campmas, BM Albi, Aug. 8; and Lepoutre, *Député-paysan et fermière,* Aug. 29.

52. For this and the following paragraphs, see Tackett, *Becoming,* chap. 6.

53. Although in theory the king's approval was not necessary for decrees voted by the current "Constituent" Assembly, in reality the failure to ratify the decrees by a monarch who remained extremely popular in public opinion seemed seriously to undercut their legitimacy.

54. Colson, "Correspondance," letter of Oct. 5, 1789; Mercier, *Le nouveau Paris* (1994), 334; and *Patriote français* (issue of Oct. 8, 1789).

55. See *Le journal de Paris* (issue of Oct. 8, 1789).

56. Jullien, "Correspondance," letter of Oct 5, 1789 (at midnight). See also Delandine, *Mémorial historique,* 6:3–4.

57. Goupilleau, "Lettres," letter of Oct. 9, 1789; Brissot, *Patriote français* (issue of Oct. 7, 1789); Romme, cited in Galante Garrone, *Gilbert Romme,* 178 (letter of Oct. 6). See also Merle, AC Mâcon, letter of Oct. 13.

58. Ménétra, "Mes réflexions," 69 and 102. See also Romme, cited in Galante Garrone, *Gilbert Romme,* 181 and 529 (letters of Sept. 8, 1789 and ca. Dec. 1789).

59. Faulcon, *Correspondance,* 2:11 (letter of Feb. 27, 1789); and Tackett, "Paths to Revolution," 547. See also Romme, cited in Galante Garrone, *Gilbert Romme,* 181 (letter of ca. Dec. 1789). Cf. Roubaud's later comments on the disappearance of "mon caractère de gaité qui longtemps a fait mon bonheur": Roubaud, "Lettres," 184 (letter of May 11, 1793).

60. Words inscribed in the parish register by the curé of Castelnau-Montratier (near Cahors): Paumès, "La Grande Peur," 197 (entry of Aug. 2, 1789).

61. Mège, "La grande peur," 141.

3. The Breakdown of Authority

1. Judd, *Members of Parliament,* 21; Galloway and Wise, *History of the House of Representatives,* 22.

2. Tackett, *When the King Took Flight,* 181–184. For the letters of the late summer and fall of 1789: AN C 91–94.

3. *L'ami du peuple,* issue of Dec. 22, 1789.

4. Mousset, *Un témoin ignoré de la Révolution,* 228; also Saint-Priest, *Mémoires,* 2:24–25.

5. See, e.g., Fréville, *L'intendance de Bretagne,* 3:292–297; and Cohen, "Les intendants au coeur de la crise," 101–109.

6. Ruault, *Gazette d'un Parisien,* 161 (letter of July 30, 1789). Among the intendants abandoning their posts were those of Caen, Soissons, Amiens, Dijon, Riom, Perpignan, Orléans, Besançon, and Bourges: Cohen, "Les intendants au coeur de la crise," 30–31; Mourlot, *La fin de l'ancien régime,* 328–330; Vidal, *Histoire de la Révolution française,* 57–62; Bart, *La Révolution française en Bourgogne,* 139; Bruneau, *Les débuts de la Révolution,* 88–89; Biard, *Missionnaires,* 27–29, and *Les lilliputiens,* esp. chap. 5. The intendants of Lyon, Toulouse, Auch, Montauban, and Poitiers all seem to have remained: Jolivet, *La Révolution dans l'Ardèche,* 156; Brégail, "Le Gers pendant la Révolution," 30 (1929), 358; Godechot, *La Révolution française dans le Midi-Toulousain,* 82; Roux, *Révolution à Poitiers,* 210–211; AN C 94, letter from Lavaur, Sept. 20, 1789.

7. *Révolutions de Paris,* issue of July 26, 1789; Bailly, *Mémoires,* 2:136 (entry of July 26, 1789); Vidal, *Histoire de la Révolution française,* 60; Bruneau, *Les débuts de la Révolution,* 90.

8. Caillet, *Les Français en 1789,* 25–27, 191–193. On the general collapse of judicial authority, see Lafon, *La Révolution française,* 35–50; Mourlot, *La fin de l'ancien régime,* 330; Pommeret, *L'esprit politique,* 69; Bruneau, *Les débuts de la Révolution,* 90. Also, Faulcon, *Correspondance,* 2:91 (journal entry of July 23, 1789); Colson, "Correspondance," letters of July 14 and 21, and Oct. 20, 1789, and May 4, 23, and 25, 1790; Ruault, *Gazette d'un Parisien,* 194 (letter of Apr. 10, 1790). Among the few courts maintaining some measure of authority were those of the *prévôts des maréchaux,* reinvigorated in the spring of 1789 to work closely with municipal authorities in repressing popular violence. But their jurisdiction was specifically limited, and even *they* were not always respected. See Seligman, *La justice en France,* 238; and research kindly shared with me by Ted Margadant. On the importance of the power vacuum in the early Revolution, see also Martin, *Violence et Révolution,* chap. 2.

9. Mirabeau, *Dix-neuvième lettre . . . à ses commettans*; Duquesnoy, *Journal,* 1:231–232 (entry of July 18). See also Gilbert Riberolles in Mège, "Notes biographiques," 126–127 (letter of Aug. 24).

10. Tackett, *Becoming,* 235–236; also the many letters sent to the National Assembly from the provinces that refer to such deputy letters: AN C 91–94.

11. See esp. Hunt, "Committees and Communes." Also, e.g., Jolivet, *La Révolution dans l'Ardèche,* 143–147, 157; Brégail, "Le Gers pendant la Révolution," 30 (1929), 355, 358; Fleury, *La ville et le district de Mamers,* 1:103–105; Arnaud, *Histoire de la Révolution,* 113–115; Bart, *La Révolution française,* 125 and 136–140; Forrest, *Revolution in Provincial France,* 64–68; Roux, *Révolution à Poitiers,* 220–226; Bruneau, *Les débuts de la Révolution,* 67–74; Dorigny, *Autun,* 2:56; and Biard, *Missionnaires,* 30.

12. AN C 93–94. Also, e.g., Seinguerlet, *Strasbourg,* 16–29; Arnaud, *Histoire de la Révolution,* 113; and Forrest, *Revolution in Provincial France,* 63–64. See also Chap. 2 in this book.

13. See the letters from municipalities in AN C 94, e.g., those of Saumur, Montluçon, and Eu.

14. Prior to the summer of 1793 the cantons would function primarily as electoral divisions. See Chap. 11 in this book.

15. See, e.g., Jolivet, *La Révolution dans l'Ardèche,* 174–191; Godechot, *La Révolution dans le Midi-Toulousain,* 124–125. Also, Margadant, *Urban rivalries;* and Ozouf-Marignier, *La formation des départements.*

16. See, e.g., Jolivet, *La Révolution dans l'Ardèche,* 161–194; and Fleury, *La ville et le district de Mamers,* 1:106–111. Also Patrick, "Paper, Posters, and People."

17. Baumont, *Le département de l'Oise,* 35–36; Fleury, *La ville et le district de Mamers,* 1:115–118; Jolivet, *La Révolution dans l'Ardèche,* 281. See also Chap. 6 in this book.

18. Lefebvre, *La fuite du roi,* 22–25.

19. See, e.g., Legendre, AM Brest 2 D 16–18, letter of June 13, 1791.

20. Lefebvre called it "la décentralisation à l'outrance": *La fuite du roi,* 22. Cf. Jones, *Peasantry,* 169; and Tocqueville, *Old Regime and the French Revolution,* esp. part 2, chap. 5.

21. See Chap. 5 in this book.

22. Ménétra, "Mes réflexions," BHVP Ms. 678, 259. See also Ruault, *Gazette d'un Parisien,* 332 (letter of Apr. 30, 1793); and the Parisian national guard leader, Charles-Alexis Alexandre, who characterized all radicals as "des amis de la liberté": Alexandre, "Fragments des mémoires," 189.

23. P. M. Jones, *Peasantry,* 168. See also Woloch, *New Regime,* 35–36, 43; and Jessenne, *Pouvoir au village,* esp. chap. 2.

24. Mirabeau in the *Courrier de Provence,* no. 26 (Aug. 10, 1789). See also Ruault, *Gazette d'un Parisien,* 162 (letter of Aug. 8, 1789); and Jolivet, *La Révolution dans l'Ardèche,* 185, 208.

25. Labrosse and Rétat, *Naissance du journal révolutionnaire,* 19, 24, and 392–397. See also Hesse, *Publishing and Cultural Politics,* 167–168; Popkin, *Revolutionary News,* esp. chap. 1; Forrest, *Revolution in Provincial France,* 93–96; and Godechot, *Révolution dans le Midi-Toulousain,* 105–107.

26. For this paragraph, see esp. Walton, *Policing Public Opinion,* esp. chap. 5; and on the radical press in general, Censer, *Prelude to Power,* esp. chaps. 2 and 4.

27. Labrosse and Rétat, *Naissance du journal révolutionnaire,* 201–202; Ruault, *Gazette d'un Parisien,* 192–193 (letter of Apr. 8, 1790).

28. Colson, "Correspondance," letter of Aug. 30, 1789.

29. Colson, "Correspondance," letter of Aug. 30, 1789; Guittard de Floriban, *Journal,* 48 and 68 (entries of Apr. 27 and July 5, 1791); Jaffé, *Le mouvement ouvrier,* 65–83; Rose, *Making of the Sans-Culottes,* 108–109; Burstin, "Problèmes du travail,"

652–655; Sewell, *Work and Revolution,* 95–98; Alpaugh, *Non-violence and the French Revolution,* appendix.

30. Colson, "Correspondance," letters of Jan. 26, 1790 and Aug. 16, 1791; Sewell, *Work and Revolution,* 97–98.

31. Noël, *Au temps des volontaires,* 170 (letter of June 22, 1792). See also S. Scott, *Response of the Royal Army,* 60–96; Carrot, *Révolution et maintien de l'ordre,* 122–131; Forrest, *Soldiers of the French Revolution,* esp. 42 and 89–124; M. Kennedy, *The Jacobin Club,* 1:178–179.

32. Bertaud and Reichel, *Atlas,* 15.

33. S. Scott, *Response of the Royal Army, 1787–93,* 92–95; Carrot, *Révolution et maintien de l'ordre,* 132–134; M. Kennedy, *The Jacobin Club,* 1:181–183; Girardot, *Le département de la Haute-Saône,* 2:94–96; and Colson, "Correspondance," letters of Sept. 5, 7, 12, and 21, 1790.

34. Markoff, *Abolition of Feudalism,* notably his conclusions, 562–569. Also, Boutier, *Campagnes en émoi,* 33–35.

35. Roux, *Révolution à Poitiers,* 244; Girardot, *Le département de la Haute-Saône,* 1:148; Dubois, *Histoire de la Révolution,* 1:101–107; Jolivet, *La Révolution dans l'Ardèche,* 189; Sol, *La Révolution en Quercy,* 1:252–253. Also P. M. Jones, *Peasantry,* 104–109.

36. The Committee on Research received complaints of poaching and woodcutting in private forests from almost everywhere in the kingdom: Caillet, *Les Français en 1789,* 142–146. See also *AHRF* 10 (1933), 167–169; AN C 94, letter from Saumur, Sept. 19, 1789; La Rochefoucauld, *Lettres,* 35 (letter of Feb. 10, 1791); Baumont, *Le département de l'Oise,* 25–26, 39, 206–207; Dubois, *Histoire de la Révolution,* 1:336–338; Girardot, *Le département de la Haute-Saône,* 2:106–108; Bruneau, *Les débuts de la Révolution,* 187.

37. Jones, *Peasantry,* 181–184; Roux, *Révolution à Poitiers,* 240–245; Jolivet, *La Révolution dans l'Ardèche,* 157; Baumont, *Le département de l'Oise,* 32–34; Bruneau, *Les débuts de la Révolution,* 93–96.

38. See Markoff, *Abolition of Feudalism,* chap. 5; Caillet, *Les Français en 1789,* 28–118; Sée, "Les troubles agraires en Haute-Bretagne," passim.

39. See Boutier, *Campagnes en émoi,* passim.

40. See, e.g., Barbier-Schroffenberg, "Extrait de la correspondance," 15 (1966), 73–75 (letters of Aug. 14 and 21, 1789).

41. In Lucenay-les-Aix (Nièvre), June 1790: Caillet, *Les Français en 1789,* 25–26.

42. Girardot, *Le département de la Haute-Saône,* 2:106; Ruault, *Gazette d'un Parisien,* 162 (letter of August 8, 1789). Cf. Dubois, *Histoire de la Révolution,* 1:105; Jolivet, *La Révolution dans l'Ardèche,* 185; AN C 94.

43. For this and the following paragraph, see esp. Bianchi and Dupuy, passim; Caillet, *Les Français en 1789,* 25, 27, 191; Dupuy, *La garde nationale,* 135–137, 172–179, and 197–199; Roux, *Révolution à Poitiers,* 226–233; Dubois, *Histoire de la Révolution,* 1:79, 91, 341; Jolivet, *La Révolution dans l'Ardèche,* 147–151; Arnaud, *Histoire de la Révo-*

lution, 192–205; Brégail, "Le Gers pendant la Révolution," 30 (1929), 365; Sol, *La Révolution en Quercy,* 240; and Pommeret, *L'esprit politique,* 68.

44. On the efforts of "youth" to establish their own contingents, see Déplanche, "French Revolution and the Origins of Modern Youth Movements," esp. chap. 3.

45. Tackett, *When the King Took Flight,* 13–14.

46. Caillet, *Les Français en 1789,* 191.

47. Ruault, *Gazette d'un Parisien,* 153–155 and 174–175 (letters of July 16 and Dec. 28, 1789); Colson, "Correspondance," letter of Sept. 15, 1789. See also Carrot, passim.

48. Tackett, *When the King Took Flight,* 44. See also Legendre, AM Brest 2 D 16–18, letter of Nov. 14, 1790.

49. For this and the following paragraph, see esp. Rose, *Making of the Sans-Culottes,* 58–70.

50. Mirabeau had expressed concern over the independence of the districts as early as July 1789: *Courrier de Provence,* no. 21 (July 31, 1789).

51. Colson, "Correspondance," letter of Sept. 6, 1789.

52. Rose, *Making of the Sans-Culottes* 69–80.

53. Ibid., 80–92.

54. Guittard de Floriban, *Journal,* 101 and 117 (entries of Oct. 20, 1791 and Jan. 13, 1792). On Dec. 4, 1791, the Café de Foy sent a deputation to the Jacobins: Aulard, *Société des Jacobins,* 3:271.

55. For this and the following paragraph, see Boutier and Boutry, *Atlas,* 9, 16, 102–103; and M. Kennedy, *The Jacobin Club,* 1:6–12, 360. See also Ruault, *Gazette d'un Parisien,* 209–210 (letter of Sept. 10, 1790).

56. Boutier and Boutry, *Atlas,* 63–64; Brinton, *Jacobins,* chap. 3; and M. Kennedy, *The Jacobin Club,* 1:371.

57. See Tackett, *When the King Took Flight,* 187; and Boutier and Boutry, *Atlas,* 50–53.

58. AD Gironde, 12 L 20.

59. Boutier and Boutry, *Atlas,* 10; M. Kennedy, *The Jacobin Club,* 1:32 and 41–45; and Brégail, "Le Gers pendant la Révolution," 31 (1930), 19–20. On the oath requirement by the club in Bordeaux, see AD Gironde, 12 L 13 (entries of Apr. 17 and May 19, 1791).

60. M. Kennedy, *The Jacobin Club,* 1; chap. 13.

61. Baker, "Politics and Social Science"; and Olsen, "A Failure of Enlightened Politics."

62. Boutier and Boutry, *Atlas,* 10; Brégail, "Le Gers pendant la Révolution," 31 (1930), 20; Ruault, *Gazette d'un Parisien,* 218–219 (letter of Jan. 28, 1791); Colson, "Correspondance," letters of Jan. 30 and Feb. 6, 1791; Gower, *Despatches,* 53–55 (letters of Jan. 28 and Feb. 4, 1791).

63. Kates, *Cercle Social,* esp. part 2. See also Ruault, *Gazette d'un Parisien,* 209 (letter of Sept. 10, 1790).

64. Mathiez, *Le Club des Cordeliers,* esp. 8–24.

65. I. Bourdin, *Les sociétés populaires,* esp. 19–39, 132–162; Mathiez, *Le Club des Cordeliers,* 24, 30–31; Rose, *Making of the Sans-Culottes,* 98–105, 110–112; and Miles, *Correspondence,* 1:220 (letters of Feb. 23 and 25, 1791).

66. Desan, " 'Constitutional Amazons,' " 13–14; and Miles, *Correspondence,* 1:246 (letter of Mar. 1, 1791). On the general issue of women's rights in the French Revolution, see esp. Godineau, *Citoyennes et tricoteuses,* chaps. 4 and 5; Hufton, *Women and the Limits of Citizenship,* chap. 1; Hunt, "Male Virtue and Republican Motherhood"; and *Inventing Human Rights,* 167–175. Also Desan, *The Family on Trial,* esp. "Introduction" and chap. 2.

67. Géraud, *Journal,* 101 (letter of Apr. 30, 1790); and Jullien, "Correspondance," letter of Aug. 5, 1792.

68. Jullien, "Correspondance," letter of Aug. 10, 1792. See also Parker, *Writing the Revolution.*

69. Hesse, *Other Enlightenment,* chap. 2.

70. Gouges, *La Déclaration des droits de la femme.*

71. I. Bourdin, *Les sociétés populaires,* 224–234; and Mathiez, *Le Club des Cordeliers,* esp. 27–34.

72. Colson, "Correspondance," letters of Feb. 8, 9, 14, and 16, 1790; Ruault, *Gazette d'un Parisien,* 181 (letter of Feb. 5); and Tackett, *Becoming,* 275–277. The event was also marked by numerous solemn masses and *Te Deum* services of thanksgiving.

73. AN C 94, letters of the towns of Lavaur, Sept. 20, 1789; and of Villefranche-en-Haute-Guyenne, Sept. 23. Also, ibid., letter of Romans in Dauphiné (Sept. 22) announcing a federation with Bourg de Péage "pour le maintien de l'ordre et pour assurer le recouvrement des impots." See also Jolivet, *La Révolution dans l'Ardèche,* 151–153; Arnaud, *Histoire de la Révolution,* 120–121; Dubois, *Histoire de la Révolution,* 1:94; Bianchi and Dupuy, *La garde nationale,* 168; and Alpaugh, "Les émotions collectives."

74. See Lefebvre, *La fuite du roi,* 112; Carrot, *Révolution et maintien de l'ordre,* 125–126; Dubois, *Histoire de la Révolution,* 1:343; Fleury, *La ville et le district de Mamers,* 1:110–111; Sol, *La Révolution en Quercy,* 1:208–211; Brégail, "Le Gers pendant la Révolution," 31 (1930), 15–18; and Corgne, *Pontivy,* 55–65.

75. See, e.g., the description of the federation ceremony in Auch in Gascony: Brégail, "Le Gers pendant la Révolution," 31 (1930), 17–18; Alpaugh, "Les émotions collectives," 67. On the general phenomenon, see also Ozouf, *Festivals and the French Revolution,* 39–42.

76. See Gorsas, *Courrier de Versailles,* issue of June 20, 1790. Also Tackett, *Becoming,* 292–293.

77. See the description by François-Xavier Lantenas in *Patriote français,* issues of June 21 and 23, 1790.

78. Colson, "Correspondance," letter of July 6, 1790. Also Tackett, *Becoming,* 298–299.

79. Ozouf, *Festivals,* 54–55.

80. Colson, "Correspondance," letter of July 18, 1790.

81. Mason, *Singing the French Revolution,* 42–46.

82. Legendre, Extracts in "Correspondance," letter of July 21, 1790; Sol, *La Révolution en Quercy,* 1:211–218; Baumont, *Le département de l'Oise,* 28–31; Boivin-Champeaux, *Notices historiques,* 1:221–223; Jolivet, *La Révolution dans l'Ardèche,* 194–195; Fleury, *La ville et le district de Mamers,* 1:113–114; and Dorigny, *Autun,* 2:59–60. See also Ozouf, *Festivals,* 52–53.

83. See, e.g., Baumont, *Le département de l'Oise,* 31; and Fleury, *La ville et le district de Mamers,* 1:114.

84. Colson, "Correspondance," letter of June 27, 1790.

4. The Menace of Counterrevolution

1. See esp. Petitfils, "Les origines de la pensée contre-révolutionnaire"; McMahon, "Counter-Enlightenment" and *Enemies of the Enlightenment,* chap. 1; and Barny, "Les aristocrates et Jean-Jacques Rousseau."

2. Roux, *La Révolution à Poitiers,* 128–129, 164–165; Pimenova, "Cahiers de la Noblesse"; and Markoff, *Abolition of Feudalism,* esp. 190–198.

3. Tackett, *Becoming,* esp. 132–138.

4. Roubaud would write of the emigrant nobles, "le triomphe de la liberté a fait leur tourment, celui de l'égalité . . . leur éternel supplice": Roubaud, "Lettres," 153 (letter of Nov. 1, 1792); see also Tulard, *La Contre-Révolution,* "Introduction."

5. For this and the following paragraph see, e.g., Lefebvre, *La fuite du roi,* 76–79 and 88–90; and Godechot, *La Contre-Révolution,* 161–167.

6. See Chap. 5 in this book.

7. For this and the following paragraphs, see Tackett, *Becoming,* esp. chaps. 4–6.

8. Tackett, *Becoming,* 158–159.

9. Irland, AD Deux-Sèvres, letter of Jan. 8, 1790.

10. For the following paragraph, see Tackett, *Becoming,* 179–195.

11. Gauville, *Journal,* 19–20.

12. Barbotin, *Lettres,* 82 (letter of Jan. 6, 1790). Cf. Boullé, AD Morbihan, 1 Mi 140, letter of Dec. 15, 1789; and T. Lindet, *Correspondance,* 156 (letter of May 8, 1790).

13. Ménard de La Groye, *Correspondance,* 201 (letter of Apr. 16, 1790).

14. Tackett, *Religion, Revolution, and Regional Culture,* 211–218.

15. Irland, AD Deux-Sèvres, letter of Apr. 16, 1790. See also his letters of Apr. 20 and May 3.

16. Gantheret, private collection, letter of June 21, 1790; Ruault, *Gazette d'un Parisien,* 203 (letter of June 22).

17. See *AP,* 16:379–386; Gorsas, *Courrier de Versailles,* issue of June 20, 1790.

18. *Gazette de Paris,* publication of protests beginning June 23, 1790 and continuing regularly for over a month. See also Rabaut Saint-Etienne, *Précis historique,* 265–267.

19. For this and the following two paragraphs, see esp. Popkin, *Right Wing Press in France;* Bertaud, *Les amis du roi;* Maspero-Clerc, *Un journaliste contrerévolution-niare;* Murray, *Right-Wing Press in the French Revolution;* Chisick, *Ami du Roi;* and Coudart, *La Gazette.*

20. Rozoi in the *Gazette de Paris,* cited in Coudart, *La Gazette,* 215.

21. Coudart, *La Gazette,* 253, 385. See also Bertaud "La presse royaliste parisienne," 207–209.

22. Gautier, cited in Bertaud, *Les amis du roi,* 184. See also Coudart, *La Gazette,* 384.

23. See, e.g., Coudart, *La Gazette,* 186–198; and *Révolutions de Paris* (issue of June 23 to 30, 1792).

24. Ruault, *Gazette d'un Parisien,* 177 (letter of Jan. 5, 1790). See also Chap. 5 in this book.

25. Legendre, AM Brest 2 D 16–18, letter of Jan. 29, 1791.

26. Chaumié, *Le réseau d'Antraigues,* 46–48; Doyon, *Un agent royaliste,* 2–69; and Tulard, *La Contre Révolution,* 51–52, 168–178.

27. Lefebvre, *La fuite du roi,* 79–80; and Jolivet, *La Révolution dans l'Ardèche,* chap. 7.

28. Moulinas, *Les massacres de la Glacière;* and Lapied, *Le Comtat,* chap. 4.

29. See, e.g., McManners, *French Revolution,* chap. 5; and Aston, *Religion and Revolution,* esp. chap. 7.

30. Vernier, "Lettres," letter of Nov. 12, 1790. See also Legendre, AM Brest 2 D 16–18, letter of Nov. 21.

31. On the regional differences and the possible explanations for such differences, see Tackett, *Religion, Revolution, and Regional Culture.*

32. See, e.g., Gaultier de Biauzat, BM Clermont-Ferrand, letter of Jan. 18, 1791; and Bouchette, *Lettres,* 622–623 (letter of Aug. 2). See also Legendre, AM Brest 2 D 16–18, letter of Feb. 2.

33. AD Aisne, L 198, deliberations of the department directory; and AD Aisne, L 604, responses of the district of Vervins.

34. See esp. the reports of the Minister of the Interior on the failure of local administrations to follow the laws on religious toleration: AN F19 311; and Tackett, *Religion, Revolution, and Regional Culture,* 275–277.

35. Lisleroy, "Correspondance," 20 (letter of July 25, 1789); Barbier-Schroffenberg, "Extrait de la correspondance," 15 (1966), 80 (letter of May 28, 1790). See also Fougeret, in Vaissière, *Lettres d'"Aristocrates,"*401 (letter of June 26, 1791).

36. See, e.g., Fougeret in Vaissière, *Lettres d'"Aristocrates,"* 416 (letter of Jan. 10, 1792); and Barbier-Schroffenberg, "Extrait de la correspondance," 15 (1966), 81 (letter of May 28, 1790).

37. Gower, *Despatches,* 47 (letter of Dec. 17, 1790); Coudart, *La Gazette,* 381.

38. On the successive waves of emigration, see Greer, *Incidence of the Emigration,* 20–28 and 114–115. On the flood of emigrants after mid-1791, see, e.g., S. Scott, *Response of the Royal Army,* 105–106; also Bruneau, *Les débuts de la Révolution,* 334; Vidal, *Histoire de la Révolution française,* 209–210; Roux, *La Révolution à Poitiers,* 453–458; and *Histoire de Lorraine,* 535.

39. Greer, *Incidence of the Emigration,* 26; Henwood and Monange, *Brest,* 100.

40. La Tour du Pin, *Mémoires,* 1:266–267; A.-C. Thibaudeau, *Biographie, Mémoires,* 133–134. See also the count de Gamache: AN D XXIX bis 36 (2), dos. 373, letter of June 26, 1791.

41. Barbier-Schroffenberg, "Extrait de la correspondance," 16 (1967–1968), 74 (letter of June 6, 1791); Médel, *Correspondance,* 165 (letter of early September 1791). Ferrières, *Correspondance,* 438 (letter of Oct. 18, 1791), describes Monsieur de Médel's departure through Paris 1791. See also Audouyn de Pompery, *A mon cher cousin,* 185–186 (letters of Oct. 17 and 28, 1791).

42. Eighteen departments are known to have had more noble than clerical emigrants: Allier, Ardèche, Aube, Cher, Côte-d'Or, Gironde, Ille-et-Vilaine, Indre, Jura, Loir-et-Cher, Lot, Meuse, Nièvre, Sarthe, Seine, Deux-Sèvres, Var, and Yonne: Greer, *Incidence of the Emigration,* 109–111.

43. From a sample of 48 Constituent nobles whose names began with A or B and whose later careers are known: Lemay, *Dictionnaire des Constituants.*

44. Lemay, *Dictionnaire des Constituants,* 465–466; Beauchet-Filleau, *Tableau des émigrés,* 36, 121.

45. On the numbers of emigrants streaming through Paris, see, e.g., A.-R.-H. Thibaudeau, *Correspondance,* 196–197 (letters of Aug. 21 and 29–30).

46. Saint-Priest, *Mémoires,* 2:24–25. For this and the following paragraphs, see Tackett, *When the King Took Flight,* esp. chaps. 2–5.

47. AN C 211–213; and Coudart, *La Gazette,* 344–349, 361.

48. Audouyn de Pompery, *A mon cher cousin,* 165 (undated letter of late June 1791).

49. Gaultier de Biauzat in Mège, *Gaultier de Biauzat,* 2:384–385 (letter of July 12, 1791). On caricatures of the king see Duprat, *Le roi décapité.*

50. For this and the following paragraphs, see Andress, *Massacre at the Champ de Mars;* and Tackett, *When the King Took Flight,* chap. 5.

51. See notably the speech by Reynaud de Saint-Jean-d'Angély: *AP,* 28:380 (July 17, 1791); and Mathiez, *La Révolution française,* 1:203. Aulard referred to the period as "une sorte de terreur": *Histoire politique,* 154.

52. A.N. D XXIX BIS 34 (dos. 350) (letter of Aug. 23, 1791).

53. Basquiat, "Lettres," letter of May 31, 1791. See also Michon, *Essai,* 181–204.

54. See, e.g., Reinhard, *La chute de la royauté,* 153–154; and M. Kennedy, *The Jacobin Club,* 1:281–296.

55. Basquiat, "Lettres," letter of Aug. 16, 1791; Geoffroy, private collection, letter of July 31; Bouchette, *Lettres*, 616–617 (letter of July 24). The deputies Fréteau de Saint-Just and Emery also claimed the activities of the Paris radicals were subsidized by foreign powers: Michon, *Essai*, 261. On the Jacobin schism see Michon, *Essai*, 271–273; and Walter, *Histoire des Jacobins*, 184–236.

56. See Tackett, *When the King Took Flight*, chap. 8.

57. Levasseur, *Mémoires*, 1:33.

5. Between Hope and Fear

1. On the initiatives of administrators and clubs see, e.g., Baumont, *Le département de l'Oise*, 40–46; Kennedy, *Jacobin Club of Marseilles*, 58–60; and Hugueney, *Les clubs dijonnais*, 18, 21, 31, 54–55.

2. Boullé, AD Morbihan, 1 Mi 140, letter of May 9, 1789; and Durand, AM Cahors, letter of July 14. See also Basquiat de Mugriet, AC Bayonne, AA 51, letter of July 15; and Tackett, *Becoming*, 150–151.

3. Guittard, *Journal*, 99 (entry of Oct. 12, 1791); Jullien, "Correspondance," letter of June 1, 1792.

4. Virgil, *The Aeneid*, book IV, lines 219–239.

5. Mercier, *Tableau de Paris*, 5:182; Colson, "Correspondance," letters of Dec. 17, 1780, Apr. 20, 1783, and Aug. 8, 1786. See also Garrioch, *Neighbourhood and Community*, 25–27, and *The Making of Revolutionary Paris*, 25–26; Farge, *La vie fragile*, 261, 266, 274–282; and Farge and Revel, *Logiques de la foule*, 95–97. On the circulation of written accounts, see Darnton, "An Early Information Society," 9.

6. For this and the following paragraph, see esp. Shibutani, *Improvised News*; DiFonzo and Bordia, *Rumor Psychology*; Allport and Postman, *Psychology of Rumor*; and Rosnow and Fine, *Rumor and Gossip*.

7. The "fears of which men are ashamed": Shibutani, *Improvised News*, 88.

8. Bloch, *Réflexions*, 42.

9. On the spread of moods along with rumors, see esp. Shibutani, *Improvised News*, 95.

10. Roubaud, "Lettres," 152 (letter of Nov. 1, 1792); Mercier, *Le nouveau Paris* (1994), 210–211. See also Colson, "Correspondance," letter of Apr. 5, 1789; Short, in *The Papers of Thomas Jefferson*, 20:585 (letter of June 29, 1791); *Révolutions de Paris* (issue of Sept. 6 to 13, 1789); Labrosse and Rétat, *Naissance du journal révolutionnaire*, 74–79; Andress, *Massacre at the Champ de Mars*, 177.

11. Colson, "Correspondance," letter of Dec. 16, 1787; see also his letters of Dec. 17, 1780 and Nov. 29, 1789. Compare the comments of Mercier on the credulity of the common people: *Tableau de Paris*, 2:297–303.

12. Colson, "Correspondance," letters of Jan. 23, 1787 and Feb. 4, 1787; Jullien, "Correspondance," letter of Sept. 22, 1789; Garat, *Mémoires*, 125. On the relation of

belief in rumors to their repetition, see DiFonzo and Bordia, *Rumor Psychology,* 234. On the effects of rumors on the elites, see also Shibutani, *Improvised News,* 95, 110; and DiFonzo and Bordia, *Rumor Psychology,* 232.

13. Miles, *Correspondence,* 1:240 and 254 (letters of Mar. 1 and 12, 1791); *Courrier de Provence,* No. 21 (issue of July 31, 1789).

14. Colson, "Correspondance," letters of Oct. 13 and 18, 1789.

15. Colson, "Correspondance," letters of Dec. 12 and 22, 1789; Ruault, *Gazette d'un Parisien,* 173–174 (letter of Dec. 28, 1789).

16. Colson, "Correspondance," letters of Dec. 6, 1789; May 4 and 25, 1790; and Jan. 23, 1791. See also Mercier, *Le nouveau Paris* (1994), 214; and *Les Révolutions de Paris,* issue of Mar. 3 to 10, 1792.

17. Alpaugh, *Non-violence and the French Revolution,* appendix; also Colson, "Correspondance," letters of May 4, 23, and 25, 1790. Andress has identified an increase in police arrests in the spring of 1791: *Massacre at the Champ de Mars,* 137–138. See also Reinhard, *La chute de la royauté,* 38–39.

18. Tackett, *When the King Took Flight,* chap. 6; Lacroix, *Actes de la Commune de Paris,* 2e Série, 5:14, 21, and 179 (entries of June 21 and 26, 1791); and *Chronique de Paris,* no. 174 (issue of June 23). Also Andress, *Massacre at the Champ de Mars,* 149.

19. De Baecque, *Le corps,* 269.

20. De Baecque, *Le corps,* 272–273; Lucas, "Denunciation," 26–27, and 29–30; and Labrosse and Rétat, *Naissance du journal révolutionnaire,* 201.

21. De Baecque, *Le corps,* 267; Lucas, "Denunciation," 30.

22. Labrosse and Rétat, *Naissance du journal révolutionnaire,* 194–197, 202; and De Baecque, *Le corps,* 273, 277, and 286. On Marat, see also Simenon, *Le déshonneur dans la République,* 227–228.

23. Labrosse and Rétat, *Naissance du journal révolutionnaire,* 201–202. Cf. Brissot's conclusion: "Publicity can never harm innocence," cited in Lucas, "Denunciation," 30.

24. Gaultier de Biauzat, BM Clermont-Ferrand, letter of Aug. 3, 1790. See also Walton, *Policing Public Opinion,* 109–110 and passim.

25. Lucas, "Denunciation," 25; De Baecque, *Le corps,* 270, 275–276; Legendre, AM Brest 2 D 16–18, letter of Dec. 1, 1789; Colson, "Correspondance," letter of Oct. 18, 1789.

26. Kennedy, *Jacobin Club of Marseilles,* 34, 180; Labroue, *Le Club Jacobin de Toulon,* 6. See also Dorigny, *Autun,* 2:106.

27. Mathiez, *Le Club des Cordeliers,* esp. 8–24.

28. Aulard, *Jacobins,* 2:468.

29. Aulard, *Jacobins,* 3:251–253 and 287 (Nov. 16 and Dec. 14, 1791). On the response of the Dijon Jacobins, see Hugueney, *Les clubs dijonnais,* 129; see also Miles, *Correspondence,* 1:207 (letter of Jan. 30).

30. The following paragraphs and quotations are based on letters in AD Gironde, 12 L 20. A full analysis will be published in a forthcoming study.

31. Marat, *L'ami du peuple* (issue of Nov. 5, 1789); Brissot, *Patriote français* (issue of Feb. 20, 1790), quoted in Martin, *Contre-Révolution,* 69.

32. *Révolutions de Paris* (issue of May 12 to 19, 1792), 290.

33. Dulaure, *Thermomètre du jour* (issue of Aug. 22, 1792). See also De Baecque, *Le corps,* 285–286; Lucas, "Denunciation," 37; and the speech by the municipal officer of Bourg, Desisles, on Aug. 26, 1792: Dubois, *Histoire de la Révolution,* 3:6.

34. *Le patriote français* (issue of Oct. 6, 1789). The register of denunciations is apparently lost.

35. Caillet, *Inventaire,* passim.

36. Baumont, *Le département de l'Oise,* 24. See also Walton, *Policing Public Opinion,* 117.

37. AD Aisne, L 604; and Caillet, *Les Français en 1789,* 192. Jacob argues that it was above all the oath crisis that first instituted the concept of "suspects": *Suspects,* 14–18.

38. Caillet, *Les Français en 1789,* 171–172.

39. *AP,* 30:698–699, "Loi sur la police de sûreté, la justice criminelle, et l'institution des jurés," Title VI; Simonin, *Le déshonneur dans la République,* 216; and information kindly given to me by Ted W. Margadant. See also Jaume, *Le discours Jacobin,* 192–193.

40. See Shapiro, *Revolutionary Justice,* esp. chap. 1 and "Conclusion."

41. Letter from the department directory of Aisne, May 28, 1791, cited in part in Caillet, *Les Français en 1789,* 192. See also Jacob, *Suspects,* 18.

42. BHVP, Ms. 678, "Réflexions" of Ménétra, 79; Mercier, *Le nouveau Paris,* 452.

43. See Chap. 6 in this book. Also Mercier, *Le nouveau Paris* (1994), 452–453.

44. See esp. Fitzpatrick and Gellately, *Accusatory Practices,* 5–6.

45. The following section is based, in part, on Tackett, "Conspiracy Obsession"; and on Tackett and Déplanche, "L'idée de complot."

46. Hofstadter, *Paranoid Style,* 3–40. On the French Revolutionary period, see esp. Campbell, Kaiser, and Linton, *Conspiracy in the French Revolution;* and Münch, "Le pouvoir de l'ombre."

47. Kaplan, *Famine Plot,* 1–2, 62. See also Farge and Revel, *Logiques de la foule,* esp. chap. 4.

48. See esp. Marcus, *Paranoia within Reason,* "Introduction"; also Fine, Campion-Vincent, and Heath, *Rumor Mills,* 103–122.

49. Cubitt, *Jesuit Myth;* and McMahon, *Enemies of the Enlightenment,* chap. 1.

50. Tackett, "Conspiracy Obsession," 697; and Diderot, letter to Necker, June 10, 1776, cited in Roche, *France in the Enlightenment,* 452.

51. Tackett, "Conspiracy Obsession," 698.

52. See ibid. Reference here is to the "general" cahiers, those written at the last stage of the electoral process of 1789, to be taken with the deputies to Versailles.

53. Marcus, *Paranoia within Reason,* 5; Fine, Campion-Vincent and Heath, *Rumor Mills,* 104–105; Delumeau, *La peur,* 16; Delpierre, *La peur et l'être,* 15. Also Palmer, *Twelve Who Ruled,* 64.

54. Colson, "Correspondance," letter of July 5, 1789; Galante Garrone, *Gilbert Romme,* 171–172; Ménard, *Correspondance,* 55 (letter of late June); Ruault, *Gazette d'un Parisien,* 155–158 (letter of July 22); *Révolutions de Paris* (issue of Aug. 2); *AP,* 8: 293–295. See also Gaultier, BM Clermont-Ferrand, 2:175, letter of July 16; Gantheret, private collection, letter of July 26.

55. *Révolutions de Paris* (issue of Sept. 2, 1789); Colson, "Correspondance," letters of Dec. 12 and 22. See also Tackett, "Conspiracy Obsession"; and Tackett and Déplanche, "L'idée du 'complot.'"

56. Ruault, *Gazette d'un Parisien,* 173–174 (letter of Dec. 28, 1789); Colson, "Correspondance," letter of Dec. 29, 1789.

57. Gaultier de Biauzat, BM Clermont-Ferrand, letter of Dec. 23, 1790. See also Geoffroy, private collection, letter of June 19, 1791; and Durand, AM Cahors, letter of May 23, 1790.

58. See, for example, Lepoutre, *Député-paysan et fermière de Flandre,* 431 (letter of June 23, 1791); and Gantheret, private collection, July 14. See also Dreyfus, "Le manifeste royal," 5–22.

59. On early rumors of a "kidnapping" of the king: Colson, "Correspondance," letter of Dec. 29, 1789; Ruault, *Gazette d'un Parisien,* 183 (letter of Feb. 23, 1790).

60. Arnaud, *Histoire de la Révolution,* 241; Legendre, AM Brest 2 D 16–18, letter of Aug. 7, 1791. See also Reinhard, *La chute de la royauté,* 37–39; Bruneau, *Les débuts de la Révolution,* 331; and Tackett, *When the King Took Flight,* esp. chap. 5.

61. *Antony and Cleopatra,* I, iii, line 12; and Sternberg and Sternberg, *Nature of Hate,* esp. chaps. 3 and 4.

62. Jullien, "Correspondance," letter of Apr. 14, 1790; Fricaud, private collection, letter of Apr. 15, 1791; De Baecque, *Le corps,* 284; Kennedy, *Jacobin Club of Marseilles,* 183–184.

63. Lepoutre, *Député-paysan et fermière de Flandre,* 505 (letter of Aug. 23, 1791); Gaultier, B. M. Clermont-Ferrand, letter of Feb. 24; Corbel, "Correspondance," letter of Dec. 3. See also Basquiat, AC Saint-Sever, letter of Apr. 9; Géraud, *Journal d'un étudiant,* 222 (letter of Oct. 21); and Dorigny, *Autun,* 2:127.

64. Bertaud, "La presse royaliste parisienne," 206; and Coudart, *La Gazette de Paris,* 315–316 and 381.

6. The Factionalization of France

1. Colson, "Correspondance," letter of Sept. 18, 1791; Guittard, *Journal,* 94–95, entries of Sept. 25, 26, and 30; Du Petit in AD Ille-et-Villaine, L 294, letter of Oct. 1; Rabusson-Lamothe, "Lettres sur l'Assemblée législative," 232–233 (letter of Oct. 4). See also the deputy Martin to the municipality of Marseille, AC Marseille, 4 D 43, letter of Oct. 23.

2. Roubaud, "Lettres," 76–77 (letter of Feb. 8, 1792). See also Colson, "Correspondance," letter of Nov. 29, 1791.

3. Markoff, *Abolition of Feudalism*, 271. See, e.g., Brégail, "Le Gers pendant la Révolution," 251; Dubois, *Histoire*, 2:282; Boutier, *Campagnes en émoi*, 133–134; and Reinhard, *La chute de la royauté*, chap. 13.

4. See, e.g., Baumont, *Le département de l'Oise*, 123–155; Dubois, *Histoire*, 2:295–298; and Girardot, *Le département de la Haute-Saône*, 2:108–110.

5. Colson, "Correspondance," letters of Jan. 3 and 25, 1792. See also Harris, *Assignats*, 171–175 (and charts on 121–122); Roux, *Révolution à Poitiers*, 490; Dubois, *Histoire*, 2:285–290; Poupé, "Le département du Var," 153; and Boutier, *Campagnes en émoi*, 135–136.

6. Markoff, *Abolition of Feudalism*, 283–286. See also, e.g., Poupé, "Le département du Var," 146–147.

7. Brégail, "Le Gers pendant la Révolution," 32 (1931), 31–34; Dubois, *Histoire*, 2:437–438; Bruneau, *Les débuts de la Révolution*, 334; and Roux, *Révolution à Poitiers*, 454–455.

8. Le Coz, *Correspondance*, 1:20 (letter of Oct. 26, 1791); Ruault, *Gazette d'un Parisien*, 262–265 (letters of Oct. 20 and Nov. 6). Also Colson, "Correspondance," letter of Oct. 12.

9. Roux, *Révolution à Poitiers*, 429–448.

10. Ramel, "Lettres," letter of Oct. 29, 1791.

11. Poupé, "Le département du Var," 149.

12. Markoff, *Abolition of Feudalism*, 276–279.

13. See, e.g., P. Jones, *Politics and Rural Society;* and Tackett, "Women and Men in Counterrevolution."

14. On the complexity of variables in urban factional formation, see Sutherland, *Murder in Aubagne*, esp. chap 1.

15. On the formation of factions, see also Garrioch, *Formation of the Parisian Bourgeoisie*, 166.

16. The districts have been described as "the hinge between department and populace," "the major point of contact between state and citizens": Woloch, *New Regime*, 39.

17. See Hunt, *Politics*, 153–155, and 160–163.

18. Azéma in "Correspondance des députés de l'Aude," 30 (1896), 163 (letter of July 13, 1792). See also Pinet, "Correspondance," letter of June 22, 1792; Cambon, "Lettres," letter of Oct. 21, 1791; and Barbaroux, *Correspondance et mémoires*, 184 (letter of June 21, 1792).

19. Legendre, AM Brest 2 D 16–18, letter of June 13, 1791. See also Wahl, *Les premières années*, 373–380.

20. Rivalries between such clubs were exacerbated since only one in a given town could be officially affiliated with the Jacobins in Paris: Kennedy, *Jacobin Clubs in the French Revolution*, 2:46–54.

21. See, e.g., Boutier and Boutry, *Atlas,* 55; and Brégail, "Le Gers pendant la Révolution," 31 (1930), 20.

22. Labroue, *Le club jacobin,* 16; Poupé, "Le département du Var," 145–147; Hugueney, *Les clubs dijonnais,* 43–44; Hanson, *Provincial Politics,* 54–63; Brégail, "Le Gers pendant la Révolution," 31 (1930), 20; and Kennedy, *Jacobin Clubs in the French Revolution,* 2:57–59.

23. Arnaud, *Histoire de la Révolution,* 192–205, 212–213. Rabaut Saint-Etienne and other Constituents from Gard also intervened in local politics in Nîmes: Rouvière, *Histoire de la Révolution française,* 2:62–65.

24. Kennedy, *Jacobin Clubs in the French Revolution,* 1:281–296.

25. E.g., the departments of Côtes-du-Nord, Ardèche, Gers, and Vienne: Roux, *La Révolution à Poitiers,* 472; Pommeret, *L'esprit politique,* 144; Jolivet, *La Révolution dans l'Ardèche,* 321; Brégail, "Le Gers pendant la Révolution," 32 (1931), 106–107. Often the most divisive issue was the competition between districts to obtain a maximum number of representatives: Girardot, *Le département de la Haute-Saône,* 2:102. But cf. also Dendena, "'Nos places maudites,'" 27. On the legislative elections of 1791 in general, see M. Edelstein, *Birth of Electoral Democracy,* chaps. 8 and 9.

26. E.g., the departments of Ain, Ariège, Aube, Calvados, Cher, Bouches-du-Rhône, Corrèze, Côte-d'Or, Dordogne, Maine-et-Loire, Nord, and Var: Kennedy, *Jacobin Clubs in the French Revolution,* 1:222–223; Reinhard, *Chute de la royauté,* 197; Dubois, *Histoire de la Révolution dans l'Ain,* 2:276–279; Arnaud, *Histoire de la Révolution,* 331–332; Babeau, *Histoire de Troyes,* 455–459; Bruneau, *Les débuts de la Révolution,* 167–172; Poupé, "Le département du Var," 112–113; Labroue, *L'esprit public en Dordogne,* 29–36; and Rouvière, *Histoire de la Révolution française,* 2:62–65.

27. Arnaud, *Histoire de la Révolution,* 192–205, 212–213. Compare also the situation in Orléans where the king's flight was critical in dividing the town between the "Feuillants" and the "democrates": Lefebvre, *Etudes orléanises,* 2:59.

28. See Shapiro, "Self-Sacrifice, Self-Interest, or Self-Defence." The only direct holdovers were the thirty-five alternate deputies to the first National Assembly who were now chosen to the Legislative—many of whom had observed the meetings from the galleries.

29. For this paragraph, see Baguenier-Desormeaux, *passim;* Tackett, "Les députés de l'Assemblée législative," 139–144; Lemay, *Dictionnaire des Législateurs;* and Lemay, "Les législateurs de la France révolutionnaire," 3–28.

30. On the myth of their lack of experience, see Mitchell, *French Legislative Assembly,* 43–44.

31. The deputies included some 57 former nobles and 26 clergymen (10 constitutional bishops and 16 other priests), a total of 83 or about 11 percent of all the deputies: based on Lemay, *Dictionnaire des Législateurs.*

32. Already in the autumn of 1791 the deputies frequently referred to the "Right" and the "Left." See, e.g., *AP,* 34:540; and 35:111–112 and 124.

33. Identification of the Jacobins is based on the various lists and the index published by Aulard, *Société des Jacobins,* 6 vols; supplemented by Lemay, *Dictionnaire des Législateurs,* 788–790; and by Mitchell, *French Legislative Assembly.* In an appendix, pp. 301–319, Mitchell prints the records of all deputies on the seven known roll-call votes between Feb. and Aug. 1792. It is clear that a "yes" vote on all of the roll calls was strongly supported by the Jacobins and that a "no" vote was strongly supported by the Feuillants. A list of Jacobins compiled from Aulard and Lemay has been corrected by removing those in the Jacobins in Oct. 1791 who (1) later signed up with Feuillants and/or (2) voted consistently "no" on roll calls in 1792. This yields a total of 122. But this list is undoubtedly incomplete, and a portion of those other deputies who consistently voted "yes" on roll-call votes must be added. Thus, ninety-one deputies not on the published Jacobin lists participated in at least five of the seven roll calls and always voted "yes." Among the ninety-one are many who are, in fact, known to have been Jacobins from other sources. Thus, e.g., Prieur, Lindet, Duquesnoy, and Bo are well-known Jacobins; and Pinet, Malassis, and Cavellier all declared themselves Jacobins in their correspondence. By 1792 there were at least 210 deputies who were either members of the Jacobins or who strongly sympathized with them and regularly supported them in the voting.

34. Perhaps 100 or so formed a loose association in October and November through meetings in the Hôtel de Richelieu: Hua, *Mémoires d'un avocat,* 74. On the voting for president, see AN C 84 (819) (through Feb. 1792). In October deputy votes for president were scattered over a large list of names. By November, however, they were beginning to cluster for a few candidates, even on the first round of voting.

35. On dating the origins of the Feuillant Club, see Mitchell, "Political Divisions," 377n.

36. Dendena, " 'Nos places maudites,' " 89–92, and 215–216. Dendena's careful analysis puts formal membership in the Feuillants at 175. But another 74 deputies voted consistently "no" in at least five of the seven roll-call votes and thus closely sympathized with the Feuillants. In late February the journalist and careful observer of the political scene, Louis-Marie Prudhomme, claimed that "le côté du roi" included "plus de deux cent cinquante" deputies: *Révolution de Paris* (issue of Feb. 18 to 25, 1792), 348. On the closing of the Feuillants, see Michon, *Essai,* 284, and Louis-Jérôme Gohier in AD Ille-et-Vilaine, L 294 (1), letter of Dec. 28, 1791.

37. Lemay, *Dictionnaire des Législateurs,* 755–756; and *AP,* vols. 34–50, passim, for the actual vote counts. After February Jacobin candidates came in as close seconds on several separate votes. None was able to win the presidency, however, until after the fall of the monarchy.

38. *AP,* 47:523–524; and *Révolutions de Paris* (issue of Feb. 18 to 25, 1792). The Jacobin Brival even accused the Right of stuffing the ballot box: *AP,* 45:117 (June 12, 1792).

39. Rabusson-Lamothe, "Lettres sur l'Assemblée législative," 318–319 (letter of Mar. 10, 1792); Roubaud, "Lettres," 80 (letter of Feb. 8, 1792); and Hua, *Mémoires d'un avocat,* 74, 166–167.

40. See Mitchell, "Political Divisions."

41. Gohier in AD Ille-et-Vilaine, L 294 (1), letter of Dec. 28, 1791. See also Aubert-Dubayet, "Aubert-Dubayet," 129 (letter of Mar. 6, 1792). On the pressures felt by Thomas Riboud, see Dubois, *Histoire de la Révolution,* 2:510–511.

42. Azéma in "Correspondance des députés de l'Aude," 30 (1896), 163 (letter of July 13, 1792).

43. Demée, "Lettres," letters of June 20 and Aug. 3, 1792. See also Codet, AD Ille-et-Vilaine, L 294, letter of Oct. 11, 1791.

44. Michon, *Essai,* 283. Rabusson-Lamothe described the Constitution as our "compass" and "Gospel": "Lettres sur l'Assemblée législative," 309 and 318–319 (letters of Feb. 25 and Mar. 10, 1792). See also Demée, "Lettres," letter of June 20.

45. Romme, "Correspondance," letter of Nov. 24, 1791; and Ellery, *Brissot de Warville,* 253. See also Condorcet, *Chronique de Paris* (issue of Nov. 26, 1791); "Correspondance des députés de l'Aude" (1896), 84 (letter of Nov. 1, 1791). Also Aulard, *Histoire politique,* 171; and Lefebvre, *La chute du roi,* 2–3.

46. E.g., see the statement of the Feuillant Claude Dorizy on Old Regime privilege: *Souvenirs,* 438; and the suspicions toward the king of the Feuillant sympathizer, Rabusson-Lamothe: "Lettres sur l'Assemblée législative," 231 and 264 (letters of Oct. 1 and Dec. 15, 1791).

47. According to Corbel, the law on emigrants was voted "à la presque unanimité": "Correspondance," letter of Dec. 3, 1791. The conservative Hua admitted that the law against the refractory clergy was voted "à une grande majorité": *Mémoires d'un avocat,* 94; and it was strongly supported by the Feuillant-sympathizing Rabusson-Lamothe: "Lettres sur l'Assemblée législative," 251 (letter of Nov. 22, 1791). Nearly all articles in the decree on free people of color were passed unanimously: Malassis and Cavellier, "Correspondance," letter of Mar. 26, 1792. On the final declaration of war: *AP,* 42:210.

48. See Baguenier-Desormeaux, passim. Both factions had an average age of about forty-one. In their social origins, e.g., 39 percent of Jacobins and 32 percent of Feuillants had exercised various liberal professions in 1789, above all as lawyers. The most important difference was in the size of their town of origin: 45 percent of Jacobins resided in towns of over 10,000 people, while only 28 percent of Feuillants came from such larger towns.

49. Overall, 46 percent of the Feuillants, but only 30 percent of the Jacobins had been department officals; while 25 percent of the Feuillants vs. 30 percent of the Jacobins had been district or municipal officials. For the deputies' positions when elected to the Legislative, see Kuscinski, *Les députés à l'Assemblée législative.*

50. Romme, "Correspondance," letter of Sept. 24, 1791; Couthon, *Correspondance inédite,* 28 (letter of Sept. 29).

51. See esp. Aulard, *L'éloquence parlementaire,* 1:80–83; and Dendena, "'Nos places maudites,'" 648–649. Based on an unpublished analysis of deputy participation in Legislative Assembly debates by Laura Sextro. Those deputies on the right—defined as Mitchell's "no-voters"—spoke a total of 4,154 times; those on the left—defined as Mitchell's "yes-voters"—spoke a total of 6,338 times: *AP,* vol. 51 (index of vols. 34–50 covering the Legislative Assembly).

52. See Ellery, *Brissot de Warville,* esp. chaps. 1 to 4; and Kates, *Cercle Social,* 5–6.

53. See Brissot's testimony at his trial in October 1793: Walter, *Actes du Tribunal révolutionnaire,* 302.

54. Roland, *Lettres,* 2:429 (letter of July 31, 1792); Dumont, *Souvenirs sur Mirabeau,* 201, 207; Garat, *Mémoires sur la Révolution,* 64–65; and Ellery, *Brissot de Warville,* 425–427. On the regular meetings among the Girondins, see Sydenham, *Girondins,* esp. chap. 4; and Reynolds, *Marriage and Revolution,* 137–147.

55. See the development on Brissot and the Brissotins by Münch, "Le pouvoir de l'ombre," e.g., 265, 336, 710–711.

56. Dumont, *Souvenirs sur Mirabeau,* 203; also Ellery, *Brissot de Warville,* esp. 256–257, 261–265.

57. For this paragraph, see Tackett, "Conspiracy Obsession in a Time of Revolution"; and Tackett and Déplanche, "L'idée de complot."

58. Romme, "Correspondance," letter of Jan. 1, 1792; Basire, *AP,* 35:361 (Nov. 25, 1791). See also Condorcet, cited in Delsaux, *Condorcet journaliste,* 183; and Couthon, *Correspondance inédite,* 49–50 (letter of Nov. 26, 1791).

59. Codet: AD Ille-et-Vilaine, L 294 (1), letter of Oct. 29, 1791; Roubaud, "Lettres," 91 (letter of Mar. 24, 1792); Aubert-Dubayet, "Aubert-Dubayet," 132 (letter of Mar. 17, 1792). Overall, references in the *AP* to internal and external plots perceived to be linked together rose from 0 in April 1790 to an average of 2 per week in July 1791, 4 per week in January 1792, and 12 per week in June 1792: see Tackett and Déplanche, "L'idée de complot."

60. Cambon, "Lettres," letter of Dec. 25, 1791; and Causse in "Correspondance des députés de l'Aude," 30 (1896), 81–82 (letter of Oct. 28).

61. Lameth, cited in Galante Garrone, *Gilbert Romme,* 273n. See also Demée, "Lettres," letter of June 20, 1792.

62. Levasseur, *Mémoires,* 1:57; Garat, *Mémoires sur la Révolution,* 51–58. See also the description of a British police spy: Miles, *Correspondence,* 1:245 (letter of Mar. 1, 1791).

63. On the origins of the conflict between Brissot and Robespierre, see esp. Walter, *Robespierre,* vol. 1, 2e partie, chap. 3; Goetz-Bernstein, *La diplomatie de la Gironde,* 87–93; and McPhee, *Robespierre,* 114–120.

64. Goetz-Bernstein, *La diplomatie de la Gironde,* 182–183; McPhee, *Robespierre,* chap 8.

65. Dumont, *Souvenirs sur Mirabeau,* 200; Brissot, *Patriote français* (issue of May 18, 1792); Hugues Destrem in "Correspondance des députés de l'Aude," 159 (letter of June 20, 1792); and Ellery, *Brissot de Warville,* 277–278.

66. Walter, *Robespierre,* 1:306–307, 331–315; Ellery, *Brissot de Warville,* 266–271; Basire, "Lettres," 106 (letter of Mar. 29, 1792). Robespierre told Garat that he had no doubts whatsoever that the Girondins were "counterrevolutionaries": Garat, *Mémoires sur la Révolution,* 53. Cf. the denunciations of Brissot by Robespierre's supporter Prudhomme in *Révolutions de Paris* (issue of May 12 to 19), 290–296. See also Linton, "Fatal Friendships."

67. Dumont, *Souvenirs sur Mirabeau,* 207.

68. Garat, *Mémoires sur la Révolution,* 5–6, 76.

69. Cambon, "Lettres," letter of Oct. 13, 1791. Also Le Coz and Codet in AD Ille-et-Vilaine, L 294, letter of Oct. 11. On anti-Jacobinism as fundamental to Feuillant rhetoric, see also Dendena, " 'Nos places maudites,' " 223, 377, and 425.

70. On the role of revenge in the Revolution, see Mayer, *Furies,* esp. chap. 5.

71. Malassis and Cavellier, "Correspondance," letter of May 19, 1792. On the use of "les noirs" in the Legislative, see also Romme, "Correspondance," letter of Sept. 24, 1791; Pinet, "Correspondance," letter of June 12, 1792; and Barbaroux, *Correspondance et mémoires,* 61 (letter of Feb. 20, 1792).

72. Tackett, "Conspiracy Obsession in a Time of Revolution."

73. See Robert Darnton's analysis of such "grub street" writers in "The High Enlightenment and the Low-Life of Literature."

74. Ruault seems to have attended the Cordeliers, when it was still a district assembly: Ruault, *Gazette d'un Parisien,* 197 (letter of April 18, 1790). On the club in general, see Mathiez, *Le Club des Cordeliers;* and De Cock, *Les Cordeliers dans la Révolution.*

75. Rose, *Making of the Sans-Culottes,* esp. 60–65; Vovelle, *Mentalité révolutionnaire,* 111–112. See also Kaplan, *Fin des corporations,* 582. Only about 1 percent were salaried employees. Note also that only about 8 to 9 percent of all active citizens seem regularly to have attended the sectional assemblies: Vovelle, *Mentalité révolutionnaire,* 111.

76. Jullien, "Correspondance," letters of Apr. 3 and Aug. 5 and 18, 1792. See also Burstin, *L'invention,* 141.

77. Lefebvre, *Gouvernement révolutionnaire,* 128; Burstin, *L'invention,* esp. chaps. 1 and 2. Also Rosanvallon, *Le peuple introuvable,* chap. 1 and Sewell, "Sans-Culotte Rhetoric," 251–252.

78. Cobb, *Police and the People,* 62.

79. On the sectional clubs, see notably Rose, *Making of the Sans-Culottes,* 146–147.

80. On the political life of the cafés in Paris, see Guittard, *Journal,* e.g., 117 (entry of Jan. 13, 1792). See also Brennan, *Public Drinking and Popular Culture.*

81. Cited in Burstin, *L'invention,* 116–117. On the newspaper hawkers, see Chap. 5 in this book.

82. Soubrany, *Dix-neuf lettres,* 7 (letter of June 20, 1792); *Révolutions de Paris* (issue of Mar. 10 to 17; and Sept. 1 to 8); and Jullien, "Correspondance," letters of July 10 and Aug. 18. See also Gilbert Romme in Galante Garrone, *Gilbert Romme,* 273 (letter of Mar. 6).

83. See Chaps. 1 and 5 in this book.

84. Ruault, *Gazette d'un Parisien,* 280 (letter of Mar. 20, 1792); Guittard, *Journal,* 130–131 (entry of March 18); Géraud, *Journal d'un étudiant,* 265 (letter of Mar. 20); *Révolutions de Paris* (issue of Mar. 17 to 24).

85. Malassis, "Correspondance," letter of June 20, 1792; Corbel, "Correspondance," letter of June 20. See also Jullien, "Correspondance," letter of June 21; Colson, "Correspondance," letter of Aug. 1; and Ozouf, *La fête révolutionnaire,* 280–316.

86. According to Mercier, describing Paris before the Revolution, "le fusil est une arme aussi étrangère aux habitants de cette ville qu'à ceux de Pékin": Mercier, *Tableau de Paris,* 5:64.

87. Couthon, *Correspondance inédite,* 85 and 95 (letters of Feb. 14 and 25, 1792). See also *Révolutions de Paris* (issue of Feb. 11 to 18); Romme, "Correspondance," letter of May 3; and Lefebvre, *La chute du roi,* 128–130. See also Dorigny, *Autun,* 2:154.

88. *Révolutions de Paris* (issue of April 7 to 14, 1792). The same paper gave a vivid description of the banquet on July 26, 1792: issue of July 21 to 28. Cf. also the banquet organized in the Bois de Boulogne two days after the abolition of the nobility in June 1790: *Le patriote français* (issue of June 23, 1790).

89. Corbel, "Correspondance," letter of Jan. 11, 1792; Viénot de Vaublanc, *Mémoires,* 215. An estimated 30,000 people had been outside during the debates on the Nancy Affair in September 1790: Gaultier, BM Clermont-Ferrand, letter of Sept. 4, 1790.

90. See also Alpaugh, *Non-violence and the French Revolution.*

91. Tackett, *When the King Took Flight,* 105–107, 111–113, 143–147. Also Alpaugh, *Non-violence and the French Revolution,* Appendix and graphs of demonstrations.

92. See the long descriptions in Jullien, "Correspondance," letter of Apr. 16, 1792; Malassis and Cavellier, "Correspondance," letter of Apr. 9; Couthon, *Correspondance inédite,* 116–117, 119–120 (letters of Apr 10 and 17); and Géraud, *Journal d'un étudiant,* 275–277 (letter of Apr. 15). Also, Ozouf, *Festivals,* chap. 3; Burstin, *Une Révolution,* 347; and Langlois, "L'invention de la liberté."

93. Couthon, *Correspondance inédite,* 116–117 (letter of Apr. 10, 1792).

94. Colson, "Correspondance," letter of Nov. 3, 1789.

95. Tackett, *Becoming,* 222; Blanning, *Origins,* 49.

96. See, e.g., Gaultier, BM Clermont-Ferrand, Ms. 788, letter of Apr. 12, 1791; also Tackett, "Constituent Assembly in the Second Year of the French Revolution," 162–169.

97. Tackett, *When the King Took Flight,* esp. chap. 6.

98. It was at this moment that French forces first officially adopted the tricolor flag: Reinhard, *La chute de la royauté,* 161.

99. Bagot in Tempier, "Correspondance des députés," 28 (1890), 76–77 (letter of Oct. 31, 1791). See also Le Maillaud, "Correspondance," letter of Oct. 5; and Clauzel, "Documents inédits," 115 (letter of Oct. 10).

100. Jaurès, *Histoire socialiste,* 3:72. On the coming of the war, see Goetz-Bernstein, *La diplomatie de la Gironde,* esp. 44–72; Reinhard, *La chute de la royauté,* chap. 12; and Blanning, *Origins of the French Revolutionary Wars.*

101. Ellery, *Brissot de Warville,* 227; *AP,* 34:309–317 (Oct. 20, 1791); Couthon, *Correspondance inédite,* 53 (letter of Nov. 29, 1791).

102. See Bell, *Cult of the Nation.*

103. Colson, "Correspondance," letter of Nov. 3, 1789; and *Les Révolutions de Paris* (issue of Sept. 8 to 15, 1792).

104. Le Maillaud, "Correspondance," letter of Oct. 5, 1791. See also, e.g., Codet in AD Ille-et-Vilaine, L 294 (1), letter of Oct. 3; and Colson, "Correspondance," letter of Oct. 4.

105. Tardiveau in Tempier, "Correspondance des députés," 28 (1890), 92–93 (letter of Nov. 28, 1791). See also Raymond Gaston, *AP,* 34:318–319 (speech of Oct. 20); and E. Rubat, "Lettres," letter of Dec. 18.

106. Brissot in the *Patriote français* (issue of Dec. 15, 1791); and at the Jacobin Club, Dec. 30, cited in Goetz-Bernstein, *La diplomatie de la Gironde,* 44–45 and 61.

107. *AP,* 37:412–13, and 491; and Colson, "Correspondance," letter of Jan. 18. See also the account of Codet in AD Ille-et-Vilaine, L 294 (2), letter of Jan. 16.

108. *AP,* 37:650; and Cahen, *Condorcet et la Révolution française,* 301.

109. On Great Power relations and the coming of the war, see esp. Goetz-Bernstein, *La diplomatie de la Gironde;* and Blanning, *Origins of the French Revolutionary Wars* and *French Revolutionary Wars.*

110. Cited in Blanning, *French Revolutionary Wars,* 58.

111. Blanning, *French Revolutionary Wars,* 58–59.

112. Ramel, "Lettres," letter of Feb. 11, 1792; also Reinhard, *La chute de la royauté,* 246–247; and Goetz-Bernstein, *La diplomatie de la Gironde,* 128–133.

113. Michon, *Essai,* 349–357; and Price, *Road from Versailles,* esp. chap. 11.

114. A. Rubat, "Lettres," letter of Dec. 18, 1791. See also Gohier in AD Ille-et-Vilaine, L 294 (1), letter of Dec. 17.

115. Walter, *Robespierre,* 1:263. See also *Révolutions de Paris,* no. 145 (issue of Apr. 14 to 21, 1792).

116. *AP,* 37:491.

117. Couthon, *Correspondance inédite,* 57 (letter of Dec. 17, 1791); and Rabusson-Lamothe, "Lettres," 277–278 (letter of Jan. 10, 1792). See also Le Coz, AD Ille-et-Vilaine, L 294 (2), letter of Jan. 9, 1792.

118. Duval, AD Ille-et-Vienne, L 294 (2), letter of Jan. 17, 1792.

119. *AP,* 42:210.

120. Blanning, *French Revolutionary Wars,* 64.

121. See Vergniaud's allusions to Marathon: *AP,* 37:490 (Jan. 18, 1792).

122. Pinet, "Correspondance," letter of May 1, 1792; Couthon, *Correspondance inédite,* 122 and 124 (letters of April 21 and 24); and *AP,* 37:547. See also Malassis and Cavellier, "Correspondance," letter of Apr. 22.

7. Fall of the Monarchy

1. For a partial list of *dons patriotiques,* see, e.g., *AP,* 42:783 and 43:759.

2. See esp. Jullien, "Correspondance," letter of Apr 30, 1792.

3. Lefebvre, *La chute du roi,* 163–164.

4. Rabusson-Lamothe, "Lettres," 341 (letter of May 10, 1792); Couthon, *Correspondance inédite,* 146–147 (letter of May 29).

5. Jullien, "Correspondance," letters of April 30, May 16, and June 1, 1792. See also Malassis and Cavellier, "Correspondance," letter of May 14; Vergniaud, *Vergniaud, manuscrits, lettres, et papiers,* 1:164 (letter of May 1792, day unspecified); Carra in the *Annales patriotiques,* cited in Buchez and Roux, *Histoire parlementaire,* 14:278 (May 15). Couthon specifically compared the situation to that of July 1789: *Correspondance inédite,* 147 (letter of May 29).

6. Pinet, "Correspondance," letter of May 8. See also Jullien, "Correspondance," letter of May 10, 1792.

7. See, e.g., Vergniaud, *Vergniaud, manuscrits, lettres, et papiers,* 1:164 (letter of May 1792, date unspecified).

8. *AP,* 44: 33–43.

9. Jullien, "Correspondance," letter of May 23, 1792; Rabusson-Lamothe, "Lettres," 349–350 (letter of May 29). See also Couthon, *Correspondance inédite,* 143 (letter of May 24); and the speeches by the Feuillants Viénot-Vaublanc and Hué, *AP,* 44:44 and 65.

10. Ruault, *Gazette d'un Parisien,* 285 (letter of May 24, 1792). See also *AP,* 44:194–196 and 478; Buchez and Roux, *Histoire parlementaire,* 14:305 (May 29); Sébire in AD Ille-et-Vilaine, L 294 (2), letter of May 28; Codet, in ibid., letter of May 30 (Apr. 30 written in error); Le Coz, in ibid., letter of June 4; Géraud, *Journal d'un étudiant,* 297 (letter of May 30); Rabusson-Lamothe, "Lettres," 349–350 (letter of May 29); Jullien, "Correspondance," undated, "Pentacost" 1792.

11. Couthon, *Correspondance inédite,* 146–147 (letter of May 29, 1792); Corbel, "Correspondance," letter of May 30.

12. Mitchell, *French Legislative Assembly,* 114–115.

13. Demée, "Lettres," letter of June 20, 1792. On debates against the refractories, see *AP,* 43:435–445 and 44:56–72.

14. The interior minister Roland claimed that 47 departments had adopted policies of this sort: Lefebvre, *La chute du roi,* 131. See also Tackett, *Religion, Revolution, and Regional Culture,* 275–282.

15. Romme, "Correspondance," letter of Apr. 10, 1792. See also Barbaroux, *Correspondance et mémoires,* 186–187 (letter of June 21); Poupé, "Le département du Var," 158–169; Boutier, *Campagnes en émoi,* 130–131; Pommeret, *L'esprit politique,* 155–157; Brégail, "Le Gers pendant la Révolution," 32 (1931), 37.

16. Colson, "Correspondance," letter of June 15, 1792; Roubaud, "Lettres," 117 (letter of June 19); Ruault, *Gazette d'un Parisien,* 289 (letter of June 24). See also Corbel, "Correspondance," letter of June 20; Jullien, "Correspondance," letter of June 16; and Couthon, *Correspondance inédite,* 157–158 (letter of June 21).

17. For this and the following paragraphs, see esp. Lefebvre, *La chute du roi,* 180–190; and Alpaugh, "Making of the Parisian Political Demonstration."

18. *AP,* 45:417–419; Ruault, *Gazette d'un Parisien,* 289–290 (letter of June 24); Rabusson-Lamothe, "Lettres," 364–365 (letter of June 21, 1792); Couthon, *Correspondance inédite,* 157–158 (letter of June 21); Jullien, "Correspondance," letter of June 20.

19. Soubrany, *Dix-neuf lettres,* 7 (letter of June 20, 1792).

20. Jullien, "Correspondance," letter of June 20, 1792; Pinet, "Correspondance," letter of June 22; Hugues Destrem, in "Correspondance des députés de l'Aude, 161 (letter of June 21); Hua, *Mémoires d'un avocat,* 132; Verneilh-Puyraseau, *Mémoires historiques,* 235–238; Alexandre, "Fragments des mémoires," 176.

21. See e.g., *AP,* 45:412; Le Coz: AD Ille-et-Vilaine, L 294 (2), letter of June 23, 1792; and Verneilh-Puyraseau, *Mémoires historiques,* 235–238.

22. Ruault, *Gazette d'un Parisien,* 290–291 (letter of June 24, 1792). See also the duchesse of La Rochefoucauld (recounting the observations of her brother Charles), *Lettres,* 103–105 (letter of June 21).

23. For this and the following paragraph, see Ruault, *Gazette d'un Parisien,* 290–291 (letter of June 24, 1792); La Rochefoucauld, *Lettres,* 103–105 (letter of June 21); Guittard, *Journal,* 154–155 (entry of June 20); Pinet, "Correspondance," letter of June 22; Couthon, *Correspondance inédite,* 157–158 (letter of June 21); Dubrueil, *Lettres parisiennes,* 47 (letter of June 21); Corbel, "Correspondance," letter of June 22; Roubaud, "Lettres," 120 (letter of June 26); Le Coz in AD Ille-et-Vilaine, L 294 (2), letter of June 23; Soubrany, *Dix-neuf lettres,* 7–9 (letter of June 20).

24. See, e.g., Codet in AD Ile-et-Vilaine, L 294 (2), letter of July 2, 1792. On the letters sent from around the country, see Reinhard, *La chute de la royauté,* 338 and 545 (map); Dendera, " 'Nos places maudites,' " 97; and *Révolutions de Paris* (issue of June 16–23); Ruault, *Gazette d'un Parisien,* 293 (letter of June 26); and Jullien,

"Correspondance," letters of June 24 and 26. Thirty-four departments were said to have sent in complaints, though only a few districts did so.

25. Guittard, *Journal,* 155 (entry of June 20, 1792).

26. Couthon, *Correspondance inédite,* 157–158, (letter of June 21, 1792); Roubaud, "Lettres," 120 (letter of June 26). Cf. also the Montagnard Pinet, "Correspondance," letter of June 22; and Soubrany, *Dix-neuf lettres,* 7 (letter of June 6); and the conservative Le Coz: AD Ille-et-Vilaine, L 294 (2), letter of June 23.

27. Pinet, "Correspondance," letter of Aug. 7, 1792. See also Jullien, "Correspondance," letter of June 26; and Jagot in Dubois, *Histoire,* 2:334–337.

28. Pinet, "Correspondance," letter of July 8, 1792. See also Destrem in "Correspondance des députés de l'Aude," 30 (1896), 161–162 (letter of July 12); R. Lindet, "Lettres," 43–44 (letter of July 13); and Choudieu, *Mémoires et notes,* 159.

29. Rabusson-Lamothe, "Lettres," 367–368, 373–374 (letters of June 26 and July 12, 1792); and Roubaud, "Lettres," 132–133 (letter of July 31). See also Demée, "Lettres," letter of July 23; and Michon, *Essai,* 408–414. There were also certain tentative efforts to reach an agreement among the deputies through the so-called *club de la réunion,* see Reinhard, *La chute de la royauté,* 350–352.

30. Vergniaud, *Vergniaud, manuscrits, lettres, et papiers,* 2:123–124 (letter of July 29, 1792).

31. Ellery, *Brissot de Warville,* 284–290; and Pinet, "Correspondance," letter of July 31, 1792.

32. The speech actually repeated much of the content of an open letter that Lafayette had addressed to the deputies two weeks earlier. At the time some of the radicals had questioned the authenticity of the letter, but now there could be no doubt. See *AP,* 45:653; Gower, *Despatches,* 195 (letter of June 22, 1792); Jullien, "Correspondance," letter of June 19; Viénot de Vaublanc, *Mémoires,* 203.

33. Pinet, "Correspondance," letter of July 6, 1792. See also Couthon, *Correspondance inédite,* 152 and 163 (letters of June 9 and 30); and Jullien, "Correspondance," letter of June 6. Some radical journalists had turned against Lafayette after the Nancy Affair in the summer of 1790: Censer, *Prelude to Power,* 110.

34. Vergniaud, *Vergniaud, manuscrits, lettres, et papiers,* 1:165 (letter of July 21, 1792) and 2:122–123 (letter of July 29); Dubreuil-Chambardel, *Lettres,* 43 (letter of July 7); Pinet, "Correspondance," letter of July 25.

35. *AP,* 46:342–344. See also Couthon, *Correspondance inédite,* 169 (letter of July 12, 1792); Pinet, "Correspondance," letter of July 13; Barbaroux, *Correspondance et mémoires,* 209–210 (letter of July 12); Corbel, "Correspondance," letter of July 13; Bancal, *Le conventionnel Bancal,* 220 (letter of July 12).

36. Guittard, *Journal,* 163 (entry of July 22, 1792); also Colson, "Correspondance," letter of July 24.

37. Ruault, *Gazette d'un Parisien,* 294 (letter of June 26, 1792).

38. Pinet, "Correspondance," letter of July 13, 1792. On the Federation Festival itself, see Demée, "Lettres," letter of July 15; Colson, "Correspondance," letter of July 15; Guittard, *Journal*, 160–161 (entry of July 14); Mareux, *Une famille de la bourgeoisie*, 273–274 (letter of July 16); Pinet, "Correspondance," letters of July 14 and 15; Etienne Rubat, "Lettres," letter of July 16; Ruault, *Gazette d'un Parisien*, 296 (letter of July 17); Bancal, *Le conventionnel Bancal*, 221 (letter of July 17); Couthon, *Correspondance inédite*, 172–174 (letter of July 17).

39. Sagnac, *La chute*, 37–39; Aulard, *Société des Jacobins*, 4:228–229 and 243 (Aug. 20 and 27, 1792); Pinet, "Correspondance," letters of July 24 and Aug. 18.

40. Sagnac, *La chute*, 33–36. On the appearance of moustaches, see Ruault, *Gazette d'un Parisien*, 297, letter of July 27, 1792.

41. Sagnac, *La chute*, 34–36, 43–45, 49–50.

42. Corbel, "Correspondance," letter of July 28, 1792.

43. Lefebvre, *La chute du roi*, 207; Vovelle in Baratier, *Histoire de Marseille*, 274–276; and Pinet, "Correspondance," letter of July 31, 1792.

44. Corbel, "Correspondance," letter of July 28, 1792; Bancal, *Le conventionnel Bancal*, 227 (letter of July 31); Ruault, *Gazette d'un Parisien*, 297 (letter of July 27); Colson, "Correspondance," letter of Aug. 1; and Guittard, *Journal*, 164–165 (entries of July 30 and Aug. 3). Also Reinhard, *Chute de la royauté*, 304–307.

45. *AP*, 47:400–401; Sagnac, *La chute*, 81–95.

46. *AP*, 47:425–427; Jullien, "Correspondance," letter of Aug. 5, 1792; Corbel, "Correspondance," letter of Aug. 4; Pinet, "Correspondance," letter of Aug. 5; Rivoallan in "Correspondance des députés des Côtes-du-Nord," 129 (letter of Aug. 4). Also Sagnac, *La chute*, 57–58; and Labroue, *L'esprit public en Dordogne*, 39–40.

47. Ruault, *Gazette d'un Parisien*, 301 (letter of Aug. 3, 1792). See also Pinet, "Correspondance," letter of Aug. 5; and Alexandre, "Fragments des mémoires," 205.

48. *AP*, 27:524–527; Rose, *Making of the Sans-Culottes*, 160; Pinet, "Correspondance," letter of Aug. 7, 1792. Also Sagnac, *La chute*, 122–124.

49. Corbel, "Correspondance," letter of July 28, 1792; and Codet, AD Ille-et-Vilaine, L 294 (2), letter of July 30.

50. Ruault, *Gazette d'un Parisien*, 298 (letter of July 27).

51. Colson, "Correspondance," letter of Aug. 10, 1792; and *AP*, 47:598–605. See also Géraud, *Journal d'un étudiant*, 317 (letter of Aug. 9); Pinet, "Correspondance," letter of Aug. 10; Corbel, "Correspondance," letter of Aug. 11; Jullien, "Correspondance," letter of Aug. 8; Bancal, *Le conventionnel Bancal*, 230 (letter of Aug. 9); Viénot de Vaublanc, *Mémoires*, 214.

52. Michon, *Essai*, 416–417, 422, 427–428; Reinhard, *La chute de la royauté*, 309–310.

53. See Michon, *Essai*, 416–417, 422–423. Among the king's secret advisers were the ex-deputies Clermont-Tonnerre, Lally-Tollendal, and Malouet and the former ministers Montmorin and Bertrand de Molleville.

54. The king was well informed of the coming confrontation: see Ruault, *Gazette d'un Parisien,* 302–303 (letter of Aug. 14, 1792); and Sagnac, *La chute,* 201: "Rien ne fut moins imprévu que la révolution du 10 août."

55. Sagnac, *La chute,* 223–225; and Mitchell, *French Legislative Assembly,* 127–132.

56. Alexandre, "Fragments des mémoires," 208.

57. *AP,* 47:400–401.

58. Jullien, "Correspondance," letter of July 26, 1792. See also Ruault, *Gazette d'un Parisien,* 296–297 (letter of July 17); and Roubaud, "Lettres," 125 (letter of July 10).

59. Sagnac, *La chute,* 64–81.

60. Jullien, "Correspondance," letters of Aug 9 and 10, 1792; Ruault, *Gazette d'un Parisien,* 302 (letter of Aug. 14).

61. Sagnac, *La chute,* 221–222, 252–253; A. Rubat, "Lettres," letter of Aug. 10, 1792.

62. The following account is based primarily on Sagnac, *La chute,* 277–303; Barbaroux, *Correspondance et mémoires,* 222–223 (letter of Aug. 10, 1792); Pinet, "Correspondance," letter of Aug. 10; Géraud, *Journal d'un étudiant,* 322–325 (letter of Aug. 11); and A. Rubat, "Lettres," letter of Aug. 10.

63. One insurgent claimed that 40 Swiss had already abandoned their posts and embraced them when the defenders in the chateau opened fire: *AP,* 47:645. See also the testimony of one of the Swiss in question: *AP,* 47:648 and the *Thermomètre du jour* (issue of Aug. 11, 1792).

64. Colson, "Correspondance," letter of Aug. 10, 1792.

65. Sagnac, *La chute,* 299–300; Rose, *Making of the Sans-Culottes,* 104–106.

66. Géraud, *Journal d'un étudiant,* 322–325 (letter of Aug. 11); Guittard, *Journal,* 168–169 (entry of Aug. 10, 1792); Ruault, *Gazette d'un Parisien,* 302–303 (letter of Aug. 14); *AP,* 47:675.

67. Jullien, "Correspondance," letter of Aug. 10, 1792; Alexandre, "Fragments des mémoires," 221.

68. Monnard, *Les souvenirs,* 43–45; Alexandre, "Fragments des mémoires," 218; Mareux, *Une famille de la bourgeoisie,* 290–297 (letter of Aug. 19, 1792); Pinet, "Correspondance," letter of Aug. 10. See also Jullien, "Correspondance," letters of Aug. 10 and 15.

69. Bancal, *Le conventionnel Bancal,* 232–234 (letter of Aug. 14).

8. The First Terror

1. Colson, "Correspondance," letter of Aug. 17, 1792; Ruault, *Gazette d'un Parisien,* 303 (letter of Aug. 28); and Braesch, *La commune,* 335. See also Corbel, "Correspondance," letter of Sept. 24; and the *Révolutions de Paris* (issue of Aug. 18 to 25).

2. Digaultray in "Correspondance des députés des Côtes-du-Nord," 28 (1890), 152 (letter of Aug. 25, 1792); and Ruault, *Gazette d'un Parisien,* 303 (letters of Aug. 14

and 28). See also Guittard, *Journal,* 169 (entry of Aug. 10); and Pinet, "Correspondance," letters of Aug. 13 and 14. Prudhomme referred to the king as "Louis-Nero" and "Louis-le-Traître" and urged that he be executed immediately: *Révolutions de Paris* (issue of Aug. 11 to 18).

3. Ruault, *Gazette d'un Parisien,* 303 (letter of Aug. 28, 1792); and Alexandre, "Fragments des mémoires," 225. See also Lebas, cited in Buchez and Roux, *Histoire parlementaire,* 35:325–326 (letter of Aug. 12).

4. See Lefebvre, *La première Terreur.*

5. Pinet, "Correspondance," letters of Aug. 11 and 18, 1792; and *AP,* esp. 47:639–646.

6. E.g., *AP,* 47:598–605 (Aug. 9, 1792).

7. Rivoallan in "Correspondance des députés des Côtes-du-Nord," 136 (letter of Aug. 13, 1792); and Le Bronsart in AM Brest, 2 D 21, letter of Sept. 8. See also Demée, "Lettres," letter of Aug. 13; and Viénot de Vaublanc, *Mémoires,* 219. Only 284 deputies were present on the night of Aug. 10 to vote for the new Conseil Exécutif; only 323 voted for the Assembly president on Aug. 19; and only 257 did so on Sept. 2: *AP,* 47:660, 48:376, 49:199. Also Reinhard, *La chute de la royauté,* 239.

8. *AP,* 48:182–184 (Aug. 15, 1792) and 185–197 (copy of documents printed and sent throughout France). See also Pinet, "Correspondance," letter of Aug. 18; and "Adresse de l'Assemblée nationale aux français" of Aug. 19 in Condorcet, *Oeuvres,* 10:567–568.

9. Aubert in "Aubert-Dubayet: Législateur," 139; Rabusson-Lamothe, "Lettres," 377–378 (letter of Aug. 16, 1792). See also Georges Couthon's reconciliation with Rabusson, his previously estranged colleague: *Correspondance inédite,* 185 (letter of Aug. 30); and the two former Feuillants, Dupont-Grandjardin, "Correspondance," 358–359 (letter of Sept. 17); and Aristide Rubat, "Lettres," letter of Aug. 21.

10. The Legislative was henceforth largely controlled by the Girondin-dominated *Commission extraordinaire des douze:* see *AP,* 45:326–327; Lefebvre, *La chute du roi,* 178; and *La première Terreur,* 29–30. The Girondin leaders Brissot, Gensonné, Guadet, Lasource, Condorcet, and Vergniaud were all members after mid-July.

11. See Reynolds, *Marriage and Revolution,* chaps. 19 and 20.

12. It was significant that the Executive Council habitually convened in Danton's Ministry of Justice. See Lefebvre, *La première Terreur,* 29–36; and Aulard, *Histoire politique,* 219.

13. "Universal" suffrage would continue to exclude women, servants, and those who had changed their residence during the previous year. See M. Edelstein, *Birth of Electoral Democracy,* esp. 259–260. On the new divorce laws, see Desan, *Family on Trial,* esp. 62–63.

14. Pinet, "Correspondance," letter of Aug. 10, 1792. Also Neufchâteau, "Recherches sur la vie," 217 (letter of Aug. 11); Colson, "Correspondance," letter of Aug. 12; and Ménétra, "Mes réflexions," BHVP, Ms. 678, 102.

15. Robespierre had resigned his position on the Paris criminal tribunal. On the early Commune and its membership, see Sagnac, *La chute,* 221–222; and Braesch, *La commune,* chap. 3. Of those members of the Commune whose professions are known, by far the largest group consisted of merchants, artisans, and shopkeepers.

16. The Commune had already complained of this on August 10: *AP,* 47:651.

17. *AP,* 48:298; and Jullien, "Correspondance," letter of Aug. 26, 1792. See also the speech by François-Paul Anthoine in the Jacobins on Aug. 12: Aulard, *Société des Jacobins,* 4:196; and Braesch, *La commune,* 416–420.

18. Braesch, *La commune,* 334, 364–383; and Caron, *La première Terreur,* chaps. 1 and 2.

19. For this and the following paragraphs, see esp. Braesch, *La commune,* 323–327, 422–425; and Lefebvre, *La première Terreur,* 64–79.

20. On the censorship of plays, see the *Thermomètre du jour* (issue of Aug. 21, 1792).

21. Ambassadors of England, Holland, and Venice all complained that they were unable to leave Paris because their local sections refused to issue them passports: Gower, *Despatches,* 209, 211, 218 (letters of Aug. 17, 23, and 28, 1792).

22. The transition from the older system with sixty independent battalions to the new arrangement with one battalion for each of the forty-eight sections took time to be implemented. See Braesch, *La commune,* 329–331; and Mitchell, *French Legislative Assembly,* 123–125.

23. *Annales patriotiques* (issue of July 21, 1792). See also Lefebvre, *La première Terreur,* 139; and Lemny, *Jean-Louis Carra,* 245–246.

24. Jullien, "Correspondance," letter of Sept. 1, 1792. See also her letter of Aug. 26.

25. Robespierre, *Correspondance,* 1:152 (letter of Aug. 20, 1792). See also Pétion's earlier efforts at reconciliation in April 1792: Walter, *Jacobins,* 249.

26. Reynolds, *Marriage and Revolution,* 195. See also *Thermomètre du jour* (issue of Sept. 5, 1792).

27. Géraud, *Journal d'un étudiant,* 357 (letter of Sept. 18, 1792). Also Condorcet, *Oeuvres,* 10:581–582, "Adresse de l'Assemblée nationale aux français" of Sept. 19; and Cahen, *Condorcet et la Révolution française,* 430.

28. William Lindsay in Gower, *Despatches,* 213 (letter of Aug. 27, 1792); and Ruault, *Gazette d'un Parisien,* 311 (letter of Sept. 14).

29. Jullien, "Correspondance," letter of Aug. 18, 1792. Also Pinet, "Correspondance," letter of Aug. 11; Mareux, *Une famille de la bourgeoisie parisienne,* 283 (letter of Aug. 19); Aulard, *Jacobins,* 4:217 (Aug. 17); and Braesch, *La commune,* 349, 360.

30. Lefebvre, *La première Terreur,* 75.

31. Pinet, "Correspondance," letter of Aug. 11, 1792; Ruault, *Gazette d'un Parisien,* 303 (letter of Aug. 14); Guittard, *Journal,* 169 (entry of Aug. 10); Colson, "Correspondance," letter of Aug. 17; Jullien, "Correspondance," letter of Aug. 18; A. Rubat, "Lettres," letter of Aug. 21; and *Révolutions de Paris* (issue of Aug. 4 to 11). The Legis-

lative also passed a decree accepting and promoting the destruction of all royal monuments: *AP,* 48:2 (Aug. 11).

32. *Thermomètre du jour* (issue of Aug. 25, 1792); and Braesch, *La commune,* 341.

33. Ruault, *Gazette d'un Parisien,* 304 (letter of Aug. 28, 1792). See also Guittard, *Journal,* 169 (entry of Aug. 10).

34. Marat, *L'Ami du peuple* (issue of Aug. 19, 1792). See also Gorsas, *Le Courrier des 83 départements* (issue of Aug. 17); Fréron, *L'orateur du peuple* (issue of Aug. 17); and Carra, *Annales patriotiques et littéraires* (issue of Aug. 13).

35. A. Rubat, "Lettres," letter of Aug. 21, 1792; Bancal, *Le conventionnel Bancal,* 236 (letter of Aug. 18); and *Thermomètre du jour* (issue of Aug. 20); and Braesch, *La commune,* 474.

36. Jullien, "Correspondance," letter of Aug. 26, 1792. See also Digaultray in "Correspondance des députés des Côtes-du-Nord," 28 (1890), 160 (letter of Aug. 26); Guittard, *Journal,* 172 (entry of Aug. 26); *Révolutions de Paris* (issue of Aug. 25 to Sept. 1); and *Thermomètre du jour* (issue of Aug. 26).

37. Lefebvre, *La première Terreur,* 21, 71, 94; Caron, *Massacres de septembre,* 428–445; and Braesch, *La commune,* 347–349.

38. Braesch, *La commune,* esp. 335 and 364–373; Lefebvre, *La première Terreur,* 75. On August 11 the Legislative gave sweeping powers to the municipalities to investigate and denounce conspiracies against *la sûreté générale: AP,* 48:41–42.

39. Pinet, "Correspondance," letter of Aug. 18, 1792. See also Colson, "Correspondance," letter of Aug. 17; Rivoallan in "Correspondance des députés des Côtes-du-Nord," 28 (1890), 135 (letter of Aug. 13); and Braesch, *La commune,* 328–331, 351–354.

40. On the prison population, see Caron, *Massacres de septembre,* 24–26.

41. See, e.g., Choudieu, *Mémoires et notes,* 171; and Colson, "Correspondance," letter of Aug. 19, 1792.

42. *AP,* 48: 180–181. Lefebvre, *La première Terreur,* 99. Also Jullien, "Correspondance," letter of Aug. 23, 1792.

43. Mareux, *Une famille de la bourgeoisie,* 308 (letter of Sept. 6, 1792). See also Guittard, *Journal,* 172–173 (entries of Aug. 25 and 27); and *Thermomètre du jour* (issues of Aug. 25 and 27).

44. See, e.g., Baumont, *Le département de l'Oise,* 175.

45. Codet, AD Ille-et-Vilaine, L 294 (2), letter of Aug. 19, 1792. See also Azéma in "Correspondance des députés de l'Aude," 30 (1896), 166 (letter of Aug. 12); Clauzel, "Documents inédits," 125 (letter of Aug. 18); and Digaultray in "Correspondance des députés des Côtes-du-Nord," 28 (1890), 165 (letter of Sept. 8).

46. Noël, *Au temps des volontaires,* 238–240 (letter of Aug. 17, 1792); and Lefebvre, *La première Terreur,* 15–19.

47. See, e.g., Boivin-Champeaux, *Notices historiques,* 1:394–398; Raymond Nicolas, *L'esprit public,* 77–79; Lefebvre, *La première Terreur,* 13–14.

48. Jullien, "Correspondance," letter of Aug. 21, 1792. See also Codet in AD Ille-et-Vilaine, L 294 (2), letter of Aug. 21; Pinet, "Correspondance," letter of Aug. 18; and Géraud, *Journal d'un étudiant,* 331 (letter of Aug. 27). Acceptance of August 10 took longer in some departments than in others: see R. Nicolas, *L'esprit public,* 71; Pommeret, *L'esprit politique,* 185–187; Dubois, *Histoire,* 3:13–18; Brégail, "Le Gers pendant la Révolution," 32 (1931), 255; Jolivet, *La Révolution dans l'Ardèche,* 376, 382–383; Corgne, *Pontivy et son district pendant,* 291; and Poupé, "Le département du Var," 182–183.

49. Arnaud, *Histoire de la Révolution,* 335–336.

50. The statistics and analysis here are based primarily on Caron, *Les massacres de septembre,* 370–391 and 396–410. All such statistics are invariably incomplete.

51. Caron, *Les massacres de septembre,* 401–402. See also Bancal's description of rumors in Montargis as he passed through this town en route to Paris: Bancal, *Le conventionnel Bancal,* 237 (letter of Sept. 18, 1792).

52. Lefebvre, *La première Terreur,* 94.

53. Baumont, *Le département de l'Oise,* 180–182 and 198. On the volunteer's terrorizing the department of Ariège, see Arnaud, *Histoire de la Révolution,* 300–306.

54. Letter by Chaudrue from La Rochelle in Géraud, *Journal d'un étudiant,* 331 (Aug. 27, 1792).

55. Lefebvre, *La première Terreur,* 103; Caron, *Les massacres de septembre,* 397–399. See also Sutherland, "Justice and Murder: Massacres in the Provinces."

56. Caron, *Les massacres de septembre,* 375; Mortimer-Ternaux, *Histoire de la Terreur,* 3:348–351. See also the efforts of Pierre-Franois Palloy to discipline the Parisian volunteers under his command, and his inability to prevent them from murdering two "suspects" in Châlons-sur-Marne: Palloy, *Livre de raison,* 182–184.

57. Lefebvre, *La première Terreur,* 108–109 and 114.

58. Lord Gower, the English ambassador, and W. Lindsay, the chargé d'affaires: in Gower, *Despatches,* 201 and 214 (letters of July 20 and Aug. 23, 1792).

59. Lefebvre, *La première Terreur,* 108–110; Blanning, *French Revolutionary Wars,* 74; Connelly, *Wars of the French Revolution and Napoleon,* 27.

60. Lefebvre, *La première Terreur,* 110–111 and 115–117.

61. Dugaultray in "Correspondance des députés des Côtes-du-Nord," 28 (1890), 158 (letter of Aug. 26, 1792); Guittard, *Journal,* 176 (entry of Sept. 2). See also Corbel, "Correspondance," letter of Sept. 1; Couthon, *Correspondance inédite,* 186–187 (letter of Sept. 1); and Tardiveau in AD Ille-et-Vilaine, L 294 (2), letter of Aug. 29.

62. Cited in Lefebvre, *La première Terreur,* 124 and 126. See also Reynolds, *Marriage and Revolution,* 194.

63. Guittard, *Journal,* 174 (entry of Aug. 29, 1792); and Jullien, "Correspondance," letter of Aug. 29. See also *Thermomètre du jour* (issue of Aug. 30); and Gohier in AD Ille-et-Vilaine, L 294 (2), letter of Sept. 1.

64. See Caron, *Massacres de septembre,* 3–4; and Porret, " 'Effrayer le crime par la terreur,' " 48, 54.

65. Colson, "Correspondance," letter of Oct. 13, 1789; Lacroix, *Actes de la Commune de Paris,* 2e série, 5:14 and 179 (entrees of June 21 and 26, 1791); *Chronique de Paris,* no. 174 (issue of June 23, 1791). Also Andress, *Massacre at the Champ de Mars,* 149; and Reinhard, *La chute de la royauté,* 37–39.

66. Guittard, *Journal,* 120 (entry of Jan. 21, 1792); Colson, "Correspondance," letter of Jan. 25. Also Rabusson-Lamothe, "Lettres," 288 (letter of Jan. 21); and Duval in AD Ille-et-Vilaine, L 294, letter of Jan. 23.

67. *AP,* 45:417.

68. Braesch, *La commune,* 353–354.

69. Codet in AD Ille-et-Vilaine, L 294 (2), letter of Aug. 19, 1792; Jullien, "Correspondance," letter of Aug. 15. See also Mareux, *Une famille de la bourgeoisie,* 290–297 (letter of Aug. 19); and Monnard, *Les souvenirs,* 46.

70. Braesch, *La commune,* 484–485, 488. Unfortunately, most of the section deliberations have been lost.

71. The principal source for this and the following paragraphs is Caron, *Massacres de septembre.* See also the descriptions in the *Thermomètre du jour* (issues of Sept. 3 to 6, 1792).

72. Caron, *Massacres de septembre,* 221–231.

73. Braesch, *La commune,* 482.

74. Caron, *Massacres de septembre,* 296n and 305.

75. Ibid., 27–43.

76. Ibid., esp. 49–70.

77. Cited in Caron, *Massacres de septembre,* 111; Monro in Gower, *Despatches,* 227 (letter of Sept. 4, 1792). Monro claimed that most of the Marseillais were still in Paris in the days after the massacres: Monro in Gower, *Despatches,* 237 (letter of Sept. 8). See also Caron, *Massacres de septembre,* esp. 106–109; and the report to Marseille by the deputy François Granet: AC Marseille, 4 D 43, letter of Aug. 20.

78. Ruault, *Gazette d'un Parisien,* 311 (letter of Sept. 8, 1792).

79. Caron, *Massacres de septembre,* 121–153. Compare the Girondin sympathizer Jacques Dulaure in the *Thermomètre du jour* (issue of Sept. 4, 1792), who concluded that "le peuple avait à pourvoir à sa légitime défense"; Prudhomme, strongly justified and praised the Massacres: *Révolutions de Paris* (issue of Sept. 1 to 8).

80. Dubreuil-Chambardel, *Lettres parisiennes,* 64 (letter of Sept. 15, 1792); Guittard, *Journal,* 175 (entry of Sept. 2); and Jullien, "Correspondance," letter of Sept. 2. See the similar statements by Couthon, *Correspondance inédite,* 191 (letter of Sept. 6); Ramel, "Lettres," letter of Sept. 5; Pinet, "Correspondance," letter of Sept. 8; Géraud, *Journal d'un étudiant,* 350–352 (letter of Sept. 4); and Monnard, *Les souvenirs,* 46. See also Dorigny, "Les Girondins et les Massacres de septembre," 105–115.

81. Ruault, *Gazette d'un Parisien,* 306–311 (letter of Sept. 8, 1792); Basire cited by Mathiez, "Recherches sur la famille et la vie privée du conventionnel Basire," 187 (letter

of early Sept. 92). For the evolving position of the Rolands, see Reynolds, *Marriage and Revolution,* 194–201.

82. Out of twenty witnesses examined for this study who gave their immediate reactions to the massacres, four condemned them outright, two avoided mentioning them, and fourteen accepted them as desirable and/or unfortunate necessities. Considered here are the letters, diaries, or speeches of Basire, Chabot, Colson, Corbel, Couthon, Demée, Digaultray, Dubreuil, Gohier, Géraud, Guittard, Rosalie Jullien, Robert Lindet, Adelaide Mareux, Pinet, Piory, Ramel, Marie-Jeanne Roland, Ruault, and Soubrany.

83. Caron, *Massacres de septembre,* 278–279.

84. Ibid., 277.

85. Pinet, Correspondance," letter of Sept. 18; Mareux, *Une famille de la bourgeoisie,* 308–309 (letter of Sept. 6); and *Révolutions de Paris* (issue of Sept. 8 to 15). See also Gohier in AD Ille-et-Vilaine, L 294 (2), letter of Sept. 17, 1792; Colson, "Correspondance," letters of Sept. 6, 9, and 19; Dubreuil-Chambardel, *Lettres parisiennes,* 67 (letter of Sept. 22, 1792); and Bancal, *Le conventionnel Bancal,* 237 (letter of Sept. 18, 1792).

86. Colson, "Correspondance," letters of Sept. 6, 9, 11, and 19, 1792; Boivin-Champeaux, *Notices historiques,* 1:418–419; and Roubaud, "Lettres," 142–144 (letter of Sept. 25). For the first time Colson himself seriously considered leaving Paris.

87. Markoff, *Abolition of Feudalism,* 271, 276–279; Caron, *Massacres de septembre,* 365–391; and Alpaugh, *Non-violence and the French Revolution,* "Appendix."

88. Dubreuil-Chambardel, *Lettres parisiennes,* 80 (letter of Nov. 17, 1792); and Mareux, *Une famille de la bourgeoisie,* 330 (letter of Dec. 18). See also Blad, "Correspondance," letter of Nov. 14; and Palasne in "Correspondance des députés des Côtes-du-Nord," 30 (1892), 116 (letter of Oct. 1).

9. The Convention and the Trial of the King

1. Le Bronsart in AM Brest, 2 D 21, letter of Sept. 8, 1792.

2. Gohier in AD Ille-et-Vilaine, L 294 (2), letter of Sept. 3, 1792; Corbel, "Correspondance," letter of Sept. 3. See also Thomas Riboud deputy from Bourg-en-Bresse, cited in Caron, *Massacres de septembre,* 125–126 (letter of Sept. 3); and Soubrany, *Dix-neuf lettres,* 14 (letter of Sept. 6).

3. Gillet, "Lettres du conventionnel," 242 (letter of Sept. 24, 1792). See also the letter from the municipality of Evreux to Robert Lindet: Lindet, *Correspondance,* 374 (Aug. 28).

4. Colson, "Correspondance," letter of Sept. 6, 1792. See also Guittard, *Journal,* 183 (entry of Sept. 23); Jullien, "Correspondance," letters of Sept. 5 and 6; and Pinet, "Correspondance," letter of Sept. 8.

5. Etienne-François Mireur in Lombard, *Un volontaire,* 133–134 (letter of Aug. 28, 1792); Brault in Picard, *Au service de la nation,* 118 (letter of Oct. 2). See also

Bricard, *Journal du cannonier,* 1–3 (journal entry of Sept 5); and François, *Journal du capitaine,* 4 (letter of Sept. 5).

6. Colson, "Correspondance," letter of Sept. 4, 1792; Guittard, *Journal,* 183 (entry of Sept. 23); Jullien, "Correspondance," letter of Sept. 2; Géraud, *Journal d'un étudiant,* 353 (letter of Sept. 4); George Monro in Gower, *Despatches,* 225 (letter of Sept. 4); Braesch, *La commune,* 466–470.

7. On the 1792 invasion of France and the battle of Valmy, see esp. Bertaud, *Valmy;* and Blanning, *French Revolutionary Wars,* 73–82.

8. Goethe, *Campaign,* entry of Sept. 4, 1792; Noël, *Au temps des volontaires,* 245 (letter of Aug. 22).

9. Goethe, *Campaign,* 116–119 (entries of Sept. 20 and 21, 1792); and Bertaud, *Valmy,* 26–40.

10. Noël, *Au temps des volontaires,* 274 (letter of Sept. 26, 1792); and Goethe, *Campaign,* 117–119 (entries of Sept. 20 and 21).

11. Sorel, *L'Europe et la Révolution,* 3:50–66; Goethe, *Campaign,* 127–132 (entries of Sept. 25–29, 1792); and Lefebvre, *Convention,* 1:118–121.

12. Goethe, *Campaign,* 154–160 (entries of Oct. 11 and 12, 1792); Noël, *Au temps des volontaires,* 280–281 (letter of Oct. 17).

13. Blanning, *French Revolutionary Wars,* 82. The Greek Constantin Stamaty compared France's plight to that of ancient Greece on the eve of Marathon and Thermopoly: Stamaty, *Correspondances,* 95–96 (letter of July 25, 1792).

14. Belot, *Journal d'un volontaire,* 78 (letter of Oct. 14, 1792).

15. Sorel, *L'Europe et la Révolution,* 3:114–117.

16. Bancal, *Le conventionnel Bancal,* 244 (letter of Oct. 16, 1792). See also Blad, "Correspondance," letter of Oct. 13; and Sorel, *L'Europe et la Révolution,* 3:149.

17. See the accounts of François, *Journal du capitaine,* 11–12 (letter of Oct. 26, 1792); and Noël, *Au temps des volontaires,* 297 (letter of Dec. 4). Also Sorel, *L'Europe et la Révolution,* 3:159–169.

18. Blad, "Correspondance," letter of Nov. 9, 1792; Boyer-Fonfrède, AD Gironde, letter of Nov. 22; Louchet, "Lettres," letter of Nov. 10; Géraud, *Journal d'un étudiant,* 375 (letter of Nov. 21). See also Pinet, "Correspondance," letter of Nov. 11.

19. Guittard, *Journal,* 189 (entry of Oct. 14, 1792); Blad, "Correspondance," letter of Dec. 3; Lefebvre, *Convention,* 1:148; Sol, *La Révolution en Quercy,* 2:436–438; Nicolas, *L'esprit public,* 87; and Bertaud, *Valmy,* 42–46.

20. Both Brissot and Danton would do so: Lefebvre, *Convention,* 1:154–158.

21. Ruault, *Gazette d'un Parisien,* 317–318 (letter of Oct. 18, 1792); Roubaud, "Lettres," 147 and 150 (letters of Oct. 9 and 25); Pinet, "Correspondance," letter of Oct. 26.

22. Corgne, *Pontivy,* 210; Jolivet, *La Révolution dans l'Ardèche,* 378; Pommeret, *L'esprit politique,* 175; Dubois, *Histoire,* 3:5; Boivin-Champeaux, *Notices historiques,* 1:392–393; R. Nicolas, *L'esprit public,* 83–84. See also Patrick, *First French Republic,* chap.

6; and M. Edelstein, *French Revolution and the Birth of Electoral Democracy,* chap. 10. Patrick, *First French Republic,* 180, argues that the actual exclusion of conservatives was rare outside Paris and a few other departments.

23. Patrick, *First French Republic,* 307–311.

24. The other deputy journalists were Robespierre, Barère, Brissot, Condorcet, Louvet, Tallien, Mercier, Audouin, Dulaure, Chénier, Fabre d'Eglantine, and Robert.

25. See the letters of Pinet, "Correspondance," and Corbel, "Correspondance," both of Sept. 22, 1792.

26. *AP,* 52:72–74; and Pinet, "Correspondance," letter of Sept. 22, 1792. See also Louchet, "Lettres," letter of Sept. 30.

27. Decreed before they declared the Republic: *AP,* 52:72 (Sept. 21, 1792).

28. Jacob, *Suspects,* 28; Braesch, *La commune,* 589, 596–598; Lefebvre, *Convention,* 1:50–51, 57, 83–85; Barbaroux, *Correspondance et mémoires,* 247 (letter of Oct. 13, 1792); Louchet, "Lettres," letter of Oct. 26; and Guyomar in "Correspondance des députés des Côtes-du-Nord," 30 (1892), 130 (letter of Oct. 27).

29. Dubois, *Histoire,* 3:47; Reynolds, *Marriage and Revolution,* 206–210; Walton, *Policing Public Opinion,* 206–216. Also Biard, *Missionnaires,* 39–42.

30. Jeanbon in *RF,* 29 (1895), 66 (letter of Oct. 3, 1792). See also Ramel, "Lettres," letter of Sept. 23; Couthon, *Correspondance inédite,* 198 (letter of Sept. 27); Blad, "Correspondance," letter of Oct. 10; Colson, "Correspondance," letter of Sept. 26; Gillet, "Lettres du conventionnel," 248 (letter of Oct. 2); Dubreuil-Chambardel, *Lettres parisiennes,* 73 (letter of Oct. 6); Louchet, "Lettres," letter of Oct. 4.

31. Saint-Martin, "L'année 1792," 50 (letter of Oct. 10, 1792). See also Dubreuil-Chambardel, *Lettres parisiennes,* 74 (letter of Oct. 6, 1792); Ruault, *Gazette d'un Parisien,* 317 (letter of Oct. 18); and Jeanbon, *RF,* 29 (1895), 65 (letter of Oct. 3).

32. Lefebvre, *Convention,* 1:148; Guittard, *Journal,* 193 (entry of Oct. 26, 1792).

33. Bancal, *Le conventionnel Bancal,* 250–251 (letter of Nov. 29, 1792); and *AP,* 53:145–147 and 506–509. See also Pinet, "Correspondance," letter of Nov. 25; Couthon, *Correspondance inédite,* 203 (letter of Nov. 3).

34. Lebas, cited in Buchez and Roux, *Histoire parlementaire,* 35:325 (letter of Oct. 26, 1792), See also Barthélemy Albouys in Sol, *La Révolution en Quercy,* 2:430 (letter of Oct. 21); Louchet, "Lettres," letter of Nov. 10; Dubreuil-Chambardel, *Lettres parisiennes,* 77–78 (letter of Nov. 10); and Gillet, "Lettres du conventionnel," 249 (letter of Nov. 24).

35. Brissot, *Correspondance et papiers,* 316–317 (letter of Nov. 28, 1792); *Révolutions de Paris,* 1792 (issue of Sept. 8 to 15).

36. *AP,* 53:331 (Nov. 3, 1792). See also Bancal, *Le conventionnel Bancal,* 243 (letter of Oct. 16); Pinet, "Correspondance," letter of Nov. 11; and Brissot, *Correspondance et papiers,* 313 (letter of Nov. 26).

37. *AP,* 55:70–73 (Dec. 15, 1792); and Pinet, "Correspondance," letter of Dec. 16. Also Sorel, *L'Europe et la Révolution,* 3:234–236.

38. *Les Révolutions de Paris* (issue of Sept. 15 to 22, 1792). See also Bancal, *Le conventionnel Bancal,* 239 (letter of Sept. 25).

39. Vinet, "Lettres du conventionnel," 63 (letter of Jan. 22, 1793). Compare Gillet's estimate of about 50 active members of the Mountain in the Convention: Gillet, "Lettres du conventionnel," 257 (letter of Dec. 10, 1792). Sydenham identified an "inner circle" of sixty Girondins: Sydenham, *Girondins,* 228–229.

40. Among other important Girondin supporters were the onetime Constituent Jacobins, Lanjuinais, Rabaut Saint-Etienne, and Salle; and four new recruits from the department of Gironde: Ducos, Boyer-Fonfrède, Grangeneuve, and Bergoeing.

41. Roland had been elected to the Convention, but he had opted to resign his seat in order to remain in the government. See Reynolds, *Marriage and Revolution,* 202, 223–229.

42. Jullien, "Correspondance," letters of Oct. 24 and Dec. 28, 1792. Mercier, the Girondin sympathizer, used almost the same phrase in referring to the Montagnards: Mercier, *Le nouveau Paris* (1994), 72.

43. See the description of Pinet, "Correspondance," letter of Jan. 11, 1793.

44. Aulard, *Société des Jacobins,* 4:219 (Aug. 19, 1792); Patrick, *First French Republic,* 288; Ruault, *Gazette d'un Parisien,* 317 (letter of Oct. 18). Ruault specified that he and Robespierre were among the few who still refused to don the cap.

45. The two groups are compared as they existed, as best one can determine, at the beginning of 1793. Before that date there was a great deal of fluidity in affiliations. In general, the Girondin leadership was somewhat younger than the Mountain leadership. Statistics are drawn primarily from Patrick, *First French Republic,* 193–194, 249–250, 259, 286–287, 292–293; and Baguenier-Desormeaux, "Origines sociales," 568–569, 572, 578–579, 582–584.

46. See esp. Lefebvre *Convention,* 1:10–17.

47. Pinet, "Correspondance," letter of Jan. 11, 1793. See also Monestier, "Lettres," letter of Dec. 28, 1792; and Marc-Antoine Jullien to his son, "Correspondance," letter of Dec. 15.

48. Lefebvre, *Convention,* 1:23–25; Cahen, *Condorcet,* 429; also the Girondin Fleury in Tempier, "Correspondance des députés" (1892), 132 (letter of Oct. 30, 1792).

49. For what follows, see esp. *AP,* 52:109 (Sept. 23, 1792); 124–127 (Sept. 24); and 130–142 (Sept. 25); and Lefebvre, *Convention,* 1:58–62. Also, e.g., Brissot, *Correspondance et papiers,* 320 (letter of Dec. 9); and Corbel, "Correspondance," letter of Dec. 28.

50. *AP,* 52:131.

51. See Brissot's address *A tous les républicains de France* of Oct. 24, 1792; Reynolds, *Marriage and Revolution,* 234–245; Walton, *Policing Public Opinion,* 206–209.

52. *AP,* 53:147–148; and Lefebvre, *Convention,* 1:73. Also Blad, "Correspondance," letter of Nov. 2; Boivin-Champeaux, *Notices historiques,* 1:431; and Roland's expression of appreciation to Marseille: AC Marseille, 4 D 44, letter of Nov. 21.

53. Braesch, *La commune,* 913; Walter, *Histoire des Jacobins,* 257; Lefebvre, *Convention,* 1:35, 203; Ruault, *Gazette d'un Parisien,* 315 (letter of Sept. 25, 1792. On the Girondins' self-exclusion from the Jacobins, see, e.g., Géraud, *Journal d'un étudiant,* 360 (letter of Oct. 4).

54. See, e.g., Soubrany, *Dix-neuf lettres,* 18–19 (letter of Jan. 15, 1793); Lebas, in Buchez and Roux, *Histoire parlementaire,* 35:335 (letter of Feb. 19).

55. Thompson, *French Revolution,* 353. See also Gillet, "Lettres du conventionnel," 245–246 (letter of Sept. 25, 1792); and Corbel, "Correspondance," letter of Dec. 28. Louvet had already ferociously attacked Robespierre during the debates on the war in the spring of 1792: see Linton, *Choosing Terror,* 120.

56. Robespierre's first letter to his constituency in Lefebvre, *Convention,* 1:63; and Pinet, "Correspondance," letter of Dec. 23, 1792. See also Jullien, "Correspondance," letter of Dec. 24.

57. See, e.g., Couppé in "Correspondance des députés des Côtes-du-Nord," 30 (1892), 117 (letter of Oct. 2, 1792); Corbel, "Correspondance," letter of Jan. 6, 1793; Jullien, "Correspondance," letter of Jan. 8, 1793.

58. Durand de Maillane, *Histoire,* 37; and Pinet, "Correspondance," letter of Jan. 8, 1793.

59. Among 25 Conventionnels whose correspondence for the period has been preserved, 19 initially opposed Robespierre and the Mountain (8 future Girondins, 8 future Montagnards, 3 from the Plain), 2 supported them (both from the Mountain), and 3 remained relatively neutral (1 from the Plain, and 2 from the Mountain). Factional alignments are taken from Patrick, *First French Republic,* appendix 4, 340–358.

60. The members of the *bureaux* through January 1793 have been reconstructed from *AP,* vols. 52–56. Of the nine members of the first Constitutional Committee, six were from the "inner circle" of Girondins (Brissot, Pétion, Vergniaud, Gensonné, Condorcet, and Paine) and only one, Danton, would have been identified with the Mountain. The two other members, Barère and Sieyès, had not yet aligned themselves with either faction.

61. Unidentified deputy speaking on Oct. 31, 1792, cited in Buchez and Roux, *Histoire parlementaire,* 19:458. See also Gillet, "Lettres du conventionnel," 256–257 (Dec. 10); and Dubreuil-Chambardel, *Lettres parisiennes,* 85 (letter of Dec. 21).

62. Vinet, "Lettres du conventionnel," 63 (letter of Jan. 22, 1793); Badinter in Furet and Ozouf, *La Gironde,* 358–360; Condorcet, *Chronique de Paris* (issues of Jan. 2 and 8); Durand de Maillane, *Histoire de la Convention nationale,* 37–38.

63. Brissot, *Correspondance et papiers,* 314 (letter of Nov. 28, 1792).

64. See esp. Jordan, *King's Trial,* 79–100.

65. The king was first mentioned in letters by Gaultier on Oct 17, 1792 (in Tempier, "Correspondance des deputes" [1892], 124); by Pinet, "Correspondance," on Oct. 23, 1792.

66. *AP,* 53:275–282.

67. For this and the following paragraph, see esp. *AP*, 54:88–337; Patrick, *First French Republic*, 39–54; and D. Edelstein, *Terror of Natural Right*, esp. 146–155.

68. Pinet, "Correspondance," letter of Nov. 21, 1792.

69. For a somewhat different emphasis, see D. Edelstein, *Terror of Natural Right*, esp. 146–154.

70. Guittard, *Journal*, 204 (entry of Dec. 7, 1792). "O que la probité est rare sur la terre," lamented Louchet: "Lettres," letter of Nov. 30. See also Blad, "Correspondance," letter of Dec. 8.

71. Blad, "Correspondance," letter of Dec. 8, 1792. See also, e.g., Blad, letter of Nov. 24; Couthon, *Correspondance inédite*, 208 (letter of Nov. 24); and Monestier, "Lettres," letter of Dec. 28.

72. Speeches by Dartigoeyte, Florent Guiot, and Albouys: *AP*, 52:89, 161, and 205.

73. The usage of the word "monstre" in the 102 speeches prepared or delivered in early December is based on a word search in a digitized version of the *AP*, 54:88–337. Note that the word "outlaw" *(hors-la-loi)* was specifically used only once in these speeches.

74. The final vote was unanimous according to Saint-Martin, "L'année 1792," 49 (letter of Dec. 3, 1792, misdated Oct. 3). See also Patrick, *First French Republic*, 47–54.

75. See *AP*, 54:740–747; 55:7–15 and 57:377; Jordan, *King's Trial*, 106–115.

76. Blad, "Correspondance," letter of Dec. 12, 1792; Monestier, "Lettres," letter of Dec. 13; Couthon, *Correspondance inédite*, 210 (letter of Dec. 13); Roubaud, "Lettres," 156 (letter of Dec. 13). See also Pinet, "Correspondance," letter of Dec. 12.

77. *AP*, 55:15; and Blad, "Correspondance," letter of Dec. 12, 1792.

78. See esp. Jordan, *King's Trial*, 126–140.

79. *AP*, 52:526 and Jordan, *King's Trial*, 144. The proposal had been mentioned but rejected in Mailhe's report on Nov. 7, 1792. See also the speech of Dec. 3 by the Girondin sympathizer Albouys: *AP*, 53:281 and 54:88–90.

80. Various Girondins spoke in support of the *appel au peuple* between Dec. 27 and Jan. 2. Louvet, Guadet, and Lanjuinais also published pamphlets in support of the measure ca. Jan. 7: see *AP*, 55:713–722; 56:passim; and 57:77. Also, for this and the following paragraph, see Patrick, *First French Republic*, 55–65; and Jordan, *King's Trial*, 144–160.

81. Their speeches against the *appel* were given between Dec. 27 and Jan. 4: *AP*, 55:706–710; and 56: passim. Marat's speech against the *appel* was published but never delivered: *AP*, 56:490–498. See also Patrick, *First French Republic*, 62–63; Pinet, "Correspondance," letter of Dec. 30, 1792; Jeanbon, *RH*, 30 (1896), 462–463 (letter of Jan. 2, 1793); Monestier, "Lettres," letter of Jan 3; Couthon, *Correspondance inédite*, 212 (letter of Jan. 5); and Soubrany, *Dix-neuf lettres*, 20 (letter of Jan. 15).

82. *AP*, 55:724–725; Gaultier in "Correspondance des députés des Côtes-du-Nord," 30 (1892), 149–151 (letters of Dec. 4 and 8, 1792); Monestier, "Lettres," letter of Dec. 28, 1792; and Dubreuil-Chambardel, *Lettres parisiennes*, 91 (letter of Jan. 15, 1793).

See also Saint-Prix, in Humbert de Soubeyran de Saint-Prix, "Hector de Soubeyran," 66 (letter of Dec. 3, 1792). On deputies carrying arms, see Blad, "Correspondance," letter of Jan. 23, 1793; and Vergniaud, *Vergniaud, manuscrits, lettres, et papiers,* 1:167 (letter of late January 1793).

83. *AP,* 56:168–170 and 181–186; Lefebvre, *Convention,* 1:198; Patrick, *First French Republic,* 61; Monestier, "Correspondance," letter of Jan. 8. Durand de Maillane, who sympathized with the Girondins, was convinced of their underlying desire to preserve the monarchy: Durand de Maillane, *Histoire de la Convention nationale,* 45.

84. Stamaty, *Lettres* (1872), letter of Jan. 3, 1793; Mareux, *Une famille de la bourgeoisie,* 329 (letter of Dec. 18, 1792). See also Colson, "Correspondance," letters of Jan. 16 and 18, 1793.

85. *AP,* 56:72–73.

86. Dubreuil-Chambardel, *Lettres parisiennes,* 88 (letter of Dec. 29, 1792). Also Blad, "Correspondance," undated letter of early Jan. 1793.

87. Monestier, "Correspondance," letter of Jan. 8, 1793; Cavaignac in Sol, *La Révolution en Quercy,* 2:392 (undated letter of Jan.); and Patrick, *First French Republic,* 89.

88. Pinet, "Correspondance," letter of Jan. 16, 1793; *AP,* 57:106–112; Patrick, *First French Republic,* 99; Jordan, *King's Trial,* 168–177. Nearly three-fourths of the deputies linked by Patrick to the Girondins would vote for the measure, but less than 2 percent of the Montagnards would so vote: Patrick, *First French Republic,* 93.

89. See esp. the printed opinions in *AP,* 57:112–326 and 342–407.

90. The word "monstre" was mentioned only 14 times by the 721 deputies announcing and justifying their votes. "Hors-la-loi" was never used; "droit des gens" was used 10 times by 6 deputies: word search of a digitized version of the *AP,* 57:112–326 and 342–407. Cf. D. Edelstein, *Terror of Natural Right,* esp. chap. 3.

91. *AP,* 57:366, 378, 391, 406.

92. *AP,* 57:342 and 384; Lebas in Stefane-Pol, *Autour de Robespierre,* 47 (letter of Jan. 21, 1793); Mercier, *Le nouveau Paris,* (1994), 319. See also Boyer-Fontfrède, AD Gironde, letter of Jan. 19; and Saint-Martin, "L'année 1792," 35 (letter of Jan. 24).

93. Patrick, *First French Republic,* 101–105; Jordan, *King's Trial,* 239–248; *AP,* 57:415 and 428.

94. On the execution, see, e.g., Guittard, *Journal,* 219 (entry of Jan. 21, 1793); Jordan, *King's Trial,* 208–221; and esp. Vaissière, *Mort du roi,* 103–129.

95. See esp. Vaissière, *Mort du roi,* 118–126; Mercier, *Le nouveau Paris* (1994), 323–325; Monestier, "Correspondance," letter of Jan. 29, 1793.

96. Mercier, *Le nouveau Paris* (1994), 323–324; Stamaty, *Lettres,* letters of Jan. 20 and 24, 1793; Colson, "Correspondance," letter of Jan. 23. See also Guittard, *Journal,* 219 (entry of Jan. 21); and Roubaud, "Lettres," 164 (letter of Jan. 22).

97. Roubaud, "Lettres," 159 (letter of Dec. 29, 1792). Compare Colson, "Correspondance," letter of Dec. 30.

98. Hunt, *Family Romance,* esp. chaps. 2 and 3.

99. *AP*, 57:384; Farge, *La vie fragile*, 209. See also Hunt, *Family Romance*, esp. 53–64.

100. Mercier, *Le nouveau Paris*, (1994), 326. See also Saint-Prix, in Humbert de Soubeyran de Saint-Prix, "Hector de Soubeyran de Saint-Prix," 67 (letter of Jan. 21, 1793); and D. Edelstein, *Terror of Natural Right*, esp. 17–25 and 140–142.

101. *AP*, 57:516 and 527; and Guittard, *Journal*, 220 (entry of Jan. 24).

102. *AP*, 57:519–520; Condorcet in *Chronique de Paris* (issue of Jan. 23, 1793). See also Saint-Prix, in Humbert de Soubeyran de Saint-Prix, "Hector de Soubeyran de Saint-Prix," 66 (letter of Dec. 3); Blad, "Correspondance," letter of Dec. 10; and Patrick, *First French Republic*, 98.

103. Guittard, *Journal*, 220 (entry of Jan. 24, 1793); *Révolutions de Paris* (issue of Jan. 19 to 26); Couthon, *Correspondance inédite*, 213 (letter of Jan. 26). See also Monestier, "Correspondance," letter of Jan. 29; and Blad, "Correspondance," letter of Jan. 26.

104. *AP*, 57:516; Lebas, in Stefane-Pol, *Autour de Robespierre*, 35:333 (letter of Jan. 21). See also Louchet, "Lettres," letter of Jan. 22; and Durand de Maillane, *Histoire*, 56.

10. The Crisis of '93

1. Vinet, "Lettres du conventionnel," 66 (letter of Feb. 25, 1793); Lebas in Stefane-Pol, *Autour de Robespierre*, 52 (letter of Apr. 21, 1793); P.-J.-L. Campmas, "Un conventionnel régicide," 213 and 247 (letters of Nov. 21, 1792 and Mar. 23, 1793); and Romme in Galante-Garrone, *Gilbert Romme*, 444 (letter of Feb. 28, 1793).

2. Brissot, *Patriote français* (issue of Oct. 7, 1789); P.-J.-L. Campmas, "Un conventionnel régicide," 247 (letter of Dec. 23, 1792); Ruault, *Gazette d'un Parisien*, 317 (letter of Oct. 18, 1792).

3. Aulard, *Etudes*, 3:25–33; Soboul, *Les sans-culottes*, 655–657; McPhee, *Robespierre*, 161; M. Robespierre, *Oeuvres*, 1:160 (letter of Feb. 15, 1793); and *AP*, 59:277 and 65:492. Chaillon first changed from "vous" to "tu" in addressing his friend in his letter of Nov. 12. The "tu" form seems virtually never to have been used in the Constituent Assembly.

4. Ruault, *Gazette d'un Parisien*, 324 (letter of Feb. 6, 1793). See also Jullien, "Correspondance," letter of Mar. 14.

5. See, e.g., Mercier, *Le nouveau Paris* (1994), 326–327; and Bancal, *Le conventionnel Bancal*, 273–274 (letter of Mar. 30, 1793).

6. *AP*, vols. 57–61, passim. Altogether during this period fifteen Convention officers were chosen from the Mountain, compared to seven from the Girondins, and two from the Plain.

7. See, e.g., *Révolutions de Paris* (issue of Feb. 16 to 23, 1793); Pinet, "Correspondance," letter of Feb. 20; Blad, "Correspondance," undated letter of late February.

8. Jullien, "Correspondance," letter of Feb. 2, 1793. See also Ruault, *Gazette d'un Parisien*, 327 (letter of Feb. 6); and Monestier, BN, letter of Feb. 2.

9. Blanning, *Origins of the French Revolutionary Wars,* 131–163; Sorel, *L'Europe et la Révolution,* 3:271–276; Lefebvre, *Convention,* 1:225–227.

10. *AP,* 56:114–116; 57:23–24.

11. *AP,* 58:112–114, 119–122. On the importance of the perceived insult to the Republic in the decision to declare war, see Pinet, "Correspondance," letter of Feb. 1, 1793.

12. Couthon, *Correspondance inédite,* 218, 223 (letters of Feb. 7 and Mar. 5, 1793); Bancal, *Le conventionnel Bancal,* 259 (letter of Feb. 21); Boyer-Fonfrède, AD Gironde, letters of Jan. 19 and Feb. 2. See also Monestier, BN, letter of Feb. 7; Dubreuil-Chambardel, *Lettres parisiennes,* 95 (letter of Mar. 5); and Blad, "Correspondance," letter of Mar. 2. In debates on military reform, both the Jacobin Dubois-Crancé and the Girondin Isnard agreed on "l'invincibilité de l'armée française": *AP,* 59:66. Among the Montagnard leadership, Robespierre, Collot, Danton, and Carnot all gave strong endorsements: Lefebvre, *Convention,* 1:239–242.

13. See, e.g., *AP,* 59:570–571, 602–603, 648–649; also Sorel, *L'Europe et la Révolution,* 3:312.

14. Pinet, "Correspondance," letter of Mar. 2, 1793; and Monestier, "Correspondance," letter of Mar. 2. See also Couthon, *Correspondance inédite,* 222 (letter of Mar. 5).

15. *AP,* 59:686–691.

16. Pinet, "Correspondance," letter of Feb. 24, 1793.

17. Blad, "Correspondance," letter of Feb. 20, 1793; *Les Révolutions de Paris* (issue of Feb. 16 to 23). See also Vinet, "Lettres du conventionnel," 66 (letter of Feb. 25).

18. Burstin, *Une Révolution,* 510.

19. For this paragraph and what follows, see esp. Burstin, *L'invention du sans-culotte;* and *Une Révolution,* 510, 514, 522, 527, 545, and 585. On moustaches, see Slavin, *Insurrection,* 115; Sutherland, *Murder in Aubagne,* 146; and Baumont, *Le département de l'Oise,* 302.

20. Jullien, "Correspondance," letter of Apr. 29, 1793. Compare with her husband, Marc-Antoine Jullien, "Correspondance," letter to his son, Dec. 15, 1792. See also the speech by Robespierre of May 8, cited in Lefebvre, *Convention,* 2:140.

21. Cited in Burstin, *Une Révolution,* 576. See also the speech by Chaumette of Feb. 27, cited in Lefebvre, *Convention,* 1:288.

22. Guittard, *Journal,* 235 (entry of Mar. 17, 1793).

23. On the general issue of women's rights in the French Revolution, see Chap. 3, note 66 in this book.

24. Guittard, *Journal,* 228–229 (entry of Feb. 25, 1793). Also Rudé, *Crowd,* 114–117; Lefebvre, *Convention,* 1:283–287; Burstin, *Une Révolution,* 531–533; Godineau, *Citoyennes et tricoteuses,* 126–127.

25. Godineau, *Citoyennes et tricoteuses,* 129; Burstin, *Une Révolution,* 564 and 566; Garrioch, *Bourgeosie,* 179–181.

26. Guittard, *Journal*, 251, 262 (entries of May 28 and July 4, 1793); Godineau, *Citoyennes et tricoteuses*, 129–135.

27. Jullien, "Correspondance," letter of May 2, 1793. For a full treatment of Jullien's activities in 1793–1794, see L. Parker, *Writing the Revolution*, esp. chap. 5.

28. Jullien, "Correspondance," letter of Apr. 29, 1793.

29. *AP*, 52:209 ("Règlement" of Sept. 28, 1792); and 58:113; Monestier, "Correspondance," letter of Feb. 2, 1793.

30. Blad, "Correspondance," letter of Apr. 15, 1793. See also Jullien, "Correspondance," letter of May 2.

31. Blad, "Correspondance," letter of May 10, 1793; Jullien, "Correspondance," letter of May 14; Godineau, *Citoyennes et tricoteuses*, 134–135. See also *AP*, 64:614–615.

32. Jullien, "Correspondance," letters of May 2 and June 11, 1793.

33. E.g., Jullien, "Correspondance," letter of Mar. 14; and Colson, "Correspondance," letter of Mar. 30, 1793. On parades through the hall, see, e.g., *AP*, 60:5–8.

34. Ruault, *Gazette d'un Parisien*, 332 (letter of May 16, 1793); Jullien, "Correspondance," letters of Mar. 10, May 5, and May 9; and *AP*, 60:1–3.

35. See, e.g., Markoff, *Abolition of Feudalism* 276; Jolivet, *La Révolution dans l'Ardèche*, 395; Fleury, *La ville et le district de Mamers*, 1:158–164; Arnaud, *Histoire de la Révolution*, 362–366.

36. See, e.g., Pommeret, *L'esprit politique*, 188–189; Jolivet, *La Révolution dans l'Ardèche*, 397–401; Girardot, *Le département de la Haute-Saône*, 2:202. For the regional distribution of unilateral actions by administrators, see Tackett, *Religion*, 277; also "The West in France," 740–743.

37. Dupuy, *Garde nationale*, 197–217.

38. Chassin, *Préparation*, 3:213 (letter of Jan. 24, 1793).

39. See Markoff, *Abolition of Feudalism*, 286 and 300. Markoff provides no separate category for recruitment riots, which are grouped with "counterrevolutionary events" (pp. 256–258). During the spring of 1793, and particularly in March, such events attained an all-time peak for the first five years of the Revolution.

40. Bertaud, *Army of the Revolution*, 94–96; Forrest, *Conscripts*, 23–25; Sol, *La Révolution en Quercy*, 2:442.

41. Blad, "Correspondance," letter of Mar. 25, 1793. See also, e.g., Arnaud, *Histoire de la Révolution*, 388–389, 409–416; Baumont, *Le département de l'Oise*, 232–234; Boutier, *Campagnes en émoi*, 212–213; Pommeret, *L'esprit politique*, 165–168; Girardot, *Le département de la Haute-Saône*, 2:206, 214.

42. Chassin, *Vendée patriote*, 17 (letter from Jolly, Mar. 24, 1793). The historian Paul Bois wrote of the long accumulating "capital" of grief and anger: cited in Martin, *Vendée*, 77.

43. See especially the letters in *AP*, 60:335–704, passim. Also, Chassin, *Préparation*, 3:378, 387; Lefebvre, *Convention*, 1:258–259; Martin, *Vendée*, 28, 45–46 and *Contre-Révolution*, 160–161.

44. See esp. *AP*, 60:558–560 and 590–594. Also Chassin, *Préparation*, 3:387.

45. Lefebvre, *Convention*, 2:53.

46. For this and the following paragraph see Lefebvre, *Convention*, 2:49; Martin, *La Vendée*, 164; Sutherland, *Chouans;* and Tackett, "The West in France."

47. On Marchais, see Lebrun, *Parole de Dieu et Révolution;* also the memoirs of curé François Chevallier in Chassin, *Préparation*, 3:333–335.

48. Chassin, *Préparation*, 358; Lebrun, *Parole de Dieu et Révolution*, 105–106; Martin, *Vendée*, 73, 82–84; Tackett, "The West in France."

49. Chassin, *Vendée patriote*, 17.

50. Chassin, *Préparation*, 3:333–334; and, more generally, 315–318, 340–345, 350; and Chassin, *Vendée patriote*, 5, 15; Lefebvre, *Convention*, 2:58–60; Martin, *Vendée*, 34.

51. On the social breakdown of competing forces, see Petitfrère, *Blancs et bleus d'Anjou,* esp. 1352–1353.

52. E.g., Chassin, *Préparation*, 3:359–360, and 504–506; and *Vendée patriote*, 16–17.

53. Chassin, *Vendée patriote*, 28.

54. Chassin, *Préparation*, 3:334 and 386.

55. See *AP*, 60:719–720 (statement by the Conseil exécutif provisoire of Mar. 30, 1793); Martin, *Vendée*, 43–46; Corbel, "Correspondance," letter of Mar. 30; and Chaillon, "Correspondance," letter of Mar. 25.

56. See esp. Martin, *Vendée*, chap. 1.

57. Sorel, *L'Europe et la Révolution*, 3:282–287; and Lefebvre, *Convention*, 1:143–146, 159–175, 244, 251–252, 316.

58. Sorel, *L'Europe et la Révolution*, 3:337–339, 347–349; Lefebvre, *Convention*, 1:290–293, 326–327, 353–354; and Blanning, *French Revolutionary Wars*, 88–106.

59. See notably Blad, "Correspondance," letter of Mar. 9, 1793; and *AP*, 59:623–621, 634–635, 667, 673, 677, 686–691.

60. Pinet, "Correspondance," letter of Mar. 10, 1793; and Boyer-Fonfrède, AD Gironde, letter of Mar. 9. See also Monestier, "Correspondance," letter of Mar. 9.

61. *AP*, 60:294–295.

62. Chaillon, "Correspondance," letter of Mar. 26, 1793; Dubreuil-Chambardel, *Lettres parisiennes*, 110 (letter of May 18); P.-J.-L. Campmas, "Un conventionnel régicide," 251 (letter of May 12). See also Guittard, *Journal*, 236–337 (entry of Mar. 19); Pinet, "Correspondance," letter of Mar. 29; and Louchet, "Lettres," letter of May 14.

63. E.g., Pinet, "Correspondance," letter of Mar. 20, 1793; Bancal, *Le conventionnel Bancal*, 268 (letter of Mar. 19).

64. Pinet, "Correspondance," letter of Mar. 13, 1793; and Gillet, "Lettres du conventionnel," 531–533 (letter of Mar. 18). See also Bancal, *Le conventionnel Bancal*, 261 (letter of Mar. 13); Boyer-Fonfrède AD Gironde, letter of Mar. 19; and *Révolutions de Paris* (issue of Mar. 16 to 23).

65. Pinet, "Correspondance," letter of Mar. 13, 1793. See also *AP*, 60:122; Bancal, *Le conventionnel Bancal*, 264 (letter of Mar. 14); Dyzèz, "Lettres," 211–212 (letter of Mar. 26); and the speech by Vergniaud, *AP*, 60:162 (Mar. 13).

66. Pinet, "Correspondance," letter of Mar. 29, 1793; and Lefebvre, *Convention*, 1:316–317 and 346–353.

67. Blad, "Correspondance," undated letter of ca. Apr. 3, 1793; and Pinet, "Correspondance," letter of Apr. 3. See also Dubreuil-Chambardel, *Lettres parisiennes*, 103 (letter of Apr. 6); and Louchet, "Lettres," letter of Apr. 2.

68. Colson, "Correspondance," letter of Apr. 3, 1793; and *Révolutions de Paris* (issue of Mar. 23 to 30). Also Guittard, *Journal*, 238 (entry of Mar. 28); Blad, "Correspondance," letter of Mar. 29; and Pinet, "Correspondance," letter of Mar. 29.

69. Biard, *Missionnaires*, 32–47 and 248–249; and *AP*, 60:9–10 and 61:306.

70. Biard, *Missionnaires*, 48–54. The two Montagnard deputies from Clermont-Ferrand differed on the advisability of sending off so many members of their "party": see Monestier, "Correspondance," letter of Feb. 23, 1793; and Couthon, *Correspondance inédite*, 222 (letter of Feb. 26).

71. See esp. Pinet, "Correspondance," letter of Mar. 10, 1793; Guittard, *Journal*, 233 (entry of Mar. 8); Jullien, "Correspondance," letter of Mar. 10; *AP*, 59:718–722, 60:1–5, 62–70, and 95–96. See also Wahnich, *La liberté ou la mort*, 59–63.

72. *AP*, 60:290–298.

73. Louchet, "Lettres," letter of Mar. 19, 1793. See also Bancal, *Le conventionnel Bancal*, 269 (letter of Mar. 19); Pinet, "Correspondance," letter of Mar. 24; Gillet, "Lettres du conventionnel," 531–533 (letter of Mar. 18); and the description in *Révolutions de Paris* (issue of Mar. 16 to 23).

74. *AP*, 60:386–390; Burstin, *Une Révolution*, 546–548. See also the Girondins: Boyer-Fonfrède, AD Gironde, letter of Mar. 19, 1793; Bancal, *Le conventionnel Bancal*, 270 (letter of Mar. 21); and Serge Aberdam in Pingué and Rothiot, *Les comités de surveillance*, 13–26.

75. *AP*, 61:63. See also Dubreuil-Chambardel, *Lettres parisiennes*, 105 (letter of Apr. 15, 1793); and Dyzèz, "Lettres," 214 (letter of Apr. 23).

76. Bancal, *Le conventionnel Bancal*, 262 (letter of Mar. 13, 1793); *AP*, 60:290; Lefebvre, *Convention*, 1:305, 331–333.

77. Gillet, "Lettres du conventionnel," 149–150 (letter of Apr. 7, 1793); also *AP*, 61:378, 396–397; Lefebvre, *Convention*, 1:359–360.

78. *AP*, 61:271–275; Lefebvre, *Convention*, 1:357, 2:3 and 6–9. See also Augustin Robespierre, in *Oeuvres de Maximilien Robespierre*, 1:163–165 (letters of Apr. 10 and 22, 1793); Couthon, *Correspondance inédite*, 232–233 (letter of May 18); Levasseur, *Mémoires*, 1:250; and Jullien, "Correspondance," letters of Mar. 12 and Apr. 16.

79. *AP*, 61:63 and 549.

80. See *AP*, vols. 62–64, passim. The substantial contingent of Montagnards sent on mission in mid-March would be summoned back at the end of April, but they

would return to the Convention only in the course of May: see Biard, *Missionnaires,* 45n and 404–407.

81. Louchet, "Lettres," letter of May 6, 1793. See also Lebas, cited in Buchez and Roux, *Histoire parlementaire,* 35:338 (letter of Apr. 21); and Jullien, "Correspondance," letter of May 23.

82. Lefebvre, *Convention,* 2:135. See also Boyer-Fonfrède, AD Gironde, letters to Bordeaux of May 7 and 15, 1793.

83. Slavin, *Insurrection,* 15–16.

84. *Patriote français* (issues of May 10 and 16, 1793).

85. The indictment was said to have been voted in a surprise evening session, when even many of those Montagnards still in Paris were absent: Pinet, "Correspondance," letter of Apr. 17, 1793; and Gillet, "Lettres du conventionnel," 166–167 (letter of Apr. 28).

86. See esp. Gillet, "Lettres du conventionnel," 164 (letter of Apr. 26, 1793); Jullien, "Correspondance," letter of Apr. 25; Pinet, "Correspondance," letter of Apr. 28; and Ruault, *Gazette d'un Parisien,* 331 (letter of Apr. 30).

87. Ruault, *Gazette d'un Parisien,* 330 (letter of Apr. 30, 1793); and Dubreuil-Chambardel, *Lettres parisiennes,* 107 (letter of Apr. 22). See also Louchet, "Lettres," letter of May 6; and *AP,* 64:152–153.

88. Lefebvre, *Convention,* 1:206; Burstin, *Une Révolution,* 545–546. Also, e.g., Barbaroux, *Correspondance et mémoires,* 347–348 (letter of Mar. 14, 1793); and Blad, "Correspondance," letter of Apr. 10.

89. Gillet, "Lettres du conventionnel," 172 (letter of May 4, 1793); Guittard, *Journal,* 243–244 (entry of Apr. 18); *Révolutions de Paris* (issue of May 6 to 13); Burstin, *Une Révolution,* 565–566; and Godineau, *Citoyennes et tricoteuses,* 134.

90. Only 325 deputies voted in the election for Commission members: *AP,* 65:138. See also Monestier, letter of May 29, 1793; Louchet, "Lettres," letter of May 28; Jullien, "Correspondance," letter of May 28; Burstin, *Une Révolution,* 570; and Godineau, *Citoyennes et tricoteuses,* 136–137.

91. *AP,* 65:320.

92. Ruault, *Gazette d'un Parisien,* 336 (letter of May 30, 1793). See also Guittard, *Journal,* 251–252 (entry of May 28); Jullien, "Correspondance," letter of May 28; and Blad, "Correspondance," letter of May 29.

93. Slavin, *Insurrection,* 68–89; Lefebvre, *Convention,* 2:147–150 and 171–181; Burstin, *Une Révolution,* 570–572; Godineau, *Citoyennes et tricoteuses,* 137–138.

94. See Jullien, "Correspondance," letter of June 2, 1793; and Garat, *Mémoires sur la Révolution,* 112–113.

95. For this and what follows, see esp. Lefebvre, *Convention,* 2:184–207 and Slavin, *Insurrection,* 90–105. Also, Monestier, BN, letter of May 29, 1793; Jullien, "Correspondance," letter of June 2; Ruault, *Gazette d'un Parisien,* 336–337 (letter of June 5); Blad, "Correspondance," letter of June 1; and *AP,* 65:638–658, although the official minutes are certainly incomplete.

96. Guittard, *Journal,* 253 (entry of May 31, 1793). See also Dubreuil-Chambardel, *Lettres parisiennes,* 111–112 (letter of June 1).

97. Blad, "Correspondance," letter of June 1, 1793. See also Guittard, *Journal,* 254 (entry of June 1).

98. Wallon, *La révolution du 31 mai,* 279; Lefebvre, *Convention,* 2:221; Slavin, *Insurrection,* 111–112; Godineau, *Citoyennes et tricoteuses,* 138. Among the Girondin leadership, only Isnard, Fauchet, Lanthenas, Lanjuinais, Barbaroux, Boyer-Fonfrède, and Vergniaud are known to have been present: *AP,* 65:690–708.

99. For this and what follows, see esp. Wallon, *La révolution du 31 mai,* 278–287; Lefebvre, *Convention,* 2:216–229; Slavin, *Insurrection,* 110–116; *Thermomètre du jour* (issue of June 4, 1793). Minutes in the *AP* are very incomplete.

100. Slavin, *Insurrection,* 114; Boissy d'Anglas in Jolivet, *La Révolution dans l'Ardèche,* 428 (letter of June 3, 1793); and Garat, *Mémoires sur la Révolution,* 141.

101. The most reliable descriptions of what followed are by those who were present: the deputy Jacques Dulaure in *Thermomètre du Jour* (issue of June 4, 1793); and the accounts of the deputies Jean-Baptiste-Michel Saladin and Jacques Brival, in Buchez et Roux, *Histoire parlementaire,* 28:30–54 and 60–67.

102. Saladin, in Buchez and Roux, *Histoire parlementaire,* 28:45.

103. Colson, "Correspondance," letter of June 5, 1793.

104. *Thermomètre du Jour* (issue of June 5, 1793); and Lefebvre, *Convention,* 2:228–229. See also Pinet, "Correspondance," letter of June 5; and Monestier, "Correspondance," letter of June 11.

105. Mercier, *Le nouveau Paris* (1994), 327.

106. Couthon, *Correspondance inédite,* 227–228 (letter of May 9, 1793); Petit, letter of May 27, cited in Lefebvre, *Convention,* 2:32–33; Dubreuil-Chambardel, *Lettres parisiennes,* 103 (letter of Apr. 6). Similar arguments were made by Monestier, "Correspondance," letter of Feb. 26; Pinet, "Correspondance," letter of Mar. 29; Boyer-Fonfrède, AD Gironde, letter of Mar. 19; and Louchet, "Lettres," letter of Apr. 6.

107. D. Edelstein, esp. 132–133. The explanation given here for the origin of a "killing Terror" is quite different from that of Edelstein.

108. Monestier, "Correspondance," letter of Feb. 26, 1793; Boyer-Fonfrède, AD Gironde, letter of Mar. 28; Corbel, "Correspondance," letter of Mar. 17; Carnot, letter of Mar. 18, cited in Lefebvre, *Convention,* 2:86. See also Blad, "Correspondance," letter of Apr. 1.

109. *Révolutions de Paris* (issue of Mar. 23 to 30, 1793). Compare Prudhomme's *Histoire générale,* published in 1797.

11. Revolution and Terror until Victory

1. Dubreuil-Chambardel, *Lettres parisiennes,* 114, (letter of June 8, 1793). See also Jullien, "Correspondance," letter of June 20; and Pinet, "Correspondance," letter of June 14.

2. Soboul, *Les sans-culottes,* 60; Godineau, *Citoyennes et tricoteuses,* 140–141; Couthon, *Correspondance inédite,* 242 (letter of June 27, 1793).

3. See, e.g., Sutherland, *Murder in Aubagne,* 148–150; Edmonds, " 'Federalism,' " 28–30, and 46; and Lucas, *Structure of the Terror,* 48–50.

4. *AP,* 60:708–712 (report on Salle); Barbaroux, *Correspondance et mémoires,* e.g., 364 (letter of May 21, 1793); Vergniaud, *Vergniaud, manuscrits, lettres, et papiers,* 2:153 (letter of May 5); Forrest, *Revolutionary Bordeaux,* 98–105; Hanson, *Jacobin Republic,* 66–68.

5. Edmonds, *Jacobinism and the Revolt of Lyon,* 187–190; Lucas, *Structure of the Terror,* 36–38; W. Scott, *Revolutionary Marseilles;* Dubois, *Histoire,* 3:205–208.

6. Hanson, *Jacobin Republic,* 63–65. Also, Lefebvre, *Gouvernement révolutionnaire,* 26–42; and Edmonds, " 'Federalism,' " 23–25, and 51.

7. Baumont, *Le département de l'Oise,* 253–255; Brégail, "Le Gers pendant la Révolution," 32 (1931), 261–264; Dubois, *Histoire,* 3:198–201 and 282–283; Fleury, *La ville et le district de Mamers,* 1:186; Girardot, *Le département de la Haute-Saône,* 2:229–230; and Jolivet, *La Révolution dans l'Ardèche,* 428–438. See also Garat, *Mémoires,* 144–145.

8. On the arrest of representatives on mission, see Forrest, *Revolutionary Bordeaux,* 112–113; Biard, *Siège de Lyon,* 10 and 19; and Hanson, *Jacobin Republic,* 69.

9. Hanson, *Jacobin Republic,* 74–76, 87–89, 93–95; and Garat, *Mémoires,* 156–157.

10. Hanson, *Jacobin Republic,* 68–72 and *Provincial Politics,* 115–156; and Corgne, *Pontivy,* 301–304.

11. Forrest, *Revolutionary Bordeaux,* 145–146.

12. E.g., Jullien, "Correspondance," letter of May 26, 1793.

13. Forrest, *Revolutionary Bordeaux,* 118–119, 145–146, and 167; Hanson, *Jacobin Republic,* 71–72, 76, 88, 90, and 95; Corgne, *Pontivy,* 303–304; Dubois, *Histoire,* 3:209; Lucas, *Structure of the Terror,* 38; and Sutherland, *Murder in Aubagne,* 165–167. Also Lefebvre, *Gouvernement révolutionnaire,* 31–32 and 43.

14. Hanson, *Jacobin Republic,* 68–72; and Forrest, *Revolutionary Bordeaux,* 145–157.

15. Edmonds, *Revolt in Lyon,* esp. Conclusion, and " 'Federalism' and Urban Revolt," 22–53. Also W. Scott, *Revolutionary Marseilles,* chap. 5; and Crook, *Journées révolutionnaires,* 71–82.

16. Jullien, "Correspondance," letter of July 8, 1793; and *AP,* 66:537. On the boycott, see Fonfrède's statement of June 2: *AP,* 66:8. There were no letters from Blad between June 5—the shortest he ever wrote—and July 20, when he announced he had "taken up my correspondence once again." The list of the seventy-five protesters is in *AP,* 75:521. See also Saint-Martin, "Journal," entry of Aug. 2, 1794.

17. See *AP,* vols. 66–77: passim. Among those elected president from June through September 1793 were Danton, Robespierre, Collot d'Herbois, Thuriot, Hérault de Séchelles, Jeanbon-Saint-André, and Billaud-Varenne. From June 13 through October 22, 1793, twenty-six of twenty-nine secretaries were Montagnards, with the three re-

maining coming from the Plain. For the vote on July 25, the only occasion during this period when all individuals receiving votes were listed, see *AP*, 69:523–524. For factional affiliations, see Patrick, *First French Republic*, 340–357.

18. See Gershoy, *Bertrand Barère*, esp. 113–115; and Palmer, *Twelve Who Ruled*, esp. 31. On the unhappiness of the Montagnards with June 2, see also Levasseur, *Mémoires*, 1:266.

19. *AP*, 66:109–112. See also Garat, *Mémoires*, 141. According to Barère, the hostage idea was first proposed by Danton: Barère, *Mémoires*, 2:94–96.

20. *AP*, 66:172. See also Durand de Maillane, *Histoire*, 131.

21. *AP*, 66:7; and Perroud, *La proscription*, 43–44. See also Dubreuil-Chambardel, *Lettres parisiennes*, 114 (letter of June 8, 1793); Saint-Martin, "Journal," entry of Aug. 2, 1794; and Garat, *Mémoires*, 142.

22. Couthon, *Correspondance inédite*, 236 and 246 (letters of June 20 and 27, 1793). See also Jullien, "Correspondance," letter of July 16; Garat, *Mémoires*, 149; and Lefebvre, *Gouvernement révolutionnaire*, 35–36.

23. Dubreuil-Chambardel, *Lettres parisiennes*, 117 (letter of June 15, 1793). See also Soubrany, *Dix-neuf lettres*, 21 (letter of July 9).

24. The Constitution of 1793 was about 5 1/2 pages in its published form; that of 1791 had been some 15 pages: *AP*, 30:151–168; and 67:143–150.

25. Taveau, "Lettres," letter of June 14, 1793; Vinet, "Lettres du conventionnel," 67–68 (letter of June 18); and Barbaroux, *Correspondance et mémoires*, 375 (letter of June 13). See also the non-Jacobin sympathizers with the Mountain: Besson, "Lettres inédites," 144–145 (letter of June 12); and François-Marie Moreau, cited in Lefebvre, *Gouvernement révolutionnaire*, 8 (letter of June 4).

26. Patrick found 95 non-Montagnard deputies who sat in committees and 37 others who served as representatives on mission. Only 119 in the Plain seem never to have so participated: *First French Republic*, 345–351.

27. Perroud, *La proscription*, 58; and Mazeau, *Le bain de l'histoire*, 38n.

28. Hanson, *Jacobin Republic*, 69–70, 77–78; and Biard, *Le siège de Lyon*, 16–17.

29. Dubreuil-Chambardel, *Lettres parisiennes*, 121 (letters of June 27, 1793). See also Dyzèz, "Lettres," 217 (letter of June 13); Couthon, *Correspondance inédite*, 241 (letter of June 25); Jullien, "Correspondance," letters of June 25 and 30; Ruault, *Gazette d'un Parisien*, 339–340 (letters of June 11 and July 8); and Garat, *Mémoires*, 146.

30. Mazeau, *Le bain de l'histoire*, esp. 214–223; Walter, *Tribunal révolutionnaire*, 37–81.

31. Ruault, *Gazette d'un Parisien*, 341–342 (letter of July 26, 1793); and Mazeau, *Le bain de l'histoire*, 82, 88–89, 94–95, 104–108.

32. *AP*, 68:710 and 715–718; and Pinet, "Correspondance," letter of July 14, 1793.

33. *AP*, 69:20; Mazeau, *Le bain de l'histoire*, 140–142; and Guittard, *Journal*, 266 and 268 (entries of July 16 and 28). See also Guilhaumou, *La mort de Marat*.

34. *AP,* 68:722–723; and 69:21–31. See also Pinet, "Correspondance," letter of July 17, 1793; Jullien, "Correspondance," letter of July 16; and Mazeau, *Le bain de l'histoire,* 102–103, 109, 112–114, and 119.

35. *AP,* 69:631; and Mazeau, *Le bain de l'histoire,* 38n and 106.

36. Reinhard, *Carnot,* 376 and 382.

37. Pinet, "Correspondance," letters of July 31 and Aug. 18, 1793; and Couthon, *Correspondance inédite,* 255 (letter of Aug. 1). See also Jullien, "Correspondance," letters of July 26 and 28.

38. *AP,* 68:513–514 and 521.

39. M. Robespierre in *Papiers inédits,* 2:14; Garat, *Mémoires,* 53, 56–58, and 154; and Barère, *Mémoires,* 2:115–116. For the dating of Robespierre's notes, see Lefebvre, *Gouvernement révolutionnaire,* 81. See also Robespierre's speech on Aug. 12: *AP,* 72:103.

40. *AP,* 70:91–103.

41. Jullien, "Correspondance," letter of June 20, 1793; and *AP,* 73:411. See also Burstin, *Une Révolution à l'oeuvre,* 600–601 and 610; and Palmer, *Twelve Who Ruled,* 64–65.

42. Blad, "Correspondance," letter of July 24, 1793; Couthon, *Correspondance inédite,* 254–255 (letters of July 25 and Aug. 1); *AP,* 70:109; and Lefebvre, *Gouvernement révolutionnaire,* 86. See also Garat, *Mémoires,* 156.

43. Mathiez, *La vie chère,* 1:239 and 266–269; Soboul, *Les sans-culottes,* 92–101; Burstin, *Une Révolution,* 610; and Mazeau, *Le bain de l'histoire,* 138–139.

44. Godineau, *Citoyennes et tricoteuses,* 147 and 154–159; and Soboul, *Les sans-culottes,* 93–94, 144, 153–154, and 226–228.

45. *AP,* 72:674; and Aberdam, "L'élargissement du droit de vote," 109. Also Desan, *Family on Trial,* 64–67.

46. Jullien, "Correspondance," letters of July 7, 21 and 26, and Sept. 16, 1793. See also L. Parker, *Writing the Revolution,* 103.

47. Burstin, *Une Révolution,* 605. See also Mathiez, *La vie chère,* 1:239 and 270–271; Lefebvre, *Gouvernement révolutionnaire,* 21–22; Soboul, *Les sans-culottes,* 58–64, 92–103, and 225.

48. Aberdam, "Un aspect du référendum," 213–214. Also M. Edelstein, *Birth of Electoral Democracy,* 289–309.

49. *AP,* 67:557; Baticle, "Le plébisite," 57 (1909) 496–499 and 504; Woloch, *New Regime,* 89; Aberdam, "Un aspect du référendum," 213–214. A small number of cantons did submit "Federalist" critiques of the Convention: Baticle, "Le plébisite," 58 (1910), 195–196. See also M. Edelstein, *Birth of Electoral Democracy,* 298.

50. Baticle, "Le plébisite," 58 (1910), 27–30. On the celebration in Grenoble, see Jullien, "Correspondance," letter of July 21, 1793.

51. Jullien, "Correspondance," letters of July 7 and 8, 1793. See also Guittard, *Journal,* 262 (entry of July 4); and Pinet, "Correspondance," letter of July 7.

52. Mathiez, *La vie chère*, 1:293; Burstin, *Une Révolution*, 597; Aberdam, "Un aspect du référendum," 219–220; and Jullien, "Correspondance," letter of July 28, 1793.

53. Pinet, "Correspondance," letter of Aug. 11, 1793; Blad, "Correspondance," letter of Aug. 12; Guittard, *Journal*, 271 (entry of Aug. 10); Aberdam, "Un aspect du référendum," 214–215; and Ozouf, *La fête révolutionnaire*, 99–100.

54. *AP*, 72:160 and 675. See also Blad, "Correspondance," letter of Aug. 17, 1793; and Aberdam, "Un aspect du référendum," 223.

55. Some were still visiting the Convention at the end of August: Blad, "Correspondance," letter of Aug. 26, 1793; and Aberdam, "Un aspect du référendum," 220 and 223.

56. *AP*, 72:101; and Mathiez, *La vie chère*, 1:293–294. See also Bertaud, *Army*, 102–104.

57. *AP*, 72:674–680; Barère, *Mémoires*, 106–107; Gershoy, *Bertrand Barère*, 176–178; Soboul, *Les sans-culottes*, 112–115; and Bell, *Total War*, 148.

58. *AP*, 72:101; Mathiez, *La vie chère*, 1:307–308; Soboul, *Les sans-culottes*, 159–163; Cobb, *Armées révolutionnaires*, 55; and Jourdan, "Discours de la terreur," 63.

59. Alpaugh, *Non-violence and the French Revolution*, appendix.

60. *AP*, 73:341–342; Cobb, *Armées révolutionnaires*, 55; and Soboul, *Les sans-culottes*, 161–162. See also Crook, *Journées révolutionnaires à Toulon*, 71–82.

61. See *AP*, 73:395; Mathiez, *La vie chère*, 1:312–315; Soboul, *Les sans-culottes*, 165–170; Cobb, *Armées révolutionnaires*, 56–57; and Burstin, *Une Révolution*, 618.

62. For this and the following two paragraphs, see esp. *AP*, 73:413–423 and 418n–419n; Mathiez, *La vie chère*, 1:321–326; and Lefebvre, *Gouvernement révolutionnaire*, 107–108.

63. *AP*, 73:423–428; Gershoy, *Bertrand Barère*, 180–181; and Simonin, *Le déshonneur*, 284–293.

64. Kuscinski, *Dictionnaire des Conventionnels*, entry "Barère." Nine of the members seem to have been present: Hérault, Prieur de la Marne, Prieur de la Côte-d'Or, Carnot, Thuriot, Robespierre, Barère, Jeanbon-Saint-André, and Saint-Just: Aulard, *Recueil des actes*, 6:282–284.

65. Garat, *Mémoires*, 114; M. Robespierre, *Papiers inédits*, 2:15.

66. They also invited in Danton, but he refused to enter the Committee, having publically announced for over a month that he would never take such a position.

67. Lefebvre, *Gouvernement révolutionnaire*, 119–120; Soboul, *Les sans-culottes*, 221–229; and Godineau, 163–177. The Convention took the occasion to abolish all women's clubs. See Chap. 12 in this book.

68. *AP*, 73:415; Lefebvre, *Gouvernement révolutionnaire*, 109; Soboul, *Les sans-culottes*, 183–188.

69. While there were at least 104 collective protests in the first three quarters of 1793, there would be only 3 from October through December: Alpaugh, *Non-violence and the French Revolution*, appendix.

70. Lefebvre, *Gouvernement révolutionnaire*, 108; Palmer, *Twelve Who Ruled*, 53–56; Gershoy, *Bertrand Barère*, 182. See also Martin, *Violence et révolution*, 186–193; and Jourdan, "Les discours de la Terreur."

71. *AP*, 73:599.

72. Cobb, *Armées révolutionnaires*, 40–48 and 57. Similar paramilitary "armies" were soon created in other regions of France.

73. *AP*, 74:303–304.

74. Jullien, "Correspondance," letter of Oct. 2, 1793. Also *AP*, 74:303–304; Lefebvre, *Gouvernement révolutionnaire*, 113–114, 118, and 131; and Burstin, *Une Révolution*, 602–603.

75. On the number of prisoners in Paris: *AP*, 72:603 (Aug. 21, 1793) and 77:692 (Oct. 27). Between these two dates the prisoner population in Paris rose from 1,634 to 3,098. See also Godfrey, *Revolutionary Justice*, 59.

76. See, e.g., Robespierre's complaint to the Jacobins on Aug. 11, 1793: Aulard, *Société des Jacobins*, 5:341.

77. Godfrey, *Revolutionary Justice*, 137 and 142–143; Greer, *Incidence of the Terror*, 113. According to Godfrey's tables I and II, during the seven months from April through September, 289 cases were tried and 70 (24 percent) led to death sentences; but in the five months from October to February 1794, 743 cases were tried and 322 (42 percent) led to death sentences. Note, however, that a significant number were acquitted or had their cases dismissed for insufficient evidence.

78. *AP*, 75:123, 131–132, 134–135; Lefebvre, *Gouvernemet révolutionnaire*, 123–124; and Palmer, *Twelve Who Ruled*, 71–72.

79. *AP*, 74:52, 106, and 109; Palmer, *Twelve Who Ruled*, 65–66; and Godfrey, *Revolutionary Justice*, 58–59.

80. *AP*, 70:104–105.

81. *AP*, 76:313–317; Palmer, *Twelve Who Ruled*, 74–75; and Soboul, *Les sans-culottes*, 238–239.

82. Jullien, "Correspondance," letter of July 28, 1793; and Dubreuil-Chambardel, *Lettres parisiennes*, 126 (letter of Sept. 11).

83. Garat, *Mémoires*, 131, remembered Hébert's vindictive fury after his arrest by the Commission. See also Soboul, *Les sans-culottes*, 215–216; and Hébert's testimony in Walter, *Actes du Tribunal révolutionnaire*, 268.

84. Jullien, "Correspondance," letter of June 30, 1793. See also Perroud, *La proscription*, 69–70.

85. *AP*, 67:105, 69:631 and 70:134; Couthon, *Correspondance inédite*, 247 (letter of July 9, 1793); Blad, "Correspondance," letter of July 20; Mazeau, *Le bain de l'histoire*, 38n. By the end of the summer some sixty Girondin sympathizers had been ordered arrested—though well over half had succeeded in escaping: Perroud, *La proscription*, 87.

86. Perroud, *La proscription*, 118.

87. *AP,* 75:399; Perroud, *La proscription,* 94–95; and Soboul, *Les sans-culottes,* 235.

88. Perroud, *La proscription,* 102 and 120.

89. *AP,* 75:522–534.

90. Apparently seventeen of the seventy-five were never found: Perroud, *La proscription,* 108, 111–112, 116–117, 141, 143, and 149. When Blad last wrote to his constituency on Oct. 2, he gave no indication of an impending arrest. See also Durand, *Histoire,* 127–128, and 170–172; Dyzèz, "Lettres," 224 (letter of Oct. 5, 1793); and Jullien, "Correspondance," letter of Oct. 5.

91. Jullien, "Correspondance," letter of Nov. 1, 1793. On the judges and jury, see Walter, *Actes du Tribunal révolutionnaire,* 236; and Godfrey, *Revolutionary Justice,* chap. 2.

92. Jullien, "Correspondance," letter of Oct. 26, 1793. Among the "small fry" were the deputies Sillery, Minvielle, and Boilleau.

93. For this and what follows, see esp. Walter, *Actes du Tribunal révolutionnaire,* 236–350.

94. Jullien, "Correspondance," letter of Nov. 1, 1793.

95. Walter, *Actes du Tribunal révolutionnaire,* 256–257 and 272–275.

96. *AP,* 78:26–27; and Walter, *Actes du Tribunal révolutionnaire,* 324–325.

97. Walter, *Actes du Tribunal révolutionnaire,* 342.

98. Jullien, "Correspondance," letter of Nov. 1, 1793; and Walter, *Actes du Tribunal révolutionnaire,* 338–339.

99. See the decree of Dec. 16, 1792: *AP,* 55:79.

100. Jullien, "Correspondance," letter of Nov. 1, 1793.

101. Walter, *Actes du Tribunal révolutionnaire,* 347–349. See also Jullien, "Correspondance," letter of Nov. 4, 1793; and Guittard, *Journal,* 290 (entry of Oct. 31).

12. The Year II and the Great Terror

1. See, e.g., Blad, "Correspondance," letter of July 20, 1793; Vinet, "Lettres du conventionnel," 68 (letter of June 18); and Chaillon, "Correspondance," letter of Sept. 30. On the destruction of personal accounts, see also the diary of Saint-Martin, "Journal," entry of 15 Thermidor Year II (Aug. 2, 1794).

2. Ruault, *Gazette d'un Parisien,* 347 (postscript to letter of Jan. 16, 1794); and Jullien, "Correspondance," letter of Feb. 24. Boisy d'Anglas sometimes hid more personal observations by writing them on the inside margins of the official bulletin of the laws sent to a friend: Jolivet, *La Révolution dans l'Ardèche,* 428.

3. Woloch, *New Regime,* esp. chaps. 5 to 8; and Lefebvre, *Gouvernement révolutionnaire,* 252–259. Also Marragon, "Lettres," letters of Dec. 28, 1793 and May 20, 1794.

4. Jullien was deeply stirred by Saint-Just's efforts: "Les malheureux sont les puissances de la terre, comme dit Saint-Just": "Correspondance," letter of May 31, 1794.

5. Guittard, *Journal,* 318 and 320–321 (entries of Feb. 4 and 18, 1794).

6. Desan, *Family on Trial,* esp. chap. 3.

7. On the suppression of women's clubs, see Guittard, *Journal,* 289–290 (entry of Oct. 31, 1793); Godineau, *Citoyennes et tricoteuses,* 169–174; and Burstin, *Une Révolution,* 564 and 624–625. On the continuing participation of women in politics after October, see esp. Godineau, *Citoyennes et tricoteuses,* 174–196; and Jullien, "Correspondance," letters of Nov. 1793 through the summer of 1794. Also, L. Parker, *Writing the Revolution,* esp. 89–104.

8. Gross, *Fair Shares for All,* esp. 32 and chaps. 2 and 3; Galante Garonne, *Gilbert Romme,* 341–346; and Biard, *Missionnaires,* esp. 282–285.

9. For this and the following paragraph see, e.g., McManners, *French Revolution and the Church,* esp. chap. 10; and Vovelle, *Révolution contre l'église.*

10. Colson, "Correspondance," letter of Dec. 25, 1792; Guittard, *Journal,* 252 (entry of May 30, 1793); Schmidt, *Tableaux de la Révolution française,* 350–351 (observation of May 30); and Lefebvre, *Convention,* 2:176.

11. Baczko, *Lumières de l'utopie,* 211–232. Jullien "Correspondance," first began using the new dating system in her correspondence on Nov. 1, 1793, writing "primidi [first day of the decade] 11 brumaire [the foggy month], 2ème de la République."

12. See Bossut, *Chaumette,* esp. chap. 11.

13. Guittard, *Journal,* 294–295, 297, and 300 (entries of Oct. 11 and 13, Nov. 10 and 20, and Dec. 10. 1793).

14. Guittard, *Journal,* 337 (entry of Apr. 13, 1794).

15. Ruault, *Gazette d'un Parisien,* 343–345, letters of Dec. 1 and undated "December" 1793.

16. Jullien, "Correspondance," letter of Nov. 18, 1793. See also Menozzi, *Interprétations politiques de Jésus.*

17. See Robespierre's speech: *AP,* 80:712–713; and the Convention's decree, 81:30; also Jullien, "Correspondance," letters of Dec. 4, 7, and 18; and Ruault, *Gazette d'un Parisien,* 344–345 (letter of "December" 1793).

18. Jullien, "Correspondance," letter of June 9, 1794; Guittard, *Journal,* 388–390 (entries of June 8 and 12); Ruault, *Gazette d'un Parisien,* 351 (letter of June 21). On festivals of the Supreme Being elsewhere in France, see Smyth, "Public Experience," 155–176.

19. See esp. Forrest, *Conscripts and Deserters.*

20. See Déplanche, "French Revolution and the Origins of Modern Youth Movements."

21. Chorus of the "Chant du départ," written by Etienne-Nicolas Méhul and Marie-Joseph Chénier in 1794. See Lefebvre, *Gouvernement révolutionnaire,* 302–303; Berthaud, *Révolution armée,* esp. 2e partie; Forrest, *Soldiers of the French Revolution,* esp. chap. 6.

22. McPhee, *Robespierre,* 180.

23. Lefebvre, *Gouvernement révolutionnaire*, 306–307; Berthaud, *Révolution armée*, esp. 2e partie, chaps. 1 and 2; and Blanning, *French Revolutionary Wars*, 107–127.

24. See esp. Palmer, *Twelve Who Ruled*, esp. chap. 4; Biard, *Missionnaires*, 286–321.

25. See Lefebvre, *Gouvernement révolutionnaire*, 193; Bertaud and Reichel, *Atlas*, 46–47.

26. Chaillon, "Correspondance," letters of 27 Nivôse, 16 Pluviôse, and 8 Prairial Year II (Jan. 16, Feb. 4, and May 27, 1794); Lefebvre, *Gouvernement révolutionnaire*, 277.

27. Sorel, *L'Europe et la Révolution*, 3:538; Palmer, *Twelve Who Ruled*, 96–97.

28. Jullien, "Correspondance," letter of Dec. 24, 1793; Guittard, *Journal*, 305 (entry of Dec. 25).

29. Martin, *La Vendée et la France*, 167–184.

30. Chaillon, "Correspondance," letters of 16, 18, 15, 30 Messidor and 3 Thermidor Year II (July 4 to 20, 1794); and Vadier, in Albert Tournier, *Vadier*, 210 (letter of July 13).

31. Guittard, *Journal*, 306–308 (entry of Dec. 30, 1793).

32. Marragon, "Lettres," letter of June 9, 1794. See also Guittard, *Journal*, 396 (entry of June 29). Also Spang, *Invention of the Restaurant*, 109–112.

33. Jullien, "Correspondance," letters of July 2 and 15, 1794; and Guittard, *Journal*, 410–412 (entries of July 14 and 15). See also Spang, *Invention of the Restaurant*, 112–118.

34. Jullien, "Correspondance," letter of July 15, 1794; and Guittard, *Journal*, 343–437 (entries between late April and early July).

35. Palmer, *Twelve Who Ruled*, 275; and McPhee, *Robespierre*, 185–186. Compare the analysis of Marisa Linton, *Choosing Terror*, esp. chap. 9.

36. Palmer, *Twelve Who Ruled*, 266.

37. McPhee, *Robespierre*, esp. chaps. 10–12; and Palmer, *Twelve Who Ruled*, 264–266, and 275.

38. Biard, *Missionnaires*, 333–335; and *Le siège de Lyon*, chap. 3.

39. Chaillon, "Correspondance," letters of Brumaire through Nivôse Year II (October 1793 through January 1794); and esp. of 24 and 30 Nivôse (Jan. 13 and 19, 1794). It would appear that two of Chaillon's sons were killed in the wars.

40. Palmer, *Twelve Who Ruled*, 220–224; Biard, *Missionnaires*, 330–333; Martin, *La Vendée et la France*, chap. 6.

41. Patrick, *First French Republic*, 340–341, identifies the "inner sixty" (actually 59); their later fate can be followed in Kuscinski, *Dictionnaire des Conventionnels*. Thirty-four of the 59 (58 percent) died from execution or suicide. Of all 179 "Girondins" and "Girondin supporters" listed by Patrick, *First French Republic*, 340–344, 41 (23 percent) died violent deaths during the Terror, another 66 (37 percent) were imprisoned and survived, and 27 (15 percent) successfully fled and survived. Only 45 (25 percent) remained untouched in the Convention. See also Perroud, *La proscription*, 126–138.

42. Tackett, "Constituent Assembly and the Terror," 39.

43. On Danton, see esp. Lefebvre, *La Première Terreur,* 36–53. On Desmoulins, see esp. Linton, "Friends, Enemies, and the Role of the Individual."

44. For this and the following, see esp. Palmer, *Twelve Who Ruled,* 287–303; and Lefebvre, *Gouvernement révolutionnaire,* chaps. 8 and 11.

45. Guittard, *Journal,* 328–330 (entry of March 24, 1794). Among deputies in the Convention, both Chaillon and Dubreuil, who habitually avoided internal politics in their letters, volunteered their conviction that those executed were guilty of treason; Dyzèz did likewise: Chaillon, "Correspondance," letters of 30 Ventôse and 3 Germinal Year II (March 20 and 23, 1794); Dubreuil-Chambardel, *Lettres parisiennes,* 134 (letter of March 25); and Dyzèz, "Lettres," 509 (letter of Mar. 15). See also Slavin, *Hébertistes to the Guillotine,* esp. chaps. 4 to 8.

46. See esp. Linton, "Fatal Friendships."

47. Lefebvre, *Gouvernement révolutionnaire,* 241; and Palmer, *Twelve Who Ruled,* 297–298. The arrest of the Dantonists was perhaps spurred above all by the radicals on the Committee, Collot and Billaud, who were never entirely happy with the execution of their former ally Hébert.

48. Chaillon, Dyzèz, and Guittard mentioned the trial and execution, but this time added no approving remarks. Dubreuil made no mention. Even Jullien, who generally supported Robespierre, expressed deep disillusionment: Chaillon, "Correspondance," letters of 12 and 17 Germinal Year II (Apr. 1 and 6, 1794); Dyzèz, "Lettres," 513 (letter of Apr. 1); Guittard, *Journal,* 334–335 (entry of April 5); and Jullien, "Correspondance," letter of Apr. 8.

49. Ruault, *Gazette d'un Parisien,* 347–349 (letter of Apr. 2, 1794).

50. Greer, *Incidence of the Terror,* 153.

51. Ibid., 26–37, 118, and 153.

52. Ibid., 39, 43, 113.

53. Lefebvre, *Gouvernement révolutionnaire,* 285.

54. Palmer, *Twelve Who Ruled,* 366; and Godfrey, *Revolutionary Justice,* 21 and 131–135.

55. See, for example, Ruault, *Gazette d'un Parisien,* 347 (letter of Jan. 16, 1794); Vadier, in Albert Tournier, *Vadier,* 204 (letter of May 2); and Marragon, "Lettres," letter of July 3.

56. Wallon, *Tribunal révolutionnaire,* 4:1–11 and 80–83; Chaillon, "Correspondance," letter of 8 Prairial Year II (May 27, 1794). See also Jullien, "Correspondance," letter of May 27; and Linton, "Stuff of Nightmares," 204–205.

57. Palmer, *Twelve Who Ruled,* 366–367; Wallon, *Tribunal révolutionnaire,* 4:262–280, 405–454, and 5:78–91; Lefebvre, *Gouvernement révolutionnaire,* 274–274, 278–279, and 286–288. See also Baczko, "Terror before the Terror," 31.

58. Greer, *Incidence of the Terror,* 119.

59. Ibid., 118; Godfrey, *Revolutionary Justice,* 133–135; Palmer, *Twelve Who Ruled,* 366; and Simonin, *Le déshonneur,* 296, 300–301.

60. Jullien, "Correspondance," letter of May 27, 1794; and Godfrey, *Revolutionary Justice,* 63 and 145–146. Georges Lefebvre described the draconian Prairial Law as "un instrument pour exterminer l'aristocratie": Lefebvre, *Gouvernement révolutionnaire,* 289.

61. Ruault, *Gazette d'un Parisien,* 352–353 (letter of June 21, 1794). On moving the guillotine to the edge of the city, see Guittard, *Journal,* 389 (entry of June 9).

62. P.-J.-L. Campmas, "Un conventionnel régicide," 246 and 328 (undated letters of "Good Friday" and "spring" 1794); and Ruault, *Gazette d'un Parisien,* 348–349 (letter of April 2). See also Fairfax-Cholmeley, "Defense, Collaboration, Counter-Attack."

63. Walter, *Neuf Thermidor,* 87–93. On Tallien, see Harder, "Reacting to Revolution."

64. For what follows, see especially Palmer, *Twelve Who Ruled,* chap. 15; Lefebvre, *Gouvernement révolutionnaire,* 315–326; Walter, *Neuf Thermidor,* esp. 96–101; Simonin, *Le déshonneur,* 249–250; and McPhee, *Robespierre,* esp. 206–214.

65. See esp. McPhee, *Robespierre,* 206–216.

66. Walter, *Neuf Thermidor,* 101 and 110–118; *AP,* 93:530–535; Lefebvre, *Gouvernement révolutionnaire,* 325–326.

67. Walter, *Neuf Thermidor,* 121–124.

68. Walter, *Neuf Thermidor,* 104; Ruault, *Gazette d'un Parisien,* 359 (letter of July 31, 1794); and Durand de Maillane, *Histoire,* 199–200.

69. Walter, *Neuf Thermidor,* 127–132; *AP,* 93:541–543 and 550–558; and Louchet, "Lettres," letter of July 29, 1794.

70. For this and what follows, see Palmer, *Twelve Who Ruled,* 375–381; Lefebvre, *Gouvernement révolutionnaire,* 329–332; Walter, *Neuf Thermidor,* 140–159; and McPhee, *Robespierre,* 217–221.

71. Guittard, *Journal,* 434–435 (entry of July 27, 1794); and Durand de Maillane, *Histoire,* 201. See also Chaillon, "Correspondance," letter of 11 Thermidor Year II (July 29); Dubreuil-Chambardel, *Lettres parisiennes,* 137 and 140 (letters of July 29 and Aug. 26); and Marragon, "Lettres," letter of Aug. 6.

72. See also C. Jones, "Overthrow of Maximilien Robespierre."

73. Dyzèz, "Lettres," 519–520 (letter of July 29, 1794). See also Saint-Martin, "Journal," entry of 15 Thermidor Year II (Aug. 2).

74. Sydenham, *Léonard Bourdon,* 238–243.

75. Guittard, *Journal,* 437–439 (entry of July 28, 1794); Ruault, *Gazette d'un Parisien,* 361 (letter of July 31). See also Louchet, "Lettres," letter of July 29.

Conclusion

1. Guittard, *Journal,* 437–441 (entries of July 27–30).

2. See, e.g., Barère's speech of July 29, 1794 (11 Thermidor Year II): *AP* 93:636. For a summary of the changes in the weeks after Thermidor, see Lefebvre, *Les Thermidoriens,* chap. 2.

3. The Dantonist sympathizers, Thuriot and Bréard; along with Treilhard, who had opposed the execution of the king.

4. E.g., Chaillon, "Correspondance," letter of July 29, 1794 (11 Thermidor Year II); Louchet, "Lettres," letter of July 29; Saint-Martin, "Journal," entry of Aug. 2 (15 Thermidor); Dubreuil, *Lettres parisiennes,* 140 (letter of Aug. 26 [9 Fructidor]). See also Baczko, *Ending the Terror;* Luzzatto, *Mémoire de la Terreur;* and Steinberg, "Trauma before Trauma."

5. See, e.g., Serna, *La république des girouettes.*

6. Garat, *Mémoires,* 205 and 218. Garat published his account in ca. March 1795, in response to attacks against him in the Convention. However, internal evidence suggests that some of his thoughts were based on notes written immediately after—or even before—Thermidor.

7. Mercier, *Le nouveau Paris* (1994), 72.

8. Greer, *Incidence of the Terror,* 120–121.

9. On the limited value of comparisons between the French Revolution and the American War of Independence, see the Introduction to this book, note 27.

10. See esp. H. Brown, *Ending the French Revolution.*

11. Mayer, *The Furies,* 171.

Sources and Bibliography

Listed here are only those sources and secondary works specifically cited or directly consulted in the present study. For a more extensive list of the correspondence of deputies to the Constituent Assembly, see the bibliography in the author's *Becoming a Revolutionary* (Princeton, NJ, 1996; and University Park, PA, 2006). For the Legislative Assembly and the Convention, see the author's "Etude sérielle de la psychologie révolutionnaire: La Correspondance des députés des Assemblées Nationales (1789–1794)" in *Archives épistolaire et histoire,* edited by Mireille Bossis and Lucia Bergamasco (Paris, 2007), 171–188.

Correspondence, Diaries, and Memoirs

Printed materials and manuscript materials have been combined here for easier reference.

Collections

AN C 91–94: letters addressed to the National Assembly from throughout France.

AN D XXIX bis 31–38: letters received by the Committee on Research.

"Correspondance des députés de l'Aude pendant la Révolution de 1791–1793." Edited by Camille Bloch. *La Révolution française* 27 (1894): 170–182; and 30 (1896): 76–86, 156–174.

"Correspondance des députés des Côtes-du-Nord à l'Assemblée législative." Edited by D. Tempier. *Société d'émulation des Côtes-du-Nord, Bulletins et mémoires* 28 (1890): 61–169.

"Correspondance des députés des Côtes-du-Nord à la Convention nationale." Edited by D. Tempier. *Société d'émulation des Côtes-du-Nord, Bulletins et mémoires* 30 (1892): 110–172.

Correspondence of deputies of Ille-et-Vilaine: AD Ille-et-Vilaine, L 294 (1–2).

Correspondence of deputies of Marseille: AC Marseille, 4 D 43–44.

Sol, Eugène. *La Révolution en Quercy.* 4 vols. Paris, 1926.

Vaissière, Pierre de, editor. *Lettres d'"Aristocrates": La Révolution racontée par des correspondances privées, 1789–1794*. Paris, 1907.

Individuals

Alexandre, Charles-Alexis. "Fragments des mémoires de Charles-Alexis Alexandre sur les journées révolutionnaires de 1791 et 1792." Edited by Jacques Godechot. *AHRF* 24 (1952): 113–251.

Aubert-Dubayet, Jean-Baptiste-Annibal. "Aubert-Dubayet: Législateur (1791–1792)." Edited by F. Vermale. *Bulletin de l'Académie delphinale,* 6e série, 9–10 (1938–1939): 115–141.

Audouyn de Pompery, Anne-Marie. *A mon cher cousin: Une femme en Bretagne à la fin du XVIIIe siècle; Correspondance de Mme de Pompery avec son cousin Kergus.* Edited by Marie-Claire Mussat and Michel Maréchal. Paris, 2008.

Bailly, Jean-Sylvain. *Mémoires d'un témoin de la Révolution.* Edited by Berville and Barrière. 3 vols. Paris, 1821–1822.

Bancal des Issarts, Henri. *Le conventionnel Bancal des Issarts: Etude biographique suivie des lettres inédites.* Edited by Francisque Mège. Paris, 1887: 209–274.

Barbaroux, Charles-Jean-Marie. *Correspondance et mémoires de Barbaroux.* Edited by Claude Perroud and Alfred Chabaud. Paris, 1923.

Barbier-Schroffenberg, Marie-Anne, baronne de. "Extrait de la correspondance de la Baronne de Barbier pendant la Révolution avec ses fils et son frère, le prince de Schroffenberg." Edited by M. de Reinach. *Société d'histoire et du Musée de la ville et du canton d'Huningue.* Bulletin 15 (1966): 58–89; 16 (1967–1968): 53–92; 17 (1969): 53–84; 18 (1970): 33–75.

Barbotin, Emmanuel. *Lettres de l'Abbé Barbotin.* Edited by Alphonse Aulard. Paris, 1910.

Barère, Bertrand. *Mémoires.* Edited by Hippolyte Carnot. 4 vols. Paris, 1842–1844.

Barnave, Antoine. *Marie-Antoinette et Barnave: Correspondance secrète (juillet 1791–janvier 1792).* Edited by Alma Söderhjelm. Paris, 1934.

Basire, Claude. "Lettres inédites de Basire à un correspondant de Dijon." *AHRF* 63 (1991), 105–111.

Basquiat de Mugriet, Alexis (sometimes jointly with Pierre-Joseph Lamarque), "Correspondance." AC Bayonne, AA 51.

Basquiat de Mugriet, Alexis. "Lettres": AC Saint-Sever, II D 31.

Belot, Denis. *Journal d'un volontaire de 1791.* Edited by Louis Bonneville de Marsangy. Paris, 1888.

Besson, Alexandre. "Lettres inédites du conventionnel Besson." Edited by Albert Mathiez. *AR* 14 (1922): 139–149.

Blad, Claude-Antoine-Augustin. "Correspondance": AM Brest, 2 D 23.

Bouchette, François-Joseph. *Lettres de François-Joseph Bouchette (1735–1810)*. Edited by Camille Looten. Lille, 1909.

Boullé, Jean-Pierre: AD Morbihan, 1 Mi 140. Reproduced through Oct. 30, 1789 in *Revue de la Révolution: Documents inédits*. Edited by Albert Macé. Vols. 10–16 (1887–89): passim.

Boyer-Fonfrède, Jean-Baptiste. "Lettres": AD Gironde, 12 L 17 (in 2 Mi 8425).

Bricard, Louis-Joseph. *Journal du cannonier Bricard, 1792–1802*. Edited by Alfred and Jules Bricard. Paris, 1891.

Brissot, Jacques-Pierre. *Correspondance et papiers*. Edited by Claude Perroud. Paris, 1912.

Cambon, Pierre-Joseph. "Lettres": AD Hérault, L 531.

Campmas, Jean-François: BM Albi, ms. 177.

Campmas, Pierre-Jean-Louis. "Un conventionnel régicide: Pierre-Jean-Louis Campmas." Edited by Emile Appolis. *La revue du Tarn*, nouv. sér., 9 (1943): 141–152; 244–254; 10 (1944): 326–335.

Cavellier, Blaise, and Romain-Nicolas Malassis. "Correspondance": AM Brest, 2 D 21.

Chaillon, Etienne. "Correspondance": BM Nantes, Fonds Dugast-Matifeux. Tome 1, vol. 44 (Mic B 48/44).

Choudieu, Pierre-René. *Mémoires et notes de Choudieu, représentant du peuple à l'Assemblée législative, à la Convention et aux armées*. Edited by V. Barrucand. Paris, 1897.

Clauzel, Jean-Baptiste. "Documents inédits sur Jean-Baptiste Clauzel, député de l'Ariège à l'Assemblée législative." Edited by G. Arnaud. *Bulletin de la Société ariègeoise des sciences, lettres, et arts* 6 (1897–1898): 115–128.

Colson, Adrien-Joseph. "Correspondance": AD Indre, 2J 10–12; excerpts in *Lettres d'un bourgeois de Paris à un ami de province, 1788–1793*. Edited by Chantal Plantier-Sanson. Paris, 1993.

Corbel du Squirio, Vincent-Claude. "Correspondance": AD Morbihan, 1 Mi 141 (R1).

Couthon, Georges. *Correspondance inédite de Georges Couthon, 1791–94*. Edited by Francisque Mège. Paris, 1872.

Delandine, Antoine-François. *Mémorial historique des Etats généraux*. 5 vols. N.p., 1789.

Demée, Louis-Michel. "Lettres": AD Orne 17 J 2 (Fonds Cochon).

Desmoulins, Camille. *Correspondance inédite de Camille Desmoulins, député de la Convention*. Edited by M. Matton. Paris, 1836.

Dorizy, Claude. "Les souvenirs inédits de Claude Dorizy, député à l'Assemblée législative de 1791." Edited by E. Jovy. *RF* 47 (1904): 436–458.

Dubreuil-Chambardel, Pierre. *Lettres parisiennes d'un révolutionnaire poitevin*. Tours, 1994.

Dumont, Etienne. *Souvenirs sur Mirabeau et sur les deux premières assemblées législatives*. Paris, 1951.

Dupont-Grandjardin, Jacob-Louis. "Correspondance de Dupont-Grandjardin avec son fils (1791–1793)." Edited by Emile Queruau-Lamerie. *Bulletin de la Commission historique et archéologique de la Mayenne* 30 (1914): 343–371.

Duquesnoy, Adrien-Cyprien. *Journal d'Adrien Duquesnoy.* Edited by R. de Crèvecoeur. 2 vols. Paris, 1894.

Durand, Antoine. "Lettres": AM Cahors, unclassed, held in B. M. Cahors.

Durand de Maillane, Pierre-Toussaint. *Histoire de la Convention nationale.* Paris, 1825.

Dyzèz, Jean. "Lettres d'un conventionnel (1793-an III)." Edited by C. Vergnol. *La revue de France* no. 6 (Nov.–Dec. 1926): 201–232, 503–527, 672–693.

Faulcon, Félix. *Correspondance de Félix Faulcon. Tome 1, 1770–89.* Edited by G. Debien. Poitiers, 1939; and *Correspondance de Félix Faulcon. Tome 2, 1789–91.* Edited by G. Debien. Poitiers, 1953.

Ferrières, Charles-Elie, marquis de. *Correspondance inédite.* Edited by Henri Carré. Paris, 1932.

Fougeret, M. de. In Pierre de Vaissière. *Lettres d'"Aristocrates": La Révolution racontée par des correspondances privées, 1789–1794.* Paris, 1907: 393–444.

François, Charles. *Journal du capitaine François, 1792–1830.* Edited by Charles Grolleau. 2 vols. Paris, 1984.

Fricaud, Claude: private collection of Dr. Robert Favre.

Gantheret, Claude: private collection of Françoise Misserey.

Garat, Dominique-Joseph. *Mémoires sur la Révolution ou exposé de ma conduite dans les affaires et dans les fonctions publiques.* Paris, 1795.

Gaultier de Biauzat, Jean-François: BM Clermont-Ferrand, Mss. 788–789; and AD Puy-de-Dôme, F 140–141. Published in part in *Gaultier de Biauzat, député du Tiers état aux Etats généraux de 1789: Sa vie et sa correspondance.* Edited by Francisque Mège. 2 vols. Clermont-Ferrand, 1890.

Gauville, Louis-Henri-Charles, baron de. *Journal du Baron de Gauville.* Edited by Edouard de Barthélemy. Paris, 1864.

Geoffroy, Claude-Jean-Baptiste: private collection of Dr. Robert Favre.

Géraud, Edmond. *Journal d'un étudiant pendant la Révolution (1789–1793).* Edited by Gaston Maugras. 2nd edition. Paris, 1890.

Gillet, Pierre-Mathurin. "Lettres du conventionnel Gillet aux administrateurs du département du Morbihan." *RF* 61 (1911): 240–268, 354–373, 435–441, 522–535; 62 (1912): 69–76, 148–174.

Goethe, Johann Wolfgang von. *Campaign in France, 1792.* In *Miscellaneous Travels of J. W. Goethe.* Edited by L. Dora Schmitz. London, 1882.

Goupilleau, Jean-François-Marie. "Lettres": BM Nantes, Fonds Dugast-Matifeux, no. 98.

Gower, Earl George Granville Leveson. *The Despatches of Earl Gower, English Ambassador at Paris, from June 1790 to August 1792.* Edited by Oscar Browning. Cambridge, 1885.

Guittard de Floriban, Nicolas-Célestin. *Journal de Nicolas-Célestin Guittard de Floriban, bourgeois de Paris sous la Révolution, 1791–1796.* Edited by Raymond Aubert. Paris, 1974.

Hua, Eustache-Antoine. *Mémoires d'un avocat au parlement de Paris, député à l'Assemblée législative.* Edited by E.-M. François Saint-Maur. Paris, 1871.

Irland de Bazôges, Pierre-Marie: AD Deux-Sèvres, Fonds Beauchet-Filleau, non-classed register of "lettres politiques, 1788–90."

Jeanbon-Saint-André, André. "Lettres de Jeanbon Saint-André et de Cavaignac à la municipalité de Montauban." *RF* 21 (1891): 338–373; 24 (1893): 156–161; 29 (1895): 63–86; 30 (1896): 461–466.

Jullien, Rosalie Ducrollay. "Correspondance": AN 39 AP; and transcription available from the Société des Amis de Rosalie et Marc-Antoine Jullien de Romans. Edited by Jean Sauvageon; abridged and incomplete excerpts in *Journal d'une bourgeoise pendant la Révolution, 1791–93.* Edited by Edouard Lockroy. Paris, 1881.

Koch, Christophe-Guillaume. "Lettres." In *L'Alsace pendant la Révolution française.* Edited by Rodolphe Reuss. 2 vols. Paris, 1880–1894: 2:242–348, passim.

La Rochefoucauld, Alexandrine-Charlotte-Sophie, duchesse de. *Lettres de la duchesse de La Rochefoucauld à William Short.* Edited by Doina Pasca Harsanyi. Paris, 2001.

La Tour du Pin, Henriette-Lucie Dillon, marquise de. *Mémoires de la marquise de La Tour du Pin: Journal d'une femme de cinquante ans, 1778–1815.* Paris, 1979.

Lebas, Philippe-François-Joseph. In Stefane-Pol, *Autour de Robespierre: Le Conventionnel Le Bas d'après des documents inédits et les mémoires de sa veuve.* Paris, 1901; and in Buchez and Roux, 35:318–365.

Le Coz, Claude. *Correspondance de Le Coz, évêque constitutionnel de l'Ille-et-Vilaine.* Edited by Abbé Roussel. Paris, 1900.

Legendre, Laurent-François: AM Brest 2 D 16–18. Extracts in "Correspondance de Legendre, député du Tiers de la sénéchaussée de Brest aux Etats généraux et l'Assemblée constituante (1789–1791)." *RF* 39 (1900): 515–558; 40 (1901): 46–78.

Le Maillaud, Jean-François. "Correspondance": AC Vannes, 262 ES.

Lepoutre, Pierre-François. *Député-paysan et fermière de Flandre en 1789: La Correspondance des Lepoutre.* Edited by Jean-Pierre Jessenne and Edna Hindie Lemay. Villeneuve d'Ascq, 1998.

Levasseur, René. *Mémoires de R. Levasseur (de la Sarthe), ex-conventionnel.* 4 vols. Paris, 1829–1831.

Lindet, Robert. "Lettres." Unpublished typescript of letters kindly given to me by François Pascal.

Lindet, Thomas. *Correspondance de Thomas Lindet pendant la Constituante et la Législative (1789–92).* Edited by Amand Montier. Paris, 1899.

Lisleroy, Marie-Alexandrine-Euphémie de. "Correspondance de Madame Auguste de Lisleroy (1789–1792)." Edited by Abbé P. Arnaud. *Revue du Vivarais* 55 (1951): 18–33, 79–92.

Lombard, Jean. *Un volontaire de 1792.* Paris, 1903.

Louchet, Louis. "Lettres": BM Rodez, from a typescript kindly given me by Peter Jones.

Maillot, Claude-Pierre: AC Toul, JJ 7.

Malassis, Romain-Nicolas. See Cavellier.

Mareux, Toussaint, et al. *Une famille de la bourgeosie parisienne pendant la Révolution d'après leur correspondance inédite.* Edited by Louis de Launay. Paris, 1921.

Marragon, Jean-Baptiste. "Lettres": BN Nouv Acq. Fr. 11822.

Maupetit, Michel-René. "Lettres de Michel-René Maupetit, député à l'Assemblée na- tionale constituante, 1789–91." Edited by Queruau-Lamerie. *Bulletin de la Com- mission historique et archéologique de la Mayenne,* 2ème sér., 17 (1901): 302–327, 439–454; 18 (1902): 133–163, 321–333, 447–475; 19 (1903): 205–250, 348–378; 20 (1904): 88–125, 176–203, 358–377, 446–472; 21 (1905): 93–124, 204–223, 325–363, 365–388; 22 (1906): 67–95, 213–239, 349–384, 454–493; 23 (1907): 87–115.

Médel, Angélique-Séraphine de. *Correspondance de Madame de Médel, 1770–1789.* Edited by Henri Carré. In *Archives historiques du Poitou* 47 (1931): 1–166.

Ménard de La Groye, François-René-Pierre. *Correspondance (1789–1791).* Edited by Flor- ence Mirouse. Le Mans, 1989.

Ménétra, Jacques-Louis. *Journal de ma vie: Jacques-Louis Ménétra, compagnon vitrier au 18e siècle.* Edited by Daniel Roche. Paris, 1982.

———. "Mes réflexions sur la révolution": BHVP, Ms. 678, 2e partie.

Mercier, Louis-Sébastien. *Le nouveau Paris.* Edited by Jean-Claude Bonnet. Paris, 1994.

———. *Paris le jour, Paris la nuit.* Edited by Michel Delon. Paris, 1990.

———. *Paris pendant la Révolution (1789–1798) ou le Nouveau Paris.* Nouv. ed. 2 vols. Paris, 1862.

———. *Tableau de Paris.* 12 vols. Amsterdam, 1782–1788.

Merle, André-Marie: AC Mâcon, D (2) 13, carton 21 bis.

Miles, William Augustus. *The Correspondence of William Augustus Miles on the French Revolution, 1789–1817.* Edited by Charles Popham Miles. 2 vols. London, 1890.

Monestier, Jean-Baptiste-Benoît. "Correspondance": BN, Nouv. Acq. Fr., 6902.

———. "Lettres": BM Clermont-Ferrand, ms. 350.

Monnard, Marie-Victoire. *Les souvenirs d'une femme du peuple: Marie-Victoire Mon- nard de Creil, 1777–1802.* Edited by O. Boutanquoi. Senlis, 1929.

Neufchâteau, François de. "Recherches sur la vie de François de Neufchâteau, à propos de ses lettres à son ami Poullain-Grandprey." Edited by Pierre Marot. *Annales de la Société d'émulation du département des Vosges* 136–141 (1960–65): 207–217.

Noël, Joseph-Louis-Gabriel. *Au temps des volontaires, 1792: Lettres d'un volontaire de 1792.* Edited by G. Noël. Paris, 1912.

Palloy, Pierre-François. *Livre de raison du patriote Palloy.* Edited by Romi. Paris, 1956.

Picard, Ernest. *Au service de la nation.* Paris, 1914.

Pinet, Jacques. "Correspondance": AM Bergerac, 3 B 43 (1–2). Extracts in "Lettres, du 10 au 14 août 1792." Edited by Etienne Charavay. *RF* 3 (1882): 97–109.

Rabusson-Lamothe, Antoine. "Lettres sur l'Assemblée législative adressées à la municipalité de Clermont-Ferrand par Antoine Rabusson-Lamothe." Edited by Francisque Mège. *Mémoires de l'Académie des sciences, belles-lettres et arts de Clermont-Ferrand* 11 (1869): 193–382.

Ramel, Pierre. "Lettres": AC Cahors, Unclassed box of deputy letters.

Robespierre, Augustin. In *Oeuvres de Maximilien Robespierre. T. 3. Correspondance de Maximilien et Augustin Robespierre.* Edited by Georges Michon. 2 vols. Paris, 1926–1941.

Robespierre, Maximilien. *Oeuvres de Maximilien Robespierre. T. 3. Correspondance de Maximilien et Augustin Robespierre.* Edited by Georges Michon. 2 vols. Paris, 1926 and 1941.

Roland, Marie-Jeanne. *Lettres de Madame Roland.* Edited by Claude Perroud. 2 vols. Paris, 1900–1902; and *Lettres de Madame Roland, Nouvelle série.* Edited by Claude Perroud. 2 vols. and supplement. Paris, 1913–1915.

Romme, Gilbert. "Correspondance": Museo del Risorgimento, Milan, Dos. 22–23; extracts of many letters reproduced in Alessandro Galante Garrone, *Gilbert Romme: Histoire d'un révolutionnaire, 1750–1795.* Paris, 1971.

———. "Lettres": BN Nouv. Acq. Fr., 4789, folios 71–90.

Roubaud, François-Yves. "Lettres de François-Yves Roubaud, député du Var à l'Assemblée législative." Edited by Edmond Poupé. *Bulletin de la Société d'études scientifiques et archéologiques de Draguignan* 36 (1926–27): 3–218.

Ruault, Nicolas. *Gazette d'un Parisien sous la Révolution: Lettres à son frère, 1783–96.* Edited by Christiane Rimbaud and Anne Vassal. Paris, 1976.

Rubat, Aristide. "Lettres": AD Ain, 1 L 114 (Ancien).

Rubat, Etienne. "Lettres": AC Mâcon, D(2) 13, carton 21 bis.

Saint-Martin, François-Jérôme Riffard de. "Journal": AN 139 AP 6 (43).

———. "L'année 1792 vue et vécue par M. Riffard de Saint-Martin, député de l'Ardèche à l'Assemblée législative et à la Convention." *La revue universelle des faits et des idées* no. 169 (1992): 47–52.

Saint-Priest, François-Emmanuel Guignard, comte de. *Mémoires: Règnes de Louis XV et de Louis XVI.* Edited by the baron de Barante. 2 vols. Paris, 1929.

Saint-Prix, Hector de Soubeyran de. In Humbert de Soubeyran de Saint-Prix, "Hector de Soubeyran de Saint-Prix, député de l'Ardèche à la Convention." *Revue historique, archéologique, littéraire et pittoresque du Vivarais* 12 (1904): 52–75, 112–124.

Short, William. In *The Papers of Thomas Jefferson.* Edited by Julian P. Boyd and John Catanzariti. Vols. 19–23. Princeton, NJ, 1982–1990.

Soubrany, Pierre-Amable. *Dix-neuf lettres de Soubrany, représentant du peuple à la Convention nationale.* Edited by Henry Doniol. Clermont-Ferrand, 1867.

Stamaty, Constantin. *Correspondances de Paris, Vienne, Berlin, Varsovie, Constanti-nople.* Edited and translated by Jules Lair and Emile Legrand. Paris, 1871.

———. *Lettres de Constantin Stamaty à Panagiotis Kodrikas sur la Révolution fran-çaise* [in Greek]. Edited by Emile Legrand. Paris, 1872. Ms. translation from the Greek by Hervé Kergall.

Taveau, Louis-Jacques-Narcisse. "Lettres": AM Honfleur D* 17.

Thibaudeau, Antoine-Claire. *Biographie, Mémoires, 1765–92.* Paris, 1875.

Thibaudeau, Antoine-René-Hyacinthe. *Correspondance inédite.* Edited by H. Carré and Pierre Boissonnade. Paris, 1898.

Toulongeon, François-Emmanuel. *Histoire de la France depuis la Révolution.* 7 vols. Paris, 1801.

Vadier, Marc-Guillaume. In Albert Tournier, *Vadier, président du Comité de sûreté générale.* Paris, 1900: 193–212.

Vergniaud, Pierre-Victurnien. "Bibliothèque de Vergniaud": BM Bordeaux, ms. 860, 263–277.

———. *Vergniaud, manuscrits, lettres, et papiers: Recherches historiques sur les Giron-dins.* Edited by C. Vatel. 2 vols. Paris, 1873.

Verneilh-Puyraseau, Jean-Joseph de. *Mémoires historiques sur la France et la Révolu-tion.* Paris, 1830.

Vernier, Théodore. "Lettres de Vernier": AC Bletterans (non-classé), in AD Jura.

Viénot de Vaublanc, Vincent-Marie. *Mémoires de M. le comte de Vaublanc.* Edited by François Barrière. Paris, 1857.

Vinet, Pierre. "Lettres du conventionnel P. Vinet." Edited by P. R. Clouet. *AHRF* 7 (1930): 63–70.

Visme, Laurent de. "Journal des Etats-Généraux": BN Nouv Acq. Fr. 12938.

Newspapers

Annales patriotiques et littéraires (Jean-Louis Carra and Louis-Sébastien Mercier)

Courrier de Provence (Count Mirabeau)

La chronique de Paris (Marquis de Condorcet)

L'ami du peuple (Jean-Paul Marat)

Le courrier de Versailles à Paris et de Paris à Versailles (Antoine-Joseph Gorsas)

Le courrier des 83 départements (Antoine-Joseph Gorsas)

Le journal de Paris (Dominique Garat)

L'orateur du peuple (Stanislas Fréron)

Patriote français (Jacques-Pierre Brissot)

Père Duchesne (Jacques Hébert)

Révolutions de Paris (Louis-Marie Prudhomme and Elisée Loustalot)

Thermomètre du jour (Jacques Dulaure)

Other Printed Sources

Actes de la Commune de Paris pendant la Révolution. Edited by Sigismond Lacroix et al. 19 vols. Paris, 1894–1955.

Archives parlementaires de 1787 à 1860, recueil complet des débats législatifs et politiques des chambres françaises. Première série (1787–1799). Edited by Jérôme Mavidal, Emile Laurent, et al. 82 vols. Paris, 1867–1913.

Brissot, Jacques-Pierre. *A tous les républicains de France.* Paris, 1792.

Buchez, Philippe-Joseph-Benjamin, and Abbé Pierre-Célestin Roux. *Histoire parlementaire de la Révolution française, ou journal des assemblées nationales depuis 1789 jusqu'en 1815.* 40 vols. Paris, 1834–1838.

Chassin, Charles-Louis, editor. *La préparation de la guerre de Vendée.* 3 vols. Paris, 1892.

———, editor. *La Vendée patriote.* 4 vols. Paris, 1893.

Condorcet, Marquis de. "Fragment de justification (juillet 1793)." In *Oeuvres.* Paris, 1847: 1:574–605.

Garat, Dominique-Joseph. *Eloge de Bernard de Fontenelle.* Paris, 1778.

Gouges, Olympe de. *La déclaration des droits de la femme et de la citoyenne.* Paris, 1791.

Lezay-Marnésia, Claude-François-Adrien, comte de. *Le bonheur.* Paris, 1785.

Mirabeau, Gabriel-Jean-Honoré, *Dix-neuvième lettre . . . à ses commettans.* Paris, 1789.

Mortimer-Ternaux. *Histoire de la Terreur, 1792–1794.* 8 vols. Paris, 1862–1881.

Papiers inédits trouvés chez Robespierre, Saint-Just, Payan, etc., supprimés ou omis par Courtois. 3 vols. Paris, 1828.

Pétion, Jérôme. *Avis aux Français sur le salut de la patrie.* Paris, 1789.

Prudhomme, Louis-Marie. *Histoire générale et impartiale des erreurs, des fautes et des crimes commis pendant la Révolution française.* 6 vols. Paris, 1796–1797.

Rabaut Saint-Etienne, Jean-Paul. *Précis historique de la Révolution française.* Paris, 1807.

Recueil des actes du Comité de salut public, avec la correspondance officielle des représentants en mission et le registre du Conseil exécutif provisoire. Edited by Alphonse Aulard et al. 28 vols. plus tables and supplements. Paris, 1899–1971.

Société des Jacobins: Recueil de documents pour l'histoire du club des Jacobins de Paris. Edited by Alphonse Aulard. 6 vols. Paris, 1889–1897.

Tableaux de la Révolution française, publiés sur les papiers inédits du département et de la police secrète de Paris. Edited by Wilhelm Adolf Schmidt. 3 vols. Leipzig, 1867–1870.

Secondary Works

Aberdam, Serge. "L'élargissement du droit de vote entre 1792 et 1795." *AHRF* 74, no. 1 (2002): 106–118.

———. "Un aspect du référendum de 1793: Les envoyés du souverain face aux représentant du peuple." In *Révolution et République: L'exception française*. Paris, 1994: 213–224.

———, editor. *Voter et élir*. Paris, 1999.

Allport, Gordon W., and L. J. Postman. *The Psychology of Rumor*. New York, 1947.

Alpaugh, Micah. "Les émotions collectives et le mouvement des fédérations." *AHRF* 85, no. 2 (2013): 49–80.

———. "The Making of the Parisian Political Demonstration: A Case Study of 20 June 1792." *Proceedings of the Western Society for French History* 34 (2006): 115–133.

———. *Non-violence and the French Revolution: Political Demonstrations in Paris, 1787–1795*. Cambridge, 2015.

———. "The Politics of Escalation in French Revolutionary Protest: Political Demonstrations, Nonviolence, and Violence in the *Grandes journées* of 1789." *French History* 23 (2009): 336–359.

Andress, David. "'A Ferocious and Misled Multitude': Elite Perceptions of Popular Action from Rousseau to Robespierre." In *Enlightenment and Revolution: Essays in Honour of Norman Hampson*. Edited by Malcolm Crook, William Doyle, and Alan Forrest. Aldershot, 2004.

———. *Massacre at the Champ de Mars: Popular Dissent and Political Culture in the French Revolution*. Woodbridge, England, 2000.

———. *The Terror: The Merciless War for Freedom in Revolutionary France*. New York, 2005.

Andrews, Elizabeth. "Between *Auteurs* et *Abonnés:* Reading the *Journal de Paris, 1787–1789*." *Proceedings of the Western Society for French History* 37 (2009), online at http://quod.lib.umich.edu/w/wsfh/.

Applewhite, Harriet. *Political Alignment in the French National Assembly, 1789–1791*. Baton Rouge, LA, 1993.

Armoogum-Ninat, Marie-Christiane. "La Grande Peur de 1789 à Sainte-Sévère (Indre)." *AHRF* 29 (1957): 122–123.

Arnaud, Gaston. *Histoire de la Révolution dans le département de l'Ariège, 1789–1795*. Toulouse, 1904.

Aston, Nigel. *Religion and Revolution in France, 1780–1804*. Washington, DC, 2000.

Aulard, Alphonse. *L'éloquence parlementaire pendant la Révolution française: Les orateurs de la Législative et de la Convention*. 2 vols. Paris, 1885.

———. *Etudes et leçons sur la Révolution française*. 9 vols. Paris, 1898–1924.

———. *L'histoire politique de la Révolution française*. 5e édition. Paris, 1913.

Babeau, Albert. *Histoire de Troyes pendant la Révolution*. 2 vols. Paris, 1873.

Baczko, Bronislaw. *Ending the Terror: The French Revolution after Robespierre*. Cambridge, 1994.

———. *Lumières de l'utopie*. Paris, 1978.

————. "Les peurs de la Terreur." In *La peur aux XVIIIe siècle: Discours, représentations, pratiques.* Edited by Jacques Berchtold and Michel Porret. Geneva, 1994.

————. *Politiques de la Révolution française.* Paris, 2008.

————. "The Terror before the Terror? Conditions of Possibility, Logic of Realization." In *FRCMPC* 4:19–38.

Baecque, Antoine de. *Le corps de l'histoire: Métaphore et politique, 1770–1800.* Paris, 1993.

————. "L'homme nouveau est arrivé: La régénération du français en 1789." *Dix-huitième siècle* 20 (1988): 193–208.

Baguenier-Desormeaux, Marie Breguet. "Origines sociales, géographiques et formations intellectuelles et professionnelles des députés des assemblées révolutionnaires." Thèse de doctorat, Université de Paris IV, 1993.

Baker, Keith Michael. *Inventing the French Revolution.* Cambridge, 1990.

————. "Politics and Social Science in 18th Century France: The Société de 1789." In *French Government and Society, 1500–1850.* Edited by J. F. Bosher. London, 1973: 208–250.

Baratier, Edouard, editor. *Histoire de Marseille.* Toulouse, 1973.

Barny, Roger. "Les aristocrates et Jean-Jacques Rousseau dans la Révolution." *AHRF* 50 (1978): 534–568.

Bart, Jean. *La Révolution française en Bourgogne.* Clermont-Ferrand, 1996.

Bastien, Pascal. *L'exécution publique à Paris au XVIIIe siècle: Une histoire des rituels judiciaires.* Seyssel, 2006.

Baticle, René. "Le plébisite sur la Constitution de 1793." *RF* 57 (1909): 496–524; 58 (1910): 5–30, 117–155, 193–237, 327–341, 385–410.

Baumont, Henri. *Le département de l'Oise pendant la Révolution (1790–1795).* Paris, 1906–1909.

Beauchet-Filleau, Henri. *Tableau des émigrés du Poitou aux armées des princes et de Condé.* Poitiers, 1845.

Bée, Michel. "Le spectacle de l'exécution dans la France de l'Ancien Régime." *Annales E.S.C.* 38 (1983): 843–862.

Bell, David Avrom. *The Cult of the Nation in France: Inventing Nationalism, 1680–1800.* Cambridge, MA, 2001.

————. *The First Total War: Napoleon's Europe and the Birth of Warfare as We Know It.* Boston, 2007.

Berchtold, Jacques, and Michel Porret, editors. *La peur aux XVIIIe siècle: Discours, représentations, pratiques.* Geneva, 1994.

Berlanstein, Lenard R. *The Barristers of Toulouse in the Eighteenth Century (1740–1793).* Baltimore, MD, 1975.

Bertaud, Jean-Paul. *Les amis du roi.* Paris, 1984.

————. *The Army of the Revolution: From Citizen Soldiers to Instrument of Power.* Princeton, NJ, 1988.

———. *Camille et Lucile Desmoulins: Un couple dans la tourmente.* Paris, 1985.

———. "La presse royaliste parisienne: L'idée de la guerre et la guerre, 1789–1792." In *Résistances à la Révolution.* Edited by Roger Dupuy and François Lebrun. Paris, 1987.

———. *Valmy, la démocratie en armes.* Paris, 1970.

Bertaud, Jean-Paul, and Daniel Reichel, editors. *Atlas de la Révolution française. Vol. 3. L'armée et la guerre.* Paris, 1989.

Bianchi, Serge. *La Révolution et la première République au village: pouvoirs, votes et politisation dans les campagnes d'Ile-de-France.* Paris, 2003.

Bianchi, Serge, and Roger Dupuy, editors. *La garde nationale entre nation et peuple en armes, mythes et réalités, 1789–1871.* Rennes, 2006.

Biard, Michel. *1793: Le siège de Lyon: Entre mythes et réalités.* Clermont-Ferrand, 2013.

———. *Jean-Marie Collot d'Herbois, homme de théâtre et homme de pouvoir (1749–1796).* Lyons, 1995.

———. *Les lilliputiens de la centralization: Des intendants aux préfets, les hésitations d'un 'modèle français.'* Seyssel, 2007.

———. *Missionnaires de la République: Les représentants du peuple en mission (1793–1795).* Paris, 2002.

Bien, David. "La réaction aristocratique avant 1789: L'exemple de l'armée." *Annales E.S.C.* 29 (1974): 23–48, 505–534.

Blackman, Robert H. "Representation without Revolution: Political Representation as Defined in the General *Cahiers de doléances* of 1789." *FHS* 25 (2001): 159–185.

Blanning, T. C. W. *The French Revolutionary Wars, 1787–1802.* London, 1996.

———. *The Origins of the French Revolutionary Wars.* New York, 1986.

Bloch, Marc. *Réflexions d'un historien sur les fausses nouvelles de guerre.* Paris, 1999.

Boivin-Champeaux, L. *Notices historiques sur la Révolution dans le département de l'Eure.* 2 vols. Evreux, 1893–1894.

Bonnet, Jean-Claude, editor. *Louis-Sébastien Mercier, 1740–1815: Un hérétique en littérature.* Paris, 1995.

Bosher, J. F. *French Finances, 1770–1795: From Business to Bureaucracy.* Cambridge, 1970.

Bossut, Nicole. *Chaumette, porte-parole des sans-culottes.* Paris, 1998.

Bourdin, Isabelle. *Les sociétés populaires à Paris pendant la Révolution.* Paris, 1937.

Bourdin, Philippe. "Bancal des Issarts, militant, député et notable: De l'utopie politique à l'ordre moral." *RH* 302 (2000): 895–938.

———. "Jean-François Gaultier de Biauzat (1739–1815): Hortensius ou nouveau Robespierre." *AHRF* 68 (1997): 31–60.

Boutier, Jean. *Campagnes en émoi: Révoltes et Révolution en Bas-Limousin, 1789–1800.* Les Treignac, 1987.

Boutier, Jean, and Philippe Boutry. *Atlas de la Révolution française. Tome 6, Les sociétés politiques.* Paris, 1992.

————. "Les sociétés politiques en France de 1789 à l'an III: Une 'machine?'" *RHMC* 36 (1989): 29–67.

Bowers, Claude G. *Pierre Vergniaud: Voice of the French Revolution.* New York, 1950.

Bozenga, Gail. "Financial Origins of the French Revolution." In *From Deficit to Deluge.* Edited by Thomas E. Kaiser and Dale K. Van Kley. Stanford, 2006: 37–66.

Braesch, Frédéric. *La commune du dix août 1792: Etude sur l'histoire de Paris du 20 janvier au 2 décembre 1792.* Paris, 1911.

Brégail, Gilbert. "Le Gers pendant la Révolution." *Bulletin de la Société d'histoire et d'archéologie du Gers* 29 (1928): 346–366; 30 (1929): 89–120, 224–258, 354–377; 31 (1930): 15–22, 97–108, 248–272; 32 (1931): 28–44, 161–172, 255–296; 33 (1932): 51–71, 138–147, 187–203, 320–339; 34 (1933): 68–83, 179–225.

Brennan, Thomas. *Public Drinking and Popular Culture in Eighteenth-Century Paris.* Princeton, NJ, 1988.

Brewer, John. *The Sinews of Power: War, Money, and the English State, 1688–1783.* New York, 1988.

Brinton, Crane. *The Jacobins: An Essay in the New History.* New York, 1930.

Brown, Howard G. *Ending the French Revolution: Violence, Justice, and Repression from the Terror to Napoleon.* Charlottesville, VA, 2006.

————. *War, Revolution, and the Bureaucratic State: Politics and Army Administration in France, 1791–1799.* Oxford, 1995.

Bruley, Georges. *Prudent-Jean Bruley.* Angers, 1901.

Bruneau, Marcel. *Les débuts de la Révolution dans les départements du Cher et de l'Indre.* Paris, 1902.

Brunel, Françoise. "Les députés montagnards." In *Actes du colloque Girondins et Montagnards.* Edited by Albert Soboul. Paris, 1980: 343–361.

Brunot, Ferdinand. *Histoire de la langue française des origines à nos jours. Tome 9, La Révolution et l'Empire.* Paris, 1967.

Burrows, Simon. *Blackmail, Scandal, and Revolution. London's French Libellists, 1758–1792.* Manchester, 2006.

Burstin, Haim. *L'invention du sans-culotte.* Paris, 2005.

————. "Problèmes du travail à Paris sous la Révolution." *RHMC* 44 (1997): 650–682.

————. *Une Révolution à l'oeuvre: Le faubourg Saint-Marcel (1789–1794).* Paris, 2005.

Cahen, Léon. *Condorcet et la Révolution française.* Paris, 1904.

Caillet, Pierre. *Les Français en 1789, d'après les papiers du Comité des recherches de l'assemblée constituante (1789–1791).* Paris, 1991.

————. *Inventaire analytique de la sous-série D XXIX bis.* Paris, 1993.

Campbell, Peter R., editor. *Origins of the French Revolution.* Basingstoke, Eng., 2006.

Campbell, Peter R., Thomas E. Kaiser, and Marisa Linton, editors. *Conspiracy in the French Revolution.* Manchester, 2007.

Caradonna, Jeremy L. *The Enlightenment in Practice: Academic Prize Contests and Intellectual Culture in France, 1670–1794.* Ithaca, NY, 2012.

————. "Prendre part au siècle des Lumières: Le concours académique et la culture intellectuelle au XVIIIe siècle." *Annales H.S.S.* 64 (2009): 633–662.

Caron, Pierre. *Les Massacres de septembre*. Paris, 1935.

————. *La première Terreur: Les mission du Conseil exécutif provisoire et de la Commune de Paris*. Paris, 1950.

————. "La tentative de contrerévolution de juin-juillet 1789." *Revue d'histoire moderne* 7 (1906–1907): 5–34, 649–678.

Carrot, Georges. *Révolution et maintien de l'ordre (1789–1799)*. Paris, 1995.

Censer, Jack R. *The French Press in the Age of Enlightenment*. London, 1994.

————. *Prelude to Power: The Parisian Radical Press, 1789–1791*. Baltimore, 1976.

Chappey, Jean-Luc. "La Révolution française dans l'ère du soupçon." *Cahiers d'histoire: Revue d'histoire critique,* no. 65 (1996): 63–76.

Chartier, Roger, Marie-Madeleine Compère, and Dominique Julia. *L'éducation en France du XVIe au XVIIIe siècle*. Paris, 1976.

Chaudron, Emile. *La grande peur en Champagne méridionale*. Paris, 1924.

Chaumié, Jacqueline. *Le réseau d'Antraigues et la Contre-Révolution, 1791–1793*. Paris, 1968.

Chaussinand-Nogaret, Guy. *La noblesse au XVIIIe siècle: De la féodalité aux Lumières*. Paris, 1976.

Chisick, Harvey. *The Ami du Roi of the Abbé Royou*. Philadelphia, 1992.

Chopelin, Paul. *Ville patriote et ville martyr: Lyon, l'Eglise, et la Révolution, 1788–1805*. Paris, 2010.

Cobb, Richard. *Les armées révolutionnaires: Instrument de la Terreur dans les départements, Avril 1793–Floréal an II*. Paris, 1961.

————. *The Police and the People: French Popular Protest, 1789–1820*. Oxford, 1970.

Cock, Jacques de. *Les Cordeliers dans la Révolution française: Textes et documents*. Lyon, 2002.

Cohen, Alain. "Les intendants au coeur de la crise de l'Ancien Régime: 1783–1791." *AHRF* 82, no. 4 (2010): 101–109.

Connelly, Owen. *Wars of the French Revolution and Napoleon, 1792–1815*. London, 2006.

Constant, J. "Voltaire et la réforme des lois pénales." *Revue de droit pénal et de criminologie* 39 (1958): 535–546.

Corgne, Eugène. *Pontivy et son district pendant la Révolution (1789-Germinal an V)*. Rennes, 1938.

Cossy, Valérie, and Deidre Dawson, editors. *Progrès et violence au XVIIIe siècle*. Paris, 2001.

Coudart, Louise. *La Gazette de Paris*. Paris, 1995.

Cousin, Bernard, editor. *Les fédéralismes: Réalités et représentations (1789–1874)*. Aix-en-Provence, 1995.

Cowans, Jon. *To Speak for the People: Public Opinion and the Problem of Legitimacy in the French Revolution*. New York, 2001.

Crépin, Annie. *Révolution et armée nouvelle en Seine-et-Marne (1791–1797)*. Paris, 2008.

Crook, Malcolm. *Journées révolutionnaires à Toulon*. Nîmes, 1989.

———. *Toulon in War and Revolution: From the Ancien Régime to the Restoration, 1750–1820*. Manchester, 1991.

Cubitt, Geoffrey. *The Jesuit Myth: Conspiracy Theory and Politics in Nineteenth-Century France*. Oxford, 1993.

Cuénin, Michel. *Le duel sous l'Ancien régime*. Paris, 1982.

Darnton, Robert. "An Early Information Society: News and the Media in Eighteenth-Century France." *AHR* 105 (2000): 1–35.

———. *The Great Cat Massacre and Other Episodes in French Cultural History*. New York, 1984.

———. "The High Enlightenment and the Low-Life of Literature in Pre-Revolutionary France." *Past and Present* no. 51 (May 1971): 81–115.

———. *Mesmerism and the End of the Enlightenment*. Cambridge, MA, 1968.

Delpierre, Guy. *La peur et l'être*. Toulouse, 1974.

Delsaux, Hélène. *Condorcet journaliste (1790–94)*. Paris, 1931.

Delumeau, Jean. *La peur en Occident*. Paris, 1978.

Dendena, Francesco. " 'Nos places maudites': Le mouvement feuillant entre la fuite de Varennes et la chute de la monarchie (1791–92)." Thèse de doctorat, Ecole des hautes études en sciences sociales and University of Milan, 2010.

Déplanche, Nicolas. "The French Revolution and the Origins of Modern Youth Movements, 1789–1790." Ph.D. dissertation, University of California, Irvine, 2012.

Deries, Madeleine. *Le district de Saint-Lô pendant la Révolution, 1787-an IV*. Paris, 1922.

Desan, Suzanne. " 'Constitutional Amazons': Jacobin Women's Clubs in the French Revolution." In *Re-Creating Authority in Revolutionary France*. Edited by Bryant T. Ragan, Jr., and Elizabeth A. Williams. New Brunswick, NJ, 1992.

———. *The Family on Trial in Revolutionary France*. Berkeley, 2004.

Desjardins, Albert. *Les cahiers des Etats Généraux en 1789 et la législation criminelle*. Paris, 1893.

Dieuleveult, Alain de. "La mort des Conventionnels." *AHRF* 55 (1983): 157–166.

DiFonzo, Nicholas, and Prashant Bordia. *Rumor Psychology: Social and Organizational Approaches*. Washington, DC, 2007.

Dorigny, Marcel. *Autun dans la Révolution française*. Vol. 2. *L'événement révolutionnaire: Du bastion royaliste à la Montagne du département (1789–1795)*. Le Mée-sur-Seine, 1989.

———. "Violence et Révolution: Les Girondins et les Massacres de septembre." In *Girondins et Montagnards*. Edited by Albert Soboul. Paris, 1980: 103–120.

Doyle, William. *The Ancien Régime*. Atlantic Highlands, NJ, 1986.

———. *The Origins of the French Revolution*. Oxford, 1988.

———. *The Oxford History of the French Revolution*. Oxford, 1989.

Doyon, André. *Un agent royaliste pendant la Révolution: Pierre-Jacques Le Maître (1790–1795)*. Paris, 1969.

Dreyfus, Jean. "Le manifeste royal du 20 juin 1791." *RF* 54 (1908): 5–22.

Dubois, Eugène. *Histoire de la Révolution dans l'Ain*. 4 vols. Bourg-en-Bresse, 1931–1934.

Dubreuil, Leon. *La Révolution dans le département des Côtes-du-Nord*. Paris, 1909.

Duport, Anne-Marie. *Terreur et Révolution: Nîmes en l'an II*. Paris, 1987.

Duprat, Annie. *Le roi décapité: Essai sur les imaginaires politiques*. Paris, 1992.

Dupuy, Roger. *La garde nationale et les débuts de la Révolution en Ille-et-Vilaine (1789-mars 1793)*. Paris, 1972.

Dupuy, Roger, and François Lebrun, editors. *Résistances à la Révolution*. Paris, 1987.

Dzimbowski, Edmond. *Un nouveau patriotisme français, 1750–1770: La France face à la puissance anglaise*. Oxford, 1998.

Edelstein, Dan. *The Terror of Natural Right: Republicanism, the Cult of Nature, and the French Revolution*. Chicago, 2009.

Edelstein, Melvin. *The French Revolution and the Birth of Electoral Democracy*. Farnham, U.K., 2014.

Edmonds, William D. "'Federalism' and Urban Revolt in France in 1793." *JMH* 55 (1983): 22–53.

———. *Jacobinism and the Revolt of Lyon, 1789–1793*. Oxford, 1990.

Egret, Jean. *The French Prerevolution, 1787–1788*. Chicago, 1977.

Ehrard, Jean, and Albert Soboul, editors. *Gilbert Romme (1750–1795) et son temps*. Paris, 1966.

Ellery, Eloise. *Brissot de Warville: A Study in the History of the French Revolution*. Boston, 1915.

Erhard, Jean. "Un étudiant riomois à Paris." In *Gilbert Romme, Correspondance, 1774–1779*. Edited by Anne-Marie Bourdin et al. 2 vols. Clermont-Ferrand, 2006: 1:41–73 and 99–105.

Fairfax-Cholmeley, Alex. "Defence, Collaboration, Counter-Attack: The Role and Exploitation of the Printed Word by Victims of the Terror, 1793–1794." In *Experiencing the French Revolution*. Edited by David Andress. Oxford, 2013: 137–154.

Farge, Arlette. *Subversive Words: Public Opinion in Eighteenth-Century France*. Pennsylvania Park, 1994.

———. *La vie fragile: Violence, pouvoirs et solidarités à Paris au XVIIIe siècle*. Paris, 1986.

Farge, Arlette, and Jacques Revel. *Logiques de la foule: L'affaire des enlèvements d'enfants, Paris 1750*. Paris, 1988.

Farge, Arlette, and André Zysberg. "Les théâtres de la violence à Paris au XVIIIe siècle." *Annales. E.S.C.* 34 (1979): 984–1015.

Fauchois, Yann. *Chronologie politique de la Révolution, 1789–1799*. Paris, 1989.

Félix, Joël. "Financial Origins of the French Revolution." In *Origins of the French Revolution*. Edited by Peter Cambell. Basingstoke, 2006: 35–62.

Figeac, Michael. *Destins de la noblesse bordelaise (1770–1830)*. 2 vols. Bordeaux, 1996.

Fine, Gary Alan, Véronique Campion-Vincent, and Chip Heath, editors. *Rumor Mills: The Social Impact of Rumor and Legend*. New Brunswick, NJ, 2005.

Fitzpatrick, Sheila, and Robert Gellately. *Accusatory Practices*. Chicago, 1997.

Fitzsimmons, Michael. *The Night the Old Regime Ended: August 4, 1789 and the French Revolution*. University Park, PA, 2003.

Fleury, Gabriel. *La ville et le district de Mamers durant la Révolution (1789–1804)*. 3 vols. Mamers, 1909–1911.

Flottes, Pierre. "Le club des Jacobins de Bordeaux et la monarchie constitutionnelle, 1790–1792." *RF* 69 (1916): 337–362.

Forrest, Alan. *Conscripts and Deserters: The Army and French Society during the Revoltion and Empire*. Oxford, 1989.

———. "The Local Politics of Repression." In *FRCMPC* 4:81–98.

———. *Paris, the Provinces, and the French Revolution*. London, 2004.

———. *The Revolution in Provincial France: Aquitaine, 1789–1799*. Oxford, 1996.

———. *Society and Politics in Revolutionary Bordeaux*. Oxford, 1975.

———. *Soldiers of the French Revolution*. Durham, NC, 1990.

Fréville, Henri. *L'intendance de Bretagne, 1689 à 1790*. 3 vols. Rennes, 1953.

Furet, François. *Interpreting the French Revolution*. Trans. Elborg Forster. Cambridge, 1981.

———, editor. *Livre et société*. 2 vols. Paris, 1965–1970.

Furet, François, and Mona Ozouf, editors. *A Critical Dictionary of the French Revolution*. Cambridge, MA, 1989.

———, editors. *La Gironde et les Girondins*. Paris, 1991.

Galante Garrone, Alessandro. *Gilbert Romme: Histoire d'un révolutionnaire, 1750–1795*. Trans. Anne and Claude Manceron. Paris, 1971.

Galloway, George B., and Sidney Wise. *History of the House of Representatives*. New York, 1976.

Garrioch, David. *The Formation of the Parisian Bourgeoisie, 1690–1830*. Cambridge, MA, 1996.

———. *The Making of Revolutionary Paris*. Berkeley, 2002.

———. *Neighbourhood and Community in Paris, 1740–1790*. Cambridge, 1986.

Genty, Maurice. *Paris, 1789–1795: L'apprentissage de la citoyenneté*. Paris, 1987.

Gershoy, Leo. *Bertrand Barère, A Reluctant Terrorist*. Princeton, NJ, 1962.

Girardot, Jean. *Le département de la Haute-Saône pendant la Révolution*. 3 vols. Vesoul, 1973.

Godechot, Jacques. *La Révolution française dans le Midi-Toulousain*. Toulouse, 1986.

———. *The Taking of the Bastille*. London, 1970.

Godfrey, James Logan. *Revolutionary Justice: A Study in the Organization and Procedures of the Paris Tribunal (1793–95)*. Chapel Hill, 1951.

Godineau, Dominique. *Citoyennes et tricoteuses: Les femmes du peuple à Paris pendant la Révolution française*. Paris, 1988.

Goetz-Bernstein, H. A. *La diplomatie de la Gironde: Jacques-Pierre Brissot*. Paris, 1912.

Goldstein, Jan. *The Post-Revolutionary Self: Politics and Psyche in France, 1750–1850*. Cambridge, MA, 2008.

Gough, Hugh. *The Newspaper Press in the French Revolution*. London, 1988.

Greer, Donald. *The Incidence of the Emigration during the French Revolution*. Cambridge, MA, 1951.

———. *The Incidence of the Terror during the French Revolution: A Statistical Interpretation*. Cambridge, MA, 1935.

Gross, Jean-Pierre. *Fair Shares for All: Jacobin Egalitarianism in Practice*. Cambridge, 1997.

Gruder, Vivian. *The Notables and the Nation: The Political Schooling of the French, 1787–1788*. Cambridge, MA, 2007.

Gueniffey, Patrice. *La politique de la Terreur: Essai sur la violence révolutionnaire, 1789–1794*. Paris, 2000.

Guilhaumou, Jacques. *L'avènement des portes-parole de la République (1789–1792): Essai de synthèse sur les langages de la Révolution française*. Villeneuve d'Asq, 1998.

———. *La mort de Marat*. Brussels, 1989.

Hampson, Norman. *Danton*. London, 1978.

———. *Prelude to Terror: The Constituent Assembly and the Failure of Consensus, 1789–1791*. Oxford, 1989.

Hanson, Paul R. *The Jacobin Republic under Fire: The Federalist Revolt in the French Revolution*. University Park, PA, 2003.

———. *Provincial Politics in the French Revolution: Caen and Limoges, 1789–1794*. Baton Rouge, LA, 1989.

Harder, Mette. "Reacting to Revolution: The Political Career(s) of J.-L. Tallien." In *Experiencing the French Revolution*. Edited by David Andress. Oxford, 2013: 87–112.

Hardman, John. *Overture to Revolution: The 1787 Assembly of Notables and the Crisis of France's Old Regime*. Oxford, 2010.

Harris, Seymour Edwin. *The Assignats*. Cambridge, MA, 1930.

Hasegawa, Teruo. "Constitution des bibliothèques privées de Poitiers à la fin du XVIIIe siècle." Thèse de 3e cycle, Université de Paris IV, 1971.

Henwood, Philippe, and Edmond Monange. *Brest: Un port en Révolution, 1789–1799*. N.p., 1789.

Hesse, Carla. *The Other Enlightenment: How French Women Became Modern*. Princeton, NJ, 2001.

————. *Publishing and Cultural Politics in Revolutionary Paris, 1789–1810.* Berkeley, 1991.

Histoire de Lorraine. Nancy, 1939.

Hofstadter, Richard. *The Paranoid Style in American Politics.* Chicago, 1965.

Horn, Jeff. *Qui parle pour la nation? Les élections et les élus de la Champagne méridionale, 1765–1830.* Paris, 2004.

Hufton, Olwen H. *Women and the Limits of Citizenship in the French Revolution.* Toronto, 1992.

Hugueney, Louis. *Les clubs dijonnais sous la Révolution.* Dijon, 1905.

Hunt, Lynn A. "Committees and Communes: Local Politics and National Revolution in 1789." *Comparative Studies in Society and History* 18 (1976): 321–346.

————. *The Family Romance of the French Revolution.* Berkeley, 1992.

————. "Male Virtue and Republican Motherhood." In *FRCMPC* 4:195–208.

————. *Inventing Human Rights: A History.* New York, 2007.

————. *Politics, Culture, and Class in the French Revolution.* Berkeley, 1984.

————. *Revolution and Urban Politics in Provincial France: Troyes and Reims, 1786–1790.* Stanford, CA, 1978.

Imbert, Jean. "La peine de mort et l'opinion au XVIII siècle." *Revue de science criminelle* (1964): 509–525.

Israel, Jonathan. *Revolutionary Ideas: An Intellectual History of the French Revolution from the Rights of Man to Robespierre.* Princeton, NJ, 2014.

Jacob, Louis. "La Grande Peur en Artois." *AHRF* 13 (1936): 123–148.

————. *Les suspects pendant la Révolution, 1789–1794.* Paris, 1952.

Jaffé, G. M. *Le mouvement ouvrier à Paris pendant la Révolution française.* Paris, 1924.

Jaume, Lucien. *Le discours Jacobin et la démocratie.* Paris, 1989.

Jaurès, Jean. *Histoire socialiste de la Révolution française.* Rev. ed. 8 vols. Paris, 1922–1927.

Jessenne, Jean-Pierre. *Pouvoir au village en Révolution: Artois, 1760–1848.* Lille, 1987.

Jolivet, Charles. *La Révolution dans l'Ardèche (1788–1795).* L'Argentière, 1930.

Jones, Colin. *The Great Nation: France from Louis XV to Napoleon, 1715–99.* London, 2006.

————. "The Overthrow of Maximilien Robespierre and the 'Indifference of the People.'" *AHR* 119 (2014): 689–713.

Jones, Peter. *The Peasantry in the French Revolution.* Cambridge, 1988.

————. *Politics and Rural Society: The Southern Massif Central, c. 1750–1880.* Cambridge, 1985.

Jordan, David P. *The King's Trial: Louis XVI vs. the French Revolution.* Berkeley, 1979.

Jourdan, Annie. "Les discours de la Terreur à l'époque révolutionnaire (1776–1798): Etude comparative sur une notion ambiguë." *FHS* 36 (2013): 51–81.

Judd, Gerrit P. *Members of Parliament, 1734–1832.* New Haven, CT, 1955.

Julia, Dominique. "Gilbert Romme, gouverneur (1779–1790)." *AHRF* 68 (1996): 221–256.

Kaiser, Thomas E., and Dale Van Kley, editors. *From Deficit to Deluge: The Origins of the French Revolution.* Stanford, 2011.

Kaplan, Steven L. *The Famine Plot Persuasion in Eighteenth-Century France.* Philadelphia, 1982.

———. *La fin des corporations.* Paris, 2001.

Kates, Gary. *The Cercle Social, the Girondins, and the French Revolution.* Princeton, NJ, 1985.

Kennedy, Emmet. *A Cultural History of the French Revolution.* New Haven, CT, 1989.

Kennedy, Michael L. *The Jacobin Clubs in the French Revolution.* 3 vols. Princeton, NJ, 1982–1988; New York, 2000.

———. *The Jacobin Clubs of Marseille, 1790–1794.* Ithaca, NY, 1973.

Kessel, Patrice. *La nuit du 4 août 1789.* Paris, 1969.

Kuscinski, Auguste. *Dictionnaire des Conventionnels.* Paris, 1917.

———. *Les députés à l'Assemblée législative de 1791.* Paris, 1900.

Kwass, Michael. *Privilege and the Politics of Taxation in Eighteenth Century France.* Cambridge, 2000.

Labrosse, Claude, and Pierre Rétat. *Naissance du journal révolutionnaire: 1789.* Lyon, 1989.

Labroue, Henri. *Le club jacobin de Toulon.* Paris, 1907.

———. *Le conventionnel Pinet d'après ses mémoires inédits.* Paris, 1907.

———. *L'esprit public en Dordogne pendant la Révolution.* Paris, 1911.

Lafon, Jacqueline-Lucienne. *La Révolution française face au système judiciaire d'Ancien régime.* Paris, 2001.

Langlois, Claude. "Les dérives vendéennes de l'imaginaire révolutionnaire." *Annales ESC* (1988): 771–797.

———. "L'invention de la liberté: le programme iconographique de la fête parisienne des suisses de Châteauvieux (15 avril 1792)." In *Iconographie et image de la Révolution française.* Montréal, 1990: 110–128.

Lapied, Martine. *Le Comtat et la Révolution française: Naissance des options collectives.* Aix-en-Provence, 1996.

Lebrun, François. *Parole de Dieu et Révolution: Les sermons d'un curé angevin [Yves-Michel Marchais] avant et pendant la guerre de Vendée.* Toulouse, 1979.

Lefebvre, Georges. *Etudes orléanaises.* 2 vols. Paris, 1962–1963.

———. *Le gouvernement révolutionnaire (2 juin 1793–9 thermidor an II).* "Cour professé à l'Ecole normale supérieure de Sèvres." Paris, 1952.

———. *The Great Fear of 1789.* New York, 1973.

———. *La Révolution française: La chute du roi.* Series "Les cours de Sorbonne." Paris, [1940].

———. *La Révolution française: La Convention.* Series "Les cours de Sorbonne." 2 vols. Paris, [1943].

———. *La Révolution française: La fuite du roi.* Series "Les cours de Sorbonne." 4 fasc. Paris, [1939].

———. *La Révolution française: La révolution aristocratique.* Series "Les cours de Sorbonne." Paris, [1937].

———. *La Révolution française: La première Terreur.* Series "Les cours de Sorbonne." Paris, [1942].

———. *Les Thermidoriens.* Paris, 1937.

Le Goff, T. J. A. "Le financement de la participation française à la guerre d'indépendance et ses conséquences: L'état et la conjoncture financière des années 1780." In *Les marines de la guerre d'indépendance américaine (1763–1783). I. L'instrument naval.* Edited by Olivier Chaline et al. Paris, 2013: 335–361.

Le Goff, T. J. A., and D. M. G. Sutherland. "The Revolution and the Rural Community in Eighteenth-Century Brittany." *Past and Present* 62 (Feb. 1974): 96–119.

Lemay, Edna Hindie, editor. *Dictionnaire des Constituants, 1789–1791.* 2 vols. Paris, 1991.

———, editor. *Dictionnaire des Législateurs, 1791–1792.* 2 vols. Ferney-Voltaire, 2006.

———. "Les législateurs de la France révolutionnaire (1791–92)." *AHRF* 79, no. 1 (2007): 3–28.

Lemny, Stefan. *Jean-Louis Carra (1742–1793): Parcours d'un révolutionnaire.* Paris, 2000.

Leuwers, Hervé. *Merlin de Douai (1754–1838): Un juriste en politique.* Arras, 1996.

Linton, Marisa. *Choosing Terror: Virtue, Friendship, and Authenticity in the French Revolution.* Oxford, 2013.

———. "Fatal Friendships: The Politics of Jacobin Friendship." *FHS* 31 (2008): 51–76.

———. "Friends, Enemies, and the Role of the Individual." In *Companion to the History of the French Revolution.* Edited by Peter McPhee. London, 2014: 261–277.

———. "The Stuff of Nightmares: Plots, Assassinations and Duplicity in the Mental World of the Jacobin Leaders, 1793–1794." In *Experiencing the French Revolution.* Edited by David Andress. Oxford, 2013: 201–217.

Lucas, Colin. "Revolutionary Violence, the People, and the Terror." In *FRCMPC* 4:57–79.

———. *The Structure of the Terror: The Example of Javogues and the Loire.* Oxford, 1973.

———. "The Theory and Practice of Denunciation in the French Revolution." In *Accusatory Practices.* Edited by Sheila Fitzpatrick and Robert Gellately. Chicago, 1997: 22–39.

Luzzatto, Sergio. *Mémoire de la Terreur: Vieux montagnards et jeunes républicains au XIXe siècle.* Lyon, 1991.

Marcus, George, editor. *Paranoia within Reason: A Casebook on Conspiracy as Explanation*. Chicago, 1999.

Margadant, Ted W. *Urban Rivalries in the French Revolution*. Princeton, NJ, 1992.

Markoff, John. *The Abolition of Feudalism: Peasants, Lords, and Legislators in the French Revolution*. University Park, PA, 1996.

Martin, Jean-Clément. *Contre-Révolution, Révolution et Nation en France, 1789–1799*. Paris, 1998.

———. *Nouvelle histoire de la Révolution française*. Paris, 2012.

———. *La Vendée et la France*. Paris, 1987.

———. *Violence et Révolution: Essai sur la naissance d'un mythe national*. Paris, 2006.

Mason, Laura. *Singing the French Revolution: Popular Culture and Politics, 1787–1799*. Ithaca, NY, 1996.

Maspero-Clerc, Hélène. *Un journaliste contrerévolutionnaire: Jean-Gabriel Peltier, 1760–1825*. Paris, 1973.

Mathiez, Albert. *Le club des Cordeliers pendant la crise de Varennes*. Paris, 1910.

———. "Etude critique sur les Journées des 5 et 6 octobre 1789." *RH* 67 (1898): 241–281; 68 (1898): 258–294; 69 (1899): 41–66.

———. *Etude d'histoire révolutionnaire: Girondins et Montagnards*. Paris, 1930.

———. "Recherches sur la famille et la vie privée du conventionnel Basire." *AR* 13 (1921): 1–22, 177–206.

———. *La Révolution française*. 3 vols. Paris, 1985 (orig. 1922–1927).

———. *La vie chère et le mouvement social sous la Terreur*. 2 vols. Paris, 1973 (orig. 1927).

Mathiot, Charles-Eugène. *Pour vaincre: Vie, opinions, et pensées de Lazare Carnot*. Paris, 1916.

Mayer, Arno. *The Furies: Violence and Terror in the French and Russian Revolutions*. Princeton, NJ, 2000.

Maza, Sarah. *The Myth of the French Bourgeoisie: An Essay on the Social Imaginary, 1750–1850*. Cambridge, MA, 2003.

Mazeau, Guillaume. *Le bain de l'histoire: Charlotte Corday et l'attentat contre Marat, 1793–2009*. Seyssel, 2009.

McMahon, Darrin M. "The Counter-Enlightenment and the Low-Life of Literature in Pre-Revolutionary France." *Past and Present* no. 159 (May 1998): 77–112.

———. *Enemies of the Enlightenment: The French Counter-Enlightenment and the Making of Modernity*. Oxford, 2001.

McManners, John. *The French Revolution and the Church*. London, 1969.

McPhee, Peter. *A Companion to the French Revolution*. Chichester, U.K., 2014.

———. *The French Revolution, 1789–1799*. Oxford, 2002.

———. *Robespierre: A Revolutionary Life*. New Haven, CT, 2012.

Mège, Francisque. "La grande peur [en Auvergne]." *Bulletin historique et scientifique de l'Auvergne,* 2e sér. (1900): 140–171, 175–240.

———. "Notes biographiques sur les députés de la Basse-Auvergne." *Mémoires de l'Académies des sciences, belles-lettres et arts de Clermont-Ferrand* 7 (1865): 437–468; 10 (1868): 81–102, 339–404.

Menozzi, Daniele. *Les interprétations politiques de Jésus de l'Ancien régime à la Révolution.* Paris, 1983.

Michon, Georges. *Essai sur l'histoire du parti Feuillant: Adrien Duport.* Paris, 1924.

Mitchell, C. J. *The French Legislative Assembly of 1791.* Leiden, 1988.

———. "Political Divisions within the Legislative Assembly of 1791." *FHS* 13 (1983–1984): 356–389.

Monnier, Raymonde. *Le Faubourg Saint-Antoine, 1789–1815.* Paris, 1981.

Montier, Amand. *Robert Lindet, député à l'Assemblée législative et à la Convention.* Paris, 1899.

Moulinas, René. *Les massacres de la Glacière.* Aix-en-Provence, 2003.

Mourlot, Félix. *La fin de l'Ancien régime et les débuts de la Révolution dans la généralité de Caen.* Paris, 1913.

Mousset, A. *Un témoin ignoré de la Révolution, le comte de Fernan Nuñez, ambassadeur d'Espagne à Paris, 1787–1791.* Paris, 1924.

Muller, D. "Magistrats français et peine de mort au XVIIIe siècle." *XVIIIe siècle* 4 (1972): 79–107.

Münch, Philippe. "Le pouvoir de l'ombre: L'imaginaire du complot durant la Révolution française (1789–1801)." Doctoral thesis, University of Laval, 2008.

Murray, William James. *The Right-Wing Press in the French Revolution: 1789–92.* Woodbridge, U.K., 1986.

Nicolas, Jean. *La rébellion française: Mouvements populaires et conscience sociale (1661–1789).* Paris, 2002.

Nicolas, Raymond. *L'esprit public et les élections dans le département de la Marne de 1790 à l'an VIII: Essai sur la Révolution française en province.* Châlons-sur-Marne, 1909.

Olsen, Mark. "A Failure of Enlightened Politics in the French Revolution: The Société de 1789." *French History* 6 (1992): 303–334.

Ozouf, Mona. *Festivals and the French Revolution.* Trans. Alan Sheridan. Cambridge, MA, 1988.

Ozouf-Marignier, Marie-Vic. *La formation des départements: La représentation du territoire français à la fin du 18e siècle.* Paris, 1989.

Palmer, Robert R. *Twelve Who Ruled: The Year of the Terror in the French Revolution.* Princeton, NJ, 1941.

Parker, Harold. *The Cult of Antiquity and the French Revolution.* Chicago, 1937.

Parker, Lindsay A. H. *Writing the Revolution: A French Woman's History in Letters.* New York, 2013.

Patrick, Alison. *The Men of the First French Republic: Political Alignments in the National Convention of 1792.* Baltimore, 1972.

———. "Paper, Posters, and People: Official Communication in France, 1789–94." *Historical Studies* 18 (1978): 1–23.

Paumès, Benjamin. "La Grande Peur en Quercy et en Rouergue: Notes et documents." *Bulletin de la Société des études littéraires, scientifiques, et artistiques du Lot* 37 (1912): 29–44, 103–117, 181–200, 229–245.

Perroud, Claude. *La proscription des Girondins, 1793–1795.* Paris, 1917.

Petitfils, Jean-Christian. "Les origines de la pensée contre-révolutionnaire." In *La Contre-Révolution.* Edited by Jean Tulard. Paris, 1990: 16–32.

Petitfrère, Claude. *Blancs et bleus d'Anjou (1789–1793).* Lille, 1979.

Peyrard, Christine. *Les Jacobins de l'Ouest.* Paris, 1996.

Pimenova, Ludmila. "Analyse des cahiers de doléances: L'exemple des cahiers de la Noblesse." *Mélanges de l'Ecole de Rome* 103 (1991): 85–101.

Pingué, Danièle, and Jean-Paul Rothiot, editors. *Les comités de surveillance: D'une création citoyenne à une institution révolutionnaire.* Paris, 2012.

Pommeret, Hervé. *L'esprit politique dans le département des Côtes-du-Nord pendant la Révolution: 1789–99.* Saint-Brieuc, 1921.

Popkin, Jeremy. *Revolutionary News: The Press in France, 1789–1799.* Durham, NC, 1990.

———. *The Right Wing Press in France, 1792–1800.* Chapel Hill, 1980.

Porret, Michel. " 'Effrayer le crime par la terreur des châtiments': La pédagogie de l'effroi chez quelques criminalistes du XVIIIe siècle." In *La peur aux XVIIIe siècle: Discours, représentations, pratiques.* Edited by Jacques Berchtold and Michel Porret. Geneva, 1994: 46–67.

Poupé, Edmond. "Le département du Var, 1790-an VIII." *Bulletin de la Société d'études scientifiques et archéologiques de Draguignan* 40 (1934–1935): 1–553.

Price, Munro. *The Road from Versailles: Louis XVI, Marie-Antoinette, and the Fall of the French Monarchy.* New York, 2002.

Quéniart, Jean. *Culture et société urbaines dans la France de l'Ouest au XVIII siècle.* Paris, 1978.

Reddy, William M. *The Navigation of Feeling: A Framework for the History of Emotions.* Cambridge, 2001.

Reinhard, Marcel. *La chute de la royauté.* Paris, 1969.

———. *Le grand Carnot.* 2 vols. Paris, 1959.

———. *Nouvelle histoire de Paris. La Révolution.* Paris, 1971.

Renouvin, Pierre. *Les assemblées provinciales de 1787.* Paris, 1921.

Rétat, Pierre. "Formes et discours d'un journal révolutionnaire: Les *Révolutions de Paris* en 1789." In *L'instrument périodique: La fonction de la presse au XVIIIe siècle.* Lyon, 1985: 139–178.

Reynolds, Sian. *Marriage and Revolution: Monsieur and Madame Roland.* Oxford, 2012.

Roche, Daniel. *France in the Enlightenment.* Cambridge, MA, 2000.

———. *The People of Paris: An Essay in Popular Culture in the 18th Century.* Trans. Marie Evans. Berkeley, 1987.

———. *Le siècle des Lumières en province: Académies et académiciens provinciaux, 1680–1789.* Paris, 1978.

Roosevelt, Grace G. *Reading Rousseau in the Nuclear Age.* Philadelphia, 1990.

Rosanvallon, Pierre. *Le peuple introuvable: Histoire de la représentation démocratique en France.* Paris, 1998.

Rose, R. Barrie. *The Making of the Sans-Culottes: Democratic Ideas and Institutions in Paris, 1789–92.* Manchester, 1983.

Rosenwein, Barbara H. *Emotional Communities in the Early Middle Ages.* Ithaca, NY, 2006.

Rosnow, Ralph L., and Gary Alan Fine. *Rumor and Gossip: The Social Psychology of Hearsay.* New York, 1976.

Rouvière, François. *Histoire de la Révolution française dans le départment du Gard.* Nîmes, 1887.

Roux, Marie de. *Histoire religieuse de la Révolution à Poitiers et dans la Vienne.* Lyon, 1952.

———. *La Révolution à Poitiers et dans la Vienne.* Paris, 1910.

Rudé, George. *The Crowd in the French Revolution.* New York, 1959.

Sagnac, Philippe. *La chute de la royauté.* Paris, 1909.

Savey-Casard, P. *La peine de mort, esquisse historique et juridique.* Geneva, 1968.

Schama, Simon. *Citizens: A Chronique of the French Revolution.* New York, 1989.

Scott, Samuel F. *The Response of the Royal Army to the French Revolution: The Role and Development of the Line Army, 1787–93.* Oxford, 1978.

Scott, William. *Terror and Repression in Revolutionary Marseilles.* London, 1973.

Sée, Henri. "Les troubles agraires en Haute-Bretagne (1790–1791)." *Bulletin d'histoire économique de la Révolution* (1920–1921): 231–373.

Seinguerlet, Eugène. *Strasbourg pendant la Révolution.* Paris, 1881.

Seligman, Edmond. *La justice en France pendant la Révolution (1789–1792).* Paris, 1901.

Sepinwall, Alyssa Goldstein. *The Abbé Grégoire and the French Revolution: The Making of Modern Universalism.* Berkeley, 2005.

Serna, Pierre. *Antonelle: Aristocrate révolutionnaire.* Paris, 1997.

———. "Le duel durant la Révolution: De la joute archaïque au combat politique." *Historical Reflections* 29 (2003): 409–431.

———. "L'encre et le sang." In *Croiser le fer: Violence et culture de l'épée dans la France moderne (XVIe–XVIIIe siècle).* Edited by Pascal Brioist, Hervé Drévillon, and Pierre Serna. Seyssel, 2002.

———. *La république des girouettes, 1789–1815.* Seyssel, France, 2005.

Sewell, William. "The Sans-Culotte Rhetoric of Subsistence." In *FRCMPC,* 4:249–269.

———. *Work and Revolution: The Language of Labor from the Old Regime to 1848.* Cambridge, 1980.

Shapiro, Barry M. *Revolutionary Justice in Paris, 1789–1790.* Cambridge, 1993.

———. "Self-Sacrifice, Self-Interest, or Self-Defence? The Constituent Assembly and the 'Self-Denying Ordinance' of May 1791." *FHS* 25 (2002): 625–656.

Shibutani, Tamotsu. *Improvised News: A Sociological Study of Rumor.* New York, 1966.

Shovlin, John. *The Political Economy of Virtue: Luxury, Patriotism, and the Origins of the French Revolution.* Ithaca, NY, 2006.

Simonin, Anne. *Le déshonneur dans la République: Une histoire de l'indignité, 1791–1958.* Paris, 2008.

Slavin, Morris. *The Hébertistes to the Guillotine. Anatomy of a "Conspiracy" in Revolutionary France.* Baton Rouge, LA, 1994.

———. *The Making of an Insurrection: Parisian Sections and the Gironde.* Cambridge, MA, 1986.

Smith, Jay M. *Nobility Reimagined: The Patriotic Nation in Eighteenth Century France.* Ithaca, NY, 2005.

Smyth, Jonathan. "Public Experience of the Revolution: The National Reaction to the Proclamation of the *Fête de l'Etre suprême.*" In *Experiencing the French Revolution.* Edited by David Andress. Oxford, 2013: 155–176.

Soboul, Albert. *Histoire de la Révolution française.* 2 vols. Paris, 1962.

———. *Les sans-culottes parisiens en l'an II: Mouvement populaire et gouvernement révolutionnaire, 2 juin 1793–9 thermidor an II.* Paris, 1962.

Sol, Eugène. *La Révolution en Quercy.* 4 vols. Paris, 1926.

Sonenscher, Michael. *Sans-culottes: An Eighteenth Century Emblem in the French Revolution.* Princeton, NJ, 2008.

Sorel, Albert. *L'Europe et la Révolution française.* 9 vols. Paris, 1885–1911.

Spang, Rebecca L. *The Invention of the Restaurant: Paris and Modern Gastronomic Culture.* Cambridge, MA, 2000.

———. "Paradigms and Paranoia: How Modern is the French Revolution?" *AHR* 108 (2003): 119–147.

Stearns, Carol Z., and Peter N. Stearns. *Emotion and Social Change: Toward a New Psychohistory.* New York, 1988.

Steinberg, Ronen. "Trauma before Trauma: Imagining the Effects of the Terror in Post-Revolutionary France." In *Experiencing the French Revolution.* Edited by David Andress. Oxford, 2013: 177–199.

Sternberg, Robert J., and Karin Sternberg. *The Nature of Hate.* Cambridge, 2008.

Sutherland, D. M. G. *The Chouans: The Social Origins of Popular Counterrevolution in Upper Brittany.* Oxford, 1982.

———. "Justice and Murder: Massacres in the Provinces, Versailles, Meaux, and Reims in 1792." *Past and Present* 222 (Feb. 2014): 129–162.

———. *Murder in Aubagne: Lynching, Law, and Justice during the French Revolution.* Cambridge, 2009.

———. "The Vendée: Unique or Emblematic?" In *FRCMPC*, 4:99–114.

Sydenham, M. J. *The Girondins.* London, 1961.

———. *Léonard Bourdon: The Career of a Revolutionary.* Waterloo, Ont., 1999.

Tackett, Timothy. *Becoming a Revolutionary: The Deputies of the French National Assembly and the Emergence of a Revolutionary Culture (1789–1790).* Princeton, NJ, 1996.

———. "Collective Panics in the Early French Revolution, 1789–1791: A Comparative Perspective." *French History* 17 (2003): 149–171.

———. "Conspiracy Obsession in a Time of Revolution: French Elites and the Origins of the Terror: 1789–1792." *AHR* 105 (2000): 691–713.

———. "The Constituent Assembly and the Terror." In *FRCMPC* [1994], 4:39–54.

———. "The Constituent Assembly in the Second Year of the French Revolution." In *Revolution, Society, and the Politics of Memory: Proceedings of the 10th George Rudé Seminar.* Melbourne, 1996: 162–169.

———. "Les députés de l'Assemblée législative, 1791–92." In *Pour la Révolution française: En hommage à Claude Mazauric.* Rouen, 1998: 139–144.

———. "La grande peur de 1789 et la thèse du complot aristocratique." *AHRF* 76, no. 1 (2004): 51–17.

———. "Paths to Revolution: The Old Regime Correspondence of Five Future Revolutionaries." *FHS* 32 (2009): 531–554.

———. *Religion, Revolution, and Regional Culture in Eighteenth-Century France.* Princeton, NJ, 1986.

———. "The West in France in 1789: The Religious Factor in the Origins of the Counterrevolution." *JMH* 54 (1982): 715–745.

———. *When the King Took Flight.* Cambridge, MA, 2003.

———. "Women and Men in Counterrevolution: The Sommières Riot of 1791." *JMH* 59 (1987): 680–704.

Tackett, Timothy, and Nicolas Déplanche. "L'idée du 'complot' dans l'oeuvre de Georges Lefebvre: Remise en cause à partir d'une nouvelle source." Online article at www.ihrf.com.

Taylor, George V. "Revolutionary and Non-Revolutionary Content in the *Cahiers* of 1789: An Interim Report." *FHS* 7 (1971–1972): 479–502.

Thompson, J. M. *The French Revolution.* New York, 1966 (orig. 1943).

Tocqueville, Alexis de. *The Old Regime and the French Revolution.* Trans. Stuart Gilbert. New York, 1955.

Tulard, Jean, editor. *La Contre-Révolution.* Paris, 1990.

Turley, Katherine M. "Channels of Influence: Patronage, Power and Politics in Poitou from Louis XIV to the Revolution." Ph.D. dissertation, University of California, Irvine, 1997.

Vaissière, Pierre de. *La mort du roi (21 janvier 1793)*. Paris, 1910.

Van Kley, Dale, editor. *The French Idea of Freedom: The Old Regime and the Declaration of Rights of 1789*. Stanford, CA, 1994.

———. *The Religious Origins of the French Revolution: From Calvin to the Civil Constitution, 1560–1791*. New Haven, CT, 1996.

Vidal, Pierre. *Histoire de la Révolution française dans le département des Pyrénées-Orientales*. 3 vols. Perpignan, 1885–1888.

Vovelle, Michel. *La mentalité révolutionnaire: Société et mentalités sous la Révolution française*. Paris, 1985.

———. *La Révolution contre l'église: De la raison à l'être suprème*. Brussels, 1988.

———. *La Révolution française, 1789–1799*. Paris, 1992.

Wahl, Maurice. *Les premières années de la Révolution à Lyon, 1788–1792*. Paris, 1894.

Wahnich, Sophie. "De l'économie émotive de la Terreur." *Annales E.S.C.* 57 (2002): 889–913.

———. *La liberté ou la mort: Essai sur la Terreur et le terrorisme*. Paris, 2003.

Wallon, Henri. *Histoire du Tribunal révolutionnaire de Paris*. 6 vols. Paris, 1880–1882.

———. *La révolution du 31 mai et le fédéralisme en 1793*. 2 vols. Paris, 1886.

Walter, Gérard. *Actes du Tribunal révolutionnaire*. Paris, 1968.

———. *La conjuration du Neuf Thermidor*. Paris, 1974.

———. *Histoire des Jacobins*. Paris, 1946.

———. *Robespierre*. 2 vols. Paris, 1961.

Walton, G. Charles. *Policing Public Opinion in the French Revolution: The Culture of Calumny and the Problem of Free Speech*. Oxford, 2009.

Wick, Daniel L. *A Conspiracy of Well-Intentioned Men: The Society of Thirty and the French Revolution*. New York, 1987.

Woloch, Isser. *The New Regime: Transformations of the French Civic Order, 1789–1820s*. New York, 1994.

Acknowledgments

THE RESEARCH for this book was begun in 1996, though it was interrupted by other projects, and it took me to dozens of archives and libraries throughout France. I was greatly assisted by a President's Fellowship from the University of California; by numerous summer travel grants from the University of California, Irvine; by a Fellowship from the National Humanities Center; by a Miegunyah Distinguished Visiting Fellowship at the University of Melbourne; and by a Research Fellowship from Senshu University, Tokyo.

It would be impossible to list all the friends and scholars who assisted me over the years. Jack Censer, David Garrioch, Lynn Hunt, Ted Margadant, Peter McCormick, Peter McPhee, Joyce Seltzer, and Donald Sutherland all read the entire manuscript. I am enormously grateful for their advice and suggestions, even when I sometimes neglected to incorporate all of their ideas. I also wish to express my gratitude to the many other friends and colleagues throughout the world who shared their thoughts and suggestions and sometimes their unpublished manuscripts, or who assisted me with local archives. Among them are Frank Bean, Mireille Bossis, Philippe Bourdin, Carolyn Boyd, Peter Campbell, Harvey Chisick, Charles Chubb, Ian Coller, Francesco Dendena, Brian Joseph Distelberg, Marc Du Pouget, Dan Edelstein, Sarah Farmer, Yann Fauchois, Gao Yi, Jan Goldstein, Carla Hesse, Peter Jones, Dominique Julia, Thomas Kaiser, Hervé Kergall, Mary Kergall, Yan Laborie, Claude Langlois, Lui Kan, Edna Hindie Lemay, Marisa Linton, Joby Margadant, Jean-Clément Martin, Charles Mitchell, Allison Okuda, Siân Reynolds, Pierre Serna, William Sewell, Tanis Thorne, and last but not least, Michel Vovelle.

Acknowledgments

Many of my students helped me with their research assistance, their own research and publications, and their enthusiasm. Among them are Micah Alpaugh, Elizabeth Andrews-Bond, Robert Blackman, Cynthia Cardona, Nicolas Déplanche, Adam Guerin, Lindsay Holowach Parker, Kenneth Loiselle, Kathryn Marsden, Morag Martin, Courtney Nguyen, Laura Sextro, and Katherine Turley Jacobson.

May I also express my appreciation to Véronique Despine at the Musée de la Révolution Française in Vizille for her assistance with the illustrations and to Philip Schwartzburg for preparing the maps.

Papers relating to aspects of this book were presented at various meetings of the George Rudé Seminar, the Society for French Historical Studies, the Western Society for French History, the Society for the Study of French History, the Washington-Baltimore Old Regime Group, and the American Historical Association. Other papers were given as invited lectures at Stanford University, the University of Paris I (Sorbonne), the Archives Nationales, the University of Chicago (campuses in Paris and in Beijing), Columbia University, the University of Melbourne, Monash University, the University of Adelaide, Peking University, Georgetown University, the University of London's Institute of Historical Research, and the Ecole normale supérieure. In the course of these meetings, I received many helpful comments, sometimes from individuals whose names I never learned.

Finally, a very special word of thanks to Helen Harden Chenut and Nicolas Tackett. I am extraordinarily fortunate to live in a family of historians, and my gratitude for their advice and support is impossible to express.

Index

Abbaye prison, 211, 214, 272, 276
Absolute monarchy, 76, 343
Academies, 27
Acquittals, 333
Actes des apôtres, 102
Active citizens, 74–75, 83, 159, 186
Administrators: royal, 24, 72–74, 91; of
    Revolution, 55, 74–76, 94, 100, 109, 122,
    134–135, 139, 145, 166, 205, 260, 267, 305, 344,
    349; of departments, 74–76, 100, 107, 116,
    146, 178, 184, 204–205, 224, 257, 282–284; of
    districts, 74–76, 100, 116, 134, 146–147, 178,
    183, 257, 283–284, 298; of municipalities, 43,
    73, 74–76, 83, 92, 116, 146–147, 196, 178, 183,
    257; of Paris, 55, 57, 64, 84–85, 88, 78, 85, 92,
    94; accused of treason, 292
Aisne, department, 110, 134
Aix-la-Chapelle, 262–263
Albi, 264
Alembert, Jean Le Rond d', 30
Alexandre, Charles-Alexis, 185, 188, 190, 193
Alps, 222–223, 280
Alsace, 52, 82, 105, 108, 110, 258, 322
Altar of the fatherland, 297, 318
Amar, Jean-Pierre-André, 244, 307
Ambush: in Paris, 55–56, 188, 190–191, 197, 200,
    346; in the Vendée, 261
American Revolution, 37, 40
Amnesty, 120, 165, 283, 306
Angers, 182, 280
Angoulême, 182, 258
Anjou, 91, 108, 258, 261
Année littéraire, 97, 103
Annexations, 226, 249, 255
Anticlericalism, 257, 315

Antraigues, Emmanuel-Henri-Louis, count d',
    105
Antwerp, 222, 322
Appeal to the people, 237–240
Aquitaine, 81
Ardennes, department, 204
Argonne Forest, 220
Ariège, department, 205
Aristocracy, 19, 22, 42, 50, 68, 122, 126–127,
    140–141, 246. *See also* Nobility
Aristocratic party, 45–47, 65, 92, 151, 344, 347
Aristocratic plot, 281
Aristocrats, as term of oprobrium, 95, 99, 104,
    111, 119, 155, 158, 173, 177, 231, 252, 254–255,
    278, 295, 300, 321, 333
Artois, count d', 57, 98–99, 105, 107, 111, 167,
    195
Assassination, 289–292, 295, 325, 347
Assembly of Notables, 41–43
Assignats, 94, 144, 154, 161, 170, 227, 328
Atheism, 315, 318
Aubert-Dubayet, Jean-Baptiste-Annibal, 154,
    195
Auch, 147
Audouin, Jean-Pierre, 213
Audouyn de Pompery, Anne-Marie, 10, 116
Austria, 11, 37, 112, 114, 128, 145, 156, 167–169,
    173, 195, 199, 204, 219, 235, 242, 264, 280, 320
Austrian Committee, 154, 157–158, 167, 174, 180
Austrian Lowlands. *See* Belgium
Authority, 24, 58, 144; royal, 42, 54, 64–65, 88,
    136, 176, 177, 179–180; of National Assembly,
    39; breakdown of, 199, 344; crisis of, 71–73;
    of Committee of Public Safety, 302, 304–305
Auvergne, 109, 152, 258

Avignon, 107, 169, 226
Azéma, Michel, 147, 150

Bagot, Jean-Louis, 167
Bailly, Jean-Sylvain, 50–51, 117, 200, 327
Bancal des Issarts, Jean-Henri, 191, 226, 249
Banquets, communal, 92, 122, 139, 163, 165
Barbaroux, Charles, 228, 230, 232, 238,
  282–283, 288, 291, 327
Barbier-Schroffenberg, Marie-Anne baronne
  de, 10, 111–112
Barère, Bertrand, 7, 16, 50, 238, 249, 254, 268,
  275, 286–287, 292, 294, 297–298, 301–306,
  341, 348
Barnave, Antoine, 8, 14, 44, 49–50, 70, 86, 119,
  152, 169, 202, 327
Barras, Paul, 7, 335, 339
Barricades, 55, 58
Barruel, abbé Augustin, 136, 97, 103
Barry, Madame du, 202
Basire, Claude, 150, 154, 214, 229, 231, 275
Basquiat de Mugriet, Alexis, 119
Bastille, 55–57, 71, 91, 98, 121, 123, 164, 181;
  Place de la, 182, 297
Bayard, Pierre Terrail, chevalier de, 103
Beauharnais, Alexandre de, 328
Beccaria, Cesare, 35
Belgium, 173, 222–223, 226, 242, 249, 262–263,
  280, 322
Belot, Denis, 221
Bergerac, 181–182
Berry, 53
Berthier de Sauvigny, Louis-Bénigne-François,
  57, 72
Besançon, 82, 182
Betrayal, 139–140, 172–173, 175, 180, 209, 239,
  265, 268, 279, 285, 291, 321, 324, 346
Billaud-Varenne, Jacques-Nicolas, 228, 231, 291,
  197, 302, 319, 335–336, 341
Biron, Armand-Louis duc de, 204, 328
Birotteau, Jean-Bonaventure, 270, 289, 327
Bishops, 19, 77, 100, 107, 110; of Paris, 316–317;
  palace of (Paris), 273
Blacks, 100–101, 158, 231
Blad, Claude-Antoine, 10, 222, 235–236, 240,
  250, 255, 258, 263, 265, 274, 285, 307
Blues, in Western France, 260
Bodyguards, royal, 118, 174–175, 185, 195
Boissy d'Anglas, François-Antoine, 275
Bonaparte, Napoleon, 322
Bordas, Pardoux, 240
Bordeaux, 13, 28, 86–87, 106, 131–133, 135, 153, 182,
  205, 228, 258, 260, 268, 283–285, 311, 325, 327

Bouchette, François-Joseph, 109, 119
Bouillé, François-Claude, marquis de, 114, 165
Boullé, Jean-Pierre, 122
Bourdon, Léonard, 264, 268, 308, 339
Bourg-en-Bresse, 282
Bourgeoisie, 18, 26, 55, 159–160, 252. *See also*
  Middle class
Bourges, 283
Bouville, Louis-Jacques, chevalier de, 104–105
Boyer-Fonfrède, Jean-Baptiste, 222, 249, 278,
  282, 285, 287, 307–308, 311
Boze, Joseph (painter), 238
Brawls, 25, 33, 345
Bread: lines, 66; shortages of, 299; price of,
  52–53, 124, 136, 161, 251. *See also* Grain
Bresse, 80
Brest, 112, 182–183, 189, 258
Breton Club, 59
Brissot, Jacques-Pierre, 9, 11, 15, 17, 35, 62–63,
  68, 117, 129, 133–134, 151–153, 155–157,
  162–164, 167–168, 174, 179, 195, 199, 224,
  227–228, 230–233, 237–239, 248–249, 255,
  270–271, 282, 306–308, 311, 328
Brissotins. *See* Girondins
Brittany, 44, 48, 59, 84, 91, 108, 116, 182, 188,
  190, 213, 258, 261, 263, 284
Bruges, 322
Brunswick, duke of, 199, 207, 219–222, 307
Brunswick Manifesto, 183–184
Brussels, 222, 322–323
Brutus, Lucius Junius, 16, 200, 235
Buffon, Georges-Louis Leclerc de, 30
Bugey, 91
Bundling, of accused in political trials, 308,
  327, 229
Burgundy, 258, 299
Buzot, François, 228, 230, 283, 291, 327

Caen, 282–285, 289, 291
Cafés, 86, 160, 251
Cahiers de doléances. See Statements of
  grievances
Cahors, 222
Ça ira!, 94, 167, 179, 204
Calendar, Revolutionary, 312, 315–316
Calonne, Charles-Alexandre de, 41, 99
Calvados, department, 289
Cambon, Pierre-Joseph, 154–155, 158, 227, 292,
  336
Campmas, Jean-François, 61
Campmas, Pierre, 246, 264, 334
Camus, Armand-Gaston, 17, 49
Cantonal assemblies, 288, 296–297

Capital punishment, 1, 34–37, 242, 268, 295–296, 327, 342

Carnot, Lazare, 4, 14, 278, 291, 298, 320

Carra, Jean-Louis, 199, 224, 228, 238, 282, 307–308

Carrier, Jean-Baptiste, 326, 335, 341

Catalina, 129

Catholic Church, 29–30, 81–82, 110, 112, 196, 235, 344; property of, 70, 75, 101, 107, 196, 262

Catholic Enlightenment, 29

Catholicism, 61, 100, 101, 105, 107–108, 140, 262, 315; as state religion, 101, 105

Cato, 16, 129

Causse, Guillaume, 155

Cavellier, Blaise, 158

Caylus, duke of, 34

Cazalès, Jacques-Antoine-Marie de, 33, 101, 158

Censorship, 44, 77, 118, 124, 198, 225

Centralization, 270, 302, 305, 328, 340

Central Revolutionary Committee (May-June 1793), 273–274, 286

Cercle social, 88

Chabot, dom François, 243, 275, 290

Chaillon, Etienne, 10, 263, 321–322, 332

Chalier, Joseph, 282, 288

Châlons-sur-Marne, 222

Champagne, 52, 114

Champ de Mars, 93, 184, 297, 318, 323; massacre of, 117, 120, 154, 165

Champion de Cicé, Jérôme-Marie, 72, 84

Champs-Elysées, 58, 93, 142, 256

Chantilly, 80

Charisma, 152–153, 158, 347

Charivaris, 82

Charleroi, 322

Charles I, of England, 234

Chartres, duke de, 222

Chasset, Charles-Antoine, 289

Châteauroux, 64, 148

Chateaus, 110, 118, 206; attacks against, 59, 82, 84

Châteauvieux, Swiss regiment of, 79, 165

Châtelet court, 72

Chaumette, Pierre-Gaspard, 88, 197, 293, 299–300, 308, 316–317

Chevallier, abbé François, 260–261

Chinon, 280

Cicero, 16–17, 129

Circumstances, 4, 158, 262, 277–278, 342, 348

Civil code, 70, 165

Civil Constitution of the Clergy, 107–110, 114

Civil rights, 28, 343

Civil War, 82, 104, 107, 119, 178, 185, 190, 257–261, 281, 292–293, 325–326, 342, 349

Classics, 16–17, 26, 129, 158, 161. *See also* Greeks; Romans

Clavière, Etienne, 170

Clergy, 4, 13, 27, 42–43, 53, 58, 60–61, 63, 65–66, 68, 82, 92–93, 107–110, 125–126, 132, 136, 140–141, 196, 258, 260, 262, 293, 295, 315, 326; conservative deputies of, 95, 100; executions of, 330; expulsion from parishes, 315; marrying of, 315–316; renounciation of priesthood, 315–316

Clermont-Ferrand, 142, 171

Cloots, Anacharsis, 168

Clothing, 46, 251; mode for deputies, 246; for women, 314

Clubs, 4, 79, 86–90, 96, 116, 118, 122, 125, 131–132, 134–135, 139, 146–158, 164, 178, 181, 204, 206, 253, 268, 297–298, 302, 303, 314, 319, 323, 344; conservative, 99, 104, 132

Coblenz, 170

Cocarde, 66, 107, 162

Cochin, Augustin, 2

Codet, Sylvain, 154, 204, 211

Collot d'Herbois, Jean-Marie, 197, 228, 302–303, 319, 332, 335–336, 341, 347

Colonies, 20, 37, 40, 46, 96, 143, 248, 313

Colson, Adrien-Joseph, 9–10, 26, 27, 31, 34–37, 40, 42, 44, 52, 54–55, 64–66, 69, 78, 84, 90, 95, 122, 124, 126–128, 130, 137, 142, 144, 166, 168, 176, 185, 188, 192, 215, 219, 241–242, 275–276, 312

Commission of Twelve, 272–274, 276, 306

Committee of a Hundred, 45, 98

Committee of General Defense, 245, 270

Committee of General Security, 268, 307, 324, 327–329, 333, 335–336, 341

Committee of Public Safety, 235, 274, 277, 285–287, 292–293, 295, 297–306, 319–320, 324, 327–329, 332–333, 335–336, 340, 346, 348; creation of, 269–270; intransigeance of, 292; moderates removed from, 292

Committee on Research, in Paris, 133

Committees in national assemblies, 225, 233, 305; of Thirty, 44; on finance, 227; on Research, 133–134, 137–140; on constitution, 51, 225, 232

Communal property, 196

Commune of Paris, 187, 197, 272–274, 293, 298, 302, 315–316, 323, 337, 340; General Council of, 197, 214; officials of, 202, 209; Insurrectional, 187, 192, 197–203, 211, 214, 225, 228, 230

Comtat Venaissin, 169

Conciliation, 328; toward Girondins after June 2, 1793, 287, 291–292, 348

Condé, 280, 291, 320

Condorcet, marquis de, 10, 89, 117, 153, 168, 184, 287, 327

Confession, 109, 146, 259

Conscription, 250, 258–259, 319

Conspiracy, 7, 37, 65, 87–88, 95, 98–99, 105, 113, 126–128, 131–134, 137–139, 141, 135–139, 145, 154, 158–160, 166, 170, 172–174, 180, 183, 186, 188, 202–206, 209–211, 217, 223, 231, 233–235, 251–253, 256, 267–268, 272, 277, 281, 291–293, 299, 301, 309, 324–326, 329–330, 332, 335–336, 344, 346–347; aristocratic, 58, 64. *See also* Grand conspiracy

Conspiracy obsession, 35, 132, 135, 139, 141, 209, 243, 348

Constituent Assembly. *See* National Assembly

Constitution, 1, 39, 44, 51, 61, 65, 67, 70–71, 94, 116–117, 120, 122, 131–132, 134, 142–143, 145–146, 151, 165, 168, 170–171, 179, 184, 225, 233–234, 236, 245, 283; of 1793, 286–288, 296–297, 305, 329; by Girondins, 247, 287

Constitutional Act. *See* Constitution: of 1793

Constitutional Clergy, 109, 196, 260, 315, 319

Convention, 1, 88, 132, 184, 193, 196, 205, 216–217, 223–243, 245–278, 280–315, 317–318, 320–326, 328–330, 332, 334–339, 340–341, 345–346; hall of, 251–252, 255; humiliated by militants, 274–276; losing legitimacy, 286; post-Thermidorian, 349

Corbel de Squirio, Vincent-Claude, 140, 163, 217, 231, 278

Corday, Charlotte, 289–291

Cordeliers club, 88–90, 117, 131, 159, 161, 182, 195, 197, 202, 251, 253, 302, 329

Correspondence, 7–11, 27, 69; self-censored of, 312, 341

Correspondence received by assemblies: National Assembly, 70, 73, 102, 116–117, 139; Legislative Assembly, 178, 204; Convention, 246–247, 263

Corruption, 129, 132, 252, 328, 252, 328

Counter-Enlightenment, 97

Counterfeiters, 36–37, 162, 203, 212

Counterrevolution, 6–7, 22, 65, 69, 85, 87, 90, 94, 96–113, 122–123, 132–133, 138, 141, 145, 157, 159, 163, 172, 182–183, 188, 195, 198, 206, 210, 212, 221, 235, 255–256, 259–261, 264, 268, 274–275, 278, 295, 297, 315, 326–327, 330, 341, 344, 346–348

Court, royal, 19, 28, 31, 154

Couthon, Georges, 8, 10, 152, 163, 167, 170, 178, 229, 236, 244, 249, 277, 287, 291, 292, 294, 335–337, 348

Crime, 34–37, 127–128, 140, 215, 242, 289, 293, 309, 311

Criminal code, 235

Criminal tribunals, 203

Crusade, 97, 103, 110, 168

Cultural revolution, 319

Curency, paper. See *Assignats*

Custine, Adam-Philippe de, 328

Danton, Georges, 8, 88, 163, 195, 228, 230–231, 263, 267, 270, 275, 286–287, 292, 294, 302, 305, 328–330, 334–336, 341

Dauphin (son of Louis XVI), 178, 184, 233, 264, 299

Dauphiné, 44, 59, 65

David, Jacques-Louis, 50, 243, 266–267, 291, 297, 318

Debry, Jean, 240, 243

Decadi, 316

Decentralization, 76, 96, 256, 267, 345

Dechristianization, 303, 315–317, 328

Declaration of duties, 98

Declaration of the Rights of Man and the Citizen, 39, 60–62, 65, 67–68, 76, 88, 92, 98, 100, 151, 164, 177, 200, 234, 240, 287, 297, 303, 310, 313, 317, 342

Declaration of the Rights of Women, 89, 254

Deism, 319

Delacroix, Charles-François, 263, 275, 292

Delegates: of primary assemblies (1793), 297–299; Central committee of, 298. *See also* Cantonal assemblies

Demagoguery, 157, 324

Demée, Louis-Michel, 151, 175

Democracy, 73, 76, 84, 86–87, 96, 122, 129, 144, 159, 161, 196, 325, 339, 345; direct, 85, 296

Demonization, 139–141, 158–159, 179, 205, 231, 326, 347

Demonstrations, 43, 78, 85, 89, 117–118, 164–165, 176–179, 184, 215, 252–254, 272–273, 299–300, 302, 346

Denunciations, 128–135, 139, 141, 150, 202, 206, 210, 268, 272, 294, 346

Department. *See* Administrators

Deperret, Charles-Romain Lauze, 291, 307

Deportation, 175, 196, 257

Deputies: in National Assembly, 70; in Legislative Assembly, 142–144, 167, 169–170; in Convention, 229–230; heavy work load of, 245–246; families of, 246; secretaries of, 246;

exhaustion of, 305, 325; death threats against, 243; carrying pistols, 150, 274. *See also* Convention; Legislative Assembly; National Assembly

Desacralization, 31

Desèze, Raymond de, 236

Desmoulins, Camille, 14, 88, 118, 129, 157, 224, 228, 294–295, 328–329

Despotism, 78, 165, 234

Diamond Necklace Affair, 31

Dictatorship, 198, 230, 269, 271, 339

Diderot, Denis, 30, 136

Digaultray, Jean-Baptiste, 192, 209

Diplomacy, 169–170, 227, 324, 341

District. *See* Administrators

Divorce, 196, 313

Dobsen, Claude-Emmanuel, 308

Domiciliary visits, 209, 265

Drôme, department, 284, 295

Drouet, Jean-Baptiste, 114–115, 243, 300

Drownings of prisoners, 326

Dubois-Crancé, Edmond-Louis-Alexis, 238, 250, 335

Dubreuil-Chambardel, Pierre, 10, 213, 216, 238–239, 264, 278, 281, 287, 289, 305

Ducos, Jean-François, 153, 285, 307–308, 311

Dueling, 22, 25, 33–34, 38, 345

Dufriche-Valazé, Charles-Eléonor, 311

Du Guesclin, Bertrand, 103

Dulaure, Jacques, 11, 133, 228, 275–276

Dumas, Mathieu, 152

Dumont, Etienne, 153, 157–158

Dumouriez, Charles-François, 170, 173, 220–222, 227, 232, 262, 264–265, 268–270, 272, 277, 291, 307, 321, 346

Duperron, Anisson, 334

Duport, Adrien-Jean-François, 119, 138, 152, 169

Duquesnoy, Adrien, 73

Durand, Antoine, 122

Durand de Maillane, Pierre-Toussaint, 17, 232, 338

Du Rozoi, Pierre-Barnabé Farmian, 103, 118

Duval d'Eprémesnil, Jean-Jacques, 45, 98, 104, 327

Dyzèz, Jean, 339

Edelstein, Dan, 3

Education, 1, 16–17, 20–21, 26–27, 63, 165, 245, 313–314

Elections: culture of, 76–77; to Estates General, 45–46, 53–54; to Legislative Assembly, 147; to Convention, 196, 205, 224; of assembly presidents, 100, 149, 232, 247;

270, 286; of Convention secretaries, 247; in Paris, 84–85; of regional administrators (1790), 74–75; of national guard officers, 84; by direct vote, 296

Emigrants, 98–100, 105, 110–113, 138–139, 145, 151, 158, 167, 170–171, 183, 195–196, 199, 221–222, 229, 235, 259, 293, 333, 344; armies of, 107, 123, 145, 178–179, 208, 271, 289, 344; property sold, 268

Emigration, 95, 102–103, 110–113, 118–119, 134, 207, 344

Emotional communities, 6, 346

Emotions, 5–8, 54, 61–63, 121–122, 140, 174, 191, 214, 242, 342, 347–348. *See also* Enthusiasm; Panic

Encyclopédie, 34

England, 40–41, 77, 153, 155, 166, 234, 238, 248, 285, 293, 299, 320, 322

Enlightened absolutism, 31

Enlightenment, 2, 9, 21, 28–33, 37, 97, 343

Enragés, 250, 261, 268, 273, 294–296, 302

Enthusiasm, 7, 51, 60, 63–64, 74, 78, 93, 122, 167–168, 181, 217, 219, 223, 250, 319–320, 324, 342–343, 345–346

Equality, 1, 6–7, 63, 78, 89–90, 92, 103, 121–122, 132, 139, 172, 177, 191, 255, 297, 314, 345

Equal justice, 1, 342

Escars: Louis-François-Marie, count d', 102; Madame d', 104

Estates General: of 1614, 43; of 1789, 39, 42–45, 53, 64, 73

Exclusionary rule, 224

Executions, 56, 162, 212, 239, 241–242, 268, 273, 278, 304, 306, 311, 324–331, 338–339, 349; in Paris, 332–333; statistics on, 330, 332

Executive authority, 177, 196, 305

Executive Council, 195–196, 198, 225

Extermination, 141, 243, 260, 278, 293, 296, 326

Fabre d'Eglantine, Philippe-François, 88, 213, 231

Factions: origins of, 150–159; influence of ideology on, 150–151, 229–230; influence of conspiracy fears on, 154, 270, 347; in assemblies, 59, 65, 69, 135, 172, 347; in National Assembly, 94, 119–120; in Legislative Assembly, 141, 149–159, 168, 174, 178, 198, 229; in Convention, 132, 228–233, 237–240, 256–257, 268–269, 270–276, 286, 314; among Montagnards, 328–330; and trial of king, 237–240, 243; effects on authority, 281; local, 75, 83–84, 144–148, 281, 205, 332,

Factions *(continued)*
345, 347; regional, 147–148, 178, 257;
religious, 110
Famine, 52–53, 79, 144, 160
Famine plot, 136, 293
Fatherland, 131, 133, 170, 235, 306, 325; in peril
(*patrie en danger*), 181, 218, 267, 278
Faulcon, Félix, 10, 16, 20, 27–28, 31, 37, 42, 44,
69, 122
Favras, marquis of, 99
Federalist rebellion, 281–285, 287–289, 307,
330, 345
Federalists, 282–285, 291–292, 295–298, 303,
325–326, 348; armies of, 282, 289; use of
committees of public safety, 283; use of
terror, 288
Federation movements, 91–92, 105, 122
Fédérés (summer 1792), 175, 181–184, 187–190,
197, 206, 213; Central Committee of, 182;
second (Fall 1792), 230–231
Fénelon, François de Salignac de la Mothe, 32
Ferrières, marquis de, 7
Fersen, Axel von, 114
Festivals: patriotic, 165, 324; of Federation
(1790), 91–95, 117, 122; of the Bastille, 181,
323; celebrating August 10, 1792, 296–297;
for war victories, 322–323; for abolition of
slavery, 313
Feudalism, 60, 80–82
Feuillants, 119–120, 148–162, 164–165, 169–170,
174–175, 177, 179–180, 184–185, 187, 195, 200,
204, 215, 228–231, 347
First Terror, 193, 215–216, 225, 242
Fiscal crisis, 40–41, 46, 81
Fleurus, battle of, 322–323
Foreigners, 268, 278; arrest of, 292
Foreign plots, 268, 317, 325
Forests, 80, 144
Foucauld de Lardimalie, Louis marquis de, 101
Fouché, Joseph, 315, 335
Foulon de Doué, Joseph-François, 57
Fouquier-Tinville, Antoine, 308–309, 341
Franche-Comté, 59, 80, 91, 108, 258
Francis II, of Austria, 170
Frankfurt, 221
Fraternal banquets, 323–324, 338
Fraternal societies, 88–90, 96, 117, 159–160, 163
Fraternity, 60, 63, 68, 90–94, 120–122, 139, 177,
227, 249, 287, 297, 324
Frederick II the Great, of Prussia, 31, 207, 226
Frederick William II, of Prussia, 207
Free Masons, 97, 103, 146
Free people of color, 88, 96, 151

Free trade, 144
Fréron, Louis-Stanislas, 88, 104, 202, 212, 224,
335
Fricaud, Claude, 140
Friends of Peace, 88
Friends of Truth, 88
Friendship, 229, 329

Galleries, 49, 87, 89, 96, 162, 164, 168–169, 174,
253–256, 272–275, 295, 300, 314, 346
Garat, Dominique-Joseph, 2, 10, 28, 32, 34,
61–62, 126, 155, 158, 287, 292, 302
Gard, department, 148
Gaultier, René-Claude, 238
Gaultier de Biauzat, Jean-François, 10, 16–17,
25, 44, 60, 109, 117, 130, 138, 140
Gautier de Syonnet, Jacques-Louis, 103
Gauville, Louis-Henri-Charles, baron de, 100
Gendarmes, 185, 188, 287, 337–338
Geneva, 221
Gensonné, Armand, 17, 153, 174, 180, 228, 238,
282, 287, 289, 307–308, 311
Géraud, Edmond, 9–10, 190, 222
Germany, 99, 105, 113, 123, 138, 145, 167–168,
173, 221, 242, 262, 280, 322, 344
Gerrymandering, 85
Gillet, Pierre, 217, 270
Girondins, 11, 132, 151, 157, 168, 170, 174,
179–180, 194, 198–199, 213, 220, 223–224,
227, 228–234, 237–241, 243–244, 247–249,
253, 255–256, 264, 268, 270–278, 281–283,
285–289, 291–292, 306–309, 312, 327–329,
347–349; contradictory positions of, 153, 239;
ministry of, 153, 157, 176–177, 181, 220; as
royalists, 239; flight of, 288–289, 306; 75
sympathizers arrested, 307, 325; trial of,
306–311, 327
Gisors, 207
Gobelins, 173
Godinot, 295
Goethe, Johann Wolfgang von, 220–221
Gohier, Louis-Jérôme, 217
Gorsas, Antoine-Joseph, 213, 224, 228, 282, 283,
306
Gossip, 30, 123–125
Gouges, Olympe de, 89, 254
Goupilleau, Jean-François-Marie, 68
Gower, Earl, 111
Grain: supply of, 65, 67, 91, 144, 202, 281, 295,
303; price of, 154, 253; trade in, 41, 92. *See
also* Bread
Grand conspiracy, 139, 154, 264–265, 276–277,
292, 325, 347

Grangeneuve, Jean-Antoine Lafargue de, 282

Granville, 322

Grasse, 223

Great Britain. *See* England

Great Fear, 58–59, 64, 69, 73, 91, 125, 127, 206

Great Terror, 11, 333, 339, 347

Greeks, ancient, 136, 163, 171. *See also* Classics

Grégoire, abbé Henri, 50, 119, 226

Grenoble, 258

Grub street, 103

Guadet, Elie, 17, 153, 156, 168, 180, 228, 238, 271, 327

Guilds, 25, 146, 345

Guillotine, 1, 36, 203, 241–242, 291, 311, 316, 321, 324, 327, 331, 333, 340, 349

Guittard de Floriban, Nicolas-Céleste, 9–10, 86, 123, 142, 178, 181, 209–210, 213, 219, 234, 253, 273, 291, 312–313, 316–318, 323–324, 338–339, 340

Guyenne, 91

Haguenau, 320

Hainaut, 59

Hanriot, François, 252, 273–275, 336, 338–339

Hawkers, newspaper, 125–127, 130, 161, 293

Hébert, Jacques-René, 197, 200, 251, 272, 294–295, 299–300, 302, 306–309, 317, 328–330

Hèle, Thomas d', 32

Helvétius, Claude-Adrien, 34

Hérault de Séchelles, Marie-Jean, 275, 286

High Court, 166

Hoarding of grain, 55, 57, 125, 144, 161–162, 184, 295, 300

Holland, 37, 40, 207, 222, 248, 262, 322

Honfleur, 288

Honor, 21–22, 25, 33–34, 102, 112, 168–170

Horace, 16

Horses, 219, 221, 321

Hostages: for the royal family, 116; for arrested Girondins, 286

Hôtel-Dieu, 93

House arrest, 276, 287, 291, 306, 342, 349

Hubris, 223, 227, 276

Human rights, 1, 61, 342

Hunting, 60, 82

Identity, 3–4, 68, 94, 167, 343

Ideology, 2–4, 6–7, 17, 29, 33, 40, 97, 158, 161, 229–230, 343

Illegitimate children, 313

Illumination (of Paris), 94, 127, 175, 200, 209, 323

Impatience, 153, 314, 348

Indulgents, 328

Inflation, 144, 161, 328

Insults, 25, 183

Insurrection, 182, 186–191, 340; of provinces, 215, 273; in Western France, 257–261, 277; of Thermidor, 336–339. *See also* Revolts

Intendants, 43, 72, 267

Intermediary Commission, 73

Interregnum: of 1789–1790, 6, 64, 74–75, 85, 196, 344; of 1792, 192–193, 196, 204, 207

Intolerance, 63, 103, 315, 343, 348. *See also* Tolerance

Invasion of France, 99, 113, 128, 173, 206–210, 212, 217, 219–221, 224, 250, 344–345

Inviolability, of king, 233, 236

Irland de Bazôges, Pierre-Marie, 10, 100–101, 113

Isnard, Maximin, 171, 272, 284, 307

Italy, 98–99, 105

Jacobins, 16, 86–90, 103, 105, 114, 119–120, 131–132, 139–141, 147–158, 162, 165, 174, 180, 182–183, 193–195, 197, 199, 202, 204, 213, 222, 228–231, 234, 246–247, 251, 254, 264, 282–283, 298–301, 302, 306–307, 309, 317, 329–330, 335–336, 347, 349

Jalès, camp of, 105, 107, 138

Jansenists, 29, 31, 54, 105, 136, 146

Jeanbon-Saint-André, André, 226, 229, 238, 320

Jemappe, battle of, 222, 265

Jesuits, 16, 136

Jesus, 315, 317

Jews, 59, 61, 82, 105

Joseph II, of Austria, 31

Journalists, 77–78, 89, 117–118, 129–130, 133, 138, 158–159, 174, 199, 224, 238, 328; patriot, 104; radical, 201; royalists, 202–203

Journées: February 28, 1791, 105; April 18, 1791, 84, 114; June 20, 1792, 176–179, 181, 198, 200, 210; August 10, 1792, 187–194, 196–197, 200–205, 207, 210, 225, 235, 238, 254, 259, 277, 296, 346, 348; February 1793, riots of, 253, 268; June 2, 1793, 274–276, 282, 286, 336, 338, 348; September 5, 1793, 300, 307, 324

Jousse, Daniel, 35

Judge. *See* Magistrates

Judicial system, 70

Judiciary, of Revolution, 344

Jullien: Rosalie, 9–10, 16, 20, 31, 64–65, 68, 89, 123, 126, 140, 160–161, 174, 176, 187, 190, 197,

Jullien *(continued)*
204, 209–211, 213, 228, 247, 252, 254–255, 256, 286, 295, 297, 303–306, 308–312, 314, 317–318, 322–324, 333; Marc-Antoine *père,* 9, 31; Marc-Antoine *fils,* 9, 312
Jurors, 304, 308–309, 341
Justices of the Peace, 77

Kant, Emmanuel, 33
Kaunitz, Wenzel Anton, prince of, 169
Kellermann, François-Christophe de, 220
Kéralio, Louise, 89, 117–118, 246
Kersaint, Armand, 248
Kings, 227, 233–234, 236, 242; foreign, 278. *See also* Louis XVI

Labor protests, 64–65, 78
Lacombe, Claire, 294–295
Lafayette, Marie-Joseph, marquis of, 22, 63, 65–66, 84–85, 87, 96, 152, 169, 173, 180, 184–185, 195, 200, 204, 209, 219, 234, 264–265, 277, 291, 321, 346
La Fontaine, Jean de, 32, 179
La Gallissonnière, count of, 34
La Glacière, Massacre of, 107
Lamartine, Alphonse de, 2
Lambertye, count of, 33
Lameth, Alexandre de, 7, 22, 70, 86, 96, 119, 152, 169
Lameth, Charles de, 22, 33, 86, 96, 152
Lameth, Théodore de, 155
Landau, 322
Land redistribution, 313–314
Language, 3, 23–24, 87, 101; seditious, 118; conspiratorial, 137; popular, 251–252; use of familiar "tu", 246–247, 252, 269; warped under Terror, 312; accents, 182
Languedoc, 84, 98, 105, 108, 111, 147, 258
Lanjuinais, Jean-Denis, 17, 283
La Rochefoucauld, Louis-Alexandre, duke of, 22, 207
La Rochefoucauld-Liancourt, François-Alexandre-Frédéric, duke of, 185
La Rochelle, 134, 182
Lasource, Marc-David Alba, 308
La Tour du Pin, Henriette-Lucie, marquise de, 112
La Tour Maubourg, Marie-Charles-César, marquis of, 34
Lavaur, 91
Lavie, Jean, 35
Lavoisier, Antoine-Laurent de, 334
Law, study of, 17, 26, 30, 35, 234

Law of nature, 233–234, 240
Law of suspects, 299, 303
Lawyers, 13, 17, 138, 171, 236, 340
Lebas, Philippe, 227, 229, 244, 239, 337, 339
Le Chapelier, Isaac-René-Guy, 327
Leclerc, Jean-Théophile, 294–295, 302
Le Coz, Claude, 145
Lefebvre, Georges, 2, 6, 160
Left, in assemblies, 65, 86, 149–150, 175, 177, 179, 180, 184, 295
Left Bank, 9, 31, 159, 163, 173, 176
Legendre, Laurent-François, 10, 104, 130, 139, 147
Legislative Assembly, 113, 120, 121, 132, 139, 141–158, 162–171, 173–181, 183–186, 188, 193–199, 202–205, 212, 214, 217, 219, 223–225, 228–229, 231, 236, 252, 265, 291; social composition of, 149–150
Lemaître, Pierre-Jacques, 105
Léon, Pauline, 294–295
Leopold II, of Austria, 169–170
Le Peletier de Saint-Fargeau, Louis-Michel, 243–244, 269, 290–291, 297, 332, 347
Lepoutre, Pierre-François, 140
Le Quesnoy, 320
Lequinio, Joseph, 238
Letters to the editor, 27, 130
Levasseur, René, 120, 155
Levée en masse, 298
Lézardière, baron de, 145
Lezay-Marnésia, Claude-François-Adrien, 21
Liberty, 1, 6–7, 61, 63, 69, 73, 76–78, 82, 90, 96, 103, 119, 121–123, 129–131, 133–134, 139, 144, 163, 168, 170–172, 191, 202, 221–223, 234, 292, 297, 300, 303, 326, 332, 345
Liberty cap, 162–164, 178, 229, 246, 251, 269, 314, 323
Liberty trees, 162–163, 167, 258, 297
Libraries: personal, 26, 30, 32; public, 27
Liège, 222, 263
Lille, 86
Limoges, 147
Limousin, 81, 260
Lindet, Robert, 235, 320
Lisleroy, Madame Marie-Alexandrine-Euphémie de, 10, 111
Literacy, 5, 24, 29, 126, 160
Locked safe, of king, 234–236
London, 248
Longwy, 208–209, 211, 219–221
Lorraine, 108, 110, 114, 208–209, 249, 258
Louchet, abbé Louis, 222, 240, 268, 271, 336
Loudun, 280

Index

Louis XIV, 31, 37, 192, 208, 223

Louis XV, 202, 223

Louis XVI, 31, 41–42, 47–49, 51, 54, 57, 59, 65–68, 70, 83–84, 90–91, 94–95, 100, 103, 105, 113–114, 120, 138, 142–143, 151–152, 154, 159, 166, 169–171, 173–191, 192–195, 201, 255, 257–259, 265, 278, 346; coronation of, 241; as father figure, 242; attempted "liberation" of, 98–99; attempts to kidnap, 65; flight of, 112–117, 119, 128, 138–140, 159, 161, 165–166, 168–169, 175, 210, 242, 265, 277, 183, 300, 347; treason of, 203, 226, 235, 239, 242; proposed removal from Paris, 185; demands that be deposed, 179, 182–184, 186; dethroning of, 117, 192–194, 197, 208, 224, 226, 230; suspension of, 194, 197, 224, 239; trial of, 115, 233–241, 308; debate on punishment of, 234, 240–242; proposed reprieve of, 341; execution of, 241–242, 245, 247–248, 271, 345; tragedy of, 241

Louvet, Jean-Baptiste, 228, 231, 238, 248

Louvre, 67, 275

Lynching, 57, 66, 128, 253; attempted, 289–290

Lyon, 13, 86, 98, 182, 282–285, 293, 303, 325–326; conspiracy of, 98, 138

Machecoul, 260

Mâconnais, 59

Magistrates, 13, 17, 19, 41–42, 72, 135, 138, 166, 260, 304, 308–309, 334, 341, 344

Mailhe, Jean-Baptiste, 233–234

Maine, 257–258, 284

Mainz, 221, 280, 291

Malassis, Romain-Nicolas, 158, 163

Malesherbes, Guillaume-Chrétien de Lamoignon de, 236, 334

Malouet, Pierre-Victor, 158

Marat, Jean-Paul, 15, 35, 71, 88, 104, 117–118, 129–130, 133, 138, 199, 201–202, 212, 224, 228, 230–232, 247, 269, 271, 273, 275, 294, 332, 347–348; assassination of, 289–292, 295, 306–307

Marathon, battle of, 221

Marchais, abbé Yves-Michel, 259

Mareux: Adélaïde, 9–10, 191, 203, 215–216; Toussaint, 9–10, 216, 239

Marie-Antoinette, 31, 66, 114–116, 124, 142–143, 154, 167, 169, 176, 178, 180, 185, 188, 194, 233, 291. See also Royal family

Marragon, Jean-Baptiste, 323

Marseillaise, la, 183, 222, 226, 320, 323

Marseillais, 182–183, 186, 190–191, 213, 231, 284

Marseille, 13, 86, 131, 140, 182–183, 189, 282–285, 293, 325

Martial law, 117–118, 225

Mask (of patriotism), 132–133, 174, 180, 231, 234, 324, 346

Masonic lodges, 86

Mass: Catholic, 92, 114, 146, 201, 315; banned in Paris, 316

Massacres, 103, 239, 300–301; in provinces, 215; of patriots, 260, 263, 326, 344; of Vendéens, 261

Massif-Central, 91, 110, 264

Maurepas, Jean-Frédéric, count of, 41

Maury, abbé Jean-Sifrein, 101, 158

Maximum, 251, 274, 328, 338

May "coup d'état" (1788), 42

May 31, 1793, 273–274

Médel, Angélique-Séraphine de, 10, 112

Memoirs, 7–8

Ménard de la Groye, François-Marie, 16, 46, 137

Ménétra, Jacques-Louis, 25, 68, 76, 135

Mercenaries, 51, 54, 137

Mercier, Louis-Sébastien, 9–10, 18, 24–26, 33–34, 36–37, 66, 78, 123, 126, 135, 160, 240–241, 243, 277, 308, 342

Merlin de Douai, Philippe-Antoine, 17

Microhistory, 8

Middle class, 4–5, 18, 33, 36, 68, 83, 160, 164, 182, 250, 251, 254, 256, 284, 313, 346. See also Bourgeoisie

Miles, William, 89, 127

Milhaud, Jean-Baptiste, 266

Militants: in Paris, 149, 159–165, 178–179, 182, 184–186, 188, 194, 197, 229, 233, 239, 251–252, 256, 264, 271–273, 282–283, 286, 293–294, 298–299, 301–303, 306, 308, 314–317, 319, 325, 340, 348; alliance with sans-culottes, 159–162, 345–346; in provinces, 293

Military, reform of, 70

Millau, 91

Millenarianism, 39, 121, 242

Ministers, 174, 188, 275, 324; royal, 75, 195, 202, 227, 236; of defense, 264; of the interior, 195, 225, 231; of foreign affairs, 173, 220; of war, 175, 319; Girondin, 176–177, 184; under the Convention, 245

Mirabeau, André-Boniface-Louis, vicount of, 34

Mirabeau, Honoré-Gabriel, count of, 11, 22, 49–50, 60, 70, 73, 77, 87, 96, 127, 129, 239, 265, 277, 346

Moderates, 87, 119, 148, 159–160, 184–185, 213, 256, 268, 301, 305, 315, 329

Monarchiens, 65–66, 100, 102

Monarchist Club, 87–88, 104, 147

Monarchy, 31, 40, 71, 153, 169, 184, 192–193, 200; reforms of, 41–43, 47, 71; constitutional, 95, 143, 200, 223, 327; fall of, 149, 152, 183–191; abolition of, 224, 226, 230, 242

Monestier, abbé Jean-Baptiste-Benoît, 236, 249, 278

Monnard, Marie-Victoire, 191

Monpellier, 182

Monro, George, 213

Mons, 222, 322

Monsters, 104, 140–141, 191, 213, 231, 235, 240, 252, 279, 289, 291, 318, 330, 333, 341

Montagnards, 132, 151, 156–157, 174, 178, 184, 194, 198–199, 228–234, 237–240, 243–244, 246–249, 254–255, 264, 266–268, 270–272, 275, 277–278, 281–288, 290–292, 295, 299–300, 303, 305–306, 314, 328, 330, 336, 341, 347–349

Montaigu, 260

Montauban, 105–106

Mont Blanc, department, 226

Montesquieu, Charles-Louis, baron of, 32, 34, 136

Montlosier, François-Dominique de, 101

Mortagne, 260

Moulins, 306

Mounier, Joseph, 65

Moustaches, 182, 251, 266

Municipalization of the revolution, 74

Municipal mobilization of 1788, 43, 46, 73, 86

Municipal revolution of, 55, 58, 73, 146–147, 152

Music, patriotic, 83, 94, 163–164, 177, 256, 297, 300, 320, 322–323

Mutinies, 55, 57, 78, 112

Namur, 222, 322

Nancy, 86; affair of, 79, 165

Nantes, 13, 182, 217, 258, 261, 263, 280, 322, 326

Napoleonic period, 76, 321

National agents, 298

National Assembly ("Constituent Assembly," 1789–1791), 48, 55–57, 60–62, 65–66, 70–75, 79–92, 96, 99–105, 107–120, 145, 147–148, 151, 160, 166, 196, 202, 223–224, 231, 234, 272, 286, 291, 327–328, 344

National guards, 65, 74–75, 81–86, 90–92, 96, 105–106, 110, 115, 117–118, 121, 125, 127, 134, 138, 173, 175–177, 180–182, 184–188, 190–191, 198, 202, 206, 209, 212–213, 222, 251, 257–258, 260–261, 273–276, 285, 293, 298, 319, 338–339, 344

Nationalism, 40, 68, 94, 146, 163, 166–168, 181, 343

Navy, 19, 40, 249, 296; reform of, 245

Necker, Jacques, 43–44, 51, 54, 57, 90, 137, 176, 200

Neerwinden, battle of, 262–264

Netherlands. *See* Holland

"New man," 62–64, 68, 98, 121, 314, 343

Newspapers, 7, 24, 26, 29, 65, 77–78, 87, 125–126, 129–131, 135, 160, 186, 195, 204, 213, 252, 289, 294; Girondin, 282; radical, 319; reactionary, 99, 102–104, 111, 116, 140–141, 172, 198, 344

Nice, 222–223, 226, 249, 255

Night of August 4, 59–61, 65, 67, 70, 80–81, 92, 100, 121

Nîmes, 283; *bagarre* of, 105

Nobility, 4, 13, 18–22, 31–33; of the robe, 19, 22, 243; liberal, 44–45, 50, 59, 97–98, 344; belief in chivalry, 97, 103, 112; conservative, 65, 77, 94–96, 100–102, 211; Estate of, 43–51, 57, 98, 102; attacks against, 82; suppression of, 70, 92, 102, 111, 118, 145; volunteers from (to save the king), 177, 185, 188–189; executions of, 330, 333

Noël, Joseph-Louis-Gabriel, 79, 204, 221

Non-violence, 186, 346

Normandy, 59, 108, 257–258, 284, 287, 291, 322, 325

Nuns, 93, 206, 326

Oaths, 48–50, 62, 73–74, 87, 91–92, 94, 122–123, 131, 133–134, 139, 143, 343; ecclesiastical, 108–110, 123, 145–146, 196, 202, 344; in Constituent Assembly, 151, 167–168; in Legislative Assembly, 193; in Convention, 244; of king, 116, 120, 138, 183; of military officers, 111–112; on Thermidor, 337

October Days, 66–68, 71, 91, 103, 127, 161, 253, 297

Officers, military, 21, 78–79, 111–112, 118, 144, 173, 207, 291, 321

Officials. *See* Administrators

Oise, department, 134, 206

Orléans, 64, 205, 215, 258, 264

Orléans, Philippe, duke d', 270, 327

Outlaws, 240, 291, 327, 338–340

Pacifism, 37

Paimboeuf, 263

Palais Royal, 44, 65–66, 88, 202, 218, 243, 294

Pamiers, 147–148

Pamphlets, flood of in 1788–1789, 44, 46–47

Index

Panic, 53, 58, 64, 99, 117, 122, 127–128, 206, 209, 166, 217, 221–222, 258, 260–261, 265, 276, 294; of May 1792, 347; of March 1793, 302, 347; of June 1794, 332–333, 347

Parallel powers, 82, 90, 118, 196, 198, 344

Paranoid politics, 7, 136–137, 155

Paris, department of, 177, 188, 207

Parish clergy, 46, 48, 59, 77, 82, 90, 107–109, 196, 259

Parisian Basin, 109

Parlement, 41–43, 72; of Paris, 35, 41, 45, 54, 72, 97, 333

Parliamentary immunity, 49, 269–271, 277

Parthenay, 264

Passage of infamy, 36–37, 311, 339

Passive citizens, 74, 85, 163, 186, 196, 198, 224

Passports, 198, 268

Pastoret, Emmanuel, 17, 35

Patrie. See Fatherland

Patriotic societies. See Clubs

Patriotism, 119, 133, 163, 169, 181, 198, 217, 219, 320, 324

Patriot party, 45, 57, 59, 69, 151, 344, 347

Patriots, 44, 109, 116, 118, 120, 128, 130, 132, 135–136, 140–141, 145, 168, 242–243, 250, 256, 260–261, 290, 292, 306, 319, 322, 332, 338

Patron-client system, 20, 31

Peasantry, 23, 26, 59–60, 79–82, 94, 144–145, 250, 252, 259, 261, 264, 276, 284, 300, 303, 319, 326, 330, 344–345

Penal code, 70, 134

People of Paris, 22–26, 54–56, 126–128, 138, 150–151, 155, 161–162, 203, 229–230, 252, 267, 274, 299, 317, 345–346

Permanent sessions: of Assembly, 175; of Convention, 265, 274, 338; of sections, 200, 302

Pétion, Jérôme, 25, 44, 50, 70, 74, 86, 119, 162–163, 176, 183, 197, 199, 228, 230, 238, 283, 306, 327

Petit, Edme-Michel, 278

Petitions, 85–86, 117, 164–165, 184, 186, 239, 252, 254, 272, 274, 299

Philosophers, 97, 103

Philosophy, 27, 29

Piedmont-Sardinia, 98–99

Pikes, 56, 67, 163, 173, 177, 187, 219, 223, 252, 269

Pillage, 56, 205–206, 215, 263

Pilnitz Declaration, 169

Pinet, Jacques, 16, 171, 174, 179–180, 181–182, 193, 196, 200, 202, 215, 223, 225, 227, 229, 231–232, 234, 240, 249–250, 263–265, 290, 292, 297

Pitt, William, 307, 332

Plain, 228, 247, 249, 270, 277–278, 288, 305, 326, 336, 340, 347

Plots. See Conspiracy

Poaching, 80, 82

Poetry, 27, 30, 97

Poitiers, 63, 86, 112

Poitou, 80, 112, 258, 260–261, 305; coalition of, 145

Poix, Prince du, 202

Poland, 169, 208, 227, 320

Polarization, 179; of Legislative Assembly, 150–158

Police, 70, 72, 80, 82, 91, 99, 124, 127–128, 134, 198, 305, 311, 334–335; spies of, 118

Political trials, 308, 329

Politics of self-destruction, 324, 327, 347

Poor, the, 104, 251–252, 281, 313–314, 323

Poor relief, 44

Popular opinion, 178, 239

Popular sovereignty, 74, 85, 103, 150, 161, 169, 196, 223, 229, 259, 282

Pornography, 30, 124

Porrentruy, 221

Portugal, 248

Power struggle, 158, 324, 347

Power vacuum, 69, 75, 122, 128, 204–205, 344–345, 348

Prairial Law, 332–334, 341, 347

Pre-Revolution, 39, 41–45, 52, 98

President: of Estates General, 48; of National Assembly, 51; of Legislative Assembly, 149; of the Convention, 232, 235, 247; Girondin domination of, 247, 270–271; Montagnard domination of, 247, 286

Press, freedom of, 1, 78, 104, 125, 130, 334

Prevotial justice, 53

Priest. See Clergy

Prieur, Claude-Antoine (de la Côte-d'Or), 298, 320

Prieur, Pierre-Louis (de la Marne), 15, 292

Primary assemblies, 224, 288, 296–299

Prisons, 120, 127, 202–203, 210–214, 304, 306, 308, 311, 327, 330, 333, 349; breakouts from, 210, 213, 214, 332; in Paris during Terror, 304; military, 321

Processions, 46, 78, 201–202, 297; through the assembly, 164–165, 173, 219, 252; religious, 259

Procope Café, 9, 86

Protestants, 28, 61, 63, 70, 81–82, 84, 97, 101, 103, 105–106, 108, 146, 226, 227; Reformation, 63, 107

Provence, 98, 182, 213, 215, 231

Provence, count of, 57, 98, 167, 195

Providence, 62, 112, 191

Provincial assemblies, 41–43, 45–46, 73

Provisional executive council, 245

Provisioning, military, 198, 262, 276, 313–314, 332

Prudhomme, Louis-Marie, 10–11, 57, 60, 62, 133, 137, 150, 161–162, 167, 227–228, 250, 265, 278

Prussia, 11, 168–169, 173, 180–181, 183, 199, 207–209, 217, 219–222, 224, 226, 235, 242, 264, 280

Psychology, 5–7, 11, 135, 139, 141, 153, 277, 348

Public opinion, 29–30, 47, 129–130, 133, 197

Public security (*Salut public*), 74, 91, 134, 151, 176, 252, 212, 221, 240, 267, 304, 332

Purges: of administrators, 267; of deputies, 277; in Convention, 269; of Girondin, 270–276, 281, 291, 348; attempted against Mountain, 230, 271; of surveillance committees, 303; of Robespierre, 349; in provinces, 349

Pyrenees, 91, 108, 147, 280

Queen. *See* Marie-Antoinette

Quercy, 80, 81, 84

Rabaut Saint-Etienne, Jean-Paul, 50, 70, 105, 238, 327

Rabusson-Lamothe, Antoine, 10, 150, 170, 173–175, 179, 195

Race, 21, 97, 102, 140

Racine, Jean, 32

Radicalism, 87, 97, 120, 142, 154–155, 159, 164, 182, 296

Radicals, in Paris, 320. *See also* Militants: in provinces

Ramel, Pierre, 145, 213

Ramond de Carbonnières, Louis, 152

Reason, 2, 6, 62, 97, 121, 137, 315, 343; goddess of, 316; cult of, 319

Recruitment, military, 181, 198, 217–218, 250, 256, 262, 265, 319–321

Red priest, 299

Referendum, 108, 178; of 1793, 288, 296; celebration of, 296–297

Refractory Clergy, 109–110, 113, 118–119, 123, 131, 134–135, 140, 145–147, 151, 166–167, 175–176, 198, 202, 211, 213, 215, 229, 252, 257, 259, 264, 278, 344

Regency, 116, 184

Regular clergy, 70, 107, 118, 146, 196

Religion, 24, 27, 29, 31, 92, 105–110–111, 122, 136, 140, 259, 315–319

Renaming, of towns, streets, etc., 316

Rennes, 182, 258

Representatives on mission: from Legislative Assembly, 198, 204; from Convention, 166, 258, 265–267, 270, 277, 282–283, 288, 314–315, 320–321, 325, 330; from Commune, 198; from Executive Council, 198

Repression, 34, 59, 79, 118, 175, 182, 243, 258, 261, 267–268, 270, 281, 293, 298–299, 301, 305, 317, 322, 324–326, 328, 330, 332, 349

Republic, 184, 222–226, 241–242, 245, 254, 256, 258, 276, 296–297, 315

Republicanism, 117–120, 129, 142, 151, 154, 161, 259–261, 271, 304

Réveillon riots, 34, 54

Revolts: popular, 24, 38, 59, 64, 84, 126; of military, 96; antiseigneurial, 146; subsistence, 53–54, 64, 66, 69, 74, 79, 81, 146, 257; of peasantry, 79–82, 96, 111, 154; anti-recruitment, 256–258, 263–265, 267; religious, 105–106, 108, 146, 257–262. *See also* Federalist rebellion; Insurrection; Vendée rebellion

Revolution, first use of word, 51

Revolutionary Army, 206, 295, 300–301, 303, 328

Revolutionary process, 123, 172, 159, 347–348

Revolutionary Republican Women, 253–255, 274, 294–295, 300, 302, 313–314

Revolutionary Tribunal, 1, 203, 261, 267–268, 271, 277, 295, 301, 304–305, 308, 310, 313, 325, 327, 330, 332–333, 336, 341–342, 348

Rhineland, 99, 110, 113, 249

Rich, the, 251–253, 256, 268, 295, 300, 314, 323

Right, in assemblies, 100, 149, 177, 179–180, 195, 231, 291

Right Bank, 9, 88, 176, 202

Riots. *See* Revolts

Rivoallan, Jean-Marie, 195

Robert, François, 88–89

Robespierre, Augustin, 337, 339

Robespierre, Maximilien, 8, 11, 13, 17, 20, 25, 36–37, 44, 50, 70, 74, 86, 119, 137, 155–157, 162, 170, 179, 181, 197, 199, 203, 224, 228, 230–238, 243, 246, 270, 275, 283, 292, 295, 300–302, 304–305, 308–309, 312, 314, 317–319, 325, 328–329, 332, 335–339, 340–341, 347–349

Rochambeau, Jean-Baptiste, count of, 169, 173

Roederer, Pierre-Louis, 177

Roland, Jean-Marie, 170, 195, 199, 209, 225, 228, 230–231, 234, 293, 327

Roland, Marie-Jeanne (Madame), 7, 16, 153, 228, 327

Romans, ancient, 129, 136, 162–163, 223, 235, 243, 254, 311. *See also* Classics

Romme, Gilbert, 8–9, 20, 25, 27, 31–32, 40, 49, 52, 55–56, 58, 62, 68, 137, 151–152, 154, 176, 314–315, 349

Roubaud, François-Yves, 10, 126, 144, 154, 176, 179, 215, 223, 236, 242

Rouen, 53

Rouergue, 81

Rousseau, Jean-Jacques, 2, 17, 29–32, 34–35, 97, 161, 295, 317, 343

Roux, Jacques, 294–295, 302

Royal family, 112–116, 145, 183, 188, 192–194, 233

Royalists, 184, 198, 200, 202, 224, 239, 243, 270, 291, 298, 301, 325

Royal Session (June 23, 1789), 49

Royer, abbé Claude, 299–300

Royou, abbé Thomas-Marie de, 103

Ruault, Nicolas, 9–10, 18, 26–28, 30–31, 34, 37, 40, 42, 44, 64–65, 69, 72, 78, 84, 90, 102, 104, 122, 128, 137, 145, 159, 162, 175–177, 183–184, 187, 192–193, 200, 213–214, 223, 247, 256, 272–273, 289, 312, 317–318, 330, 333–334, 339, 342

Rubat, Aristide, 169

Rumor, 6, 53–54, 57–59, 77, 99, 105, 123–128, 130, 135, 138–139, 141, 162, 170, 173–174, 186, 202, 205–206, 210–211, 214–215, 265, 273, 281, 291, 293, 299, 324, 332, 346–347

Russia, 52, 169

Sables-d'Olonne, Les, 257

Saint-Antoine, neighborhood, 54, 176, 182, 188

Saint-Bartholomew's Day Massacre, 127, 141, 174

Saint-Cloud, 91, 114

Saint-Denis, 58, 317

Sainte-Menehould, 114

Saint-Just, Antoine de, 9, 229, 234, 238, 287, 305, 306, 313, 320, 322, 329, 335–337, 339, 348

Saint-Lawrence's Day Massacre, 191, 210, 239

Saint-Marcel, neighborhood, 176, 184–185, 188, 190

Saint-Martin, François-Jérôme Riffard de, 226, 287

Saintonge, 288

Saint-Sulpice, 312, 316, 316; Place de, 323; seminary of, 206

Saladin, Jean-Baptiste-Michel, 275

Salle, Jean-Baptiste, 238, 327, 282, 291

Salm, 249

Salon française, 104–105

Salt tax (*gabelle*), 60

Sans-culottes, 4, 160–162, 164, 182, 184, 188, 197, 251–252, 256, 265, 269, 271, 282, 286, 298, 302, 316, 340, 349; alliance with radical militants, 159–162, 345–346

Santerre, Antoine-Joseph, 176, 188

Saumur, 280

Savoy, 222, 226, 242, 322

Scaffold, 311, 340, 342

Schoolboys, 93, 173, 197, 241, 297

Scientific revolution, 29

Scipio, 16

Secretaries: in National Assembly, 100; in Convention, 232, 267, 286

Sections of Paris, 4, 85, 96, 118, 159, 163–164, 173, 175–176, 179, 181, 183–184, 186, 198, 211, 219, 239, 246, 251–254, 256, 271–274, 282, 294, 297–300, 302, 315, 329, 337, 344; assemblies of, 85, 90, 125, 160; central bureau of, 186; clubs of, 160

Sedition, 330

Seigneurial: courts, 60, 72; dues, 60, 80–81, 94, 111, 144–145, 259; lords, 24, 80–81, 136, 145; property, 100; rights, 20, 102, 196, 216; system, 59–60, 80, 100

September Massacres, 193, 198–199, 203, 205, 211–216, 217, 225, 230, 247, 267, 296, 300, 333, 346

Serre, Joseph, 238

Servan, Joseph-Marie, 170, 181

Seven Years War, 40, 220

Sieyès, abbé Emmanuel-Joseph, 48–50, 87

Simond, Philibert, 247

Slavery, 20, 37, 79, 96, 143, 162, 164, 345; abolition of, 1, 313–314

Soboul, Albert, 2

Social contract, 325

Social welfare, 1, 313, 324, 339

Society of 1789, 87

Soissons, 80, 181

Sorbonne, 97

Soubrany, Pierre, 161

Sovereignty, 62, 226

Spain, 40, 71, 166–167, 227, 249, 263, 322

Spartans, 254

Speech, freedom of, 1, 334

Stamaty, Constantine, 239, 241

Statements of grievances, 33, 36, 46, 53, 62, 71, 82, 96–97, 137

Statue of liberty, 316

Strikes, 338

Suffrage: universal male, 1, 74, 85, 88, 184, 196, 225, 251; for women, 5, 89, 294, 296

Supreme Being, cult of, 317–319, 335

Surveillance, 87, 90, 131, 186

Surveillance committees, 1, 118, 166, 268–269, 265, 277, 325, 330, 334; of Commune, 198–199, 202, 212, 225; of sections, 198, 202; during Terror, 303, 305

Suspects, 74, 85, 135, 184, 198, 200, 206, 210, 268, 295, 299–300, 302–303, 327, 330, 349

Swiss Guards, 185, 188–191, 193, 197, 200–201, 210, 212; massacre of, 190–191

Switzerland, 153, 163, 221–222, 242, 249

Symbols: of royalism, 200; of Old Regime, 206

Tacitus, 16

Talent, 1, 33, 44

Talleyrand, Charles-Maurice de, 7, 87

Tallien, Jean-Lambert, 231, 335–337

Tardiveau, François-Alexandre, 168

Target, Guy-Jean-Baptiste, 17

Taveau, Louis-Jacques, 288

Tax: farmers, 40, 333; collectors, 72, 81, 334; excise, 60, 81; municipal, 81

Taxation, 5, 18, 20, 24, 32, 39–43, 47–48, 59, 70, 74–75, 80–81, 88, 91, 94, 144, 170, 205, 227, 245, 251, 253, 256, 258–259, 268

Te Deum, 62, 222

Temple, the, 192, 233, 235, 241

Tennis Court Oath, 49–50, 168

Terror: word used before year II, 35, 38, 68; of 1791, 113, 115–120; as tragedy, 172, 241; origins of, 342–348, 261–262, 265, 267–270, 277; as "order of the day," 299–302, 309, 341; fever of, 324; goals of, 329; grassroots, 135; in other revolutions, 348; incited against all monarchies, 227; institutions of, 301–305, 347–348; killing, 243, 278; non-linear development of, 347; psychology of, 5, 7, 11, 141, 342, 348; pushed by enragés, 295–296; promoted to preserve Revolution, 277–278; used by federalists, 281; on the battlefield, 321; dismantling of, 341

Texier, Jean, 28

Thermidor, 11, 335–342, 349

Thibaudeau, Antoine-Claire, 63, 112

Third Estate, 13, 17, 20–21, 34, 43–51, 137

Thomas, Jean-Jacques, 246–247

Thouret, Jacques-Guillaume, 327, 334

Thuriot, Jacques-Alexis, 301, 304

Tilly, Jacques-Pierre-Alexandre, count of, 22

Tithes, 60, 81–82, 100, 259

Tocqueville, Alexis de, 2, 76

Tocsin, 187, 200, 211, 217, 273, 338

Tolerance, religious, 1, 61, 63, 100, 110, 314, 317, 334, 342. *See also* Intolerance

Torture, 34–36, 57, 291

Total War, 298, 320

Toulon, 131, 147–148, 182–283, 285, 296, 299, 322–323, 325

Toulouse, 86, 258

Touraine, 257

Tournai, 223

Tours, 260

Treason, 35, 37, 117, 119–120, 134–135, 139, 154–156, 158, 173, 179, 183, 186, 191, 195, 202, 208–210, 210, 223, 231, 234–235, 265, 285, 293, 299, 305–306, 309, 324, 327, 328, 342

Tribunals, 135, 162–163, 205; in early Revolution, 74–75, 82; during September Massacres, 212; of August 17, 203, 225, 267. *See also* Revolutionary Tribunal

Triumvirate, 119, 152, 335

Tronchet, François-Denis, 236

Troyes, 148

Tuileries Gardens, 142, 190, 202, 275, 323, 329, 336

Tuileries Palace, 67, 84, 105, 113, 115, 145, 175, 177–179, 183, 185–191, 194, 200, 202, 224, 255, 259, 297; assault on, 203, 205, 213, 235, 348; ministerial files found in, 195, 203; king's safe in, 234–236

Tulle, 148

Turenne, Henri, vicount de, 103

Uncertainty, 6, 39, 69, 76, 90, 95, 122–124, 137, 139, 159, 170, 192, 205, 262, 265, 294, 345–346, 348

Unity, 332; law on, 311

Vadier, Marc-Alexis, 139, 147–148, 323

Valence, 91, 284

Valenciennes, 280, 291, 320

Valmy, Battle of, 220–222, 224, 265, 270, 280

Var, department, 146

Varennes, 83; king's flight to, 90, 115, 119–120, 140, 159, 161, 165–166, 168–169, 183, 242, 265, 277, 300

Varlet, Jean-François, 302

Vauban, Sébastien Le Prestre de, 208

Venality of office, 60

Vendée, department, 257

Vendée rebellion, 257–261, 271, 274, 279–282, 284–285, 291–292, 296–297, 307, 322, 326, 330, 344–345, 348

Index

Vendetta, 25, 345

Ventôse decrees, 313

Verdun, 208, 211, 219–221

Vergennes, Charles Gravier, count of, 41

Vergniaud, Pierre-Victurnien, 8, 10, 13, 17, 20, 27, 31, 40, 153, 168, 170, 179–180, 193, 227–228, 230, 238, 270, 282, 287, 289, 307–309, 311, 329

Vernier, Théodore, 10, 17, 62, 108

Versailles, 19, 36, 46–51, 54, 57, 59, 65, 66, 92, 97, 110, 124, 253, 297

Veto, 65–66, 85, 164–166, 175–179, 181, 196, 236

Vice, 232, 271

Viénot de Vaublanc, Vincent-Marie, 152, 164

Vierzon, 64

Vigilantes, 72, 128, 205–207

Villefranche-de-Rouergue, 91

Vinet, Pierre, 228, 288

Virtue, 232, 271, 325, 335, 339, 343

Vivarais, 59, 80, 91

Voltaire, 9, 30–32, 34, 37, 136, 162, 317

Volunteers: of 1792, 206–207, 215–219, 221, 249, 262; of 1793, 256–258, 264, 267; of 1794, 319; summoned by Girondins, 271

Voting: in provincial assemblies, 43; in Estates General, 43, 46–48; in National Assembly, 49; in Convention on king's trial, 239–240

War: declaration of, 171, 248–249, 255, 263; just, 37; of "liberation," 262, 276, 227, 242; to end war, 227, 249; "revolutionized," 321; mass mobilization for, 298

Wealth: of middle class, 13–16; of nobility, 20; of lower classes, 23–24

Weather, in 1788–1789, 51–53, 69

Whites, in Western France, 260

White Terror, 349

Women, 1, 5, 16–17, 24–25, 36, 55, 58, 66–67, 87, 89–90, 92–94, 117, 127, 163–164, 173, 176, 186–187, 209, 212, 221, 239, 252–255, 272–275, 294–298, 300, 323, 345; clubs of, 89, 314; inheritance rights of, 90; property rights of, 90, 294, 313; rights over children, 313

Working class, 23, 33, 54, 144, 160–161, 172, 182, 229, 251, 281, 284, 299, 313, 315, 345, 348

World revolution, 226–227

Youth, 83, 94, 186, 206, 319